Language and Communication:
Comparative Perspectives

Comparative Cognition and Neuroscience
Thomas G. Bever, David S. Olton, and Herbert L. Roitblat, Series Editors

Antinucci: Cognitive Structures and Development in Nonhuman Primates

Boysen/Capaldi: The Development of Numerical Competence: Animal and Human Models

Brown: The Life of the Mind

Kendrick/Rilling/Denny: Theories of Animal Memory

Kesner/Olton: Neurobiology of Comparative Cognition

Nilsson/Archer: Perspectives on Learning and Memory

Ristau: Cognitive Ethology: The Minds of Other Animals: Essays in Honor of Donald E. Griffin

Roitblat/Herman/Nachtigall: Language and Communication: Comparative Perspectives

Schulkin: Preoperative Events: Their Effects on Behavior Following Brain Damage

Schusterman/Thomas/Wood: Dolphin Cognition and Behavior: A Comparative Approach

Zentall/Galef: Social Learning: Psychological and Biological Perspectives

Zentall: Animal Cognition: A Tribute to Donald A. Riley

Language and Communication: Comparative Perspectives

Edited by

Herbert L. Roitblat
University of Hawaii at Manoa

Louis M. Herman
University of Hawaii at Manoa

Paul E. Nachtigall
Naval Ocean Systems Center, Hawaii

1993

LAWRENCE ERLBAUM ASSOCIATES, PUBLISHERS
Hillsdale, New Jersey   Hove and London

Copyright © 1993 by Lawrence Erlbaum Associates, Inc.
All rights reserved. No part of this book may be reproduced in
any form, by photostat, microform, retrieval system, or any other
means, without the prior written permission of the publisher.

Lawrence Erlbaum Associates, Inc., Publishers
365 Broadway
Hillsdale, New Jersey 07642

Library of Congress Cataloging-in-Publication Data

Language and communication : comparative perspectives / edited by
 Herbert L. Roitblat, Louis M. Herman, Paul E. Nachtigall.
 p. cm.
 Includes bibliographical references and index.
 ISBN 0-8058-0946-5 (cloth). — ISBN 0-8058-0947-3 (paper)
 1. Language and languages. 2. Animal communication.
 I. Roitblat, H. L. II. Herman, Louis, M. III. Nachtigall, Paul, E.
 P106.L3134 1993
 156'.36—dc20 92-39728
 CIP

Books published by Lawrence Erlbaum Associates are printed on
acid-free paper, and their bindings are chosen for strength and
durability.

Printed in the United States of America
10 9 8 7 6 5 4 3 2 1

Contents

1. **Cognitive Processing in Artificial Language Research** 1
   Herbert L. Roitblat, Heidi E. Harley, and David A. Helweg

   Animal language research and its controversies 2
   The value of animal language research 6
   Some general issues in cognitive processing 8
   Meaning and reference. 9
   Syntax. 12
   Pragmatics 17
   Conclusion 19

2. **Beyond Animal Language** 25
   Gary Bradshaw

   The path to language 28
   Limitations of the Signature Characteristic Strategy 30
   Beyond Animal Language 34
   Conclusion 39

3. **Similarities and Differences in Human and Animal** 45
   Language Research: Toward a Comparative
   Psychology of Language
   Stan A. Kuczaj II and Virginia M. Kirkpatrick

   What is the study of language?. 45
   Is human language an appropriate standard for
     comparative language research? 48
   Questions generated by the human language standard 49
   What are the language units of various language
     systems? 50
   How meaningful are the symbolic units of various
     language systems?. 52
   Do nonhuman language systems involve syntax?. 55
   What functions do the languages of other species
     serve? 57

Contents

Concluding remarks 58

4. **Knowing How to Use Language: Developing a** 65
   Rapprochement Between Two Theoretical Traditions
   William Bechtel

   Symbol processing versus associationism. 66
   Ryle's distinction between knowing how and knowing
      that 68
   The promise of connectionism to explain knowing
      how. 69
   The contribution of animal language research 75
   Conclusion 81

5. **A Proposal for Computer Modeling of Animal** 85
   Linguistic Comprehension
   Earl Hunt

   The theoretical issue raised by animal linguistic
      comprehension. 85

6. **Language Acquisition and the Power of Expression** 95
   Lois Bloom

   The "tool use" metaphor 98
   Language as expression 99
   Language, emotion, and cognition. 101
   Expression of beliefs, desires, and feelings 104
   Allocating cognitive resources for emotional expression
      and words 105

7. **Animal Language Research Needs a Broader** 115
   Comparative and Evolutionary Framework
   Peter L. Tyack

   The evolution of domain specific cognitive processes 117
   Capability versus skill 124
   Problems in applying language analogies to animals 125
   Vocal learning and imitation. 129
   Signature whistles in wild dolphins 131
   Vocal imitation in adult captive dolphins 134

Contents

    Do dolphins imitate signature whistles to call specific individuals? 136
    Ethological suggestions for animal language research 138

8. **Frequency-modulated Whistles as a Medium** **153**
   for Communication with the Bottlenose Dolphin
   (*Tursiops truncatus*)
   John Sigurdson

    Method 156
    Conclusions 170

9. **Linguistic Phenomena in the Natural** **175**
   Communication of Animals
   Charles T. Snowdon

    Phonetic variation and categorization 177
    Social components of communication 181
    Syntax 184
    Referential communication 186
    Summary and conclusions 189

10. **Meaning, Reference, and Intentionality** **195**
    in the Natural Vocalizations of Monkeys
    Robert M. Seyfarth and Dorothy L. Cheney

    Subjects 196
    Semanticity in the weakest sense 197
    Semanticity in a stronger sense 201
    Semanticity in the strongest sense 209
    Summary 214

11. **Cognition and Communication in an African** **221**
    Grey Parrot (*Psittacus erithacus*): Studies on a
    Nonhuman, Nonprimate, Nonmammalian Subject
    Irene Maxine Pepperberg

    Background 221
    Experimental design 229
    Behaviors during training 231

Contents

Testing procedures 233
Results and discussion 235
Concluding remarks 237

12. **Behavior Control by Exclusion and Attempts** 249
at Establishing Semanticity in Marine Mammals Using
Match-to-sample Paradigms
Ronald J. Schusterman, Robert Gisiner, Brigit K.
Grimm, and Evelyn B. Hanggi

Control by Exclusion 253
A Hypothetical experiment on semantic comprehension:
Harbor seal and stimulus equivalence 268
General discussion 270

13. **Auditory Sequence Complexity and Hemispheric** 275
Asymmetry of Function in Rats
Kevin N. O'Connor, Herbert L. Roitblat, and Thomas
G. Bever

Method 277
Results 280
Summary and discussion 288

14. **Hemispheric Priming as a Technique in the** 293
Study of Lateralized Cognitive Processes in
Chimpanzees: Some Recent Findings
William D. Hopkins and Robin D. Morris

Methodological issues 296
Statistical issues 299
The time course of hemispheric activation 302
Summary and conclusion 305

15. **Cognitive Factors Affecting Comprehension** 311
of Gesture Language Signs: A Brief Comparison of
Dolphins and Humans
Palmer Morrel-Samuels and Louis M. Herman

Artificial gestural language 311
General features of gesture recognition 312

viii

Contents

Cerebral asymmetry during gesture recognition 316

16. **Chimpanzee Competence for Comprehension** 329
    Video-formatted Task Situation
    Duane M. Rumbaugh, William Hopkins, David A.
    Washburn, and E. Sue Savage-Rumbaugh

    Perceptions of quantities 333

17. **Acquisition of Personal Pronouns by a Chimpanzee** 347
    Shoji Itakura and Tetsuro Matsuzawa

    Discrimination of the letters of the alphabet 348
    Individual recognition 348
    Description of the subject and the object of action 349
    Acquisition of personal pronouns 351
    Discussion and conclusions 359

18. **"Language Training" and its Role in the** 365
    Expression of Tacit Propositional Knowledge by
    Chimpanzees (*Pan troglodytes*)
    Roger K. R. Thompson and David L. Oden

    A profound disparity? 365
    Representational differences between physical and
        relational matching 367
    Evidence for tacit if not explicit propositional
        knowledge in infant chimpanzees. 370
    The chimpanzee infants and their general environment
        370
    Matching training and testing 371
    Perceptual sensitivity to physical and relational
        similarities and differences 373
    Explicit training on relational matching 377
    What does language training do? 379

ix

Contents

19. **The Effects of Language on Information Processing 385
and Abstract Concept Learning in Dolphins, Monkeys,
and Humans**
Melissa R. Shyan and Anthony A. Wright

> Evidence from dolphin and human comparative
>   research 386
> Evidence from monkey and human comparative
>   research 392
> Where do we go from here? 396
> Conclusions. 398

20. **Representational and Conceptual Skills of Dolphins 403**
Louis M. Herman, Adam A. Pack, and Palmer
Morrel-Samuels

> Receptive language competencies. 404
> Behavioral mimicry: Imitating the behavior
>   of a model 414
> Matching-to-sample 421
> Conclusions. 428

21. **A Bottlenosed Dolphin's Responses to Anomalous. 443
Sequences Expressed Within an Artificial Gestural
Language**
Mark D. Holder, Louis M. Herman, and Stanley
Kuczaj II

> The use of anomalous sequences in language
>   research 444
> Akeakamai's language and the construction of
>   anomalous sequences 445
> Testing responses to anomalous sequences 446
> Relational anomalies. 449
> Nonrelational anomalies 451
> Responses to sequences given by a naive signer 453
> Summary 454

22. Language Learnability in Man, Ape, and Dolphin 457
E. S. Savage-Rumbaugh

The strong-L learning view 458
Reference and syntax...................... 459
Receptive and productive competence............ 462
Critical differences between dolphin and child linguistic
   experience........................ 464
A theory of language acquisition 467
Summary 469

Preface

This book is the result of a conference on language and related cognitive processes in animals. The purpose of this conference was to bring together scientists working on language and communication, to review the work done on language in apes and dolphins, and to place this work in a larger perspective of animal communication and cognition.

The conference convened an international group of distinguished scientists interested in exploring the neurological, cognitive, social, and behavioral aspects of communication in animals. A broad spectrum of perspectives was represented, including naturalistic investigations of animals in their natural habitat as well as strictly controlled laboratory investigations. Similarly, a broad range of species was described including rats, parrots, monkeys, apes, dolphins, and humans.

Investigations of animal communication and language impinge on some very fundamental psychological and philosophical issues concerning human nature and the mind. The history of such investigations has frequently been punctuated by confrontation and conflict. This conference made clear, however, that this period of deep and frustrating conflict is largely behind us. New methodologies and new perspectives are continuously emerging that allow consideration of issues that previously could not be resolved. Emerging technology such as video equipment and advanced database systems allow one to exhaustively record in an accessible format the evidence on which scientific conclusions must be based. Investigation of animal language and communication is a small, but again vigorously exciting area of scientific investigation, as the chapters in this volume clearly attest.

The conference was supported by a grant (N00014-89-J-1093) to the University of Hawaii from the Office of Naval Research. We thank ONR for their support. Above all, we thank Dr. Donald Woodward for having the vision to develop and direct an advance research initiative program in marine mammal cognition and for inspiring this meeting. His intellectual leadership will continue to have a powerful influence on this field for many years.

Contributors

William Bechtel
Department of Philosophy
Georgia State University
Atlanta, GA 30303

Thomas G. Bever
Department of Psychology
University of Rochester
Rochester, NY 14627

Lois Bloom
Teacher's College
Columbia University
New York, NY 10027

Gary Bradshaw
Institute of Cognitive Science
Campus Box 345
University of Colorado
Boulder, CO 80309

Dorothy L. Cheney
Department of Psychology
University of Pennsylvania
3815 Walnut Street
Philadelphia, PA 19104

Robert Gisiner
Naval Ocean Systems Center-Hawaii
Laboratory
Kailua, HI 96734

Brigit K. Grimm
Long Marine Lab
University of California
100 Shaffer Road
Santa Cruz, CA 95060

Evelyn B. Hanggi
Long Marine Lab
University of California
100 Shaffer Road
Santa Cruz, CA 95060

Heidi Harley
Department of Psychology
University of Hawaii
2430 Campus Road
Honolulu, HI 96822

David Helweg
Department of Psychology
University of Hawaii
2430 Campus Road
Honolulu, HI 96822

Louis M. Herman
Department of Psychology
University of Hawaii
Honolulu, HI 96822

Mark D. Holder
Department of Psychology
Memorial University of
Newfoundland
St. John's Newfoundland
Canada A1B 3X9

William Hopkins
Language Research Center
Georgia State University/Yerkes
3401 Panthersville Rd.
Decatur, GA 30034

Earl Hunt
Department of Psychology
NI-25
University of Washington
Seattle, WA 98195

Shoji Itakura
Department of Psychology
University of Tokyo
3-8-1 Komaba
Meguro-ku
Tokyo 153, Japan

Virginia M. Kirkpatrick
Department of Psychology
Southern Methodist University
Dallas, TX 75275

Stanley Kuczaj
Department of Psychology
Southern Methodist University
Dallas, TX 75275

Tetsuro Matsuzawa
Department of Psychology
Primate Research Institute
Kyoto University
Inuyama
Aichi 484, Japan

Palmer Morrel-Samuels
EDS Center for Advanced Research
2001 Commonwealth Blvd.
Ann Arbor, MI 48105

Robin D. Morris
Language Research Center
Georgia State University/Yerkes
3401 Panthersville Rd
Decatur, GA 30034

Paul E. Nachtigall
Naval Ocean Systems Center-Hawaii
Laboratory
Kailua HI 96734

Kevin N. O'Connor
Department of Psychology
Tobin Hall
University of Massachussetts
Amherst, MA 01003

David L. Oden
Department of Psychology
La Salle College
Philadelphia, PA 19141

Adam A. Pack
Department of Psychology
University of Hawaii
Honolulu, HI 96822

Irene Pepperberg
Department of Ecology and
Evolutaionary Biology
University of Arizona
Tucson, AZ 85721

Herbert L. Roitblat
Department of Psychology
University of Hawaii
Honolulu, HI 96822

Duane Rumbaugh
Language Research Center
Georgia State University/Yerkes
3401 Panthersville Rd.
Decatur, GA 30034

E. Sue Savage-Rumbaugh
Language Research Center
Georgia State University/Yerkes
3401 Panthersville Rd.
Decatur, GA 30034

Ronald Schusterman
Long Marine Lab
University of California
100 Shaffer Road
Santa Cruz, CA 95060

Robert Seyfarth
Department of Psychology
University of Pennsylvania
3815 Walnut Street
Philadelphia, PA 19104

Melissa Shyan
Department of Psychology
Butler University
4600 Sunset Avenue
Indianapolis, IN 18352

John Sigurdson
Naval Ocean Systems Center-Hawaii
Laboratory
Kailua, HI 96734

Charles Snowdon
Department of Psychology
Birge Hall
University of Wisconsin
Madison, WI 53706

Roger Thompson
Whitely Psychology Laboratories
Franklin & Marshall College
P. O. Box 3003
Lancaster, PA 17604

Peter Tyack
Woods Hole Oceanographic Institute
Woods Hole, MA 02543

David A. Washburn
Language Research Center
Georgia State University/Yerkes
3401 Panthersville Rd
Decatur, GA 30034

Anthony A. Wright
Graduate School of Biomedical
Sciences
University of Texas Health Sciences
Center
Houston, TX 77025

1 Cognitive Processing in Artificial Language Research

Herbert L. Roitblat, Heidi E. Harley, and David A. Helweg

> *It was immensely foolish not to have anticipated the intense fervor this work would generate. Yet it was not easy to prepare for the occasion because so few other issues in recent academic psychology had had a comparable effect. The attention given the work by the media kept the emotion dancing. While most work in psychological laboratories proceeds without the slightest attention or diversion from the outside world, the chimpanzee language work was held continually before the public eye. This did little to quell the emotion and equally little, unfortunately, to maintain the quality of the work.* (Premack, 1986, p. 1)

In this chapter we outline some alternative conceptualizations of the research on teaching artificial language to animals. In order to make our perspective clear, we state our biases at the outset:

1. No animal has a communication system like that of a normal adult human.

2. There are many similarities and also substantial differences between the performance of animals and the performance of young children in the

age range at which they produce utterances with a mean length of utterance (MLU) of approximately 1.0 to 3.0 morphemes.

3. Much of animal performance has been compared with an idealized model of human language acquisition and performance that is probably untenable.

4. Learning, formulaic patterns, and language rituals play important roles in human and animal language acquisition.

5. The question of whether animals have been shown to have (a full adult human) language is ill formed and of little heuristic value.

6. More interesting questions concern the psychology of the systems that animals in language-training experiments acquire.

We refer frequently to "animal language." We use this term as a shorthand for the use by animals of (frequently tiny) artificial language-like systems. We do not wish to beg the question of whether the performance of animals actually constitutes a language in any particular sense, but it seems too awkward always to use the kind of qualifications that do not prejudge the issues.

ANIMAL LANGUAGE RESEARCH AND ITS CONTROVERSIES

Historically, the field of animal language research has been racked by frequent controversy. These controversies often provide dramatic spectacles for the participants and the observers, but they frequently place greater emphasis on the supposed intellectual and social shortcomings of the participants than on the merits of the argument. The reasons for such controversies are complex; nevertheless, they can be summarized into five major categories: (a) sociology, (b) methodology, (c) justificationism, (d) reductionism, and (e) the problem of resemblance.

Sociology

Little work in psychology has engendered as much emotional involvement and heated argument as has research in animal language. The very enterprise attacks beliefs that some individuals hold very dear, for example, those concerned with what it means to be a human, or with what it means to know a word. The

1. Cognitive processing in artificial language

research has taken tremendous investments of time, effort, and in some cases even personal money.

All of the projects are long-term, with payoffs, in the form of conclusive data, typically delayed for several years (if ever forthcoming). Most projects have focused on individual animals and on the development of a warm personal relationship with those animals. These factors make it very difficult to view the research and its criticism with the kind of objective detachment people would like for a scientific discipline.

Methodology

Animal language research presents particularly difficult methodological task. Research typically involves single subject designs, in which the variable of interest either is learned or is related to learned variables. Development of proper control procedures is difficult, especially with the limited numbers of subjects typically available for each project. Experiments frequently take many months or years to conduct and often require changes in the nature or approach toward the research during the training period. Researchers who are used to conducting experiments in which they have access to large numbers of subjects, have tighter controls over environmental and methodological variables, and can conduct pilot experiments before investing their experimental subjects in a procedure frequently have difficulties accepting typical animal language research designs.

Justificationism

In addition to these methodological and sociological factors that have contributed to the acrimony in animal language research, the controversy has often been fueled by what we consider to be ill-formed questions. Many of these questions have been the result of a quest for some kind of "positivist ideal"(Premack, 1986). This ideal is based on the assumption that fundamental scientific questions can be answered by simple crucial experiments. One has merely to conduct the crucial experiment and all issues will be settled. By judiciously sticking close to ones observations one can develop sound theories and prove that they are correct.

The positivist ideal is a form of justificationism (Lakatos & Musgrave, 1970). Justificationism is the epistemological position that scientific theories can somehow be justified or proved. Implicit in this position is the belief that theory-free observations can prove the validity of scientific theories. As long as the observations are made under sensible conditions, one can be sure that they are infallibly valid and can use them to justify or verify scientific statements.

Unfortunately, neither positivism nor justificationism has fared very well as an epistemological position (see Bechtel, 1988, for an overview of these approaches and the issues). The reasons for this failure are manifold, and space limitations prevent a more complete discussion. They can be summarized by noting that there is no infallibly valid inductive theory that guarantees the correctness of observations or the validity of statements about those observations. Sound deductive logic can transmit truth infallibly from premises to conclusions, but there is no infallible inductive method and no means of guaranteeing the soundness and pertinence of observations. Theories transcend observations in at least three ways, each of which requires a fallible induction: (a) a theory is a universal extension of a finite number of observations; (b) a theory is a precise formulation based on observations accurate only within limits of experimental error; (c) a theory attempts to specify the mechanism underlying observed phenomena, but the phenomena are not those mechanisms. Ultimately, theories depend on the semantic interpretation of the concepts used in the theory and there can be no simple correspondence between finite observations and the concepts of a the theory (see Suppe, 1989).

Although many investigators hold implicitly to the positivist ideal, as a description of the scientific enterprise it is more science fiction than science fact (e.g., see Lakatos & Musgrave, 1970). Science does not proceed by the hypothetico-deductive method, but by fits, starts, and reorganization. Criticism is the engine that drives scientific progress (see Roitblat, 1982). It is naive to believe that fundamental questions about the nature of such phenomena as language can be settled once and for all, even by distinguished scientists. The point of this discussion for present purposes is that it is probably mistaken to expect that any particular research program will be able to settle with finality the issues in animal language research. The implication that the programs fail because they do not provide irrefutable data is to demand a standard of rigor that is unachievable in any area of science. It is in the nature of science that experiments are subject to interpretation and that the interpretations must be arguable. Methodology is far easier to criticize than to perform. Interdisciplinary collaboration is essential to make the best use of the critical and research skills available.

1. Cognitive processing in artificial language

Reductionism

Our biological perspective leads us to reject one approach to understanding the competencies of animals that can be called nothing-but-ism. In this approach, the competencies of an animal are dismissed as *nothing but* the operation of such factors as temporal or conditional discrimination. The approach seeks to reduce phenomena of animal language to allegedly simpler phenomena.

We avoid such reductionistic approaches for two reasons. First, the mere fact that one can describe some performance in terms used for simpler phenomena is not the same as explaining the phenomenon in terms of those processes. All learning can be described, for example, as changes in response tendencies in particular situations. This description does not imply that learning *is* the connection of response tendencies with situations. Learning, even as studied in the laboratory, consists of processes with a great deal more complexity than the formation of S-R (stimulus-response) connections (see Roitblat, 1987).

In understanding one phenomenon scientists often attempt to reduce it to simpler phenomena. For example, we may seek to explain the language-like competencies of animals as nothing but the result of conditional discriminations. This analysis implies that conditional discriminations are adequate to explain the phenomenon, are well understood, and are simple, at least relative to the phenomena we wish to reduce. None of these assumptions is necessarily true, and the mere fact that the candidate phenomenon for reduction can be studied in less intelligent or less complex (note the biological irony) organisms than chimpanzees or dolphins fails to imply that the relation is a reduction (see Churchland, 1986, for a discussion of reductionism).

Second, human linguistic processes are not themselves ineffable. Human competence is the result of the operation of biological mechanisms. Human performance may be intelligent, but the mechanisms themselves need not be. Somehow humans compile "intelligent" linguistic behavior out of nothing but "stupid" biological mechanisms. Animals may or may not employ the same mechanisms that humans use, but it would be misleading to dismiss these phenomena as unimportant when they can be attributed to "nothing but" the mechanisms that instantiate it. We want to know how animals perform their tasks. Linguistic competence remains linguistic competence even if we do understand the mechanisms that produce it. Psychologists often erroneously reject as not psychological any phenomenon that they can actually understand in terms of the mechanisms that produce it.

Resemblance

Finally, the last major factor we wish to highlight concerns resemblance. Critics and proponents of the progress in animal language research have often argued about the resemblance between animals' capacities versus those of human language users. There is no unambiguous way to decide how similar two phenomena must be before they can be said to resemble one another. One person might say, "That woman over there looks just like Meryl Streep," to which a second person might reply, "No her lips are broader, her hair is shorter, and her eyes are larger." Finally, the first person might reply, "Yes, but she looks just like Meryl Streep." Both conversants know that they are not looking at Meryl Streep, but rather at someone who resembles her. We cannot definitively decide which of these conversants is correct. A simple yes or no answer, even if we could establish some criterion by which to provide an answer, would be inadequate. This is not just scientific waffling, but is a fundamental issue. Animal language (or whatever animals in animal language projects have) is not adult human language, and may never be, but opinions about its resemblance to adult human language are fundamentally and forever just opinions. We think that such yes/no questions about the existence or nature of language are best avoided.

THE VALUE OF ANIMAL LANGUAGE RESEARCH

Evolutionary Questions

We consider animal language research to be well worth pursuing. These phenomena contribute to our understanding of such issues as the evolution of linguistic competencies (Roitblat, 1987). There are two ways one can study evolution. One way is to examine the fossil record for evidence of change and for the presence of the features in which one is interested. Although some concomitants of linguistic competence can be found in the fossil record (e.g., Marshack, 1984), language itself leaves no record. The other way to investigate the evolution of a capacity is to examine the distribution of these features in current living species. Although no current species is truly ancestral to any other living species, much can be learned by assuming (tentatively) that common features in two species are the result of their presence in a common ancestor. This assumption must be tentative because evolution is a continuing process and because environmental demands often support convergent evolution.

1. Cognitive processing in artificial language

Examination of communalities among species has the added benefit of forcing us to view human language as an example of possibly several alternative systems. One difficulty with studying language in humans is that our familiarity with our own language makes it difficult to avoid glossing over problematic areas and makes it easy to miss hidden assumptions. For example, Braine (1976) has noted that many researchers concerned with language development in children have presupposed the presence of adult linguistic categories such as verb and adjective. These categories are so salient to adult language users that it takes special effort to gain the perspective necessary to see that it might be otherwise, for example, that children may use "grammatical" categories that are described for each lexical item separately, and only later induce abstract class categories for the representation of these rules (see Maratsos, 1988).

Perspectives and Detachment

Research on animals is useful because it encourages us to view cognitive problems with greater detachment and allows us to avoid the seduction of hidden assumptions. We can attempt explanations with greater parsimony because we have no a priori reason to believe that animals must solve their problems in the same way we solve ours. Animal research, in short, allows us to be critical in ways that are difficult when dealing with our fellow human beings. This criticism comes at a cost, however. The cost is being too ready to dismiss examples of complex cognitive functioning in animals as the result of processes that are viewed as simpler. Morgan's (1894) canon enjoined psychologists from seeking complex explanations of an animal's behavior as long as mechanisms lower in psychological scale were adequate. On the other hand, Marshall (1971) noted that if we apply the same standards to human language that we apply to animal language, we would find that humans do not talk either! There is thus a slippery path to tread between abject parsimony and flaky entelechy. It is too easy to find "stupid" explanations for phenomena that may be produced by very sophisticated mechanisms (see Roitblat & Herman, 1988). Parsimony cannot be abandoned, but neither should it be applied willy-nilly. Morgan's canon requires phenomena to be arrayed along a psychological scale so that higher-order phenomena can be replaced by sufficient lower-order phenomena, but such scales have, in fact, been impossible to produce (Hodos & Campbell, 1969). Furthermore, attributing a corpus of behavior to a collection of independent but simple mechanisms may be less parsimonious than attributing the same corpus to a single coherent, though abstract, mechanism. Complex collections of simple mechanisms are not necessarily simpler than a single complex mechanism. Deciding which alternative is simpler requires an adequate theory of the phenomenon and of the alternative mechanisms. The relative simplicity must be considered in light of this theory, because there is no theory-free infallible way to make these decisions. In the following sections of this chapter we offer some suggestions for alternative mechanisms and for their analysis.

SOME GENERAL ISSUES IN COGNITIVE PROCESSING

The language-like systems in which animals have been schooled have tended to consist of strings of tokens or lexical items. The animals either are required to produce these strings or to respond in appropriate ways to strings that are presented to them. We would like to know how the animals process these strings, how they represent the tokens that make up the strings, and how they represent the instructions or intentions that the strings are designed (by the human experimenters) to communicate. In addressing these questions we would also like to know the extent to which the strings do actually communicate, that is, transfer new information.

Animals presumably employ at least implicit rules of some sort in dealing with these strings. Considering the representation of the tokens, the rules that animals employ could be quite direct in the sense that they specify certain specific relations between individual tokens and events or behaviors, or they could be more abstract, in the sense of representing relations among classes of tokens and classes of events. Examples of token-specific rules include such phenomena as classical and instrumental conditioning. For example, an animal could learn that a particular token (e.g., a tone) signals the impending delivery of food, or that a particular action performed in the presence of another token leads to a desirable outcome (see Roitblat, 1987, for a discussion of the representations used in classical and instrumental conditioning). Examples of abstract rules (i.e., rules concerning abstract categories) include the kinds of grammatical rules that relate sentence structure to noun-phrases and verb-phrases, where the type "noun-phrase" can stand for a wide variety of possible instantiating noun-phrases. Obviously, the difference between token-specific and abstract rules is not a dichotomy, but a matter of degree. We would like to know under what conditions and to what extent animals employ abstract representations. There is considerable evidence, in fact, that animals do employ relatively abstract representations even in situations outside of artificial language experiments (Bever, 1984; Roitblat, 1988). In the next section we return to the issue of how tokens are represented.

Just as tokens can be represented in different ways, so too can strings of tokens be represented differently. Most of the studies on animal language have employed some type of syntax that employs word order as a significant

1. Cognitive processing in artificial language

component. For example, a dolphin is expected (trained) to respond differently to tokens in different orders such as FRISBEE SURFBOARD FETCH and SURFBOARD FRISBEE FETCH (Herman, Richards, & Wolz, 1984). These two strings contain exactly the same tokens, but they are apparently represented differently by the animal because they lead to different patterns of responding. In the first case the animal takes the surfboard to the Frisbee, and in the second, it takes the Frisbee to the surfboard. We would like to know to what extent and how abstractly the animal represents these strings so that it can respond differentially to them. The strings could be processed and represented in a strictly token-by-token linear fashion (e.g., a chain or finite-state grammar), as wholistic entities (e.g., holophrases), or they could be represented as examples of more complex patterns (e.g., phrase structures of different complexities). We return to the question of how strings are represented later.

MEANING AND REFERENCE

Semantics is central to human language. As a result, one of the central questions in animal language programs is the semantic status of the tokens or lexemes of the animal's artificial language. We do not view this question as an all-or-none issue: Do animals' symbols carry semantic content. Rather we see the problem as one of identifying the degree to which the tokens carry semantic content, or the kind of meaning they carry. We can identify at least four semantic grades that a token may occupy. A token may *elicit* a particular action; it may *occasion* a particular action; it may *refer* to specific items or events; or it may *mean*.

The tokens or lexemes of an animal's artificial language are intended by the experimenters to be symbols for objects, actions, relations, and so forth. In some sense the tokens in an animal's artificial language stand for (represent) something, but there are several different kinds of things those tokens can represent. At the simplest level, a token could simply elicit a certain kind of action the way an unconditioned stimulus in classical conditioning elicits an unconditioned response. At this level the token need not represent anything for the animal; rather, the activity is biologically and relatively inflexibly tied to the stimulus in a more-or less mechanical fashion.

At the next level, the token may stand for a particular kind of action. The token acts as a cue or an occasion on which the animal performs a certain action. The representation of action has its own difficulties (see Roitblat, 1988), but these difficulties are largely separable from those concerning the representational status of artificial language tokens. It is significant, however, to note that animals seem to represent their own behaviors at different levels of abstraction; a simple stimulus-response kind of mechanism is inadequate even to describe relatively simple behaviors (e.g., phenomena such as behavioral contrast are resistant to stimulus-response analyses, as is maze running).

At the level of occasioning, the tokens do not represent the performance of an action; rather, they signal the occasion on which the action is to be performed. This level implies a relatively fixed relation between the token and the behavior, but one not as fixed as tokens at the elicitation level. The animal typically must learn that a particular token occasions a particular action, so in this sense the relation between token and action is flexible, but once learned, the token stands for a specific action in a more or less constrained context. The representation is assumed to be relatively impoverished (it is not, for example, a description of the behavior) and of limited scope and flexibility.

At the third grade, a token could be used referentially. The key difference between this level and the previous is one is that a referential token is used as a flexible representation of the item or action. It can play a number of roles in a variety of contexts. A characteristic of referential use of a lexeme includes the ability to use the lexeme to express or comprehend an arbitrary variety of statable relations. A referential lexeme can be used to request an item, to report on its location, to describe it, etc. For example, Lana learned to use lexemes in order to request specific items, but then had to be specially trained to respond to questions about the names of the items she requested (Rumbaugh & Gill, 1977). Following this initial training, however, Lana was able to generalize this naming skill to other lexemes and other items, suggesting that she had learned to broaden the denotative scope of her lexemes.

The concept of "reference" is used in several different ways in linguistics. For example, we can refer to an apple, denoting thereby something like an example of the category of apples (see Lakoff, 1987), we can refer to the apple as a particular example of the apple category (e.g., "the apples from Washington are particularly good at this time of year"), or we can refer to that apple as a spatiotemporally localized example of an apple. On the standard view (e.g., Strawson, 1959), a token refers when it allows one to pick out, select, or distinguish an item or class of items from a set of alternatives. This view implies that communication is an essential part of reference. In fact, Strawson (1950/1971) argued that referring is something that people do, not utterances. An utterance refers just in case it allows the hearer to disambiguate or select an item from a set of alternative items. An utterance refers, in other words, precisely when it communicates.

1. Cognitive processing in artificial language

At the fourth level, the animal's lexemes not only communicate, they have meaning. In the classic view the meaning of a term is the set of objects to which it refers; reference and meaning are synonymous (e.g., Russell, 1903). This association between meaning and reference is untenable (see Lakoff, 1987, and Martinich, 1984; for thorough reviews of this issue). For this conceptualization of meaning to be sensible, every meaningful token would have to refer to an object that existed. That object would, of necessity, have to be specified with some degree of precision, but in addition, any word that referred to a nonexistent object would have to be meaningless. One classic conundrum revolves around statements such as "The golden mountain does not exist." If the golden mountain really does not exist, then the statement about the nonexistent object cannot refer to anything and so must be meaningless. A second classic conundrum involves deciding the referent of meaningful words, such as the words in this very sentence, including "conundrum," "involves," "deciding," "meaningful," etc. These words have no referent, but they seem to have meaning nevertheless.

The classic view that meaning and reference are identical is derived from a *correspondence* theory of meaning. This correspondence theory is the same one that underlies the so-called positivist ideal dismissed earlier. In general, the idea is that the meaning of a term, whether it is a scientific concept in search of justification or a term in natural language in search of meaning corresponds to a certain ostensive or operational state of affairs. The meaning is taken to be identical to the ostensive or operational situation. Meaning, like theories, must transcend these specifics, however. For example, an operational definition defines a concept by the operations used to measure it. The standard example is that intelligence *is* that which is measured by intelligence tests. Operational definitions, although useful, are incomplete, precisely because there is no way to combine multiple operational definitions for the same concept. In terms of operational definitions, two intelligence tests provide two different incommensurable meanings to the concept of intelligence--two operations, two definitions, two meanings. If we believe that two operations can converge on the same concept we must believe that the meaning of the concept is deeper than the specific operations. The meaning of the concept must be different from the operations that define it if two sets of operations are to address the same meaning.

Pinning down the nature of meaning may not be critical to our analysis of animal language, because no animal, so far as we are aware, has yet approached this semantic grade. For present purposes it is sufficient to note that meaning and reference are not identical and that future work may be needed to address this issue.

SYNTAX

Finite-State Grammar

The grammar of a language, whether natural or artificial, is the set of rules that govern its production and its comprehension. A language's grammar includes rules for the semantics of the symbols and for their arangement. An organism could represent its rules in a number of different ways, and psycholinguists have sought to discover the ways in which individuals represent the rules of their language. One of the key dimensions along which grammars can be organized concerns the abstractness of the rule categories contained in the grammar. A language or language-like system can be represented in terms of rules that specify the relations among specific lexical items or among classes of constituents (including lexical items among others) arranged in hierarchies of increasing abstractness and complexity (see, e.g., Pinker, 1979; for a related discussion concerning a hierarchy of human grammars).

Some early models of grammar attempted to describe language use in terms of a finite-state grammar. Token strings in a finite-state grammar are produced or interpreted in a strict left to right order. For example, the sentence "The boy asked the pretty girl for a . . ." would be more likely to continue with the word "date" than with the word "serendipity." The words selected early in the sentence constrain the appropriate choice of words later in the sentence. These constraints raise the possibility that sentences could be understood and represented in a similar left-right manner, in which the choice of each successive word is constrained by the previously selected word. In the simplest form of this kind of grammar, the rule base consists of descriptions of how one token leads to another. The production of token A, for example can be followed by either the production of token B (with some probability), the production of the token C, or a repeat of token A. In general, a finite-state grammar consists of a specification of a set of states, rules for traversing from one state to another, and rules for producing symbols given each state or each transition (see for example, Miller, 1958; Reber, 1967; Servan-Schreiber & Anderson, 1990).

Humans are sensitive to such finite-state systems. Miller (1958) asked human subjects to learn seven serially presented strings of nine items or fewer. For one group the strings were produced according to a finite-state grammar.

1. Cognitive processing in artificial language

For another group the strings were randomly produced from the same set of elements. Strings were better recalled by the group that received grammatically produced strings. The only difference between the two sets of strings was presumably the redundancy introduced by using the grammar to produce the items in the list. The subjects' ability to take advantage of this redundancy implies that they were sensitive to this kind of grammar and could use its redundancy to simplify or schematize their representations of the strings. This is not to say that the subjects could articulate the rules that produced the strings, only that they were capable of using the rule information implicitly. In fact, attempting to articulate the rules while learning structured strings may actually interfere with acquisition of the appropriate rules (Reber, 1967; see also Reber, Kassin, Lewis, & Cantor, 1980).

Because humans are capable of taking advantage of the organization provided by a finite-state rule system, their grammatical capacity must be at least as powerful as a finite-state grammar. So far as we are aware, no animal projects have explicitly investigated whether their animals are similarly sensitive to rule-based versus non-rule-based strings. The only such studies of which we are aware, compared very simple rules with more complex rule-governed sequences. Serial anticipation experiments, for example, require rats to run down a straight alleyway for differing amounts of food reward. Under some conditions rats learn to run quickly in anticipation of large rewards and to run slowly in anticipation of small or no rewards. The ease of anticipating the small rewards depends on the complexity of the sequence. Monotonic sequences are generally easy to learn, whereas nonmonotonic sequences are generally difficult to learn. When the animal is repeatedly trained with the sequence 14 - 7 - 3 - 1 - 0 or 0 - 1 - 3 - 7 - 14, in which each number indicates the number of food pellets waiting at the end of a run, then the animal learns easily to run slowly in anticipation of the 0-pellet element and more quickly in anticipation of the other elements (Hulse & Campbell, 1975). In contrast, rats trained with random sequences that either began or ended reliably with the 0-pellet elements did not learn (i.e., the rat did not slow down in anticipation of the 0-pellet element). Furthermore, the rats were better at anticipating the terminal 0-pellet element when it followed a monotonically decreasing sequence than when it followed a regular reliable nonmonotonic sequence, 14-1-3-7-0 (Hulse & Dorsky, 1977). Both the monotonic and the nonmonotonic sequences could be described by extremely simple finite-state grammars, yet the rats were better at learning the monotonic sequence with its simpler "grammar" than the grammatically more complex nonmonotonic sequence. The monotonic sequence is simpler only if the rat can be sensitive to the abstract relation between successive elements that each succeeding element is smaller than the preceding element until 0 is reached. By changing from a rule based on the elements to a rule based on abstract quantities the theory loses parsimony in terms of the elements presumed to be represented, but gains parsimony in the simplicity of the rules.

These experiments show that rats are capable of learning some abstract rules. Tasks that are easier to represent in terms of these abstract rules are easier for the rats learn. In fact, there is evidence that the rats employ even more abstract representations of this task. On some probe trials one element in the monotonic sequence was replaced by a 0-pellet element. If the rat were employing a finite-state rule then when the animal reached the 0-pellet element it should reset the sequence to begin again with the 14-pellet element or should be otherwise disrupted. Instead, rats seem not to be affected by these probe replacements. They continue to perform the remainder of the sequence as if they had received the correct number of food pellets on the probe trial. The rats clearly use more than the immediately preceding element to anticipate the following element in the sequence (Roitblat, Pologe, & Scopatz, 1983).

Even rats appear to show some capability of using representations that are more than the mere chaining of elements and that take advantage of the underlying rule structure of their experience. It would be an interesting research question to investigate the extent to which language-trained animals can take advantage of the underlying structure of events and use information in finite-state or more complicated rule systems.

Slot and frame grammar

Another kind of grammar that animals could employ is a so-called slot and frame grammar. Utterances in a slot and frame grammar are organized around certain formulaic patterns. Children typically learn many whole, at first unanalyzed phrases (Dore, Franklin, Miller, & Ramer, 1976; MacWhinney, 1982), which they later segment into words and organize into structural patterns in the form of frames with fillable slots (Peters, 1986). The child can memorize sets of phrases such as all gone, all clean, all done, all dressed. Braine (1976) noted that his subject Andrew learned 12 such phrases with *all* in the first position. He called this a positional associative pattern. The child then organizes these separate frames into a schema of all + x. Longer frames with more replaceable elements are also used.

As the length of utterances increases and as the number of lexical items increases, the child may need some simplifying mechanism to reduce the

1. Cognitive processing in artificial language

memory load. Linguistic organization may be a product of limitations on cognitive processing. At some point it becomes less burdensome to extract abstract hierarchical classifications for utterances than to keep track of individual utterance types. When the child has collected some critical number of limited scope patterns for combining words she will integrate them into a smaller, more manageable number of patterns (Peters, 1986). Vertical integration (Ewing, 1982) occurs when the child integrates limited patterns such as big/little + X and hot + X into a more abstract pattern PROPERTY + X. Horizontal integration occurs when two patterns are combined into one longer pattern, for example, big/little + X and see + X into see big/little + X.

Thompson and Church (1980) identified a set of six frames (they called them stock sentences) in the productions of the chimpanzee Lana:

1. Please machine give <*incentive*>.

2. Please <*name*> <give | move into room><*incentive*>.

3. Please <*name*> <move behind room | put in machine><*incentive*>.

4. Please Lana <want eat | want drink><*incentive*>.

5. Please <*name*><tickle | groom | swing | carry out of room> Lana.

6. Please machine make <*event*>.

Lana produced her utterances by pressing keys on a Yerkish keyboard. Thompson and Church argued that in one context, without a human present, 91% of Lana's utterances were consistent with one of these six frames and only 1% were correct productions of nonstock sentence frames. When a human was present, 66% of her utterances were still consistent with one of these sentence frames and 14% were correct utterances that were not consistent with these frames. The remaining utterances in the corpus were judged to be errors. Subsequent analysis of a later corpus of Lana's utterances (Pate & Rumbaugh, 1983) suggests that Lana was not ultimately limited to these stock frames, but analysis of this argument remains instructive.

First, all of the stock phrases consist of requests. The high percentage of requests suggested to Thompson and Church (1980) that the task was largely an instrumental reinforcement situation in which a chain of elements had to be produced in order to receive some reward (see also Seidenberg & Petitto, 1987).

Second, the stock frames consist of constant and variable elements. The most obvious constant element is the substring *Please machine*, and the most obvious variable element is the incentive that Lana is requesting. Thompson and Church argued that the relationship between the incentive and the lexigram selected was determined by paired associate learning between the lexigram and the incentive, and the sentence frame was determined by situational cues. This latter determination requires some additional explication. Whereas it is true, that the situational cues determined the sentence frame that Lana employed, the relationship between the supposed situational cues and the particulars of the frame is more complex than Thompson and Church implied. For example, utterances that were inconsistent with the current situation were not rewarded. Furthermore, virtually no other legal sentences were possible with the set of lexical items they analyzed. Other lexigrams were apparently available to Lana, but these appear to have been used only rarely in the corpus. One appropriate conclusion from this analysis is that the situation and the set of functionally available lexical items constrained the set of utterances to focus on requests for food (first) and other rewards (second), and the rules of the system constrained the range of possible sequences. It should be noted that many utterances were consistent with the same situation. Thompson and Church simply selected among the alternative consistent utterances at random. Because they do not report the relative frequency of each of the alternative utterances or the probabilities attached to each frame by their computer simulation, it is unclear whether selecting at random (with unknown probability) is reasonable. Third, an instrumental account fails to specify why the animal should use alternative synonymous utterances. Frames 2, 3, and 4 are each appropriate in the same situations. Frame 4 would appear to provide the least cognitive load, because it contains the fewest variables (eat vs. drink and the desired incentive). It should therefore be preferred on an instrumental account over its competitors.

Finally, recordings of utterances in any constrained situation of finite duration can always be described in terms of some limited number of frames, especially when the frames can vary in the number of options they contain. For example, it may be equally valid to separate the frames into nine categories by breaking frames 2, 3, and 4 into two frames each on the basis of the type of the request (e.g., give vs. move into room). In the absence of relative frequency information (concerning finer-grained categorizations of utterances) and in the absence of information about the range of possible acceptable utterances, it is difficult to assess the appropriateness of the claim that Lana used a slot and frame grammar, because it is difficult to know what data might have been inconsistent with such an analysis.

1. Cognitive processing in artificial language

Despite these caveats, the slot and frame analysis may actually be the most appropriate for explanation of this corpus of Lana's utterances. The frames constrained the range of possibilities of the variable elements, but the choice of some variable elements constrained the choice of other variable elements. For example, there are variable foods, such as apple, banana, and cabbage, that always are preceded by a lexigram for PIECE OF as opposed to unit foods, such as M&M, nuts, and raisins, that do not take the PIECE-OF lexigram. With foods, Lana was required to use the WANT EAT lexigrams, but with liquids she was required to use the WANT DRINK lexigrams. Because the lexigram for the incentive is entered last in each of the frames in which food and drink were incentives, the incentive the animal would later select determined the choice of the earlier-selected action symbol, or she simply selected an incentive from the set available that was consistent with the action symbol already chosen and with the situation. The mutual constraint among the incentive and other lexical units in the utterance makes implausible the idea that Lana simply selected a sentence frame at random from those that were consistent with the situation. The production of a legal utterance required internal consistency as well as situational relevance. For example, assuming that both a food and a drink were available, Lana had to select the correct frame and the correct slot-fillers in that frame to be internally consistent from the request to the specification of the incentive. No random rule could have produced 91% correct utterances without this kind of consistency information.

Thompson and Church's (1980) analysis appears to suggest that Lana's rules were specified with regard to the lexical items themselves. They argued that she memorized certain strings of lexigrams and that these strings included positions that could be filled with one of several alternative substrings of lexigrams. Their analysis would also seem to imply that Lana was capable of at least a limited kind of slot and frame grammar. In contrast, Premack (1986) and later Schusterman and Gisiner (1988) argues that dolphins employ a slot and frame grammar with rules specified relative to classes of lexemes. Their analysis apparently presupposes the kind of vertical integration (Ewing, 1982) that allows the individual to abstract categories from specific examples. In their analysis, the strings that were "understood" (i.e., to which the dolphin Ake responded correctly) could be described.

PRAGMATICS

Several investigators have been struck by the instrumental function of most animal communication (e.g., Thompson & Church, 1980; Seidenberg & Petitto, 1988). Most of the "sentences" investigated in the animal language projects have tended to be requests. In contrast to this focus on the instrumental use of language (i.e., to induce some work on the part of the receiver), adult human language has many more functions than just obtaining incentives. For example, adult humans are capable of commenting on features and events of the world around them. This focus on instrumental use of language may reflect pragmatic differences between human conversation and animal language studies, or it may be an indication that animal language is nothing but a chain of behavior that animals must emit in order to receive rewards.

In response to the instrumental criticism, several studies have attempted to divorce the receipt of reinforcers from the communicative function of the language system. For example, dolphins have been trained to answer questions about the objects in their environment (Herman & Forestell, 1985). Objects were shown to the dolphin and placed in her tank. She was then presented with a sequence of signs that could be glossed as BALL QUESTION. The dolphin was then rewarded for responding to one paddle if the ball were present in the tank and to another paddle if the ball were absent. Although this procedure also yielded reinforcement, and could be conceived as another instrumental task, the important point for present purposes is that the animal could respond to the sign for ball in a different way if it appeared in the question string than if it appeared in a command string. It is no longer sensible to argue that the sign for ball is the occasion on which to approach balls and that the animal does so because it has been rewarded in the past for doing so. In fact, the animal can respond to question strings containing signs for objects that are familiar to the animal in the command context but had never before been used in a question string, indicating that the rules that govern the animal's performance concern entities more abstract than the particular objects and the particular signs (see earlier discussion).

Although adult humans employ language in many more ways than merely as instrumental means to reinforcement, the instrumental role is a very important use of language. The fact that animals use language primarily in an instrumental mode need not imply anything strong about their capacity to use language. Individuals tend to discuss material in which they are interested, and the nature of the training situations ensures that one of the animals' primary interests is in obtaining food or other rewards. Because obtaining rewards is one of animals' most important interests, it hardly seems surprising that their linguistic activity concerns rewards. Finally, we already know that animals do not "talk" naturally (i.e., if left to themselves), therefore, it is not surprising that it takes special effort for them to communicate.

1. Cognitive processing in artificial language

Another pragmatic factor that may limit animals' abilities to demonstrate their language competencies is the redundancy that is present in most human languages, but absent from the artificial languages in which animals are schooled. English, for example, contains articles that aid in the identification of sentence parts. If the same markers were used in animal language, there would be a tendency to attribute performance to the discriminative properties of the markers (e.g., Lana's original Yerkish keyboard coded semantic categories by the color of the key). We do not know how important these markers are in the acquisition of natural human languages. Although these markers may not be necessary to language acquisition, their widespread presence in human languages suggests that they play some important role.

CONCLUSION

We have argued that all-or-none questions about the existence of language in animals are ill formed and of little heuristic value. These questions inevitably devolve into arguments analogous to that over whether the glass is half full or half empty. We find it much more interesting to enquire into the linguistic skills that animals have or have not generated and the degree to which these have been developed. To be sure, such questions require a theory of linguistic skills. Although there is no single theory that receives widespread support, we have offered some suggestions toward the development of such a theory, for example, by considering grammars written on items of varying levels of abstraction or with different computational power.

Although it is reasonably clear that no animal has yet demonstrated linguistic skills comparable to those of an adult human, their skills may be more fruitfully compared with those of a 2- to 3-year-old child. Although it would be at best premature to say that chimpanzee or dolphin language skills are identical to those of a young child, the methods used for studying language in young children are also useful for the investigation of language in animals.

Many questions remain for investigation. Addressing these questions will provide valuable information for understanding language in general and animals in particular. Grappling with such issues as the degree to which an animal shows evidence of using symbols referentially or the power of its grammar helps us to gain perspective on such issues as reference and grammar from a more distant and perhaps more objective perspective. This perspective can only help in understanding the nature of our own cognitive processes.

REFERENCES

Bechtel, W. (1988). *Philosophy of science. An overview for cognitive science.* Hillsdale, NJ: Lawrence Erlbaum Associates.

Bever, T. G. (1984). The road from behaviorism to rationalism. In H. L. Roitblat, T. G. Bever, & H. S. Terrace (Eds.), *Animal cognition* (pp. 61-75). Hillsdale, NJ: Lawrence Erlbaum Associates.

Braine, M. D. S. (1976). Children's first word combinations. *Monographs of the Society for Research in Child Development,* 41(1).

Churchland, P. S. (1986). *Neurophilosophy.* Cambridge, MA: MIT Press.

Dore, J., Franklin, M., Miller, R., & Ramer, A. (1976). Transitional phenomena in early language acquisition. *Journal of Child Language,* 1, 205-219.

Ewing, G. (1982). Word order invariance and variability in five children's three-word utterances: A limited-scope formula analysis. In C. E. Johnson & C. L. Thew (Eds.), *Proceedings of the Second International Congress for the Study of Child Language,* Washington, DC: University Press of America.

Herman, L. M. & Forestell, P. H. (1985). Reporting presence or absence of named objects by a language-trained dolphin. *Neuroscience and Biobehavioral Reviews,* 9, 667-681.

Herman, L. M., Richards, D. G., & Wolz, J. P. (1984). Comprehension of sentences by bottlenosed dolphins. *Cognition,* 16, 129-219.

Hodos, W. & Campbell, C. B. G. (1969). Scala naturae: Why there is no theory in comparative psychology. *Psychological Review,* 76, 337-350.

Hulse, S. H. & Campbell, C. E. (1975). "Thinking ahead" in rat discrimination learning. *Animal Learning and Behavior,* 3, 305-311.

Hulse, S. H., & Dorsky, N. P. (1977). Structured complexity as a determinant of serial pattern learning. *Learning and Motivation,* 8, 488-506.

1. Cognitive processing in artificial language

Lakatos, I. & Musgrave, A. (1970). *Criticism and the growth of knowledge.* New York: Cambridge University Press.

Lakoff, G. (1987). *Women, fire and dangerous things: What categories reveal about the mind.* Chicago: University of Chicago Press.

Maratsos, M. (1988). The acquisition of formal word classes. In Y. Levy, I. M. Schlesinger, & M. D. S. Braine (Eds.), *Categories and processes in language acquisition* (pp. 31-44). Hillsdale, NJ: Lawrence Erlbaum Associates.

MacWhinney, B. (1982). Basic processes in syntactic acquisition. In S. A. Kuczaj, II (Ed.), *Language development,* vol. 1. Hillsdale, NJ: Lawrence Erlbaum Associates.

Marshack, A. (1984). The ecology and brain of two-handed bipedalism: An analytic, cognitive, and evolutionary assessment. In H. L. Roitblat, T. G. Bever, & H. S. Terrace (Eds.), *Animal Cognition* (pp. 491-511). Hillsdale, NJ: Lawrence Erlbaum Associates.

Marshall, J. C. (1971). Can humans talk? In J. Morton (Ed.) *Biological and social factors in linguistics* (pp. 24-52). London: Logos.

Martinich, A. P. (1984). *Communication and reference.* New York: Walter de Gruyter.

Miller, G. A. (1958). Free recall of redundant strings of letters. *Journal of Experimental Psychology,* 56, 485-491.

Morgan, C. L. (1894). *An introduction to comparative psychology,* London: Walter Scott.

Pate, J. L. & Rumbaugh, D. M. (1983). The language-like behavior of Lana chimpanzee: Is it merely discrimination and paired associate learning? *Animal Learning and Behavior,* 11, 134-138.

Peters, A. M. (1986). Early syntax. In P. Fletcher & M. Garman (Eds.), *Language acquisition, 2nd Edition* (pp. 307-325). New York: Cambridge University Press.

Pinker, S. (1989). Language acquisition. In M. I. Posner (Ed.), *Foundations of cognitive science* (pp. 359-399). Cambridge, MA: The MIT Press.

Premack, D. (1986). *Gavagai: Or the future history of the animal language controversy.* Cambridge, MA: The MIT Press.

Reber, A. S. (1967). Implicit learning of artificial grammars. *Journal of Verbal Learning and Verbal Behavior,* 6, 855-863.

Reber, A. S., Kassin, S. M., Lewis, S., & Cantor, G. W. (1980). On the relationship between implicit and explicit modes in the learning of a complex rule structure. *Journal of Experimental Psychology: Human Learning and Memory,* 6, 492-502.

Roitblat, H. L. (1982). The meaning of representation in animal memory. *The Behavioral and Brain Sciences,* 5, 353-406.

Roitblat, H. L. (1987). *Introduction to Comparative Cognition.* New York: Freeman.

Roitblat, H. L. (1988). A cognitive action theory of learning. In J. Delacour & J. C. S. Levy (Eds.), *Systems with learning and memory abilities* (pp. 13-26). Amsterdam: North Holland.

Roitblat, H. L. & Herman, L. M. (1988). Animal Thinking: The development and status of research and theory on animal cognition. In D. Topping & D. Crowell (Eds.), *Proceedings of the Third International Conference On Thinking* (pp. 269-290). Hillsdale, NJ: Lawrence Erlbaum Associates.

Roitblat, H. L., Pologe, B. & Scopatz, R. A. (1983). The representation of items in serial position. *Animal Learning and Behavior,* 11, 489-498.

Rumbaugh, D. M. & Gill, T. V. (1977). Lana's acquisition of language skills. In D. M. Rumbaugh, (Ed.), *Language learning by a chimpanzee: The Lana project* (pp. 165-192). New York: Academic Press.

Russell, B. (1903). *The principles of mathematics 2nd ed.* New York: W. W. Norton.

1. Cognitive processing in artificial language

Schusterman, R. J. & Gisiner, R. (1988). Artificial language comprehension in dolphins and sea lions: The essential skills. *The Psychological Record*, 38, 311-348.

Seidenberg, M. & Petitto. L. (1987). Communication, symbolic communication, and language: Comment on Savage-Rumbaugh et al. *Journal of Experimental Psychology: General*, 116, 279-287.

Servan-Schreiber, E. & Anderson, J. R. (1990). Learning artificial grammars with competitive chunking. *Journal of Experimental Psychology: Learning, Memory, and Cognition*, 16, 592-608.

Strawson, P. F. (1950/1971). On referring. In P. F. Strawson *Logico linguistic papers*. London: Methuen.

Strawson, P. F. (1959). *Individuals*. London: Methuen.

Suppe, F. (1989). *The semantic conception of theories and scientific realism*. Urbana, IL: University of Illinois Press.

Thompson, C. R. & Church, R. M. (1980). An explanation of the language of a chimpanzee. *Science*, 208, 313-314.

2 Beyond Animal Language

Gary Bradshaw

At the Hawaii Animal Language Workshop, we were presented with a dazzling array of animals engaged in complex behaviors: chimps who understand spoken language, a parrot that counts, sea lions that comprehend sentences, and dolphins that report on the presence or absence of objects. Yet, the research presented at the workshop is only a subset of recent work in animal language, which offers further remarkable accomplishments by animals.

After encountering such a splendid array of painstakingly nurtured trees, it is easy to lose track of the larger forest. What does it mean when investigators have shown that a chimpanzee can use pronouns, or can count, or reports about abstract relationships? As in all fields of research, the real value lies not in isolated studies but in the larger body of research. The purpose of this chapter is to consider this larger picture. I discuss questions such as, where did so many different experimental methodologies come from, how do they relate to one another, and where is the field heading? My goal is to provide one perspective on this research, and to identify some of the many significant contributions that have been made by animal language investigators. During this process, I describe what seems to be the *driving strategy* for much of this research. The prospects of this strategy is discussed, and an alternative is proposed that avoids many problems inherent in our current strategy.

To begin our exploration of current research, I consider the experimental paradigms that have been developed in animal language research.

2. Beyond animal language

Table 2.1.
Experimental Animal Language Paradigms

Language system	Tasks	Measures
Sign language Keyboards Vocal speech Magnetic chips	Production tasks Sentence production Labeling Counting Object attributes	Production measures MLU Production accuracy Vocabulary assessment Counting accuracy
Animals Chimpanzees Gorillas Orangutans Dolphins Sea Lions Parrots	Tool requesting Reporting Pronoun utilization Comprehension tasks Request comprehension	 Comprehension measures Comprehension errors

Loosely speaking, an experimental paradigm can be understood as a framework that structures and organizes an experimental program (Kuhn, 1970). The paradigm includes a task or set of related tasks, appropriate controls, and a set of behavioral measures. For animal language projects, important features of the paradigm include the type of language system (gestural, vocalic, etc.), training procedures, the type of task that is studied (language production or comprehension), the species of animal subjects, and measures of performance. Table 2.1 presents a number of different alternatives for these components, illustrating the diverse array of activities that have been performed under the umbrella of animal language research.

This diversity of animal language paradigms stands in sharp contrast to other areas of psychological research where only a few paradigms are actively pursued at any given time. Typically many studies are performed using the same paradigm, whereas in animal language research most paradigms have been pursued by a single investigator with one or two subjects. On the surface, exploring a diverse set of paradigms seems like an effective strategy. Researchers can divide up a large goal up into a number of different subtasks, separately pursue each subtask, then synthesize their efforts into a greater whole.

Unfortunately, the complexity of experimental paradigms and the animals we investigate cloud the interpretation of isolated studies. Small changes in the task can result in different strategies on the part of subjects. Subjects with different backgrounds will exploit their unique histories to approach experimental tasks in different ways. Even when investigators replicate one another's research, they often attend to different characteristics of the results, and so reach different conclusions. Thus, the results of a single study are seldom as clear and interpretable as we would like. This situation has led most psychological researchers to a strategy of replication and thorough exploration of a limited number of paradigms.

Sue Savage-Rumbaugh discussed many of the problems of individual studies in her historical account of her explorations of reference in chimpanzees (Savage-Rumbaugh, 1986). After training her two chimps, Sherman and Austin, to request food using the keyboard, a natural conclusion was that the chimpanzees understood their symbols as "words." Upon further investigation, Savage-Rumbaugh discovered that symbol use did not transfer to other tasks, even though the new tasks seemed to be minor variations of the original to human observers. This reflected an unexpected limitation of her initial paradigm. Fortunately, through extensive work with a carefully designed program of related tasks, the chimpanzees were able to overcome many of their initial limitations of word understanding, and closely approximated humans in their symbolic use of words. Without cross-validation, these problems would never have appeared, and our understanding of the factors leading to word reference in animals would have been grievously flawed.

Given the limited utility of isolated studies, the question arises as to why animal language researchers have violated the normal experimental program by developing and exploring a diverse array of experimental paradigms. This diversity leads to difficulties in assembling a coherent picture of research findings. When only a few widely spaced trees have been studied, appreciating the forest is difficult. I next turn to a description of the strategies that animal language researchers have employed to generate experimental questions and paradigms, to understand how the current situation developed.

2. Beyond animal language

THE PATH TO LANGUAGE

Curiously, the diversity of animal language paradigms arises from a common goal: to show that animals can learn a close approximation to human language. This goal was explicitly stated in early papers describing animal language research (Gardner & Gardner, 1974; Terrace, 1980), but recent efforts usually present more restricted ambitions, omitting any mention of the long-term goals driving the research. Nevertheless, it seems clear that most of these research projects are also aimed at the goal of language.

Given that a common goal exists, we might expect that animal language researchers would agree on the most direct way to meet that goal, define an appropriate paradigm, and work feverishly with their animals to meet the defining tests of language competency. To understand the diversity we have observed, it is necessary to consider this goal in greater detail. In particular, I consider the question of what it means to learn a close approximation to human language.

Human language is, among other things, a complex and sophisticated skill. Indeed, language is doubtless the most elaborate skill humans acquire. Language acquisition begins shortly after birth and continues for decades. During school years, children acquire roughly 5000 words per year or about 13 new words per day. The vocabulary of high school graduates averages about 80,000 words, names, and idiomatic expressions (Miller & Gildea, 1987), while exceptional adult vocabularies may include as many as 200,000 words (Just & Carpenter, 1987). The grammars of languages are also remarkably elaborate and detailed. The authoritative description of English grammar, *A Grammar of Contemporary English* (Quirk, Greenbaum, Leech, & Svartvik, 1972), is 972 pages long.

The best demonstration of language competency is to replicate adult language skill in animals. Such a full-scale demonstration will be the ultimate proof that will win over the field's stoutest critics, or at least quiet them. Nevertheless, working only to achieve this competency is not a good idea, and has never been attempted by animal language researchers. There are two serious problems with the full-scale demonstration strategy. The first problem derives from the time required to bring an animal to adult levels of performance. If humans take two decades to master language to this level, can we expect an animal to take any less time? Few researchers and no funding agencies have the necessary patience to bring animals up to adult language abilities before reports are made of the research, tentative conclusions drawn, and so forth.

A second problem with the full-scale demonstration strategy is more serious than the first. The strategy is based on a premise that the only interesting outcome of animal language projects is a complete replication of adult language in animals. Imagine training an animal for 20 years, who comes to understand and produce language with astonishing success. Confident of the animal's linguistic prowess, you arrange for testing by a blue-ribbon panel. During the hours-long grilling, your animal performs well, but makes an occasional mistake. The panel then informs you that the animal failed the test because of improper utilization of the subjunctive clause. The full scale demonstration strategy implies that any deviation from adult skill, no matter how small or inconsequential, results in a negative answer. For these reasons, animal language researchers have wisely pursued a different goal.

As an alternative to full-scale demonstrations, investigators have sought to demonstrate that their animals are on the *path to language*, though they may not yet have reached the lofty heights of adult humans. If animals can be shown to possess the important and central characteristics of language, limitations in vocabulary or grammar can be considered of secondary importance. Presumably these limitations could be overcome by additional practice, so that our animals might someday be ready for full-scale tests.

To carry out this alternative strategy, we must identify important characteristics of language. An immediate obstacle arises because we do not know what language really is: No complete theory of language exists that can be used to identify a comprehensive set of skills and knowledge necessary and sufficient for language. Unwilling to wait until linguists complete their description of language, animal language researchers have turned to psycholinguistics for assistance in identifying important properties of language. The presumption is that demonstrations of similarity between animal and human language behavior counts as evidence that animals are mastering human language.

This background permits us to understand the development of many different animal language paradigms. Different paradigms exist because psycholinguists have established many different characteristics of language behavior. Each of these characteristics can be used as a basis for comparison between animal and human language. Animal language researchers have relied on two popular sources to identify language characteristics: developmental psycholinguistics and comparisons of language and communication. References to the work of Elissa Newport, Lois Bloom, Roger Brown, and Charles Hockett abound in animal language papers. Reports often include psycholinguistic

2. Beyond animal language

measures such as the mean length of utterance for animals (Patterson, 1979; Miles, 1983; Fouts, 1972, etc.) and the developmental "stage" of language development (Gardner & Gardner, 1971, 1974), as well as discussions of linguistic features such as displacement (Herman & Forestell, 1985; Herman, Richards, & Wolz, 1984; Savage-Rumbaugh, Pate, Lawson, Smith, & Rosenbaum, 1983).

Comparing animals and humans on selected attributes is known as the *signature characteristic* approach because the method relies on finding similarities in behaviors that bear the distinctive mark of language.

The signature characteristic strategy leads to an agenda for research where investigators seek to demonstrate as many psycholinguistic characteristics as possible in their animals. The logic of this agenda is straightforward: the more significant properties of language exhibited by our animals, the closer they must be to human language. Unfortunately, even though this is the predominant strategy in contemporary animal language research, it suffers from several important flaws. We now turn to a discussion of these problems.

LIMITATIONS OF THE SIGNATURE CHARACTERISTIC STRATEGY

Three major problems with the signature characteristic strategy are: (a) signature characteristics need to be continually revised to reflect new developments in language and communication; (b) signature characteristics are necessary but not sufficient for language; and (c) measurements of these characteristics are often simple indices that indirectly reflect complex behaviors in people but not necessarily in animals. I discuss each of these limitations in turn.

Signature Characteristics are Subject to Revision

Signature characteristics are developed as a way to summarize important features of language and to contrast them with other systems. Characteristics are necessarily no better than our understanding of psycholinguistics. As research in linguistics and psychology proceeds, our understanding improves, and signature characteristics must be updated. Research performed on an early set of characteristics loses its relevance when formerly important characteristics are discarded.

The most obvious example of this problem concerns Hockett's (1958, 1960) criteria for language. Hockett identified 16 characteristics of language behavior, such as *displacement* (the ability to refer to objects remote in space and time) and *productivity* (the set of messages is vast and open-ended), that he felt could be used to discriminate language from other types of animal communication. Since that time, developments in several fields have undermined his analysis. Hockett proposed a set of *discriminative* characteristics to distinguish language from animal communication. These characteristics depend not only on our understanding of language, but also on our understanding of animal communication. Since Hockett proposed his criteria, both fields have continued to develop. Several attempts have been made to salvage these criteria through revisions. Altmann (1967) proposed some variations on these criteria, then Hockett and Altmann (1968) joined forces for a major revision. Later, Ristau and Robbins (1982) modified the list. Related sets of criteria were proposed by Brown (1973), Limber (1977), and by Chomsky (1979).

In spite of these revisions, the criteria are once again out of date. Research by Seyfarth and Cheney (this volume, chapter 10; Seyfarth, Cheney, & Marler, 1980) and others has shown that characteristics long thought to be rare in animal communication are quite common. Linguistic analyses of grammar (Sells, 1985) have also been extended so that a set of distinctive criteria identified today would look quite different from those proposed only a few years ago.

Other signature characteristics of language, such as the stages of language development identified by Roger Brown (1973), have also been revised in the light of further evidence (see Bates, Bretherton, & Snyder, 1988). Children do not all follow the same developmental sequence in language acquisition, a fact not easily appreciated from the small number of children initially studied by Brown.

Revisions of signature characteristics will continue until our understanding of language is complete. The difficulty of duplicating a system that has not been fully described again hinders our efforts (see also Savage-Rumbaugh, 1986, this volume, chapter 22). Under the circumstances, researchers who spend years of effort to replicate signature characteristics of language in animals are likely to find that linguists and psycholinguists remain unimpressed because the abilities demonstrated are no longer considered important or central to language.

2. Beyond animal language

Signature Characteristics are Necessary but not Sufficient for Language

Psycholinguists and animal language researchers utilize signature characteristics for different purposes. Psycholinguists use signature characteristics for descriptive functions: How can complex linguistic phenomena be concisely summarized? For this purpose, a partial description is much better than none at all. Psycholinguists are content to work with characteristics that seem necessary without claims that the features they identify are sufficient. Indeed establishing necessity is taxing enough.

Animal language researchers, on the other hand, would like sets of signature characteristics to be both necessary and sufficient for language. If this were true, these characteristics could be treated as a checklist. When an animal had mastered all of the necessary items, it would be judged to have language. Unfortunately, there is good evidence that most sets of signature characteristics are far from complete. Again we turn to Hockett for the simplest example.

Hockett's criteria are intended to discriminate animal communication from language. Unfortunately, a communication system that met all of Hockett's criteria would not necessarily qualify as a language. Consider computer programming languages that have been developed in the past two decades. No linguist would certify any of these systems as a true language. One important difference between the two is that computer languages are not nearly as complex as natural languages. Yet computer languages meet all of the criteria for language proposed by Hockett. Passing the Hockett suite of tests is necessary for language, but not sufficient.

Signature characteristics drawn from the developmental literature have a similar problem. An animal that exhibits all known characteristics of a 3-year-old cannot be said to have adult language any more than a 3-year-old can. This qualification should not be taken as a statement that parallels in development between animals and children are uninteresting: All I propose is that these parallels do not count as strong evidence for adult language competency.

Measurements of Signature Characteristics are Specialized to Humans

The final problem with the signature characteristic strategy arises from the methods that psycholinguists use to measure these characteristics. Strong pressure exists to simplify measurements, so data coding can be done quickly and easily. Simplicity cannot be obtained at the expense of validity, however. The measure must reflect the intended characteristic. A simple and frequent compromise is to use *indirect* measures: characteristics that are simple to extract and are correlated with the true factors of interest.

Roger Brown proposed one of the best-known indirect measures in psycholinguistics: the *mean length of utterance (MLU)*, obtained by finding the average number of morphemes present in 100 utterances. The MLU was proposed as an indirect index of grammatical development. Brown noted that MLU increases for sentences of increasing grammatical complexity, and described several developmental factors that impact on the complexity of children's utterances. The true factor of interest is grammatical complexity, which can be indirectly measured in children by looking at their MLU.

Terrace (1983) has written extensively about the problems of using MLU to measure linguistic skill in animals. The crux of his argument is that MLU loses its validity when repetitive word strings are frequent. Children seldom produce strings such as Nim's 16-word utterance *give orange me give eat orange me eat orange give me eat orange give me you* (Terrace, 1983), so Brown ignored the problem when creating the MLU. In signing chimps, however, these strings are quite common, so reliance on MLU to measure grammatical development is inappropriate. Measures taken from psycholinguistic research must be revalidated to ensure that they reflect the signature characteristics (such as grammatical complexity) that are of interest.

Revalidation and adaptation of measurements does not invalidate the signature characteristic strategy, but complicates the strategy considerably. New measures often must be developed to tap into a characteristic. Before the measures can be used with animals, they must be validated against human behavior. Wholesale adoption of psycholinguistic measures is unjustified, and has led to serious problems in past research.

In summary, significant problems arise in pursuit of a strategy of replicating signature characteristics of human language in animals. The characteristics are not stable, so that research based on one set of characteristics may be rendered unimportant by new developments in language or communication. Characteristics are intended to be necessary for language, but cannot be considered complete or sufficient. Finally, measures of characteristics are often indirect, and cannot be used without extensive revalidation and adaptation.

2. Beyond animal language

Although the signature characteristic strategy has more limited goals than the full-scale demonstration strategy, it has a similar vulnerability: Research can be discounted as trivial for failure to meet any number of characteristics of language. In this sense, language is still understood as an all-or-none phenomenon, and deviations from adult-human competency lead to an evaluation of "no significant contribution." Criticisms of the field of language research may be caricaturized as "This animal behaves in manner X which is unlike people. Therefore the animal does not possess true language, and so the research is worthless."

Having reviewed the problems of both the full-scale demonstration and signature characteristics strategies, a natural question is: What alternatives do researchers have to reach the goal of language competency in animals? Unfortunately, no one has developed a viable alternative. Instead, we might consider whether the goal is a wise one. Every investigator will have to answer this for her- or himself, but I must express some personal skepticism over the wisdom of this goal. Two basic problems arise in replicating human language skill in animals. First, we do not understand language very well, so we do not know what we are trying to teach to our animals. Second, our understanding of animal cognition is far from complete, so we do not know where significant problems in imparting this skill might lie. When the Gardners and Premack inaugurated the modern animal language period in the 1960s, the field of animal cognition did not exist. Without a broad understanding of language or animal cognition, pursuing a goal to replicate language in animals seems premature.

Fortunately, research performed in service of animal language can be used for other purposes as well. In the next section, I describe some of the many contributions that animal language research has made to animal cognition and illustrate the potential of these projects to further this vital effort.

BEYOND ANIMAL LANGUAGE

An alternative to the language goal is to consider animal cognition: What do we know about animal thinking? In contrast to the dim prospects for the language goal, we find that research on animal language provides a wealth of important data for understanding animal cognition. Indeed, it seems likely that animal language projects will be a major part of the foundation of animal cognition. The quality and quantity of data that can be derived from animal language projects cannot easily be matched by any other paradigm. I first consider the ways in which animal language projects can be used to develop animal cognition. Next I review some of the available data that provides striking information about animal cognition. Future explorations are then proposed that exploit animal language systems to provide additional data.

How Animal Language Research Informs Animal Cognition

Working to establish language skills in animals, researchers have developed a rich communication system between human and animal. This communication system can be used in two ways to help understand animal cognition. The first way is direct evidence, where the communication system itself is the object of study. The second way is indirect, where the communication system is exploited to investigate other issues.

Direct evidence comes from studying the performance of animals in their language tasks. The analysis focuses on identifying the cognitive prerequisites needed for task performance. Object and event classification is one example. The cognitive question is: Do animals organize the world around them in human-like ways? Here we can study the categories used by animals. Will a chimpanzee recognize sparrows, eagles, chickens, and penguins as birds? Are Reese's Pieces considered to be M&M's? What about a Hershey bar? Such categorization is partly a function of training and vocabulary, so we must be cautious when animal categories seem more inclusive than human ones. A more important question about animal conceptual structure is: Do animals utilize a hierarchical structure to encode objects and actions, where concepts at the "base level" (Rosch, 1978) seem most central? Relevant evidence can be derived from language tasks (Savage-Rumbaugh, Rumbaugh, & Boysen, 1978). It matters little whether the task is to request items, report on them, or understand a request. By studying the groupings of objects under the same symbolic label and the confusions made between objects, it is possible to learn about how other animals organize their psychological worlds.

Indirect evidence about animal cognition can be obtained when the communication system is used as a tool to explore specific characteristics of animal thought. Here the task must be more carefully designed to provide the evidence we seek. Instead of laboriously training an animal to perform a new task, we can use the communication system to make a simple request. Premack (1983) performed experiments of this sort in which the language system was used to discover whether chimps can recognize the similarity of relations (see also Thompson, & Oden, this volume, chapter 18). Here the focus is more obviously on animal cognition than on language; the language system is being exploited for its ability to quickly provide evidence about cognition.

2. Beyond animal language

What We Have Learned About Animal Cognition

Thinking is often described in terms of the representation of information and the processes that act on those representations. I use this model to structure some of the contributions of animal language research. Unfortunately, a comprehensive sketch is beyond the scope of this chapter, so the discussion is limited to a few prominent contributions.

Representation of knowledge is usually broken down into two major issues: the *form* and *content* of knowledge. Human cognitive psychology has primarily concerned itself with the form of knowledge, and how that form supports processes. Animal language research only indirectly reflects issues of form, but instead provides substantial data on the contents of an animals' representation. Even from everyday experience, we know that pets can identify their owners in spite of changes in clothes, hair style, soap smell, and so on. Thus we can conclude that dogs and cats can represent people in a somewhat abstract manner. They are not tied to any particular sensory stimulus, but can recognize underlying constancies through surface changes.

In language tasks, animals have been asked to identify objects, describe their attributes, report on object presence or absence, count the number of objects present, and so on. These activities reflect coding of the external world. From the success of animals on this diverse set of tasks, we can conclude that animals represent the environment in a manner similar to human coding. For example, the distinction between figure and ground is essential to most of these activities. The observed similarities are probably unsurprising: interacting with the physical world constrains perception in very specific ways.

A more interesting representational issue is to investigate the representation of imperceptible information: Can animals understand what is hidden from their direct senses? Perhaps the most obvious source of "hidden" information is the mind itself. The mind is certainly unobservable, yet presumably affects the behavior of human trainers that the chimpanzee interacts with. To this end, Premack's work on deception (Woodruff & Premack, 1979) represents an important development. Because the chimps can sort out the good trainers from the bad, it seems likely that they can represent unobservable information, such as mental states, in a manner similar to humans. Savage-Rumbaugh also reports several interactions between Sherman and Austin (Savage-Rumbaugh, 1986; Savage-Rumbaugh, et al., 1978;) that indicate the chimpanzees were aware of the knowledge of their cohort, and used the language system to communicate in order to change the others' mental state.

The representation of unobservable information implicates inference processes that must have been used to create that information. The revelations about mental processes probably represent the most remarkable contributions of animal language projects. Premack (1976) presented evidence for causal inferences by chimpanzees. Sherman and Austin apparently made similar inferences when they learned that pushing a lexigram caused a vending machine to operate, regardless of whether or not it contained food. This insight seemed necessary and sufficient for learning to use appropriate lexigrams to dispense foods (Savage-Rumbaugh, 1986, pp. 90-94).

Reasoning of this sort can often be driven by sensory information. Humans also engage in a deeper form of reasoning, where we make inferences about the world, then reason using those inferences as data. For example, a child might infer that a parent is angry, then attempt to placate the the parent through good behavior. This type of reasoning uses mental states instead of perceptual information as inputs, and so represents a "higher" level of reasoning (Anderson, 1983).

We find only a small amount of evidence that animals can reason at this heady level. Jesse, one of Premack's chimps who had learned to withhold any response that would clue the hostile trainer to the location of food, suddenly learned to deceive the trainer (Woodruff & Premack, 1979). This shift is evidence for reasoning about the situation, including the inferences made about the trainer's mental state. Unfortunately, cases like this in the literature are isolated and scarce. We next turn to a discussion of how animal language projects can help to quickly fill this void.

Future Explorations of Animal Thinking

The same representation/process framework is used to structure my suggestions about data that could be readily obtained from animals in language projects. First consider what we might learn about knowledge representation. People exploit several different representation schemes to encode world knowledge, such as images, linear strings, propositions, and schemata (Anderson, 1983). We can ask whether animals also share these representations. Of particular interest is evidence for meaning-based knowledge representations: propositions and schemata. These forms of representation are abstract, removed from direct sensory input.

Propositions can be identified by showing that the meaning or gist of a message is retained, not the sensory input that led to that meaning. A simple

2. Beyond animal language

form of linguistic gist is the "deep structure" of a sentence. People seldom remember whether a fact was presented in the active or passive form because the meaning of these two forms is similar. Explorations of propositional storage contrast retention of the studied form with a form that was not directly studied. The typical finding is that the advantage of re-exposure to the studied form quickly disappears (e.g., Begg, 1971; Sachs, 1967), though the meaning is retained. A simpler form of this experiment is simply to demonstrate the equivalence of the two forms of input. If animals can be trained to recognize the equivalence of active and passive forms of expression, we would have strong evidence for a purely meaning-based level of knowledge representation.

The most obvious process explorations center around problem solving (Newell & Simon, 1972). Some problems, such as those faced by Kohler's apes (1927), do not require internal representation and manipulation of world states. As the animal considers and carries out actions, the environment "stores" the world state. Problems of this sort are reversible: If an action is taken, it can be undone without penalty. More complex problems do not have this reversibility. Sacerdoti (1977) illustrated this property with a problem where a robot is asked to paint a ladder and a room. If the ladder is painted before the room is painted, the ladder cannot be used to paint the room. There is no simple way to "unpaint" the ladder after it has been painted, so the robot reaches an impasse. In order to avoid situations of this sort, a problem solver must represent the world internally, consider the consequences of proposed actions, notice impasses of this sort, and restructure the order of actions to avoid the problem.

Anderson (1983) has been very clear that he believes animals incapable of this sort of reasoning. Certainly the requirements of these problems are quite different than those where the environment is self-representing. Teaching animals to solve these problems is challenging, because often solutions are prohibited by custom, not by necessity. The robot could paint the ladder and then use the ladder to paint the ceiling, although it would get paint all over itself, the floor, and so on. We feel this solution is unaesthetic, but not truly impossible. Explaining our aesthetics to animals as constraints on their solution is not a trivial matter. However, some problems studied by developmental psychologists illustrate how the environment can "prohibit" certain solutions.

Imagine we have a bucket that serves as a receptacle for various objects. One of the objects, such as a ball, completely fills the bucket. We ask our animal to put the ball in the bucket, then request that another object be placed in the bucket. If the animal first removes the ball from the bucket, then retrieves the second object and places it inside the bucket, we have clear evidence about reasoning about problem requirements. If the animal retrieves the object, sets it aside, removes the ball, and places it inside the bucket, the evidence seems positive, but is less clear. If the animal insists on stuffing the second object in the bucket while the ball is still there, evidence suggests the animal is not reasoning about world states internally.

Evidence about the problem-solving ability of animals is of particular interest, as it reflects on the capability of animals to perform complex linguistic processes. Many of the criticisms of animal language research have proposed that the animal is using simple processes, such as cues from the experimenter, in their "linguistic" performance (Umiker-Sebeok & Sebeok, 1981). These criticisms could be countered by clear evidence that animals had the capacity to perform complex processes on internal representations, which is exactly what is required in problem solving and in language understanding. However, evidence about problem solving is more overt, and therefore less subject to criticism, than processing of linguistic strings.

Doubtless more data are available in current language projects relevant to these questions than I am aware of. Hopefully, these suggestions will lead investigators to consider their projects in a larger context, so the picture of animal cognition can be rapidly expanded.

CONCLUSION

Developing human linguistic skill in animals has long been a dream. Such a system would enable rich communication with our biological cousins, change our perception of the relationship between human and animal, and allow us to explore the thinking of other species through mere conversation. Unfortunately, this dream still seems beyond our grasp: We do not completely understand language, much less how to teach this subtle, extensive skill to chimps, dolphins, sea lions, or parrots. What is within our reach, and indeed within our grasp, are artificial communication systems that bear interesting similarities to human language.

Rather than dismiss existing animal language projects for their failure to duplicate human language, or expend our energy in efforts to close this vast gap, we might instead consider whether the artificial communication systems that have been developed possess merit on their own. From a perspective of human cognition, the answer is already a resounding yes. The complex abilities demonstrated by animals in language projects reveals continuity in cognitive processes between man and animal. Although humans are still special and

2. Beyond animal language

unique in the animal kingdom, the margin of difference is eroded, and hopefully some of our arrogance disappears as well. Using these communication systems, we can explore animal cognition in ways that are otherwise difficult or impossible. In the process, we understand more clearly the general nature of cognition, and through a distorted mirror learn more about ourselves.

From my remarks, a natural conclusion is that animal language researchers are insensitive to these issues, caring only about the development of human language skill in animals. Nothing could be farther from the truth. Many researchers have been aware of the broader implications of their research, although some researchers show more sensitivity to these issues than others. Nevertheless, the dominant purpose for animal language research seems to have been to demonstrate language skill in animals. This may in part be due to the ease of justification of linguistic research to funding agencies and journal editors, but for whatever reason, the goal of human language capabilities is probably unattainable and unnecessary. Animal language research has long been providing invaluable data about animal cognition, though it is not often presented in that way.

The gap between contemporary accounts of human cognition and animal language is broad and deep. This chapter has attempted to narrow this gap, if only slightly, by showing how research in animal language can be analyzed using a human cognitive approach, and how this perspective can pose interesting questions about animal thinking. If the fields of animal language and human cognition can develop new connections, the opportunity for mutual enrichment is great.

ACKNOWLEDGMENT

I am grateful to Stephanie Doane, Walter Kintsch, Lise Menn, Alan Bell, and Herbert Roitblat for their comments on this paper. Remaining errors are the sole responsibility of the author.

REFERENCES

Altmann, S. A. (1967). The structure of primate social communication. In S.A. Altmann (Ed.), *Social communication among primates* (pp. 325-362). Chicago: University of Chicago Press.

Anderson. J. R. (1983). *The architecture of cognition.* Cambridge, Ma.: Harvard University Press.

Bates, E., Bretherton, I., & Snyder, L. (1988). *From first words to grammar.* Cambridge: Cambridge University Press.

Begg, I. (1971). Recognition memory for sentence meaning and wording. *Journal of Verbal Learning and Verbal Behavior,* 10, 176-181.

Brown, R. (1973). *A First language: The early stages.* Cambridge, MA: Harvard University Press.

Chomsky, N. (1979). Human language and other semiotic systems. *Semiotica,* 25, 31-44.

Fouts, R. S. (1972). The use of guidance in teaching sign language to a chimpanzee (Pan troglodytes). *Journal of Comparative Psychology,* 80, 515-522.

Gardner, B. T., & Gardner, R. A. (1971). Teaching sign language to a chimpanzee, VI. Replies to wh questions. *Psychonomic Science,* 25, 49.

Gardner, B. T., & Gardner, R. A. (1974). Comparing the early utterances of child and chimpanzee. In A. Pick (ed.), *Minnesota Symposium in Child Psychology* (Vol. 8, pp. 3-23). Minneapolis, MN: University of Minnesota Press.

Herman, L. M., & Forestell, P. H. (1985). Reporting presence or absence of named objects by a language-trained dolphin. *Neuroscience and Biobehavioral Reviews,* 9, 667-681.

Herman, L. M., Richards, D. G., & Wolz, J. P. (1984). Comprehension of sentences by bottlenosed dolphins. *Cognition,* 16, 129-219.

Hockett, C. F. (1958). *A course in modern linguistics.* New York: Macmillan.

Hockett, C. F. (1960). Logical considerations in the study of animal communication. In W.E. Lanyon & W. N. Tavolga (Eds.), *Animal sounds and animal communication* (pp. 392-430). Washington, DC: American Institute of Biological Sciences.

2. Beyond animal language

Hockett, C. F., & Altmann, S. A. (1968). A note on design features. In T. A. Sebeok (Ed.), *Animal Communication* (pp. 574-575). Bloomington, IN: Indiana University Press.

Just, M. A., & Carpenter, P. A. (1987). *The psychology of reading and language comprehension.* Newton, MA: Allyn & Bacon.

Kohler, W. (1927). *The mentality of apes.* London: Routledge & Kegan Paul.

Kuhn, T. S. (1970). *The structure of scientific revolutions* (2nd ed). Chicago: University of Chicago Press.

Limber, J. (1977). Language in child and chimp? *American Psychologist,* 32, 280-295.

Miles, H. L. (1983) Apes and language: The search for communicative competence. In J. de Luce & H. T. Wilder (Eds.), *Language in primates: Perspectives and implications* (pp. 43-62). New York: Springer-Verlag.

Miller, G. A., & Gildea P.M. (1987). How children learn words. *Scientific American,* 257, September, 94-99.

Newell, A., & Simon H. A. (1972). *Human problem solving.* Englewood Cliffs, NJ: Prentice Hall.

Patterson, F. G. (1979). *Linguistic capabilities of a lowland gorilla.* Unpublished doctoral dissertation, Stanford University, 1979.

Premack, D. (1976) *Intelligence in ape and man.* Hillsdale, NJ: Lawrence Erlbaum Associates.

Premack, D. (1983). The codes of man and beasts. *Behavioural and Brain Sciences,* 6, 125-167.

Quirk, R., Greenbaum, S., Leech, G., & Svartvik, J. (1972). *A Grammar of contemporary English.* New York: Harcourt Brace Jovanovich.

Ristau, C. A., & Robbins, D. (1982). Language in the great apes: A critical review. *Advances in the Study of Behavior,* 12, 141-255.

Rosch, E. (1978). Principles of categorization. In E. Rosch & B. B. Lloyd (Eds.), *Cognition and categorization* (pp. 27-48). Hillsdale, NJ: Lawrence Erlbaum Associates.

Sacerdoti, E. D. (1977). *A structure for plans and behavior.* New York: Elsevier North-Holland.

Sachs, J. (1967). Recognition memory for syntactic and semantic aspects of connected discourse. *Perception and Psychophysics,* 2, 437-442.

Savage-Rumbaugh, E. S. (1986). *Ape language from conditioned response to symbol.* New York: Columbia University Press.

Savage-Rumbaugh, E. S., Rumbaugh, D. M., & Boysen, S. (1978). Linguistically mediated tool use and exchange by chimpanzees (*Pan troglodytes*). *Behavioral and Brain Sciences,* 4, 539-554.

Savage-Rumbaugh, E. S., Pate, J. L., Lawson, J., Smith, S. T., & Rosenbaum, S. (1983). Can a chimpanzee make a statement? *Journal of Experimental Psychology: General,* 112, 457-492.

Sells, P. (1985). *Lectures on contemporary syntactic theories: An introduction to government-binding theory, generalized phrase structure grammar, and lexical-functional grammar.* Chicago: University of Chicago Press.

Seyfarth, R. M., Cheney, D. L., & Marler P. (1980). Vervet monkey responses to three different alarm calls. Evidence of predator classification and semantic communication. *Science,* 210, 801-803.

Terrace, H. S. (1980). *Nim: A chimpanzee who learned sign language.* New York: Knopf.

Terrace, H. S. (1983). Apes who "talk": Language or projection of language by their teachers? In J. de Luce & H. T. Wilder (Eds.), *Language in primates perspectives and implications* (pp. 19-42). New York: Springer-Verlag.

Umiker-Sebeok, J., & Sebeok, T. A. (1981). Clever Hans and smart simians. The self-fulfilling prophecy and kindred methodological pitfalls. *Anthropos,* 76, 89-165.

2. Beyond animal language

Woodruff, G., & Premack, D. (1979). Intentional communication in the chimpanzee: The development of deception. *Cognition*, 7, 333-362.

3 Similarities and Differences in Human and Animal Language Research: Toward a Comparative Psychology of Language

Stan A. Kuczaj II and Virginia M. Kirkpatrick

Despite the considerable and oftentimes contentious disputes that characterize the literature that comprises comparative language research, scholars interested in human language and scholars interested in animal language share common interests that are often clouded by argumentative jargon. In this chapter, we outline these common interests and offer suggestions to facilitate communication among the disparate camps of language scholars.

WHAT IS THE STUDY OF LANGUAGE?

The ultimate goal of all scholars of language is to determine the processes involved in language use, a task that is complicated by the fact that language is a multifaceted phenomenon. The multifarious nature of language is evident in both its properties and its functions. The systems of language include the physical forms and combinatorial properties that yield language units (e.g., phonological systems in human languages), the assignment of meaning(s) to language units (e.g., semantic systems in human languages), the combination of meaningful units with one another to produce more complex meaningful units (e.g., morphological systems in human languages), and the arrangement of units in strings to produce meaningful multi-unit expressions (e.g., syntactic systems in human languages). Although scholars may disagree on the extent to which these systems are independent of one another (or even change their own mind, as they revise their theories—witness the changing emphasis placed on the role of the semantic system in syntactic phenomenon in Chomsky's early versions of transformational grammar (Chomsky, 1957, 1965) and his later theory of universal grammar (Chomsky, 1976, 1981, 1988)—none would presume to understand language qua language if they understood but one (or even two or three) of these systems. A viable theory of language must account for all of its systems. Otherwise, prima facie it is an incomplete theory.

Just as language incorporates a variety of systems, language is used to serve a variety of functions. Many of these functions are communicative in nature. For example, speakers of a human language can faithfully communicate facts, feelings, ideas, needs, opinions, and wants. They can also communicate hypothetical and possible situations, or deliberately deceive their listeners. Hence, the communicative function of language is not a single straightforward phenomenon. Instead, the communicative function is multidimensional. To further complicate matters, language serves functions other than communication. For example, language may influence the categories that are used to make sense of the world, perhaps the very nature of thought itself. At this point, certain readers may be thinking that whatever the functions of language are, influencing thought is not one of them. Other readers may be wondering why communication is considered a function rather than a system. Regardless of the additions, deletions, or substitutions one wishes to make to our lists of language systems and our lists of language functions, we suspect that all will agree that language involves some set of systems and serves some set of functions. Unless accounts of language systems simultaneously account for language functions, or vice versa, it is necessary to consider both systems and functions if one is to account for language.

Although the preceding discussion has been couched in terms of the properties and functions of human language, we believe that it is relevant for animal language research as well. The study of language, be it human language or animal language, is the study of language properties and language functions. For this reason, a comparative psychology of language is not only possible, but essential. Cross-species comparisons are necessary to answer questions such as:

3. Toward a Comparative Psychology of Language

1. What are the similarities and differences that exist in regard to the *properties* of the language systems of various species?

2. What are the similarities and differences that exist in regard to the *functions* of the language systems of various species?

3. Does the manner in which the young of a species acquires its language reflect cross-species universal developmental patterns and processes or species-specific developmental phenomena?

4. Are the differences that exist between species qualitative or quantitative in nature?

These questions are the types of questions that a comparative psychology of language must address. In fact, we believe that a vigorous and rigorous comparative study of language will lead to a better understanding of human language as well as animal language. Two assumptions underlie this belief (and also guide our work). Our first assumption is that language acquisition and language use by humans involve the processing and organization of both linguistic and non-linguistic information. This assumption is relatively straightforward, for there is universal agreement among scholars of language that the specification of the processing and organizational abilities involved in human language is essential for an understanding of human language acquisition and use. However, there is also considerable disagreement concerning the precise nature of such abilities. As we shall see, the lack of a universally accepted theory of human language use and acquisition has implications for all language research, regardless of the species being studied.

Our second assumption is that animals other than humans are capable of using "language-like" systems. We have placed language-like in quotations because the term is ambiguous, due in large part to the mysterious and complex nature of human language. It is this ambiguity that has led to many of the controversies in comparative language research. For example, detractors of animal language research often use the complexity of human language to belittle an animal's language ability.

> No species of animal has spontaneously come to use anything like human language; *apes and dolphins, whatever they do in captivity, appear not to use anything like language in the wild.* Some controversial studies...have claimed that (other species) are capable of being taught languages...It might be questioned whether the

languages used in these experiments are fully human-like...They may be communication systems that use none of the distinctive features of human language (Cook, 1988, p. 22, italics added).

The complexity of human language also comes into play in the arguments of advocates of animal language research. Typically, such arguments acknowledge both the complexity of human language and the inability of any animal other than humans to acquire any human language in toto, but suggest that at least some animals may be able to master specific (albeit limited) language-like skills.

Although human linguistic ability is unique, it has features that also enter into the communications systems of other animals, who therefore also can be said to have linguistic ability....Animals have animal languages. Their languages obviously do not share all the characteristics of human language. (Lieberman, 1989, p. 222)

Note that both Cook and Lieberman acknowledge the uniqueness and complexity of human language. The fact that the complexities of human language are used in the arguments of both detractors and proponents of animal language research reflects the mysterious nature of these complexities. We simply do not understand human language to a sufficient degree to unequivocally compare the language abilities of animals with those of humans. Even if we did, we know far too little about the language abilities of animals to make unequivocal comparisons. Comparative work is sorely needed.

IS HUMAN LANGUAGE AN APPROPRIATE STANDARD FOR COMPARATIVE LANGUAGE RESEARCH?

Perhaps human language is not the appropriate standard by which to judge the language skills of other species. The notion that human language is *the* standard for such comparisons most certainly reflects an arrogant attitude, akin to ethnocentric arguments that a particular human culture, language or religion is superior to all others. Prejudice has no place in science, and we should like to emphasize that human language is but one standard with which to compare the language skills of other species. And as already noted, the complexities of human language make it difficult to operationally define the criteria used to decide if an organism does or does not possess human language (or something like it).

3. Toward a Comparative Psychology of Language

Despite these problems, we believe that human language is an appropriate standard (although not the only standard) for comparative language research. Although there are more questions than answers in the literature concerned with human language, more is known about human language than about the language of any other species. The comparative study of language requires comparisons, and human language will and should be involved in many of these comparisons.

In addition, human language will continue to be a standard by virtue of its apparent uniqueness. Most scholars of language assume that human language is unique among the language systems available to terrestrial species (and perhaps to extraterrestrials as well). Although we have also made this assumption, it is important to remember that the uniqueness of human language is an assumption, not an established fact. It is true that no other species has been found to possess, either spontaneously or after extensive training, a language that shares all of the properties and functions of human language. This is support for the uniqueness hypothesis, but does not demonstrate that human language is unique. We do not know that all other species lack natural language systems akin to those of humans. Until the natural language systems of all species have been identified and understood, it is not possible to transform the uniqueness hypothesis into an axiom. Similarly, it has not been demonstrated that all other species cannot learn or be trained to use language systems as complex or meaningful as those of humans. To date, then, there is little positive evidence to support the notion that other species possess (either spontaneously or after training) language systems like those of humans. However, there is also insufficient negative evidence to rule out the possibility that other species could have (or be taught) such systems. The hypothesis that human language is unique is just that, a hypothesis. It has not been disproven (and perhaps never will be), but neither has it been proven beyond a shadow of doubt.

QUESTIONS GENERATED BY THE HUMAN LANGUAGE STANDARD

Although we have emphasized the hypothetical status of human language uniqueness, this is not the central question around which comparative language research should evolve (see also Roitblat, 1987). Rather than focusing on the question of human language uniqueness, we need to better determine both the processes and nature of language systems in all species, including humans. Arguing whether or not particular animals or species evidence human language abilities is relatively fruitless at this point, a sentiment shared by at least some scholars of comparative cognition.

Let us not think just about semantic issues in mentalistic terminology or how to draw lines as to what animals reach what abstract level. Let us...refer to specific abilities (e.g., selective attention, communication of resource location, mirror self-recognition), and keep the referents of our concepts at the fore. Let us retain an open-minded delight in animal abilities, a respect for what they may be experiencing, and a balance between skepticism and incredulity. (Burghardt, 1985, p. 918)

We suggest that language researchers (regardless of the species that they study) concentrate on determining what the presence or absence of particular abilities tells us about an organism's capacity to acquire, process, and organize particular types of information. Doing so will allow us to compare competencies of one species with those of another (including humans) without needlessly trying to justify an animal's abilities in human terms. Only then will a truly comparative psychology of language be possible.

Specific questions that we would like to see addressed (or in many cases, further addressed) include the following:

WHAT ARE THE LANGUAGE UNITS OF VARIOUS LANGUAGE SYSTEMS?

This question is a basic one, for the determination of a language's units is a prerequisite for other questions. For human languages, the prototypic units are specific sounds, sound categories, and sound combinations. However, certain human languages consist of gestural units rather than phonological units, and we suspect that the human language capacity is sufficiently flexible to permit other types of units as well.

Given the importance of determining a language's units for comparative language research, we know surprisingly little about such units outside of the realm of human language. Part of the problem is in knowing where to look. Payne's (1989) recent work on elephants' use of infrasound is illustrative of this problem. Concentrating on sounds that human beings can normally hear underestimates the range of sounds that elephants can hear and produce. Similar problems exist when we study any species that has auditory capacities above or below the normal human range. Given that it has not been demonstrated that language units must be auditory in nature, the problem of knowing where to look for such units may not be resolved by determining the auditory capabilities of all species. To reinforce this caveat against looking for

3. Toward a Comparative Psychology of Language

language units only in the auditory realm, we remind the reader that not all human languages use sounds as their primary units. This is also true of certain animal languages, one example being the symbolic dance of the honeybee (Gould, 1975; Lindauer, 1955; von Frisch, 1967).

Even if one has determined where to look for a language's units, the daunting task of isolating the units remains. For example, consider the phonological units that characterize most human languages. A speaker of a human language must distinguish important differences between sounds but ignore unimportant differences. This ability depends on the categorization of speech sounds, not on any simple ability to discriminate physical differences among sounds. In human languages, a *phoneme* is a category of sounds that are not physically identical, but that speakers of the language treat as functionally equivalent. Human languages differ in terms of the manner in which speech sounds are classified and in terms of the number of phonemes they employ. For example, the [k] sound in *ski* and the [k] sound in *key* are from the same English phoneme. English speakers do not discriminate these two sounds, despite the fact that the [k] sound in *key* is aspirated (it concludes with a short puff of breath) and the [k] sound in *ski* is not. In contrast, the two [k] sounds belong to different phonemes in Chinese. Consequently, speakers of Chinese can readily discriminate the aspirated [k] and the unaspirated [k].

Every human child has the capacity to learn the phonemes of any human language. This capacity appears to involve the interaction of innate predispositions and experience. Human infants do not learn to categorize speech sounds into phonemes, but instead seem predisposed to engage in categorical perception of speech sounds (Eimas, 1985). Hence, categorical perception qua process does not depend on experience. Nonetheless, experience with speech sounds is an important aspect of phonological development. Young infants make phonemic discriminations that adult speakers of their language community do not (Streeter, 1976; Trehub, 1976), a phenomenon that seems necessary if children must have the capacity to learn any set of human language phonemes. The capacity to make phonemic discriminations diminishes toward the end of the first year of life, the result being that 1-year-old children and adult speakers of the language the children will learn utilize virtually the same set of phonemic distinctions. Children's experience with their native language somehow restricts their ability to make phonemic discriminations. At present, both innate predispositions and experience are implicated in the acquisition of human language phonology, but neither type of factor has been specified.

The search for units in nonhuman languages parallels that for human languages. First, the nature of the units must be determined. Units could be discrete individual sounds, determined by absolute physical properties and requiring the ability to produce and recognize identical units. Or units could be categorical, as in the case of human phonemes, requiring the ability to recognize equivalence despite physical differences. Categorical perception has been demonstrated in nonhuman species (Snowdon, 1987), and may be the norm for language units. At present, there exists little empirical evidence to verify this possibility. Nor is there sufficient theoretical rationale to conclude that language units must be categorical. The advantage of categorical language units depends on whether one is "speaking" or "listening." Languages that use categorical units allow for both within- and across-speaker variability in regard to the production of individual units, but require the listener to accurately categorize sounds despite such variability. Hence, languages that use categorical units place more of a burden on listeners than on speakers. Language systems that require identical units place the primary burden on the speaker, who must faithfully produce each unit. In such cases, the listener would have to make an identity decision (e.g., X is X) rather than a categorical decision (e.g., X is a type of Y). Given the human predisposition for categorical language units, it is important to keep in mind that other types of language units are possible. Searching for a variety of types of language units will increase our understanding of the possible types of language units, which will in turn increase our understanding of the comparative significance of categorical units.

The ability to produce and perceive the units of a language is but one aspect of language knowledge. Language also involves the ability to combine units with one another to produce more complex units, one example being phonological rules in human languages. In addition, language involves the attachment of meaning to units. It is this latter phenomenon to which we now turn.

HOW MEANINGFUL ARE THE SYMBOLIC UNITS OF VARIOUS LANGUAGE SYSTEMS?

The smallest meaningful units of human languages are morphemes, which can be free (e.g., the free morpheme *idea* in English) or bound (e.g., the bound morpheme *s* in *ideas*). Free morphemes can stand alone, whereas bound morphemes must be attached to free morphemes.

What does it mean to say that an organism knows a morpheme? Although the answer to this question can also be answered in terms of the use of

3. Toward a Comparative Psychology of Language

morphemes to communicate (e.g., referential communication) or in terms of the permissable uses of morphemes in combinations with one another to produce multi-unit constructions (what are called syntagmatic relations in human language), we concentrate here on the notion of a morpheme as a discrete meaningful unit.

The simplest way in which an organism can be said to know a morpheme is found in the ability to discriminate one morpheme from another. Such an ability involves perceptual discrimination skills, and is a prerequisite for morpheme learning. An organism that cannot discriminate one morpheme from another would not be able to assign meanings to individual morphemes, for there would be no stable units. Hence, one task facing language researchers is the determination of the types of units that various species are able to discriminate. This is not an easy task, as anyone who has been exposed to an unfamiliar human language can attest. Segmenting a language stream into morphemes is difficult unless one knows the language. Given that few of us are fluent in animal language systems, the problem of determining the morphemes is a real one.

In addition to discriminating units from one another, the ability to know a morpheme depends on the ability to recognize a unit as one that has or has not been previously experienced. In human morpheme acquisition, such mnemonic ability is a prerequisite for consolidating and refining the meanings of morphemes, determining the range of communicative functions into which morphemes enter, and determining the syntagmatic relations of morphemes. Unless an organism can remember units qua units, all other aspects of morpheme-meaning relationships become moot. Thus, another task facing comparative language scholars is the determination of the types of units various species can remember. This is not a frivalous concern, for an organism may be able to discriminate two units but not be able to remember the units. The ability to remember various discriminable units may have varying ecological significance for various species. Thus, species may differ in terms of the types of units they can discriminate, and in terms of the types of units they can store, organize, and recall from memory. All of this has implications both for the types of morphemes various species can learn and for the ability of humans to understand the morphemes of other species.

Although the ability to use a morpheme presupposes both perceptual discrimination and memory skills, the presence of such skills does not entail an ability to use morphemes. By definition, a morpheme involves the attachment of meaning to a unit. In other words, the use of morphemes depends on the capacity for symbolic representation, the ability to allow a symbol (morpheme) to represent something else.

In human languages, morphemes are conventional and arbitrary. They are conventional in that the speakers of a language use the same sound or combination of sounds to refer to a given object, class of objects, or idea. For example, speakers of English use the term *dog* to refer to the wide variety of mammals that constitute man's best friend. The symbols are arbitrary in that there is no necessary relation between sounds and their meanings. Consider the morpheme *dog* once again. There is no reason that this sound pattern must refer to the particular class of animals that it does. Speakers of English could just as easily refer to what we call dogs as *morts* or *gatels*. Indeed, it comes as no surprise that different languages use different sound combinations to refer to the same meaning; the English *dog* is *hund* in German, *perro* in Spanish, and *chien* in French.

The issue of whether discrete units function as morphemes in animal language systems is far from resolved. In most cases, too little is known to reach a conclusion. For example, virtually nothing is known about the morphemic status of the units in cetacean language systems (Dalheim & Awbrey, 1982; Ford, 1989; Herman & Tavolga, 1980; Smith, 1986). As noted earlier, one problem lies in determining the units themselves. An equally difficult problem exists when one attempts to determine the meanings of individual units. As Quine (1960) noted, context is usually sufficiently ambiguous to result in multiple equally possible interpretations about the meaning of morphemes in human language systems. Of course, the problem is magnified when the information available from context is impoverished, as it often is when comparative language scholars study other species in their natural habitat.

Despite these problems, there is evidence that at least some species use morphemic units in their natural language systems (e.g., see Lindauer's 1955 discussion of the dance of the honeybee; Leger & Owings' 1978 analysis of the alarm calls of ground squirrels; Gouzoules, Gouzoules, & Marler's 1984 consideration of the agonistic screams of rhesus monkeys; and Seyfarth & Cheney's 1982 discussion of the alarm calls of vervet monkeys). In addition, the results of numerous training studies suggest that various species may be able to learn arbitrary symbols that function as morphemes (Gardner and Gardner, 1969; Herman & Forestell, 1985; Rumbaugh, 1977). All in all, these findings suggest that species other than humans have the capacity for symbolic representation, and are capable of using conventional and arbitrary morphemes.

3. Toward a Comparative Psychology of Language

However, it is not yet clear how closely the symbolic representational skills of other species compare with those of humans (Savage-Rumbaugh, 1981; Terrace, 1985).

To date, considerations of the morphemic status of units learned by animals in training studies have focused on the referential status of such units (e.g., Herman Forestell, 1985; Savage-Rumbaugh, Rumbaugh, Smith, & Lawson, 1980; Terrace, 1985). Determining the referential status of morphemes in trained artificial languages is necessary if we are to discover the symbolic capacity of language trained animals, particularly if symbolic capacity is not evident in the animals' natural behavior. Similar efforts to discover the referential status of morphemes in natural language systems are equally important for increased understanding of the symbolic capacity of non-language-trained species (e.g., Seyfarth & Cheney, 1982).

Although we encourage continued investigations of the referential status of morphemes in both artificial and natural languages, there are other questions concerning the meanings of such morphemes that should also be addressed. For example, an important aspect of vocabulary growth in human children involves the creation of a semantic system, a phenomenon that requires children to relate word meanings to one another (Kuczaj, 1982). This involves paradigmatic relations, which are semantic relations that structure the semantic system. Examples of paradigmatic relations include lexical opposition and hyponymy. Lexical opposition includes gradable contrasts such as *hot* and *cold*, and ungradable contrasts such as *male* and *female*. Hyponymy involves subordinate-superordinate relationships, such as that between *cow* and *mammal*. The acquisition of these and other paradigmatic relations result in the formation of a semantic system, a system of interrelated sets of units and meanings. At present, little is known about the ability of nonhuman species to employ paradigmatic relations. One task facing comparative language scholars is the determination of the paradigmatic relations different species employ. Species could differ in terms of the ability to use paradigmatic relations in general, or in terms of specific paradigmatic relations. Until we know more about the ability of nonhuman species to use paradigmatic relations, the comparative study of morphemes will be incomplete.

DO NONHUMAN LANGUAGE SYSTEMS INVOLVE SYNTAX?

Despite considerable disagreement concerning the nature and characteristics of human language, the following definition is one with which most scholars of human language would concur: Human language is a symbolic, rule-governed system that is both abstract and productive, a system that enables its speakers to produce and comprehend a wide range of utterances.

Language is a rule-governed system in that each human language is constrained by a set of rules that reflect the regularities of the language. For example, in English morphemes such as *the* and *a* must precede the noun to which they refer: *the boy ate a hot dog* is correct, but *boy the ate hot dog a* is not. The rule system is abstract because it goes beyond the association of individual sounds and morphemes, and instead involves the manipulation of abstract classes of morphemes. Thus, rather than saying that *the* must precede *boy*, we may state that articles (the class containing morphemes such as *the* and *a*) must precede nouns (the class containing morphemes such as *boy*). All of this makes possible perhaps the most important characteristic of human language, its productivity.

Human language is productive in the sense that a finite number of linguistic units (sounds and morphemes, and the abstract classes of which morphemes are members) and a finite number of rules are capable of yielding an infinite number of utterances. The productivity of language is important not because a given speaker will produce an infinite number of sentences, for this is impossible, at least if the speaker is mortal. Even though no speaker of any human language will ever produce all of the possible sentences in the language, the capability to do so is quite important. The productivity inherent in all human languages permits the production and comprehension of *novel* sentences, an important aspect of the communicative diversity speakers of human languages enjoy. All of this is made possible by the syntactic characteristics of human languages.

Although the literature of concern is replete with disagreements about the syntactic capabilities of nonhuman species, two conclusions seem warranted at this time. First, no nonhuman species has evidenced syntactic abilities comparable to those of humans. Second, nonhuman species are capable of employing syntax, even if their syntactic accomplishments do not rival those of humans.

Marler (1977) suggested two types of syntax relevant for comparative language research. Phonetic syntax involves the combination of units to produce another unit that has a different meaning than its individual parts, and seems most equivalent to the combination of phonemes to produce words in human languages. Lexical syntax involves the rearrangement of individual

3. Toward a Comparative Psychology of Language

words in sequences to produce different and more complex meanings, and seems closer to the typical notions of human syntax than does phonetic syntax. Marler suggested that phonetic syntax would be more common in animal language systems than would lexical syntax, which might be limited to human languages.

Phonetic syntax certainly exists in animal languages (e.g., Cleveland & Snowdon, 1982), but would seem to be better compared with the human phonological system than the human syntactic system. Lexical syntax has also been observed in natural animal languages (Cleveland & Snowdon, 1982; Robinson, 1984), albeit in a much more limited sense than in human languages. In addition, dolphins have been found to use lexical syntax in their comprehension of artificial languages in which word order is important (Herman, Richards, & Wolz, 1984). Clearly, additional work is needed to discover the syntactic characteristics of animals' natural languages and to determine the limits of various species' abilities to learn lexical syntax in artificial languages. Both types of information are necessary for comparisons with human syntactic abilities. In addition, it seems necessary to distinguish two types of lexical semantics. One type, which we call lexical syntax, involves the manipulation of units that can meaningfully stand alone (free morphemes) to produce more complex strings of units, such as sentences in human languages. The other type, which we shall call morphological syntax, involves the combination of morphemes to produce other units (not strings of units). For example, human languages allow the combination of bound morphemes (*ing*) and free morphemes (e.g., *eat*) to produce combinations in which the more complex meaning depends on the meanings of its parts (e.g., *eat* + *ing*). Comparative studies of syntax should also consider the extent to which various species are capable of using lexical syntax and morphological syntax.

WHAT FUNCTIONS DO THE LANGUAGES OF OTHER SPECIES SERVE?

An overwhelming proportion of work on language functions has focused on communication. This is not surprising, considering the significance of the communicative function. Due to space constraints, we do not dwell here on this literature. Nonetheless, we should like to emphasize that it is impossible to understand a language system's communicative functions unless one knows the morphemes and syntax of the language. For example, consider how little is known about the communicative functions of killer whale vocalizations (Ford, 1989). Killer whales appear to be very social creatures, and very likely may communicate with one another via vocalization. However, too little is known about the morphemes and syntax of killer whale language to gauge its status as a communication system.

The noncommunicative functions of language include the effects of morphemes on categorization, the use of language to facilitate problem solving, and the effects of language systems on thought. These functions are controversial, regardless of whether human or animal language is involved. The notion that human language influences human thought has a long and controversial history, but the evidence is accummulating to support the notion that human language is an important aspect of human thought (see Kuczaj, Borys, & Jones, 1989, for a discussion of this literature). Little is known about the influence of animal language on animal thought. This is not surprising given how much remains to be discovered about animal language (and animal thought, for that matter). Nonetheless, it has been hypothesized that qualitative differences in human thought and animal thought are due at least in part to the lack of language in animals (Terrace, 1981). Although we do not believe that all nonhuman species have been demonstrated to lack language, we suspect that Terrace is correct in his assumption that an organism with language possesses different cognitive capacities than does an organism without language.

Along these lines, Premack (1983) suggested that language training may influence the cognitive abilities of language trained animals. Although this is a real possibility, we concur with Roitblat's assessment of the influence of language training on thought. "There is little doubt that language-trained animals perform differently from non-language-trained animals, but it remains unclear what aspects of the language-training experience are influential in producing this difference" (Roitblat, 1987, p. 315).

CONCLUDING REMARKS

We have offered a number of suggestions (admittedly not exhaustive) to guide comparative language resuarch. We close our chapter with two additional observations.

First, comparative language research is incomplete unless it incorporates developmental considerations into its investigations. Developmental investigations are necessary to determine the relative significance of innate predispositions and experience, including the roles that others play in an individual's language development.

3. Toward a Comparative Psychology of Language

Second, comparative language research will require naturalistic observational investigations, experimental investigations, and training studies. Naturalistic observational investigations are necessary to determine what animals actually do in their natural habitat. Experimental investigations are necessary to test hypotheses, including those derived from naturalistic observational studies. Training studies are necessary to determine competences and capabilities that may not be evident in a species' natural behavior. These types of investigations should not be isolated intellectual endeavors, but instead interactive enterprises. This is true for the study of human language as well as animal language.

> Language is a complex, rule-governed domain of human behavior that is not explicitly taught to children. The knowledge acquired by young speakers of a language contrasts sharply with other knowledge-based competencies that are usually taught (e.g., reading, writing, arithmetic, word processing, piano playing). The limits of our knowledge about language and the acquisition process are evident when we attempt to help children who have failed to acquire language during the normal developmental span. We would be in a better position to help such children if we knew: (1) which aspects of language can be taught. . ., and (2) what types of experiences and strategies are most facilitating to what children (Schiefelbusch, 1989, p. 2).

Thus, comparative language research should involve the comparison of types of investigations using the same species as well as comparisons of the language systems and capabilities of different species.

REFERENCES

Burghardt, G. M. (1985). Animal awareness: Current perceptions and historical perspective. *American Psychologist*, 40, 905-919.

Caldwell, M., & Caldwell, D. (1965). Individualized whistle contours in bottle-nosed dolphins (*Tursiops truncatus*), *Nature*, 207, 434-435.

Chomsky, N. (1957). *Syntactic structures*. The Hague: Mouton.

Chomsky, N. (1965). *Aspects of the theory of syntax*. Cambridge, MA: MIT Press.

Chomsky, N. (1981). *Lectures on government and binding.* Dordrecht, Netherlands: Foris.

Chomsky, N. (1988). *Language and problems of knowledge: The Nicaraguan lectures.* Cambridge, MA: MIT Press.

Cleveland, J., & Snowdon, C. (1982). The complex vocal repertoire of the adult cotton-top tamarin (*Sanguinus oedipus oedipus*). *Zeitschrift für Tierpsychologie,* 58, 231-270.

Cook, V. (1988). *Chomsky's universal grammar.* Oxford: Basil Blackwell.

Dalheim, M., & Awbrey, F. (1982). A classification and comparison of vocalizations of captive killer whales (*Orcinus orca*). *Journal of the Acoustical Society of America,* 72, 661-670.

Eimas, P. (1985). The perception of speech in early infancy. *Scientific American,* 252, 46-52.

Ford, J. (1989). Acoustic behaviour of resident killer whales (*Orcinus orca*) off Vancouver Island, British columbia. *Canadian Journal of Zoology,* 67, 727-745.

von Frisch, K. (1967). *The dance language and orientation of bees.* Cambridge, MA: Harvard University Press.

Gardner, R., and Gardner, B. (1969). Teaching sign language to a chimpanzee. *Science,* 165, 664-672.

Gould, J. (1975). Honeybee recruitment: The dance-language conroversy. *Science,* 189, 685-693.

Gouzoules, S., Gouzoules, H., & Marler, P. (1984). Rhesus monkey (*Macaca mulatta*) screams: Representational signaling in the recruitment of agonistic aid. *Animal Behavior,* 32, 182-193.

Herman, L., & Forestell, P. (1985). Reporting presence or absence of named objects by a language-trained dolphin. *Neuroscience and Biobehavioral Reviews,* 9, 667-681.

3. Toward a Comparative Psychology of Language

Herman, L., Richards, D., & Wolz, J. (1984). Comprehension of sentences by bottlenosed dolphins. *Cognition*, 16, 129-219.

Herman, L. & Tavolga, W. (1980). The communication systems of cetaceans. In L. Herman (Ed.), *Cetacean behavior: Mechanisms and functions*, (pp. 149-209). New York: Wiley Interscience.

Kuczaj, S. (1982). On the nature of syntactic development. In S. Kuczaj (Ed.), *Language Development, Vol. 1, Syntax and semantics* (pp. 37-72). Hillsdale, NJ: Lawrence Erlbaum Associates.

Kuczaj, S., Borys, R. & Jones, M. (1989). On the interaction of language and thought: Some thoughts and developmental data. In A. Gellatly, D. Rogers, & J. Slaboda (Eds.), *Cognition and social worlds*, (pp. 168-189). Oxford: Oxford University Press.

Leger, D., & Owings, D. (1978). Response to alarm calls by California ground squirrels: Effects of call structure and maternal status. *Behavioral Ecology Sociobiology*, 3, 177-186.

Lieberman, P. (1989). Biological constraints on universal grammar and learnability. In M. Rice and R. Schiefelbusch (Eds.), *The teachability of language*, (pp. 199-225). Baltimore: Brooks.

Lindauer, M. (1955). Schwarmbienen auf Wohnungssuche. *Zeitschrift für Vergleichende Physiologie*, 37, 263-324.

Marler, P. (1977). The structure of animal communication sounds. In T. H. Bullock (Ed.) *Recognition of complex acoustic signals* (17-35). Berlin: Dahlem.

Payne, K. (1989). Elephant talk. *National Geographic*, 176, 264-277.

Premack, D. (1983). The codes of man and beasts. *The Behavioral and Brain Sciences*, 6, 125-167.

Quine, W. (1960). *Word and object*. Cambridge, MA: MIT Press.

Robinson, J. (1984). Syntactic structures in the vocalizations of wedge-capped capuchin monkeys (*Cebus olivaceus*). *Behaviour*, 90, 46-79.

Roitblat, H. L. (1987). *Introduction to comparative cognition.* New York: W. H. Freeman.

Rumbaugh, D. (Ed.) (1977). *Language learning by a chimpanzee: The Lana project.* New York: Academic Press.

Savage-Rumbaugh, E. S. (1981). Can apes use symbols to represent their world? In T. Sebeok & R. Rosenthal (Eds.), *The clever Hans phenomenon: Communication with horses, whales, apes, and people* (pp. 35-59). New York: New York Academy of Sciences.

Savage-Rumbaugh, E. S., Rumbaugh, D., Smith, S., and Lawson, J. (1980). Reference: The linguistic essential. *Science,* 210, 922-925.

Schiefelbusch, R. (1989). An introduction to teachability issues. In M. Rice & R. Schiefelbusch (Eds.), *The teachability of language* (pp. 1-9). Baltimore: Brooks.

Seidenberg, M., & Petitto, L. (1979). Signing behavior in apes: A critical review. *Cognition,* 7, 177-215.

Seyfarth, R., & Cheney, D. (1982). How monkeys see the world: A review of recent research on East African vervet monkeys. In C. Snowdon, C. Brown, and M. Petersen (Eds.), *Primate communication,* (pp. 239-252). New York: Cambridge University Press.

Smith, W. (1986). Signaling behavior: Contributions of different repertoires. In R. Schusterman, J. Thomas, & F. Wood (Eds.), *Dolphin cognition and behavior: A comparative approach* (pp. 315-330). Hillsdale, NJ: Lawrence Erlbaum Associates.

Snowdon, C. (1987). A naturalistic view of categorical perception. In S. Harnad (Ed.), *Categorical perception,* (pp. 332-354). New York: Cambridge University Press.

Streeter, L.A. (1976). Language perception of two-month old infants shows effects of both innate mechanisms and experience. *Nature,* 259, 39-41.

Terrace, H. (1981). Animal versus human minds. *Behavioral an Brain Sciences,* 5, 391-392.

3. Toward a Comparative Psychology of Language

Terrace, H. (1985). In the beginning was the "Name." *American Psychologist,* 40, 1011-1028.

Trehub, S. E. (1976) The discrimination of foreign speech contrasts by infants and adults. *Child Development,* 47, 466-472.

4 Knowing How to Use Language: Developing a Rapprochement Between Two Theoretical Traditions

William Bechtel

Animal language research has a critical role to play in advancing our understanding of the cognition by helping to construct a crucial bridge between two quite different theoretical perspectives. The rationalist tradition posits rule-based processing of language-like representations as a primitive cognitive activity, whereas the associationist tradition tries to account for cognitive performance in terms of more basic operations. In this chapter, I discuss this conflict of perspectives briefly and discuss why each tradition, on its own, encounters a serious difficulty in attempting to explain cognition and language use. I then introduce a distinction between knowing how and knowing that proposed by Gilbert Ryle. Knowing how is very different from knowing that in that it does not require a representational medium in which propositions can be represented.

In the spirit of Ryle, I argue that using language is something we learn and know how to do, but does not rely on knowing that. At least in cognitive domains, knowing how has been largely ignored due to the lack of adequate models of what it might involve. I next sketch how recently developed connectionist models may provide a framework for modeling about knowing how. While the connectionist approach draws from the associationist tradition, if it can explain what is involved in knowing how to manipulate symbolic representations, it can help bridge the conflict between the rationalistic and associationist traditions. Finally, I discuss how research on animal language such as that presented elsewhere in this volume can provide an important guide in building models of what is involved in knowing how to use a language.

SYMBOL PROCESSING VERSUS ASSOCIATIONISM

Modern philosophy (in philosophy, the modern period was the 17th and 18th centuries) gave birth to two radically opposed frameworks for thinking about cognition: rationalism and empiricism. Aspects of the difference between these two perspectives still divide researchers today. Consider rationalism first. Rationalists focused primarily on the capacities for reasoning exhibited by humans. This capacity is intimately connected with the ability to use language. Thus, Descartes viewed the flexible use of language needed to conduct such reasoning as a distinctive ability of humans and attributed it to a special substance, *res cogitans*. He differentiated this substance from *res extensa*, of which ordinary physical objects are composed, thus advancing a dualist ontology. By making reasoning a basic activity of a substance, Descartes foreclosed any attempt to decompose that activity, that is, to show how it could arise from more basic operations (on the role of decomposition in explanation of a function, see Simon, 1969, and Bechtel & Richardson, 1992).

At least in this one respect, symbolic, rule-processing models in contemporary cognitive science can be seen as a modern heir of the rationalist legacy. These models assume that information is encoded in language-like representations and is manipulated according to rules that are much like those of logic. For example, in a production system, the rules take the form of conditional statements, and if information in working memory satisfies the antecedent of any rule, the operations specified in the consequence are performed. By treating symbol processing as a basic cognitive activity, the symbolic tradition, like the rationalists, forecloses inquiry directed at explaining the primitive processes hypothesized. In building a cognitive model, a researcher will specify representations and rules to operate on them, but will not attempt to explain how rules are applied to representations. Researchers turn the problem of explaining how rules get applied over to biology (Pylyshyn, 1984). (In an artificial intelligence simulation, the architecture of the computer and the process of compiling a program into machine code are responsible for insuring the proper execution of rules given the representations currently stored in memory.

4. Knowing How to Use Language

In many respects the most extreme presentation of this rationalist view that symbol manipulation is fundamental to cognition is found in Fodor (1975), who argues that thinking requires a representational system, a language of thought comparable to a natural language. In part, Fodor (1987, Fodor & Pylyshyn, 1988) defended this view by pointing to three features of thought:

1. Its productivity (the possibility of thinking an unlimited number of thoughts),

2. Its systematicity (thinking one thought implies the possibility of thinking related thoughts), and

3. Its inferential coherence (the applicability of logical operations to all propositions with the same structure).

He contended that these features can only be accounted for by postulating an internal language-like representational system. He maintained further that if organisms that do not use a natural language are cognitive, then they too must possess a language of thought.

Empiricism begins at the opposite extreme. Rather than postulating reasoning capacities, classical empiricists such as Locke postulated a variety of ways of associating simple sensory experiences so as to build up our knowledge of the world. The challenge for this associationist approach has been to show how the kind of knowledge and reasoning humans, at least, are capable of, can result from such associations. For example, they need to show that problem solving and logical inference can be accounted for in this manner. In eschewing the use of elaborate systems of rule-processing and in trying to account for complex behavior in terms of learned relations between stimuli and behavior, behaviorism constitutes an heir of this associationist tradition. The difficulties that arise in attempting to account for complex behaviors on the basis of simple relations are seen in Skinner's (1957) attempt to account for linguistic behavior using operant conditioning alone. The program seems to succeed best in explaining use of language directly prompted by environmental stimuli. But human language use, as Descartes and Fodor have emphasized, is much more flexible and does not seem to be linked directly to environmental factors. At minimum, it seems necessary to provide an account of intermediate stages of processing within the cognitive system. But even allowing for intermediate processing may not be enough; according to the symbolic theorists, the only kind of processing system capable of modeling human cognition (including language use) is a rule-based system.

From a descriptive perspective, the symbolic theorist clearly possesses a tool sufficiently strong to describe human cognitive performance. From an explanatory perspective, however, it is the associationist approach that seems to be on the right track. One cannot explain a capacity by postulating it and treating it as unanalyzable. One must discover its basic components and show how the capacity can be built up from them. However, so far associationists do not seem to have succeeded in providing mechanisms adequate to explain cognition and language use.

RYLE'S DISTINCTION BETWEEN KNOWING HOW AND KNOWING THAT

A promising start for overcoming the impasse between symbolic and associationist approaches is found in Ryle's (1949) notion of knowing how. His distinction is manifest in our use of language. In general, the expression *knowing that* requires completion by a proposition which specifies what it is that the person knows. For example, we might say that someone knows that oxygen impedes fermentation. Here the proposition *oxygen impedes fermentation* specifies what the person knows. On the other hand, the expression *knowing how* is completed by an infinitive specifying an activity. Thus, we might say that someone knows how to ride a motorcycle.

When Ryle introduced this distinction he was objecting to the preoccupation of philosophers with facts and theoretical knowledge that would be represented in propositions. He maintained that propositional knowledge represented only one aspect of human intelligence. Intelligence is also required to perform a variety of activities, and it makes sense to judge whether one performed these activities intelligently or stupidly. For example, we speak of someone driving intelligently or taking a computer apart in a stupid manner. Many of Ryle's examples of knowing how were cognitive in nature, such as making or appreciating jokes, talking grammatically, playing chess, and arguing, suggesting that knowing how may characterize cognitive capacities as well. Ryle made this point explicitly: "Indeed even when we are concerned with their intellectual excellences and deficiencies, we are interested less in the stocks of truths that they acquire and retain than in their capacities to find out truths for themselves and their ability to organise and exploit them, when discovered" (1949, p. 28).

Ryle's distinction is fairly widely known. It has been employed in discussions of animal language research by Ristau and Robbins (1982), but in a manner contrary to Ryle's intent. Ristau and Robbins treat knowing how to use

4. Knowing How to Use Language

a linguistic idiom as a lesser accomplishment than true language use, which requires knowing that one is using language to communicate. Moreover, most philosophers and cognitive scientists have continued to focus on symbolic representations of information (e.g., propositions) as the objects of knowledge. In cognitive psychology, the notion of procedural knowledge partly corresponds to Ryle's notion of knowing how. Models of procedural knowledge, however, have generally employed rule systems in which the information needed to execute a procedure is encoded symbolically. This approach, of course, does little to explain what kinds of mechanisms underlie the use of language-like representations; rather it assumes the capacity. It also fails to recognize the radical character of Ryle's suggestion that a form of knowledge that does not rely on symbolic representation might be more basic.

A major reason why Ryle's perspective has not been pursued is that there have not been plausible models of cognitive performance that have not relied on symbolic representations and rule-governed manipulations of these representations. If there were such models, then we might be able not only to allow for a domain of knowing how that was not dependent on symbolic representations, but also to consider the possibility that representing information symbolically is something we know and learn how to do. I turn now to a development in cognitive science that is promising in this regard.

THE PROMISE OF CONNECTIONISM TO EXPLAIN KNOWING HOW

When investigators first began to break with the strictures of behaviorism and to model the internal operations of the mind, there was an alternative to the more rationalistic symbol-processing approach. This alternative approach tried to model cognitive processes using networks of very simple processing units, which can assume different levels of activation and send excitations and inhibitions to other such units much in the manner neurons do in the brain. The behavior of such systems is determined by the connections through which excitations and inhibitions are passed between units. These connections can be weighted, and the weights can be adjusted depending on the activity occurring in the network; this capacity of a network to adjust its weights and so alter its performance is referred to as learning. The important point about these networks is that because weights determine how they behave, whatever knowledge the network acquires is encoded in these weights. There are no propositional representations as such. The network approach, more closely linked with associationism than rationalism (because connections represent ways of associating whatever the simple processing units represent), was

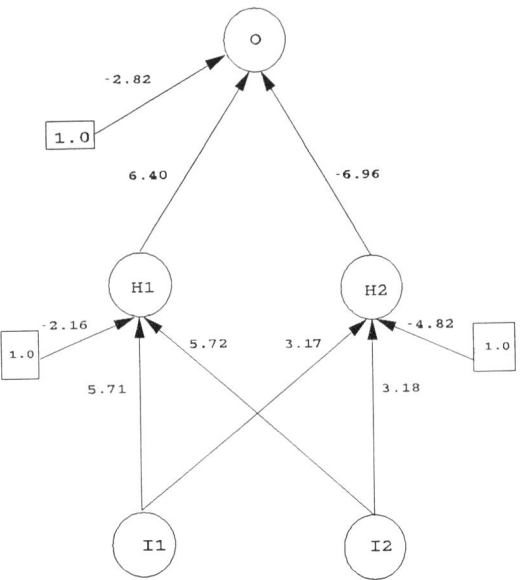

Figure 4.1. A three-layer connectionist network capable of learning the exclusive-or (XOR) problem.

severely criticized as insufficient to account for cognition (Minsky and Papert, 1968) and was temporarily eclipsed. It has reemerged in recent cognitive science under the names connectionism, parallel distributed processing, and neural networks (Rumelhart, McClelland, & the PDP Research Group, 1986).

To obtain a brief introduction to connectionist processing and learning, consider the three- layer network shown in Figure 4.1. Inputs are supplied to the two units on the bottom layer. They pass their activations to the two units in the next layer, which then pass their activations to the single unit in the top layer. The units in the middle and top layers take activations between 0 and 1, as determined by a continuous, nonlinear function of the net input to the unit. This net input is determined by summing, over all units sending activation to the unit in question, the products of the activations of the units sending to the unit and the weight of the corresponding connections. The network is trained using a back-propagation procedure: It is supplied an input pattern and produces an output pattern on its top layer, it is informed of the discrepancy between each output activation and the target activation for that unit, and weight changes are made in such a manner as to decrease the discrepancy gradually. When each of

4. Knowing How to Use Language

a set of input patterns has been presented once each, a training epoch has been completed.

If the inputs to this network are assumed to represent the truth values of two propositions (with 1 designating true), this network can be trained to calculate any Boolean function. In particular, this network was trained on the exclusive or (XOR) function which has an output of true (1) whenever just one of the inputs is true and false (0) otherwise. Thus, XOR employs the following truth table:

Proposition A	Proposition B	A XOR B
1	1	0
1	0	1
0	1	1
0	0	0

After considerable training (generally several hundred epochs), the network acquires weights like those in Figure 4.1 and is able to generate the correct response for each input set. The first point to note is that the network's ability to carry out this task resides simply in the weights on the connections. There is no propositional knowledge (knowing that) that the network utilizes in order to solve XOR problems. The second point to note concerns the behavior of the hidden units (those located between the input and output units). In this simulation, the hidden units have each become responsive to quite different pieces of information. By examining the weights shown in Figure 4.1, we can ascertain that H1 has become an OR detector; it becomes active when either of the input units is active and sends a positive input to the output unit. H2, on the other hand, has become an AND detector; it becomes active when both input units are active and sends a inhibitory signal to the output unit. The hidden units capture appropriate information, but they do not do employ a propositional

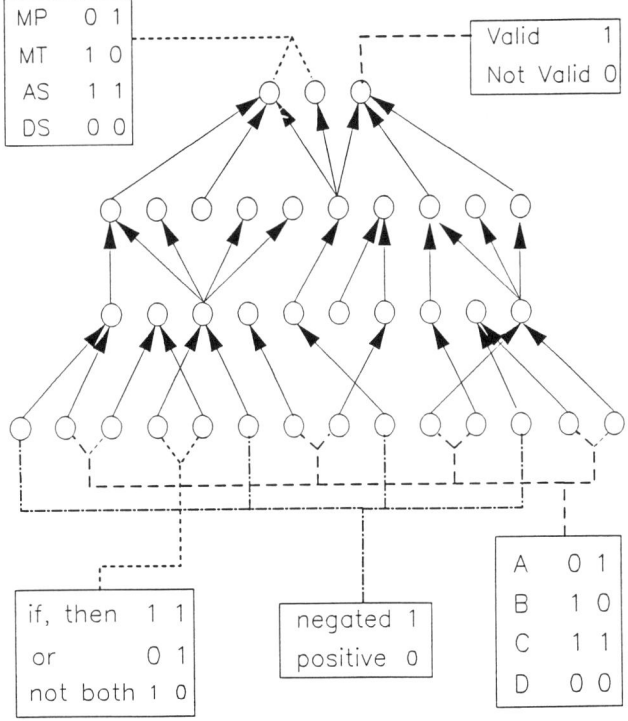

Figure 4.2. A connectionist network for solving logic problems.

format such as would be used in a traditional artificial intelligence program or in a model of cognitive performance developed by a language of thought theorist.

This simple network knows how to evaluate the XOR function, and this capacity can easily be expanded. I have, for example, developed networks for solving problems in the propositional logic. These simulations reveal one of the important characteristics of connectionist networks: generalization from training sets to additional cases. The network (see Figure 4.2) consists of an input layer on which the argument was encoded, two layers of hidden units, and an output layer on which it was trained to produce the argument name and judge its validity. This network was initially trained on 192 logic problems and, after reaching perfect performance on them, was tested on an additional set of 192 problems. It got 76% of these correct (chance would be 12.5%). After training on the first two sets combined, it was tested on the remaining 192 problems and

4. Knowing How to Use Language

reached a performance of 84% correct. I have also trained a similar network to complete enthymemes (arguments with missing premises or conclusions). The same arguments were used as in the previous simulation, and the network was trained on 384 of the problems. It was then tested on the remaining 192 and supplied the missing part 80% of the time. This performance is not perfect, but it indicates that simple networks can learn how to perform such a task. (For a more detailed report, see Bechtel & Abrahamsen, 1991.)

Besides illustrating the capacities of simple networks, this logic network is interesting because arguments typically consist of propositions, and what the network has learned to do is produce behavior that can be interpreted as manipulating propositions, but the network only knows how to do this. The information for performing the task is encoded in weights, not symbolically encoded in rules that the system knows. The proposal I want to advance is that dealing with linguistic material may be something that language users know how to do and that this performance rests on an internal structure something like that found in these networks.

Many connectionist researchers have tried to model linguistic behavior because the use of language is often seen as a major cognitive accomplishment. In order to respond to critics who contend that connectionist networks do not accomplish anything cognitive, they counter by demonstrating how such networks can deal with language. One of the earliest examples is a network developed Rumelhart and McClelland (1986), which learns to generate phonological representations of the past tense of English verbs from phonological representations of the present tense. In the process this simulation exhibits the U-shaped learning pattern similar to that shown by human children. While details of this model have been criticized (Pinker & Prince, 1988), the most serious issue is whether the rather simple architectures of current networks are sufficient to model language.

One of the major features of language that presents a challenge to connectionists is variable binding, which must occur when two expressions in a propositional structure need to be satisfied by the same individual. A simple example of such a context is the rule: If someone is 16 and has taken a driver training course, then that person can take a driving test. Here it is critical that the same person who wants to take the driving test be 16 and have taken the course. Variable binding is a task easily accomplished by symbolic systems, but is very difficult for connectionist networks. One proposal for doing it is found in Touretzky and Hinton (1988), but these investigators require a very detailed architecture in order to do quite modest variable binding. As interesting as their model is, I would contend that this strategy of explicitly designing structures in networks explicitly to handle variable binding may face the same difficulty as the symbol processing approach: It requires building into the system an elaborate structure to permit linguistic behavior without any indication of how such a structure might have evolved. In advancing this as a criticism, I do not want to deny that cognitive systems may be highly structured. The human cognitive system is clearly not a totally connected feedforward network such as I employed in the logic simulation. However, what is attractive about connectionism from a theory-building perspective is the promise of building up from a simpler system to complex structures in such a manner that we can come to understand what are the building blocks of our cognitive system. This is lost if we build into the network that is to model the psychology of language the sophisticated structure observed in language itself.

An alternative strategy is to build in a much simpler structure and to see if, through interaction with a structured environment, the system can learn to behave appropriately. On this view language is a structured system that initially appears external to the organism; the organism learns to interact with it. This strategy is illustrated in Servan-Schreiber, Cleeremans, and McClelland's (1988) recurrent network, which learns to predict symbolic sequences generated by a finite-state grammar from exposure to examples of strings formed according to that grammar. From the perspective advanced here, what is significant is that the network reached the state of knowing how to perform the task of predicting strings specified by a finite state grammar but did not encode propositionally, or in a specially contrived architecture, the rules of that grammar. We can therefore study how the network learned to perform in this highly structured domain, by acquiring an appropriate set of weights.

The development of connectionist systems that know how to perform cognitive tasks, including tasks involving language, seems to point a way to integrating the symbolic and associationist perspectives. Some cognitivists have criticized connectionism as representing merely a return to associationism. It is certainly true that connectionist models have an associationistic character to them. But it is also the case that they provide a vehicle for modeling very rich internal structures not usually considered in classical associationist accounts. If connectionists can also generate models that know how to use symbols, then they may be able to account for the kind of symbolic reasoning that has been the forte of rationalism. One result of this approach is that rule-based symbol processing will have a much smaller role than in symbolic models where it is taken to be foundational to all cognition. Yet humans at least use symbol systems and engage in the sorts of reasoning Descartes and Fodor describe. For

4. Knowing How to Use Language

the most part, this activity may employ external symbols, as when we write or speak, or when we solve logic or math problems by writing them on paper and explicitly manipulate the written symbols. (Many humans eventually learn to perform these activities without explicitly external symbols, a process that may involve utilization of an internal representation of symbols that were initially external. Modeling this process may require developing ways of representing symbol structures in networks.) The connectionist reconciliation of symbol processing and associationism would interpret symbol manipulation as an activity a person learns how to do, but would not treat such language-like processing as a basic cognitive operation (See further discussion in Bechtel & Abrahamsen, 1991).

THE CONTRIBUTION OF ANIMAL LANGUAGE RESEARCH

So far I have not said anything explicit about how animal language research can inform the rapprochement. In this section I sketch a proposal for a fruitful two-way interaction between connectionist model builders and animal language researchers. In one direction, animal language research can reveal some of the ways in which linguistic capacities might develop, and connectionists can attempt to build models that behave similarly. These models can be viewed as tentative explanatory accounts of the competencies displayed by the organism as it masters components of language. These proposed explanations can lead to interaction in the other direction, as models suggest further aspects of the learning process that have not been noted before and prompt more detailed investigations of animal behavior.

The question might be raised as to why connectionists should be interested in the rather simple language systems used by nonhuman organisms rather than more elaborate human languages. One good reason is that fully developed human linguistic performance is so complex and so integrated that it seems nearly impenetrable. Explaining the performance requires decomposing it, but it is very difficult methodologically to decompose the performance in a manner that reveals its actual components and how they interact. When model builders turn to human language, they sometimes try to build in highly complex structures corresponding to those found in the language itself rather than building simple systems that learn how to use those structures. An example of the kind of difficulty one faces in dealing with the linguistic performance of the adult human is seen in Fodor's discussion of the systematicity of both thought and language. Fodor contended that it would be unimaginable for a language user to understand an expression such as "John loves Mary" but not "Mary loves

John." If one accepts such systematicity as basic to cognitive systems, one may be led, like Fodor, to postulate an elaborate internal representation system. But developmentally, there is evidence that children learning a language do learn to process one sentence type while still lacking understanding of closely related sentences. This suggests a different perspective than Fodor's. Because language exhibits such systematicity, a mature speaker of language must develop so as to process any of the related set of sentences, but this does not mean that we need to posit a systematic internal processing system at the outset.

Animal language research allows us to begin with simpler linguistic systems that may reveal components of more fully developed human linguistic performance. By first modeling these systems, connectionists can reduce the tendency to build too much special structure into the system but yet develop systems that can begin to exhibit linguistic abilities. This will provide a useful heuristic strategy for discovering the component capacities figuring in language use. To be more concrete, I briefly indicate examples of work in animal language that might provide a basis for two-way interactions between language researchers and connectionist modelers.

Teaching Chimpanzees to Use Language Intentionally

One of the serious questions raised with respect to the first generation of chimpanzee language projects was whether chimpanzees had learned that their symbols could be used to refer to objects in a variety of linguistic contexts, or whether they had simply learned to use them as required in specific tasks to procure rewards (Savage-Rumbaugh, Rumbaugh, Smith, & Lawson, 1980). In philosophy, the term *intentionality* is used to refer to the fact that symbols have content, that they are about things. Since Brentano (1874/1973) construed intentionality as the mark of the mental, philosophers of mind have been greatly worried about how one might explain it (for discussion, see Bechtel, 1988). A notorious challenge to most symbolic accounts of cognition, raised by Searle (1980), is that a system might use symbols properly without understanding what they meant. For example, a computer programmed to process natural language might do so without any knowledge of what the language referred to. Such a system would lack genuine intentionality. Extrapolating, Searle might charge that Washoe, Nim, and Lana lacked genuine intentionality, at least in their use of signs or lexigrams. In this regard, Savage-Rumbaugh's (1986) research with Sherman and Austin is particularly interesting. These chimpanzees were taught to use a set of lexigrams in a variety of different tasks such as naming and requesting. They were then taught the task of sorting some basic-level lexigrams according to the superordinate lexigrams for food and tool and then

4. Knowing How to Use Language

tested on others. They experienced no difficulty on this task, which required them to sort in terms of the lexigrams' referents since the lexigrams for a category were not physically similar. Thus, the training regime used by Savage-Rumbaugh was sufficient to teach Sherman and Austin how to use symbols intentionally.

This suggests that a connectionist who wished to show how networks could master intentional use of language might do well to consider a training regime much like that employed by Savage-Rumbaugh. The reason to think that a network might master the preliminary tasks Savage-Rumbaugh taught is that each seemed to require extracting particular information from a context. For example, to learn to request a food by name correctly, the chimpanzees had to notice that pressing a lexigram had a specific consequence, namely, activating the dispenser for the named food (see Gauker, 1990, for a related view). Once the causal relation between pressing the lexigram and the dispensing of food became salient, the chimpanzees mastered the task. Networks do well at extracting such information as is evidenced by the XOR model already described (which extracted the OR and AND information) and by Hinton's (1986) network, which learned kinship relations in two hypothetical families from statements of particular relations.

Savage-Rumbaugh's account of Sherman's and Austin's learning intentional use of symbols through learning component tasks raises additional questions for investigation: (a) What is involved in the chimpanzee mastering each of the component tasks, and (b) is mastery of these component tasks sufficient to achieve intentional use of symbols? Here is where developing connectionist models may be extremely fruitful. With a network, unlike an animal, we can observe the changes in weights that occur as a task is mastered. Second, if we succeed in training a single network to perform the separate tasks that Savage-Rumbaugh taught Sherman and Austin, we can then investigate whether for that network this learning is sufficient to perform the categorization task and if so, precisely how what is learned in the component tasks figures in learning the categorization task. (There are, of course, a variety of network designs that might be employed and different ones might perform quite differently.) If such modeling succeeded, we would gain instructive clues as to the internal structures involved in knowing how to use symbols.

Teaching Dolphins to Comprehend Symbolic Instructions

Most chimpanzee language projects (an exception is described later) have emphasized the productive use of language and have not attended to comprehension. Yet, it is clear that humans learn to comprehend language before they produce it. In this light, the research of Herman and his associates (chapters 15, 20, 21 in this volume) in teaching Atlantic bottlenosed dolphins is particularly interesting. What the dolphins have mastered to date is responding appropriately to commands in an artificial language. Attempts to model the dolphins' behavior in networks might be particularly instructive in explaining what is involved in knowing how to comprehend language.

Clearly, a major part of what is involved in learning to comprehend language is learning to pick out different pieces of information in linguistic input. What connectionist researchers need to do is explore what sorts of networks can extract pertinent bits of information in linguistic input. Here they might begin by trying to model how the dolphins have extracted the information they need. What makes the linguistic system Herman has developed particularly interesting is that, even though it is quite simple when compared to English, it does require the animal to attend to both a simple phrase structure and semantic information. The same handsign in different positions in a sequence may denote either the direct object or the indirect object of an action. Nor can position be encoded merely as a slot in a fixed sequence. As a result of modifiers, the indirect object may be in position 1 or 2, while the direct object may be in position 2, 3, or 4. Thus, the second sign could represent either the direct or the indirect object.

Although it is not clear in advance what sort of connectionist network might master this task, a plausible first candidate is Elman's (1990) recurrent network architecture which uses the values obtained on hidden units in previous processing as part of the input to the next processing cycle. This was the sort of network used by Servan-Schreiber et al. (1988) to predict symbolic sequences generated by a finite-state grammar (see earlier discussion). Thinking in terms of such a network suggests an interesting perspective on a difficulty Herman identified in learning of relational sentences. One dolphin, Akeakamai, made most of her errors with the indirect object, especially when the indirect object specified was moveable and so could also have been a direct object. Herman attributed this to a limitation in working memory but it is not clear why a memory as traditionally understood would experience more difficulty when moveable objects were used as indirect objects. A recurrent network does not have an analogue of working memory, but it does exhibit more difficulty

4. Knowing How to Use Language

responding appropriate when information is presented earlier in a string than when it is presented later, and is especially likely to experience greater problems with information such as names of moveable objects that could fill either of two semantic roles. By trying to model sensitivity to phrase structure in a recurrent network we could identify whether it confronts the same limitations when there is ambiguity as to whether a name specifies a direct or an indirect object and so gain further understanding of the difficulties in processing phrase structures. With such a network, we might also discover ways of training that overcome this limitation, which might then be tried in further dolphin research.

Spontaneous Language Learning in a Language-Rich Environment

One thing that appears to many people to differentiate chimpanzee and dolphin use of language from that of humans is that humans do not require explicit training in order to learn language. This is one factor that has made Savage-Rumbaugh's recent work with the pygmy chimpanzee Kanzi so noteworthy. Kanzi was present during a period when Savage-Rumbaugh was trying to teach his mother to use the lexigram system, using much the same strategies as had succeeded with Sherman and Austin. During this period, Kanzi would seemingly play with the lexigram board, often running over to food dispensers after having pressed keys (apparently) at random. When his mother was temporarily removed from the project, Savage-Rumbaugh discovered that Kanzi had actually mastered the connection between certain lexigrams and their referents and did not require specific training. Accordingly, she adopted a strategy of observational learning with Kanzi. Kanzi's caretakers used lexigrams as well as spoken English in his presence as they went about daily activities. Lexigrams were generally available, and Kanzi was free to use them as he chose. Many of Kanzi's daily activities were outside, and he rather quickly mastered the use of lexigrams to inform his caregivers of locations he wished to visit. Generally, when he made his desires known, they were acknowledged. Subsequently, Savage-Rumbaugh noted that Kanzi seemed to comprehend spoken English and indeed confirmed in blind tests that Kanzi understood spoken English words: He could respond to a spoken word by identifying either the proper lexigram or a picture of the object. More recently (this volume, chapter 22), she has reported that Kanzi responded correctly to an impressive number of novel spoken sentences such as *Make the doggie bite your ball!* by performing the required action.

Although Kanzi's spontaneous learning makes it harder to use his accomplishments to distinguish component skills that are involved in eventual mastery of language, the research with him still provides an avenue for decomposing linguistic performance. First, his learning is still slower than a human child, and his final level of development is less than that of a human being. Thus, by trying to understand and model his achievements we are able to look at some elements that may figure in fluent human language use in isolation. Second, by focusing on how he learned, and what elements were required for his learning, we may gain insights into how to build a simulation that also learns language observationally. In attempting to develop models that can learn spontaneously, it will be useful to focus on the differences between those animals that learned observationally and those that seemed to require explicit training. Because at least one common chimpanzee seems to have acquired some language skills through observational learning as well, the difference between Kanzi and the common chimpanzees does not seem to be a species difference alone. A difference that is likely to be important is the chimpanzee's age when training begins. Most research has employed animals that were already more mature than Kanzi at the outset of training, while observational learning has only been noted when exposure to language begins very early. Although this suggests that the difference may be due to differences in the brain at different ages, it is not clear how to model this in connectionist networks. Another difference, however, lies in the nature of the linguistic input the animals received. In using language around Kanzi, his caretakers emphasized utterances that were potentially very meaningful to him. On the one hand, this meant that what was said in his presence contained information that was useful for Kanzi to extract. Thus, if Kanzi could discover a reliable relation between a certain sort of utterance and an action that occurred shortly thereafter, he could begin to learn that language presented useful information. On the other hand, even when language comprehension and production were not serving purely utilitarian goals for Kanzi, the somewhat simplified system to which he was exposed provide him with a system whose properties he could explore simply for its own sake.

This suggests that if connectionists were to try to model Kanzi's acquisition of language through observational learning, they need to concentrate not just on the design of the network, but also on the sorts of nonlinguistic tasks the network would perform, the character of the language to which it was exposed, and the relevance of that language to the nonlinguistic tasks. That is, we would want to begin with language from which it might extract information useful for other tasks in which it was engaged and at the same time present it with enough of the systematicity of language so that it could begin itself to identify that systematicity and adapt its behavior to it. Networks are quite sensitive to the sorts of regularities that are available to them in the environment

4. Knowing How to Use Language

as long as attending to that information can improve the network's performance. The challenge is to create this combination of circumstances. If they can be achieved, it may be possible to show that both networks and language users can learn through observation how to use a systematic system without building that very systematicity into the system.

CONCLUSION

One of the exciting prospects of animal language research is that we might finally discover a means to decomposing linguistic performance. This does not mean denying the reality of linguistic performance, but showing how it is achieved through interaction of more basic cognitive capacities. If this were done, we might finally achieve a rapprochement between the rationalistic symbolic tradition, which has treated language-like processing as basic to cognition, and associationism, which has long emphasized searching for more basic cognitive primitives. Using Ryle's term, this would involve showing that linguistic systems are systems we know how to use but in which the internal processes that make this possible are not themselves linguistic. I have argued that connectionism offers the resources for the appropriate kind of internal modeling. But connectionism must avoid the danger of proceeding directly to human language and then trying to build in too much explicit linguistic structure so as to master such developed languages. It needs help from animal language research so as to decompose linguistic performance. It can also provide animal language researchers with potentially useful models of the internal processing that is responsible for the performance the animals exhibit. Thus, a two-way interaction between connectionists and animal language researchers might facilitate development of a model of the cognitive structures underlying language that does not assume linguistic capacity at the outset but in the end generate true linguistic competence.

ACKNOWLEDGMENTS

I received extremely valuable comments and suggestions on earlier versions of this chapter from Adele Abrahamsen, Christopher Gauker, James Pate, Herbert Roitblat, and Sue Savage-Rumbaugh. I am most appreciative of their help.

REFERENCES

Bechtel, W. (1988). *Philosophy of mind: An overview for cognitive science*. Hillsdale, NJ: Lawrence Erlbaum Associates.

Bechtel, W. & Abrahamsen, A. (in press). *Connectionism and the mind: An introduction to parallel processing in networks.* Oxford: Basil Blackwell.

Bechtel, W. & Richardson, R. C. (1992). *Discovering complexity: Decomposition and localization as scientific research strategies.* Princeton: Princeton University Press.

Brentano, F. (1973). *Psychology from an empirical standpoint* (A.C. Pancurello, D. B. Terrell, & L. L. McAlister, Trans.). New York: Humanities. (Originally published 1874).

Elman, J. (1988). Finding structure in time. *Cognitive Science,* 14, 179-211.

Fodor, J. A. (1975). *The language of thought.* New York: Crowell.

Fodor, J. A. (1987). *Psychosemantics: The problem of meaning in the philosophy of mind.* Cambridge, MA: MIT Press.

Fodor, J. A., & Pylyshyn, Z. W. (1988). Connectionism and cognitive architecture: A critical analysis. *Cognition,* 28, 3-71.

Gauker, C. (1990). How to learn a language like a chimpanzee. *Philosophical Psychology,* 3, 31-53.

Hinton, G. E. (1986). Learning distributed representations of concepts. *Proceedings of the Eighth Annual Conference of the Cognitive Science Society.* Hillsdale, NJ: Lawrence Erlbaum Associates.

Minsky, M. A., & Papert, S. (1969). *Perceptrons.* Cambridge, MA: MIT Press.

Pinker, S., & Prince, A. (1988). On language and connectionism: Analysis of a parallel distributed processing model of language acquisition. *Cognition,* 28, 73-193.

Pylyshyn, Z. (1984). *Computation and cognition: Towards a foundation for cognitive science.* Cambridge, MA: MIT Press/Bradford Books.

Ristau, C. A., & Robbins, D. (1982). Language in the great apes: A critical review. *Advances in the Study of Behavior,* 12, 141-255.

4. Knowing How to Use Language

Rumelhart, D. E., & McClelland, J. L. (1986). On learning the past tense of English verbs. In J. L. McClelland, D. E. Rumelhart, & the PDP Research Group (Eds.), *Parallel distributed processing: Explorations in the microstructure of cognition: Volume 2. Psychological and biological models* (pp. 216-271). Cambridge, MA. MIT Press/Bradford Books.

Rumelhart, D. E., McClelland, J. L., & the PDP Research Group (1986). *Parallel distributed processing: Explorations in the microstructure of cognition: Volume 1. Foundations.* Cambridge, MA: MIT Press/Bradford Books.

Ryle, G. (1949). *The concept of mind.* New York: Barnes and Noble.

Servan-Schreiber, D., Cleeremans, A., & McClelland, J. L. (1988). *Encoding sequential structure in simple recurrent networks* (Tech. Report No. CMU-CS-88-183). Pittsburgh: Carnegie Mellon University.

Savage-Rumbaugh, E. S. (1986). *Ape language: From conditioned response to symbol.* New York: Columbia University Press.

Savage-Rumbaugh, E. S., Rumbaugh, D. M., Smith, S. T., & Lawson, J. (1980). Reference: The linguistic essential. *Science, 210,* 922-925.

Searle, J. (1980). Minds, brains, and programs. *Behavioral and Brain Sciences, 3,* 417-424.

Simon, H. A. (1969). *The sciences of the artificial.* Cambridge, MA: MIT Press.

Skinner, B. F. (1957). *Verbal behavior.* New York: Appleton-Century-Crofts.

Touretzsky, D. S., & Hinton, G. E. (1988). A distributed connectionist production system. *Cognitive Science, 12,* 423-466.

5 A Proposal for Computer Modeling of Animal Linguistic Comprehension

Earl Hunt

THE THEORETICAL ISSUE RAISED BY ANIMAL LINGUISTIC COMPREHENSION

In 1950, psychology was privileged to have two revealed truths. One was that it was impossible to teach an ape to communicate with humans using a human-like language. The idea that one might communicate to dolphins using such a language was strictly reserved for Doctor Doolittle stories. The other revealed truth was that language was acquired by a general learning process that was not qualitatively different in rat and human, but that was so quantitatively elaborate in humans that human linguistic behavior superficially appeared to be qualitatively different from animal communication (Skinner, 1957).

The revealed truth, circa 1970, was that the revealed truth of 1950 was false. By then it had clearly been shown that apes could comprehend messages in a human-like language. Research on comprehension[1] in dolphins was soon to

---

[1] Throughout I shall restrict my comments to comprehension. The issue of nonhuman animals producing language-like behavior is considerably harder to deal with.

follow. Paradoxically, it was, and still is, widely believed that humans learn language by a species-specific mechanism specialized for acquiring natural language alone. There are two important codicils to this second revealed truth. The first is that the laws developed to account for the shaping of behavior in rats, pigeons, and humans have little to do with language acquisition (Chomsky, 1959). The second codicil is that whatever the apes and dolphins are comprehending, it is not language.

In the 1990s things are much more muddled. Truth Number 1 (1970 variety) has clearly been shown to be true. Other chapters in this volume document the fact that at least four species (chimpanzees, pygmy chimpanzees, bottlenosed dolphins, and California sea lions) can respond to very complex messages, providing that they have been appropriately trained by humans. Whether or not the animals are comprehending language is much less clear, simply because we have no clearcut definition of language (Bradshaw, this volume, chapter 2). In terms of establishing empirical observations, research in the area I call *animal linguistic comprehension* has been a stunning success.

But what does it all mean? This is not at all clear. One way to look at the theoretical meaning of animal linguistic comprehension data is to accept them as evidence of the use of a reduced form of human natural language. From this, one is tempted to conclude that the language acquisition mechanism is not species specific. This does not follow logically. Furthermore, it seems to be incompatible with most of what we know about human speech. There is a speech-specific area in the human brain. It is not unreasonable to speculate that this area may exist in rudimentary form in a species closely related to humans such as the chimpanzee, but it seems unlikely to exist in a very distantly related species such as the dolphin or sea lion. On the other hand, it is arbitrary in the extreme to assert that the behavior exhibited in animal linguistic comprehension "isn't language" and therefore is irrelevant to language learning. Such an approach simply sweeps inconvenient facts under a definitional rug.

In this highly speculative chapter, I want to challenge the second revealed truth of 1970: that a speech-specific mechanism is required to account for linguistic behavior. To what extent can the data from animal linguistic communication research be accounted for by general discrimination learning mechanisms? I sketch one theoretical approach to this question, although I certainly do not resolve the issue. Raising the question in this manner is not meant to be an attack on the animal linguistic research. What I want to do is to fit it in with a particular theoretical perspective. In order to do so, a few remarks about the "special nature of language" are in order.

5. Computer Modeling of Linguistic Comprehension

The linguistic revolution of the 1955-1970 period was based on the assumption that general associationist laws of learning could not explain language acquisition. The linguistic argument was largely presented as an "isn't it obvious" recitation of examples rather than as a proof of the inadequacy of associationist models. Somewhat late in the 1950-1970 period Minsky and Papert (1969) indirectly strengthed the linguistic argument by presenting formal proofs that a restricted form of associationism could not account for certain discriminations that humans clearly do make. Minsky and Papert's argument was principally directed at the discriminations that are made in perception. However, they did show that the associationist models they considered could not perform discriminations that are closely related to linguistic discriminations, such as the notion of parity. This work has to be considered when debating the need for special learning mechanisms for language. As a matter of historical fact, though, linguists and psycholinguists had accepted the need for special linguistic mechanisms well before Minsky and Papert's work was published.

Minsky and Papert's mathematical conclusions applied only to the restricted associationistic learning mechanisms that they defined as formal systems. These results are mathematical facts, and as such, cannot be challenged. Minsky and Papert also made a much wider informal argument, in which they doubted that more complex associationist models of discrimination learning could account for classification behavior based on the structure of the object being classified. This conclusion, although accepted widely at the time, is very probably false.

The argument against accepting Minsky and Papert's pessimistic informal conclusion is based on a line of research variously known as neural net modeling, connectionism, or parallel distributed processing (PDP) research (Rumelhart & McClelland, 1986). I use the term PDP modeling, because it is more descriptive than connectionism and does not have the superfluous biological connotation of neural net modeling. In the remainder of this paper, I shall sketch what the PDP approach is and outline how it might be applied to a theoretical analysis of the animal linguistic studies.

What Are PDP Models?

PDP models are loose collections of theories based on pattern recognition and learning. The models fall into two general classes, which I call *implicit rule learning* and *instance-based learning* models. The models are best explained graphically, with the aid of a few mathematical formalisms.

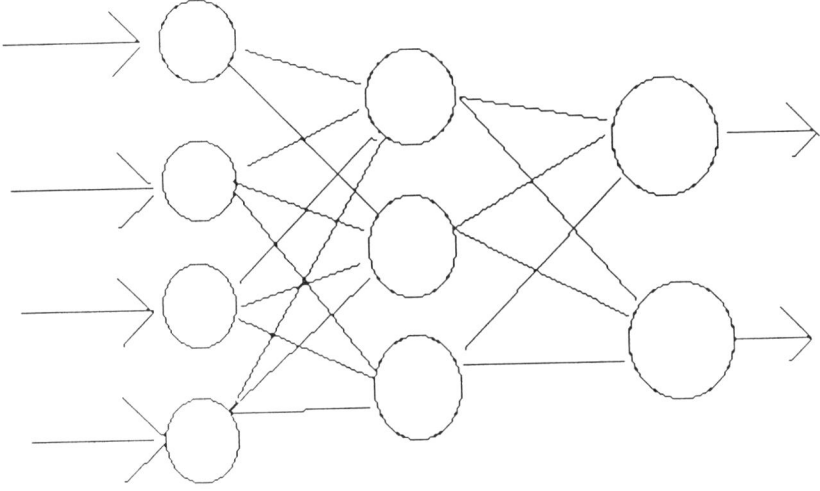

Figure 5.1. A 3-layer PDP model.

Implicit rule models are based on the idea that an organism can detect primitive features and define classification rules based on nonlinear combinations of these features. (The term "nonlinear" is the key. Minsky and Papert considered only linear combinations.) The idea is shown graphically in Figure 5.1, which depicts a system consisting of three layers of nodes. Each node should be considered as a center of (neural?) activation. The first (left-hand) layer consists of feature detectors. These are directly connected to the environment. The third (right-hand) layer consists of response units. When these are raised to some level of activation, an overt response is made.

The stimulus-response rules that the system follows are determined by the transmission of activation from the first layer to the third, via the second. Because the second layer units are not directly connected to the external environment, they are generally referred to as "hidden" units. The transmission of activation through the network is nonlinear, because each unit can receive as input any amount of transmission but can output values only in a restricted range (e.g., zero to one). The transmission from one unit to another can be weighted either positively or negatively. Formally, let $x_i(t)$ be the output of node i and let $y_j(t)$ be the input to node j. If node j is a first level (feature detection) node, the input is determined by the environment. Finally, let $w_{ij}(t)$

5. Computer Modeling of Linguistic Comprehension

be the weight of the connection between node i and node j. The input-output relations are:

$$y_j(t) = \sum_i w_{ij}(t) x_i(t) \qquad (1)$$

and

$$x_j(t+1) = f(y_j(t)) \qquad (2)$$

where $f(y_j(t))$ must fall between limits A and B, that is, $A \le f(y_j(t)) \le B$.

A stimulus is defined by a configuration of activation levels in the feature detection layer. Similarly, a response is defined by the activation levels in the response layer. A discrimination problem is a mapping from the set of all possible stimuli to the set of all possible responses.

What is the relevance of this for psychology, and, in particular, studies of animal linguistic communications? In linguistic comprehension studies (e.g., Herman, Richards, & Wolz, 1984; Schusterman & Krieger, 1986), humans train animals to perform complex discriminations. Schusterman (1989) has characterized the resulting problems as contingent discrimination problems. In what appear to be the most challenging of these problems, the animal has to learn what appears, at least superficially, to be the syntax of a simple phrase structure grammar. The theoretical question asked here is whether or not PDP models can be created to account for both learning and performance. This in turn requires a definition of *learning* and *performance*.

A discrimination problem can be performed by a PDP model if a network can be constructed that achieves the appropriate stimulus-response mapping. It turns out that all discrimination problems can be solved. This follows from some standard results in mathematical logic. It can be proven that any computable function can be expressed as a combination of the logical functions NOT and OR, and both NOT and OR can be computed by networks such as the one shown in Figure 5.1. To illustrate these complexities in an elementary way, Figure 5.2 shows a PDP network realization of the logical function EXCLUSIVE OR (X or Y but not both) XOR problem. Note that this is, in Shusterman's (1989) terms, a contingent discrimination. The response to X depends on the presence or absence of Y, and vice versa. Somewhat more complex networks can be designed to accommodate limited temporal contexts, that is, making the response to X dependent on the immediately prior stimulus. Also, the solution is a mapping based on a nonlinear weighting of features. The problem itself could not be solved by the associationist devices Minsky and Papert analyzed.

It should be noted that it is very hard to create networks that can encompass the depth of nested expressions sometimes found in human language. However, such nesting is far beyond any study I know of that has ever been attempted with a nonhuman animal.

What is "learning" in a PDP system? The network begins with a random set of weights. The system is then presented with a stimulus. It will eventually make some response. Mathematically, this means that the system will have computed a vector representing the output of the response units (the rightmost units of Figures 5.1 and 5.2). The vector is compared to a desired vector, and an error correction message is sent to the system. The system uses this information to adjust the weights. More formally, let $R(t)$ be the response vector at time t, $D(t)$ be the desired response vector, $X(t)$ be the outputs of all units other than the response vector, and $W(t)$ be the weight matrix. A learning algorithm, $f(x)$, computes a new set of response weights:

$$W(t+1) = f(R(t),D(t),X(t),W(t)). \tag{3}$$

A discrimination problem is said to be solvable with algorithm $f(x)$ if a network of weights can be constructed by algorithm f for all possible initial weight settings, $W(0)$.

The development of learning algorithms is one of the major research activities in PDP studies today. One algorithm, called *back propagation* (Rumelhart McClelland, 1986), has proven to be particularly useful in the sense that it has been shown to solve a wide variety of discrimination problems. Gluck and Bower (1988) have pointed out that the back propagation algorithm is also of interest to psychologists because the computations used in its first stage, in which the executed response is compared to the desired response, are closely related to a learning algorithm that Rescorla and Wagner (1972) proposed as a model of classical conditioning.

Networks such as the one depicted in Figure 5.1 are *rule-learning* models, in the sense that the response is a nonlinear sum of the collection of

5. Computer Modeling of Linguistic Comprehension

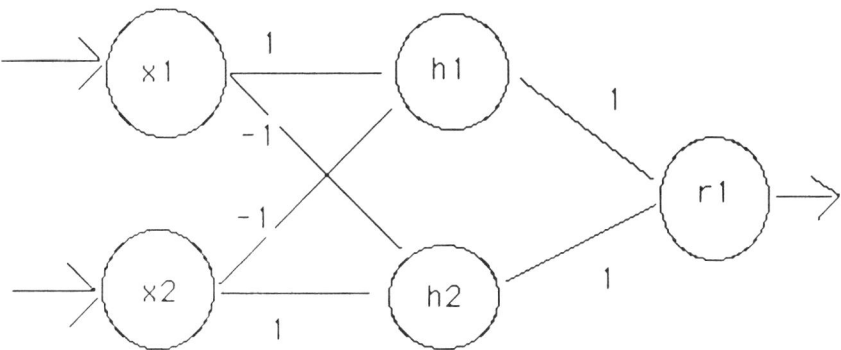

Figure 5.2. A PDP network realization of the logical function exclusive or (XOR).

features in the input. At any one time the model's history of learning is entirely contained in the set of weights. There is no representation of specific stimulus-response-reward episodes. It is also possible to develop instance-based PDP models. These models record specific learning episodes by establishing bonds between the features of the stimulus, the response made, and the feedback received. When a new situation is presented, it is compared to old situations and an "analogous response" is created. This gives instance-based models the capability of responding to novel situations (Hintzman, 1986). Although not as much research has been done on the computational properties of instance-based models as has been done on rule-realization models, these models should not be ruled out as explanations of biological learning, especially in creatures with large brain systems.

The Connection to Animal Linguistic Comprehension

The background having been established, the theoretical proposal can now be sketched. Can PDP models be constructed to account for the data on animal linguistic comprehension? Intuitively, this is a researchable question. However, the design of the research requires some thought.

Most of the research workers in the modern animal linguistic comprehension field keep superb records of training sequences. Thus, in principle, it would be possible to recreate the training sequences used for every animal in captivity. The straightforward way to proceed would be to use these training sequences as input to PDP networks to see if a network could be found that would recreate both the animals' asymptotic performance and their performance during training.

In practice it is unlikely that this will ever happen. There are two reasons for pessimism. One is the sheer logistical difficulty of dealing with masses of data, even computer-readable data developed with different recording systems and notations. The second reason is more fundamental. Although there is voluminous data on every animal that has been trained, there are very few such animals. Furthermore, in spite of the high degree of experimental rigor practiced in all the laboratories that I know of in this field, it is undoubtedly the case that on any one trial the experimental animal may be distracted and may respond to something not noted in the training record. This means that there is little hope of achieving what is essentially a statistical test of a theory, given the very sparse number of training records available, even though each of those records is individually very rich.

Fortunately, there is a solution to the problem. Each of the animals that has been a subject in these studies has its own unique training history. However, that training history was generated by the experimenters' applying a set of principles to define the trial-by-trial stimulus sequence. This means that every individual training sequence can be regarded as having been sampled from the set of training sequences that the experimenters regard as equivalent. It should be possible to recover the principles used to generate the actual training sequence and use them to generate very large sets of theoretically equivalent sequences. These sequences could then be used in attempts to create PDP models of the animal linguistic comprehension data.

I strongly believe that this can be done, although I am the first to admit that this is a conjecture. Suppose the effort were successful. What would it tell us?

First, it would provide a theoretical connection between the animal linguistic comprehension literature and other literature on learning. This is important, because at this moment the animal linguistic comprehension work stands rather apart from other scientific endeavors. That is a serious problem; therefore the present theoretical endeavor should be worthwhile from the viewpoint of those interested in animal linguistic comprehension.

Second, the effort would be a useful step forward in research on PDP systems. Efforts to understand the psychological significance of PDP research have been hampered by a lack of clearcut ties between the behavior of the

5. Computer Modeling of Linguistic Comprehension

models and the sorts of behavior that we observe in both humans and animals. This has particularly been the case for PDP research on language learning, which has been heavily attacked on the grounds that the training sequences used to simulate children's language learning do not resemble the environment actually experienced by the child (Pinker and Prince, 1988). The animal linguistic comprehension phenomena are both rich enough and well documented enough to provide an interesting and unexplored research question.

Finally, success in this effort would document a case in which interesting "fragments" of language were captured by a PDP system. This would show that it was not necessary to postulate a special speech mechanism in order to explain some linguistic phenomena. Of course it would not show that there is no special speech mechanism in humans. Neither would it show that they don't need one. To show that, one would have to define more precisely what language is. And that, as Bradshaw (this volume, chapter 2) has shown, seems to be an endless debate.

REFERENCES

Chomsky, N. (1959). Review of B.F. Skinner, *Verbal Behavior Language, 35*, 26-57.

Gluck, M. A. & Bower, G.H. (1988). Evaluating an adaptive network model of human learning. *Journal of Memory and Language, 27*, 166-195.

Herman, L. M., Richards, D. G. & Wolz, J. P. (1984). Comprehension of sentences by bottlenosed dolphins. *Cognition, 16*, 129-219.

Hintzman, D. L. (1986). "Schema abstraction" in a multiple trace model. *Psychological Review*, 93, 411-428.

Minsky, M. & Papert, S. (1969). *Perceptrons: An introduction to computational geometry.* Cambridge, MA. MIT Press.

Pinker, S., & Prince, A. (1988). On language and connectionism: Analysis of a parallel distributed processing model of language acquisition. *Cognition*, 28, 73-193.

Rescorla, R. A. & Wagner, A. R. (1972). A theory of Pavlovian conditioning: Variations in the effectiveness of reinforcement and nonreinforcement.

In A. H. Black & W. F. Prokasy (Eds.) *Classical conditioning II: Current research and theory* (pp. 64-99). New York: Appleton-Century-Crofts.

Rumelhart, D. E., & McClelland, J. L. (1986). On learning the past tense of English verbs. In McClelland, Rumelhart, & the PDP Research Group (Eds.), *Parallel distributed processing: Explorations in the microstructure of cognition: Volume 2. Psychological and biological models* (pp. 216-271). Cambridge, MA. MIT Press/Bradford Books.

Schusterman, R. J. (1989). Please parse the sentence: Animal cognition in the procrustean bed of linguistics. *The Psychological Record*, 39, 3-18.

Schusterman, R. J. & Krieger, K. (1986). Artificial language comprehension and size transposition by a California sea lion (*Zalophus californianus*). *Journal of Comparative Psychology*, 100, 348-355.

Skinner, B. F. (1957). *Verbal behavior.* New York: Appleton-Century-Crofts.

6 Language Acquisition and the Power of Expression

Lois Bloom

The study of language acquisition in human children typically proceeds in one or another of two directions. One is to determine how children acquire knowledge about language. Studies with a focus on the language the child is learning are ordinarily concerned with acquisition of words, semantics, syntax, or discourse. For example, in studies of the development of syntax, child sentences are examined for evidence of the structures the child knows and the conditions in which the child knows to apply them. Another direction in child language studies is to determine how children acquire language as a "tool" for socially and strategically influencing the activities of other persons and getting things done in the world. Studies that focus on the instrumental function of language examine the uses of language in everyday contexts. In both these perspectives on language acquisition, researchers typically take what Searle (1984) has called a "third person perspective." Speech is observed as it occurs in real time, and features of utterance and context are compared to discover what the child knows of language and how it is used in interactions with other persons. Such a perspective puts heavy emphasis on those things that are external to the child and therefore observable, such as speech and social behaviors.

An alternative is a view of language acquisition that proceeds from a first-person perspective in explicitly addressing the contents of the states of mind that underlie actions and, especially, acts of expressing and interpreting.

These states of mind include the beliefs, desires, and feelings that we express as we relate to one another in everyday contexts. Language has evolved in societies for making such expression possible. It follows, then, that children learn language in the effort to make known to others the contents of their own beliefs, desires, and feelings and to attribute beliefs, desires, and feelings to other persons. These are the unobservable facts in language acquisition and they determine that knowledge of the lexicon, syntax, semantics, and discourse will be acquired. Furthermore, language can succeed in influencing other persons in social contexts only because language makes such internal mental contents manifest and puts them in a public place (Taylor, 1979, 1985). Expression is central in this perspective. All the functions of language, including its instrumental and designative functions, depend on the fact that what one has in mind determines what is said and what is understood of what others say.

A first-person perspective, then, begins with the assumption that the actions of speaking and interpreting are determined by psychological attitudes of belief, desire, and feeling directed toward some mentally present content (e.g., entities and events). The centrality of expression in this view ties language acquisition to the two important aspects of the mental life of the young child: cognition and emotion.

Young children on the threshold of language are already quite successful, and have been for some time, in using affect for expression. The importance of emotional expression in infancy has been well documented in the last two decades of research in infant communication and emotional development. Caregivers readily respond to the young infant's cries, whimpers, smiles, and chortles and depend on these signals for their caregiving practices. Since Darwin, we have assumed that these capacities for emotional expression are biologically determined. They have important signal value for protecting and extending the species, and they have reactive value as well for the regulation of physiological arousal and discharge. The question we asked in the research I refer to in this chapter is: How is language acquired in the second year of life in relation to this system of affect expression that is already in place?

One of the best known "facts" of language development is that children differ widely in age of onset and rate of acquisition. For this reason, we used three reference points to define the transition from prelexical vocalizing and emotional expression in infancy to language. These allowed us to equate the children for language achievement rather than age in our analyses. The first reference point was the child's first words, which ordinarily appear sometime around the first birthday, plus or minus several months. The second was a

6. Language Acquisition and Expression

vocabulary spurt, which is the sharp increase in the number of words in a child's vocabulary that has been observed repeatedly at least since Stern and Stern (1907). These two reference points, first words and a vocabulary spurt, generally define the beginning and end of the single-word period and the child's discovery of words. The third was the transition to multiword speech and the beginning of grammar, which ordinarily happens sometime around the second birthday. We have used these reference points in the second and third years of life in our studies of the emergence of language as the development of expression.

In asking how children acquire the power of expression through language, we have drawn a distinction between *observable* and *unobservable* phenomena. Unobservable phenomena, when we use language, consist of the representations we have in mind and our attitudes toward them as we talk and listen. These representations are data structures that we construct out of what we perceive in the immediate "here and now" and what we recall from what we know and have stored in memory. Our psychological attitudes toward these representations consist of the momentary feelings, desires, and beliefs that we have in mind toward them. These data structures are intentional states in the philosophical sense of Danto (1973), Dennett (1978), Fodor (1979), Searle (1983) and Taylor (1985). They have been the recent focus of attention in linguistics, for example, the "mental spaces" of Fauconnier (1985), and cognitive science, for example, the "mental models" of Johnson-Laird (1983). The important point about such mental phenomena for the acquisition of language is this. These representations that underlie actions of expressing and interpreting are hidden within the individual. They require expression: to make them manifest, to give them form in an embodiment, to make them public (Danto, 1973; Taylor, 1979). It is this that drives the acquisition of language.

We have made such unobservable phenomena the focus of our research in our studies of the emergence of language. The assumption that children learn language for expression and articulation of these underlying representations is the focus of our theoretical perspective. Before going on to show how we translated theory into method, it may be instructive to compare this perspective to another widespread assumption in language research with both human children and animals. The prevailing metaphor in much language acquisition research today is "tool use" with an emphasis on the designative and instrumental functions of language. The emphasis in this perspective is on observable phenomena in communication: language happens between persons and the effect of language is to influence the actions of other persons.

Bloom

THE "TOOL USE" METAPHOR

When the focus is on the instrumental function of language, the assumption is that we use language and children learn language to get things done in the world. The emphasis in research is on pragmatics, means-end relations, and the social functions of speech (e.g., Bates, Benigni, Bretherton, Camaioni, & Volterra, 1979). This perspective explains why Vygotsky (1930/1978), who stressed the (a) communicative function, (b) organizing function, and (c) practical importance of speech is the current child language "guru". In fact, the use of language as a tool was cited by Vygotsky as the factor that distinguished human from animal language: "Although children's use of tools during their preverbal period is comparable to that of apes, as soon as speech and the use of signs are incorporated into any action. . . the specifically human use of tools is thus realized, going beyond the more limited use of tools possible among the higher animals" (1930/1978, pp. 24-26).

This same sentiment regarding the instrumental function of speech for distinguishing animal and human language motivated de Laguna (1927/1963) as well: "Speech is the great medium through which human cooperation is brought about. . . . The problem which we have before us, then, is to compare and differentiate the type of social control effected by the cries of animals with that effected by speech in human society" (pp. 19, 21).

This was a popular position among the contemporaries of Vygotsky and de Laguna who were also writing at the time. Language was considered "the most important of the instruments of civilization . . . used to aid the process of thinking and to record . . . achievements" by Ogden and Richards (1923/1946, p. 24). According to Wittgenstein (1934-1935/1958), "there is no one relation of name to object, but as many as there are uses of sounds or scribbles which we call names" (pp. 172-173). The anthropologist Malinowski (1923) put forth a "situational theory of meaning" and in his "contextualist view": "Speech. . . is primarily used for the achievement of a practical result [and] . . . is meaningless without the context of the activity in which it is enveloped. . . words which cross from one actor to another do not serve primarily to communicate thought: they connect work and correlate manual and bodily movements" (Malinowski, 1935, Vol. 1, pp. 8-9).

An apt summary of the tool use metaphor at that time is "words are tools, and the "meaning" of a tool is its use" (Sampson, 1980, p. 224).

6. Language Acquisition and Expression

This instrumental view of language was, in fact, a response to the rise in behaviorism and the increased emphasis on observable phenomena in the early part of this century. Indeed, de Laguna called her model of language and its acquisition "social behaviorism." The view of language as a social "tool" was also a reaction to the earlier idea of language as expression that flourished in the previous century.

LANGUAGE AS EXPRESSION

The view that language is the expression of ideas has a long history, dating back in psychology at least to Wundt and in philosophy to Humboldt, Husserl, and Frege among others (as summarized, for example, in Taylor, 1985). de Laguna's thesis was an explicit denunciation of the centrality of expression in language as it was articulated in particular by Wundt at the turn of the century and by the 19th century anthropologist Tylor (1871), who had written:

We must cease to measure the historical importance of emotional exclamations, of gesture signs, and of picture-writing, by their comparative insignificance in modern civilized life, but must bring ourselves to associate the articulate words of the dictionary in one group with cries and gestures and pictures, as being all of them means of manifesting outwardly the inward workings of the mind" (quoted in de Laguna, 1927/1963, p. 17).

The most explicit articulation of this thesis for the study of child language and its acquisition belongs to Clara and Wilhelm Stern (1907): "A word is an expression of a unified content of consciousness. A sentence . . . is the expression of a unified position either taken, or about to be taken concerning a content of consciousness" (translated and quoted in Blumenthal, 1970, p. 91).

The purpose of this chapter is to revive this idea in proposing that children learn language for expression rather than as an instrument for getting things done in the world. To be sure, words influence what other persons do, but such effects are subordinate to the expressive power that the individual achieves through language. It is obviously true that "[s]peech is the . . . one indispensable instrument for creating the ties of the moment without which unified social action is impossible" (Malinowski, 1923, p. 310). However, the social and interpersonal functions of language absolutely depend on the centrality of expression. This fact was recognized by Heider (1958), the founder of attribution theory in social psychology, who proposed that the psychology of persons guides the psychology of the interpersonal. Attribution theory made clear that the beliefs, feelings, and desires of individuals must be taken into account in the effort to understand and explain coordinated social activity. Language is the preeminent capacity we have for expressing these ideas that we form about ourselves and other persons and the expectations for action and interaction that follow from them. Thus, expression is not only one of the functions of language but it is basic to all its functions, including the social, designative, and instrumental functions.

The centrality of expression is common to both the language of humans and the language of animals. The tool use metaphor has had a prominent place in the history of animal language studies, and using a tool presupposes a goal with some psychological attitude toward that goal. At the minimum, this would include belief that it exists, is attainable, a desire to attain it, and feelings about the result of attaining it or difficulty in attaining it. The fundamental fact that expression is central to both human and animal languages is obvious. Once we acknowledge that fact and make it explicit in our research, the question then turns from similarities and differences in the languages themselves to understanding how humans and animals are similar and different in the representations their language expresses.

In our research with human children we have inquired into the developments that make these representations possible in our efforts to explain how it is that a language is learned. The sources for the beliefs, desires, and feelings of the young language-learning child, and for animals as well, are in the data of perception and knowledge. Developments occur in the knowledge base in memory and in the sorts of cues individuals can use for accessing data from memory for the representations they express. These developments, in turn, depend on the development of a notation system for such mental contents. Human children are, at first, constrained to nonlinguistic perceptual and physiological cues for recall from memory. This is true for animals observed in the wild as well, not having been exposed to words and signs. Nevertheless, young human infants and animals in the wild do use affective expressions for the sorts of mutual attribution that establish intersubjectivity and sustain the individual in a social world.

Once language begins to be acquired, human infants can use words and signs for recall. We know from the animal language studies reported in other chapters in this book that animals are capable of similar notation systems. Dolphins and sea lions can make use of signs, and chimpanzees can make use of spoken words as cues for recall in guiding their actions. Several chapters in this

6. Language Acquisition and Expression

book address, at least implicitly, the cognitive underpinnings for interpretive and expressive acts by animals. By making the view of language as expression explicit, we can explore both the limitations and the possibilities for what an animal of any species can hold in mind for language.

In sum, the power of expression comes with the ability to take something that is hidden within the individual and make it public (Taylor, 1985). Hidden within the individual are the contents of feelings, beliefs, and desires. Two modes of expression that allow us to attribute such internal properties to the expressor are affect and language. Affect expression is in place in early infancy and its forms are biologically determined. Language is the system of expression provided by society and culture for making public what is internal to the individual. Before language, affect expresses how the infant feels about such mental contents. By learning language, infants come to express and articulate what these contents are about and to attribute such contents to other persons.

LANGUAGE, EMOTION, AND COGNITION

The study of language is typically fragmented. We study different aspects of language as though they are indeed separate domains. This is so, perhaps, because we tend to be intimidated by the complexity of language and the enormity of the task of its acquisition. However, domains of language are integrated and not separate for the child (Bloom, 1976; Bloom & Lahey, 1978). Once pointed out, such integration is often taken for granted. For example, before Bloom (1968/1970) the study of meaning had been virtually overlooked in contemporary psycholinguistic research. Some may well wonder today that meaning was not considered admissible evidence in studies of language acquisition until the systematic use of context to explore the role of semantics for syntax acquisition in that study.

The same situation exists today with respect to the relation between emotion and language and the relative contributions of cognition to both. For example, the upsurge of research and theory in cognitive science in the last two decades studiously avoided the cognition of emotional experience until only recently. Similarly, the cognitive activity involved in emotional experience and expression has only gradually been recognized in studies of emotion. Beginning with the early work of Arnold (1960) and others, the emphasis on the role that cognition plays in emotion has grown steadily. More contemporary theory and research have made clear that emotional experience entails the cognitive activity of evaluating the situation in relation to some goal (e.g., Campos, Barrett, Lamb,

Goldsmith, & Stenberg, 1983; Oatley & Johnson-Laird, 1987; Stein & Levine, 1987).

The study of emotional development and the study of language development have proceeded separately from one another, even though both have to do with the mind of the young child and its development. Similarly, in the history of animal language studies, emotion originally played a large role in efforts to understand animal communication. In contrast, contemporary laboratory research on animal language pays little attention to emotional experience and expression.

This separation of emotion and language is due to the fact that emotion, for a long time, was considered disorganizing and disruptive; more "primitive;" and less worthy as an object of study in general. In linguistics, the emphasis on spoken words and sentences dictated the avoidance of any consideration of the relevance of emotion to language. When emotion is considered as an object for linguistic study, the emphasis is generally on the words that name the emotions.[1] Of course, language provides names for the emotions and children learn these names, but children also have to talk about the objects of their emotions: their causes, circumstances, and consequences. And emotion and language have mutual effects on each other because of the cognition that both require. In fact, recent research and theory in emotional development have stressed the organizing and regulating functions of emotional experiences. Jean Piaget himself described the relationship between affectivity and intelligence as a "functional" one: Affectivity plays "the role of an energy source on which the functioning but not the structures of intelligence... depend. ... like gasoline, which activates the motor of an automobile but does not modify its structure" (1954/1981, p. 5). A related development, in turn, is the reciprocal regulation of affectivity and its expression by language and our research has demonstrated the mutual influence between affectivity and language (Bloom & Beckwith, 1989; Bloom, Beckwith, & Capatides, 1988; Bloom & Capatides. 1987).

The question we asked in studying the developmental relationship between affect expression and language was, What are infants expressing before and after language begins? In attempting to answer the question, we were unaware of any explicit theoretical or empirical claims that expressions of the discrete emotions (e.g., anger, joy, sadness) would relate in any interesting ways

---

[1]For exceptions, see Schieffelin (1979, 1990) and Ochs and Schieffelin (1989) for accounts of emotion in language and its acquisition.

6. Language Acquisition and Expression

to language development. For this reason, we coded two gradient properties of affect expression: valence (hedonic tone) as positive, negative, or neutral, and intensity of display, with three degrees of relative fullness of expression. Three sources of cues were used for coding affect expression: facial expressions, body tensions and posture, and affective vocalizations such as whining and laughing. Affect expression was coded continuously as infant and mother played with toys and shared a snack. The onset of a change in affect expression was associated with a time code, and the onset time of one affect expression was also the offset time of the previous expression because affect expression was coded continuously in the stream of activity. The time code enabled us to count expressions, determine their duration, and the like. Speech was transcribed in a separate pass through the video recording, with onset and offset times of each utterance, by independent coders. The computer was able to read the time codes subsequently to integrate the two channels of expression, affect and speech, and recover the original temporal relation between them. The persons responsible for transcription and coding were uninformed of the goals and hypotheses in these studies.

Positive, negative, and occasional mixed or equivocal affect displays were considered to be instances of emotional expression without attributing the expressions to discrete emotion categories (joy, anger, sadness, and the like). The children whom we studied expressed emotionally toned affect in these episodes of free play and eating a snack an average of 16% of the time at 9, 13, 17, and 21 months (Bloom, Beckwith, & Capatides, 1988). A similar result was obtained in studies of somewhat older children (Cole, Barrett, & Zahn-Wexler, 1990) and younger infants as well (Malatesta, Culver, Tesman, & Shepard, 1989). Thus, the prevalence of neutral affect is an important feature of expression in infancy.

Here I can only briefly summarize some of the results of our research that may be informative for animal language studies. At a macro level of analysis, we looked at the infants' affect expressions and words and attributed to them the contents of desires and beliefs that the expressions were presumably about. Our goal was to understand what infants' words and affect expressions express and changes in expression with development (in Bloom, Beckwith, Capatides, & Hafitz, 1988). At a more micro level, we looked at the timing relations between saying a word and expressions of affect in the period of early word learning to determine how the limited cognitive resources of the young language-learning child are deployed for the two sorts of expression (in Bloom & Beckwith, 1989). I next discuss each of these studies briefly.

Bloom

EXPRESSION OF BELIEFS, DESIRES, AND FEELINGS

We were interested in what infants have in mind when saying words or expressing emotion at the two reference points we used for identifying the transition to language and equating the children for achievements in language rather than age. The first was First Words (the beginning of the single-word period, mean age = 13 months) and the second was a Vocabulary Spurt (toward the end of the period, mean age = 19 months). For this purpose, we attributed an underlying data structure to each expression. These consisted of a psychological attitude of belief or desire directed toward the elements and relations between them that were the child's focus of attention. The behavioral data we used in making these attributions were what the child and mother were doing in the situation and the focus of the baby's attention in the moments surrounding the expression (see Bloom et al., 1988, for a fuller description of these procedures). At First Words, emotional expressions were far more frequent than words, as would be expected. At Vocabulary Spurt, words were eight times more frequent than they had been at First Words, but this was neither surprising nor interesting because an increase in numbers of words was the criterion for the Vocabulary Spurt.

However, although the number of words and representations attributed to words increased, the frequency of emotional expressions and representations attributed to emotional expressions remained essentially the same from First Words to Vocabulary Spurt. Thus, the frequency of emotional expression did not change between the two language achievements for the group of infants as a whole. This result means that words did not replace affect expression in the period of word learning and speech was not something these children did instead of expressing emotion. Rather, they were beginning to learn language as a new system of expression for the contents of their beliefs and desires while they continued to express their feelings about these contents through displays of affect.

The next analysis determined whether the infants expressed a desire (had as a goal to change the world) or expressed a belief (in the way the world was, to them). Desires were expressed more often than beliefs with both emotional expressions and words. The ratio of desires to beliefs was 2 to 1 for emotional expression at both First Words and the Vocabulary Spurt. Just as the frequency of emotional expression did not change, the ratio of attributed desires to beliefs did not change between the two language achievements. However, at the time of first words, the ratio of desires to beliefs attributed to words was much less, 1.3 to 1, and increased to 2 to 1 (the same ratio as for emotional expressions) at Vocabulary Spurt. Thus, early words expressed what the infants saw or imagined the world to be relatively more often than they expressed what or how they wanted the world to be. When words first appeared, then, they were less likely to be used as tools for achieving goals.

The third analysis had to do with whether desires expressed in words and affect concerned the infants themselves or their mothers as the actors in anticipated events. At both First Words and Vocabulary Spurt, for both words and emotional expression overall, the desires these infants expressed were most often desires concerning themselves as actors rather than their mothers. They expressed what they wanted to do or were in the process of doing to change the world more often than they expressed what they wanted their mothers to do. The result was the same for words at both times, with a ratio of 4 to 1 for self to mother representations in desire attributions. Thus, the children in this study learned words to express desires concerning their own actions in regard to their own purposes and goals. Their words were not used primarily as tools for getting other persons to do things.

ALLOCATING COGNITIVE RESOURCES FOR EMOTIONAL EXPRESSION AND WORDS

At the minimum, an emotional expression requires: (a) a representation in attention of what the feeling is about, which results from an evaluation of the circumstances in the situation relative to the individual's plans and goals; (b) the subjective feeling; and (c) the display. Similarly, saying a word requires (a) a representation in attention that draws on data from perception and data recalled from memory; (b) recalling the word from memory; and (c) encoding. The cognitive requirements for these two sorts of expression-affect and speech-might be expected to compete with one another for the young child's limited cognitive resources. In order to explore the mutual effects between them, we looked at the way saying a word and expressing emotion occurred together in the single-word period (Bloom & Beckwith, 1989). Recall that these children were expressing neutral affect most of the time (84% on average). Most of the children's words were also said while they were expressing neutral (nonemotional) affect. At First Words, the time they spent saying words with emotionally toned valence did not differ from what was expected, given the time spent in emotional expression overall (time computed as the percentage of video tape frames, with 30 frames per second). However, by the Vocabulary Spurt, the time spent saying words with overlapping emotional expression was greater than predicted. This meant that the children's emotional expressions were closely associated with saying words.

However, two factors influenced the ability to say words with overlapping emotional expression. One was the intensity of emotional expression: Words were more likely to be said with low intensity than with heightened intensity levels of emotional expression. Another factor was emotional valence: Words were more likely to be said with positive affect than with negative affect. The positive evaluation of a situation relative to a goal means that the goal has been or will be achieved and less cognitive activity should be required (Rothbart, 1973). The cognitive activity underlying negative emotion also entails evaluating the situation relative to goals but, in addition, often includes creating a new plan. In the case of anger, for example, a goal is blocked and a plan is required to remove the obstacle to the goal. In the case of sadness, the goal is lost and a plan is needed for abandoning the goal or generating a new one (e.g., Oatley & Johnson-Laird, 1987; Stein & Levine, 1987). In sum, positive affect expression at low levels of intensity co-occurred with saying words, but negative affect expression and heightened levels of both positive and negative affect tended not to occur with words.

In addition, the words the children were learning contributed to the overlap of emotional expression and speech. Words said at the same time as emotional expression tended to be words the children learned earliest, used most frequently, and/or person words (e.g., *Mama* and *baby*) and parts of well-known play and other routines. Earlier learned, more frequent words are presumably the words children know best, with relative ease of recall and automaticity of expression. We might expect such words to be easiest to say at times when children are also experiencing and expressing emotion. In addition, the words said at the same time that the children expressed emotion were words for the circumstances and objects that caused the emotion, for example *Mama, more,* and *baby*. They were not words that were labels for the different emotions.

We proposed that the cognitive activity needed for saying words competes with the cognition required for the experience and expression of emotion. One result of this would be suppression of emotional expression at times of word learning and/or use. At a local level, we looked at the timing of speech and affect expressions in a series of lag sequential analyses. Using the occurrence of a word as the target lag, we determined the extent of differences from baseline levels of emotional expression in each of the 15 1-sec lags before and after the word. The result, at both First Words and at Vocabulary Spurt, was a substantial suppression of emotional expression beginning approximately 5 seconds before the onset of a word, with greater effect at First Words than at Vocabulary Spurt.

6. Language Acquisition and Expression

We are interpreting this preword dip below the baseline level of emotional expression as the time when the mental activity associated with the expression of emotion is, essentially, suspended. This is the time the child uses for the cognitive work that recalling and saying a word involves. This effect was greater when words were first acquired (at First Words) than later in the period (at Vocabulary Spurt) when saying words and affect expression (positive emotion primarily) were integrated.

The peak in affect expression came in the moments just after words were said. Two implications of this result are noteworthy. Once the word is said, the child's cognitive resources are freed for the cognitive work that the experience and expression of emotion involves. Given that most of the children's emotional expression was positive, this burst of emotional expression just after a word is reminiscent of the smile of recognition observed with younger infants by McCall (1972) and Zelazo (1972), and smiles following mastery (Sroufe & Waters, 1976) or assimilation after "concentrated attention" (Kagan, Lapidus, & Moore, 1978). Thus, words and emotional expression were closely associated in time, but emotion was more likely to be expressed in the seconds immediately after a word.

Perhaps even more important, the peak in emotional expression in the moments after saying words means that these children were learning words that expressed what their feelings were about. Cognitive theories of emotion stress the importance of goals and plans, and changes in the environment that influence success or interfere with an individual's goals or plans. If these are the facts that produce emotional experience (e.g., Oatley, 1988) and underlie knowledge about what emotions are (e.g., Stein & Levine, 1989), then children could be expected to want to talk about goals and plans and circumstances that interfere with or facilitate their achieving a goal. Moreover, we know that when the mothers in our study responded to their 1-year-old children's emotional expressions, they talked about their goals and actions and the situations that were associated with different feeling states. They did not provide labels for the emotions themselves (Capatides, 1990).

The two lag analyses also show that the expression of emotion once again dipped below baseline after the postword peak in emotional expression. Although we have not looked as yet at other events surrounding the children's words, we know that their mothers invariably responded to what they said. We speculate that this inhibition of emotional expression in the postword lags can be attributed to the children's listening to their mothers responding to what they themselves had just said.

In sum, children's early words in the second year of life do not name their emotions and so they cannot tell us what they are feeling. Rather, they continue to rely on expression of emotion through facial and postural displays of affect while the words they are learning express and articulate what their feelings are about. As children approach the second year of life, all they have learned about objects, persons, and the self inform the beliefs, desires, and feelings that they have. These cannot be expressed by displays of affect alone. Other modes of expression are required. Language is the preeminent mode of expression that evolved in societies and cultures to embody and make public what is internal to the individual. The success of language as a social activity depends on the ability of individuals to share what is otherwise hidden within them. The goals and plans, beliefs and desires, the feelings that we have are, themselves, unobservable. For the young child, to make these manifest and public requires that words and procedures for sentences and discourse will be learned.

One purpose of this chapter was to draw attention to the unobservable facts of language in seeking to know why and how a language will be acquired by any species. A second purpose of this chapter was to underscore the cognitive requirements for both language and emotional expression to show how these can compete for the limited cognitive resources of the young language-learning child. The effects described in this chapter were local and reciprocal. Saying words inhibited emotional expression (in the moments before a word) and words were not said with heightened intensity and/or negative emotional expression. The third purpose was to make clear that the language of emotion is the language of everyday events: talk about the objects, causes, and circumstances of emotional experience. The words that name particular emotions are a relatively small part of it. Finally, in making explicit the centrality of expression for language acquisition, we can begin to see how language and emotion come together in the mental life of individuals to determine the social life of individuals together.

ACKNOWLEDGMENTS

This chapter was drawn from material in a forthcoming book, *The Transition from Infancy to Language: Acquiring the Power of Expression*, by Lois Bloom. Both the theoretical perspective and the data presented here resulted from collaborations with Richard Beckwith, and I am happy to acknowledge his considerable input while, at the same time, making clear that I alone am responsible for any errors of fact or interpretation. Financial support for the research discussed here was generously provided by the Spencer Foundation and

6. Language Acquisition and Expression

the National Science Foundation and preparation of this chapter was facilitated by a James McKeen Cattell Sabbatical Award.

REFERENCES

Arnold, M. (1960). *Emotion and personality, Psychological aspects* (Vol. 1). New York: Columbia University.

Bates, E., Benigni, L., Bretherton, I., Camaioni, L. & Volterra, V. (1979). *The emergence of symbols: Communication and cognition in infancy.* New York: Academic Press.

Bloom, L. (1970). *Language development: Form and function in emerging grammars.* Cambridge MA: The MIT Press. (Originally appeared as a Ph.D. dissertation, Columbia University, 1968).

Bloom, L. (1976). An integrative perspective on language development: Keynote address. In Papers and reports on child language development, Department of Linguistics, Stanford University.

Bloom, L. & Beckwith, R. (1989). Talking with feeling: Integrating affective and linguistic expression in early language development. *Cognition and Emotion,* 3, 313-342.

Bloom, L., Beckwith, R., & Capatides, J. (1988). Developments in the expression of affect. *Infant Behavior and Development,* 11, 169-186.

Bloom, L., Beckwith, R., Capatides, J., & Hafitz, J. (1988). Expression through affect and words in the transition from infancy to language. In P. Baltes, D. Featherman, & R. Lerner (Eds.), *Life-span development and behavior* (Vol. 8, pp. 99-127). Hillsdale, NJ: Lawrence Erlbaum Associates.

Bloom, L., & Capatides, J. (1987). Expression of affect and the emergence of language. *Child Development,* 58, 1513- 1522.

Bloom, L., & Lahey, M. (1978). *Language development and language disorders.* New York: John Wiley & Sons.

Blumenthal, A. (1970). *Language and psychology: Historical aspects of psycholinguistics.* New York: John Wiley.

Campos, J., Barret, K., Lamb, M., Goldsmith, H., & Stenberg, C. (1983). Socioemotional development. In M. Haith & J. Campos (Eds.), P. Mussen (Series Ed.), *Handbook of child psychology: Vol. 2. Infancy and developmental psychobiology* (pp. 783-915). New York: John Wiley & Sons.

Capatides, J. (1990). *Mothers' socialization of their children's experience and expression of emotion.* Ph.D. dissertation, Columbia University.

Cole, P., Barrett, K., & Zahn-Wexler, C. (1990). Emotion displays in two-year-olds during mishaps. *Child Development,* in press.

Danto, A. (1973). *Analytical philosophy of action.* Cambridge: Cambridge University Press.

deLaguna, G. (1963). *Speech: Its function and development.* Bloomington, IN: Indiana University Press. (Originally published in 1927)

Dennett, D. (1978). *Brainstorms.* Montgomery, VT: Bradford Books.

Fauconnier, G. (1985). *Mental spaces: Aspects of meaning construction in natural language.* Cambridge, MA: MIT. Press.

Fodor, J. (1979). *The language of thought.* Cambridge, MA: Harvard University Press.

Heider, F. (1958). *The psychology of interpersonal relations.* Hillsdale, NJ: Lawrence Erlbaum Associates.

Johnson-Laird, P. (1983). *Mental models: Towards a cognitive science of language, inference, and consciousness.* Cambridge, MA: Harvard University Press.

Kagan, J., Lapidus, D., & Moore, M. (1978). Infant antecedents of cognitive functioning. *Child Development,* 49, 1005-1023.

6. Language Acquisition and Expression

Malatesta, C., Culver, C., Tesman, J., & Shepard, B. (1989). The development of emotion expression during the first two years of life. *Monographs of the Society for Research in Child Development*, Serial No. 219, 54.

Malinowski, B. (1923). The problem of meaning in primitive languages. In C. Ogden & I. Richards (Eds.), *The meaning of meaning* (pp. 296-336). New York: Harcourt Brace.

Malinowski, B. (1935). *Coral gardens and their magic* (Vols. I and II). London: Allen & Unwin.

McCall, R., (1972). Smiling and vocalization in infants as indices of perceptual-cognitive processes. *Merrill-Palmer Quarterly*, 18, 341-347.

Oatley, K. (1988). Plans and the communicative function of emotion. In V. Hamilton, G. Bower, & N. Frijda (Eds.), *Cognitive perspectives on emotion and motivation* (pp. 345-364). Dordrecht: Kluwer Academic.

Oatley, K., & Johnson-Laird, P. (1987). Towards a cognitive theory of emotions. *Cognition and Emotion*, 1, 29-50.

Ochs, E., & Schieffelin, B. (1989). Language has a heart. *Text*, 9, 7-25.

Ogden, C., & Richards, I. (1946). *The meaning of meaning*. New York: Harcourt Brace. (Originally published in 1923)

Piaget, J. (1954/1981). *Intelligence and affectivity: Their relationship during child development* (T. Brown & C. Kaegi, Trans.). Palo Alto, CA: Annual Reviews Inc.

Rothbart, M. (1973). Laughter in young children. *Psychological Bulletin*, 80, 247-256.

Sampson, G. (1980). *Schools of linguistics*. Stanford, CA: Stanford University.

Schieffelin, B. (1979). *How Kaluli children what to say, what to do, and how to feel: An ethnographic study of the development of communicative competence*. Ph.D. dissertation, Teachers College, Columbia University.

Schieffelin, B. (1990). *The give and take of everyday life: Language socialization of Kaluli children.* Cambridge: Cambridge University Press.

Searle, J. (1983). *Intentionality: An essay in the philosophy of mind.* Cambridge: Cambridge University Press.

Searle, J. (1984). *Minds, brains and science.* Cambridge, MA: Harvard University.

Sroufe, A., & Waters, (1976). The ontogenesis of smiling and laughter: A perspective on the organization of development in infancy. *Psychological Review*, 83, 173- 189.

Stein, N., & Levine, L. (1987). Thinking about feelings: The development and origins of emotional knowledge. In R. Snow, & M. Farr (Eds), *Aptitude, learning, and instruction, Vol. 3, Cognition, conation, and affect* (pp. 165-197). Hillsdale, NJ: Lawrence Erlbaum Associates.

Stein, N., & Levine, L. (1989). The causal organization of emotional knowledge: A developmental study. *Cognition and Emotion*, 3, 343-378.

Stern, C., & Stern, W. (1907). *Die Kindersprache.* Leipzig: Barth.

Taylor, C. (1979). Action as expression. In C. Diamond & J. Teichman (Eds.), *Intentions and intentionality, Essays in honor of G. E. M. Anscombe* (pp. 73-89). Ithaca, NY: Cornell University Press.

Taylor, C. (1985). *Human agency and language, philosophical papers* (Vol. 1). Cambridge: Cambridge University Press.

Tylor, E. B. (1871). *Primitive cultures.* London: John Murray.

Vygotsky, L. (1930/1978). *Mind in society, The development of higher psychological processes.* M. Cole, V. John- Steiner, S. Scribner, & E. Souberman (Eds.), Cambridge MA: Harvard University Press. (Originally published in 1930, *Tool and symbol*).

Wittgenstein, L. (1958). *The blue and brown books.* (Originally published in 1934-35)

6. Language Acquisition and Expression

Zelazo, P. (1972). Smiling and vocalizing: A cognitive emphasis. *Merrill-Palmer Quarterly*, 18, 349-365.

7 Animal Language Research Needs a Broader Comparative and Evolutionary Framework

Peter L. Tyack

In 1960, Jane Goodall went to live with chimpanzees in their natural habitat like an anthropologist living with some tribe of forest people. It took her years to gain the trust of her subjects, but eventually she and those who followed were able to get close enough to watch these apes interact with each other and with humans (Goodall, 1986). Since 1947, animal psychologists have taken the equally radical step of raising chimps as part of their families in order to see how well chimps could learn human language (Hayes, 1951). Both kinds of study bear promise for the study of animal cognition, but each has suffered from a peculiar insularity. Psychologists have studied for decades how well chimps can learn artificial or human languages, scarcely interacting with the parallel inquiries into the social behavior, parental care, and communication systems of wild chimps. Progress in animal cognition will be much faster if psychological and cognitive studies of animal behavior develop tighter links with biological disciplines of ethology, neurobiology, and behavioral ecology (Kamil, 1988; Snowdon, 1983). Kummer, Dasser, and Hoyningen-Hüne (1990) point out that cognitive ethologists have much to learn from psychology's emphasis on proximate mechanisms, on behavioral development, and on experimental methods. On the other hand, cognitive ethology emphasizes the larger context in which all behavior is embedded. It can contribute a strong tradition of emphasizing function and evolution of animal behavior, and of methods to study animals in their natural environments. In order to understand the evolutionary origins of animal cognition, we require a synthesis of these two disciplines.

The cooperation of biologists and psychologists studying foraging behavior has a synergy that accelerates scientific progress. Behavioral ecologists have developed formal models of how foragers can optimize the costs and benefits of foraging (e.g., Stephens & Krebs, 1986). Data from animals feeding in the wild and in controlled experiments are consistent with complex foraging strategies. Optimal foraging models have been taken up by comparative psychologists in attempts to test more specifically the proximate mechanisms by which animals follow or approximate decision rules (e.g., Kamil & Roitblat, 1985). While food-reinforced conditioning was a staple of comparative psychology, optimal foraging finally provides a theory that allows the integration of data describing how contingencies of food reinforcement affect subsequent behavior with the typical ecological problems faced by a species. Evolutionary biologists have also targeted new areas little explored by comparative psychologists. For example, W. D. Hamilton described the evolutionary importance of kinship in animal social behavior (Hamilton, 1964). This has stimulated behavioral and cognitive research into the proximate mechanisms for kin recognition in animals. These collaborations show great promise for elucidating the evolutionary origins of specific cognitive skills and mechanisms.

Similar collaborations have been less productive in the study of language and communication in animals. The controversy accompanying the interpretation of animal language experiments should be no surprise. It does not just stem from the religious and ideological intensity with which some humans guard the separation between human and animal. If linguists and psychologists cannot agree about how we learn and generate the language of our own species, questions of comparing animal language to human language can only be less well formulated. Part of the problem lies in a history of divergent goals between psychologists and linguists. There has been a strong tradition within psychology of seeking to minimize the building blocks of psychological theory to a few general principles associating sensory stimuli and behavioral responses. Although this theory in principle could describe complex behavior, few linguists have been taken with such parsimony; they would much rather trade in associationism for a richer theory that is more practical for working with language.

7. A Comparative and Evolutionary Framework

THE EVOLUTION OF DOMAIN SPECIFIC COGNITIVE PROCESSES

During the past decade or so, there has been a trend within psychology away from an exclusionary insistence on general principles of learning, memory, and intelligence. Rather than viewing learning or memory as content independent, more psychologists have been willing to consider domain-specific intelligences (Cheney & Seyfarth, 1990; Gardner, 1983) or innately specified cognitive modules (Fodor, 1983). The domain specific view emphasizes that learning may be channeled by innate predispositions to facilitate the solution of particular problems. For an example that ranchers have known as bait shyness, some animals are more likely to associate a taste or smell than a sound with becoming sick, even hours later, and this may help them learn to avoid noxious food after only one exposure (Garcia & Koelling, 1966). This view is more consistent with an evolutionary view[1] and is more easily integrated than general theories of learning with both the neurobiological and ethological views of cognitive processes. The classic ethological studies of learning, such as imprinting, orientation, and avian song learning, are domain specific. The neural substrates that birds use to learn song are better understood than substrates for more general learning abilities. Auditory information from the ears projects to nuclei involved in song processing. These nuclei project to integrative nuclei which project to motor nuclei driving the syrinx, thus closing the loop of vocal control.

Sensory perception clearly involves domain-specific cognitive processing. Visual information flows along clear pathways between brain areas specialized for vision. Lesions of these areas involve vision-specific deficits. Just as some stimuli may more easily associated with some responses, some stages of visual processing are more accessible than others. Animals cannot be trained to identify stimulation of one retinal cell rather than another. Visual information is processed to represent features of objects in the world before most integration with nonvisual information. Different areas of visual cortex in cats map different functional representations of visual features. These specialized mechanisms appear to be necessary for solving the complex problem of extracting meaningful representations of the outside world from stimulation of the retinal surface.

---

[1]However, see Lieberman (1991) concerning problems reconciling a strong modular view with evolutionary theory.

Human language has been proposed as another candidate for treatment as a modular cognitive system (Fodor 1983). Many linguists argue that humans have a language acquisition module in the brain, which is activated during a critical period of development and is required to enable the acquisition of language given the limited and unsystematic exposure to speech that children have. Lieberman (1991) debates both how independent language is from other cognitive processes, and whether we must inherit a universal grammar in order to learn language. However, most linguists appear to agree that humans rely on a combination of both general and specialized processes to perceive and generate phonemes, words, and sentences. When humans parse phonemes, they rely on some auditory processes shared with other mammals and other more species-specific linguistic processes (Kuhl, 1987). As with vision, specific neural substrates are defined for many language abilities. For example, damage to Broca's area of cerebral cortex is associated with Broca's aphasia, which is characterized by deficits in speech and syntax. An aphasia characterized by difficulties in naming rather than syntax or vocal control of speech sounds is associated with damage to Wernicke's area of cortex.

If the development, production, and comprehension of language depend in humans on a somewhat idiosyncratic collection of specialized cognitive processes and neural circuits along with more general ones, then this raises questions about animal language. When animals are trained with language, are we testing whether they have similar specialized circuits to perform similar tasks, or are we forcing them to use more general-purpose cognitive systems? Areas homologous to Broca's and Wernicke's area have been identified for some primate species (Deacon, 1988), but it is unclear how involved these areas are either in natural communication or in trained performance for animal language experiments. No such homologous areas have been identified for birds or marine mammals. Species in both of these taxa use vocal learning in their natural systems of communication. It is unknown whether animals in animal language experiments use neural circuits analogous to those used by humans for language.

The training in language experiments may on the other hand enlist primarily general learning and cognitive abilities. The further such experiments diverge from homologies with human language and its underlying neural circuits, the more strained the language analogy becomes. To the extent animals are trained using domain-independent learning, animal language experiments would better be framed as animal thought experiments. This view would emphasize the role of training in facilitating an animal's ability to report internal states by communication. Even Fodor (1983), who emphasizes the modularity

7. A Comparative and Evolutionary Framework

of the mind, argues that there must also be domain independent central mechanisms that integrate representations from the different domains.

Even if animal language experiments are viewed as a window on central mechanisms, investigators must search carefully to find the right match between natural communication abilities and the artificial language training. Each species may require careful tailoring of an artificial language in order to open the communication channel fully. I would argue that the only way to make sense of these questions is to perform a broad evolutionary comparison of language-specific capabilities and more general cognitive capabilities as evolutionary traits. We must go below surface similarities of trained language acts to investigate how these languages are acquired and processed. Convergences between domain specific views of cognition, neural studies of cognitive function, and the ethological views of cognitive capabilities as adaptations may facilitate the required interdisciplinary efforts. However, it is critical to bear in mind that cognitive capabilities in animals including *Homo sapiens* have been shaped by evolution.

Evolution is a historical process, and a science of evolution must use different methods from sciences such as physics that aim for general laws. If behavior and cognition derive from evolutionary processes, then the quest in psychology for context independent laws of learning may be ill-founded. Evolution does not proceed like an engineer who can start new designs from scratch and whose choices for subunits are only limited by his purchasing power. Evolution must work with the materials that are at hand, and this often leads to a messy mixture of parts that originally served different purposes. Old parts may be changed to take on new functions, and these may function in parallel with new parts. Lieberman (1991) emphasizes that some of the neural building blocks for human language stem from brain circuits evolved in our reptilian ancestors, while others are found in the expanded neocortex that evolved recently in our species. Some of these neocortical circuits may have evolved specifically to serve linguistic functions.

Criticisms of the adaptationist program notwithstanding (Gould & Lewontin, 1979), ethology has profited greatly by assuming that many behavioral and cognitive capabilities are similar to morphological or physiological adaptations. While the design features of cognitive adaptations may be more difficult to identify than those for an eye or a wing, this point of view would suggest that some cognitive capabilities are honed by evolution to develop specific functional skills. This functional view stresses that if one wants to understand an adaptation, whether cognitive, behavioral, or morphological, one must understand both the problems it evolved to solve and the building blocks available to a phylogenetic lineage for achieving the solution. Adaptations in the Darwinian sense evolve through natural selection of different genotypes, and ethologists have traditionally focused on innately determined behaviors. However, learning mechanisms may evolve in just the same fashion. Genetic predispositions may even guide learning for those species that require learning for behavioral development. Imprinting and song learning in birds are classic ethological examples, and many linguists argue that language acquisition in humans is guided by similar predispositions. Many of the most complex behavioral and cognitive skills involve sensitive periods for learning, extended periods of development, and may even require training by or observation of parents and other conspecifics. The interplay of innate factors with development and learning will be particularly complex for higher cognitive functions, but this does not free them from the evolutionary process.

If we are to understand the evolution of cognitive processes in animals and humans, four basic biological questions must be explored. While these questions must be answered for the study of any kind of adaptation, they were identified as the backbone of classical ethology (Tinbergen, 1951). The four avenues of exploration are mechanism, development or ontogeny, function, and evolution. Tinbergen argued that the isolation of behavioral scientists studying proximate explanations of behavior from those studying the ultimate evolutionary causes impeded both avenues of study. Studying a learning mechanism without understanding its function is like trying to solve how a clock works without knowing what the clock is for (Cosmides & Tooby, 1987). On the other hand, simply matching contemporary behavioral acts to those predicted by a model of an adaptive problem provides only a caricature of an evolutionary analysis.

Whereas individual behavioral acts may have obvious consequences for natural selection, it is perilous to overemphasize the stage on which natural selection plays so much that one loses sight of the fact that individual acts of behavior do not evolve. Between their ears, animals carry sophisticated mechanisms to select information from their environment, compare this to past information and internal states, and respond with strategies to achieve goals. These mechanisms filter a bewildering array of potential environmental inputs to produce an equally complex and variable array of behavioral responses. Classical ethology provides examples of tight linkages between fixed action patterns that are elicited by an innate releasing mechanism when a feature detector is triggered by a particular suite of environmental cues. However, one cannot assume that the evolution of behavioral mechanisms always proceeds by

7. A Comparative and Evolutionary Framework

linkages so tight between situation and response that one can ignore intervening sensory and cognitive mechanisms.

There are many situations where selection may favor more opportunity for an animal to modify its responses based on its environment. Students of birdsong have suggested a threshold in song repertoire size may exist, beyond which it is cheaper to build a mechanism to learn to imitate songs rather than to encode the acoustic structure genetically. Given the enormous variety of situations an animal may encounter throughout its life and the variety of appropriate responses depending on its condition, the potential simplifications of cognitive mechanisms more flexible than the fixed-action-pattern/innate-releasing-mechanism link should be obvious. Tierney (1986) reviewed neurobiological evidence that also questions assumptions that individual behaviors are programmed by specific genes and that more canalized behaviors are simpler, less costly, and phylogenetically primitive to less canalized behaviors. There are other classes of novel or unpredictable situations that may require learning and other plastic forms of cognition. Many individual animals encounter situations that are unpredictable for their population or species. Even if an animal inherits a sophisticated ability to navigate, it is likely to have to learn where home is. Optimal foraging studies show that, even though a species may have a limited range of prey species and distributions, each individual can improve its foraging behavior by tailoring it to the conditions prevailing at any one moment. On the other hand, trial and error learning may not be the algorithm of choice for avoiding a deadly predator, because one may not survive the first trial. Depending on these kinds of considerations, a behavior may be selected to be more or less canalized.

Many authors have argued that the social environment of hominids may have been particularly important for the evolution of human intelligence and even consciousness. If hominids lived in groups where success demanded both cooperation and competition with the same individuals, this could have led to particularly unpredictable social strategies and counter-strategies, creating something of an arms race for intelligence in the sense of abilities to forecast the outcome of interactions (Humphrey, 1976). Animals that form individual specific social relationships and that face a similar tension between competition and cooperation in reciprocal relationships may also encounter selective pressures to evolve more complex forms of social cognition. Cooperation that is maintained by taking turns with asymmetric costs and benefits requires the players to monitor for cheaters who take the benefits of cooperation but do not reciprocate and pay the costs when their turn is due (Axelrod, 1984; Trivers, 1971). There is evidence that humans have evolved domain specific cognitive processes to analyze these social interactions. Cosmides (1989) made sense out of otherwise puzzling deviations of humans from the rules of formal propositional logic by suggesting that when humans evaluate social contracts, their behavior deviates from logic in order better to detect cheaters. Her results suggest that when humans reason about social problems, their thought may be guided by Darwinian algorithms to solve these adaptively important problems.

Analysis of the evolution of behavior cannot evade study of cognitive mechanisms. The study of sociobiology suffered from attempts to bypass this level of understanding to find a shortcut to understanding the evolution of behavior. On the other hand, because adaptive mechanisms must evolve from parts initially often serving other functions, the mechanistic details of proximate solutions to adaptive problems are often obscure. The functional cognitive level is required to link these two widely separate levels of understanding. Physiology plays a critical role relating organ structure to organ function. Physiologists lump complex suites of anatomical and biochemical features to form more readily interpretable functional descriptions such as digestive or circulatory systems. The study of cognitive processes provides a similar functional language to bridge the gap between the details of a neural mechanism and the behavioral function(s) it serves (Cosmides & Tooby, 1987). Tinbergen (1951) was correct to reject the lack of integration between these often separate disciplines and to "argue the necessity of studying both causation and adaptiveness" (p. 152).

The general problems of studying adaptation are compounded by several difficulties specific to cognition. It is difficult enough to discriminate genetic and environmental influences on developmental maturation, and learning adds yet another layer of processes by which the environment can alter behavioral traits. One must both investigate the range of environments in which the functional trait can develop and also investigate how flexible the developed trait is to fine tuning through learning in particular environments. Cognitive mechanisms that generate adaptive behavior in an animal's normal environment may generate maladaptive behavior in other environments. The very sensitivity of flexible mechanisms to environmental change and novelty may render them vulnerable to derailing in environments very different from those in which they evolved.

Darwin (1859/1979) appreciated that natural selection can lead to the evolution not just of beautifully designed bodily traits such as eyes or a wings but also of behavioral traits that function so well as to seem intelligent and purposive. Darwin (1871/1981) also recognized that selection is not limited to

7. A Comparative and Evolutionary Framework

individual behaviors, but may favor the evolution of higher mental faculties such as intelligence and intentionality to the point of self-awareness in humans. It requires great care to discriminate animals whose individual behaviors merely appear goal directed from animals that reason intelligently to achieve their goals. Here is where experimentation with artificial and novel problems is most useful. It is ironic that experiments training animals with artificial languages have been framed more as language experiments than as experiments to gain access to more general cognitive processes such as intentionality, intelligence, or even awareness. While language-like skills may open a window on these general cognitive processes, there is a strong tradition emphasizing that human language itself is not a general skill but has many idiosyncratic and species-specific features.

One way to test whether animal species have adaptive specializations in particular cognitive skills involves broad comparative analysis of both the skill and its underlying neural structures. For example, Shettleworth (1990) reviewed data on differences among birds in spatial memory related to whether they store food or not. The hippocampus has been implicated in spatial memory in both birds and mammals, and Krebs (1990) showed that two regions of the hippocampus are enlarged in food storing species. Comparative analysis also reveals strong associations between song learning in birds and its neural substrates. For example, male marsh wrens (*Cistothorus palustris*) in western North America produce about four times as many different songs as the eastern subspecies (Kroodsma & Verner, 1987). There is a well-defined song perception and control system in the brains of songbirds, and it expands in volume and capability during the song season. The song control nuclei in western marsh wrens are larger than in eastern marsh wrens (Kroodsma & Canaday, 1985). Male-male competition appears to be higher in western versus eastern marsh wrens, and natural selection appears to have favored the evolution of larger song repertoires and investment in larger neural structures in the western subspecies. Marler (1990) emphasized the synergy between behavioral and neural studies of song development in birds. Extensive data indicate that specific areas of the human brain are involved in different linguistic functions, but little attempt has been made to compare homologous structures in different species involved in animal language studies. This is critical for determining whether so-called language skills in other species are homologous or analogous (in the evolutionary sense) to those of our own species (Deacon, 1988).

Detailed investigation of the interplay between innate and environmental factors in development is critical for understanding the evolution of cognitive traits. We need to attend more to how animals acquire trained language skills-what forms of training are necessary and sufficient. One of the striking features of language aquisition in humans is how little formal training children get when they solve arguably the most complex intellectual task of their lives. By focusing on the data children receive and their performance as they acquire language, one can rule out some possible models of language comprehension and production. As children learn a language, their errors[2] (i.e., "runned" for ran) reveal that they are not just imitating grammatical constructions by rote, but that they try out grammars approximating normal usage. Even though seldom corrected for making ungrammatical sentences, most children converge on a productive grammar that seldom generates sentences recognized by adults as ungrammatical. Pinker (1984) argues that given this lack of correction, the only way children can acquire a well-formed grammar is by innate restraints on which grammars are considered. If only a subset of the grammars that could describe adult language is learnable by children, then the learnability constraint can be used to narrow the search for which grammars humans actually use.

CAPABILITY VERSUS SKILL

Most animal language researchers tend not to examine the training process and responses of animals during training as much as has been exploited by students of human language acquisition. However, the natural tendency for teachers to take credit for the performance of their pupils is evident. Some animal language experiments reveal cognitive abilities not shown for the same species in the wild. Many researchers conclude that their language training has created cognitive skills not present in wild conspecifics (Herman, 1980; Premack, 1983; Savage-Rumbaugh, Lawson, Smith, & Rosenbaum, 1983). Certainly some aspects of the skills trained in the laboratory differ from those developed in nature, but we are just beginning scratch the surface of animal cognition, and are certainly in no position to argue for the creation in the lab of fundamental cognitive abilities that are not expressed in the wild. To clarify this distinction, I distinguish between a capability, or a faculty capable of development, and a skill, or a fully developed ability to perform a particular task.

---

[2]The errors children make as they learn a language can help reveal the kind of grammar they are trying out. If artificial languages included the exceptions so typical of natural language, similar errors would help demonstrate that animals actually are applying syntactic rules.

7. A Comparative and Evolutionary Framework

Although it is often more practical to study animals in captivity, few ethologists would not feel the need to verify captive results in the wild. On the other hand, anyone who has attempted to study chimps, parrots, or dolphins in the wild knows how hard it can be simply to find them, much less uncover their mental abilities, while trying to keep up with them in their own habitat. Under these circumstances, if one does not find strong evidence for the existence of a cognitive capability, one cannot conclude that this is strong evidence for the absence of the capability. We know less about the cognitive skills developed by animals in the wild than in the laboratory, so I think it dangerous to assume that a skill discovered in the lab does not have an undiscovered counterpart in the wild. I expect negative results to be the norm in studies of animal cognition. The cognitive ethologist must turn poorly controlled naturalistic observation into a convincing demonstration of a cognitive capability, and the comparative psychologist must select the appropriate age, sex, species, and match of artificial conditions in order to tap selective attention and domain specific intelligences evolved to solve particular problems.

Language acquisition in humans can be modified by many environmental factors. Behavioral development may also be disrupted by artificial conditions in other species that also rely on learning during prolonged periods of parental care. For example, white-crowned sparrows (*Zonotrichia leucophrys*) do not learn songs from tape recordings after 50 days of age, but they continue to learn songs if given the chance to interact with live tutors (Baptista & Petrinovich, 1986). The ethologist is far more likely to expect the fullest development of cognitive capabilities through the process of behavioral development with conspecifics than through being raised and trained by humans, no matter how intelligent and devoted the trainers are. This is not to say that people cannot train specific skills that are not seen in the wild, just that an animal's cognitive capabilities are likely to be most finely tuned to developing functional skills in the environment in which they evolved (for a psychologist's development of this point for humans, see Bowlby, 1969).

PROBLEMS IN APPLYING LANGUAGE ANALOGIES TO ANIMALS

Psychological tests are notoriously culture bound (Cole & Scribner, 1974). If it is difficult for psychologists to rate the cognitive abilities of a human who is from a different culture and speaks a different language, how much more difficult is it for humans to know that they correctly understand what skills are used in the performances of a different species? This is particularly problematic when a psychologist compares the language-like performance of a trained animal to a linguistic gloss of the same performance. Precisely what an animal needs to know or do in order to perform successfully is seldom obvious, and the surface similarity of the linguistic gloss to the performance may be more misleading than helpful. If the animal does correctly respond to the command JUMP OVER FRISBEE, does it really understand JUMP as a verb or FRISBEE as a grammatical object? At what point does the language analogy become inappropriate?

Ethologists have confronted similar problems when they attempt to draw parallels between human language and natural communication in animals (Snowdon, 1990). For example, early work on the development of song in birds emphasized that, as in humans, the young must hear the sounds of conspecific adults during a critical period in order to develop normal song (e.g., Marler, 1970). Babbling in humans and subsong in birds both appear to reflect a process in which the young match their own vocal output to an internal auditory template. Subsequent work on birdsong reveals enormous variety in development in different species. Although some species match some aspects of language development in humans, other closely related species show completely different patterns. Although lateralization of brain function has been demonstrated for both bird song and human language, the structures involved are by no means homologous. Early parallels between birdsong and language may have been overgeneralized and overenthusiastic.

The power of animal language experiments may be unnecessarily limited if researchers only compare animal use of artificial languages to human use of natural human languages. A comparative approach to understanding the evolution of language capabilities requires not just comparing each animal group to humans, but rather comparing all combinations of phylogenetically and ecologically related taxa. Human language involves a complex and idiosyncratic mixture of perceptual, cognitive, and motor capabilities. It is unlikely that many other species have exactly the same mixture, or use the capabilities in precisely the same way. Furthermore, animals are typically conditioned to learn artificial languages using controlled training protocols. Human children learn the rules of human language with far less controlled input and less formal training. The comparative use of linguistic terms such as syntax simplifies interpretation of animal language research to the popular press, but it may force an inappropriate analogy between a subsystem of human language with an animal system involved in some very different task. Clear progress in further animal language research will also benefit from a more careful analysis of the specific cognitive capabilities and training required to acquire and to use the artificial language.

7. A Comparative and Evolutionary Framework

For example, all human languages can create an unlimited number of utterances out of a few tens of morphemes by using syntax to rearrange phonemes into words and sentences. There are no data indicating this level of syntactic rearrangement of phoneme-like chunks of signals in any animal, but other animals can order signals into complex series. Both accomplished songbirds, such as the long-billed marsh wren *(Cistothorus palustris*, Verner, 1976) and the humpback whale *(Megaptera novaeangliae*; Payne, Tyack, & Payne, 1983), can produce organized strings of hundreds of signals (individual songs in the wren, song units in the whale) lasting tens of minutes before they repeat. Songs of both birds and whales are reproductive advertisement displays. Their structure appears to have evolved through sexual selection involving male-male competition and female choice of a mate. Male songbirds can increase the acoustic complexity of their display through large song repertoires, and some even produce structured sequences of many songs within their repertoire. Experimental studies show that songbird females of some species tend to prefer males with larger song repertoires. Individual humpback whales do not have large song repertoires at any one time, but all of the whales singing on a breeding ground slowly change the song over time. The song changes so pervasively that after several years, no sounds are left unchanged. Because the same whales still use these different songs in the same interactions, it appears that this variation in the acoustic structure of song does not reflect changes in the message in any linguistic sense (Tyack, 1981). Rather, humpbacks appear to use song change as birds use large song repertoires: to increase the acoustic complexity of their advertisement display.

In human language, syntax is intimately tied to the semantic content of the message. Some animal songs clearly have syntax-like ordering, but not necessarily with a semantic component. It may make no more sense to compare these songs to language than to compare the marks on a peacock's tail to some strange hieroglyphic writing. As Darwin (1859/1979) appreciated, advertisement displays may better be compared to the aesthetic domain than the linguistic. Music may be a more appropriate analogy (if not evolutionary homology) than language for song in birds and whales. Gardner (1983) argued for differences in the cognitive processes and neural structures that mediate the production and comprehension of music compared to language. In right-handed humans, language is lateralized primarily in the left hemisphere of the brain, while most musical abilities are lateralized in the right hemisphere. These two processes can function independently; exposure to tones interferes with recall of a tune much more than exposure to verbal stimuli (Deutsch, 1975). Many autistic children or aphasic adults with severely compromised language have excellent musical abilities. Some animal species may have evolved sophisticated syntactic capabilities with no parallel development of semantics or other specifically linguistic abilities. If one were to train these animals in a language paradigm, the research might never uncover their highly developed abilities to learn complex sequences of sounds.

Another problem with testing linguistic models of animal behavior involves radically different standards for demonstrating the applicability of linguistic terms. If an animal language experiment yields results that deviate from random in the direction predicted by a formal linguistic model, the experimenter typically states that the animal understands the model. However, the skeptic may compare the same performance to humans and conclude that the results are negative. Random expectations are a particularly weak straw man in animal behavior, so it would be better to allow several stronger models to compete in this kind of experiment. However, there is little benefit in splitting hairs over whether particular patterns of animal cognition are distinguishable from human cognition. This is particularly true because what we know of human cognition is a moving target. For example, while babbling was initially thought to involve a process of matching vocal articulation to an auditory template, recent studies of manual babbling in deaf infants indicates that babbling may represent a more amodal expressive language capability (Petitto & Marentette, 1991). Rather than argue whether an animal has "true" babbling, syntax, or whatever, we would do better to focus on which particular models best fit the performance of each species.

Distinguishing between good alternate models is much more difficult than comparison to a null hypothesis of random behavior. Even for human language, linguists cannot agree which formal models of grammar best predict our language production. For animal communication, this problem extends well beyond fine details separating similar models. For example, in order to test whether animals can learn syntactic rules, an artificial language with a formal syntax may be taught to animals. Either their utterances or their responses to sequences of commands may be used to test whether the animals have learned the grammar. Typically these grammars are simple and non-recursive, and may simply involve serial learning of a chain of tokens.

Demonstration that an animal's performance is closer to that predicted by a grammar than by a random model does not provide a strong test of whether the animal is using the grammar. Animals may produce what appear to be highly significant sequences of vocalizations when there is no contingency between one vocalization and the next. In a study of natural sounds from wild dolphins, Markov analysis of a transition matrix for dolphin vocalizations

7. A Comparative and Evolutionary Framework

showed significant deviations from random (Solow & Tyack, 1990). In animal language terms, this would appear to support the hypothesis that dolphins organize their vocalizations in a finite state or simple chaining type of grammar. However, if one separates the sequences into different behavioral states, in this case fast travel and slow travel, then the sequences appear random within each state. The data are completely consistent with the interpretation that the probabilities of each vocalization are conditionally dependent on behavioral state and are completely independent of the preceding vocalization. If one ignores or does not know about the behavioral states, and if one only tests a model assuming serial dependence, then one could easily mistakenly "confirm" a sequential grammatical model where in fact there may be no serial dependence of any sort.

VOCAL LEARNING AND IMITATION

Given the difficulties in both defining and testing for the presence of such general abilities as language or syntax for comparative analysis, it may help to focus on more specific cognitive capabilities that may be components of higher level processes. Demonstrating the presence or absence of component capabilities in different species will also facilitate the search for optimal study animals for particular problems. It is easier to specify capabilities with better defined input/output relations than language. There is also strong reason to target specific learning abilities that foster or allow language acquisition in humans. One such capability that appears to be very limited among animals is vocal learning: the capacity to modify what one says on the basis of what one hears. This capacity is clearly necessary for human speech. While four families of birds are capable of vocal learning, no terrestrial nonhuman mammal has been unequivocally shown to modify its vocal repertoire based on what it hears. Many primates are skilled at "aping" or imitating gestures and expressions, but despite decades of intensive research, there is no strong evidence for any vocal learning in nonhuman primates (Newman & Symmes, 1982). Imitation has been identified as particularly important in the acquisition of language and other aspects of culture that are not trained and shaped by overt reinforcement (Lieberman, 1991).

The absence of vocal learning has been a robust result from some animal language experiments. For example, it appears that one cannot teach a chimp to speak, even if it is raised at home from a very young age (Hayes, 1951). One explanation is that chimps are anatomically incapable of producing some human speech sounds (Lieberman, 1984), but this failure may also reflect a more central inability. Vocal learning is one of the skills necessary for speech, that appear to have evolved de novo in our hominid ancestors. Just as comparison of language in deaf and hearing humans can help address the question of how easily language can be divorced from the vocal channel in humans (Klima & Bellugi, 1979; Meier, 1991; Petitto & Marentette, 1991), so comparisons of language-like communication in species capable or incapable of vocal learning may address the same question across species.

Although it is not clear precisely how to specify and test for animal analogs of linguistic concepts such as syntax, vocal learning is well defined in terms of input and output. However, testing for vocal learning in the development of natural sounds is time-consuming and difficult. One way to target promising taxa is to look for species that can imitate manmade sounds. If an animal can imitate a sound that is not normally part of its repertoire, then it must have learned to modify its normal vocalizations to match the model. Animals that have evolved this rare capability may use it in developing their natural vocalizations. Even though we know little about vocal development in most marine mammal species, there are a surprising number of reports of marine mammals imitating manmade sounds: Hoover, a harbor seal at the New England Aquarium, imitated human speech well enough to have a recognizable New England accent (Ralls, Fiorelli, & Gish, 1985). Captive dolphins from many aquaria have been reported to learn to imitate computer generated tones and pulses (e.g., Richards, Wolz, & Herman, 1984; Sigurdson, this volume, chapter 8). Logosi, a beluga whale at the Vancouver Aquarium, was able to imitate his own name (Eaton, 1979). These reports include both seals and whales, which have different terrestrial ancestors. Presumably, this means that both groups independently evolved this capability.

It is difficult to differentiate learning from maturation, especially if all members of a species develop similar repertoires (Tinbergen, 1951). For example, young vervet monkeys produce calls higher in pitch than those produced by adults (Seyfarth & Cheney, 1986). As the young monkeys grow older, these calls become more similar to those of adults. This could simply be a result of growth of the vocal tract rather than a consequence of learning. It would be easier to test for vocal learning in species where different individuals produce different sounds.

The bottlenose dolphin (*Tursiops truncatus*) is perhaps the most promising marine mammal species for the study of vocal learning. These dolphins have a global distribution and number in the tens of thousands in the coastal waters of the southeastern United States. Hundreds of bottlenose dolphins also live in captivity, where their vocalizations and acoustic

7. A Comparative and Evolutionary Framework

environment can be studied in great detail. Bottlenose dolphins have also been the subject of many cognitive experiments including animal language experiments at the Kewalo Basin Marine Mammal Laboratory in Honolulu (Herman, Richards, Wolz, 1984). Since the mid 1960s, it has been known that captive bottlenose dolphins produce individually distinctive pure tone sounds called signature whistles (Caldwell & Caldwell, 1965). Unlike the click sounds used for echolocation, which are processed in midbrain areas such as the inferior colliculi, whistles are processed in the cerebrum, particularly temporal cortex (Bullock & Ridgway, 1972). These whistles function both to broadcast individual identity and to maintain contact between individuals such as between mothers and calves.

One puzzling question to me as an ethologist was why dolphins appear to have evolved highly developed skills of vocal mimicry when they tend to produce only one highly stereotyped whistle. Do dolphins use vocal learning and imitation in the development of their natural vocalizations? If so, when and in what contexts? Sigurdson (this volume, chapter 8) suggests that even during training for mimicry, bottlenose dolphins may only actively imitate or match acoustic models for limited periods of time under limited circumstances. I have taken two approaches to studying vocal learning and imitation in bottlenose dolphin whistles. One involves finding situations where one can identify the vocal repertoire of individual dolphins repeatedly in the wild. The other studies the vocal repertoires of captive dolphins during social interaction.

SIGNATURE WHISTLES IN WILD DOLPHINS

Randall Wells of the Chicago Zoological Society (Brookfield Zoo) and Woods Hole Oceanographic Institution has been studying wild bottlenose dolphins near Sarasota, FL since 1970 (Wells, Scott, & Irvine, 1987). Dolphins in this area have distinctive marks that allow most individuals to be identified. In this coastal habitat, individual dolphins often have such predictable home ranges that one can set out each day to look for particular animals. Wells has resighted some individuals for decades and knows several generations of matrilineal ties.

One of my graduate students, Laela Sayigh, and I have worked with Wells to study the signature whistles of these wild dolphins. It is seldom possible to determine which dolphin makes a whistle when they are swimming freely, so we record them when they are restrained in a net corral. When the dolphins are held in the corral, we can attach underwater microphones, or hydrophones, to their heads with suction cups. This is not a very natural context for these animals, but it allows us to sample the results of normal whistle development among wild dolphins. Moreover, dolphins swimming freely within the net corral or recorded immediately after release produced whistles very similar to those produced while they were restrained.

Whistles have been recorded from many of the Sarasota dolphins over a period of 15 years. These recordings confirm that wild dolphins, like captive ones, produce individually distinctive signature whistles, and that signature whistles are stable for over a decade (SayighB, Tyack, Wells, & Scott, 1990). Sayigh has concentrated on studying whistle exchanges between dolphin mothers and their young calves. When a mother-calf pair in the net corral was ready for processing, we restrained the pair together. Typically, one of the pair was held in shallow water while the other dolphin was being measured in a rubber raft. The animals were always in acoustic contact even when they could not see one another. Mothers and their calves typically started a well-defined whistle exchange as soon as they were restrained.

Young dolphins both in the wild and in captivity have variable whistles when born, but develop a stereotyped signature whistle within the first year of life. David and Melba Caldwell have recorded whistles from captive dolphins on the day they were born, but these whistles remain faint, "quavery," and unstereotyped for 4-6 months (Caldwell & Caldwell, 1979). Sayigh has recorded similar whistles while following wild mothers and calves, but one can seldom be sure which dolphin produces which whistle under these circumstances. The whistles of wild calves can be recorded using contact hydrophones from when they are first caught at an age of 1 year until well after they leave their mothers at ages typically ranging from 3 to 6 years. Analysis of whistles from over 40 mother-calf pairs shows that by the first year of age, wild calves have developed a stereotyped whistle pattern that remains more or less fixed over subsequent observations as many as 10 years later (Sayigh et al., 1990). This is similar to the pattern reported for captive dolphins (Caldwell, Caldwell, & Tyack, 1990).

When she compared whistles from male and female calves, Sayigh discovered that almost all of the female calves developed whistles that were very different from those of their mothers, but most of the male calves developed whistles that were remarkably similar to their mother's whistle. This sex differences in signature whistle structure may reflect differences in the life histories of males versus females. In Sarasota, when a young adult female first has a calf, she tends to associate with a group of adult females including her own mother. If the grandmother and daughter with calf (not to mention other related females within the same group) had similar whistles, it could be difficult

7. A Comparative and Evolutionary Framework

for a young calf to maintain contact with its mother. Males, on the other hand, disperse from their natal group. There may thus be little advantage for males to develop signature whistles different from their mothers. There may even be benefits to allowing recognition of relationships between mother and son or between brothers. Recognition of mother-son relationships could limit inbreeding. Adult males form coalitions that compete with other males for access to females (Connor, Smolker, & Richards, in press); recognition of brother-brother relations might facilitate the role of kinship in mediating interaction within and between coalitions.

This sex difference suggests that calf whistles are modified as a consequence of exposure to the mother's whistle. Males modify their initially unstereotyped whistles to become more like those of their mother, while females modify their initially unstereotyped whistles to become more distinct. The two sexes may inherit different predispositions for learning their signature whistles. Any alternative explanation that rules out vocal learning would have to model how the X chromosome from the father triggers the formation of a new and distinctive whistle structure in a young female, while the Y chromosome from the father limits the young male to produce a whistle structure encoded in the mother's contribution to its genes. The simplest genetic model would posit that whistle structure is an X-linked additive trait. Male calves, with only one X chromosome from the mother, would inherit their whistle structure from the mother, while the whistles of female calves would be influenced by the X chromosomes from both parents. Wells is currently establishing paternities of calves in the Sarasota population, and we will compare whistles of mothers, fathers, and calves in order to test these competing hypotheses.

Sayigh and I are also conducting a series of playback experiments to test whether mothers and their independent calves recognize each others' signature whistles. When in the net corral, dolphins can be gently restrained by hand, and their position with respect to a playback speaker and other dolphins can be controlled. Dolphins responded strongly to some playbacks, both vocalizing and turning toward the playback speaker. We are using a matched pair design in which each of two mothers (or calves) are played the same stimulus tape containing whistles of one of their calves (or mothers), then the other. The prediction is that dolphins will show a stronger response to the whistles of the animal with which they shared a strong bond than to the matched animal. Similar tests are being conducted for bonds other than the mother-calf bond.

VOCAL IMITATION IN ADULT CAPTIVE DOLPHINS

Even before the Caldwells' pioneering work on signature whistles, many studies reported that dolphins use whistles to establish vocal or physical contact with one another (McBride & Kritzler, 1951; Wood, 1954). Captive dolphins whistle when separated and respond to whistles either by whistling themselves or by approaching the whistler. As we observed with wild dolphins, captive females and their young calves will exchange whistles until reunited. Data from both captivity and the wild strongly indicate that individual-specific social relationships are very important to bottlenose dolphins. Even when other animals in the group are also whistling, a mother and calf, for instance, presumably can use their signature whistles to find one another.

It has been difficult to investigate the social functions of signature whistles because it is so difficult to tell which dolphin is whistling underwater, even within a small captive group. I developed a small telemetry device, called a *vocalight* (Tyack, 1985), and a miniature computer data logger (Tyack & Recchia, 1991) to overcome this obstacle. Either device is attached to a dolphin's head or back with a suction cup. The vocalights are made in a variety of colors. Every time a dolphin produces a sound, its vocalight lights up. If several animals are in a pool, each can be equipped with a vocalight that produces a different color. To identify which dolphin has made a particular sound, a poolside observer simply calls out the color that was illuminated when the sound was heard. Both the whistles (recorded underwater with hydrophones) and the observers' identifications are recorded simultaneously for later analysis. It is difficult for an observer to follow more than two or three dolphins simultaneously, so dataloggers are used for larger groups. We attach a datalogger to each dolphin to record the level of sound 20 times/second for up to 45 minutes. The dataloggers are synchronized to a time code recorded simultaneously with both audio and video records from the pool.

The vocalights were first used with two captive bottlenose dolphins named Scotty and Spray at Sealand, a marine park in Brewster, MA, on Cape Cod. Here the dolphins could be studied while they were interacting in the water, rather than recorded in air or in isolation as had been typical for earlier studies of signature whistles. Scotty and Spray each produced a stereotyped whistle very much like the signature whistles described by the Caldwells. However, the Caldwells reported that signature whistles made up over 90% of the whistle repertoire of each bottlenose dolphin, yet only 48% and 67% of the whistle samples from Scotty and Spray, respectively, were their own signature whistles (Tyack, 1986). Both Scotty and Spray produced highly variable

7. A Comparative and Evolutionary Framework

whistles and each also produced whistles almost identical to the presumed signature whistle of its poolmate. The most common whistle from each animal was its signature whistle, but each imitated the other's whistle at rates near 20%. The male, Scotty, produced more imitations than Spray, and both listening and inspection of spectrograms indicate that his imitations of Spray's signature whistle were more precise than Spray's imitations of Scotty's whistle. Scotty was recorded 2 years after Spray died, and when Spray was not present, he whistled less frequently, produced shorter whistles, and did not imitate Spray's whistle (Tyack, 1991).

In considering possible functions for imitation of signature whistles, I was helped by data from a foray by an ethologist to Louis Herman's marine mammal lab at Kewalo Basin. For several years, Herman used acoustic cues as well as gestural cues for language training with his dolphins. When Douglas Richards joined Herman's lab, he already had ethological experience studying acoustic communication. After Richards joined the lab, they showed that the dolphins not only responded to the acoustic cues as commands, but they also were imitating them quite precisely. Similar imitation had been reported earlier (e.g., Caldwell & Caldwell, 1972).

As Sigurdson (this volume, chapter 8) points out, these whistle mimicry results suggest a useful medium for dolphin language research focussing on signal production as well as comprehension. Even though apes failed at vocal imitation, ape language researchers were so committed to establishing a two-way communicative link with their subjects that they switched to gestural communication. It is ironic that the animal language research on marine mammals has not taken advantage of their imitative capabilities to establish two-way use of an artificial vocal communication system. Once training problems are overcome, the kind of system being developed by Sigurdson should allow humans to listen and respond to the dolphins as well as vice versa.

Richards et al. (1984) showed that a dolphin can be trained to label arbitrary objects by imitating arbitrary manmade sounds. When they gave a dolphin the command to imitate a sound, they would simultaneously play the model sound and hold up an object associated with that sound. For example, for the tune of "Mary had a little lamb," one might show a frisbee, and for "Row, row, row your boat," one might show a pipe. After the dolphin got used to this, they started occasionally to show the object but not to play the model sound. In order to respond with the right sound, the dolphin had to remember which sound was associated with which object. After sufficient training, the dolphin succeeded in learning how to label each manmade object with an arbitrary manmade tune.

I am currently testing the hypothesis that imitated signature whistles are also vocal labels used as names, and that untrained dolphins imitate whistles of particular individuals in order to call them. This shares an obvious analogy with the research on imitation of manmade sounds. The vocal labeling study by Richards et al. demonstrates that dolphins have the cognitive capabilities required to use signature whistles as names. If dolphins do imitate signature whistles to name a particular individual, they must be able to make similar associations between each dolphin in their group and the appropriate signature whistle. We are currently using the dataloggers to study the precise behavioral contexts when captive dolphins produce their own signature whistles and when they imitate the signature whistles of others. We are also investigating the responses of other dolphins when a dolphin produces its own whistle, imitates the whistle of the listener, or imitates the whistle of some other dolphin. Neither study addresses the question of how referential is the use of these vocal labels (Savage-Rumbaugh, 1986; Savage-Rumbaugh Rumbaugh, Smith, & Lawson, 1980;).

DO DOLPHINS IMITATE SIGNATURE WHISTLES TO CALL SPECIFIC INDIVIDUALS?

We also have consistent evidence for vocal imitation of signature whistles among the wild dolphins of the Sarasota community. These dolphins tend to imitate the whistles of animals with whom they share strong social bonds. Mothers and calves have been recorded to imitate one another, as do pairs of adult males that have formed a coalition and are almost always sighted together. The signature imitation research is in progress, but I describe preliminary data from one whistle exchange that illustrates how dolphins may use signature whistles to call specific individuals. This exchange was recorded on 21 June 1984, before we had adopted the policy of processing calves together with their mothers during the temporary captures in Sarasota. This whistle exchange occurred between a dolphin in the processing raft and one of five that were in the net corral. The whistles from the animal in the raft were recorded using a suction cup contact hydrophone, all other whistles were recorded from one hydrophone in the water approximately 6 m from the raft and up to 80 m from the furthest part of the net corral.

Six dolphins were encircled in the net corral. The first one to be put into the raft was Nicklo, a 34-year-old adult female. Nicklo maintained a stable

7. A Comparative and Evolutionary Framework

whistle rate of approximately 18 whistles/minute throughout her time in the raft. This rate was higher than that of any of the animals in the net corral. Nicklo produced over 520 signature whistles, 39 variant whistles, and no imitations during the first half of her hour in the raft. Halfway into the recording, measuring, and sampling process, Nicklo began imitating the signature whistle of Granny, the oldest dolphin in the corral (40 years old in 1984). During the second half of the hour, Nicklo produced 472 signature whistles, 47 imitations of Granny, and 6 variant whistles. Nicklo continued to imitate the signature whistle of Granny until she was released from the raft. She did not imitate the signature whistle of any other animal in the group, including her own 3.5-year-old female calf. As the oldest female in the group, Granny was most likely to have had experience with this new and potentially threatening situation, and on this basis would be most likely to be of assistance.

Signature whistles from the 5 dolphins in the net corral were also analyzed. Because these were recorded together on the same underwater channel, we were not able to identify which dolphin made which whistle, and thus would not have been able to detect imitation of whistles among these dolphins. Furthermore, another mother had signature whistle contours so similar to her 3.5 year old male calf that we did not attempt to discriminate between them. None of the animals in the corral imitated the whistle of Nicklo.

In order to test whether the whistles of Nicklo became synchronized with whistles from any of the dolphins in the net, we tallied how often each kind of whistle from Nicklo occurred within the same 3 second window as whistles from each of the dolphins in the net corral. The time window was chosen to be short enough that dolphins seldom produced more than one whistle per window. The only whistles that synchronized with Nicklo were the signature whistles of Granny during the period immediately after Nicklo started imitating Granny's signature whistle. A caveat is in order regarding statistical analysis of these windows. Successive whistles from the same dolphin are seldom independent, but depend on both what kind of whistle came before and how long ago it occurred. Therefore, treatment of successive 3 second windows as independent may inflate the sample size of independent observations for statistical analysis.

These data clearly support the prediction of the signature labeling hypothesis that a dolphin will show a differential response following imitation of its signature whistle. Before Nicklo first imitated Granny's whistle, there was no temporal association between Granny and Nicklo whistles. As soon as Nicklo started imitating Granny's whistle, Granny and Nicklo whistles were strongly associated. Granny showed a higher response to Nicklo's imitations of her own whistle than to Nicklo's signature whistle. The association between Granny and Nicklo whistles was stronger than that of Nicklo and any other dolphins in the net, including Nicklo's own calf. Nicklo thus imitated the whistle of the oldest dolphin in the group (perhaps the most able and likely to help her), and only that dolphin responded to the imitations. Some of Nicklo's imitations preceded and some followed Granny's production of her own signature whistle. This demonstrates that Granny did not just respond to imitation and Nicklo did not just imitate Granny immediately following a Granny whistle.

Although dolphins can play with imitating novel sounds, they harness learning primarily to develop stable whistles. It may seem counterintuitive to use flexibility in the service of developing a stable sound, but this is how humans learn words. People who speak a language must share the same referents to words, but the precise sounds we use are learned and arbitrary. English speakers learn to say *house*, while French speakers say *maison*. If dolphins learn to develop their signature whistles and learn to imitate the whistles of others in order to name them, then learning allows a remarkably open-ended system of communication in these social animals.

ETHOLOGICAL SUGGESTIONS FOR ANIMAL LANGUAGE RESEARCH

When comparative psychologists want to study a particular cognitive skill in the laboratory, they would do well to search the animal kingdom for taxa that solve similar problems. For studies of spatial memory, animals such as nutcrackers (*Nucifraga* sp), which store and retrieve tens of thousands of seeds per year, might be more promising than species such as pigeons (*Columba livia*), which seldom are faced with spatial memory problems of similar magnitude (Shettleworth, 1990). If animal language research is taken as an attempt to study how the communication skills of animals can be modified by learning, then the selection of apes, dolphins, parrots, and sea lions makes some sense. All four groups are highly social, with relatively long periods of parental care, and with well developed imitative capabilities. Any species where the young are taught would also be a promising candidate for animal language research.

More careful examination of behavioral development in young animals raised by their own parents may also target particular age or sex classes as optimal for language training. In most songbird species, males provide more evidence for vocal learning than females, and they learn best during critical periods of development. Data on whistle imitation suggest that male dolphins

7. A Comparative and Evolutionary Framework

might be better subjects for the study of vocal imitation than females. Not only does a male calf in the wild tend to learn his signature whistle by imitating his mother, but also the imitations of adult males appear more precise than those of adult females. The captive male Scotty produced more frequent and more accurate imitations than did the female Spray (Tyack, 1991). However, both sexes do show strong evidence for vocal learning, and females can produce quite accurate imitations.

Animal language training may be improved by closer matching to development of natural communication systems in each species. There are obvious problems with starting training after a critical period for learning has passed, but there are more subtle problems as well. Cognitive capabilities may be channeled to solve particular tasks by perceptual limitations, selective attention, domain-specific intelligences, and motivational factors. Close feedback between laboratory experiment and field work are of obvious utility for matching an experimental protocol to an animal's capabilities. I discuss four different ways in which better matches may be developed: stimuli used in artificial languages, training techniques, context of testing, and more emphasis on the communicative and expressive elements of artificial languages.

Care must be taken to match artificial languages to the perceptual and motor abilities of the subjects. It is by now obvious that the inability of chimps to speak says little about their language abilities. While they are physically incapable of producing many speech sounds, they can learn and use manual gestural languages. Perceptual limitations are not so obvious, but may be equally important. For example, it appears that discrimination of the human speech sounds /pa/ from /ba/ relies in part on a categorical perception that is shared among mammals, whereas humans use specially evolved mechanisms to parse sentences in normal speech (Kuhl, 1987). For artificial languages to proceed beyond minimal complexity, they must rely on features that animals can discrimate rapidly with little error. If discrimination of /pa/ from /ba/ relies on auditory processing shared among most mammals, this may be a useful feature for artificial languages, but if humans require special mechanisms to parse phoneme strings within speech, artificial languages for other species may require special attention for more discriminable features. Attention to the natural signals of each species may help identify such features. For example, the coo calls of Japanese macaques (*Macaca fuscata*) divide into groups with early or late maxima in frequency, and these two classes of coo occur in different contexts (Green, 1975). Japanese macaques discriminate this feature with ease, while closely related species require extensive training for the same discrimination (Zoloth et al., 1979).

Some psychologists choose highly artificial settings or stimuli for tests. If the experimental protocol requires novel objects or contexts, then artificiality may be advantageous, but many animals may perform best on problems similar to those for which their cognitive capabilities evolved. If students of artificial intelligence want to program a robot to find, identify, and manipulate things, they could simplify their task by narrowing down the robot's symbol set and outside world to very few different kinds of simple geometrical shapes that do not move about on their own. It is by no means certain that training an animal to use a formal language describing a similar static and highly constrained object world is simpler for the animal than a more natural world. Perceptual abilities are likely to be tuned to an animal's natural environment. Pigeons learn to form "complex" natural concepts of visual images of water, trees, or even one individual human, just as quickly as "simple" geometric shapes (Herrnstein, Loveland & Cable, 1976). Psychologists may have to search carefully to find the right match of settings and stimuli in order to open a communication channel and gain access to more general cognitive abilities of different species.

Animal language researchers would do well to match their training techniques to observations of how their subjects acquire their own natural systems of communication. Some communication skills may be learned better through social reinforcement than food reinforcement. Animal language training in parrots advanced only after application of an innovative social modeling paradigm in which a human alternated with the parrot in responding to spoken English (Pepperberg, this volume, chapter 11). As has been reported for white-crowned sparrows learning song from conspecifics, more intense social interaction with tutors may engage learning processes that are otherwise hidden (Baptista & Petrinovich, 1986).

Selection of naturalistic settings for experimental testing may also improve performance. For example, Terrace, Saunders, and Bever (1979) trained a chimpanzee (*Pan troglodytes*) to sign using American Sign Language. The chimp was trained and tested by many different people during controlled test sessions in a small bare room, under the assumption that this impoverished environment would minimize distractions and cueing. They concluded that the chimp seldom signed spontaneously and that many of the chimp's multisign utterances were cued by the trainer. The regularities in the chimp's multisign utterances were thus as likely to be a consequence of the trainers' understanding of syntax as the chimp's. However, this same chimp was later tested in both Terrace's restrictive testing environment and while interacting and playing with people. In the Terrace test setting, the chimp primarily responded to the trainer, but in the more relaxed setting, most of the signs were spontaneous and only

7. A Comparative and Evolutionary Framework

11% were imitations (O'Sullivan & Yeager, 1989). After the fact, Terrace (1979) concluded that motivation to sign had been a problem in his study and that the chimp would have made better progress if his sign training had been more integrated into communication throughout the day rather than limited to formal sessions in an impoverished environment.

If pigeons can easily form a concept of an individual person, if parrots can learn language skills most easily by role playing with a human, and if chimps show more communicative use of signs while playing with people, then this suggests that more explicitly interactive use of human-animal relationships might further animal language research. As we learn more about the social behavior of species involved in animal language research and about how their communication mediates social interaction, there will be more opportunity for humans to intervene both with playback experiments and for humans to play roles interacting with animals as more active agents. Close observation of captive primates (e.g., de Waal, 1989) and field experiments with wild primates (e.g., Cheney & Seyfarth, 1990) reveal that monkeys and apes know and communicate a surprising amount about their complex social relationships. If the social domain is a primary one for communication and cognition in these species, then animal language researchers would do well to develop a richer repertoire for manipulating and communicating about their interspecies social relationships.

An ethologist with an evolutionary and cognitive bent may find it difficult to interpret experiments in which an animal is trained with an artificial language to communicate about an artificial object-oriented world constructed by humans. How can he or she integrate the observation that, say, a chimp or a parrot can label a triangle or square and tell us what color a ball is? How can one compare to natural observations, experiments where people train animals to produce or understand strings of commands, such as GO THROUGH A HOOP, after earlier exposure only to different requests such as JUMP OVER A FRISBEE? The ethologist interested in the adaptive functions of particular cognitive skills is more interested in how animals develop representations of and communicate about their own natural world, including their social world.

Study of signature whistles suggests that dolphins use vocal learning and imitation to develop a flexible and open-ended way to communicate primarily about individual-specific social relationships. This contrasts with the marine mammal language experiments, in which dolphins or sea lions are trained to manipulate objects (JUMP OVER HOOP) or to treat people or other dolphins as they do other objects (FETCH BALL [to] PHOENIX). Although these animals clearly can be trained to label objects, to report their presence or absence, and to comprehend sequential commands about objects and actions, all of these experiments use artificial languages as a one-way street to get the animals to perform. This training opens a clear window on some aspects of dolphin or sea lion cognition, but the animals are never given a chance to use the language to alter the contingencies of any human behavior other than tossing a fish. Describing the experiments as "language" experiments thus stretches the usage of language as a communication system. The marine mammal experiments are in this way very different from both the primate (e.g., Savage-Rumbaugh, this volume, chapter 22) and parrot research (Pepperberg, this volume, chapter 11).

The term "animal language" sometimes seems to be used as a cipher for animal awareness. Humans certainly use language to refer to the mental states of themselves and others. Consciousness is required for all but highly unusual language use (and exceptions such as infant speech, talking in ones sleep or talking in hypnosis may more accurately reflect alterations of consciousness rather than its absence). Kihlstrom (1987) identified consciousness primarily as a link of cognition to a representation of the self as either an agent or an experiencer. This would suggest that consciousness is particularly important for the ability it provides of mental scenario building, including the ability to represent ones own performance as others may see it. Alexander (1990) suggested that consciousness evolved to prepare humans for the flow of novel social circumstances for reciprocation that characterize human societies. Language may have evolved in parallel as a way to frame and to manipulate such social understandings. Animals that form individual-specific social relationships and that face a similar tension between competition and cooperation in reciprocal relationships may also encounter selective pressures to evolve more complex forms of social cognition. If consciousness and language coevolved in humans in large measure as a response to human sociality, then higher cognitive functions related to sociality in other animals may have evolved in parallel with abilities to communicate about them. One might expect "animal language" also to frame representations of self and self interest compared to other conspecifics or other elements of the environment.

There is a danger in taking such a formal view of artificial languages and language training that the communicative context is overshadowed. There is a striking lack of overlap between psychological studies of artificial languages and ethological studies of animal communication. Communication is a social phenomenon, and the study of natural communication systems in animals is primarily a study of social behavior. Most animal signals mediate social

7. A Comparative and Evolutionary Framework

interactions, yet few animal language studies emphasize the social domain. Animals are more typically trained to use artificial languages primarily to request, describe, or manipulate objects. Researchers following this approach run the risk that their subjects are less able to tap potentially domain-specific communication skills. Animals may be much better at recognizing their mother, have a much richer concept of mother, and be much more motivated to communicate about this kind of natural social relationship than to communicate about discriminating an "x" from a "+."

Language training should not be a purely formal exercise, but should be a tool for opening a two way channel of communication with animals. As with children early on in language development, animals may use signs to obtain favored foods or objects. This may be a useful way to start language training, but it is limited in its communicative scope. Savage-Rumbaugh et al. (1980) suggested that if chimps can get away with being behaviorists, they will, but that they can also engage in symbolic reference if trained to do so. If we create more ways for animals to communicate with us (and possibly deceive us) about desires or plans, including those involving their social environment, and about individuals they associate with, including the trainers, we may both increase their motivation and start to learn more about the social functions of cognition.

Natural animal communication tends to be manipulative and goal oriented. Much of the goal directedness of natural animal behavior is a consequence of adaptation through natural selection of genetically determined behavior patterns. Testing animals under artificial circumstances may help to discriminate whether apparently intentional and intelligent behavior observed under natural conditions represents a "clever" adaptation or an intelligent and intentional animal. If animals can show similar planning in the laboratory using artificial systems of communication, this will help to address these difficult issues of intentionality and intelligence. In the past, the researchers who have been most sensitive to these issues have not been preoccupied with comparisons to human language. Köhler (1925) created experiments to detect insight and to investigate whether chimps appear to understand the problems being solved by other chimps. Menzel and Halperin (1975) showed that captive chimps appear to be able to convey or withold information on the location of hidden objects, apparently intentionally, but the researchers were unable precisely to specify the mode of communication.

In order for animal language research to address these questions, animals should be tested within a social and communicative context. Data both from the natural communication of primates (Cheney & Seyfarth, 1990) and animal language experiments (Bennett, 1978) suggest that animal utterances are more like commands aimed to elicit behavior than like statements aimed to produce or change beliefs in the other party. However, few carefully controlled animal language experiments have given the animals scope for this kind of communication. Humans are disposed to attribute intentions, beliefs, and desires to others, but we have scarce evidence that other animals make similar social attributions. The work of Premack and Woodruff (1978) on whether apes attribute mental states to others and of Woodruff and Premack (1979) on deception suggest that these questions can be addressed by controlled psychological experiments.

Griffin (1981) emphasized that just as language is a medium by which humans can learn about each other's mental experiences, so too animal language training has similar potential for opening a window on the minds of animals. Animal language research has often focused more on narrow comparisons with human language than on these more general cognitive questions. The ability to communicate with people using language is a mixed blessing for cognitive scientists; talking, by itself, may often be a shallow and misleading probe of cognition. A major theme of psychology in this century has been how few of our internal psychological processes are fully accessible for conscious reflection, and how inaccurate the conscious report of human subjects may be. Even in humans, analysis of consciousness cannot proceed independently of nonconscious cognitive processes. Psychological research on humans clearly indicates that nonconscious cognitive processes have impacts on conscious processes and that different cognitive processes are more or less penetrable by conscious thought (Kihlstrom, 1987). However, to the extent that animal language experiments can give us access to intentionality, attribution, and the ability to synthesize information across domains in animals, they will remain important general tools in the study of animal cognition.

It is difficult to integrate animal language experiments into comparative study of the evolution of animal cognition. We require more information on the functions in nature of the cognitive capabilities revealed by these experiments in order to understand their evolutionary origins. It is only by shuttling back and forth between cognitive experiments and observational study that we can hope to understand the full complexity and diversity of animal cognition. The work of Richards and co-workers, for instance, gave me more confidence that dolphins had the cognitive capabilities required to imitate signature whistles in order to label or call other individuals. Conversely, results on the imitation of signature whistles may help comparative psychologists to

7. A Comparative and Evolutionary Framework

understand the functions in nature of cognitive skills they have uncovered in the laboratory. Further progress in animal cognition requires a tighter synthesis of the functional and evolutionary studies of organismal biologists, mechanistic study by neurobiologists, and study of development and cognitive processes by comparative psychologists.

REFERENCES

Alexander, R.D. (1990). Epigenetic rules and Darwinian algorithms. *Ethology and Sociobiology*, 11, 241-303.

Axelrod, R. (1984). *The evolution of cooperation.* New York: Basic Books.

Baptista, L. F. & Petrinovich, L. (1986). Song development in the white-crowned sparrow: Social factors and sex differences. *Animal Behavior*, 34, 1359-1371.

Bennett, J. (1978). Some remarks about concepts. *Behavioral and Brain Sciences*, 1, 557-560.

Bowlby, J. (1969). *Attachment.* New York: Basic Books.

Bullock, T. H. & Ridgway, S. H. (1972). Evoked potentials in the central auditory system of alert porpoises to their own and artificial sounds. *Journal of Neurobiology*, 3, 79-99.

Caldwell, M. C. & Caldwell, D. K. (1965). Individualized whistle contours in bottlenosed dolphins *(Tursiops truncatus). Nature*, 207, 434-435.

Caldwell, M. C. & Caldwell, D. K. (1972). Vocal mimicry in the whistle mode by an Atlantic bottlenosed dolphin. *Cetology*, 9, 1-8.

Caldwell, M. C. & Caldwell, D. K. (1979). The whistle of the Atlantic bottlenosed dolphin *(Tursiops truncatus)* - ontogeny. In H. E. Winn & B. L. Olla (Eds.), *Behavior of marine animals, Vol. 3, Cetaceans* (pp. 369-401). New York: Plenum Press.

Caldwell, M. C., Caldwell, D. K., & Tyack, P. L. (1990). A review of the signature whistle hypothesis for the Atlantic bottlenose dolphin, *Tursiops truncatus.* In S. Leatherwood, & R. Reeves (Eds.), *The bottlenose dolphin: Recent progress in research* (pp. 199-234). San Diego: Academic Press.

Cheney, D. L. & Seyfarth, R. M. (1990). *How monkeys see the world.* Chicago: University of Chicago Press.

Cole, M. & Scribner, S. (1974). *Culture & thought, a psychological introduction.* New York: Wiley.

Connor, R. C., Smolker, R. A., & Richards, A. F. (in press). Dolphin alliances and coalitions. In A. H. Harcourt, & F. B. M. de Waal (Eds.), *Coalitions and alliances in humans and other animals.* Oxford: Oxford University Press.

Cosmides, L. (1989). The logic of social exchange: Has natural selection shaped how humans reason? Studies with the Wason selection task. *Cognition*, 31, 187-276.

Cosmides, L. & Tooby, J. (1987). From evolution to behavior: evolutionary psychology as the missing link. In J. Dupre (Ed.), *The latest on the best* (pp. 277-306). Cambridge MA: MIT Press.

Darwin, C. (1859/1979). *On the origin of species by means of natural selection.* Cambridge: Harvard University Press.

Darwin, C. (1871/1981). *The descent of man, and selection in relation to sex.* Princeton: Princeton University Press.

Deacon, T. W. (1988). Human brain evolution: 1. Evolution of language circuits. In H. J. Jerison & I. Jerison (Eds.), *Intelligence and evolutionary biology,* (pp. 363-381). NATO ASI Series G: Ecological Sciences, Vol. 17, . Berlin: Springer Verlag.

Deutsch, D. (1975). The organization of short-term memory for a single acoustic attribute. In D. Deutsch & J. A. Deutsch (Eds.), *Short term memory* (pp. 107-151). New York: Academic Press.

Eaton, R. L. (1979). A beluga whale imitates human speech. *Carnivore*, 2, 22-23.

Fodor, J. A. (1983). *The modularity of mind.* Cambridge, MA: MIT Press.

7. A Comparative and Evolutionary Framework

Garcia, J. & Koelling, R. A. (1966). The relation of cue to consequence in avoidance learning. *Psychonomic Science*, 4, 123-124.

Gardner, H. (1983). *Frames of mind.* New York: Basic Books.

Goodall, J. (1986). *The chimpanzees of Gombe.* Cambridge, MA: Harvard University Press.

Gould, S. J. & Lewontin, R. C. (1979). The spandrels of San Marco and the Panglossian paradigm: A critique of the adaptationist paradigm. *Proceedings of the Royal Society of London*, 205, 281-288.

Green, S. (1975). Variations of vocal pattern with social situation in Japanese monkey (*Macaca fuscata*): A field study. In L. A. Rosenblum (Ed.) *Primate behavior*, (Vol. 4, pp. 1-102). New York: Academic Press.

Griffin, D. R. (1981). *The question of animal awareness.* Los Altos, CA.: Kaufmann.

Hamilton, W. D. (1964). The genetical theory of social behavior. *Journal of Theoretical Biology*, 7, 1-52.

Hayes, C. (1951). *The ape in our house.* New York: Harper.

Herman, L. M. (1980). Cognitive characteristics of dolphins. In L. M. Herman (Ed.), *Cetacean behavior: Mechanisms and functions* (pp. 363-429). New York: Wiley-Interscience.

Herman, L. M., Richards, D., & Wolz, J. (1984). Comprehension of sentences by bottlenosed dolphins. *Cognition*, 16, 129-219.

Herrnstein, R., Loveland, D. H. & Cable, C. (1976). Natural concepts in pigeons. *Journal of Experimental Psychology: Animal Behavior Processes*, 2, 285-311.

Humphrey, N.K. (1976). The social function of intellect. In P. P. G. Bateson & R. A. Hinde (Eds.), *Growing points in ethology*, (pp. 303-317). New York: Cambridge University Press.

Kamil, A. C. (1988). A synthetic approach to the study of animal intelligence. In D. W. Leger (Ed.), *Comparative perspectives in modern psychology:*

Nebraska symposium on motivation. (Vol. 35, pp. 257-308). Lincoln: University of Nebraska Press.

Kamil, A. C. & Roitblat, H. L. (1985). Foraging theory: implications for animal learning and cognition. *Annual Review of Psychology,* 36, 141-169.

Kihlstrom, J. F. (1987). The cognitive unconscious. *Science,* 237, 1445-1452.

Klima, E. S. & Bellugi, U. (1979). *The signs of language.* Cambridge MA: Harvard University Press.

Köhler, W. (1925). *The mentality of apes.* New York: Harcourt Brace.

Krebs, J. R. (1990). Food-storing birds: Adaptive specialization in brain and behaviour? *Philosophical Transactions of the Royal Society, London. B,* 329, 153-160.

Kroodsma, D. E. & Canaday, R. A. (1985). Differences in repertoire size, singing behavior, and associated neuroanatomy among marsh wren populations have a genetic basis. *Auk,* 102, 439-446.

Kroodsma, D. E. & Verner, J. (1987). Use of song repertoires among marsh wren populations. *Auk,* 104, 63-72.

Kuhl, P.K. (1987). The special-mechanisms debate in speech research: Categorization tests on animals and infants. In S. Harnad (Ed.), *Categorical perception* (pp. 355-386). Cambridge: Cambridge University Press.

Kummer, H., Dasser, V. & Hoyningen-Hüne, P. (1990). Exploring primate social cognition: some critical remarks. *Behaviour,* 112, 84-98.

Lieberman, P. (1984). *The biology and evolution of language.* Cambridge, MA: Harvard University Press.

Lieberman, P. (1991). *Uniquely human.* Cambridge, MA: Harvard University Press.

Marler, P. (1970). Birdsong and human speech: could there be parallels? *American Scientist,* 58, 669-674.

7. A Comparative and Evolutionary Framework

Marler, P. (1990). Song learning: the interface between behaviour and neuroethology. *Philosophical Transactions of the Royal Society, London, B,* 329, 109-114.

McBride, A. F. & Kritzler, H. (1951). Observations on pregnancy, parturition, and post-natal behavior in the bottlenose dolphin. *Journal of Mammalogy,* 32, 251-266.

Meier, R. P. (1991). Language acquisition by deaf children. *American Scientist,* 79, 60-70.

Menzel, E. W., Jr. & Halperin, S. (1975). Purposive behavior as a basis for objective communication between chimpanzees. *Science,* 189, 652-654.

Newman, J. D., & Symmes, D. (1982). Inheritance and experience in the acquisition of primate acoustic behavior. In C. Snowdon, C. H. Brown, & M. Peterson (Eds.), *Primate communication* (pp. 259-278). Cambridge: Cambridge University Press.

O'Sullivan, C. & Yeager, C. P. (1989). Communicative context and linguistic competence: The effects of social setting on a chimpanzee's conversational skill. In R. A. Gardner & B. T. Gardner (Eds.), *Teaching sign language to chimpanzees* (pp. 269-279). Albany: State University of New York Press.

Payne, K. B., Tyack, P. & Payne, R. S. (1983). Progressive changes in the songs of humpback whales. *AAAS Selected Symposia Series* (pp. 9-59). Boulder, CO: Westview Press.

Petitto, L. A. & Marentette, P. F. (1991). Babbling in the manual mode: Evidence for the ontogeny of language. *Science,* 251, 1493-1496.

Pinker, S. (1984). *Language learnability and language development.* Cambridge, MA: Harvard University Press.

Premack, D. (1983). The codes of man and beast. *Behavioral and Brain Sciences,* 6, 125-167.

Premack, D. & Woodruff, G. (1978). Does the chimpanzee have a theory of mind? *Behavioral and Brain Sciences,* 1, 515-526.

Ralls, K., Fiorelli, P., & Gish, S. (1985). Vocalizations and vocal mimicry in captive harbor seals, *Phoca vitulina*. *Canadian Journal of Zoology*, 63, 1050- 1056.

Richards, D. G., Wolz, J. P., & Herman, L. M. (1984). Vocal mimicry of computer-generated sounds and vocal labelling of objects by a bottlenosed dolphin, *Tursiops truncatus*. *Journal of Comparative Psychology*, 87, 10-28.

Savage-Rumbaugh, E. S. (1986). *Ape language: From conditioned response to symbol*. New York: Columbia University Press.

Savage-Rumbaugh, E. S., Pate, J. L., Lawson, J., Smith, S. T., & Rosenbaum, S. (1983). Can a chimp make a statement? *Journal of Experimental Psychology: General*, 112, 457-492.

Savage-Rumbaugh, E. S., Rumbaugh, D. M., Smith, S. T. & Lawson, J. (1980). Reference: the linguistic essential. *Science*, 210, 922-925.

Sayigh, L. S., Tyack, P. L., Wells, R. S. & Scott, M. D. (1990). Signature whistles of free-ranging bottlenose dolphins *Tursiops truncatus*: stability and mother-offspring comparisons. *Behavioral Ecology and Sociobiology*, 26, 247-260.

Seyfarth, R. M. & Cheney, D. L. (1986). Vocal development in vervet monkeys. *Animal Behavior*, 34, 1640-1658.

Shettleworth, S. J. (1990). Spatial memory in food storing birds. *Philosophical transactions of the Royal Society, London. B*, 329, 143-151.

Snowdon, C. T. (1983). Ethology, comparative psychology, and animal behavior. *Annual Review of Psychology*, 34, 63-94.

Snowdon, C. T. (1990). Language capacities in nonhuman animals. *Yearbook of Physical Anthropology*, 33, 215-243.

Solow, A. & Tyack, P. L. (1990). Inhomogeneity and apparent organization in animal behavior. *Biometrics*, 46, 837-840.

Stephens, D.W. & Krebs, J. R. (1986). *Foraging theory*. Princeton, NJ: Princeton University Press.

7. A Comparative and Evolutionary Framework

Terrace, H. S. (1979). *Nim: A chimpanzee who learned sign language*. New York: Washington Square Press.

Terrace, H. S., Petitto, L. A., Saunders, R. J., & Bever, T. G. (1979). Can an ape create a sentence? *Science*, 206, 891-902.

Tierney, A. J. (1986). The evolution of learned and innate behavior: Contributions from genetics and neurobiology to a theory of behavioral evolution. *Animal Learning and Behavior*, 14, 339-348.

Tinbergen, N. (1951). *The study of instinct*. New York: Oxford University Press.

Trivers, R. L. (1971). The evolution of reciprocal altruism. *Quarterly Review of Biology*, 46, 35-57.

Tyack, P. (1981). Interactions between singing Hawaiian humpback whales and conspecifics nearby. *Behavioral Ecology and Sociobiology*, 8, 105-116.

Tyack, P. (1985). An optical telemetry device to identify which dolphin produces a sound. *Journal of the Acoustical Society of America*, 78, 1892-1895.

Tyack, P. (1986). Whistle repertoires of two bottlenosed dolphins, *Tursiops truncatus*: Mimicry of signature whistles? *Behavioral Ecology and Sociobiology*, 18, 251-257.

Tyack, P. L. (1991). Use of a telemetry device to identify which dolphin produces a sound: when bottlenosed dolphins are interacting, they mimic each other's signature whistles. In K. Pryor & K.S. Norris (Eds.) *Dolphin societies: Methods of study*, (pp. 319-344). Berkeley: University of California Press.

Tyack, P. L. & Recchia, C. A. (1991). A datalogger to identify vocalizing dolphins. *Journal of the Acoustical Society of America*, 90, 1668-1671.

Verner, J. (1976). Complex song repertoire of male long-billed marsh wrens in eastern Washington. *Living Bird*, 14, 263-300.

de Waal, F. (1989). *Chimpanzee politics.* Cambridge, MA: Harvard University Press.

Wells, R. S., Scott, M. D., & Irvine, A. B. (1987). Structural aspects of dolphin societies. In H. H. Genoways (Ed.) *Current mammalogy,* (vol. 1, pp. 247-305). New York: Plenum Press.

Wood, F. G., Jr. (1954). Underwater sound production and concurrent behavior of captive porpoises, *Tursiops truncatus* and *Stenella plagiodon. Bulletin of Marine Science of the Gulf and Caribbean,* 3, 120-133.

Woodruff, G. & Premack, D. (1979). Intentional communication in the chimpanzee: the development of deception. *Cognition,* 7, 333-362.

Zoloth, S. R., Petersen, M. R., Beecher, M. D., Green, S., Marler, P., Moody, D. M., & Stebbins, W. C. (1979). Species-specific perceptual processing of vocal sounds by monkeys. *Science,* 204, 870-873.

8 Frequency-modulated Whistles as a Medium for Communication with the Bottlenose Dolphin (*Tursiops truncatus*)

John Sigurdson

The frequency-modulated (FM) whistles of dolphins have received considerable attention from field and laboratory researchers over the last several decades. A large variety of FM patterns has been documented among dolphins (Dreher & Evans, 1964; Caldwell & Caldwell, 1979), and this between-subject variability has led to the conjecture that the whistles are a major component in a system of intraspecies communication. While there is no dispute that the whistles serve in some communicative capacity, the sophistication of that system remains an open question. The variety and relative frequencies of whistles recorded from multiple animals engaged in navigation, play and foraging led Dreher and Evens (1964) to suggest a complex system with some similarities to human language, but the test of such a hypothesis requires the identification of the individual producing the sounds and the order in which they are produced (Wood, 1973). Presently, new technology is being applied with success to the sorting of sounds made by individual animals (Tyack, 1986) and to analysis of the ontogeny of the whistle production (Sayigh, Tyack, Wells, & Scott, 1990).

The failure to decipher the natural communication of dolphins has prompted investigators to attempt to train specific artificial, acoustic communication systems that take advantage of the dolphin's presumed abilities, but use stimuli that are easier for humans to classify and produce than the dolphin's natural whistle repertoire. These systems typically resemble simplified human communication systems and involve sequences of elements in which the meaning of a sequence is conveyed not only by the elements present but by their order as well.

Early attempts to establish such systems used human voice and modified human voice to command the animal to perform various motor actions (Lilly, 1962, 1965), but they met with little success (Wood, 1973). More reliable performance was obtained with human voice converted to whistles (Batteau & Markey, 1967) and with whistles that resembled common electronic wave forms (Herman, Richards, Wolz, 1984). Recent proposals suggest bidirectional communication systems wherein both the commands to the animal and its responses are acoustic. The proposed acoustic element is either a code sequence of discrete tones of different absolute frequencies (McKay, 1981) or a single, continuous, FM sine wave (Richards, Wolz & Herman, 1984). Other possibilities exist. For example, the absence of uncorrelated harmonics in the whistles of *Tursiops* makes the use of phoneme-like elements unlikely, but the animal can produce simultaneous whistle and broad-band emissions, and such combinations may serve to increase the number of distinguishable elements in a set of signals.

The present research examines the ability of the dolphin to acquire and manipulate a set of artificial FM whistles as a prerequisite for a bidirectional, acoustic communication system. The usefulness of such a set depends on its size, and the practical size depends on the distinctiveness of the elements to the animal as demonstrated by its ability to both discriminate and produce them reliably. Individual dolphins have not been shown to produce large sets of distinctive signals spontaneously, and the problems encountered in attempts to establish artificial sets (Batteau & Markey, 1967; Caldwell & Caldwell, 1972; Richards et al., 1984) have led to increased interest in the contingencies that control the whistle response.

Richards et al. (1984) used artificial FM models differing in center frequency, duration and FM pattern to demonstrate instrumental control over those dimensions of the whistle response. A female dolphin discriminated between four models by producing whistle responses that agreed sufficiently along the three dimensions of their respective models to allow human judges to classify them without confusion. Selected whistle responses to five other models were presented.

8. Whistles as a communication medium

Although the variety of models used in that study may have been sufficient to demonstrate the flexibility of the whistle response, there are several apparent problems with attempting to expand the repertoire of responses with models of that type. While the use of center frequency as a relevant dimension may facilitate discrimination, it may interfere with reliable production if the dolphin exhibits a preferred frequency range for production as their animal did. In acquisition, the animal's initial responses to a model with a relatively low center frequency were in its preferred range, and only slowly did the center frequency change toward that of the model. Established responses with center frequencies that were out of the animal's preferred range changed slowly toward the preferred range or jumped a whole octave in that direction. A second problem stems from the model set of sine-, triangle-, and square-wave patterns that would be difficult to expand without loss of distinctiveness between the members. Finally, better resemblance between the whistle responses and their respective models would be required if the distinctiveness of the responses were to be maintained in the context of a larger set.

The problems that Richards et al. (1984) observed with absolute frequency as a relevant dimension led to the decision to use only relative frequency (or FM pattern) in the present research. A set of distinctive FM models was developed and a dolphin was trained to produce whistle responses that resembled the models. The models were generated by a computer and the animal's responses were compared with the model by the computer.

The artificial FM models of the present study satisfy several simultaneous criteria. Their design attempts to incorporate the best features of the code sequences suggested by McKay (1981) and the continuous FM pure tones used by Richards et al. (1984). The code sequences of constant-frequency tones yield a large number of distinctive signals and minimize the system complexity required for generation of models and analysis of responses. However, signals of this type are infrequent in the spontaneous repertoires of dolphins, and the stability of responses with multiple, discrete-frequency levels may suffer the problems of drift already described. Alternatively, continuous FM signals are closer in form to the natural signals observed in wild and captive dolphins (Caldwell & Caldwell, 1972; Dreher & Evans, 1964; Evans, 1967; Lilly, 1962; Ridgway, 1983; Tyack, 1986), and there is promise for that form if the problems regarding absolute-frequency and distinctiveness can be overcome.

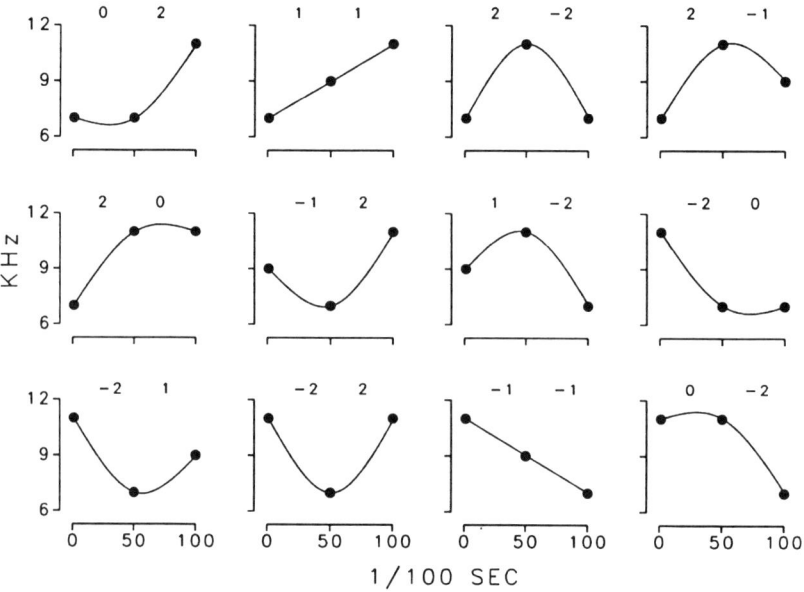

Figure 8.1. Anchor points and spline fits of simple acoustic models.

METHOD

The present set of models is formed by starting with all possible 27 sequences of 3 frequency levels taken over 3 time periods. To eliminate any dependency on absolute frequency and duration for the identification of a particular pattern, only the 12 models that contain at least one high- and one low-frequency level are retained in the subset as shown in Figure 8.1. Like a code-sequence, each model is uniquely described by either the sequence of relative levels (e.g., 1 3 3) or the pair of whole integer slopes between adjacent points (e.g., 2 0). Although dolphins can make such triangle-like signals (Richards et al., 1984), the preferred form would be a smooth contour similar to their spontaneous whistles. A natural cubic-spline fit of 100 points through the original 3 anchor points produces a continuous contour while maintaining the exact relationships between the original frequency levels and time. Other smoothing techniques

8. Whistles as a communication medium

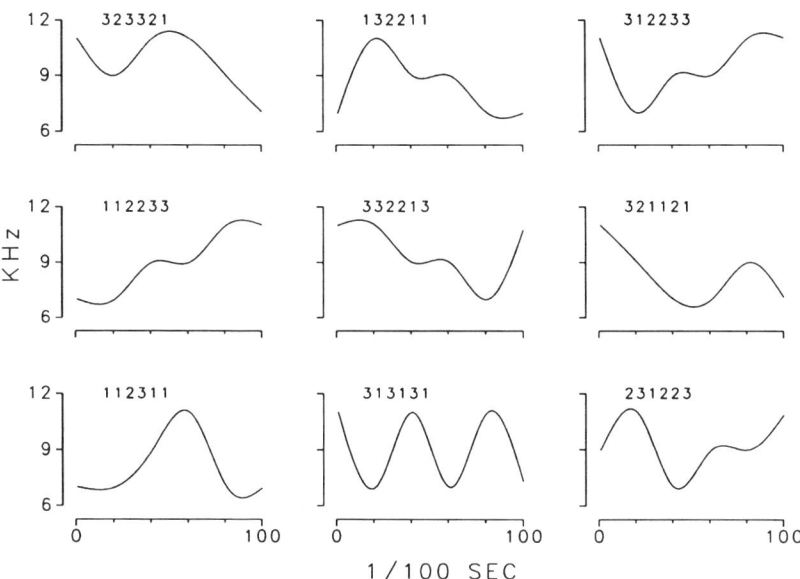

Figure 8.2. Spline fits of selected complex acoustic models.

were found to distort the slope relations between adjacent anchor points. These "simple" signals are either straight line functions or contain a single critical point where the slope equals 0.

"Complex" signals with 2 or more critical points are formed with two sets of 3 by 3 points placed side by side to yield 3 frequency levels by 6 time periods. Here, the number of possible sequences is over 700, but the majority are eliminated by applying the same criterion as was applied to the simple curves plus the added constraint of having no more than two consecutive levels of the same frequency. The cubic-spline fit to these 6 anchor points produces forms of greater complexity as illustrated in Figure 8.2. The complex forms add about a dozen, distinctly different wave-forms as well as a much larger set containing a complete systematic variation of each level at each time period. Finally, the models are expressed in absolute frequencies ranging from 7 to 11 kHz. To minimize signal-processing overhead, each model is represented in 3, ordered tables in computer memory. For model generation, each model has 100 voltage-values for delivery to a voltage-controlled-oscillator (VCO) at 10-msec intervals for a continuous 1-s model. For point-to-point comparison of the animal's response with a specific model, 100 absolute-frequency values of each model are available. Finally, for rapid recognition of the animal's response as one of all possible models, the unique slope sequence for each model is stored. This economical representation allows all three representations of the complete set of models to be stored in the memory of a 512-kb personal computer for rapid access.

Each training trial began with the computer-generated presentation of one model. The dolphin's whistle response was then compared point-for-point with that model. The whistle response was required not to overlap the model in time and to fall within broad, parameters for acceptable duration ($0.6 < t < 2$ s), frequency-range (25 kHz $>$ f $>$ 4 kHz), and amplitude (above 60 dB) to be accepted for analysis. If accepted, the response was scaled to the frequency range and duration of the model and an error score was computed for the difference between the FM patterns of the model and the response.

Once trained, a given whistle response must be recognized uniquely as one of all models. Recognition was accomplished by first classifying an acceptable response as either simple or complex by the number of critical points and then setting an appropriate number of anchor points (3 or 6) at equal intervals across the signal. With the frequency at each anchor point expressed in units that are equal to one-half the frequency range of the response, the slopes between points are computed to the nearest integer and the table of slopes is searched for a matching sequence. The use of the half-range units makes the recognition process insensitive to the frequency range and duration of the response and follows from the constraint of allowing only models with at least one high and one low frequency level. Minor distortions from the ideal FM pattern are permitted by allowing slope deviations within rounding error of whole integer values for simple signals and compensated rounding points for complex signals. No scaling beyond that of the anchor points is required for the recognition process, but additional protection against minor signal roughness and dropouts is included for both point-to-point evaluation and recognition.

Apparatus and Training Techniques

The dolphins in this study were a mature male (Tt-011-M) and female (Tt-580-F) between 20 and 30 years old. The animals were housed in floating enclosures with open-mesh sides and bottoms in Kaneohe Bay, Hawaii. A 20 by 30 ft enclosure was equipped with the training apparatus and two 20 by 30 ft connected enclosures provided additional living space.

8. Whistles as a communication medium

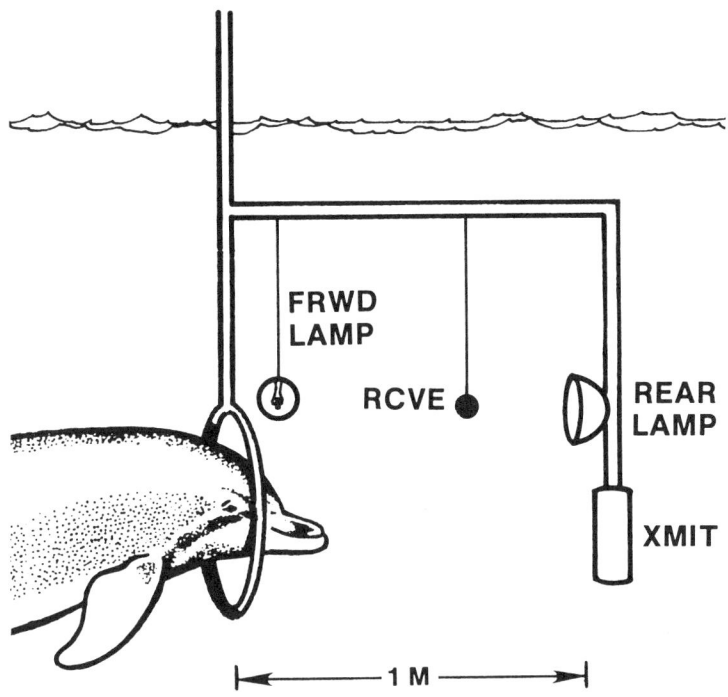

Figure 8.3. Underwater hoop-station for training acoustic responses.

The underwater apparatus is shown in Figure 8.3. A photodetector (not shown) detects the presence of the animal in the stationing hoop. The animal was trained to enter the hoop when the rear lamp was illuminated and to avoid it when the lamp was off. In subsequent acoustic training, a trial was initiated by illumination of the rear lamp, and the entry of the animal into the hoop caused the presentation of an acoustic model. The model and acoustic responses of the animal were recorded and analyzed by the computer. If the error score of a response was less than a set criterion, the rear lamp was extinguished and the forward lamp was illuminated to signal the impending delivery of reward (usually two smelt). On nonrewarded trials, the main lamp was extinguished and the trial was terminated. A typical training session consisted of 40 discrete trials with intervals between trials of 20, 35, or 50 s occurring in a quasi-random order.

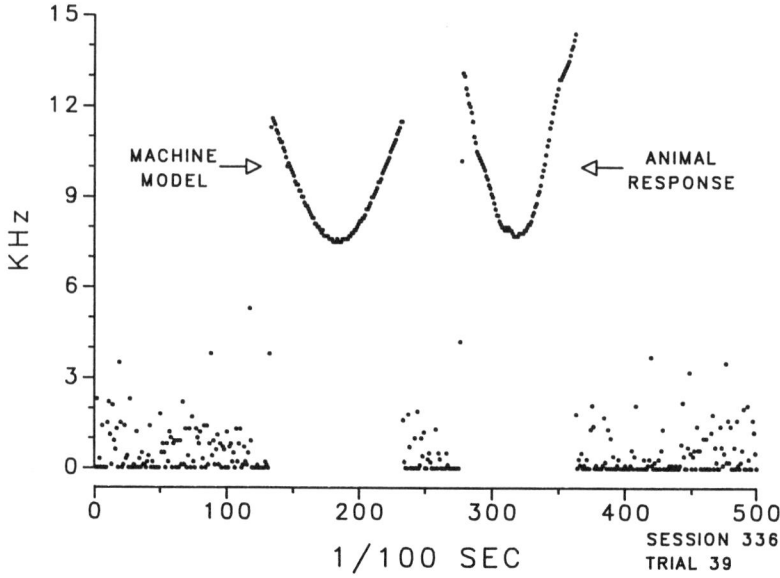

Figure 8.4. Unprocessed data-input-stream for a training trial.

A Compaq Plus microcomputer with a Tecmar Labmaster board provided the basic control and data acquisition capabilities. For model transmission, the output from a voltage-controlled oscillator (VCO) was compensated to match the characteristics of the transmitting hydrophone, amplified by a David Hafler P-230 amplifier and broadcast into the water with a Massa, TR-25C hydrophone. Underwater sounds were monitored with a Gould CH-17 hydrophone (later, an International Transducer 1032) and passed to a three-stage amplifier and level-shift detector. The number of input voltage swings above 2.5 V and below -2.5 V were accumulated in a standard digital counter and the count was recorded in a ring-buffer every 10 msec. The signal capture and storage design was optimized for the continuous recording of FM pure-tones with maximum data reduction while suppressing the broad-band clicks of the snapping shrimp in Kaneohe Bay. The characteristics of this noise source have been described by Au, Carder, Penner and Scronce (1985). These impulsive clicks, being much shorter than the 10 msec integration time, are recorded as relatively low values in the counter and are easily eliminated in the initial stages of analysis. Figure 8.4 shows the actual input stream for a single trial with a well-trained animal emitting a FM whistle.

8. Whistles as a communication medium

The production of models and the continuous capture and storage of signals were carried out by by a time-synchronous background program while analyses and coordination were controlled by a multitasking foreground program wirtten in POLYFORTH II (native).

Tt-011-M Training and Results

The male dolphin was trained on the basic procedures with the hoop and lamp, but without acoustic stimuli. Subsequently, he was induced to produce crude whistles in response to a simple FM model that swept from 11 to 7 kHz over a 1-s period (down-ramp). Structured, 40-trial sessions were initiated when the animal's responses began to meet the evaluation criteria for analysis already described. When the performance with this model reached asymptote, the animal was switched to a simple up-ramp and then a U-shaped model in successive conditioning series. In each series, the FM pattern of the animal's response was brought to resemble that of the model by first holding the error criterion below the animal's mean error score and subsequently adjusting the criterion in increments to achieve better approximations of the model.

The acquisition of the down-ramp response is shown in Figure 8.5. The improvement in performance over sessions is described in the lower graph by the decline of the mean error score over sessions. The upper graph indicates the percent of trials on which the error score for a whistle response was below the maximum-error criterion and reward was delivered to the animal. Intertrial-control measures of the attentiveness of the animal were monitored throughout the session by reporting the percent of trials on which the latency of response to the lamp was less than the shortest intertrial interval and no entries to the hoop occurred during the intertrial interval. The mean error scores declined slowly over sessions with a constant criterion, and eventually 80-90% of the responses were rewarded. Lowering the maximum-error criterion at session 120 caused a temporary disruption of performance, followed by recovery but little further improvement in the quality of signal as measured by the mean error score. The asymptotic performance is shown in Figure 8.6. For each trial the down-ramp model is plotted as it was recorded in the water, and the animal's response, scaled to the frequency range and duration of the model, is overlaid on the model for comparison. The reliability of the response is high and its resemblance to the model, while good overall, deviates from the model at the onset of the response.

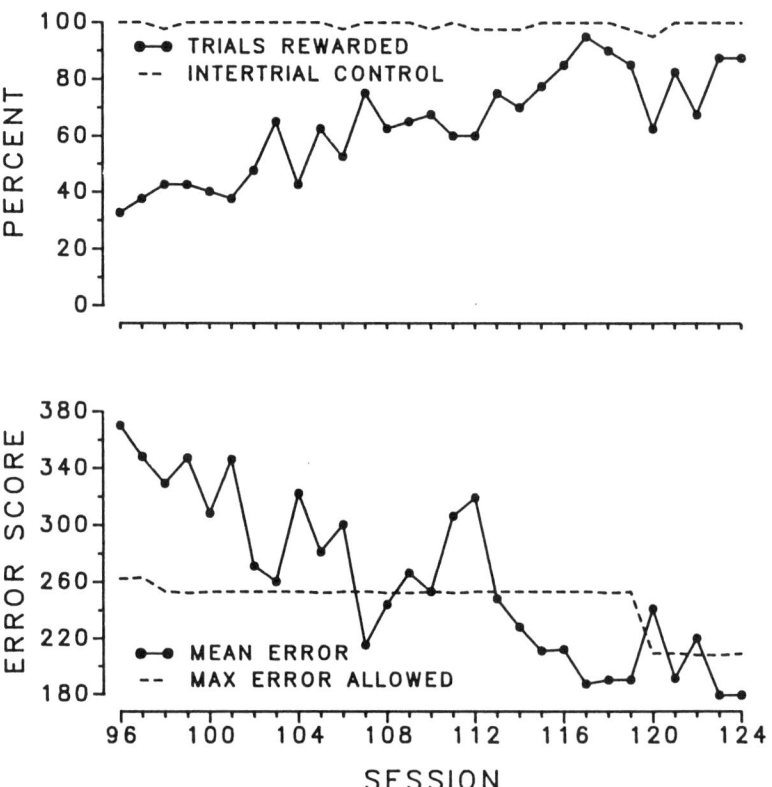

Figure 8.5. Tt-011-M's acquisition of the down-ramp response.

In the following session the model was switched from the down-ramp to an up-ramp. Despite the change of the model, the animal continued to emit the down-ramp response and the percent of reinforced trials fell to zero. The animal eventually stopped emitting the down-ramp and gradually modified its response to resemble the new up-ramp model. In this and the following series, the error score computations were modified to improve the consistency of scoring for highly deviant responses. Although this change caused the range of error scores to differ between the series, the relative scores within each series closely follow the fit of response and model.

8. Whistles as a communication medium

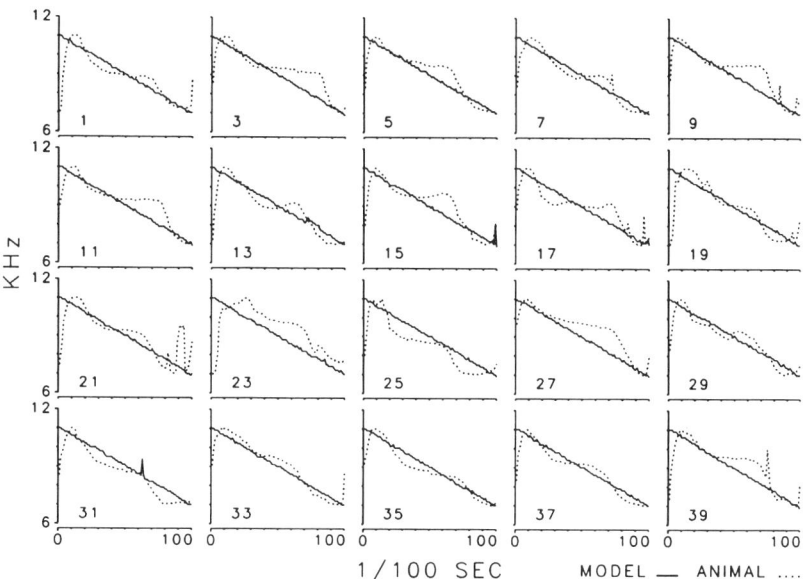

Figure 8.6. Tt-011-M's asymptotic performance of the down-ramp response on odd numbered trials.

Figure 8.7 shows the eventual acquisition of response to the up-ramp model and Figure 8.8 shows the asymptotic performance. In the early sessions, the FM pattern of the animal's response gradually diverged from that of the model at a criterion level that allowed no reinforcement. Relaxation of the criterion to allow the best 10% of responses to be reinforced produced a convergence of the animal's whistle response with the model. Reinstating the original, stricter criterion produced some improvement in the resemblance of the response to the model and a sharp reduction of between-session variability. Again, the final performance is highly reliable but the early portion of the response deviates from the model.

The U-shaped model was introduced at the end of the up-ramp series. Again, there was no immediate change of the previously rewarded response and the animal continued to produce the up-ramp whistle for several sessions. The later stage of acquisition with the U-shaped model is described in Figure 8.9 and the asymptotic performance in Figure 8.10. As in the acquisition of responding to the ramp models, the response gradually came to resemble that of the model. The terminal performance reached high reliability as before and the response closely matched that of the model. Subsequently, the down-ramp was

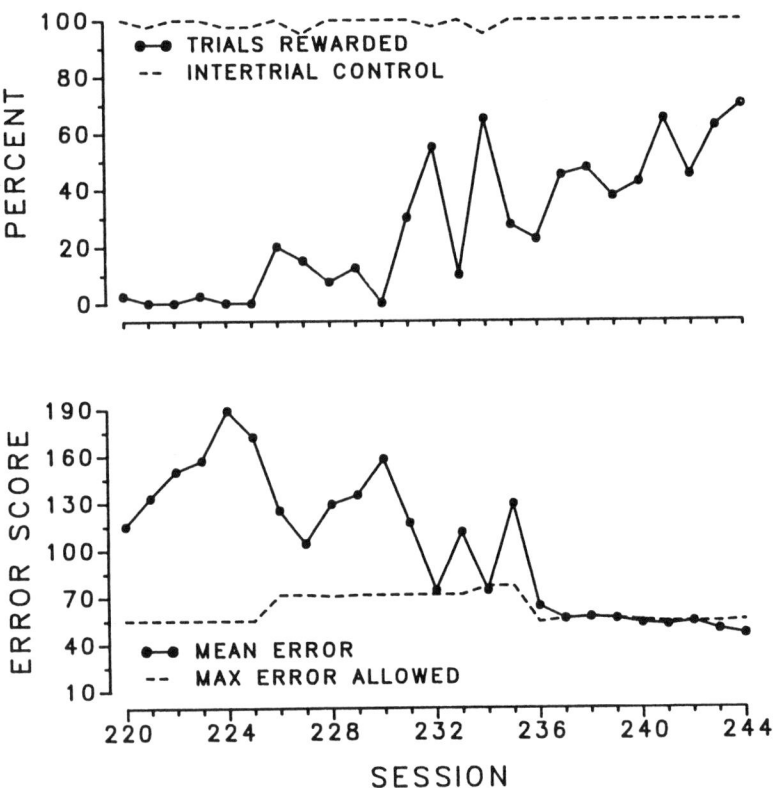

Figure 8.7. Tt-011-M's acquisition of the up-ramp response.

reintroduced and, as before, there was little change of ongoing responding and no detectable benefit from the prior experience with that model.

Tt-011-M Discussion

The results demonstrate the ability of the animal to vary the FM pattern of its response to conform to very different arbitrary wave forms and to maintain that responding with reliability. This confirms the reliability reported by Richards et al. (1984) and goes beyond that work by producing substantially better resemblance between the responses and their models. Although the capability to produce accurate facsimiles of arbitrary signals is important for the systematic development of large sets of distinctive signals, the animal must be responsive

8. Whistles as a communication medium

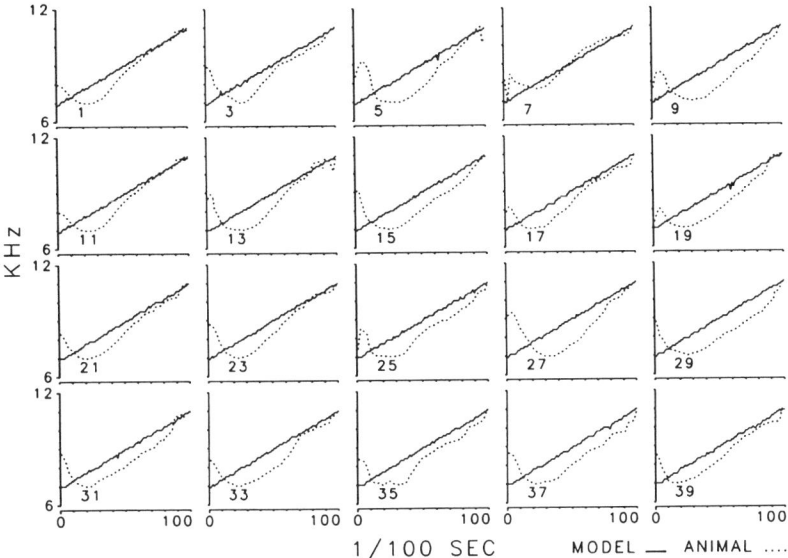

Figure 8.8. Tt-011-M's asymptotic performance of the up-ramp response on odd-numbered trials.

to the parameters of the model as well. In the present study, the relatively slow acquisition of an acceptable response and the persistence of the previously rewarded response following a change of the model indicate only conditioned responding and minimum stimulus control over the animal's response. This use of simple conditioned responses instead of any model-copying process appeared even though use of the latter concept would have produced more immediate and consistent reward at every phase of training. A subsequent test was made to evaluate the animal's ability to discriminate between FM signals. Three complex models were tested as discriminative stimuli in a three-position, paddle-pressing problem. The discrimination problem was solved after extensive training, but there was no apparent transfer of the successful experience with acoustic discrimination when the animal was returned to the sound-production task.

Tt-580-F Training and Results

A variety of procedures were used to elicit the initial acoustic responses from the male and a better method was desired for initial training of the female. Also, within-session observations of the male indicated frequent improvement in the

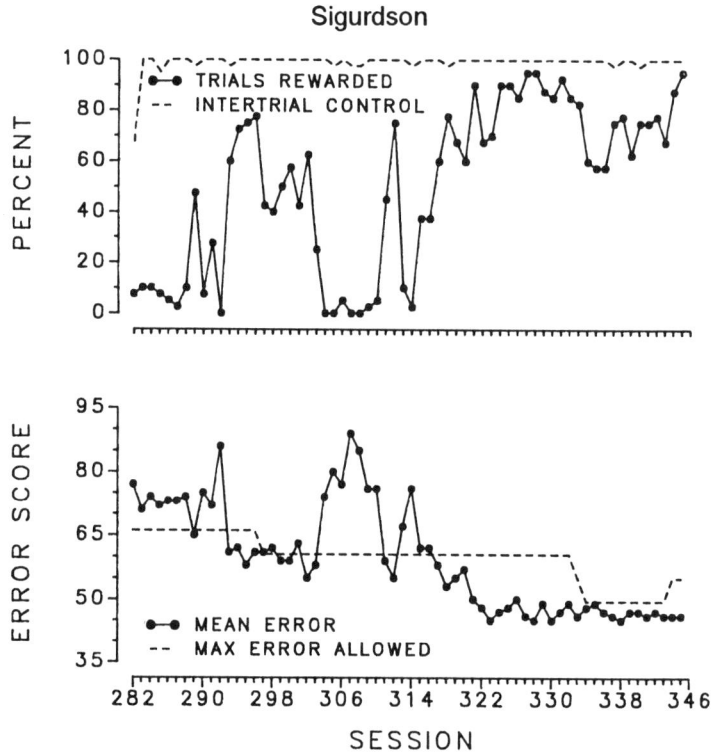

Figure 8.9. Tt-011-M's acquisition of the U-shaped response.

resemblance of the response to the model during longer runs of rewarded trials, and often, encounters with successive nonreward produced responses with poorer resemblance to the model. This suggested the possibility that the relative frequency of reward in the presence of the model (an implicit classical contingency) was exerting an influence on performance beyond that attributable to the pairing of acceptable responses with reward (the explicit instrumental or shaping contingency). To test an alternative method of training that incorporated this hypothesis, the apparatus was removed and a single hydrophone was suspended in the center of the pen. An auto-shaping design (Brown & Jenkins, 1968) was employed wherein the down-ramp model was presented at intervals of either 1, 2, or 3 min in quasi-random order. Initially, a classical contingency was in effect: each presentation of the model was followed by 5 s of silence to allow recording of any responses and then, regardless of the behavior, the delivery of two smelt. Subsequent to the first distinctive acoustic response, reward became contingent on the resemblance of the response to the model. Every fifth trial of the first session is shown in Figure 8.11.

8. Whistles as a communication medium

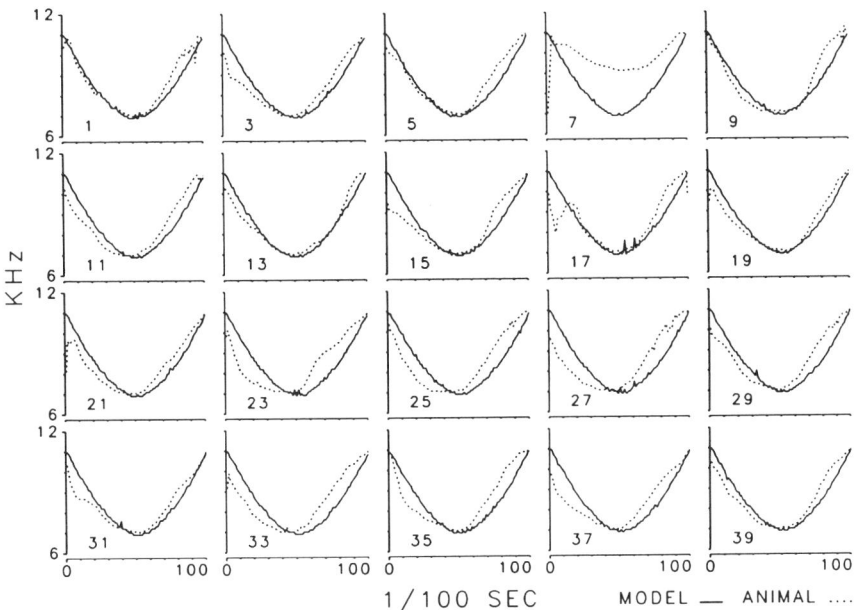

Figure 8.10. Tt-011-M's asymptotic performance of the U-shaped response on odd numbered trials.

Slight broadband acoustic activity occurred on trials 1 and 5, but little or none occurred on the other trials prior to trial 10. On the tenth trial, a loud, down-swept, broadband "creak" emerged and, subsequently, reward was delivered only when a down-swept response followed the model. The combined frequency and repetition rate of the broadband impulses that produced the creak were recorded by the computer system. The switch from the classical to the instrumental contingency on trial 11 caused reward to be omitted on about 70% of the subsequent trials as the animal was shaped to produce signals that were more similar to the duration and general frequency characteristics of the model. In subsequent sessions, the animal showed no tendency to switch spontaneously from the down-swept broadband signals to down-swept pure-tone signals like the model. Therefore, the broadband response was extinguished, and a pure-tone response was shaped to resemble the down-ramp model with same session and trial procedures as those used for the male.

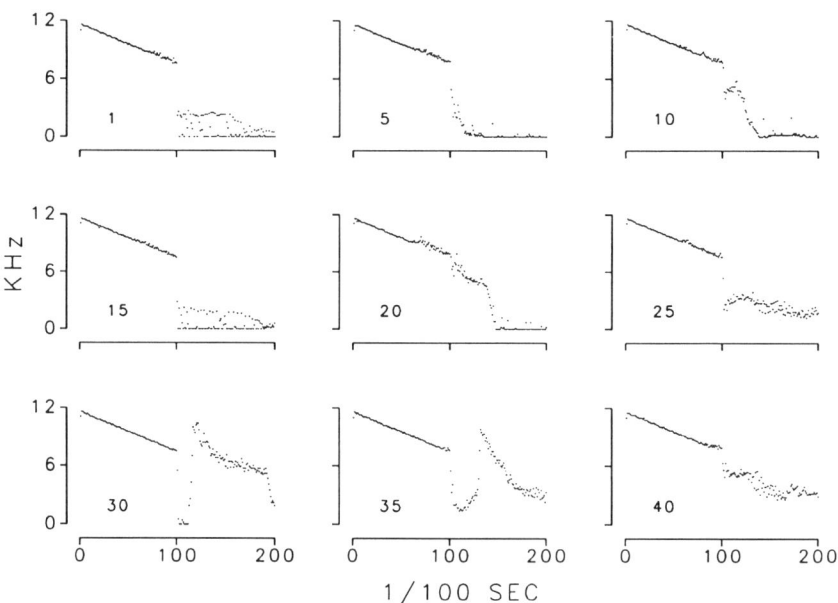

Figure 8.11. Tt-580-F's acquisition of acoustic response on an auto-shaping schedule.

When the whistle response showed no further improvement in its resemblance to the down-ramp model, half of the down-ramp trials were replaced in quasi-random order with U-shaped-model trials. The method of response evaluation remained the same, and the animal was still allowed only one response before moving on to the next trial—a noncorrection procedure. The animal continued to produce the down-ramp response to both models for several sessions, then the variable intertrial intervals were shortened to 15, 20, and 25 s and a time-out of 30 s was imposed after each inappropriate response. A discrimination appeared after several sessions with the animal falling silent on the U-shaped-model trials while continuing to make appropriate responses to the down-ramp. After two more sessions, a crude approximation of the new model suddenly emerged on the U-shaped-model trials. A full correction procedure (each trial was repeated until the error score criterion was met) and considerable training were required to achieve the level of performance shown in Figure 8.12. The reliability of the conditional discrimination exceeded 90% and the consistency of the FM patterns was very high as in the single-model case with the male. The resemblance between the responses and their respective models is

8. Whistles as a communication medium

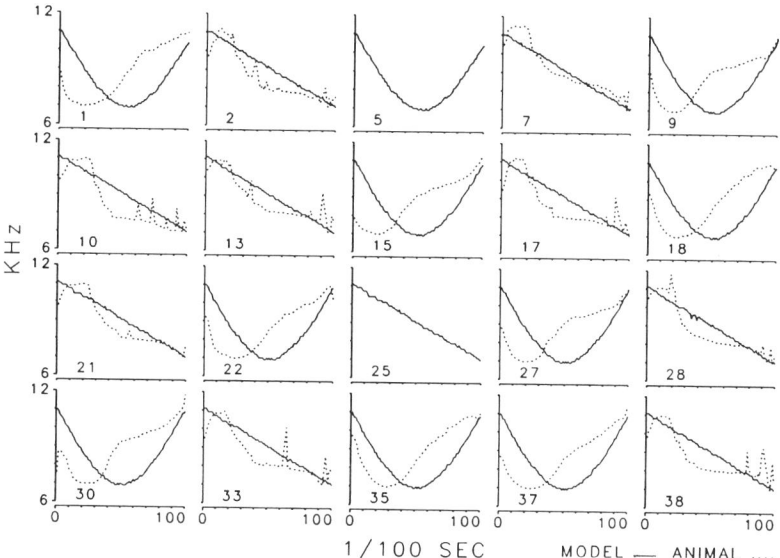

Figure 8.12. Tt-580-F's performance on a conditional discrimination of the down-ramp and U-shaped models.

sufficient to distinguish between the two alternatives, but further improvement would be required to maintain their distinctiveness within a larger set of FM signals. The errors that occurred throughout acquisition are noteworthy as well. Occasionally, runs of errors occurred wherein the response associated with the opposite model was given on successive correction opportunities. Also, while producing responses of the correct type, the animal would suddenly alter the duration or frequency range of its response and continue with the new parameters for an indefinite time.

Tt-580-F Discussion

Exposure to the classical contingency of the auto-shaping design was intended only to initiate general acoustic responding and facilitate subsequent shaping of the response, but something unexpected occurred. Unlike the typical result of classical conditioning, the pairing of the model (the conditional stimulus) with the fish (the unconditioned stimulus) produced a crude reproduction of the conditional stimulus rather than some unconditioned response to food. Current work seeks to determine whether the result was caused by adventitious reinforcement of chance responses in the early trials or if a different and possibly higher-order process such as model copying or imitation was at work. Additional evidence for such a process is suggested by the sudden emergence of the U-shaped model in the two-model training. Following the switch to the instrumental contingency on the 11th trial, further change of the response parameters toward those of the model was only gradual, and remedial training was required to elicit pure-tone whistle responses.

Several possible explanations for the performance of the female are apparent and may apply to the male's performance as well. The switch from the classical to the instrumental contingency reduced the initial perfect correlation between the model and reward and established a consistent and superseding relationship between response and reward. Early in the shaping process, the parameters of the response differed from those of the model, but the liberal criterion at earlier stages allowed those responses to be rewarded and it was their parameters, rather than those of the model, that became the guide for subsequent responding. If it was the model's reliability in predicting reward in the first 10 trials that led the animal to emit a similar signal in an attempt to gain reward, then that model-copying process may have been undermined by the instrumental contingency and the animal was left to sample a relatively complex response space by trial and error with only its prior successes as a guide. Although the application of the shaping procedure produced initial progress, the gradual tightening of the criterion induced errors and subsequent nonreward which, in this situation, may have acted like a partial-reinforcement schedule that increased the persistence of earlier rewarded responses. Thus, the difficulty of readily achieving highly accurate replicas of the models with conventional shaping techniques may have been due more to the lack of relevant guidance and the resultant persistence of earlier response tendencies than to an inability of the animal to produce the desired signal. From this point of view, a wide latitude with regard to absolute frequency and duration of response may still be desirable in later stages of training, but the use of such liberal criteria early in training may have rewarded responses that differed too widely from the model. Work in progress indicates that setting these parameters closer to those of the models facilitates performance. Also, the use of acoustic models may require that several signals be used in the same context to allow the FM pattern to be discerned as the relevant stimulus dimension.

CONCLUSIONS

The term *vocal-mimicry* was used by Richards et al. (1984) to mean the production of a response that is similar to a model-signal, but unlike those in the

8. Whistles as a communication medium

spontaneous repertoire. The present analysis suggests that the appearance of vocal mimicry, so defined, does not necessarily indicate a currently active, "copying" or "imitative" process. In the present study, the asymptotic performance in both the single- and two-model training would qualify as vocal mimicry, but further analysis indicates a conditional discrimination that uses only general characteristics of the model for discrimination and previously established responses rather than an active, model-copying process. The extent to which these factors are at work in other field and laboratory reports of acoustic mimicry cannot be determined without more complete testing and reporting, but the available information suggests their presence.

The present results show that the sound producing mechanism of the dolphin is sufficiently flexible and reliable to allow a set of FM patterns of significant size and that synthetic signals may be used as models for those FM patterns. The acquisition performance of the female in the auto-shaping experiment and the early movement of the response parameters toward those of the models in both animals suggests the presence of an active, model-copying process. The acquisition of the U-shaped response by the female suggests the generalization of that process to new models. Richards et al. (1984) also reported an instance of the animal producing an approximation to a novel model, and their acquisition data suggest that the animals use the models as guides for responding, but the resemblance of the responses to the models at asymptote indicates that their animal experienced a process similar to the one seen here. In both studies, the initial progress seems to be achieved by copying the more general aspects of the model, but continued differential reinforcement leads the animal to disregard the finer details of the model and depend on its previous successes as a guide. Work in progress uses this understanding to develop methods that strengthen the model-copying behavior throughout training to establish and maintain an expanded repertoire of distinctive signals for the study of language-like behavior in dolphins.

REFERENCES

Au, W. W. L., Carder, D. A., Penner, R. H., & Scronce, B. L. (1985). Demonstration of adaptation in beluga whale echolocation signals. *Journal of the Acoustical Society of America*. 77, 726-730.

Batteau, D. W. & Markey, P. R. (1967). *Man/dolphin communication*. Report on contract N00123-67-C-1103, 15 December 1966 - 13 December 1967, China Lake: U. S. Naval Ordnance Test Station.

Brown, P. L. & Jenkins, H. M. (1968). Auto-shaping of the pigeon's key-peck. *Journal of the Experimental Analysis of Behavior*, 11, 1-8.

Caldwell, M. C. & Caldwell, D. K. (1972). Vocal mimicry in the whistle mode by an Atlantic bottlenosed dolphin. *Cetology*, 9, 1-8.

Caldwell, M. C. & Caldwell, D. K. (1979). The whistle of the Atlantic Bottlenose dolphin (Tursiops truncatus) - Ontogeny. In H. E. Winn & B. L. Olla (Eds.), *Behavior of marine animals, Vol. 3: Cetaceans* (369-401). New York: Plenum.

Dreher, J. J., & Evans W. E. (1964). Cetacean communication. In W. N. Tavolga (Ed.), *Marine bioacoustics* (vol. 1, pp. 373-393). New York: Pergamon.

Evans, W. E. (1967). Vocalization among marine mammals. In W. N. Tavolga (Ed.), *Marine bioacoustics* (vol. 2, pp. 159-186). New York: Pergamon.

Herman, L. M., Richards, D. G., & Wolz, J. P. (1984). Comprehension of sentences by bottlenosed dolphins. *Cognition*, 16, 129-219.

Lilly, J. C. (1962). Vocal behavior of the bottlenose dolphin. *Proceedings of the American Philosophical Society*, 106, 520-529.

Lilly, J. C. (1965). Vocal mimicry in Tursiops. Ability to match numbers and durations of human vocal bursts. *Science*, 147, 300-310.

McKay, R. S. (1981). Dolphin interaction with acoustically controlled systems: Aspects of frequency control, learning, and non-food rewards. *Cetology*, 41, 1-12.

Richards, D. G., Wolz, J. P. & Herman, L. M. (1984). Vocal mimicry of computer-generated sounds and vocal labeling of objects by a bottlenosed dolphin, *Tursiops truncatus*. *Journal of Comparative Psychology*, 94, 1, 10-28.

Ridgway, S. H. (1983). Dolphin hearing and sound production in health and illness. In R. R. Fay & G. Gourevitch (Eds.), *Hearing and other senses: Presentations in honor of E. G. Wever* (pp. 247-296). Groton, CT: Amphora Press.

8. Whistles as a communication medium

Sayigh, L. S., Tyack, P. L., Wells, S. W., & Scott, M. D. (1990). Signature whistles of free-ranging bottlenose dolphins *Tursiops truncatus*: Stability and mother-offspring comparisons. *Behavioral Ecology and Sociobiology,* 26, 247-260.

Tyack, P. (1986). Whistle repertoires of two bottlenosed dolphins, *Tursiops truncatus*: Mimicry of signature whistles? *Behavioral Ecology and Sociobiology,* 18, 251-257.

Wood, F. G. (1973). *Marine mammals and man.* Washington, DC: Luce.

9 Linguistic Phenomena in the Natural Communication of Animals

Charles T. Snowdon

At the beginning of the 20th century, there were two groups of people who went off to the far corners of the world to discover new cultures and learn their languages. One group, the missionaries, wanted to convert these newly discovered people to Christianity. When they made contact with a group, they attempted to learn the language so that they could translate the Bible and then they worked to teach the people the missionaries' language. They attempted to impose Western models of clothing and of social mores on these people. Frequently the people gave up their own cultural traditions and lost much of their own language.

The other group, the anthropologists, participated in the lives of the people they were studying without attempting to impose Western values or lifestyles. They learned the language of the people in order to understand their culture better and did not try to teach their own language to the people. The information that the anthropologists returned with has been extremely important in illustrating to us our own cultural restrictions. There are alternative ways of dividing sex and age roles; there are alternative patterns of family organization and alternative social organizations. The anthropologists greatly expanded our understanding of the possibilities of human social behavior. We may still choose to follow the ways of our culture but we are now aware of alternatives.

There is a parallel between the missionary and anthropologist approaches to distant cultures and how psychologists and ethologists go about studying language in nonhuman animals. The comparative psychologists have adopted the missionary position. Chimpanzees, bonobos, or dolphins are taken away from their normal social environment and provided with human companions as social surrogates. In an environment radically different from the ones in which they evolved, they are given extensive training on learning symbols, sequences of symbols, and the appropriate responses to make to these symbols. The results have been nothing short of spectacular. There is clear evidence that these animals can learn to use arbitrary symbols as referents to real objects, that they can comprehend different word orders appropriately, that they can respond to novel utterances with appropriate behavior. The dolphins, chimpanzees, and bonobos almost seem human. But they ultimately disappoint us by not achieving what a human child can achieve linguistically.

The ethologists, on the other hand, can be viewed as cross-species anthropologists, seeking to find in animal societies the sorts of information that anthropologists sought in novel human cultures. How do groups organize their social lives? How do they organize their economic lives? How do they communicate with one another? The linguistic ethologist seeks to understand the language of the animals rather than to make the animals understand language. Because we do not have expectations that the animals will have a human-like language, we are not disappointed when they turn out not to be human-like.

Each position has its costs and benefits. The comparative psychologist shows us what animals are capable of doing regardless of what they might do if left to their own devices. Perhaps we would never know from study of the natural language of a dolphin or a bonobo that they could understand word order and acquire a large vocabulary. The results of the comparative psychologist are easily accessible to the general public because they are framed in terms that all human beings can understand. However, this knowledge of the linguistic capacity of animals comes at the cost of removing animals from their natural social environments and at the cost of a great amount of labor in the daily training of animals.

The linguistic ethologist may never know the upper limits of the linguistic capacities of a species. The ethologist must play detective to decode the utterances of another species and must develop clever observational and experimental methods to determine whether signals are used symbolically or if there is a meaningful syntax to animal's utterances. There may be as much labor

9. Linguistic Phenomena in Natural Communication

involved in careful observation and decoding of an animal language as the comparative psychologist spends in training an animal on a human language analogue. The results of the linguistic ethologist, because they are stated in terms of the signals used by the animals, are less accessible to the general public. But the inferences made by the linguistic ethologist may tell us more about the evolutionary precursors of various linguistic phenomena: What are the environmental conditions that might have lead to symbolic communication? What are the circumstances that lead to syntactic structures? What ontogenetic influences affect the acquisition of proper phonology, comprehension or usage? The linguistic ethologist can tell us about the evolution of language and language-like phenomena. As the anthropologists were able to offer new insights about our own culture based on comparative findings from other cultures, a linguistic ethologist should also offer us some new ideas about thinking about human language based on comparative results from the study of other animals.

Although I am a psychologist, I am more comfortable aligned with the linguistic ethologists. I am interested in finding what is linguistically interesting in the natural communication systems of nonhuman animals. In order to do this I study animals in natural social groupings either in the field or in complex captive environments. I do not attempt to make pets or friends of animals, but attempt to be a neutral observer who describes and decodes the animals' utterances. Because I do have a strong interest in discovering language parallels, I have tried to maximize these parallels by choosing to study species that have highly developed vocal communication systems. Most of my own research has been with several species of the family Callitrichidae, a group of small, arboreal, clawed primates found throughout South America. These are colloquially known as marmosets and tamarins, and I attempt in this chapter to illustrate some of the complexity of their natural communication systems, focusing on several topics: phonetic variability and categorical perception, social influences on communication, syntax, and referential communication. I add some additional examples from the work of others on other species of South American primates and a few examples of work from birds. A linguistic ethologist would not want to be limited to the study of one or a few species, because it would be likely that different linguistic precursors would develop at different times under different environmental pressures in different species.

PHONETIC VARIATION AND CATEGORIZATION

One of the first places to look for complexity in vocal communication is in the complexity of the structure of vocalizations. In the past 15 years there have been several demonstrations in birds and primates that vocalizations that were previously treated by human observers as unitary call types actually displayed subtle variations, and these variations appeared to be correlated with equally subtle differences in the context in which calls were given. Further studies using playback techniques demonstrated that these variations were perceived by the birds or monkeys themselves and thus truly represented an increased vocabulary size for these species.

In birds, Ficken and Ficken (1967), Kroodsma (1981), Lein (1978), Morse (1967), and Smith, Pawlukiewicz and Smith (1978) all described variations in songs that indicated different contexts. Frequently one song variant was used at the periphery of territories, presumably in defense against intruders, while another song variant was used in the central parts of territories or near nests, presumably as a way of communicating with ones mate.

An important primate study was Green's (1975) study of coo vocalizations in Japanese macaques (*Macaca fuscata*). Green described 7 variants of coo calls that were used in 10 different contexts. The distribution of call type by context was far from random. Green hypothesized that the coo variants indicated differing strengths of motivation for social contact with another monkey. Thus, the underlying basis of the variation in call types was assumed to be a unitary motivational state. Subsequently, Lillehei and Snowdon (1978) found similar coo variants in young stumptail macaques (*Macaca arctoides*), and Zoloth, Petersen, Beecher, Green, Marler, Moody and Stebbins (1979) found that Japanese macaques could learn to discriminate between two of the coo variants. Japanese macaques learned the discrimination much more rapidly than did other species, suggesting to Zoloth et al. a species-specific perceptual processing system.

Subsequently, several other demonstrations of subtle variations in call types have appeared. Cleveland and Snowdon (1982) described four variants of long calls (song analogues) in cotton-top tamarins (*Saguinus oedipus*). One call type was used at the start of territorial encounters, another at the peak of vocal displays in territorial encounters, a third variant was used for intragroup cohesion and by animals separated from the rest of the group, and the final variant was itself highly variable and characteristic of reproductively immature animals within a group. Subsequently, Snowdon, Cleveland. and French (1983) demonstrated that tamarins could discriminate between two of the long call variants. They used a technique to play back calls to subject monkeys through hidden speakers. Thus, all social cues and cues from other sensory modalities

9. Linguistic Phenomena in Natural Communication

were eliminated, and any differences in responses observed could be directly attributed to differences in call structure alone.

Cleveland and Snowdon (1982) also described 8 chirp variants (short frequency modulated calls) in cotton-top tamarins. These chirp variants represented multiple underlying motivational states. One was used in mobbing, another as an alarm call, two variants were associated with food, another with territory defense, and another as a general call to maintain contact between group members. Bauers and Snowdon (1990) used a playback technique to show that cotton-top tamarins could discriminate between the two variants that were most similar in acoustic structure, giving contextually appropriate responses to each.

Pola and Snowdon (1975) described four variants of trill vocalizations in the pygmy marmoset (*Cebuella pygmaea*). Two of the variants (the Open Mouth Trill and the Closed Mouth Trill) differed on a single acoustic parameter: duration. Closed Mouth Trills had a mean duration of 176 msec while Open Mouth Trills had a mean duration of 334 msec. Observation of the usage of these two trill types indicated that the Closed Mouth Trill was used in calm relaxed conditions as the animals moved through the environment. The most common response to a Closed Mouth Trill was an antiphonal trill. In contrast, the Open Mouth Trill was found to precede an aggressive or agonistic encounter. There appears to be no single motivational state that underlies the different trill variants.

The findings of species-specific perceptual processing in Japanese macaques discriminating between coo variants and the results of several studies on human speech perception suggested that we try a similar perceptual study on pygmy marmosets. Because the trill structure was quite easily defined acoustically, Snowdon and Pola (1978) constructed a pygmy marmoset trill synthesizer and played back a wide variety of trill variants to pygmy marmosets. The presence of an antiphonal trill within 5 s of a trill playback was used as evidence of the marmoset's labeling the trill as a Closed Mouth Trill. When trill structure was held constant except for duration, all trills up to 248 msec were treated as equivalent to natural Closed Mouth Trills in eliciting a high rate of antiphonal responses. However, as soon as the trill duration was increased by 9 msec to 257 msec the response disappeared. There was clear evidence of categorical labeling of the two trill types. When we tested human subjects with the same array of stimuli, we found no evidence of categorical labeling or discrimination. These results from pygmy marmosets along with those from Japanese macaques and human categorical perception support the notion of species-specific perceptual mechanisms for species-specific vocal communication systems. Snowdon and Pola (1978) could not test within and between category discrimination of different trills. Hence their labeling study is merely suggestive of categorical perception.

The finding of categorical labeling of synthesized calls by pygmy marmosets was rather puzzling. Pygmy marmosets appeared to be less precise in distinguishing between different versions of their own trills than human subjects were. Why should this be? One possibility concerns the conditions of testing. The pygmy marmosets were presented with a stimulus that mimicked the average acoustic variables of a Closed Mouth Trill in the colony but did not mimic the values of any particular animal. Practical speech perception for human beings has a strong social component, though this has rarely been formally tested in human subjects. We attend not only to the phonemes of speech, but we can also attend to the age, sex, and individual identity of the speaker, and our responses to speech sounds are often, in normal speech at least, a joint response to the phonemes perceived and to the perception of a particular speaker. Might not this be the case for pygmy marmosets as well?

Snowdon (1987) reported an alternative version of the study with pygmy marmoset trills. Three individual animals were selected that had very different trill structures, and the individual features of each were synthesized, with duration of the trill being varied in a systematic way. In this replication the monkeys were asked not just to identify whether they heard a Closed Mouth Trill or not, but whether they heard a Closed Mouth Trill from a particular individual. To determine this we made use of another finding from pygmy marmosets (Snowdon & Cleveland, 1980) that animals responded to a trill of a given individual only if that trill were played back through a speaker in that individual's cage. They rarely responded antiphonally when an individual's trill was played back through a speaker in a part of the colony where that individual would not be found. In the present study, a synthesized trill was considered as representative of a given individual if there was a significant increase in antiphonal responding when the synthesized trill was played back from the stimulus animal's home cage versus when the same synthesized trill was played back from some other part of the colony. The marmosets responded differently according to their prior experience with familiar individuals. Thus, they responded to a stimulus animal, which had extremely short trills, only to the shortest of the synthesized trills, while they responded only to longer synthesized trills mimicking animals that typically produced longer trills. These results show an apparent within category discrimination of trills when those trills were synthesized to represent calls of familiar individuals. The sharp boundary indicative of categorical labeling appeared only when monkeys were tested with average stimuli that represented no familiar individual.

These results of Snowdon (1987) indicate that pygmy marmosets do not display the strict form of categorical perception. To my knowledge no similar study has been done with human subjects, but if it could be shown that humans adjust the category boundaries of speech perception to match their expectations of sounds produced by familiar speakers while retaining broader ranges of tolerance for sounds of unfamiliar speakers, it would seriously question the uniqueness of categorical perception of speech. Several authors (Diehl & Kluender, 1987; Macmillan, 1987; Massaro, 1987) have questioned seriously the phenomenon of categorical perception through other types of evidence. Snowdon (1987) also suggests that perception of calls cannot be considered to be hard-wired, but rather that animals acquire through experience with other individuals expectations for how the trills of these animals ought to sound.

SOCIAL COMPONENTS OF COMMUNICATION

There is an ongoing debate concerning whether animal signals are primarily emotive and reflexive or whether animals display in their communication higher level cognitive abilities such as using syntax or using signals as symbols. In the classical ethological view, communication was viewed as a fixed action pattern given in response to a very specific releasing stimulus. One argument against a reflexive or fixed action pattern view of communication would be to show that animals adjust communication according to different social contexts. If animals communicate differently to the same stimuli according to different social contexts, then the animals cannot be responding simply to internal motivational states.

There are several examples that animals are responsive to their social environments. I present a few examples here, and others are presented by Seyfarth and Cheney (this volume, chapter 10). Snowdon and Hodun (1981) studied trill calling of a group of pygmy marmosets in their natural habitat in the Peruvian Amazon. One puzzle from our previous studies on trill vocalizations in captive marmosets was the finding that there were three trill types that differed greatly in acoustical structure (Closed Mouth Trill, Quiet Trill, and J-Call; from Pola & Snowdon, 1975) but that appeared to have similar usage, in contrast to the smaller degree of difference in acoustic structure found in the Closed Mouth Trill versus Open Mouth Trill described earlier. The Closed Mouth Trill, Quiet Trill, and J-Call differed structurally in ways that would be predicted to increase their localization by recipients. The Quiet Trill is very difficult to localize with few temporal or frequency cues for sound localization. The J-Call, on the other hand, has great frequency modulation and is a pulsed call with several time-of-arrival cues within the call and should be quite easy to localize. The Closed Mouth Trill is intermediate in the structural features used in sound localization. We hypothesized that in the wild it might be adaptive for animals to use the most cryptic calls when they are close together and can use visual or olfactory localization cues. As animals become more separated from one another, they should use calls with more structural features for sound localization.

To test this hypothesis we mapped the 3-dimensional home range of the pygmy marmoset, and every time we recorded a marmoset giving one of the trills we noted its location on the map and immediately searched for the nearest marmoset that we could see. The results were quite clear. More than 50% of all Quiet Trills were used when animals were within a meter of each other, and all Quiet Trills were given within 5 m of a monkey that we could locate. On the other hand, J-Calls were used at greater distances and were the only trills heard when monkeys were more than 20 m from the nearest monkey. The Closed Mouth Trills had a distribution that was intermediate between those of the Quiet Trills and the J-Calls.

Thus, the monkeys are adjusting the acoustic structure of their calls according to how far away they are from other monkeys. To do this an individual must be monitoring where it is located with respect to other marmosets, and thus adjusting its call structure to the distance it is located from its group.

In another example, Snowdon and Cleveland (1984) recorded the trill vocalizations of a group of three pygmy marmosets and found that there was a clear sequence of turn-taking. The animals did not call at random, but instead a significant number of sequences of three calls recorded included a call from each of the three members of the group. That is, the animals took turns in calling. There are two possible sequences of turn-taking among three animals: Animal 1 followed by Animal 2 followed by Animal 3 (123), 231, or 312 (versus 132, 321, or 213). The group of pygmy marmosets used the first sequence of calling almost twice as frequently as the second ordering. The turn-taking behavior and the prevailing use of one sequence of turn-taking rather than the other indicates that these monkeys are responding to their social companions.

9. Linguistic Phenomena in Natural Communication

Furthermore, the achievement of turn-taking in children is considered to be an indicator of significant cognitive complexity (passing from egocentricity to the ability to understand another individual's perspective). Therefore the pygmy marmosets should be credited with the same degree of cognitive complexity represented in children's turn-taking.

A third example of patterned communication responding to social companions comes from a study by McConnell and Snowdon (1986), who simulated territorial encounters in captive groups of cotton-top tamarins. By opening doors between adjacent rooms, we could increase the sound intensity of within-group calls of an unfamiliar group. Within approximately 30 sec one individual would alert and orient toward the open doors, and then all animals in both groups would commence a sequence of vocal interactions. There was a clear pattern in the sequencing of these calls. The responses of tamarins depended on where the previous call originated. If the previous call was from their own group, they escalated to a more intense call type, but if the previous call was from the other group, they imitated that call. Again, the social familiarity of the previous caller affected the response of the current caller.

Two additional examples come from the work of Marler and his colleagues on audience effects on the calling behavior of chickens (*Gallus gallus*). Domestic cocks give food calls in response to food in the presence of their mates (Marler, Dufty & Pickert, 1986a), but when tested with food in the presence of another male or when tested alone they failed to give food calls. When they were presented with food in the presence of a novel female they gave even higher rates of food calls than they did in the presence of their own mates (Marler, Dufty, and Pickert, 1986b). In a subsequent study on alarm call vocalizations elicited by passing a model of hawk overhead, Karakashian, Gyger and Marler (1988) found additional audience effects. When cocks were tested in the presence of any conspecifics (their mate, another female, another male, or a hen with chicks) they gave a significant number of alarm calls. However, when presented with the same hawk stimuli while alone, alarm calls were very rare. When tested in the presence of bobwhite quail, alarm calls were also very rare. Thus, whether a male alarm calls is conditional upon the presence of an audience of conspecifics, but the male does not discriminate between mate and novel female or male versus female as he does when he gives food calls.

The authors have argued that both of these demonstrations of chickens being responsive to their social companions require a cognitive explanation. The food calls are often given in the context of courtship where a male provides small pieces of food to females, so it makes sense that the male should call only in the presence of females. Alarm calls can elicit mobbing responses from conspecifics, so it also makes sense for cocks to alarm call only when other chickens are present. A solitary animal is better protected in not calling. Although the explanation of these audience effects in chickens may not indicate complex cognitive skills, they also cannot be explained in terms of simple fixed action patterns.

Each of these examples is instructive for both those who study human speech and those who use language analogues with animals. I know of no studies in human speech indicating that we adjust our speech patterns to the location of our listeners, although I am convinced that we do make adjustments similar to those of the pygmy marmosets. There are relatively few studies on sequences of turn-taking or conversations in humans or in the animals trained to use language analogues. Aside from the study of Premack and Woodruff (1978) on how Sarah responded to the "good" versus "bad" caretaker, there have been few studies on how language trained animals respond to different social companions. The studies of how animals communicate in their natural social groups can suggest a variety of novel studies both for humans using language and for animals using language analogues.

SYNTAX

One of the major criteria of language is the presence of syntax, and part of the debate of whether chimpanzees have an understanding of language has been the issue of whether chimpanzees can form sentences (Terrace, Petitto, Saunders & Bever, 1979). Although a functional generative grammar may be impossible to demonstrate in animals, other simpler forms of grammar (finite-state grammar, slot and frame grammar and phrase structure grammar; see Roitblat, Harley, & Helweg, this volume, chapter 1) may exist. There have been demonstrations of finite-state and slot and frame grammars in animals.

Hailman, Ficken and Ficken (1985) showed that the structure of the "chick-a-dee" call of the black-capped chickadee (*Parus atricapillus*) contained four types of notes (labeled A, B, C, and D) that followed predictable sequences. In a sample of 3500 chickadee calls Hailman et al. found 362 different sequences of the notes, but only 11 failed to follow a simple rule system. The grammar is: If the call begins with an A, it can be repeated several times; the next note is a D, which can be repeated several times; then the call ends. If the call begins with a B, it can be repeated. It then moves to C, which can also be repeated, then switches to a D, which can be repeated. Using information theory analysis, Hailman et al. showed that there is a potential of 6.7 bits of

9. Linguistic Phenomena in Natural Communication

information in a chickadee call compared with 11.8 bits per word in English (based on relative frequency of use of English words; Shannon, 1951; cf. Pierce, 1980). English and chickadee are generative in that they are capable of producing an infinite number of sequences. The main problem with the chickadee work so far is that there is no evidence that they make use of the potential generativity of their grammar.

Ratcliffe and Weisman (1986) studied the song of black-capped chickadees and rearranged the patterns of notes in the song; finding that chickadees could discriminate between the normal and abnormal sequences.

Robinson (1979) described vocal sequences in the calls of the titi monkey *(Callicebus moloch)*, a monogamous, territorial species from South America. Titi monkeys give complex calls in response to the approach of intruders, and these calls were organized hierarchically into phrases which then made up longer sequences. When Robinson rearranged the sequences and played them back to titi monkeys, they showed significantly higher rates of "moaning" vocalizations which Robinson said were responses to disturbances. This difference in moaning rate indicates that titi monkeys discriminated between normal and abnormal sequences.

Cleveland and Snowdon (1982) found that the call units of cotton-top tamarins consisted of short frequency-modulated calls (chirps) and longer unmodulated calls (whistles). Many of the calls in the vocal repertoire were combinations of several different vocal units. These sequences could be described by a simple structural grammar: (1) In a sequence all chirps preceded all whistles. (2) Chirps or whistles can be repeated several times. (3) Within a sequence each successive call has a lower frequency than the preceding call.

Marler (1977) distinguished two types of syntax, a phonetic syntax that is equivalent to the formation of different words from phonemes (such as dog vs God), and a lexical syntax which is the formation of phrases or sentences from separate words (such as "the man bit the dog."). In lexical syntax, the meaning of the individual words (or vocal units) is retained with the phrase representing the summation of the individual components. Marler argued that this type of syntax would be quite rare in animals, although it is quite common in humans. Lexical syntax has been found in natural communication systems of at least two species of monkeys. Cleveland and Snowdon (1982) found two examples of lexical syntax in cotton-top tamarins. One was a combination of an alarm call with a whistle used in calm situations. This combination was typically emitted after an alarm call when animals took cover and froze, and preceded animals beginning to move freely again. The second example was a combination of a territorial call given mainly by males with a territorial call given primarily by females. The combined call was given equally by both sexes at the peak of arousal in a territorial conflict (McConnell & Snowdon,1986). Robinson (1984) studied the wedge-capped capuchin monkey (*Cebus olivaceus*) in Venezuela and found several calls that were used in isolation and as part of a sequence. Forty percent of all the calls recorded were given in sequences, and in several cases the sequences represented the additive properties of the meaning of the individual components.

Although these examples of grammar do not begin to show the complexity of human grammar, they do indicate that both birds and monkeys have rule-based systems for combining sounds in orderly sequences, the beginnings of a more complex grammatical system.

REFERENTIAL COMMUNICATION

Much of the focus of the other chapters in this volume is on symbols, words, and reference. Many have argued that true language is based fundamentally on words-symbolic representations of objects or events external to the organism producing the utterance. Seyfarth and Cheney (this volume, chapter 10) have provided several elegant and conclusive demonstrations of referential communication in vervet monkey (*Cercopithecus aethiops*) alarm calls and grunt vocalizations.

To determine whether our cotton-top tamarins had predator alarm calls that were specific to different predators as has been shown for vervet monkeys, Hayes and Snowdon (1990) presented several pairs and groups of monkeys with a live boa constrictor (a natural predator of cotton-top tamarins) and with clusters of flowers as a control. The responses of adult monkeys were highly variable. Monkeys stared at the snake for a longer period of time than they did at the flowers, and a minority of animals showed an increased rate of mild alarm calls and mobbing responses, although we never saw a full mobbing response as has been described for tamarins in the field (Bartecki & Heymann, 1987; Heymann, 1987; Neyman, 1977). Subsequently, we tested a subset of the original subjects with a white rat to serve as a control for a moving animate object, and we found the same degree of staring and the same number of alarm and mobbing responses. We also tested some of our cotton-top tamarins with a live hawk (controlled by a trained falconer) and again observed a mixed pattern of responses. Some monkeys gave alarm vocalizations while others approached

9. Linguistic Phenomena in Natural Communication

and investigated the hawk. What might be the cause of these varied responses to predators?

Monkeys born and raised in our colony had never been exposed to a snake, rat, or hawk before in their lives. Our colony has no windows and there was no possibility for the monkeys to have seen any of these animals before. Some of the monkeys we tested were from zoos and other research colonies where there was a possibility of seeing snakes, rats, or hawks. When we separated the data of monkeys known to be naive to snakes or rats, we found that these monkeys rarely showed strong alarm or mobbing responses to the snake and furthermore, that their responses habituated from the first to second presentation of the snake. The lack of a consistent mobbing or evasive response to the presentation of a snake or a hawk, the equivalence in response to a snake and to a laboratory rat, and the habituation of response from the first to the second trial all suggest that cotton-top tamarins must learn how to respond to predators, a finding in accord with developmental data presented by Seyfarth and Cheney (1986) and with demonstrations of observational learning of snake fear in rhesus macaques (*Macaca mulatta*) by Mineka and Cook (1988).

Interestingly, there was a much higher incidence of alarm and mobbing calls among immature animals in our groups, suggesting the possibility of an initial predisposition to fear of snakes in tamarins that needs reinforcement through social learning in order to be maintained. This parallels findings of Mineka and Cook (1988) showing that rhesus macaques could be easily trained through observation to fear snakes, but could not be trained to fear flowers. Seyfarth and Cheney (1986) have argued that social reinforcement and observational learning are mechanisms by which young vervet monkeys learn to give appropriate alarm calls to appropriate predators. Although we have not been able to find a specific referential call for predators in cotton-top tamarins, we have found a similar ontogenetic basis for acquiring appropriate responses to predators.

Another type of referential communication that has received active study in natural communication systems in animals is food calls. Dittus (1984) described a call of the toque macaque (*Macaca sinica*) that was said to be given to the discovery of highly preferred fruits such as figs when they became ripe. While most of the "food calls" were associated with the discovery of ripe fruits, they were also heard on days when the first clouds appeared after the dry season or when the sun first came out after the monsoon season, suggesting that these calls may not be specific to food, but instead serve as "elation calls" indicating that something good has occurred.

Marler, Dufty and Pickert (1986 a, 1986b) described food calls given by domestic cocks in the presence of a hen. They found that the rate of food calling related to the quality and amount of the food present. In a subsequent study, Gyger and Marler (1988) tested chickens in a larger environment where the female could move to be out of sight of the food, and they reported that on nearly 50% of the times when a "food call" was given that there was no food present. They interpreted these results to mean that the cocks were "deceiving" the hens by giving food calls when no food was present. However, there is an alternative explanation that does not rely on deception. The "food call" may simply not have been a "food call" in the first place, but a request for affiliation that may often be given in the presence of a food. Before we conclude that the existence of reference is widespread among animals, we need to consider alternative explanations.

Elawson, Tannenbaum, and Snowdon (in press) have studied food-associated calls in cotton-top tamarins. Cleveland and Snowdon (1982) described two types of chirps given in association with food—the C-chirp and the D-chirp. We have recorded animals before and after the presentation of foods of different types, and we found that 97% of all of the food-associated calls were, in fact, associated with food. The C-chirp was given as an animal approached food or while it was at the food dish selecting a food. The D-chirp was given while the animal was at the food dish or after it had taken a food item to another part of the cage. We have found that different foods elicit different rates of chirps, but these rates vary among individuals. One monkey will give most of its food-associated chirps to kiwi fruit while another gives most of its chirps to tuna. We have tested the same animals in a two-alternative forced-choice preference paradigm with each possible pairing of foods. Most of the monkeys displayed a clear transitive ordering of food preferences, but each monkey had a different individual preference order. When the preference rankings of individual monkeys were compared with the number of food calls they gave when presented with each food item, there was a clearly positive correlation. Thus, the food-associated calls appear to be related to an individual's food preferences, a preference scale not likely to be shared by other members of the group.

Is this then evidence of referential communication? I think not. The more parsimonious explanation is that the food-associated calls of tamarins reflect each individual's motivation for food types. Furthermore, since the rate of calling is nearly perfectly correlated with each individual's preference hierarchy, it is unlikely that the food calls of tamarins can be seen as deceptive. Although it is important to demonstrate that nonhuman animals display some

9. Linguistic Phenomena in Natural Communication

attributes of human language, it is equally important that we consider more parsimonious alternatives before concluding that referential communication and deception might be widespread among nonhuman animals.

SUMMARY AND CONCLUSIONS

There are two equally valid approaches to the study of animal language—the comparative psychologist's and the linguistic ethologist's approaches. Each provides a different type of information, with the comparative psychologist telling us the limits of the linguistic capacities of animals and the ethologist telling us what animals have evolved to do spontaneously in their natural environments. One benefit of the ethologist's studies is that we frequently discover communicative skills of animals that have not been previously studied or looked for in human beings. Thus, one value of the ethological approach is to expand our range of knowledge and thinking about linguistic phenomena.

I have emphasized several aspects of the natural communication skills of animals. Many birds and primates have larger vocabularies than previously thought, being able to use subtle variations in call structure to indicate subtle differences in what they are communicating about. There is evidence that animals can discriminate these subtle differences in their calls and that they can label sounds categorically. However, pygmy marmosets were shown to use different category boundaries to classify calls of socially familiar conspecifics, indicating that social environment affects perception.

Other social factors affect communication. Monkeys can alter the structure of their calls to increase sound localization by other group members as they get further away from the rest of the group, and they show turn-taking behavior and follow a clear sequence of turn-taking. Monkeys in territorial encounters give different types of calls according to which group the preceding call came from and what call was heard. Chickens are sensitive to the presence of other animals, with cocks giving more food calls when the mate or a novel hen is present than when another cock is present. They give more alarm calls when conspecifics are present than when alone or when another species is present. All of these examples indicate that animals can alter their communication as a function of their social environment.

Simple syntax has been shown in birds and monkeys, with one possible case of generative grammar in the chickadee, although its functional significance has not yet been established. Both lexical and phonetic syntax are present in some species of monkeys. Finally, referential communication has been a major theme, but some skepticism needs to be raised about food calls serving a referential, semantic, or deceptive function. Although it is important to demonstrate the cognitive complexity of nonhuman animals and the presence of protolinguistic capacities in their natural communication systems, we need also to be careful not to overgeneralize animal results as being parallels to human language.

ACKNOWLEDGMENTS

The author's research and the preparation of this manuscript were supported by USPHS grant MH 29,775 and a NIMH Research Scientist Award MH 00,177.

REFERENCES

Bartecki, U. & Heymann, E. W. (1987). Field observations of snake-mobbing in a group of saddleback tamarins, *Saguinus fuscicollis nigrifrons*. *Folia Primatologica*, 48, 199-202.

Bauers, K. & Snowdon, C. T. (1990). Discrimination of chirp vocalizations in the cotton-top tamarin, *American Journal of Primatology*, 21, 53-60..

Cleveland, J. & Snowdon, C. T. (1982). The complex vocal repertoire of the adult cotton-top tamarin (*Saguinus oedipus oedipus*). *Zeitschrift fur Tierpsychologie*, 58, 231-270.

Diehl, R. L. & Kluender, K. R. (1987). On the categorization of speech sounds. In: S. Harnad (Ed.), *Categorical Perception* (pp. 226-253). New York: Cambridge University Press.

Dittus, W. P. J. (1984). Toque macaque food calls: Semantic communication concerning distribution of food in the environment. *Animal Behaviour*, 32, 470-477.

Elawson, A. B., Tannenbaum, P. L., & Snowdon, C. T. (in press). Food associated calls communicate food preferences in cotton-top tamarins. *Animal Behavior*.

9. Linguistic Phenomena in Natural Communication

Ficken, M. S. & Ficken, R. W. (1967). Singing behaviour of blue winged and golden winged warblers and their hybrids. *Behaviour*, 28, 149-181.

Green, S. (1975). Variation of vocal pattern with social situation in the Japanese monkey (*Macaca fuscata*): A field study. In L. A. Rosenblum (Ed.), *Primate behavior* (Vol. 4, pp. 1-102). New York: Academic Press.

Gyger, M. & Marler, P. (1988). Food calling in the domestic fowl, *Gallus gallus*: The role of external referents and deception. *Animal Behaviour*, 36, 358-365.

Hailman, J. P., Ficken, M. S., & Ficken, R. W. (1985). The "chick-a-dee" call of *Parus atricapillus*: A recombinant system of animal communication compared with written English. *Semiotica*, 56, 191-224.

Hayes, S. L. & Snowdon, C. T. (1990). Predator recognition in cotton-top tamarins (*Saguinus oedipus*), *American Journal of Primatology*, 20, 283-291.

Heymann, E. W. (1987). A field observation of predation on a moustached tamarin (*Saguinus mystax*) by an anaconda. *International Journal of Primatology*, 8, 193-194.

Karakashian, S. J., Gyger, M., & Marler, P. (1988). Audience effects on alarm calling in chickens (*Gallus gallus*). *Journal of Comparative Psychology*, 102, 129-135.

Kroodsma, D. E. (1981). Geographic variation and functions of song types in warblers (*Parulidae*). *Auk*, 98, 743-751.

Lein, M. N. (1978). Song variation in a population of chestnut-sided warblers (*Dendroica pennsylvanica*): Its nature and suggested significance. *Canadian Journal of Zoology*, 56, 1266-1283.

Lillehei, R. A. & Snowdon, C. T. (1978). Individual and situational differences in the vocalizations of young stumptail macaques. *Behaviour*, 65, 270-281.

Macmillan, N. A. (1987). Beyond the categorical/continuous distinction: A psychophysical approach to processing modes. In S. Harnad (Ed.),

Categorical perception, (pp. 53-85). New York: Cambridge University Press.

Marler, P. (1977). The structure of animal communication sounds. In T. H. Bullock (Ed.), *Recognition of complex acoustic signals (Report of the Dahlem Workshop)* (pp. 17-35). Berlin: Dahlem Konferenzen.

Marler, P., Dufty, A., & Pickert, R. (1986a). Vocal communication in the domestic chicken: I. Does a sender communicate information about the quality of a food referent to a receiver? *Animal Behaviour, 34,* 188-193.

Marler, P., Dufty, A., & Pickert, R. (1986b). Vocal communication in the domestic chicken. II. Is a sender sensitive to the presence and nature of a receiver? *Animal Behaviour, 34,* 194-198.

Massaro, D. W. (1987). Categorical perception: A fuzzy logical model of categorization behavior. In S. Harnad (Ed.), *Categorical perception,* (pp. 254-283). New York: Cambridge University Press.

McConnell, P. B. & Snowdon, C. T. (1986). Vocal interactions between unfamiliar groups of captive cotton-top tamarins, *Behaviour, 97,* 273-296.

Mineka, S. & Cook, M. (1988). Social learning and the acquisition of snake fear in monkeys. In T. Zentall & B. G. Galef, Jr. (Eds.), *Social Learning: Psychological and Biological Perspectives* (pp.51-74), Hillsdale, NJ: Lawrence Erlbaum Associates.

Morse, D. H. (1967). The context of songs in black-throated green and blackburnian warblers. *Wilson Bulletin* 79, 64-74.

Neyman, P. A. (1977). Aspects of the ecology and social organization of free-ranging cotton-top tamarins *(Saguinus oedipus)* and the conservation status of the species. In D. G. Kleiman (Ed.), *The Biology and Conservation of the Callitrichidae* (pp. 39-71), Washington, DC: Smithsonian Institution Press.

Pierce, J. R. (1980). *An introduction to information theory: Symbols, signals and noise* (2nd ed. revised), New York: Dover.

9. Linguistic Phenomena in Natural Communication

Pola, Y. V. & Snowdon, C. T. (1975). The vocalizations of pygmy marmosets (*Cebuella pygmaea*) *Animal Behaviour*, 23, 826-842.

Premack, D. & Woodruff, G. (1978). Does a chimpanzee have a theory of mind? *The Behavioral and Brain Sciences*, 1, 515-526.

Ratcliffe, L. & Weisman, R. G. (1986). Song sequence discrimination in the black-capped chickadee (*Parus atricapillus*). *Journal of Comparative Psychology*, 100, 361-367.

Robinson, J. G. (1979). An analysis of the organization of vocal communication in the titi monkey (*Callicebus moloch*). *Zeitschrift fur Tierpsychologie*, 49, 381-405.

Robinson, J. G. (1984). Syntactic structures in the vocalizations of wedge-capped capuchin monkeys (*Cebus olivaceus*). *Behaviour*, 90, 46-79.

Seyfarth, R. M. & Cheney, D. L. (1986). Vocal development in vervet monkeys. *Animal Behaviour*, 34, 1640-1658.

Shannon, C. E. (1951). Prediction and entropy of printed English. *Bell System Technical Journal*, 30, 50-64.

Smith, W. J., Pawlukiewicz, J., & Smith, S. L. (1978). Kinds of activities associated with singing patterns of the yellow-throated vireo. *Animal Behaviour*, 26, 862-884.

Snowdon, C. T. (1987). A naturalistic view of categorical perception. In S.Harnad (Ed.), *Categorical perception* (pp. 332-354). New York: Cambridge University Press.

Snowdon, C. T. & Cleveland, J. (1980). Individual recognition of contact calls in pygmy marmosets, *Animal Behaviour*, 28, 717-727.

Snowdon, C. T. & Cleveland, J. (1984). "Conversations" among pygmy marmosets. *American Journal of Primatology*, 7, 15-20.

Snowdon, C. T., Cleveland, J., & French, J. A. (1983). Responses to context- and individual-specific cues in cotton-top tamarin long calls. *Animal Behaviour*, 31, 99-111.

Snowdon, C. T. & Hodun, A. (1981). Acoustic adaptations in pygmy marmoset contact calls: Locational cues vary with distance between conspecifics. *Behavioral Ecology and Sociobiology*, 9, 295-300.

Snowdon, C. T. & Pola, Y. V. (1978). Interspecific and intraspecific responses to synthesized pygmy marmoset vocalizations, *Animal Behaviour*, 26, 192-206.

Terrace, H. S., Petito, L. A., Saunders, R. J., & Bever, T. G. (1979). Can an ape create a sentence? *Science*, 206, 891-902.

Zoloth, S. R., Petersen, M. R., Beecher, M. D., Green, S., Marler, P., Moody, D. B., & Stebbins, W. C. (1979). Species-specific perceptual processing of vocal sounds by monkeys, *Science*, 204, 870-872.

10 Meaning, Reference, and Intentionality in the Natural Vocalizations of Monkeys

Robert M. Seyfarth and Dorothy L. Cheney

When humans use words like "apple" or "eagle," we recognize the referential relation that holds between such signs and the things for which they stand. Referential relations can, for instance, be distinguished from causal relations: The word "eagle" does not cause a particular bird to appear or result in a particular pattern of behavior. Instead, the word "stands for," or "conjures up images of," an object even when that object cannot be seen.

Representational capacity occupies a pivotal role in studies of human language, animal communication, and the mechanisms that underlie them because it concerns not only how organisms communicate but also how they classify features of their environment. Given the extensive research that has documented the ability of captive nonhuman primates to learn referential communicative signals in the laboratory (e.g., Premack, 1976), we focus in this chapter on the vocalizations used by nonhuman primates under natural conditions. We begin by asking whether monkeys, apes, or any other animals ever use sounds to denote objects and events in the world around them. If so, are their vocalizations semantic in the same sense that human words are semantic? Do animals understand the referential relation that exists between calls and the things for which they stand? Finally, we consider whether monkeys ever use vocalizations to influence another animal's beliefs as well as its behavior.

In this chapter we ask whether the vocalizations used by East African vervet monkeys (*Cercopithecus aethiops*) under natural conditions can usefully be called semantic. Data are drawn from a population of vervets that we and our colleagues studied over a 12-year period in Amboseli National Park, Kenya (Cheney & Seyfarth, 1990a). Additional data, supplementing those on vervet monkeys, come from experiments recently conducted on captive rhesus (*Macaca mulatta*) and Japanese macaques (*M. fuscata*) housed at the California Primate Research Center, University of California, Davis (Cheney & Seyfarth, 1990b).

SUBJECTS

Vervet monkeys in Amboseli National Park live in stable social groups composed of a number of adult males, adult females, and their juvenile and infant offspring. Each group occupies a territory that averages around 0.3 km^2 in size. Territories remain relatively stable from one year to the next and are aggressively defended against incursion by the members of other vervet groups.

As in most Old World monkey species, female vervets remain throughout their lives in the groups where they were born, maintaining close social bonds with female kin through frequent grooming, proximity, and the formation of alliances. Males, in contrast, leave their natal group at around sexual maturity and join a neighboring group, often in the company of brothers or natal group peers. Within each group, males and females can be ranked in linear dominance hierarchies that accurately predict the outcome of competitive interactions over access to food, water, and social companions. Offspring acquire dominance ranks immediately below those of their mothers, such that all members of a family share adjacent ranks (Cheney & Seyfarth, 1990a).

In the wild, group composition, patterns of dispersal, and social behavior among rhesus and Japanese macaques are similar to those among vervet monkeys (e.g., Lindburg, 1971; Sade, 1972; Kawai, 1958; reviewed in Melnick & Pearl, 1987). At the California Primate Research Center, rhesus and Japanese macaques are housed in groups that retain many of the features of each species' natural social organization. Each of the four groups used in our research (two of each species) lived in an outdoor enclosure constructed from two modified corncribs (hereafter called "arenas") connected by an intercage unit. Each group was composed of one or two sexually mature males, three to

10. Meaning reference and intentionality

five sexually mature females, and the females' juvenile and infant offspring. In each group at least two adult females were close genetic relatives (mother and daughter or half-sisters). One rhesus group had been constituted in 1984; animals in the three other groups had lived together for at least 10 years.

SEMANTICITY IN THE WEAKEST SENSE

There are at least three senses in which an animal vocalization might be called semantic. In the weakest sense, we can describe an animal vocalization as semantic whenever different calls signal the presence of different external objects or events, and when each call elicits the same response as would its referent even when the referent itself is absent (see, for example, Hockett, 1966).

As an example, consider the alarm calls given by vervet monkeys to different sorts of predator. In East Africa, vervet monkeys give acoustically different alarm calls to at least three different predators (Struhsaker, 1967): leopards (*Panthera pardus*), eagles (the martial eagle, *Polemaetus bellicosus* and the crowned eagle, *Stephanoaetus coronatus*), and snakes (usually the python, *Python sebae*). Each alarm call type (Figure 10.1) elicits a different, apparently adaptive response from other monkeys nearby. When vervets are on the ground a leopard alarm causes them to run into trees, where they are safe from a leopard's attack. Eagle alarm calls cause them to look up in the air or run into bushes; when the monkeys are in trees, eagle alarms often cause them to run out of trees and into bushes on the ground (martial and crowned eagles can capture vervets when the monkeys are in trees). Finally, snake alarms cause the monkeys to stand on their hind legs and peer into the grass around them (Struhsaker, 1967). Subsequent experiments have shown that alarm calls alone, even in the absence of an actual predator, elicit the same responses (Seyfarth, Cheney & Marler, 1980). Thus each alarm call type accurately replaces (i.e., elicits the same response as) the object for which it stands, even when that object is not itself present.

The behavior of young vervets provides further evidence that monkeys may be using alarm calls to denote particular predators. When an infant vervet first begins giving alarm calls, he gives alarms to many species, small hawks or pigeons, for example, that do not prey on monkeys and pose no danger to him. Such "mistakes" by infants, however, are not entirely random. Infants give leopard alarms only to terrestrial mammals, eagle alarms only to birds, and snake alarms only to long, snake-like objects (Figure 10.2). As they grow older, infants and juveniles increasingly restrict their leopard, eagle, and snake alarm

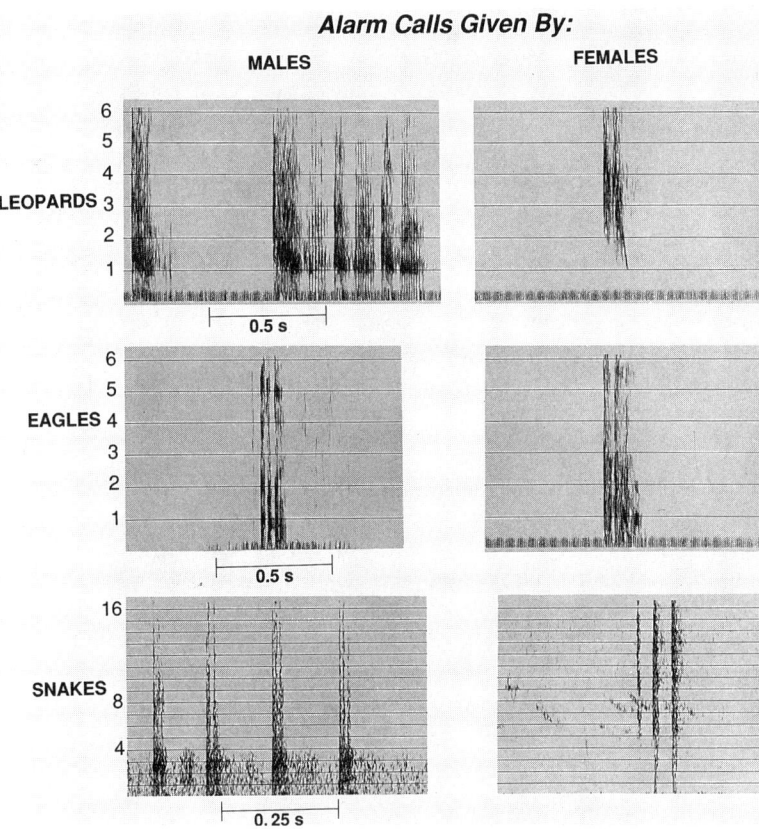

Figure 10.1. Spectrograms of alarm calls given by adult male and female vervet monkeys to leopards, martial eagles, and pythons. In each spectrogram, X-axis indicates time, Y-axis indicates frequency in units of 1 kHz. From *How monkeys see the world: Inside the mind of another species* by D. L. Cheney & R. Seyfarth, 1990, Chicago: University of Chicago Press. Reprinted by permission.

calls to the few species within each broad category that actually prey on vervet monkeys (Seyfarth & Cheney, 1980, 1986).

The behavior of infant vervets recalls similar behavior by human infants, who for a brief period during development may overgeneralize the meaning of a word, saying "dadoo" to refer to any male person or "ball" when

10. Meaning reference and intentionality

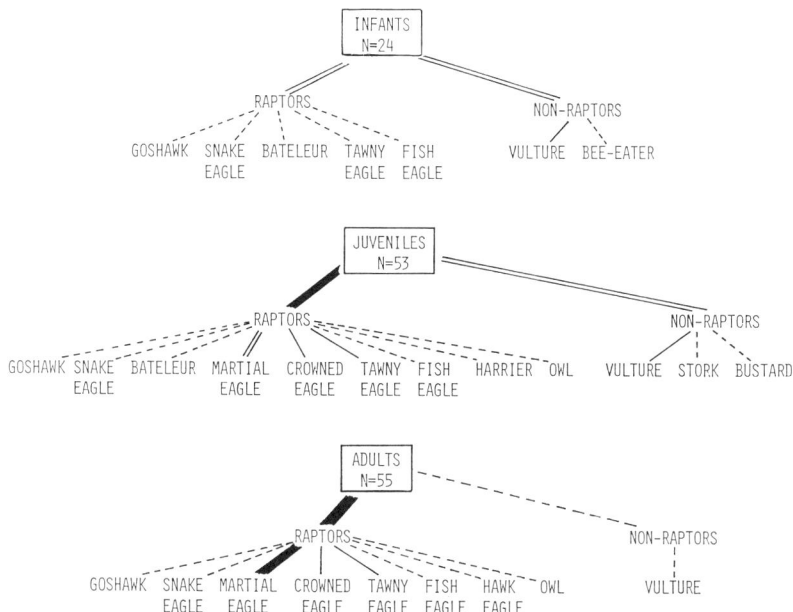

Figure 10.2. The stimuli that elicited eagle alarm calls from vervet monkeys of different ages. Data were collected over two 9-month periods in 1983 and 1985-1986. Infants are animals less than one year old; juveniles are 1-4 years old; and adults are over 4; N = number of alarm calls from animals in each age class. Broken lines indicate < 5 alarms, single lines 6-10 alarms, double lines 11-15 alarms, and thick solid lines > 15 alarms. From "Vocal development in vervet monkeys" by R. M. Seyfarth & D. L. Cheney, 1986, *Animal Behavior*, 34, 1640-1658.. Copyright, 1986, Animal Behavior Society. Reprinted by permission.

pointing to any round object (e.g., de Villiers & de Villiers, 1978). And, just as the human child's behavior helps us understand what she has in mind and shows that meaning is not always the same for children and adults, the infant vervet's behavior suggests that the monkeys have some particular class of objects in mind when they use their different alarm calls.

Seyfarth and Cheney

There are at least two alternatives to this "semantic" interpretation of vervet monkey alarm calls. The first (e.g., Marshall, 1970) argues that each call type does not denote a different predator but instead reflects different levels of fear and excitement. In our experiments, however, variation in the length and amplitude of alarm calls, assumed to mimic variation in the caller's emotional state, had little apparent effect on the responses each call elicited from other monkeys (Seyfarth, Cheney, & Marler, 1980).

A second alternative hypothesis (e.g., Smith, 1977, 1981) suggests that different alarm calls do not denote different predators but instead signal what the caller is likely to do next. Of course, given the close link between predator type, alarm call type, and the most appropriate escape response, there will inevitably be a predictable relationship between a specific call and the signaler's subsequent behavior. In itself, however, this does not rule out the possibility that vocalizations also serve a referential function. Recall, for example, that vervet eagle alarm calls can elicit a number of different responses. Animals on the ground may look up or run into a bush, while animals in a tree may run down from the tree; in either circumstance a listener can also do nothing. Moreover, vervets in a tree may run down from a tree even when the caller himself is on the ground and is responding by looking up. In this case, the most parsimonious explanation would seem to be that calls denote a type or class of danger rather than the caller's behavior, and that an individual's particular circumstances strongly influence the exact nature of its response (Seyfarth & Cheney, 1990).

Given these results, we have called the alarm calls of vervet monkeys semantic signals in order to emphasize that, contrary to earlier interpretations, vervet alarms do not simply reflect different levels of excitement or provide information solely about what the caller will do next. Instead, they function to denote objects in the environment in a manner that is at least to some degree independent of the caller's behavior. Of course, this is not to say that information about external referents is the only information conveyed by the vervets' vocalizations. Features such as alarm call amplitude, length, rate of delivery, and the number of individuals calling almost certainly provide listeners with information about how close a predator is and whether it poses immediate danger (e.g., Owings & Hennessy, 1984). Moreover, our understanding of a call's meaning will almost certainly be enriched as we learn more about the acoustic features correlated with a caller's level of motivation or arousal (e.g., Marler, Evans, & Hauser, in press). We emphasize the importance of external referents, in other words, not to minimize the role of emotion or the caller's subsequent behavior as determinants of call meaning, but instead to suggest that

10. Meaning reference and intentionality

the communication of monkeys, long known to be highly expressive, can be denotative as well.

Our definition of semanticity is limited, however, because it is based exclusively on what animals do in the wild and makes no reference to the mechanisms that underlie their behavior. From the data reviewed thus far we can conclude that vervet monkeys behave as if their calls, like some words, denote objects and events in the environment, but we cannot say whether vervets understand the referential relation that exists between their calls and features of the environment, or whether vervets, in responding to another animal's alarm call, interpret this vocalization as a representation of the caller's knowledge. As a result, we cannot say whether the parallel between vervet monkey alarm calls and human words is anything more than a superficial resemblance.

SEMANTICITY IN A STRONGER SENSE

Suppose, however, we adopt a stronger definition of semanticity and argue that an animal's vocalization is semantic only if an individual, given the opportunity to compare two calls, judges them to be the same or different on the basis not just of their acoustic properties but of what they denote. This sort of classification happens so often in language that we take it for granted. When we are asked, for example, to compare two words like "treachery" and "deceit" we judge them to be roughly the same because they refer to the same thing even though their acoustic properties are quite different. By contrast, when asked to compare two words like "treachery" and "lechery" we judge them to be different even though their acoustic properties are very similar.

The "ape language" projects provide a number of elegant cases in which animals have learned to assess and compare signs according to their meaning. To cite just one example, Premack (1970, 1976) used an artificial lexicon of plastic chips to study communication and intelligence in chimpanzees. His most famous subject was an adult female, Sarah. To test whether Sarah really understood the meaning of her symbols, Premack first asked her to describe the features of an actual apple. Was it red? Was it round? Did it have a stem? Then Sarah was asked the same questions about the symbol for apple, in this case a blue triangle. She described the blue triangle as being red, round, and having a stem. Premack then reversed the question and asked Sarah to begin with an object and describe properties of the name for that object. Shown an apple, Sarah correctly answered that the sign for this object was triangular not round, blue not green, and small not big.

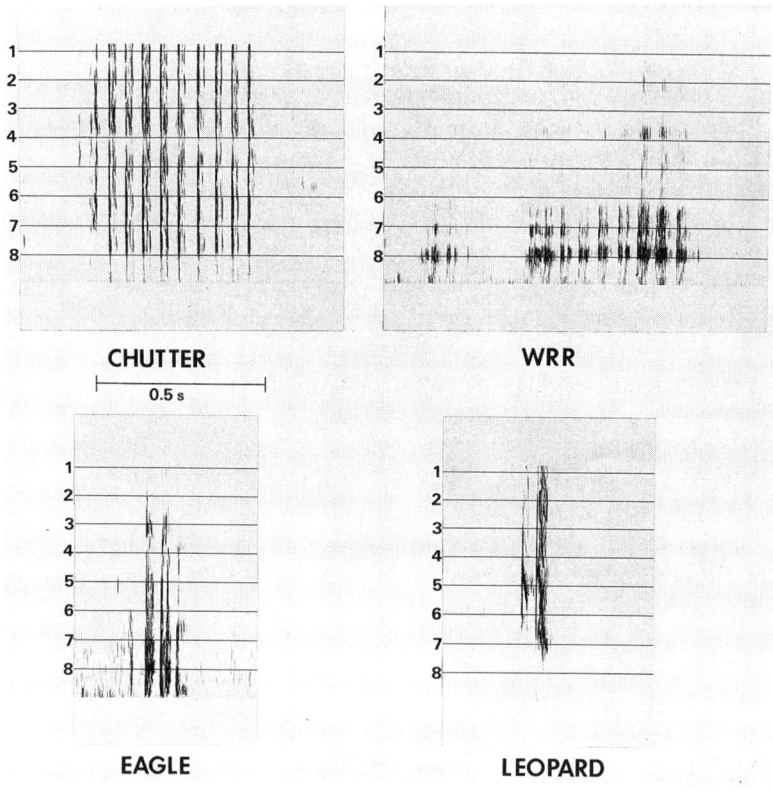

Figure 10.3. Spectrograms of chutter and wrr vocalizations given by one adult female, and alarm calls to leopards and eagles given by another. Legend as in Figure 10.1. From "Assessment of meaning and the detection of unreliable signals by vervet monkeys." by D. L. Cheney & R. M. Seyfarth 1988, *Animal Behavior*, 36, 477-486. Copyright, 1988, Animal Behavior Society. Reprinted by permission.

To test whether vervet monkeys also assess vocalizations according to the things for which they stand, we designed a series of experiments in which subjects were asked to compare two calls with different acoustic properties. In some tests the calls referred to similar objects or events; in other tests their referents were different. If vervets compare vocalizations, that is, make a

10. Meaning reference and intentionality

same/different judgment between them, on the basis of their referents, subjects should have judged two calls as "same" even when the calls were acoustically different. By contrast, calls with different referents should always have been judged as "different".

In one series of experiments, we used as stimuli two different calls given by female and juvenile vervets to members of other groups: a short, staccato chutter and a wrr, a long, loud trilling call. Although the two calls are acoustically quite different (Figure 10.3), each occurs only in the presence of another group (Struhsaker, 1967; Cheney & Seyfarth, 1982). Wrrs are usually given when a neighboring group has first been spotted, and they seem to function to alert other animals to the proximity of another group. Roughly 45% of all intergroup encounters involve only the exchange of wrrs (Cheney, 1981). Other encounters, however, escalate into aggressive threats, chases, and even physical contact. When groups come together under these conditions, females and juveniles often give the acoustically different chutter vocalization (Cheney & Seyfarth, 1988).

Although wrrs and chutter are acoustically distinct, they have broadly similar referents. To test whether subjects compare vocalizaitons according to their acoustic properties or their referents, we designed experiments in which a subject would repeatedly hear animal X's wrr when there was no other group present. Under these conditions, when the subject had habituated to X's wrr, we played animal X's chutter to see if she had also habituated to this acoustically different vocalization. If the two calls have similar meanings, and if monkeys use meaning to judge the relationship between calls, habituation to X's repeated wrrs should also produce habituation to X's chutter. Alternatively, if monkeys use some other feature (like the calls' acoustic properties) to judge similarity or difference between calls, these features, and not the calls' referents, should determine whether habituation is transferred from X's wrr to X's chutter.

In conducting our experiments, we borrowed a method that has been used successfully in research on preverbal human infants (e.g., Eimas, Siqueland, Jusczyk, & Vigorito, 1971). On day 1, as a control, a subject was played a particular female's chutter in order to establish the baseline strength of the subject's response to this vocalization. Then, on day 2, the subject heard the same female's wrr repeated eight times at roughly 20-min intervals. We measured subjects' responses and found that they did, in fact, habituate. Finally, roughly 20 min after the last playback in the habituation series, the subject heard the same female's chutter again (the test condition). The magnitude of the decrement in response between control and test conditions measured the extent

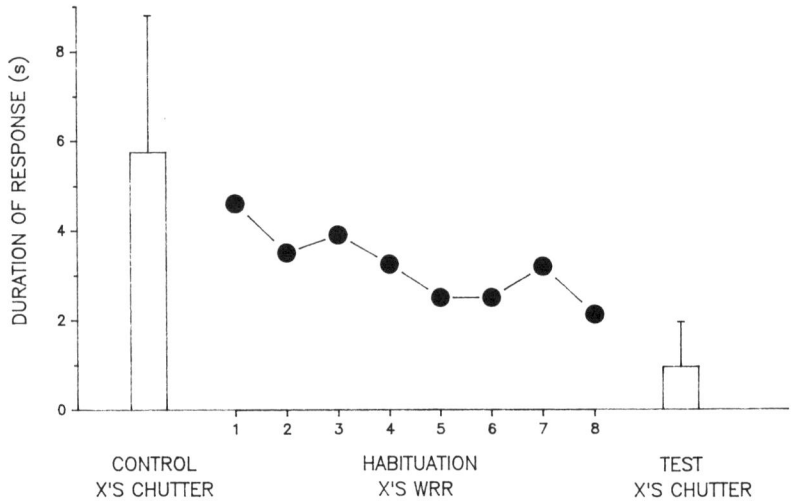

Figure 10.4. Results of habituation tests using wrrs and chutters given by the same individual. Histograms show the duration, in seconds (mean + SD) of 10 subjects' responses to playback of a given individual's intergroup chutter following repeated exposure to the same individual's wrr (test) compared with subjects' responses to the same chutter in the absence of such exposure (control). Mean duration of subjects' responses during habituation trials is also shown. Subjects responded for significantly shorter durations to test than to control calls. From "Assessment of meaning and the detection of unreliable signals by vervet monkeys. "by D. L. Cheney & R. M. Seyfarth 1988, *Animal Behavior*, 36, 477-486. Copyright, 1988, Animal Behavior Society. Reprinted by permission.

to which subjects judged the habituating and test stimuli to be the same: a large decrement indicated that subjects regarded the two calls as similar; little or no decrement indicated that the calls were different.

Since vervets and other primates take note of the signaler's identity when attending to calls (e.g., Hansen, 1976; Cheney & Seyfarth, 1980), we also wanted to determine whether subjects would transfer habituation from one individual to another. Hence in a second series of experiments we varied our procedure by playing two different individuals' calls. On day 1, we established

10. Meaning reference and intentionality

baseline data on the strength of a subject's response to individual Y's chutter. Then, on day 2, we played X's wrr to the subject eight times. After the subject had habituated to X's wrr we then tested to see if she had also habituated to Y's chutter.

A third test examined whether vervets would also transfer habituation if the identity of the signaler remained the same but the call's *referent* was changed. We therefore repeated the procedure described for the first set of experiments but now, instead of wrrs and chutters, we used leopard and eagle alarm calls as stimuli.

Results provided clear evidence that vervet monkeys compare different calls on the basis of their meaning and not just their acoustic properties. In all experiments, subjects rapidly habituated to repeated presentation of the same vocalization. When they were presented with the same individual's wrr and chutter, two acoustically different calls with roughly the same referent, they transferred habituation across different call types (Figure 10.4). In other words, if a subject had habituated to animal X's wrr, she also ceased responding to X's intergroup chutter.

By contrast, when subjects were asked to compare two calls whose referents were different, they did not transfer habituation across call types (Figure 10.5). If a subject had ceased responding to X's leopard alarm call, she nevertheless still responded at normal strength to X's eagle alarm.

Habituation was also not transferred when the calls had the same referent but were given by two different individuals. Even if a subject had ceased responding to individual X's wrr, individual Y's chutter still elicited the same response as it had under normal conditions (see Cheney & Seyfarth, 1988, for details of this and further experiments).

Compared with our earlier research on the vervets' alarm calls, these tests address the question of meaning and reference more directly, by asking animals to compare two vocalizations and to reveal the criteria they use in making their comparison. Like humans (e.g., Yates & Tule, 1979), vervet monkeys appear to process vocalizations according to an abstraction—their meaning—and not just according to acoustic similarity. The fact that subjects failed to transfer habituation when played the calls of two different individuals suggests that they took into account both the signal's meaning and the signaler's identity when attending to a call.

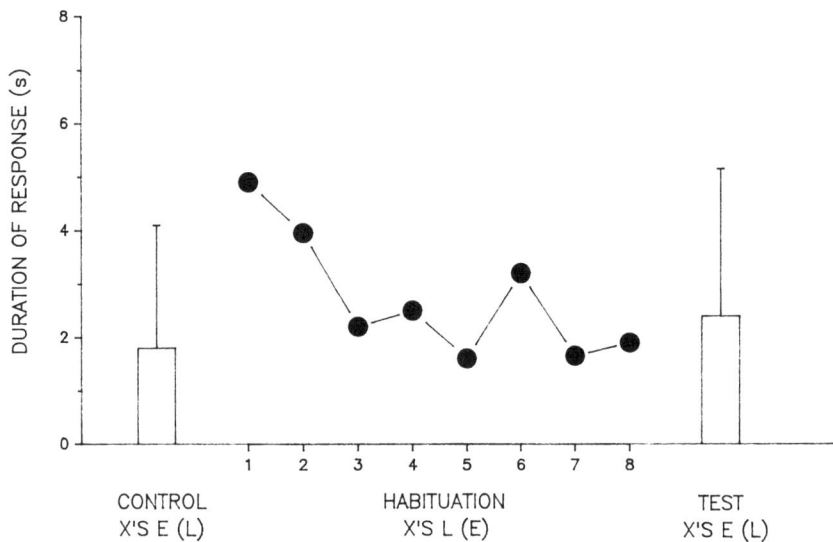

Figure 10.5. As in Figure 10.4, except results shown are for 10 subjects tested with one individual's leopard (or eagle) alarm after repeated exposure to the same individual's eagle (or leopard) alarm.

For further evidence that vervet monkeys make judgments about vocalizations according to the objects and events they denote, consider the monkeys' responses to the alarm calls of a sympatric bird, the superb starling (*Spreo superbus*). Like vervets, starlings have at least two distinct alarm calls, neither of which bears any acoustic resemblance to the vervets' own alarms. One starling alarm, a harsh, noisy chatter, is given to a variety of terrestrial predators. The second, a clear rising or falling tone, is given to hawks and eagles that attack from the air.

Vervet monkeys appear to recognize the difference between these calls, because they respond differently to each. When we carried out playback experiments using starling terrestrial predator alarms, starling raptor alarms, and starling song as stimuli, monkeys responded by running toward trees when they heard terrestrial predator alarms and looking up when they heard raptor alarms. By contrast, the monkeys showed no particular response when they heard the starlings' song (Cheney & Seyfarth, 1985).

10. Meaning reference and intentionality

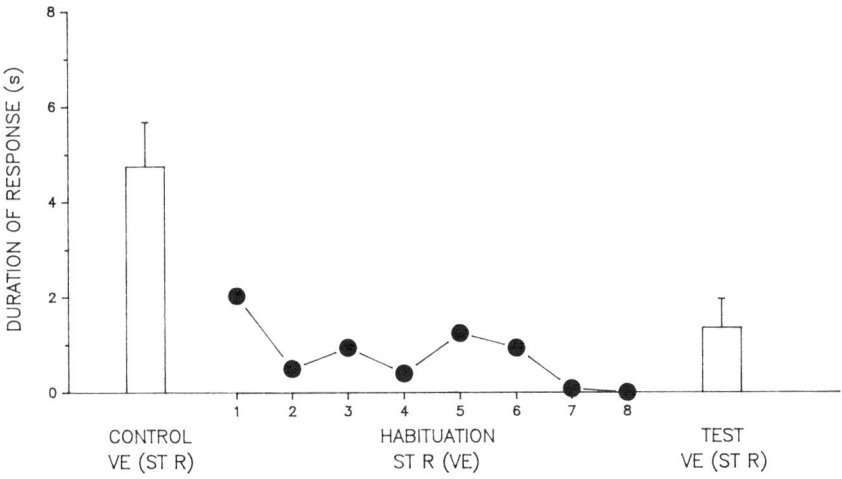

Figure 10.6. Results of habituation tests using vervet and starling eagle alarm calls. Histograms show the duration, in seconds (mean ± SD) of eight subjects' responses to playback of a vervet eagle (or starling raptor) alarm followed by repeated exposure to a starling raptor (or vervet eagle) alarm (test) compared with subjects' responses to the same alarm call in the absence of such exposure (control). Subjects responded for significantly shorter durations to test calls than to control calls. VE = vervet eagle alarm; ST R = starling raptor alarm; VL = vervet leopard alarm; ST T = starling terrestrial predator alarm. From "The assessment by vervet monkeys of their own and another species' alarm calls" by R. M. Seyfarth & D. L. Cheney, 1990, *Animal Behaviour*, 38, 754-764. Copyright, 1990, Animal Behavior Society. Reprinted by permission.

As noted earlier, however, such playbacks say nothing about the mechanisms that underlie the vervets' discrimination among different alarm call types. To investigate such mechanisms in more detail, we once again used a habituation/dishabituation paradigm that asked subjects to compare two vocalizations. We reasoned that if vervet monkeys not only distinguish between the starling's different alarm calls but also classify starling alarms according to the types of predator they denote, then subjects should transfer habituation from the alarm calls of one species to the alarm calls of another provided the calls have the same referent. For example, vervets who have habituated to the raptor alarm calls of starlings should cease responding to the raptor alarms of vervets, and vice versa. By contrast, subjects who have habituated to one species' terrestrial predator alarm should not transfer habituation to the other species' raptor alarm.

Once again, results suggested that vervet monkeys assess and compare vocalizations according to the calls' meaning and not just their acoustic properties. For example, when subjects had habituated to repeated presentation of a vervet's (or starling's) raptor alarm call, they transferred habituation to the raptor alarm of the other species (Figure 10.6). The monkeys behaved as if vervet eagle alarms and starling raptor alarms, despite their different acoustic properties, were in at least one respect similar to one another. In contrast, when subjects were asked to compare starling raptor alarm calls with vervet leopard alarms (Figure 10.7), no transfer of habituation occurred (for further details and results of other tests, see Seyfarth & Cheney, 1990).

This, of course, makes perfectly good biological sense. Given the high rates of predation in the vervets' environment (Cheney & Seyfarth, 1990a), there is every reason for them to have learned that sympatric species like starlings can be just as effective as other vervets in warning of an imminent attack. At the same time, it is interesting to note that when the monkeys were asked to compare two of their own species' vocalizations (wrrs and chutters), caller identity played an important role in the assessment of call meaning. By contrast, when the monkeys made a comparison that involved the calls of another species, caller identity seemed less important.

Taken together, the results of experiments using wrrs, chutters, vervet alarm calls, and starling alarm calls are difficult to explain without assuming that monkeys have some representation of the objects and events denoted by different call types and that they compare and respond to vocalizations on the basis of these representations. Apparently, when one monkey hears another monkey (or even a nearby bird) vocalize, the monkey forms a representation of what that call means. And if, shortly thereafter, the monkey hears a second vocalization, the two calls are compared on the basis of their representations, not just their physical similarity.

This is not to say that monkeys are necessarily aware of the distinction between signs and the objects they denote, or aware of their ability to compare vocalizations according to their referents. We cannot assume that an individual who can make same/different judgments about two calls on a habituation test will be able to make conscious use of this distinction in his daily life. Indeed,

10. Meaning reference and intentionality

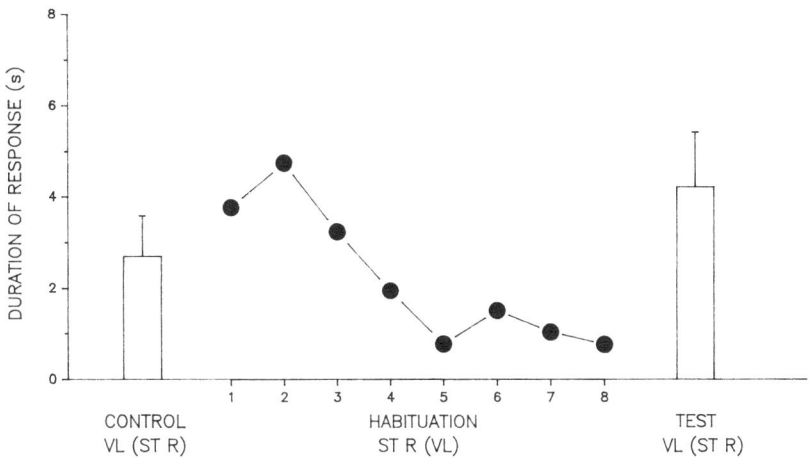

Figure 10.7. As in Figure 10.6, except results shown are for 7 subjects tested with a vervet leopard (or starling raptor) alarm after repeated exposure to a starling raptor (or vervet leopard) alarm.

there is evidence that infant chimpanzees that can perceive a relational distinction when tested with an habituation procedure are nevertheless unable to apply their apparent knowledge of this distinction in a match-to-sample test (Oden, Thompson, & Premack, 1988). Habituation data alone, therefore, do not prove that monkeys understand the relation *wrr denotes another group* or *eagle alarm denotes an eagle* in the same way that a chimpanzee understands the relation *blue triangle means apple*.

SEMANTICITY IN THE STRONGEST SENSE

Human language involves more than just a recognition of the referential relation between words and the objects or events they denote. When communicating with one another we also attribute mental states like knowledge, beliefs, or desires to others, and we recognize that there is a causal relation between mental states and behavior: what an individual thinks influences what he does. Similarly, as listeners we interpret words not only as signs for things but also as representations of the speaker's knowledge. We are, moreover, acutely sensitive to the relation between words and the mental states that underlie them. If we detect a mismatch between what another person says and what he thinks, we immediately consider the possibility that he is trying to deceive us.

Human language thus provides us with a definition of semanticity in its strongest sense. Having shown that monkeys make judgments about vocalizations based on their referents, we now consider whether animals ever attribute mental states to one another, know that these mental states can affect behavior, and as a result vocalize not only to influence what other animals do but also to influence what they think.

To attribute beliefs, knowledge, or ignorance to another individual is to have what Premack and Woodruff (1978) term a *theory of mind*. A theory of mind is a theory because, unlike behavior, mental states are not directly observable, although they can be used to make predictions about behavior. Many animals are adept at monitoring each other's behavior. What is not known is whether they are equally adept at monitoring each other's states of mind (see discussion by Dennett, 1987). To cite just one example, the alarm calls of many birds and mammals are not obligatory, but depend on social context. Individuals often fail to give alarm calls when there is no functional advantage to be gained by alerting others—for instance, when they are alone or in the presence of unrelated individuals (e.g., ground squirrels, Sherman, 1977; downy woodpeckers, Sullivan, 1985; vervet monkeys, Cheney & Seyfarth, 1985; roosters, Gyger, Karakashian, & Marler, 1986). However, while this audience effect clearly requires that a signaler monitor the presence and behavior of group companions, it does not demand that the signaler also distinguish between ignorance and knowledge on the part of his audience. Indeed, in all species studied thus far, signalers call regardless of whether or not their audience is already aware of danger. Vervet monkeys, for example, will continue to give alarm calls long after everyone in their group has seen the predator and retreated to safety (for further discussion see Cheney & Seyfarth, 1990a).

According to Grice (1957), true communication does not occur unless both signaler and recipient take into account each other's states of mind. By this criterion (from which we derive the definition of semanticity in its strongest sense), it is highly doubtful that any animal signal could ever be described as truly communicative. Does this matter, though? It could easily be argued that there is little selective advantage to be gained from determining whether or not one's audience is ignorant or knowledgeable before uttering an alarm call; as long as the call functions to inform others of danger, the audience's state of mind is irrelevant. In at least some species, however, individuals who give alarm calls put themselves at greater risk than those who remain silent, because their alarm calls attract the attention of predators (see, e.g., Sherman, 1977, 1985 for ground squirrels). Under these conditions, an individual would be at an advantage if he could determine whether or not an alarm call was necessary before giving a vocalization.

Pedagogy as Evidence for a Theory of Mind

An individual who cannot recognize the difference between his own and another individual's knowledge and beliefs will be incapable of selectively teaching or informing others of information that he possesses, simply because he will be unable to recognize ignorance in others. There is very little evidence, however, that the behavior of monkeys is ever influenced by other individuals' states of mind. Consider, for example, the development of antipredator behavior in young vervet monkeys. As noted earlier, when infant vervets first begin giving alarm calls they often make "mistakes," giving alarm calls to species like vultures or storks that pose no danger to them. Adults nonetheless respond to infant alarm calls, albeit in some cases quite briefly. For example, if an infant gives an eagle alarm in response to a pigeon, adults will look up and then quickly go back to what they were doing. By contrast, if an infant is the first member of his group to give an eagle alarm in response to a genuine predator (a martial or crowned eagle), adults will look up and then give an alarm call themselves (Seyfarth & Cheney, 1986). At first glance these "second alarms" by adults seem to be explicitly instructive, becausethey reinforce the infant's behavior when it is correct. Adults, however, are no more likely to give second alarms after correct alarm calls by infants than they are after correct alarm calls by other adults. Even though infants make many more errors than adults, adults make no special effort to reward them when they are correct. We would expect such special efforts if adults attributed ignorance to infants.

A similar picture emerges when we consider infants' responses to alarm calls. Here again, young infants make many mistakes. When we played tape-recorded alarm calls to infants younger than 6-months of age, adult-like responses were rare. Instead, infants either ran toward their mothers or responded in a way that actually increased their vulnerability to predation. An infant, for example, might look up when he heard a snake alarm or run into a bush when he heard a leopard alarm (Seyfarth & Cheney, 1986). In analyzing the responses of infants and mothers to playbacks of alarm calls, we looked carefully to see whether an infant's behavior affected what his mother did—whether, in this respect, mothers ever corrected their infants' errors. We found no such evidence.

In both of these cases, the vervets' behavior draws our attention to the distinction between active pedagogy and more passive observational learning.

Perhaps because adult monkeys do not recognize the difference between what they know and what an infant knows, adults do not go out of their way to instruct infants about predators and the proper response to alarm calls. As a result, infants are left to learn by observation, which is a much slower and less efficient way to transmit information.

Informing as Evidence for a Theory of Mind

As a more direct test to determine whether monkey mothers ever modify their behavior depending on their offspring's knowledge, we carried out a series of experiments on two groups of rhesus and two groups of Japanese macaques. In captivity, both rhesus and Japanese macaques often give alarm calls when they see technicians carrying nets, and they also give coo-like food calls when they are fed preferred foods like fruit (personal observation; Green, 1975).

We began each trial by locking all but two members of a given group into one of the cage's arenas. The two remaining animals, a mother and her juvenile offspring, were locked in the intercage unit at the edge of the other arena. In the "knowledgeable" condition, mother and offspring were seated next to each other. Each could see the other and both could see the empty test arena. In one set of trials, both individuals then watched a human place a highly preferred food (apple slices) in a food bin in the test arena. After observing the placement of food, the offspring, but not the mother, was released into the test arena where it had access to the food bin.

In the "ignorant" condition, mother and offspring were again locked in the intercage unit, but the offspring was seated some distance from the mother, visually isolated and physically separated from her by a steel partition. Now only the mother could see the apple slices being placed in the food bin. After the food had been placed in the bin, the offspring, but not the mother, was once again released into the arena.

In a second set of trials, mothers were presented with a "predator" in the form of a technician wearing a surgical mask and brandishing a net as if to capture her. After 10 s of exposure, the technician hid behind a barrier next to the test arena. In the "knowledgeable" condition the mother was seated next to her offspring so that both mother and offspring saw the technician. In the ignorant condition, as before, the offspring was separated from the mother behind a steel partition and only the mother could see the technician. In both conditions, the offspring was released into the test arena immediately after the technician had disappeared.

10. Meaning reference and intentionality

If monkeys are sensitive to the mental states of others, that is, if they take their audience's knowledge into account when giving food or alarm calls, the mothers should have uttered more calls (or in some other way have altered their behavior) when their offspring were ignorant than when they were already informed. On the other hand, if informants are unaffected by their audience's mental states, the mothers' behavior should have been similar regardless of whether or not their audience had also seen the food or danger.

In both experiments the mothers' behavior seemed unaffected by their offspring's knowledge. In the food experiments, mothers and offspring did exchange vocalizations at low rates, but there was no difference in calling rate between mothers whose offspring were knowledgeable and those whose offspring were ignorant. In the predator experiments, mothers did not alarm call at higher rates when their offspring were ignorant, nor did they orient toward or look at their offspring more when the offspring were ignorant than when the offspring had also observed the predator (Cheney & Seyfarth, 1990b).

In each experiment, the mothers' apparent failure to communicate information to their ignorant offspring had measurable consequences. In the food experiments, the mean latency for finding and eating food was significantly shorter for knowledgeable offspring than for ignorant ones (Figure 10.8). In other words, even though mothers had ample opportunity to recognize a mismatch between their own knowledge and that of their offspring, they took no apparent steps to redress this imbalance—for example, by giving coo vocalizations while looking at the food bin. In the predator experiments, offspring who knew the technician was present spent significantly more time sitting huddled near the barrier separating them from their mothers than did ignorant offspring, who were more likely to wander around the cage (Figure 10.9). Once again, the primary factor in the amount of anxiety shown by offspring was their own knowledge, and not their mothers'.

Of course, these negative results do not allow us to distinguish between the inability to attribute states of mind to others and the failure of this ability to alter behavior. It is certainly possible that monkeys do recognize the difference between their own knowledge and the knowledge of others, but that their behavior is simply unaffected by this knowledge. Whenever knowledge in another species is defined operationally, through behavior, there is a danger of concluding that an ability is absent when it is simply not manifested. Negative results are of interest, however, when compared with information transmission in humans. Although human cultures vary in their emphasis on active informing and pedagogy (see, e.g., Boyd & Richerson, 1985), in no culture are these

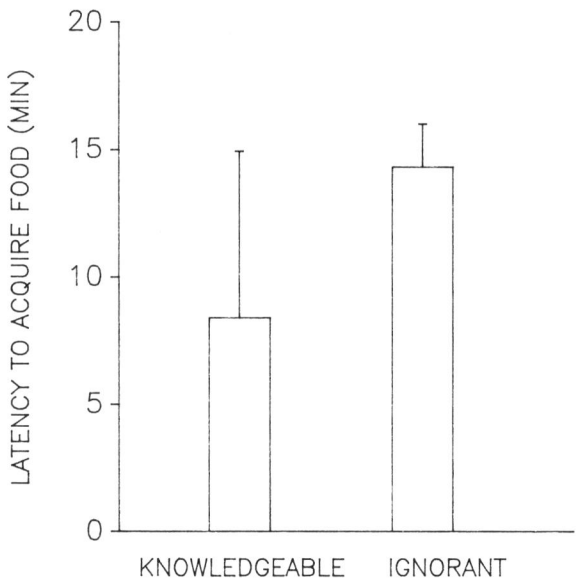

Figure 10.8. The latency (in minutes) with which knowledgeable and ignorant subjects acquired food. Histograms show means ± standard deviations for seven knowledgeable and seven ignorant juveniles. Knowledgeable subjects acquired food significantly faster than ignorant ones. From "Attending to behaviour versus attending to knowledge: examining monkeys' attribution of mental states" by D. L.Cheney & R. L. Seyfarth, 1990, *Animal Behaviour*, 40, 747-753. Copyright, 1990, Animal Behavior Society. Reprinted by permission.

modes of transmission absent. In contrast, pedagogy has yet to be documented conclusively in any nonhuman primate species, including chimpanzees (for reviews see Cheney & Seyfarth, 1990a; Visalberghi & Fragaszy, 1990). Even if nonhuman primates are capable of distinguishing ignorance and false beliefs in others, therefore, their apparent failure to act on this knowledge is striking.

SUMMARY

Vervet monkey vocalizations qualify as semantic signals in the weak sense that they provide listeners with information about objects and events in the

10. Meaning reference and intentionality

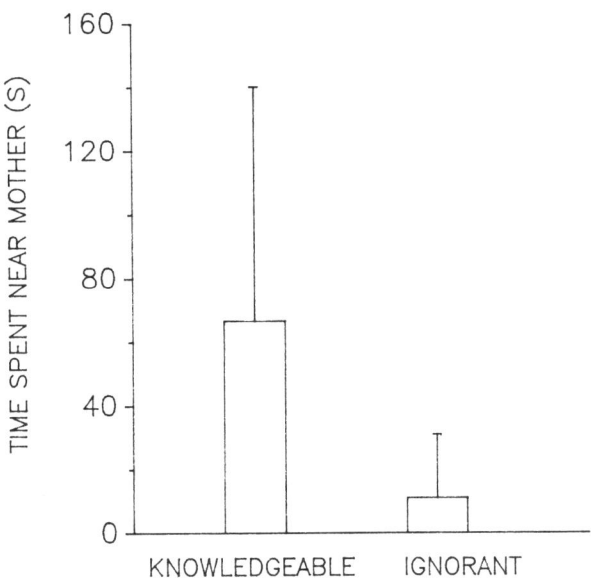

Figure 10.9. The number of seconds spent by knowledgeable and ignorant subjects within arm's reach of their mothers. Legend as in Figure 10.8. Knowledgeable subjects spent significantly more time near their mothers than did ignorant ones.

environment. Vervet calls are also semantic in the stronger sense that their production and interpretation depend on the mental states of both signaler and recipient. For example, when monkeys in habituation experiments are asked to compare two vocalizations, they do so not just according to the calls' acoustic properties but also according to their referents. To a vervet, the world is composed of two fundamentally different sorts of things: objects, such as leopards, snakes, or other groups; and vocalizations, which serve as representations of these objects. Monkeys respond to objects according to their physical features; they respond to vocalizations according to the things for which they stand.

Although vocalizations are semantic in this stronger sense, the calls of vervets and other monkeys seem not to be semantic in the strongest sense of being given with an intent to modify the mental states of listeners, or to draw listeners' attention to the signaler's own mental state. Adult monkeys, for example, make no special effort to correct infants that use and respond to vocalizations incorrectly. Similarly, there is no evidence that adults distinguish between juveniles that are unaware of food or danger and those that already know that food and danger are present. We suggest that monkeys cannot communicate with an intent to modify the mental states of others because they do not recognize that such mental states exist.

ACKNOWLEDGMENTS

Research supported by NSF grant 85-21147 and NIH grant NS 19826. We thank the Office of the President, Republic of Kenya for permission to conduct research in Amboseli National Park; A. Hendrickx and W. A. Mason for support and administrative assistance at the California Primate Research Center; and C. T. Snowdon, R. K. R. Thompson, M. D. Hauser, and Peter Marler for comments on the manuscript.

REFERENCES

Boyd, R. & Richerson, P. (1985). *Culture and the evolutionary process.* Chicago: University of Chicago Press.

Cheney, D. L. (1981). Intergroup encounters among free-ranging vervet monkeys. *Folia Primatologica, 35,* 124-146.

Cheney, D. L. & Seyfarth, R. M. (1980). Vocal recognition in free-ranging vervet monkeys. *Animal Behaviour, 28,* 362-367.

Cheney, D. L. & Seyfarth, R. M. (1982). How vervet monkeys perceive their grunts: Field playback experiments. *Animal Behaviour, 30,* 739-751.

Cheney, D. L. & Seyfarth, R. M. (1985). Social and nonsocial knowledge in vervet monkeys. In L. Weiskrantz (Ed.), *Animal intelligence* (pp. 187-201). Oxford: Clarendon Press.

Cheney, D. L. & Seyfarth, R. M. (1988). Assessment of meaning and the detection of unreliable signals by vervet monkeys. *Animal Behaviour, 36,* 477-486.

Cheney, D. L. & Seyfarth, R. M. (1990a). *How monkeys see the world: Inside the mind of another species.* Chicago: University of Chicago Press.

10. Meaning reference and intentionality

Cheney, D. L. & Seyfarth, R. M. (1990b). Attending to behaviour versus attending to knowledge: examining monkeys' attribution of mental states. *Animal Behaviour*, 40, 747-753.

Dennett, D. C. (1987). *The intentional stance*. Cambridge, MA: MIT Press/Bradford Books.

Eimas, P. D., Siqueland, P., Jusczyk, P., & Vigorito, J. (1971). Speech perception in infants. *Science*, 171, 303-306.

Green, S. (1975). Communication by a graded vocal system in Japanese monkeys. In L. A. Rosenblum (Ed.), *Primate Behavior* (Vol. 4, pp. 1-102), New York: Academic Press.

Grice, H. P. (1957). Meaning. *Philosophical Review*, 66, 377-388.

Gyger, M., Karakashian, S. J. & Marler, P. (1986). Avian alarm-calling: Is there an audience effect? *Animal Behavior*, 34, 1570-1572.

Hansen, E. W. (1976). Selective responding by recently separated juvenile rhesus monkeys to the calls of their mothers. *Developmental Psychobiology*, 9, 83-88.

Hockett, C. F. (1966). Logical considerations in the study of animal communication. In W. E. Lanyon & W. N. Tavolga (Eds.), *Animal sounds and communication* (pp. 390-430). Washington: American Institute of Biological Sciences.

Kawai, M. (1958). On the system of social ranks in a natural group of Japanese monkeys. *Primates* 1, 11-48.

Lindburg, D. G. (1971). The rhesus monkey in northern India: An ecological and behavioral study. In L. A. Rosenblum (Ed.), *Primate Behavior* (Vol. 2, pp. 1-106). New York: Academic Press.

Marshall, J. C. (1970). The biology of communication in man and animals. In J. Lyons (Ed.), *New Horizons in Linguistics* (pp. 229-241). Harmondsworth, U.K.: Penguin.

Melnick, D. & Pearl, M. C. (1987). Cercopithecines in multimale groups: Genetic diversity and population structure. In B. Smuts, D. L. Cheney,

R. M. Seyfarth, R. W. Wrangham & T. T. Struhsaker (Eds.), *Primate Societies* (pp. 121-134). Chicago: University of Chicago Press.

Oden, D. L., Thompson, R. K. R. & Premack, D. (1988). Spontaneous transfer of matching by infant chimpanzees (*Pan troglodytes*). *Journal of Experimental Psychology: Animal Behavior Processes*, 14, 140-145.

Owings, D. & Hennessy, D. (1984). The importance of variation in sciurid visual and vocal communication. In J. O. Murie & G. R. Michener (Eds.), *Biology of ground dwelling squirrels: Annual cycles, behavioral ecology, and sociality* (pp. 169-200). Lincoln: University of Nebraska Press.

Premack, D. (1970). A functional analysis of language. *Journal of the Experimental Analysis of Behavior*, 14, 104-125.

Premack, D. (1976). *Intelligence in ape and man*. Hillsdale, NJ: Lawrence Erlbaum Associates.

Premack, D. & Woodruff, C. (1978). Does the chimpanzee have a theory of mind? *Behavioral and Brain sciences*, 1, 515-526.

Sade, D. S. (1972). A longitudinal study of social behavior of rhesus monkeys. In R. H. Tuttle (Ed.), *The functional and evolutionary biology of primates* (pp. 378-398). Chicago: Aldine Publishing Co.

Seyfarth, R. M. & Cheney, D. L. (1980). The ontogeny of vervet monkey alarm calling behavior: A preliminary report. *Zeitschrift fur Tierpsychologie*, 54, 37-56.

Seyfarth, R. M. & Cheney, D. L. (1986). Vocal development in vervet monkeys. *Animal Behavior*, 34, 1640-1658.

Seyfarth, R. M. & Cheney, D. L. (1990). The assessment by vervet monkeys of their own and another species' alarm calls. *Animal Behaviour*, 38, 754-764.

Seyfarth, R. M., Cheney, D. L. & Marler, P. (1980). Vervet monkey alarm calls: Semantic communication in a free-ranging primate. *Animal Behavior* 28, 1070-1094.

10. Meaning reference and intentionality

Sherman, P. W. (1977). Nepotism and the evolution of alarm calls. *Science,* 197, 1246-1253.

Sherman, P. W. (1985). Alarm calls of Belding's ground squirrels to aerial predators: Nepotism or self-preservation? *Behavioural Ecology & Sociobiology,* 17, 313-323.

Smith, W. J. (1977). *The behavior of communicating.* Cambridge, MA: Harvard University Press.

Smith, W. J. (1981). Referents of animal communication. *Animal Behaviour,* 29, 1273-1275.

Struhsaker, T. T. (1967). Auditory communication among vervet monkeys (*Cercopithecus aethiops*). In S. A. Altman (Ed.) *Social communication among primates* (pp. 281-324). Chicago: University of Chicago Press.

Sullivan, K. (1985). Selective alarm-calling by downy woodpeckers in mixed-species flocks. *Auk,* 102, 184-187.

de Villiers, J. G. & de Villiers, P. A. (1978). *Language acquisition.* Cambridge, MA: Harvard University Press.

Visalberghi, E. & Fragaszy, D. M. (1990). Do monkeys ape? In S. T. Parker & K. R. Gibson (Eds.), *"Language" and intelligence in monkeys and apes* (pp. 247-273). Cambridge: Cambridge University Press.

Yates, J. & Tule, N. (1979). Perceiving surprising words in an unattended auditory channel. *Quarterly Journal of Experimental Psychology,* 31, 281-286.

11
Cognition and Communication in an African Grey Parrot (*Psittacus erithacus*): Studies on a Nonhuman, Nonprimate, Nonmammalian Subject

Irene Maxine Pepperberg

BACKGROUND

Rationale for Using Animal-Human Communication to Study Animal Cognition

Various techniques can provide data for cross-species comparisons of cognitive abilities. Researchers use protocols that range from operant laboratory procedures (see Kamil, 1988; Roitblat, Bever, & Terrace, 1984) to field studies that examine how animals respond to different types of auditory playbacks (e.g., Cheney & Seyfarth, 1985, Seyfarth & Cheney, this volume, chapter 10). The technique that my students and I use, which involves interspecies communication, is still considered somewhat unconventional (e.g., Seidenberg & Petitto, 1987) although it has been in existence for over two decades. Our studies on an African Grey parrot (*Psittacus erithacus*), like the pioneering projects on chimpanzees (*Pan troglodytes*, Gardner & Gardner, 1978; Premack,

1976, Rumbaugh, 1977) and dolphins (*Tursiops truncatus*, Herman, 1980), use a two-step procedure in which the parrot is first taught a communication code based on certain aspects of human language. The resultant capacity for animal-human communication then provides a channel for assessing the bird's cognitive abilities (see Pepperberg, 1981, 1986, 1990c, 1991).

Animal language studies are special because of their potential to provide, in a form that can easily be evaluated, data about the relative cognitive capacities of animals. Unlike some systems used for testing, interspecies communication provides a direct means of evaluating subjects: For example, in contrast to operant or playback experiments, respectively, two-way communication studies do not require the subject to determine, through trial and error, the question (e.g., is it match-to-sample or oddity-from-sample?) that the experimenter wishes to ask, nor create certain circumstances (e.g., habituation; Petrinovich & Patterson, 1978) that could inadvertently affect the results. A system that uses an interspecies communication code instead enables researchers to communicate to their subjects the precise nature of the questions being asked and to query their animal subjects in as direct a manner as they now query human participants in related studies.

Projects involving animal-human communication also (a) take into account data that animals will more likely learn a task and respond appropriately in a laboratory situation if they are within a social context similar to their field environment (Baptista & Petrinovich, 1984; Menzel & Juno, 1985; Pepperberg, 1981; Petrinovich & Baptista, 1987; Todt, 1975; West & King, 1985); (b) facilitate comparisons among widely divergent species, including humans, because every system has a common basis in a human code; (c) provide an open and arbitrary system in which the subject can create subtle variations in response that encourage the researcher to examine the nature as well as the extent of the information perceived by the subject; and (d) provide enough flexibility to allow subjects to respond in novel and possibly innovative ways that can imply competence beyond that required by the intended task (from Pepperberg, 1987a; 1991). Such data can, at the least, provide the impetus for subsequent studies to determine whether the implied competence does indeed exist (Pepperberg, 1988a; Pepperberg & Kozak, 1986).

Countering the Possible Drawbacks to the Use of Animal-human Communication as an Investigative Tool

Despite the advantages described earlier, interspecies communication does have two potential drawbacks as an investigative tool. Both drawbacks are inherent

11. Cognition and Communication in a Parrot

in the method, as they are related to the language-like nature of the communication code. The drawbacks are (a) the propensity for researchers to lose sight of the code as an investigative tool and argue as to the extent to which it is equivalent to human language and (b) the possibility that learning such a code enables animals to reason at levels beyond their native abilities. A brief discussion of these factors, however, shows that they are far less problematic than they might at first appear.

Because all interspecies communication codes are based on some form of human language, investigators often emphasize direct comparisons between human and nonhuman linguistic abilities rather than between human and nonhuman cognitive abilities. Thus data and discussions about relative cognitive capacities are often lost amidst open-ended debates as to the extent to which a particular animal has acquired "language" or how well particular studies or procedures demonstrate linguistic competence (e.g., Herman, 1989; Nelson, 1987; Premack, 1986; Savage-Rumbaugh, 1987; Schusterman & Gisiner, 1989; Seidenberg & Petitto, 1987). The reason for such debates is an assumption that the extent to which an animal can learn and use such a code is a direct indication of its cognitive capacities (see Premack, 1976; Terrace, 1979). But training techniques and the codes themselves vary considerably with respect to the subject species and vary even among projects that study the same species; such variation in experimental design invalidates any comparison of cognitive capacity based solely on facility in using a particular interspecies communication code. It would, for example, be foolish to claim that a parrot exhibits a greater cognitive capacity than a dolphin because it vocally produces its code, and a lesser capacity than a chimpanzee because it does not read symbols. Nevertheless, even widely divergent codes may, in properly designed experiments, be used to obtain data on cognitive tasks that can be directly compared across species; for example, although the parrot vocalizes and some chimpanzees manipulate plastic symbols, both have been shown to have a comparable understanding of concepts of similarity and difference (Pepperberg, 1987c; Premack, 1976, 1983). To exploit the power of interspecies communication, researchers must therefore focus on how an animal's use of such a code facilitates investigations of its cognitive abilities, rather than on what the animal's use of the code itself might imply about such abilities.

Researchers are also concerned that language, or language-like training, facilitates conceptual thinking and would thus enable a subject in a communication project to demonstrate a competence beyond its native abilities (e.g., Premack, 1983, 1986). I have argued elsewhere (e.g., Pepperberg, 1987b, 1987c, 1990a, 1990c, 1991; Pepperberg & Funk, 1990Pepperberg & Kozak,

1986) that, for the specific tasks so far studied, such as concepts of same/different, training is unlikely to allow an animal to acquire a concept it would otherwise be incapable of learning. Human children, for example, are now thought to form many concepts well before they acquire language (see Mandler, 1990), although the effect on concept learning of their exposure to language is not taken into account. Language training does, however, affect the type of task that can be administered and facilitates testing of abilities that a researcher might otherwise be incapable of examining: An animal that can, for example, be "told" the point of the task (e.g., that responses should be made on the basis of presence or absence of some feature) is more likely to succeed than one that must learn by trial and error (see Hearst, 1984; Newman, Wolff, & Hearst, 1980).

The potential drawbacks of an interspecies communication protocol can, therefore, be turned to an investigator's advantage. Once researchers accept that is it less important to debate whether an animal has human language and whether language affects thinking than to teach such a communication code as an investigative tool, the potential exists for learning more about the nature of cognitive processing in animals. Specifically, certain tasks, such as the one I describe next, are considerably easier to administer to a subject that has learned an interspecies communication code.

Use of Animal-Human Communication Techniques for Cross-Species Comparisons of Cognitive Abilities

Interspecies communication has already provided comparative data for species as disparate as dolphins (Herman, 1987; Herman & Forestell, 1985); chimpanzees (Gardner & Gardner, 1978, 1984; Matsuzawa, 1985; Premack, 1983; Savage-Rumbaugh, Rumbaugh, Smith, & Lawson, 1980); sea lions (*Zalophus californianus*; Schusterman & Gisiner, 1988; Schusterman & Krieger, 1984, 1986), an orangutan (*Pongo pygmaeus*; Miles, 1983), and an African Grey parrot (Pepperberg, 1990c). For the nonhuman primates and the parrot, the animal-human communication codes use both production and comprehension modes, and capacities that I have compared in this manner include categorization (Pepperberg, 1983), labeling of specific numerical quantities (Pepperberg, 1987b), and abstract concepts of same/different (Pepperberg, 1987c). Research with marine mammals is predominantly limited to the comprehension mode so that direct comparisons of psittacine and cetacean/pinniped abilities have been more difficult and were, until the study reviewed in this chapter, restricted to a comparison of these animals' concepts of absence (Pepperberg, 1988a). Because avian data on a recursive task (one that

11. Cognition and Communication in a Parrot

requires some form of sequential processing of information) would provide additional comparisons with the abilities of both terrestrial and aquatic mammals, I designed an experiment for the African Grey parrot, Alex, that used interspecies communication to study recursive competence (Pepperberg, 1990a).

Recursive Competence and Cognitive Capacities

Although recursive tasks vary considerably in their design (see Granier-Deferre & Kodratoff, 1986; Pepperberg, 1990a), a common procedure is to present to a subject several different objects and one of several different possible questions or commands concerning the attributes of these objects. The complexity of the task overall is based on the number of different objects and the potential number of different questions or commands that can be presented, as well as the complexity of the individual questions or commands (i.e., their context and the number of attributes used to specify the target and the number of responses from which to choose). Each question thus contains several parts, the combination of which uniquely specifies which object is to be targeted and what action is to be performed. The subject must divide the question into these parts (e.g., what is the topic of information being targeted, what it is to do, and to which object it is to respond) and (recursively) use its understanding of each part to answer correctly. The subject then demonstrates its competence by reporting on only a single aspect (e.g., color, shape, or material) of, or performing one of several possible actions (fetching, touching) on, an object that is one of several differently colored and shaped exemplars of various materials.

Examining some questions from a recursive task may clarify these points. A relatively complex question, for example, would concern the shape of a blue wooden exemplar ("What shape is the object that is blue and wood?"): All blue objects of other materials, all wooden objects of other colors, all categories other than those concerning shape would have to be excluded, and the information about the appropriate instance of shape would have to be accessed and then encoded after the object was isolated. The question can be made less complex in two ways. In one, the number of features that define the target could be decreased ("What shape is the object that is wood?"); that is, the conjunction of search features could be eliminated.[1] In the other, the subject could be asked

---

[1] A subject that is searching for targets defined by the conjunction of two features may, under some conditions, perform the search as a parallel, rather than as a sequential (recursive) task (Langley & Riley, 1988). Including conjunction in a task, therefore, may not affect its recursive complexity.

to fetch the exemplar ("Bring the object that is blue and wood"), so that no additional information would have to be accessed after the target was found. The task retains its recursive nature despite such simplifications, because there is still the need to process information sequentially about the topic of the question, the type of response required, and the specific object that is targeted.

Unlike other types of tasks (e.g., operant match-to-sample), recursive tasks require a subject not only to come to a decision by evaluating (or processing) current information based on some representation of prior experiences (e.g., Kamil, 1984; Roitblat, 1984), but also to choose, from among various possible sets of rules that have been acquired or have been taught, the set that appropriately governs the current processing of this data. I have argued elsewhere (Pepperberg, 1990a) that both forms of processing are required for a rigorous test of cognitive ability (see also Granier-Deferre & Kodratoff, 1986). The following analysis will clarify just how recursive tasks provide strong tests of such abilities.

To respond to a recursive task, a subject must engage in a stepwise procedure. First, the subject must use the elements of the question, for example, transient vocalizations or hand signals, to chose from among a set of possible responses. This choice requires the subject to comprehend the particular labels or symbols in the question that represent the several possible actions (e.g., fetch, touch) or object attributes (e.g., shape, number). The subject must then use its understanding of additional symbols to determine the subset of information to which it should selectively attend (e.g., exemplars that are blue and wood) in the context of any number of different situations (i.e., for any specific collection of objects; Granier-Deferre & Kodratoff, 1986). Finally, the subject must determine an appropriate course of action and encode its response into an appropriate physical motion or verbal representation of an object or attribute. The tasks cannot be solved by responding with respect to a single set of criteria (e.g., match-to-sample based on shape). Nor can the tasks be interpreted as performance of a single action determined by a relatively simple 1:1 correlation (e.g., "Pick up X," where the only variable is X). The tasks are not based on responses to single questions (e.g., "What's this?") for even a large number of different exemplars, nor to chaining two independent responses to different objects ("Do X to A and Y to B"; Premack, 1986). And, although recursive tasks are related to conditional tasks ("If tray green, do match-to-sample; if tray black, do oddity"), the number of concepts involved and the number of options for response are considerably greater in a recursive task: Whereas, in a conditional task, *green* can be interpreted as a symbol for *same* simultaneously with *black* as a symbol for *different*, in the recursive task previously described

11. Cognition and Communication in a Parrot

there are several conditional discriminations each for choice of topic (quantity, shape, color, etc.), choice of action (bring, label, touch), and choice of object on which to operate, all within a number of different contexts (see Thomas, 1980; for further discussion, see Pepperberg, 1990a).

Although several studies had tested the competence of chimpanzees and marine mammals on tasks involving some form of recursion (e.g., Essock, Gill, & Rumbaugh, 1977; Herman, 1987; Schusterman & Gisiner, 1988), the experiment described in this chapter was the first such study on an avian subject. The recursive task in this study was in most ways functionally equivalent to those used with chimpanzees and marine mammals, but differed in two aspects. First, the design capitalized on Alex's ability to work within the vocal mode. Second, unlike some studies that concentrated on single-topic tests (see discussion in Pepperberg, 1990a), each trial was presented intermittently during training and testing of other unrelated topics (e.g., number competency, photograph recognition). This procedure ensured Alex's exposure to numerous possible exemplars and questions during each session (described later, also Premack, 1976, p. 129-130), thus decreasing the possibility of his using nonlinguistic cues and requiring him to chose his responses based on his entire repertoire of more than 80 vocalizations, including labels for foods, locations, and quantity that were not related to the recursive task. This protocol would thus also minimize errors caused by proactive interference, by separating the types of stimuli and responses (see Schusterman, Gisiner, & Hanggi, 1988). If Alex were successful on this task, he would demonstrate capacities comparable to those of nonhuman primates and marine mammals.

Competence in Comprehension: a Prerequisite for a Recursive Task

The recursive task described earlier places significant demands on a subject's ability to comprehend symbols; data from our previous experiments (Pepperberg, 1983, 1987b, 1987c, 1988a, 1988b, 1990b), despite their emphasis on the productive rather than the receptive mode, suggested that Alex's comprehension abilities would be adequate. Alex could, for example, not only produce vocal responses to vocal questions (e.g., vocally label colors, shapes, and materials of various objects; Pepperberg, 1978), but also comprehend the categorical relevance of his labels so as to differentiate questions and therefore target the appropriate subset of information for a given situation. For example, he could comprehend and respond differentially to vocal questions of "What color?" or "What shape?" for objects that simultaneously incorporated even novel variations of both attributes (e.g., respond "green wood" or "2-corner wood"; "yellow hide" or "5-corner hide" for, respectively, green wooden "footballs" or yellow rawhide pentagons; Pepperberg, 1983). Similarly, during a study on numerical concepts, Alex could be shown a collection comprised of objects of two different types (X's and Y's) and, based on the question he heard, respond with the number of either X's or Y's (Pepperberg, 1987b).

Research on Alex's concepts of similarity and difference provided additional evidence for his ability to comprehend and respond to more than one question at a time. In these studies (Pepperberg, 1987c, 1988a) he was shown two exemplars that could vary with respect to color, shape, and material and then was asked "What's same?" or "What's different?" Based on the exemplars and the question, he had to determine what (if anything) was same or different and then produce vocally the label not for the appropriate color, shape, or material markers, but for the relevant category (i.e., not "yellow," but "color"). If nothing was same or different, he would respond "none". Specific probe questions for which there were two possible correct answers (e.g., "matter" and "shape" for "What's same?" with respect to a pair of blue and yellow wooden triangles) were used to demonstrate that he was responding to the content of the question. If he were ignoring the content of the question and answering on the basis of prior training and the physical aspects of the exemplars alone, he would have determined the single attribute that was either similar or different and responded with the one wrong answer (in this example, "color"). Instead, he was correct about 80% of the time (Pepperberg, 1987c, 1988a). Moreover, because Alex's tests always included questions on all possible topics, he always had to comprehend the topic of a question to determine from which set of responses his answers should come; for example, he could be shown two keys and asked "What's same?", "What's different?", or "How many?" (Pepperberg, 1990a).

Finally, additional evidence for Alex's capacity for comprehension came from our study of his requesting behavior. Here we showed that he comprehended his own utterances. When presented with an object other than one he had requested, he would, more than 75% of the time, refuse the alternative object. He would say "No" and often repeat his initial request (Pepperberg, 1987a, 1988b).

Summary

According to some researchers (e.g., Case, 1985; Premack, 1983, 1986; Rogoff, 1989), what distinguishes the more complex from the simpler levels of cognitive competence is not just the ability to solve a particular problem by evaluating

11. Cognition and Communication in a Parrot

current information based on some representation of prior experience, but rather the ability to transfer this information to related problems and to choose the set of rules, from among many, that appropriately guides the response to the situation (Pepperberg, 1990a). A recursive task, which is most easily administered to animals that can comprehend and respond to some form of a human-based code, provides the means to administer such a test.

EXPERIMENTAL DESIGN

At the time this experiment began, Alex had been the focus of studies on interspecies communication and animal cognition for over a decade (e.g., Pepperberg, 1981). He could produce vocal (English) labels for seven colors [green, rose (red), blue, yellow, grey, purple, orange], several shapes (2-, 3-, 4-, 5-, and 6-corner for, respectively, football-shaped, triangular, square, pentagonal, and hexagonal forms), seven materials [cork, wood, hide (rawhide), paper, chalk, wool, rock (Playdoh forms)], and could label various items of metal [key, chain, grate, tray, truck (toy cars)], wood [peg wood (clothes pin), block], and plastic or paper (cup, box) (Pepperberg, 1987a, 1990c). He could use these labels to identify, request, refuse, and respond to questions concerning abstract categories of color, shape, material, and quantity for more than 100 different objects, including ones that differed somewhat from training exemplars (Pepperberg, 1978, 1981, 1983, 1987a, 1987b, 1987c, 1988a, 1988b).

Alex acquired the abilities described above through training procedures that are based on a modeling technique, and the same procedures were used in the study on recursive tasks. All training is conducted by live, interacting human tutors who demonstrate referential, contextual use of each targeted vocalization (the model/rival or M/R approach), and provide as rewards those exemplars that relate to the skill or task being taught (i.e., objects or collections about which Alex has been queried). Such protocols provide the closest possible association of each object or action and the label or concept to be learned (Pepperberg, 1981, 1983, 1987a, 1987b, 1987c, 1988a, 1988b; note Greenfield, 1978).

The recursive task was presented as follows (Pepperberg, 1990a): In each trial, Alex was shown a different collection of seven exemplars. Each collection was chosen from among 100 objects of various combinations of shapes, colors, and materials. He was allowed to touch each object briefly with his tongue so that certain materials that often appeared visually similar (e.g., Playdoh and rawhide forms) could be more easily distinguished. These objects were then scattered onto the surface of a circular tray. Only if an object was obscured by the placement of other objects was the arrangement altered in any way. Each object was generally spaced less than 2" from any other object. Alex was asked one of four possible vocal questions concerning one aspect of one of the seven possible items. Thus for a collection that contained a circular purple key, a football-shaped ("2-corner") yellow wood, a triangular piece of green rawhide, a square of blue paper, a pentagonal orange Playdoh "rock," a red hexagonal piece of plastic, and a grey metal box, Alex could be asked "What color is the key?", "What shape is the rock?", "What object is blue?", or "What object is 2-corner?"—or various permutations of these questions. Every question contained three pieces of information: (a) information about the topic under study (e.g., an attribute of one item in a collection vs. the quantity of the collection); (b) information that designated (in the form of the label for a particular instance of a category, e.g., "wood" and not "3-corner") the one object of seven that was the specific target of the search; and (c) information that designated (in the form of a different category label, e.g., color, rather than shape or material) the particular category from which the response should be chosen. To respond correctly, Alex would have to process each piece of information without error, then recognize and encode as a vocal label (e.g., "blue") the information about the appropriate instance of the targeted category. Some or all of these behaviors likely occur as separate (and thus recursive) steps, with each step adding to the complexity of the task (see Premack, 1983).

To ensure that factors other than Alex's understanding of the task would not affect his performance, we took the following precautions. So that the tray on which the exemplars were placed would not become associated solely with the comprehension task, the tray was covered in the same green felt that had been used for the studies on numerical concepts (Pepperberg, 1987b) and object permanence (Pepperberg & Kozak, 1986). The number of items on the tray also varied between two and seven, and we continued to ask questions of "How many?" as well as questions as to the colors and shapes of specific exemplars and the materials of particular colored or shaped exemplars. We also included training on more complicated tasks (e.g., "What color is the 4-corner metal key?") for subsequent studies. We recorded which objects were included in each training trial so that neither the same collection nor the same question would be asked during testing. And, so that Alex could not tell which of the four comprehension questions was to be asked from the composition of objects on the tray, such trials all contained seven objects, including shape trials for which there were only five labelable choices. During testing, chance was (conservatively) calculated on the number of possible labelable choices, not the number of objects or all the possible vocalizations that Alex could produce, which would have given a value for chance of about 1/100. Note that all

11. Cognition and Communication in a Parrot

utterances, other than his requests for information or for other objects, were recorded during testing (discussed later). Furthermore, all trials had some objects that varied in both color and shape even if only one of these categories was being targeted. Finally, to ensure that this task would not be associated with specific trainers, students who were examiners for other tasks were used as trainers for this task.

BEHAVIORS DURING TRAINING

Alex does on occasion react to novel situations with behaviors that can, when integrated into our procedures, serve to facilitate training or, alternatively, must be accommodated if training is to proceed smoothly. For example, when Alex was learning to identify either the color or shape of a given exemplar (e.g., a green wooden square; Pepperberg, 1983), his most common error on preliminary trials was to produce markers for both attributes. He appeared not to be attending to our specific questions of "What color?" or "What shape?" but to be responding instead as if we had asked the more customary "What's this?" Training in that study thus emphasized the content of the specific questions being posed. During that study we also realized that Alex would be most attentive if training sessions were interspersed with other activities (see also Pepperberg, 1987b, 1987c; 1988a). To determine the possible behavioral constraints for learning the recursion task, we therefore conducted, at widespread (1-2 week) intervals, three probe trials before we began formal training. These three trials constituted a pretest identical in form to the recursive task we would ultimately use in the study.

Alex's first responses to each of the probes were correct, which suggested that there were no behavioral constraints to prevent him from learning the procedure very quickly and that protracted training might not be necessary. Accurate responses to three trials did not, however, provide a strong enough rationale to eliminate the training step, and we initiated formal training in November 1986.

Despite his perfect responses on the feasibility probes, Alex's accuracy decreased considerably after we began the formal training. The reasons for this decrease, however, appeared to be behavioral and unrelated to his comprehension of the task: He would (a) label and grab favored objects before we asked questions, or (b) respond to many questions with either the label "green" (while pulling at the green wool tray liner) or "tray" (while biting at the tray itself). These utterances had to be counted as errors, but they were not directly related to his comprehension of the task. To ensure that such factors would not interfere with further training, we determined the causes for such behaviors and developed appropriate counterstrategies.

We knew from other studies that Alex often engaged in such behaviors when tasks involved series of similar questions or familiar exemplars (Pepperberg, 1987a, 1987b). During previous studies, when familiar objects were repeatedly used as rewards, Alex ceased to work, began to preen, or interrupted with many successive requests for other items ("I want X") or changes of location ("Wanna go Y"; see Pepperberg, 1983, 1987b, 1987c, 1988a, 1988b). Similar "boredom" behavior has been observed in other animal subjects (Davis, 1984; Davis & Bradford, 1986; Moran, Joch, & Sorenson, 1983; Putney, 1985).

Our earlier studies had also shown that introducing novel objects would serve to refocus Alex's attention, but such a procedure was not possible for the present set of experiments. During the study on same/different, for example, the length of time Alex would attend to exemplars increased and his accuracy improved on transfer trials, which by definition incorporated novel (i.e., conceivably more interesting) exemplars (Pepperberg, 1987c). But in the recursion study, although the combination of exemplar features for each task had to be novel, the exemplars themselves had to be of familiar colors, shapes, and materials because Alex had to be able to label and comprehend the labels for all their attributes. Note that training labels for new attributes (e.g., pink) would have confounded other concurrent studies (e.g., Pepperberg, 1987b, 1987c) for which we needed attributes that Alex could not label.

Rather than altering the set of exemplars, we adjusted our protocols in three ways. First, we continued to intersperse recursion trials among other training and testing tasks. Second, we emphasized, through our modeling procedure, that a correct response would allow Alex not only to obtain the object he had identified, but also to request any additional favored exemplar or activity (e.g., "I want cork," "You tickle me," as already described; also see Pepperberg, 1988b). Third, we altered the syntactic form of our questions in any given trial to provide additional novelty; for example, we would alternate "Alex, what color is the key?" with "Key, Alex, what color?"

Altering the syntax of the questions may have affected the results of this study in other ways. For example, such alterations would have prevented Alex from using word order to assist his comprehension. Furthermore, exchanging the order of the categories and labels may have avoided both proactive and retroactive interference effects, where the information in the first

11. Cognition and Communication in a Parrot

label or category could interfere with that of the second, and vice versa. In some comprehension studies on marine mammals, for example, retroactive interference effects were observed when sentence meaning was affected by word order (e.g., Schusterman & Gisiner, 1988; Schusterman et al., 1988).

TESTING PROCEDURES

We initiated formal testing when our training techniques successfully eliminated the interruptive behaviors just described-that is, when Alex's responses on three consecutive sessions did not include irrelevant vocalizations of "tray," "green," or his grabbing of preferred items before testing began. He reached this criterion in February 1987. We subsequently included a single comprehension question in his tests, which included queries on all topics that had been studied to date (discussed later). Test sessions were held one to four times per week, and formal comprehension testing was completed at the end of December 1987.

Although details of the procedure are available elsewhere (Pepperberg, 1990a), it is worthwhile to emphasize how the test protocol avoided trainer-induced cuing. First, the design prevented either Alex or the examiners from predicting which questions (or answers) would appear on a given day. Tests included only one question on each possible topic under examination (e.g., "What's this?", "What color?", "What shape?", "What's same?", "How many?", "What's blue?", or "What color is the key?"), and test questions were randomly ordered by a student not involved in testing.[2] Test questions were then presented intermittently during training sessions on current (and thus unrelated) topics over the course of several days. Thus the opportunity for a particular object (or collection of objects) in any series to be tested might occur only once per week. Consequently, a response of "gree" would not inadvertently be accepted for "three," which might happen if all the responses were expected to be numerical. Second, because the seven objects in the comprehension trials were less than 2 in. apart on a 12-in. tray, the parrot could not be cued with eye

---

[2]When testing involved only object identification, each exemplar to be identified was assigned a number and the test order was determined by a random number table. When the number of exemplars exceeded 10, a trainer not involved in testing picked the exemplars out of the toy box and wrote down the order of her choice. In the present study and in those of numerical concepts and same/different (Pepperberg, 1987b, 1987c, 1988a), all the test questions were listed on a page, the list itself was covered, and a trainer other than the examiner randomly ordered the list.

gaze. (Trainers, for example, could not cue each other in a trial in which one student presented a tray to another with the question "What color is the bleep?") Third, to further lessen the possibility of trainer-induced cuing, only those students who had not trained Alex on the comprehension task conducted tests (Pepperberg, 1981).

Using multiple-topic tests and intermingling test and training sessions had several advantages other than preventing trainer-induced cuing. Such procedures also ensured that Alex was never tested exclusively on a single topic (e.g., number labels) in one session, nor tested successively in one session on the same question ("What's same?") or questions that would have one particular correct response (e.g., "color"). These procedures thus not only increased the complexity of the task, but ensured that our results were unaffected by "expectation cuing": Questions having a relatively restricted range of answers could enable a subject to perform somewhat better than would otherwise be justified by its actual knowledge of the topic (see Pepperberg, 1983). A question would be repeated in a session if Alex's initial answer was incorrect, or if he requested another object or other information (Pepperberg, 1981, 1983, 1987a, 1987b, 1987c, 1988a).

The number of times a collection was presented to Alex was therefore related to his accuracy, which was determined as follows: When the secondary trainer questioned the bird, the principal trainer was present, but sat in a corner of the room. The principal trainer had her back to Alex during presentation of the test objects, and therefore did not know what was being presented. The secondary trainer asked the question. Alex responded, and the principal trainer repeated what she heard him say. If that was the correct response (the appropriate label), then Alex was praised and given the object to which the question referred or was allowed to request an alternative. There were then no additional presentations of the same material during that test; that is, there was only a single, first-trial response. If the identification was incorrect or indistinct, the examiner removed the tray of objects, turned his/her head, and emphatically said "No!" The test materials were then immediately repeatedly presented until a correct identification was made; errors were recorded and scored as discussed later.

Alex thus found, and appeared to learn, that an incorrect identification (including substitution of the name of a more desired object for the one presented) was fruitless; instead, a quick, correct identification allowed him to request and obtain the preferred item. Because immediately repeated presentation of an object or collection of objects during a test occurred when the response to the initial presentation was incorrect, the testing protocol penalized use of a "win-stay" strategy: Repetition of a previously correct response (e.g., the name of the previous exemplar) elicited no reward (Pepperberg, 1981).

Occasionally it was the examiner who stood corrected. In about 1 in 20 trials (particularly during student exam periods), an examiner would err and scold Alex for a correct response. Alex would repeat his correct response, despite our procedures, which encouraged a lose-shift strategy. The examiner would then recognize her error, and the bird would get his reward. Note that although this is not a formal blind test, it produced the same results.[3]

RESULTS AND DISCUSSION

Alex's scores on the four questions involving recursion ("What color is object-X?", "What shape is object-Y?", "What object is color-A?", or "What object is shape-B?") averaged better than 80%. His accuracy was apparent whether our calculations were based on the percentage of first trials that were correct (39 of 48 trials; 81.3%) or on the percentage obtained by dividing the total number of correct identifications (i.e., the predetermined number of questions) by the total number of presentations required (48 of 57 trials; 84.2%). (The latter score is higher because he was always correct after an initial error.) Because chance values for the binomial tests differed with respect to the topic of the question—1/7 for color questions and 1/5 for shape questions—scores were also calculated and found significant (p values for first presentations < .0001) with respect to the topic of the question: Alex's responses for first trials and all trials, respectively, for questions concerning color were 75.0% and 80.0%, and for questions concerning shape, 87.5% and 88.9%. The chance values of 1/5 and 1/7 were conservative in that they were based on the number of possible responses to the targeted category (rather than to all categories) and they ignored the possibility that Alex could have produced any of his labels (e.g., those for objects not on the tray or for food items, which were never included in a test). The value of 1/5 was used for shape trials even though there were seven objects because the number of possible responses with respect to shape was five (see Herman, Richards, & Wolz, 1984; Schusterman & Gisiner, 1988, for

---

[3]Other forms of blind tests have also been performed: Alex has several idiosyncratic labels for objects ("banerry" for apple, "truck" for toy metallic cars, "rock corn" for dried corn, "wheat" for cereal, "cork nut" for almond). People unfamiliar with Alex and with these labels have queried him on these objects; he was correct on 5/6 first trials.

discussions on appropriate values for chance). Scores were also calculated for the individual questions ($p < .001$, Figure 11.1); a complete list of these questions and Alex's responses can be found elsewhere (Pepperberg, 1990a).

Not only was Alex's overall accuracy quite high, but even his errors demonstrated some degree of higher order cognitive processing. For all but 1 of the 48 questions ("What shape is hide?", for which he gave the appropriate color), the first single label that he uttered was always that of the appropriate category, whether or not it was the correct instance of that category. Such a response pattern demonstrated that he was likely choosing appropriately—from among all the possible subsets of information—the category to which he should attend. All other responses he produced were not single labels, but rather were phrases: either repetitions of parts of our questions (e.g., "What color?") or requests for other objects or actions (e.g., "I want X"; see Pepperberg, 1987b, 1987c, 1988b), and were not scored as identification errors (see discussion in Pepperberg, 1988b).

The types of errors that Alex made not only suggested that he was using some form of cognitive processing, but might also tell us something about the specific processes involved. Errors in the task he was given could have arisen from three sources. First, errors might arise from confusion of labels that sound very much alike. Second, errors might have come from Alex's misunderstanding of the labels that directed the targeted search. Third, errors might have occurred if Alex had correctly selected the object of the search, but then mislabeled the attribute in question.

Of the nine errors, four likely involved some level of phonological misprocessing. These errors involved either comprehension or production of labels that, at least to humans, sound very similar. On one question, for example, Alex replied with the color of the "rock" (a Playdoh form) instead of that of the wooden "block". Similarly, his initial production of "box" was "bock," which may explain his confounding of "box" and "rock" in two other questions ("What object is blue?", targeted once for the rock and once for the box). Although "grey" and "green" may not sound very much alike in standard American English, Alex will sometimes produce "gree" instead of "green" in a manner that might be mistaken for "grey." By our criteria (Pepperberg, 1981), such a response will always be counted incorrect, and was the source of another error. Thus, about half of the errors—and somewhat less than 9% of the total responses—could be attributed to possible problems with phonological processing (both for the trainers and Alex), rather than cognition. This type of confusion is significant and not unexpected, because it demonstrates that Alex is

11. Cognition and Communication in a Parrot

interpreting acoustic cues in an orderly manner, possibly with respect to the lengths of the formants and the speaking rates of his trainers. These findings are similar to those seen for humans (note Lieberman & Blumstein, 1988; Miller, 1981).

Errors that arose from the second and third sources could not easily be distinguished by the protocol of our task. Thus, if the question was "What color is the wood?" and Alex said the wrong color, he could have understood both "color" and "wood" and mislabeled its color, or correctly identified the color of a different object. (As noted above, only one of his errors was outside of the targeted category, so that the category label was not a likely source of confusion. And, because we altered the syntactic form of our questions, word order was not likely to have caused either proactive or retroactive interference.) Our previous data, however, suggest that the errors were (except for the block-rock-box confound) likely to be mislabeling an attribute after he had correctly targeted the exemplar: Alex's accuracy in labeling attributes (color, shape, or material) of individually presented objects averages about 80% (Pepperberg, 1987a, 1990b), and he therefore had to be close to 100% on comprehending the label of the target to maintain his present comparable score.

CONCLUDING REMARKS

The data from this study provided evidence that Alex did comprehend the labels in his repertoire and that he was indeed capable of performing a task that involved some form of recursive processing. The results thus demonstrate certain similarities in abilities between at least one avian subject and other animals. The implications of such research are, however, considerably broader. The data suggest intriguing possibilities for future studies and, in particular, how interspecies communication can be a tool for evaluating and comparing further the cognitive abilities of various animals.

It is not difficult to suggest the more obvious studies in which interspecies communication could play a facilitatory role. One could, for example, test whether a parrot can exhibit symbolic comprehension comparable to that of some of the language-trained marine mammals; such a study is, in fact, already in progress. Preliminary work shows that Alex may be capable of responding to recursive questions that involve combinations of modifier and object labels. He has, for example, successfully replied to 17 of 21 questions such as "What shape is the green wood?" or "What color is the 3-corner paper?" Such tasks, because they require not only recursive competence but also the ability to define an object by the conjunction of two features (see footnote 1),

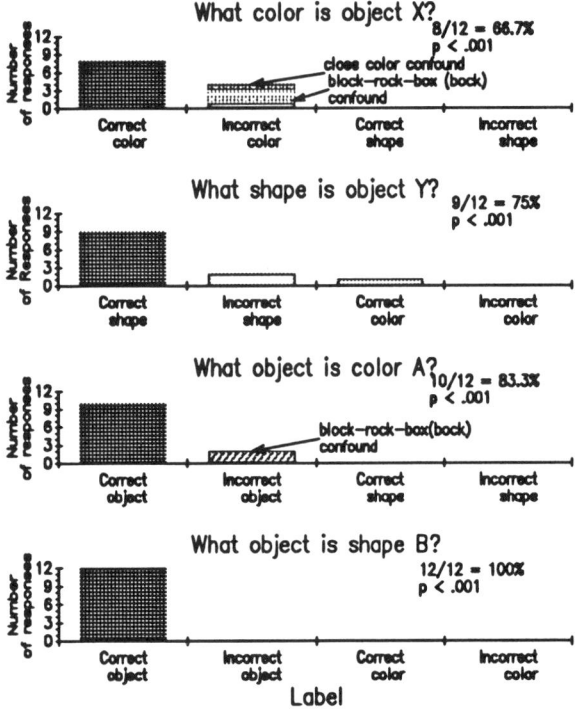

Figure 11.1. (a) Alex's responses to questions about the color of one of seven exemplars placed on a tray. Each exemplar is a different color, and the targeted exemplar is uniquely designated by its object or material label (e.g., "key" or "wood"). Chance is 1/7, based on the number of possible color responses. One error was a response of "gree" (a vocalization that sounds halfway between "green" and "grey") when the correct response was "grey". In another question, he gave the color of the "rock" rather than that of the "block". (b) Alex's responses to questions about the shape of one of seven exemplars placed on a tray. Each exemplar is a different shape, and the targeted exemplar is uniquely designated by its object or material label (e.g., "key" or "wood"). Chance is 1/5, based on the number of possible shape responses, even though there are seven objects present. Once Alex erred by providing the color, rather than the shape label.

- 238 -

11. Cognition and Communication in a Parrot

demand that the subject exhibit a more advanced overall capacity for comprehension than has been shown here (see discussions in Granier-Deferre & Kodratoff, 1986; and Herman, 1987, on conjunction and recursive tasks).

Other investigations might involve demonstrating that marine mammals and parrots can achieve levels of cognitive processing comparable to those already exhibited by the great apes. Only a single study exists, for example, that examines the ability of nonprimate species on tasks related to transitive inference or analogic reasoning (e.g., von Fersen, Wynne, Delius, & Staddon, 1991; see Premack, 1986). Nor have researchers as yet investigated fully the numerical abilities of nonprimates, such as their capacity to both sum and label a summed quantity (see Boysen & Berntson, 1989).

Whether nonprimate subjects can succeed on such tasks is not the real issue. Nor is it important that techniques could be developed to allow such studies to be conducted with animals who have not received language-like training. Rather, what is important is that two-way communication can facilitate such studies if researchers move beyond using interspecies communication for comparisons of human and nonhuman linguistic abilities and the debates that such comparisons engender. Variability in experimental design may limit our capacity to investigate linguistic comparisons, but data from studies using animal-human communication can potentially provide comparable information

---

Figure 11.1. (cont.) To two other questions, he responded with the wrong shape. (c) Alex's responses to questions about the material or object label of one of seven exemplars. Each exemplar is of a different material or has a unique label ("block"), and the targeted exemplar is designated by its unique color. Chance is 1/7, based on the number of different colored objects. Alex's two errors appear to be confounds of the labels "box" and "rock": Once he responded with "box" when the answer to "What object is blue?" is "rock," and once (to the same question) with "rock" when the answer is "box". (d) Alex's responses to questions about the material or object label of one of seven exemplars. Each exemplar is of a different material or has a unique label ("truck"), and the targeted exemplar is designated by its unique shape. Chance is 1/5, based on the number of different shaped objects for which Alex has labels. He made no errors.

on cognitive processing because all such studies are based on a similar (human) code. In sum, we must focus on the opportunity that interspecies communication provides to develop procedures that will allow us to examine and compare the bases of cognitive processing and representation for various species.

By arguing that interspecies communication ought to be used as a tool for studying comparative cognitive rather than linguistic processes, I may seem to have ignored some alternative, equally viable goals. Some researchers, for example, suggest that the study of animal communication—and, particularly, the extent to which animals can learn and use human codes—may also provide insights into the evolutionary precursors of human language (e.g., Griffin, 1985). I believe, however, that insights into the precursors of human language are more likely to come from studying how animals use their codes in their natural habitat than from attempts to teach them elements of a human code in an artificial laboratory environment (see Premack, 1986; Roitblat, 1987). Given that evolution essentially involves "the control of development by ecology" (Van Valen, 1976: p. 180)—how habitat does or does not favor certain adaptations—there are only a few cases in which it makes sense to study a process outside of its natural milieu; for example, when the goal is to examine which aspects of the ecology can individually exert this control. Thus, although the extent to which animals acquire a human code can provide truly valuable insights into the extent to which their natural abilities can be channeled in a particular direction (Savage-Rumbaugh, Sevcik, Hopkins, & Rubert, 1986; cf. Premack, 1983), such a measure is as much one of underlying cognitive capacity as of linguistic competence. Using a human-based code to examine cognitive abilities that can be used for linguistic as well as other behaviors, rather than the linguistic capacities themselves, thus seems the more fruitful approach.

ACKNOWLEDGMENTS

This research was supported by NSF Grants BNS 84-14483, 86- 16955, and the NSF Research Experiences for Undergraduates Program. Preparation of this chapter was supported by NSF grant BNS 88-20098. I thank Katherine Dunsmore Brese, Denise Neapolitan, Kathryn Spangler, Laura O'Brien, Daniel Rutledge, Dorianne Conn, and especially Nada Wolff for their assistance as secondary trainers. Gordon Gallup, Donald Kroodsma, Anthony Wright, Robyn Bright, Paul Nachtigall, Herbert Roitblat, and two reviewers for the *Journal of Comparative Psychology* provided valuable comments on earlier versions of this material.

REFERENCES

Baptista, L. F., & Petrinovich, L. (1984). Social interaction, sensitive phases, and the song template hypothesis in the white-crowned sparrow. *Animal Behaviour*, 32, 172-181.

Boysen, S. T., & Berntson, G. G. (1989). Numerical competence in a chimpanzee (*Pan troglodytes*). *Journal of Comparative Psychology*, 103, 23-31.

Case, R. (1985). *Intellectual development: Birth to adulthood*. New York: Academic Press.

Cheney, D. L., & Seyfarth, R. M. (1985) Social and non-social knowledge in vervet monkeys. In L. Weiskrantz (Ed.), *Animal intelligence* (pp. 187-201). Oxford: Clarendon Press.

Davis, H. (1984). Discrimination of the number three by a raccoon (*Procyon lotor*). *Animal Learning & Behavior*, 4, 121-124.

Davis, H., & Bradford, S. A. (1986). Counting behavior in rats in a simulated natural environment. *Ethology*, 73, 265-280.

Essock, S. M., Gill, T. V., & Rumbaugh, D. M. (1977). Language relevant object- and color-naming tasks. In D. M. Rumbaugh (Ed.), *Language learning by a chimpanzee* (pp. 193-206). New York: Academic Press.

von Fersen, L., Wynne, C. D. L., Delius, J. D., & Staddon, J. E. R. (1991). Transitive inference formation in pigeons. *Journal of Experimental Psychology: Animal Behavior Processes*, 17, 334-341.

Gardner, B. T., & Gardner, R. A. (1984). A vocabulary test for chimpanzees. *Journal of Comparative Psychology*, 98, 381-404.

Gardner, R. A., & Gardner, B. T. (1978). Comparative psychology and language acquisition. In K. Salzinger & F.L. Denmark (Eds.), *Psychology: the state of the art* (pp. 37-76). New York: New York Academy of Sciences.

Granier-Deferre, C. & Kodratoff, Y. (1986). Iterative and recursive behaviors in chimpanzees during problem solving: A new descriptive model inspired from the artificial intelligence approach. *Cahiers de Psychologie Cognitive*, 6, 483-500.

Greenfield, P. M. (1978). Developmental processes in the language learning of child and chimp. *Behavioral and Brain Sciences*, 4, 573-574.

Greenfield, P. M., & Savage-Rumbaugh, E. S. (1984). Perceived variability and symbol use: A common language-cognition interface in children and chimpanzees (*Pan troglodytes*). *Journal of Comparative Psychology*, 98, 201-218.

Griffin, D. R. (1985). The cognitive dimensions of animal communication. In B. Holldobler & M. Lindauer (Eds.), *Experimental behavioral ecology and sociobiology* (pp. 471-482). New York: Fischer-Verlag.

Hearst, E. (1984). Absence as information: some implications for learning, performance, and representational processes. In H. L. Roitblat, T. G. Bever, & H. S. Terrace (Eds.), *Animal cognition* (pp. 311-332). Hillsdale, NJ: Lawrence Erlbaum Associates.

Herman, L. M. (1980). Cognitive characteristics of dolphins. In L. Herman (Ed.), *Cetacean behavior: Mechanisms and functions* (pp. 363-430). New York: Wiley.

Herman, L. M. (1987). Receptive competencies of language-trained animals. In J. S. Rosenblatt, C. Beer, M-C. Busnel, & P.J.B. Slater (Eds.), *Advances in the study of behavior*, (Vol. 17, pp. 1-60). New York: Academic Press.

Herman, L. M. (1988). The language of animal language research: A reply to Schusterman and Gisiner. *Psychological Record*, 38, 349-362.

Herman, L. M. (1989). In which Procrustean bed does the sea lion sleep tonight? *Psychological Record*, 39, 19-50.

Herman, L. M., & Forestell, P. H. (1985). Reporting on the presence or absence of named objects by a language-trained dolphin. *Neuroscience and Biobehavioral Reviews*, 9, 667-681.

11. Cognition and Communication in a Parrot

Herman, L. M., Richards, D. G., & Wolz, J. P. (1984). Comprehension of sentences by bottlenosed dolphins. *Cognition*, 16, 129-219.

Kamil, A. C. (1984). Adaptation and cognition: Knowing what comes naturally. In H. L. Roitblat, T. G. Bever, & H. S. Terrace (Eds.), *Animal cognition* (pp. 533-544). Hillsdale, NJ: Lawrence Erlbaum Associates.

Kamil, A. C. (1988). A synthetic approach to the study of animal intelligence. In D.W. Leger (Ed.), *Nebraska symposium on motivation: comparative perspectives in modern psychology*, Vol. 35 (pp. 257-308). Lincoln, NB: University of Nebraska Press.

Langley, C., & Riley, D. A. (1988). *Feature versus conjunctive search in pigeons.* Paper presented at the annual meeting of the Psychonomic Society, Chicago.

Lieberman, P., & Blumstein, S. E. (1988). *Speech physiology, speech perception, and acoustic phonetics.* Cambridge: Cambridge University Press.

Mandler, J. M. (1990). A new perspective on cognitive development in infancy. *American Scientist*, 78, 236-243.

Matsuzawa, T. (1985). Use of numbers by a chimpanzee. *Nature*, 315, 57-59.

Menzel, E. W., Jr., & Juno, C. (1985). Social foraging in marmoset monkeys and the question of intelligence. In L. Weiskrantz (Ed.), *Animal intelligence* (pp. 145-157). Oxford: Clarendon Press.

Miles, H. L. (1983). Apes and language. In J. de Luce & H.T. Wilder (Eds.), *Language in primates* (pp. 43-61). New York: Springer-Verlag.

Miller, J. L. (1981). Effects of speaking rate on segmental distinctions. In P. D. Eimas & J.L. Miller (Eds.), *Perspectives on the study of speech* (pp. 39-74). Hillsdale, NJ: Lawrence Erlbaum Associates.

Moran, G., Joch, E., & Sorenson, L. (1983). *The response of meerkats (Suricata suricatta) to changes in olfactory cues on established scent posts.* Paper presented at the annual meeting of the Animal Behavior Society, Lewisburg, PA.

Nelson, K. (1987). What's in a name? Reply to Seidenberg and Petitto. *Journal of Experimental Psychology: General*, 116, 293-296.

Newman, J., Wolff, W. T., & Hearst, E. (1980). The feature-positive effect in adult human subjects. *Journal of Experimental Psychology: Human Learning and Memory*, 6, 630-650.

Pepperberg, I. M. (1978). *Object identification by an African Grey parrot (Psittacus erithacus)*. Paper presented at the midwestern meeting of the Animal Behavior Society, W. Lafayette, IN.

Pepperberg, I. M. (1981). Functional vocalizations by an African Grey parrot (*Psittacus erithacus*). *Zeitschrift fur Tierpsychologie*, 55, 139-160.

Pepperberg, I. M. (1983). Cognition in the African Grey parrot: Preliminary evidence for auditory/vocal comprehension of the class concept. *Animal Learning & Behavior*, 11, 179-185.

Pepperberg, I. M. (1985). Social modeling theory: A possible framework for understanding avian vocal learning. *Auk*, 102, 854-864.

Pepperberg, I. M. (1986). Acquisition of anomalous communicatory systems: Implications for studies on interspecies communication. In R. J. Schusterman, J.A. Thomas, & F.G. Wood (Eds.), *Dolphin cognition and behavior: A comparative approach* (pp. 289-302). Hillsdale, NJ: Lawrence Erlbaum Associates.

Pepperberg, I. M. (1987a). Interspecies communication: A tool for assessing conceptual abilities in the African Grey parrot (*Psittacus erithacus*). In G. Greenberg & E. Tobach (Eds.), *Language, cognition and consciousness: Integrative levels* (pp. 31-56). Hillsdale, NJ: Lawrence Erlbaum Associates.

Pepperberg, I. M. (1987b). Evidence for conceptual quantitative abilities in the African Grey parrot: Labeling of cardinal sets. *Ethology*, 75, 37-61.

Pepperberg, I. M. (1987c). Acquisition of the same/different concept by an African Grey parrot (*Psittacus erithacus*): Learning with respect to color, shape, and material. *Animal Learning & Behavior*, 15, 423-432.

11. Cognition and Communication in a Parrot

Pepperberg, I. M. (1988a). Comprehension of "absence" by an African Grey parrot: Learning with respect to questions of same/different. *Journal of the Experimental Analysis of Behavior*, 50, 553-564.

Pepperberg, I. M. (1988b). An interactive modeling technique for acquisition of communication skills: Separation of "labeling" and "requesting" in a psittacine subject. *Applied Psycholinguistics*, 9, 31-56.

Pepperberg, I. M. (1990a). Cognition in an African Grey parrot (*Psittacus erithacus*): Further evidence for comprehension of categories and labels. *Journal of Comparative Psychology*, 104, 41-52.

Pepperberg, I. M. (1990b). Referential mapping: A technique for attaching functional significance to the innovative utterances of an African Grey parrot. *Applied Psycholinguistics*, 11, 23-44.

Pepperberg, I. M. (1990c). Some cognitive capacities of an African Grey parrot (*Psittacus erithacus*). In P. J. B. Slater, J. S. Rosenblatt, C. Beer, & M. Milinski (Eds.), *Advances in the study of behavior*, Vol. 19. New York: Academic Press.

Pepperberg, I. M. (1991). A communicative approach to animal cognition: A study of the conceptual abilities of an African Grey parrot. In C. Ristau (Ed.), *Cognitive ethology: the minds of other animals* (pp. 153-186), Hillsdale, NJ: Lawrence Erlbaum Associates.

Pepperberg, I. M., & Funk, M. (1990). Object permanence in four species of psittacine birds: an African Grey parrot (*Psittacus erithacus*), an Illiger macaw (*Ara maracana*), a parakeet (*Melopsittacus undulatus*), and a cockatiel (*Nymphus hollandicus*). *Animal Learning & Behavior*, 18, 97-108.

Pepperberg, I. M., & Kozak, F. A. (1986). Object permanence in the African Grey parrot (*Psittacus erithacus*). *Animal Learning & Behavior*, 14, 322-330.

Petrinovich, L., & Baptista, L. F. (1987). Song development in the white-crowned sparrow: Modification of learned song. *Animal Behaviour*, 35, 961-974.

Petrinovich, L., & Patterson, T. L. (1979). Field studies of habituation: I. The effects of reproductive condition, number of trials, and different delay intervals on the responses of the white-crowned sparrow. *Journal of Comparative and Physiological Psychology*, 93, 337-350.

Premack, D. (1976). *Intelligence in ape and man*. Hillsdale, NJ: Lawrence Erlbaum Associates.

Premack, D. (1983). The codes of man and beast. *Behavioral and Brain Sciences*, 6, 125-176.

Premack, D. (1986). *Gavagai! or the future history of the animal language controversy*. Cambridge, MA: Bradford Books, MIT Press.

Putney, R. T. (1985). Do willful apes know what they are aiming at? *Psychological Record*, 35, 49-62.

Rogoff, B. (1990). *Apprenticeship in thinking: Cognitive development in a social context*. Oxford: Oxford University Press.

Roitblat, H. L. (1984). Representations in pigeon working memory. In H. L. Roitblat, T. G. Bever, & H. S. Terrace (Eds.), *Animal cognition* (pp. 79-98). Hillsdale, NJ: Lawrence Erlbaum Associates.

Roitblat, H. L. (1987). Metacomparative psychology. *The Behavioral Brain Sciences*, 10, 675-676.

Roitblat, H. L., Bever, T. G., & Terrace, H. S. (Eds.) (1984). *Animal cognition*. Hillsdale, NJ: Lawrence Erlbaum Associates.

Rumbaugh, D. M. (1977). *Language learning by a chimpanzee*. New York: Academic Press.

Savage-Rumbaugh, E. S. (1987). Communication, symbolic communication, and language: Reply to Seidenberg and Petitto. *Journal of Experimental Psychology: General*, 116, 288-292.

Savage-Rumbaugh. E. S., Rumbaugh, D. M., Smith, S. T., & Lawson, J. (1980). Reference: the linguistic essential. *Science*, 210, 922-925.

11. Cognition and Communication in a Parrot

Savage-Rumbaugh, E. S., McDonald, K., Sevcik, R. A., Hopkins, W. D., & Rubert, E. (1986). Spontaneous symbol acquisition and communicative use by pygmy chimpanzees (*Pan paniscus*). *Journal of Experimental Psychology: General*, 115, 211-235.

Schusterman, R. J., & Gisiner, R. (1988). Artificial language comprehension in dolphins and sea lions: the essential cognitive skills. *Psychological Record*, 38, 311-348.

Schusterman, R. J., & Gisiner, R. (1989). Please parse the sentence: Animal cognition in the Procrustean bed of linguistics. *Psychological Record*, 39, 1-18.

Schusterman, R. J., & Krieger, K. (1984). California sea lions are capable of semantic comprehension. *The Psychological Record*, 34, 3-23.

Schusterman, R. J., & Krieger, K. (1986). Artificial language comprehension and size transposition by a California sea lion (*Zalophus californianus*). *Journal of Comparative Psychology*, 100, 348-355.

Schusterman, R. J., Gisiner, R. C., Hanggi, E. B. (1988). *Priming short-term memory on a language task in sea lions*. Paper presented at the annual meeting of the Psychonomic Society, Chicago.

Seidenberg, M. S., & Petitto, L. A. (1987). Communication, symbolic communication, and language: Comment on Savage-Rumbaugh, McDonald, Sevcik, Hopkins, and Rupert (1986). *Journal of Experimental Psychology: General*, 116, 279-287.

Terrace, H. S. (1979). Is problem-solving language? *Journal of the Experimental Analysis of Behavior*, 31, 161-175.

Thomas, R. K. (1980). Evolution of intelligence: An approach to its assessment. *Brain, Behavior, and Evolution*, 17, 454-472.

Todt, D. (1975). Social learning of vocal patterns and modes of their application in Grey parrots. *Zeitschrift fur Tierpsychologie*, 39, 178-188.

Van Valen, L. (1976). Energy and evolution. *Evolutionary Theory*, 1, 179-229.

West, M. J., & King, A. P. (1985). Learning by performing: An ecological theme for the study of vocal learning. In T. D. Johnston & A. T. Pietrewicz (Eds.), *Issues in the ethological study of learning* (pp. 245-272). Hillsdale, NJ: Lawrence Erlbaum Associates.

12 Behavior Control by Exclusion and Attempts at Establishing Semanticity in Marine Mammals Using Match-to-sample Paradigms

Ronald J. Schusterman, Robert Gisiner, Brigit K. Grimm, and Evelyn B. Hanggi

Match-to-sample (MTS) is a sequential "if . . . then" or conditional discrimination. There are several characteristics of the MTS procedure that make it suitable for studying such aspects of animal cognition as short-term memory, perceptual categorization or concept formation, counting, abstraction and some aspects of language, especially semantic comprehension. (For reviews of MTS paradigms as they relate to concept formation, abstraction, and semanticity, see Schusterman & Gisiner, 1989; Sidman & Tailby, 1982; Carter & Werner, 1978.) When visual cues are used in MTS, a sample stimulus is displayed, usually in a central position, equidistant from subsequent choice stimuli. The sample stimulus is followed by comparison or choice stimuli. The comparison stimuli are presented simultaneously on two or more side panels. If the physical characteristics of sample and comparison configurations are different, the relations between these types of stimuli are considered "arbitrary" (Cumming & Berryman, 1965). In animal language research, sample stimuli as well as comparison stimuli may be presented in a variety of ways (Schusterman

& Krieger, 1984). In the original and simplest case, there are two sample stimuli and two comparison stimuli. In this chapter, the two sample stimuli are designated as A_1 and A_2 and two comparison stimuli are designated as B_1 and B_2. Reinforcement contingencies are arranged by the experimenter so that an animal's choice of B_1 is correct and reinforced in the presence of A_1, but not in the presence of A_2, while its selection of B_2 is correct and reinforced in the presence of A_2 but not in the presence of A_1. For example, a monkey may be trained to match a set of geometric figures as samples (A_1 = circle; A_2 = triangle) to pictures of animals as comparisons (B_1 = hawk; B_2 = leopard).

Several investigators have attempted to study semanticity and/or symbolic learning in a variety of animal taxa by using some version or other of a conditional discrimination within an MTS paradigm (for a review, see Roitblat, 1987). Animal language researchers frequently say that samples have a "symbolic" relation to comparison stimuli. However, these animal language researchers have not always explicitly stated what operations in their experiments allowed them to infer that their animal subject was developing a comprehension of anything more than an "if . . . then" relation between the sample or so-called symbol and the corresponding comparison or so-called referent. For example, Savage-Rumbaugh (1988) used a conditional discrimination within an MTS paradigm to determine whether a pygmy chimpanzee (*Pan paniscus*) could differentiate spoken words and relate them to the appropriate geometric figures or lexigrams. The pygmy chimpanzee, Kanzi, had to select by touching one of three lexigrams contingent on the word he heard (produced by a person or by a speech synthesizer) through headphones. Even after Kanzi had learned to match a set of spoken word samples to the corresponding lexigram comparisons, it should not be assumed that his behavior was symbolic and that the spoken words and the geometric forms were symbols. Instead, we should consider that perhaps Kanzi had only learned a conditional relation that has no intrinsic symbolic significance. In this context a determination of whether Kanzi was acting symbolically awaits further testing.

Recently Sidman (in press) and his colleagues (see, e.g., Sidman & Tailby, 1982) have suggested that if stimuli are serving as symbols, then they should be interchangeable or equivalent with the things they designate. That is, in linguistic parlance the symbol and referent should each stand for one another, and in discrimination learning parlance, the conditional-discrimination procedure should have generated equivalence relations. In the monkey example we used earlier, the monkey is trained to match Set-A geometric form samples to Set-B picture comparisons (AB). If the Set-A and corresponding Set-B stimuli are equivalent, then the monkey should be able to do the opposite, that

12. Behavior control by exclusion

is, match Set-B samples to corresponding Set-A comparisons without any additional training. This is called a test of *symmetry*. The new conditional discriminations (BA matching) must emerge without having been explicitly trained. If the conditional relations are not equivalence relations, then the monkey will not pass the test. Failure by the monkey would indicate that the conditional relations between stimulus classes within Sets A and B had not become equivalent, and that conditional relations between geometric forms or lexigrams and pictures of animals had not, as yet, achieved symbolic status. The concept of equivalence relations in general and the test of symmetry in particular are important because they can be applied precisely to behavioral phenomena that appear symbolic. According to Sidman (in press), although it may not be possible to determine which is cause and which is effect, the question of whether verbal behavior is necessary for equivalence relations to emerge would be answered negatively if such relations could be demonstrated unequivocally with nonhuman animals. Distinguishing between truly symbolic animal behavior and animal behavior based on unidirectional stimulus relations may enable animal language researchers to determine the relationship between "naming," "rule governance," and equivalence relations.

Our chapter is divided into two sections. First, we show how animals, once they have learned the original conditional discrimination (if A_1 then B_1 and if A_2 then B_2) with much difficulty, will then consistently select a novel comparison (designated as Y_1) errorlessly or nearly so in the presence of a novel sample (designated as X_1) instead of selecting the familiar or trained comparisons B_1 or B_2. (Trials testing whether an animal is responding appropriately will be designated as X(Y,B) and A(B,Y), with the letter outside the parenthesis representing the sample; the first letter within the parenthesis represents the appropriate comparison and the second letter represents the alternate comparison.) We further show that such behavior probably does not reflect an immediate association between a new signal and an "unnamed" object as has been claimed for dolphins in "language" learning experiments (Herman, Richards, & Wolz, 1984). Rather, selection of novel comparison objects probably depends on control by "exclusion" ("if *not* A_1, then Y_1, etc."). It is only many trials later that the effects of exclusion emerge as a novel conditional performance in contexts where the basis for exclusion is no longer immediately available, for example, when two novel comparison stimuli are available instead of only one. Thus, we propose that what appears to be immediate or errorless learning of an association or a relationship between the novel sample and the novel comparison is not. Rather, the association is learned following choices of the novel comparison by the exclusion principle. First, the animal chooses the novel comparison stimulus because its behavior is controlled by the exclusion

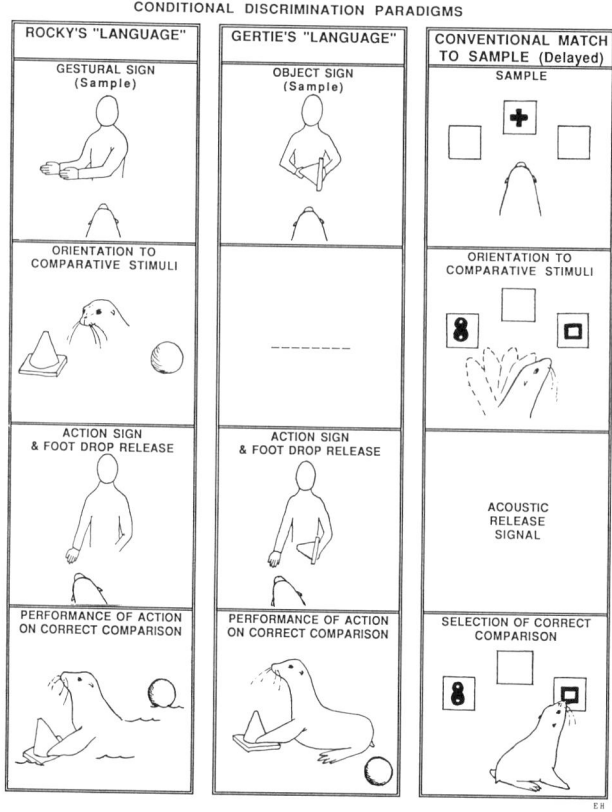

Figure 12.1. Three different types of conditional discrimination paradigms used with sea lions. All paradigms shown begin with presentation of a "symbolic" sample and end with a response to a comparison stimulus.

principle. Then, only after an animal's choices of the novel comparison have been reinforced in the presence of the novel sample, does a relationship develop between the two stimuli. Second, we develop a thought experiment using Sidman's equivalence relations model (1986) to show how a conditional discrimination is an initial stepping stone in developing simple semantic relations (Catania, 1980). In this part of the chapter we apply the idea of stimulus class equivalences to teaching a harbor seal to understand and say human words that refer to real world objects.

12. Behavior control by exclusion

CONTROL BY EXCLUSION

Even large-brained anthropoid apes such as chimpanzees have difficulty learning that sample A_1 and comparison B_1 are paired associates just as sample A_2 and comparison B_2 are paired associates. Learning to relate A_1 to B_1 and A_2 to B_2 invariably takes hundreds or even thousands of trials depending on the specific MTS procedure (e.g., see Nissen, Blum, & Blum, 1948). So it would be quite significant if individuals of a species could consistently form such associations immediately and virtually without error. Herman et al. (1984) reported just that, using bottlenose dolphins (*Tursiops truncatus*) as subjects. Without stating the problem in those terms, these investigators used conditional discriminations within an MTS paradigm to study what they called sentence comprehension. In the case of one dolphin named Akeakamei (or Ake for short), arm/hand gestures served as discriminative stimuli for actions and as sample conditional cues for objects and the location of objects in a pool. One of their many interesting findings was that "It was sometimes sufficient to pair a new signal with an unnamed object for the dolphin to associate the two immediately. Successful association was indicated by the dolphin continuing to respond appropriately to the previously unnamed object in the presence of the new signal and of other objects" (Herman et al., 1984, p. 157). Schusterman and Krieger (1984), using a 6-year-old female California sea lion (*Zalophus californianus*) named Rocky, replicated several aspects of the dolphin study. After requiring 716 trials to relate one gesture (A_1) with the object "pipe" (B_1) and a different gesture (A_2) with the object "ball" (B_2) (see column 1 in Figure 12.1 for an outline of this MTS procedure), Rocky immediately appeared to relate a novel gesture with a novel object (e.g., a "ring") by selecting it consistently instead of selecting either the ball or the pipe. The previously learned relations between the arbitrary gestures for pipe and ball remained intact when each of these old comparison stimuli were paired with each other or with the newer object "ring." In other words, dolphins and sea lions seem to acquire new conditional relations immediately and without error when the available comparison stimulus objects are previously trained ones.

In the next part of this chapter we summarize several experiments that document more completely how dolphins and sea lions might seemingly associate signals or sample stimuli and their "referents" or comparison stimuli immediately and without error.

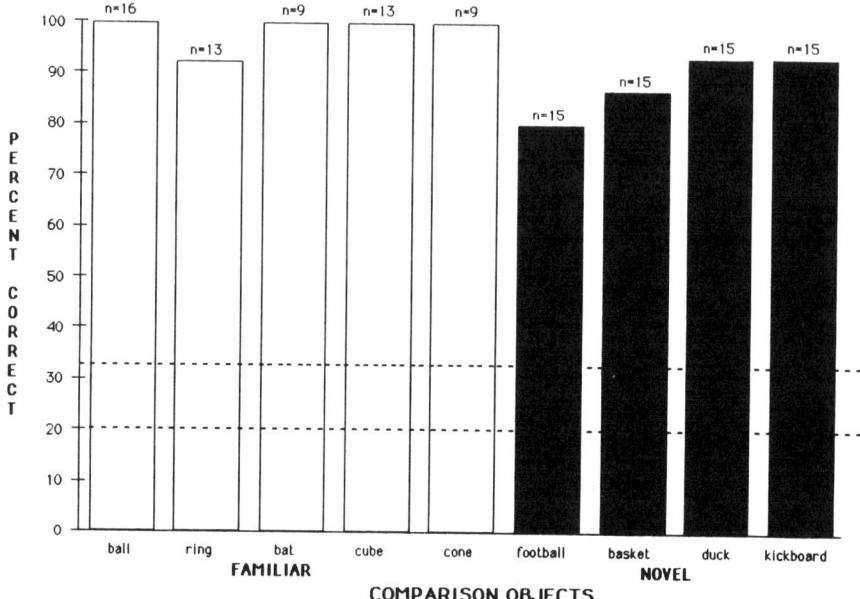

Figure 12.2. Correct choices of familiar and novel objects by Gertie. On each test trial a single novel object was available with several familiar ones. Correct responses were conditional on the object shown to Gertie. The number of MTS trials for each comparison object is displayed above the bars. The parallel dotted lines indicate the range of chance performance based on the number of comparisons available on any given trial.

Rocky's Initial Experiments

Detailed descriptions of the general methods, training procedures and apparatus are given by Schusterman and Krieger (1984, 1986) and Schusterman and Gisiner (1988). Over a period of about 2 years we conducted tests of novel conditional relations with sea lion Rocky within the context of an artificial language comprehension program. In all tests a new sample or gesture was introduced along with a new object. In most tests, the new object was presented with a single previously trained comparison object, and Rocky's task was to

12. Behavior control by exclusion

choose the previously trained comparison following the presentation of its associated or conditional signal and to choose the novel comparison conditionally on the presentation of the new signal. All correct responses were reinforced with a piece of fish. Eleven unique novel signals with their related objects were introduced this way, tested against all other familiar objects resulting in 54 different X(Y,B) combinations and 54 different A(B,Y) combinations. The first eight trials of each combination constituted a test. In order to ensure that both exploratory and fearful motivations toward the novel object were minimized, Rocky was always given a series of habituation trials prior to novel vs. familiar comparison testing when the novel object was first paired with its novel signal. On these habituation trials no object signals were given. Instead, Rocky was signaled to perform one of usually three different actions (FETCH, FLIPPER TOUCH, or MOUTH). Because the novel object was the only one in the pool she performed this action on the novel object. To control for context cues, similar trials were conducted with a trained object and were intermixed with novel object trials. Rocky invariably hesitated to touch novel objects on the first presentation, but after a few reinforced presentations, she performed actions on a novel object as readily as on a familiar or previously trained object.

The first column in Figure 12.1 illustrates the type of MTS task we used to determine whether Rocky selected novel over trained comparison items when the gestural sign was also novel. First she was given the novel object sign, which usually resulted in her orientation to the novel object. After repositioning, Rocky was given an action sign and released from station, which usually resulted in her performing an action on the novel object. Position of the novel and trained comparisons was randomized. Rocky was given an approximately equal number of successive novel X and trained A gestural signals with simultaneously available novel Y and trained B comparisons. She consistently made the correct choice (75% correct on the first eight trials) during 42 of 54 different X(Y,B) (novel correct) and 51 of 54 different A(B,Y) (familiar correct) tests (p's $< .01$, binomial test). Failure to make correct selections of the novel object usually occurred when the novel gesture was given and Rocky had to choose between the most recently trained object and the novel object (10 of 12 cases). This finding suggests that errorless associations between novel gestures and corresponding objects are more apparent than real. Therefore, it seems likely that recently trained objects had not been completely trained, that is, relations between these objects and their signs had not been fully formed.

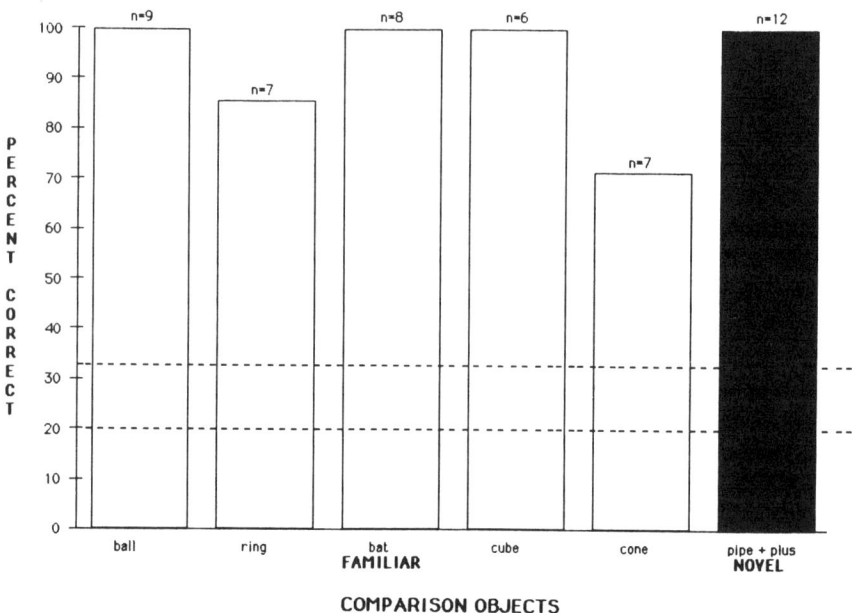

Figure 12.3. Gertie's correct choices of familiar and novel objects "pipe" and "plus" (combined). On each trial both novel comparisons were available along with several familiar ones. Correct responses were conditional on the object shown to Gertie. The number of MTS trials for each comparison object is displayed above the bars. The parallel dotted lines indicate the range of chance performance based on the number of comparisons available on any given trial.

Gertie's Experiments on Novel Paired Associates

Experiment 1. Gertie, a 6-year-old female California sea lion, performed in an MTS procedure which was somewhat different than the procedure used with Rocky. For complete descriptions of this procedure, see Schusterman and Gisiner (1988). Instead of being reinforced for selecting a comparison object conditional on a gestural sign, Gertie was reinforced for choosing an object conditional on being shown a duplicate object (regardless of its orientation). The top panel of column 2 in Figure 12.1 depicts the sample object displayed to

12. Behavior control by exclusion

Figure 12.4. The MTS apparatus for testing sea lions. In the first panel the sea lion views the sample. During simultaneous MTS the comparisons are shown on the side panels four seconds after the sample has been presented. This is shown in the middle panel. In the delay procedure, the sample is hidden before the comparisons are shown. In the last panel the sea lion makes a correct choice following an acoustic release signal.

Gertie. This is followed by a gestural hand signal and a release. The last panel shows Gertie performing the signaled action on the appropriate comparison object.

Following an approximately 3 year artificial language comprehension program (Schusterman & Gisiner, 1988) in which Gertie learned to select eight different object shapes conditionally on being shown similar or different sample objects, we inserted a series of nondifferentially reinforced probe trials of the type X(Y,B) into standard conditional discrimination baseline sessions. We probed with four different novel or untrained objects to which Gertie was first habituated in much the same way as Rocky had been. Although the displayed objects were shown in a variety of orientations or angular planes, the comparisons floated on the surface of the water in the same plane. There were about six probes per day for 10 days superimposed on a baseline of about 60 trials. Each of the four novel objects was tested 15 times with displays of novel X samples, novel Y comparisons, and the previously trained or familiar B comparisons. On any given probe trial there was only one appropriate novel object and from two to four familiar or trained comparison objects.

On the first trial of each type of X(Y,B) probe Gertie selected the correct or novel object (four of four cases). Figure 12.2 shows Gertie's performance on both X(Y,B) probes and familiar A(B,Y) trials. The figure clearly shows that Gertie selected the novel Y comparison when novel X samples were displayed almost as consistently as she selected the familiar or B comparisons when trained A samples were shown. Gertie had some difficulty in finding the football because it was so small and inconspicuous and on several trials she appeared to search for it before selecting one of the available familiar objects. Selection of novel objects was significantly better than chance ($p < .01$, binomial test).

Although it seems unlikely, one could interpret Gertie's immediate selection of novel objects as identity matching, that is, the sea lion had acquired an identity or similarity concept. Another interpretation of her performance is that when *not* presented with an A sample she eliminated the B comparisons and chose the Y comparison by exclusion. Dixon (1977) first proposed the idea that humans might use a rule such as "any stimulus that is correct for spoken word A is incorrect for a different spoken word" (p. 441), and most recently the phenomenon of exclusion has been applied to MTS tasks with severely retarded persons (e.g., McIlvane & Stoddard, 1985). A similar finding from the Russian literature is cited by Slobin (1966), who states that teaching 2-year-old children the names of objects is easiest if the object is a new object among a collection of familiar ones that have already been named. In order to test whether sea lion Gertie was using exclusion or a sameness concept to select novel objects in an MTS procedure we performed another experiment in which two different novel objects served as samples and both were available as comparisons.

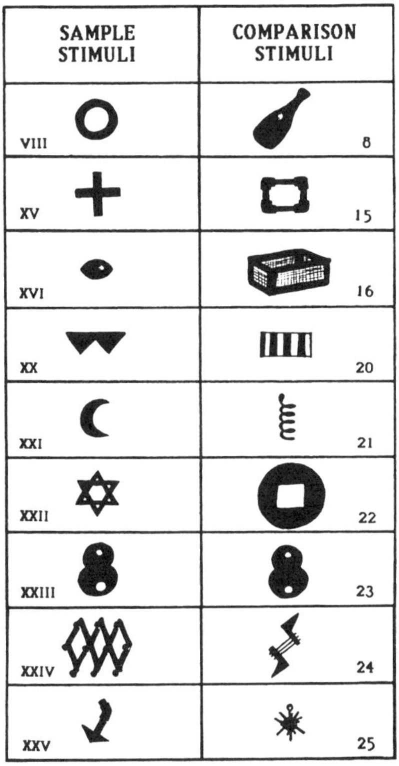

12. Behavior control by exclusion

SAMPLE STIMULI	COMPARISON STIMULI
VIII ○	🥔 8
XV ✚	▢ 15
XVI ●	🗃 16
XX ▼▼	||||| 20
XXI ☾	⟿ 21
XXII ✡	⬤ 22
XXIII 8	8 23
XXIV ⋙	⚡ 24
XXV ↵	✴ 25

Figure 12.5. Representations of sample objects and their related comparisons. Roman numerals refer to sample stimuli and arabic numerals refer to comparison stimuli.

Experiment 2. This experiment was similar in all respects to the previous one except that on X(Y,B) probes two novel object comparisons were available along with from two to four familiar comparisons. Two probes were given each day for 6 days. The "pipe" and "plus" objects, following habituation, were each displayed as samples on six probe trials. On the first "pipe" probe Gertie went to the pipe and on the first "plus" probe she selected the plus. However, thereafter when Gertie was presented with the pipe as a sample she consistently selected the plus and when shown the plus she selected the comparison plus two times and the comparison pipe three times. As Figure 12.3 shows, Gertie selected novel comparisons each time a novel sample was displayed ($p < .01$). However, she showed no indication of identity matching in this MTS context. Figure 12.3 also shows that Gertie selected novel comparisons correctly at a slightly higher level than she selected trained comparisons. The results of this experiment support the idea that Gertie's choice of novel comparison stimuli was based on her exclusion of the trained comparison stimuli. This means that in animal language research when new "names" for objects are added, such conditional cues may not even be used initially. Instead a sea lion, dolphin, or chimpanzee may use exclusion or the process of elimination to select novel objects when given a new "name" or new conditional cue.

More Traditional MTS Experiments

Prior to beginning the following experiments our general procedure of using MTS within the context of artificial language comprehension was to initiate a trial or set of trials by throwing the comparison or "named" objects into the pool before displaying samples consisting of either gestures (Rocky) or an object (Gertie), after which the sea lions were released from station to find and act on the designated object (see Schusterman & Krieger, 1984, 1986; Schusterman & Gisiner, 1988). In order to control display of the sample or conditional cues more precisely, particularly in relation to the presentation of the comparison stimuli, we developed an apparatus and procedure that conformed to more traditional MTS tasks with animals (for a review see Roitblat, 1987). Figure 12.4 shows Rocky working on the MTS task that we currently use for studying "symbolic" learning and memory in California sea lions.

The apparatus is used to test sea lions on land and consists of three hinged wooden boards on casters. The center board is 1.2 X 1.2 m and contains an approximately centered 30-cm-square display box, 10 cm deep for presenting sample objects. The two side boards are 61 cm wide and 1.2 m high and also contain centered 30-cm-square display boxes, 10 cm deep for presenting comparison stimulus objects. During training and testing the side boards are angled about 20o. As can be seen in Figure 12.4, a sea lion can be trained to station its head on or near a headstand about 51 cm high and about 46 cm from the sample display and 76 cm from the comparisons. Stimulus objects like those shown in Figures 12.4 and 12.5 are hung from white cords, which are clipped to the top of hinged lids on the display boxes. The backs of the display boxes are painted flat white and most objects are three dimensional and all are painted flat black. During an intertrial interval (which lasts about 10-15 s) two operators behind the three wooden boards place objects into position while the sliding opaque panels in front of the display boxes remain closed. A trial begins when

12. Behavior control by exclusion

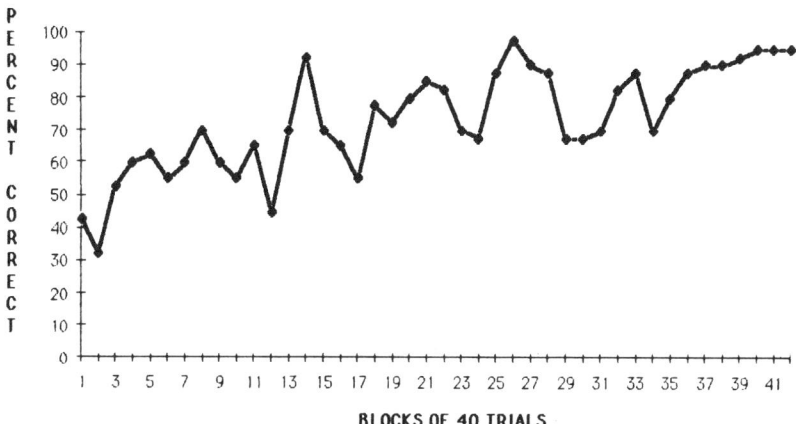

Figure 12.6. Rio's acquisition of the initial conditional discrimination in the MTS apparatus shown in Figure 12.4.

the panel in front of the sample box is slid horizontally to expose the object (see the first panel of Figure 12.4).

Exposure times for the sample were 4 s. In the delay conditions the sample box is closed for a period following the sample presentation. At the end of delay the two side panel doors are opened vertically and simultaneously by means of a pulley system mounted behind the three boards. In the simultaneous condition the sample panel remains open while the panels to the boxes containing the comparison stimuli are opened. As soon as the comparisons stimuli are visually accessible the sea lions orient to them and soon after this are released from station by an electronic acoustic release signal. Release signals are given after a variable delay generally ranging between 2 and 6 s. On release sea lions put their nose into one of the two comparison boxes thereby indicating their choice (see the third column in Figure 12.1 and see the last panel of Figure 12.4). Correct responses are immediately followed by an acoustic tone and then by a piece of fish thrown from behind the boards. Incorrect responses are immediately followed by a "no" signal and are not food reinforced. Note that the sea lions are never required to move toward or in any way overtly respond to

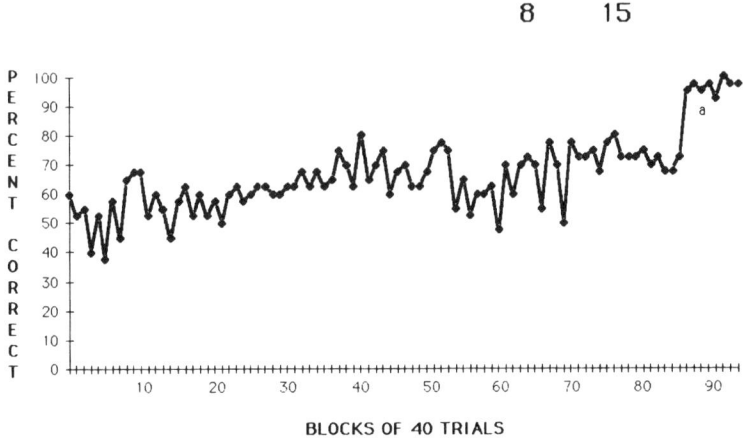

Figure 12.7. Rocky's acquisition of the initial conditional discrimination in the MTS apparatus shown in Figure 12.4.

the sample object (for contrast between our sea lion MTS training and conventional pigeon MTS training see Carter & Werner, 1978).

Experiment 1: Acquisition. A 3-year-old female sea lion, Rio, was first given training on a prototype of the apparatus shown in Figure 12.4. She was trained on an MTS task with two sample stimuli represented by Roman numerals VIII and XV in column 1 of Figure 12.5 and two comparison stimuli represented by Arabic numerals 8 and 15 in column 2 of Figure 12.5. A simultaneous condition was used, but as a variant on the usual MTS sequence, comparison stimuli were presented 4 s before the sample was presented. Using an acquisition criterion of 90% correct choices on two consecutive blocks of 40 daily trials, Rio appeared to learn relations between samples VIII and XV and their paired associate comparisons 8 and 15, respectively, within 1560 trials (see Figure 12.6). During the first 800 trials many different prompts were used, including eliminating position and comparison object preferences.

Rocky was trained to learn relations between sample VIII and comparison 8 and between sample XV and comparison 15 primarily in the apparatus shown in Figure 12.4. During the first 1240 trials the comparison stimuli were displayed before the samples. This sequence was changed

12. Behavior control by exclusion

gradually until a simultaneous condition was instated with the sample shown alone for 4 s and then accompanied by the simultaneous display of the comparisons. Using the same criterion we used with Rio, Rocky appeared to learn the relations between samples VIII and XV and their associated comparisons 8 and 15, respectively, within 3440 trials. Immediately after acquisition Rocky performed the MTS task consistently better than 85% correct responses even with delays of 1-5 s between the disappearance of samples and the appearance of comparisons (see Figure 12.7).

Experiment 2: Introduction of Novel Paired Associates. It appears that, like humans in language comprehension or naming tasks (Dixon, 1977), sea lions, dolphins, and perhaps chimpanzees use an exclusion rule to select novel "referents" in the presence of novel signs. The question we pose here is whether the same phenomenon can be demonstrated in sea lions on more controlled MTS tasks similar to those used to determine whether an exclusion rule controlled the behavior of handicapped teenagers (Stromer, 1986). The importance of taking a comparative perspective on exclusion is twofold. First, if animals use an exclusion principle, then this principle is not likely to be mediated by verbal behavior. Second, if the phenomenon is widespread and better understood, it can be used appropriately to train new conditional relations errorlessly in a variety of animal species for the purposes of studying cognition.

In the experiment, Rio was tested in a simultaneous condition in the apparatus shown in Figure 12.4. The sequence of sample-comparison pairs that was tested beginning with XX-20 and ending with XXIV-24 is seen in Figure 12.5. We should note that unlike the other three pairs, pairs XXII-22 and XXIII-23 were tested on alternate days. Generally, a new paired relation was first tested against the originally acquired conditional relations (VIII-8 and XVI-16), followed by testing against the next trained pair, etc. Test trials were superimposed on a baseline of already trained relations. Thus, Rio's task on test trials could be described as a requirement to choose the novel comparison instead of the trained comparison when a novel sample was displayed and to choose the trained comparison and not the novel one following the presentation of its related sample. All correct responses were reinforced with a piece of fish. Deciding when a sample-comparison became trained, or when the association between the two new stimuli had actually formed, was difficult (discussed later) and usually a novel pair was pitted against a familiar pair for between 400 and 600 trials. Thus, Rio was given between 200 and 300 novel or X(Y,B) trials and an equal number of familiar or A(B,Y) trials. Unlike the MTS task in the artificial language comprehension program, we did not habituate Rio to novel comparisons.

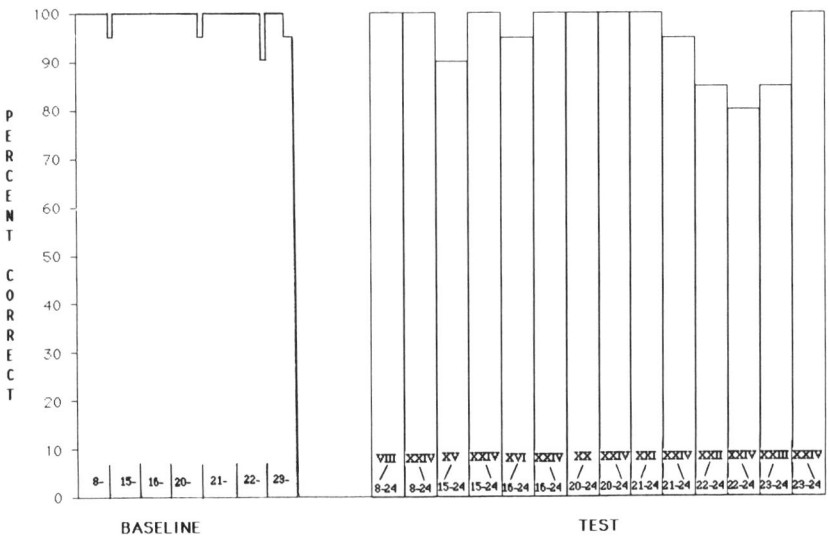

Figure 12.8. Rio's performance on the first 20 trials of novel pairing XXIV and 24. Baseline trials are compressed. Each baseline segment constitutes the percent correct choices and the indicated comparison stimulus or other trained comparisons. Thus, the first segment represents stimulus 8 as compared with all other trained stimuli - - - 15, 16, 20, 21, 22, 23, respectively. Baseline performance is contrasted with test trials where one comparison is novel. Testing stimuli are identified at the bottom of the bars, with a line connecting each sample to its correct paired comparison.

Figure 12.8 shows Rio's performance on the first 20 trials of novel pairing XXIV-24 tested with trained paired associates. Rio's performance on each of the four earlier novel pairings was quite similar to that shown in Figure 12.8. In this figure, performance on trained baseline paired associates is contrasted to performance on test trials when the comparison stimulus was newly introduced. During test trials, when novel relations were pitted against trained ones (i.e., the comparison stimuli consisted of one trained and one untrained or novel object), Rio's performance was nearly as good as that shown

12. Behavior control by exclusion

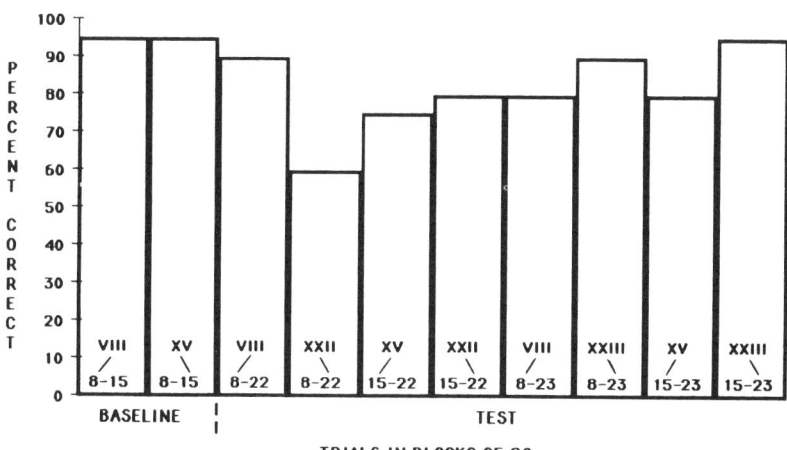

Figure 12.9. Rocky's performance on the first 20 trials of two novel pairings, XXII and 22, and XXIII and 23, tested with trained paired associates. (See Figure 12.8).

on "baseline" when only trained relations were used (i.e., when both comparison stimuli consisted of trained objects). On several of these "novel" conditional discriminations Rio made no errors at all. On the first trial of each unique pairing of novel and trained comparison stimuli, Rio, as expected, chose the novel comparison appropriately on 18 of 26 trials ($p = .05$, binomial test) and chose the trained comparison appropriately on 19 of 24 trials ($p < .01$, binomial test).

The procedures used for testing Rocky on the introduction of novel paired associates was similar to those used for Rio with the following exceptions. Rocky was given a conventional delayed MTS procedure with delays ranging from 1 to 5 s, and she was tested only with novel pairs XXII-22 and XXIII-23 against trained pairs VIII-8 and XV-15 on alternative days.

Rocky's results are shown in Figure 12.9, and although her preference for the appropriate comparison stimulus is apparent at the introduction of sample-comparison XXIII-23, she shows no strong preference for novel comparison stimulus 22. These results are best explained by Rocky's fearful

- 265 -

behavior toward novel comparison objects. Although Rocky oriented to the novel comparison when first shown the novel samples, she always hesitated and then chose the trained or familiar but incorrect comparison. Indeed, initially Rocky never selected the novel comparison (0 of 4 cases) in the presence of the novel sample but always selected the trained comparison in the presence of the trained sample (4 of 4 cases). Had Rocky been habituated to the novel comparison stimuli so that she was not afraid to approach them, we think she would have behaved more like Rio in her selection of novel comparisons.

Experiment 3: Pitting Two Novel Paired Associates Against One Another. Rio and Rocky were given probes with the novel paired associates XXII-22 and XXIII-23 during the early and middle parts of the previously described testing phases. On the probes, the sea lions were forced to choose between the two novel comparisons in the presence of their corresponding samples. Choices were not differentially reinforced. If the animals were rapidly learning the relations between novel samples and novel comparisons, then they should have responded better than chance over the course of these probe trials. Instead, both sea lions showed chance performance during these novel-novel probes. Rocky responded appropriately on 9 of 20 trials (45%) and Rio responded appropriately on 53 of 92 trials (58%). Performance on all baseline pairings remained above 90% correct responses.

Experiment 4: "Blank" Sample Probes. Again, although the sea lions perform well and in many cases errorlessly on X(Y,B) trials, on $X_1(Y_1, Y_2)$ and on $X_2(Y_2, Y_1)$ trials performances initially remain at chance. Thus performance on the basis of what we have called exclusion does not necessarily reflect paired associate learning. Immediately following the previously described experiment, we decided to further check the influence of samples XXII and XXIII on Rocky's choice of the associated novel comparisons 22 and 23. In this experiment, on any given one of eight trials, novel comparisons 22 or 23 were displayed in one compartment while trained comparisons 8 or 15 were displayed in the other compartment. On all eight trials, the sample compartment was empty and when its panel slid open to begin a trial only the white background was shown for 4 s. On these "blank" sample probes, Rocky chose the novel comparisons on 8 of 8 trials ($p < .01$, binomial test). In a control experiment with 8 blank sample probes and two trained comparisons to choose from (8 and 15), Rocky distributed her choices randomly between the trained comparisons; choosing one six times and the other two times. These results strongly argue that initially, sea lions choose novel comparisons in the absence of trained samples instead of choosing them in the presence of the novel sample. Only later is the relation between new sample and new comparison

12. Behavior control by exclusion

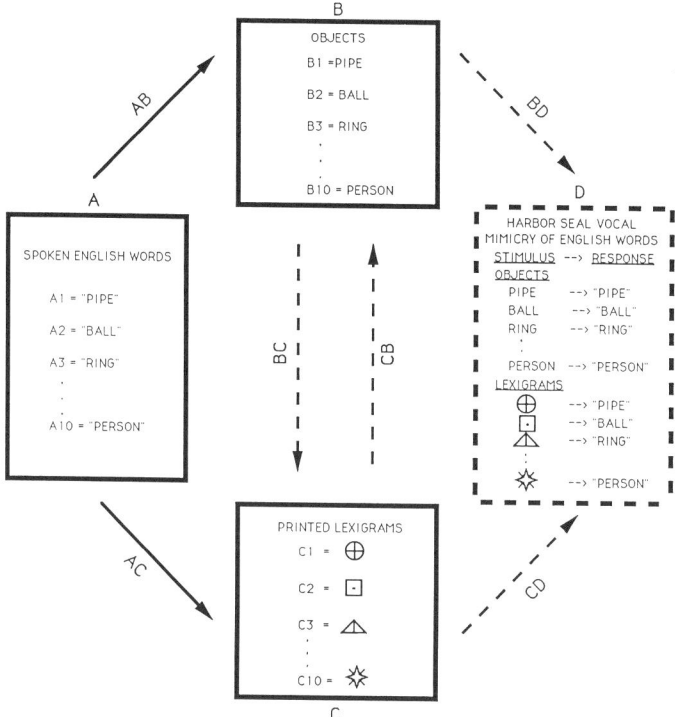

Figure 12.10. An equivalence paradigm for teaching a harbor seal semantic relations. Each of the three enclosed boxes A, B and C represent a set of 10 stimuli. Arrows AB, AC, BC and CB, each representing a set of conditional relations, point from sample to comparison stimuli. Solid arrows (AB and AC) represent relations that are explicitly taught to the seal and broken arrows represent conditional relations that are expected to emerge subsequently. For a given sample stimulus, the appropriate comparison is designated by the same number. Broken box D represents mimicked sounds by the seal which "name" stimulus sets B and C. Broken arrows from these stimulus sets to vocal mimicry of English words represent object naming (BD) and lexigram naming (CD).

stimulus learned. Another way of saying this is that an animal not presented with a trained sample will not choose the trained comparison but will instead choose the novel comparison by exclusion.

Although these experiments are far from definitive, they do suggest that in a variety of MTS contexts, some marine mammals are likely to choose the novel comparison object, not because they have learned that a relation exists between the novel "symbol" and the new object, but simply because they exclude the trained object in the absence of the trained symbol by a process of elimination.

A HYPOTHETICAL EXPERIMENT ON SEMANTIC COMPREHENSION: HARBOR SEAL AND STIMULUS EQUIVALENCE

Recently it has been reported that male harbor seals (*Phoca vitulina*) produce sounds that mimicked English words (Ralls, Fiorelli, & Gish, 1985), suggesting that it may be possible to teach harbor seals to produce and understand names for objects as has been reported with dolphins (Herman et al., 1984). In a concrete, but totally hypothetical, illustration, a male harbor seal may be shown two objects simultaneously or played two recordings of spoken English words in rapid succession-perhaps objects like a ball and a pipe in the first instance or the words "ball" and "pipe" in the second case. The seal must use a third stimulus, the sample or instructional cue, to determine to which object or which word the animal should respond. Sidman and Tailby (1982) and others have noted that the term "MTS" sometimes refers to a procedure and sometimes it refers to the results of a procedure. These two different meanings of MTS bear on fundamental issues in animal cognition (e.g., see the controversy between Herman, 1988, 1989, and Schusterman & Gisiner, 1988, 1989). For example, if a harbor seal performed appropriately on a matching task and its opposite, a mismatching or oddity task, the behavior does not necessarily imply that the seal has a "sameness" or "oddity" concept. The critical test of concept formation comes when the seal must match *novel* stimuli solely on the basis of their identity relationship. As in identity MTS, there is a tacit assumption in symbolic MTS that each paired associate of sample and comparison stimulus is related not merely by an if...then.. relation, but by equivalence (Sidman & Tailby, 1982). Thus, in the harbor seal example, it is easy to assume that each spoken English word sample and each object stands in an equivalence relation to one another (e.g., the seal makes both of these relationships: if spoken word "ball" then object ball, *and* if object ball, then spoken word "ball"). However, as Sidman and Tailby (1982) have shown, the arbitrary relationship between so-called symbols and their referents like identity matching remain in a unidirectional if-then relation and cannot be considered to form an equivalence class relationship unless there are explicit and independent tests. Simple behavioral variables may be mistakenly identified as evidence of complex

12. Behavior control by exclusion

cognitive processes, such as symbol manipulation, if the assumption of stimulus equivalence is in fact invalid (Mackay & Sidman, 1984).

If, as a result of the training on a series of conditional discriminations within MTS paradigms (if A_1 then B_1, if A_2 then B_2, etc., or if spoken word "ball" then object ball, if spoken word "pipe" then object pipe, etc.), there is the emergence of untrained relationships between dissimilar stimulus patterns, then the equivalence of stimulus classes can be said to exist. Stimulus equivalence has three defining characteristics: reflexivity, symmetry, and transitivity.

Reflexivity. Reflexivity emerges from generalized identity matching of the type: If A_1, then A_1; if A_2, then A_2; and if B_1, then B_1; if B_2, then B_2; etc. Thus, if hypothetically, it takes several trials before a naive harbor seal can consistently match the spoken word "ball" to itself, but then the seal matches the spoken word "pipe" to itself on the first trial and the spoken word "ring" to itself on the first trial, and if the seal also shows some difficulty in matching the object "ball" to itself, but then immediately can match the object "pipe" to itself and "ring" to itself, etc., then we can conclude that this seal who was taught a set of sample-comparison relations (spoken English words and objects) has demonstrated that these relations were reflexive by showing himself capable of matching the two kinds of stimuli to themselves. Moreover, ideally, to develop additional critical tests of class equivalency, another set of sample-comparison relations is needed (see Sidman & Tailby, 1982, for a description of the mathematical definition of equivalence relations and the way conditional tests are derived from such a definition). These could consist of spoken English words and printed lexigrams. Reflexivity would be further demonstrated if the subject could match each lexigram to itself.

Symmetry. Symmetric relations are shown when two or more dissimilar stimuli are related bidirectionally or reciprocally (e.g., if A_1, then B_1; if B_1 then A_1). Figure 12.10 illustrates a basic equivalence paradigm. The seal that has learned to match comparison stimulus B_1 to sample stimulus A_1 or comparison stimulus C_2 to sample stimulus A_2 must then, without additional training, be able to match A_1 as a comparison to B_1 as a sample and A_2 as a comparison to C_2 as a sample. Symmetry requires sample and comparison stimuli to be functionally interchangeable, or, stated another way, within the context of semantics, symmetry occurs when "conditional cues have become more than conventional discriminative stimuli . . [i.e.], when signs and their referents are shown to be immediately interchangeable" (Schusterman & Gisiner, 1989, p. 14).

Transitivity. The emergence of transitive stimulus relations from conditional discriminations requires three stimulus sets as illustrated in Figure 12.10. Transitivity is shown when previously untrained stimulus relations emerge following the training of a third set of stimulus relations-if A_1, then B_1; if B_1, then C_1; and if A_1, then C_1. Suppose our seal, having learned to select a pipe when it hears the word "pipe," and having learned to select the appropriate lexigram (C_1) when it hears the word "pipe", now without explicit training, chooses the object pipe when presented with the corresponding lexigram and chooses the lexigram (C_1) when shown a pipe. We may conclude that for the seal, the spoken word "pipe", the object pipe and the lexigram form a single equivalent class despite showing no physical similarity. The seal's emergent ability to do new types of matching tasks, BC and CB, will have confirmed the development of 10, three-member classes of equivalent stimuli: $A_1B_1C_1$ $A_2B_2C_2$, ... and $A_{10}B_{10}C_{10}$, (see Figure 12.10). Moreover, one might want to conclude that by passing the stimulus equivalence test, this seal clearly shows that the conditional relations between words and their referents as well as lexigrams and their referents involve semantic relations. Indeed, if the male harbor seal can mimic English spoken names of the objects (BD) and lexigrams (CD), then the original teaching of 20 conditional relations to the seal will have resulted in the creation of 20 novel conditional relations and 20 naming relations or a total of 40 novel performances. In this hypothetical experiment symmetry and transitivity could be tested indirectly with a male harbor seal trained to mimic English words by determining whether the test subject vocalizes appropriately to objects or to printed lexigrams or both (see Figure 12.10).

GENERAL DISCUSSION

Our results on "errorless" acquisition by California sea lions of conditional relations between symbolic or arbitrary samples and comparisons, as a function of pitting novel or untrained comparisons against previously trained or conditioned comparisons (conditioned to an arbitrary sample), are virtually identical with similar results when 2-year-old children are trained to name objects (Slobin, 1966) and with those recently obtained on humans (both retarded and normal) in a variety of MTS paradigms (e.g., McIlvane & Stoddard, 1985). Such results suggest that in a variety of MTS contexts, but most assuredly in the two-comparison context, sea lions choose the novel comparison, not because of their common property of novelty or because of their previous "language training" as earlier suggested (Herman et al., 1984; Schusterman & Krieger, 1984), but because they exclude the trained comparison stimulus in the absence of a trained sample and thus select the untrained or novel comparison by default. The behavioral basis for the exclusion

12. Behavior control by exclusion

phenomenon may be a quite fundamental conditioning process, because it is only following preferences of untrained comparisons by exclusion that these marine mammals may start learning the relation between a novel sample and a novel comparison stimulus.

We have attempted to show that semantic comprehension in seals, sea lions and dolphins and other animals as well may begin with arbitrary conditional relations between signals (samples) and referents or objects (comparisons) and that initially the choice of appropriate referents is controlled by exclusion. It is only after an unspecified number of trials [perhaps about 150-200 X(Y,B) trials] that the effects of exclusion emerge as a novel conditional performance in contexts where the basis for exclusion is no longer immediately available. However, the ability to learn conditional relations is only an intermediary step in the hierarchy of learning abilities necessary to do semantic relations. Thomas (1980), for example, suggested that biconditional or symmetrical concepts are the highest forms of intellectual functioning. Symmetrical conceptualization may be critical for the emergence of semanticity. As Sidman and Tailby (1982) have stated so cogently: "Pointing to a picture in response to a printed word denotes . . . (semantic) . . comprehension only if the word and picture are related by equivalence and not merely by conditionality. Stimulus classes formed by a network of equivalence relations establish a basis for referential meaning. The equivalence paradigm provides exactly the test needed to determine whether or not a particular conditional discrimination involves semantic relations" (p. 20).

Although the ability of dolphins, apes, monkeys, and several other vertebrate taxa to respond to complex classes of stimuli is not in doubt, their ability to "refer" to objects, events, and relations and, in general, to manipulate symbols is very controversial. The origin and nature of symbolic activity, which invariably involves the logical properties of reflexivity, symmetry and transitivity, may be rooted in the way animals acquire rules to deal with social and nonsocial stimulus objects, events, and relationships. Sidman (1986) has shown that in humans conditional discriminations can lead to a semantic correspondence between each sample and its matching comparison stimulus, that is, a stimulus class equivalency within an MTS paradigm. Can dolphins and sea lions or for that matter chimpanzees do the same?

ACKNOWLEDGMENTS

This research was supported by contract N00014-85-K-0244 from the Office of Naval Research to Ronald J. Schusterman. We acknowledge the contributions of student volunteers in the Sea Lion Cognition Group at Long Marine Laboratory. We especially thank Barbara Emery for her help in preparing this manuscript.

REFERENCES

Carter, D. E. & Werner, T. J. (1978). Complex learning: A critical analysis. *Journal of the Experimental Analysis of Behavior*, 29, 565-601.

Catania, A. C. (1980). Autoclitic processes and the structure of behavior. *Behaviorism*, 8, 175-186.

Cumming, W. W. & Berryman, R. (1965). The complex discriminated operant: Studies on match-to-sample and related problems. In D. I. Mostofsky (Ed.). *Stimulus Generalization* (pp. 284-330). Stanford, CA: Stanford University Press.

Dixon, L. S. (1977). The nature of control by spoken words over visual stimulus selection. *Journal of the Experimental Analysis of Behavior*, 7, 433-442.

Herman, L. M. (1988). The language of animal language research: Reply to Schusterman & Gisiner, *Psychological Record*, 38, 349-362.

Herman, L. M. (1989). In which procrustean bed does the sea lion sleep tonight? *The Psychological Record*, 39, 19-42.

Herman, L. M., Richards, D. G., & Wolz, J. P. (1984). Comprehension of sentences by bottlenosed dolphins. *Cognition*, 16, 129-219.

Mackay, H. A. & Sidman, M. (1984). Teaching new behavior via equivalence relations. In P. H. Brooks, R. Sperber, & C. McCaulay, (Eds.), *Learning and cognition in the mentally retarded* (pp. 493-513). Hillsdale, NJ: Lawrence Erlbaum Associates.

McIlvane, W. J. & Stoddard, L. T. (1985). Complex stimulus relations and exclusion in severe mental retardation. *Analysis and Intervention in Developmental Disabilities*, 5, 307-321.

12. Behavior control by exclusion

Nissen, H. W., Blum, J. S., & Blum, R. A. (1948). Analysis of matching behavior in chimpanzee. *Journal of Comparative and Physiological Psychology*, 41, 62-74.

Ralls, K. F., Fiorelli, P., & Gish, S. (1985). Vocalizations and vocal mimicry in captive harbor seals, *Phoca vitulina*. *Canadian Journal of Zoology*, 63, 1050-1056.

Roitblat, H. L. (1987). *Introduction to comparative cognition.* New York: W. H. Freeman.

Savage-Rumbaugh, E. S. (1988). A new look at ape language: Comprehension of vocal speech and syntax. In D. Leger (Ed.), *Comparative perspectives in modern psychology. Nebraska Symposium on Motivation, 1987* (vol. 35, pp. 201-256). Lincoln, NE: University of Nebraska Press.

Schusterman, R. J. & Gisiner, R. (1988). Artificial language comprehension in dolphins and sea lions: The essential cognitive skills. *Psychological Record*, 38, 311-348.

Schusterman, R. J. & Gisiner, R., (1989). Please parse the sentence: Animal cognition in the procrustean bed of linguistics, *Psychological Record*. 39, 3-18.

Schusterman, R. J. & Krieger, K. (1984). California sea lions are capable of semantic comprehension. *Psychological Record*, 34, 3-23.

Schusterman, R. J. & Krieger, K. (1986). Artificial language comprehension and size transposition by a California sea lion (*Zalophus californianus*). *Journal of Comparative Psychology*, 100, 348-355.

Sidman, M. (in press). Equivalence relations: Where do they come from: In D. E. Blackman & H. Lejeune (Eds.), *Behavior analysis in theory and practice: Contributions and controversies* (pp. 213-245). Hillsdale, NJ: Lawrence Erlbaum Associates.

Sidman, M. (1986). Functional analysis of emergent verbal classes. In T. Thompson & M. D. Zeiler (Eds.), *Analysis and integration of behavioral units.* Hillsdale, NJ: Lawrence Erlbaum Associates.

Sidman, M. & Tailby, W. (1982). Conditional discrimination vs. matching to sample: An expansion of the testing paradigm. *Journal of the Experimental Analysis of Behavior*, 37, 5-22.

Slobin, D. (1966). The acquisition of Russian as a native language. In F. Smith & G. A. Miller (Eds.), *The genesis of language: A psycholinguistic approach* (pp. 129-148). Cambridge, MA: MIT Press.

Stromer, R. (1986). Control by exclusion in arbitrary matching-to-sample. *Analysis and Intervention in Developmental Disabilities*, 6, 59-72.

Thomas, R. K. (1980). Evolution of intelligence: an approach to its assessment. *Brain, Behavior and Evolution*, 17, 454-472.

13 Auditory Sequence Complexity and Hemispheric Asymmetry of Function in Rats

Kevin N. O'Connor, Herbert L. Roitblat, and Thomas G. Bever

Language in humans is characteristically manifested by the left cerebral hemisphere. This fact must reflect properties of the left hemisphere that make it a relatively natural site for language behavior. The same fact may be taken as the basis for a stronger claim: Certain properties of the left hemisphere are unique to humans and causally related to the existence and nature of language. There are several ways to gain perspective on such a claim, such as the study of cerebral asymmetries in nonhumans and of nonlinguistic behaviors, particularly those bearing some structural similarity to language. If we find that asymmetries occur for these behaviors, and in nonhumans, we must conclude that functional hemispheric differences as such are not unique to humans, nor are they the sufficient cause of the existence of language.

The comparative study of auditory sequence learning and perception provides one approach to the study of this problem. The study of simple sequential stimuli in nonhuman species may reveal general psychological mechanisms underlying the structure of natural serial systems such as human language, and general features of brain organization, such as asymmetries in function. A preliminary goal for such research is to develop tasks and methods suited for comparative research. Monaural and dichotic presentation of acoustic stimuli have revealed asymmetries in hemispheric function on a variety of tasks in humans, in which both the direction and degree of hemispheric asymmetry

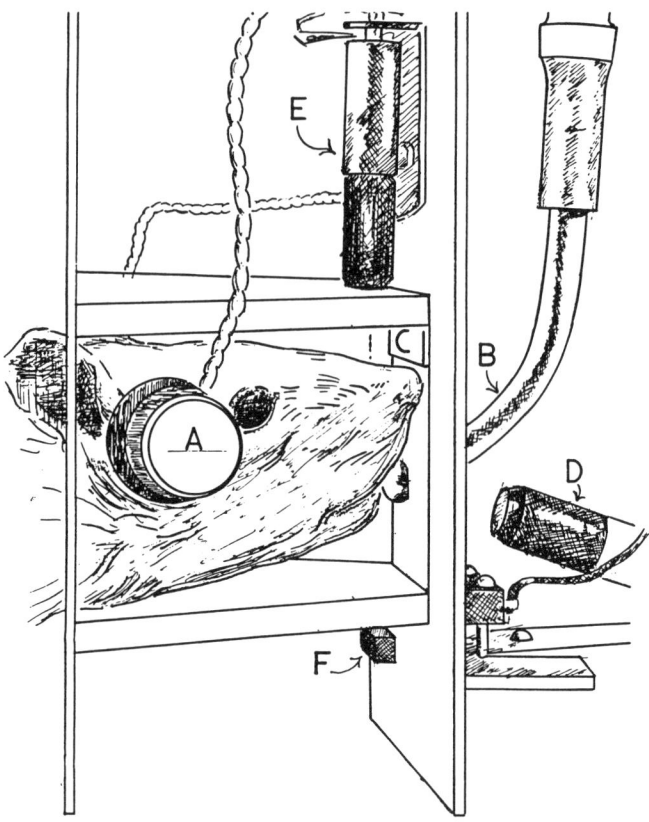

Figure 13.1. The dichotic hood is illustrated: (A) earphone, (B) drinking tube, (C) response key, (D) key lamp, (E) hood lamp, (F) light detector.

are related to the complexity of an acoustic stimulus. Discriminations involving simple, serially presented or temporally varying information, on the other hand, tend to be particularly dramatic in subjects with unilateral brain damage (Chedru, Bastard, & Efron, 1978; Gordon, 1967; Lackner & Teuber, 1973; Van Allen, Benton, & Gordon, 1967), but have also been revealed in studies using intact human subjects and monaural and dichotic techniques (Efron and Yund, 1974; Halperin, Nachson, & Carmon, 1973; Mills & Rollman, 1979a, 1979b; Murphy & Venables, 1970; Sidtis, 1980; Simon, 1967; Vroon, Timmers, & Tempelaars, 1977).

Functional asymmetries in rats

The monaural and dichotic techniques involve presenting different, sometimes conflicting signals simultaneously to both ears through headphones. The term *monaural* generally refers to the presentation of some stimulus of interest to one ear, while a different stimulus (typically white-noise) is simultaneously presented to the other ear. The word *dichotic* refers to a technique in which the two stimuli are similar, such as two different vowels or tones. Because the information originating at the level of the auditory receptors in one ear is projected to both sides of the brain in mammals, though asymmetrically in favor of the contralateral side, these forms of stimulus presentation are believed to interfere or perhaps compete with each other within a hemisphere. Superiority is assigned to the hemisphere contralateral to the ear that "performs better."

The experiments described in this chapter address the problem of auditory sequential complexity and hemispheric asymmetries in intact rats using the monaural presentation technique. As is the case with humans, an ear advantage would imply superior performance by the contralateral side of the brain. If auditory processing in rats parallels that found in humans we would predict an asymmetry to be revealed on the task; further, we would expect the degree and direction of the asymmetry to depend on sequence complexity.

METHOD

Intact albino rats (*Rattus norvegicus*) were used in these studies. They were trained and tested in an operant chamber modified by the addition of a hood just large enough to accommodate a rat's head (see Figure 13.1). Auditory stimuli were presented to each ear of the rat through subminiature speakers mounted on the hood. The hood underwent modification in design in each of the experiments, in order to improve the control of sound delivery. In the first (3-tone) experiment, the hood consisted of a tapered cubicle with a single light-sensing circuit at the distal end with the speakers mounted on the sides opposite the position of the ears. In Experiment 2 (1-tone) and 3 (2-tone) the hood consisted of a cylinder with two cutouts large enough to accommodate each ear, and each with its own light-sensing circuit. Additionally, in Experiment 3, a rectangular cap with attached speaker was mounted over each cutout, providing an enclosed delivery system for each ear.

In all these experiments a single-response "go/no-go" procedure was used. On each trial the subject was signaled to insert and correctly orient its head in the listening hood (monitored by the light sensing circuits) for the duration of the stimulus presentation. The discriminative stimulus or sequence was then presented followed by a 3-s response interval. A response made during this interval was reinforced with water if it followed a stimulus designated as positive and punished with a time-out if it followed a negative stimulus. The tone stimuli consisted of square waves generated by a microcomputer and amplified. Broad-band thermal noise was presented continuously to the contralateral ear receiving tone stimuli. Noise was presented bilaterally during the training sessions in order to train the rat to fixate its head during the stimulus. Movement of the head or responses made during the stimulus resulted in a 5-s time-out before representation of the stimulus.

The subject's task in Experiment 1 (N = 8) was to discriminate a sequence consisting of a specific series of three tones (1.1, 1.5, and 2.33 kHz) in nonmonotonic order, from all other possible combinations (26) of the three elements. The subjects in Experiment 2 (N = 8) were required to discriminate a high pitch (2.33 kHz) from a low pitch (1.1 kHz) tone, one presented on each trial. Six subjects from Experiment 2 were then successfully transferred to a task in which they were required to discriminate a sequence comprising two different tones (1.1 and 2.33 kHz) from the other four combinations of the these elements. The tones in Experiments 1 and 2 were 0.5 s in duration (with 0.5-silent intervals between the elements). To promote transfer in Experiment 3, the tones were briefer, 0.25 s in duration, with an equivalent silent interval between them. In all experiments an equal number of positive and negative trials were randomly presented within each session and ear presentation was counterbalanced in blocks of trials across sessions and subjects. Subjects were tested for 36 sessions in Experiments 1 and 3, and for 30 sessions in Experiment 2.

Correct and incorrect responses, and their latency, were recorded on each trial. It was noted early in Experiment 1 that responses to positive sequences (hits) were, on average, faster than those to negative sequences (false alarms), a common finding supporting the notion that false alarms are executed with less confidence. This prompted us to employ a powerful analysis based on signal detection theory (SDT) which exploits both response accuracy and latency information (Carterette, Friedman, & Cosnides, 1965; Emmerich, Gray, Watson, and Tanis, 1972; Kulics, 1977). The use of latency information as an index of confidence or response criterion may be useful in cases of a difficult discrimination (Green & Swets, 1966), and also addresses the problem of obtaining a sufficient number of probability values for accurate determination of a receiver operating characteristic (ROC).

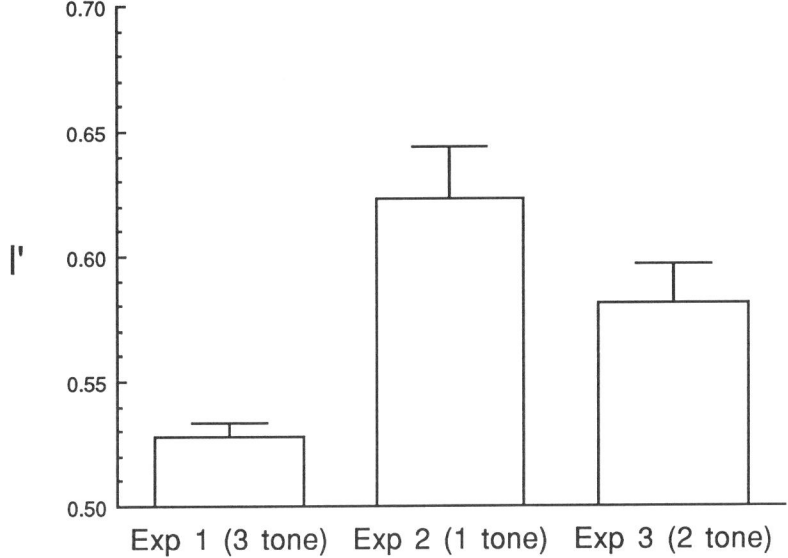

Figure 13.2. Discriminative performance is expressed in mean l' values for each of the experiments. Bars = 1 standard error.

For this analysis, a key press was defined as either a hit or a false alarm depending on whether it followed a positive or negative tone. Hit and false alarm probabilities were calculated for each 300-ms epoch during the 3-s response interval. The corresponding cumulative probability values in each bin were then plotted on unit axes to yield an ROC. These ROCs are linear when plotted on normal deviate (double-probability) scales (O'Connor, 1990), supporting the usual assumption of underlying Gaussian signal and noise functions of SDT. The area falling under the ROC was calculated as a measure of discrimination and will be referred to as l'. Random performance is revealed by a characteristic falling on the positive diagonal, bisecting the unit square and yielding an l' value of 0.5, while better than random performance is shown by values between 0.5 and 1 (optimal performance).

RESULTS

Figure 13.2 illustrates that the rats were able to discriminate a three-tone sequence but their performance was poor relative to the two-tone, and particularly the single-tone task. A right ear (RE) advantage emerged early in training on the three tone task. This result was apparent across both subjects and sessions, and manifested itself during roughly the first half (18) of the total number of training sessions. The mean performance of 14 out of 18 sessions was better for the RE, and these differences were significant Wilcoxon $t(18) = 21.5, p < .05$]. This bias was fairly consistent over subjects—seven out of eight rats exhibited better RE performance for the first 18 sessions (sign test, $p < .05$).

During the second half of the experiment there was no longer a bias in favor of the RE; in fact, 13 out of these 18 sessions showed better LE performance (Sign test, $p < .05$), though these differences were not significant ($t(18) = 64.5, p > .05$). The possibility of a reversal in asymmetry is supported by an examination of ear bias over sessions and subject. Over the entire experiment, the number of sessions showing superior RE performance within six session blocks is: 4-4-6-2-0-3 (the value of zero in the fifth block is part of a seven session run of superior LE performance). The number of subjects (out of eight) showing better RE performance within six session blocks is 7-6-5-2-3-4.

Further evidence for an RE, and so, inferred left hemisphere (LH) advantage on the 3-tone task early in training comes from an analysis of discriminative performance for certain negative sequences. Because of the apparent difficulty of discriminating three sequential tones, subjects may have adopted a simpler strategy, such as basing a decision on some subset of the entire sequence (Roitblat, Scopatz, & Bever, 1987). For example (letting the series ABC denote the positive sequence), subjects may have rejected negative sequences on the basis of only a single element (such as those ending in C), or two elements (rejecting all negative sequences ending in elements other than BC, but not those ending in BC). To address this question, discrimination between the positive sequence and various subsets of the entire set of negative sequences was assessed. The entire set of negative sequences was first subdivided on the basis of whether single or double tonal elements matched those of the positive sequence in the same positions. In the case of single elements this produced subsets of negative sequences with element A, B, or C in the first, second or third position respectively, with eight sequences of each type. These sequences may be denoted as Axx, xBx, or xxC, where the letter x stands for any other element, except, of course, those producing the positive sequence. For two element matches, the subsets consisted of sequences ABx,

Functional asymmetries in rats

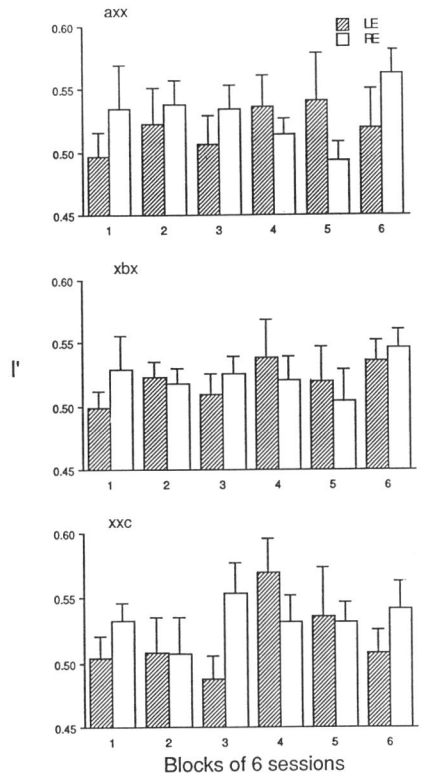

Figure 13.3. l' values calculated over subjects for individual negative sequences containing one matching element are shown.

xBC, and AxC, each subset comprising two sequences. Discrimination was then assessed by determining l' scores between the positive sequence and each subset of the negative sequences.

The results of this analysis are depicted in Figure 13.3 and 13.4 for single- and double-element cases, respectively, in blocks of six sessions across the entire experiment. The analysis indicated that performance was reliably above chance (.5) levels for both single- and double-element subsets, though better in the case of single-element matches, evidence that subjects were not simply basing their decisions on some subset of the entire positive sequence. Inspection of these figures also suggests that this ability was better when stimuli were presented to the RE during the first half of the experiment. For single-element matches, a comparison of the performance over all negative cases yielded a significant difference between the ears for the first three six-session blocks [$t(9) = 3, p < .02$], but not the last three blocks [$t(9) = 16, p > .05$]. This difference is greatest during the first six sessions; analysis of performance of subjects within blocks revealed an effect of ear presentation closely approaching significance only in this case [$F(1,7) = 4.94, p < .10$].

Ear differences in the case of two element matches also appear more prominent in the first half of the experiment, with the bias again in favor of the RE. A comparison of performance for all negative cases revealed a significant difference between the ears for the first three blocks [$t(9) = 7$, one-tailed $p < .05$], but not the last three [$t(9) = 18.5, p > .05$]. This difference is again most apparent during the first six sessions of the experiment, wherein performance is significantly better for RE presentations [$F(1,7) = 7.18, p < .05$].

Because the l' measure is based partly on response latency it seems reasonable to ask whether the dichotic difference may have been due to a simple underlying cause such as a latency difference dependent on hemispheric initiation of responses. One reason for rejecting such an explanation is that the l' measure is sensitive to relative response speed, that is, the latency of hits relative to false alarms. A simple response or motoric difference between the hemispheres would cause a shift in both hit and false alarm distributions, so should leave l' unaffected. In any case, an examination of mean overall response latency (the average of hits and false alarms) revealed no consistent difference in mean latency over the course of the experiment.

Analysis of both overall performance and discrimination of negative sequences resembling the positive stimulus in form supports superior discrimination for stimuli presented to the RE early in training, for a 3-tone sequence discrimination. This implies better performance by the LH. The results of this study, therefore, support an LH superiority for learning an abstract sequence discrimination not obviously related to natural communicative behavior in the rat. If, as in humans, this advantage is dependent on stimulus complexity, then a simple auditory discrimination should produce either a diminution or reversal of the asymmetry found on the complex task. Experiment 2 was designed to examine this question using a simple, high-low tone discrimination task.

Functional asymmetries in rats

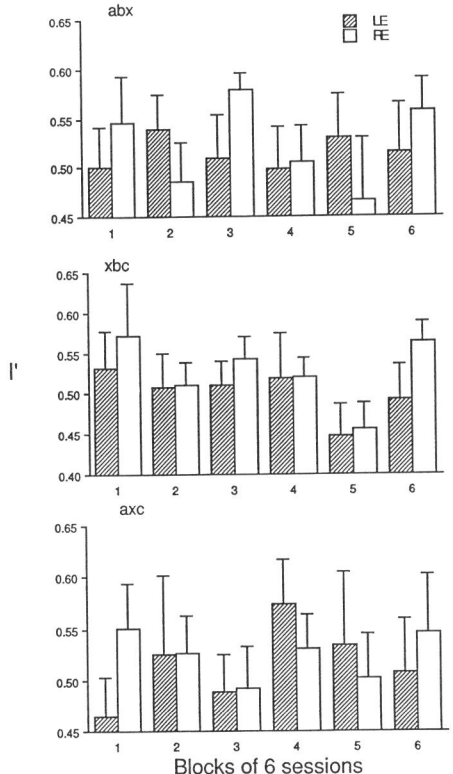

Figure 13.4. l' values calculated over subjects for individual negative sequences containing two matching elements are shown.

Figure 13.2 shows that performance on this task was quite good relative to that in Experiment 1. There was no apparent difference in mean performance between the ears in the first or second half of the experiment: On 8 of the first 15 sessions, performance is superior for RE presentations (sign test, $p > .05$), and on 10 out of the second 15 sessions performance is better for LE presentations (sign test, $p > .05$). Neither did individual performance show a clear ear bias. Six out of eight rats exhibited better performance for RE presentations (one subject showed no difference) during the first half of the experiment, but the magnitude of these differences was not large (one-tailed $t = 6, p > .05$).

The strongest support for congruence of the findings from Experiment 2 with results from human studies would be a significant difference in favor of LE presentations, implying better RH performance. It is difficult to make a case when no clear differences are found, even though such a result is not uncommon in humans. In lieu of a strong LE bias, it seems reasonable to ask whether the asymmetries found on the sequence discrimination task in Experiment 1 were larger that those found in Experiment 2. The first 18 sessions were chosen for this comparison, because of the consistent ear bias found in Experiment 1 during this period. In Experiment 1, 14 out of the first 18 sessions showed larger l' values for the RE (Sign test, $p < .05$), differences which were significant [$t(18) = 21.3, p < .01$]. In Experiment 2, 10 out of 18 did and the differences were not significant [$t(18) = 70, p > .05$]. A comparison of the first 18 sessions of the two experiments revealed the ear differences by session on the three tone task to be significantly larger than those from the single tone task [$t(18) = 16.5, p < .05$].

If this relationship holds, we would expect training on a 2-element tone sequence to result in an RE bias greater than that found on a single tone discrimination, but smaller than the bias previously demonstrated using a three element sequence. We decided to examine this question with the rats having undergone training in Experiment 2. Six of these rats successfully adapted to the modified chamber and were transferred to a two tone discrimination employing tones of the same frequency. Transfer from a 1- to 2-tone task in these subjects permitted comparison of asymmetries for two types of negative sequence of interest during acquisition: (a) sequences closely resembling the previously positive and negative stimuli in form (doublets or sequences with a single repeating element, AA or BB), and (b) a novel sequence composed of two different elements (BA). Responses made to doublets early in training should reflect the strategy used for single tone discrimination in Experiment 2, resulting in little or no asymmetry. The negative sequence composed of two different tones should be handled as a novel case. Discrimination of this type, then, should result in a greater degree of asymmetry early in training with a bias in favor of RE presentations.

Not surprisingly, overall performance on this task was better than that of Experiment 1, but poorer than that in Experiment 2, as Figure 13.2 reveals. An examination of performance by session though, revealed little difference dependent on ear: Ten out of 18 sessions were better for the RE, in both the first and second half of the experiment. Individual performance also did not show a large difference. As in the previous two experiments, there is a bias in favor of RE presentations for performance early in training, though the differences are

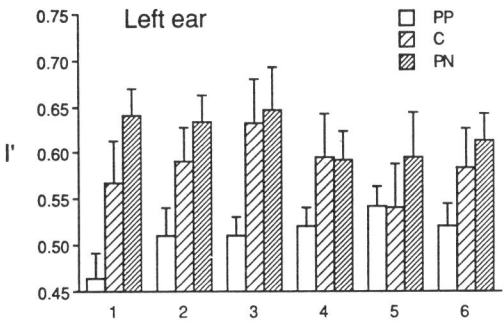

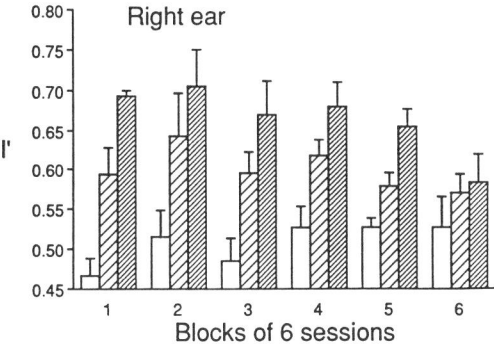

Figure 13.5. l' values calculated for each of the negative cases over subjects are displayed. PP = previously positive, PN = previously negative, C = combination.

not large as in Experiment 1. Four out of six rats show superior performance for RE presentations during the first half of the experiment, though the magnitude of these differences was not significant $[t(6) = 5, p > .05]$.

An examination of negative cases revealed a stronger RE bias. The results for each negative case are presented in Figure 13.5. Before discussing ear differences some remarks regarding general performance dependent on negative sequence type should be made. First, there was a large and significant difference in discrimination depending on stimulus type $[F(2,10) = 9.58, p < .005]$. The smallest value of l' emerged for the repetition (doublet) of the single tone that had been positive in the first experiment. The best performance, not surprisingly, is reserved for the doublet comprising the single tone that had previously been negative. Values of l' for the negative sequence comprising the combination of both tones are intermediate to these other two. Second, the differences in the degree to which the negative cases are discriminated decline over the course of the experiment; there is a significant interaction between block of training and stimulus type [$F(10,50) = 3.18, p < .005$]. These results indicate that training in Experiment 2 influenced responding primarily during early sessions, but had a declining effect as the experiment progressed.

Inspection of Figure 13.5 reveals overall better performance when stimuli were presented to the RE. Thirteen out of a total of 18 blocks show better performance for RE presentations (sign test, one-tailed $p < .05$), and the magnitude of these differences was significant [$t(18) = 43$, one-tailed $p < .05$]. Though there is no main effect of ear of presentation ($F(1,5) = 1.95, p > .05$), the interaction between ear and stimulus type approaches significance [$F(2,10) = 3.75, p < .10$].

Recall that the largest ear difference was predicted for the negative sequence bearing the least resemblance to the stimuli in Experiment 2, that is, the sequence composed of two different elements. The largest ear difference, however, occurs with the doublet of the tone that was previously negative; for every block except the last one, performance is better for RE presentations [$t(6) = 1$, one-tailed $p < .05$]. There is also a bias in favor of the RE for discrimination of the doublet that was previously positive (five out of six blocks) and for the sequence composed of two different elements (four out of six blocks), but these differences are not significant.

Examination of individual performance once again reveals an RE bias during the first half of the experiment, which is also dependent on stimulus type, and again is largest for the doublet that was previously negative. Five out of six subjects show superior discrimination of this stimulus for RE presentations during sessions 1 through 18, and the magnitude of these differences is significant [$t(6) = 1$, one-tailed $p < .05$]. The magnitude of ear differences during the first block of six sessions is also biased in favor of the RE. For the sequence composed of two different elements, and the previously positive and previously negative doublets, five, four and five of the rats, respectively, demonstrated better discrimination for RE presentations. Regardless of stimulus type, then, in a total of 14 out of 18 cases (six subjects × three negative cases), subject performance was better for RE presentations (Sign test, $p < .05$), and these differences were large [$t(18) = 37.5, p < .05$].

Functional asymmetries in rats

Table 13.1.
l' (RE - LE)

Experiment	Rat	First 18	Total Sessions
1 (3 tones)	2	.045	.003
	3	.053	.025
	4	.017	-.001
	7	.053	.035
	L	-.039	-.005
	C	.011	-.018
	G	.034	.014
	M	.035	.030
Mean		.026	.011
SE		.011	.007
2 (1 tone)	19	.080	.059
	13	.001	-.008
	20	.028	.029
	11	.012	.011
	16	-.011	-.014
	12	-.034	.029
	17	-.009	-.034
	15	-.007	.001
Mean		.008	.009
SE		.012	.010
3 (2 tones)	19	.030	-.005
	13	.059	.049
	20	-.032	.019
	11	.048	.050
	16	.016	-.022
	12	.004	.040
Mean		.021	.022
SE		.012	.012

The analysis for individual negative cases reveals a RE, and therefore, probable LH advantage for discrimination of an auditory sequence comprising two tones. If hemispheric asymmetry is dependent on sequence complexity, increasing with complexity as seems to be the case in humans, then we should find the greatest asymmetry in Experiment 1 and the smallest in Experiment 2. Differences in l' between ear presentations are listed for each subject in Table 13.1, both for the first 18 sessions and over each of the entire three experiments, together with the mean and standard error of the differences. Inspection of the mean differences for the first half of each experiment, those in which the most consistent ear bias was found, shows that they lie in the right direction. It is also apparent from looking at Table 13.1 that there is an overall bias in favor of the RE. Questions of the precise relationship between complexity and hemispheric asymmetry aside, the point should be made that the LH of the rat may be generally superior to the right hemisphere at auditory processing.

SUMMARY AND DISCUSSION

Three experiments examined ear differences on single-, two- and three-tone monaural sequence discriminations in rats. Performance was evaluated using signal detection theory and revealed: (a) superior overall performance for RE presentations, particularly early in training; (b) the greatest degree of asymmetry emerging on the three tone discrimination—performance was better early in training for RE presentations; (c) ear differences were significantly greater on the three tone than the one tone task early in training; and (d) the average of the ear differences early in training was positively related to sequence length and task difficulty.

Degree of asymmetry, then, was found to increase with sequence complexity and was biased in favor of the RE. The trend of increasing asymmetry with task complexity is found in humans, but the assignment of lateral superiority, particularly for tasks involving complex auditory information, has been more problematic and may depend on the experience and skills a subject brings to the task. In the case of music, early work demonstrated a LE advantage for identification of melodic sequences (Kimura, 1973), but the subjects of the studies were not musically sophisticated. Later work showed an RE superiority for musically sophisticated subjects, while less skilled subjects showed an overall LE superiority (Bever & Chiarello, 1974; Gordon, 1975). The few studies that show an overall LE superiority for musicians use familiar and short melodies (see Bever, 1975, for review). The inferred hemispheric differences are thought to depend on differences in processing strategy that reflect the relative strengths of each hemisphere. Musically unsophisticated

Functional asymmetries in rats

subjects may depend on a simple process, perhaps Gestalt in nature, which does little in the way of sequential structural analysis, and so show right-hemisphere (RH) superiority. The inferred LH superiority in the case of musically skilled subjects may reflect an analysis of the structural relations between the sequential elements.

These results suggest that humans would perform better on the same three-tone discrimination when the stimuli are presented to the LE, implying better RH performance, and they do (O'Connor, 1990). A three-tone discrimination is evidently handled better by the LH in humans, but the RH in rats. One might conclude that these results imply a different hemispheric organization for the two species, but the data are interpretable in terms of different processing strategies, on the basis of unitary versus relational processing (Bever, 1980). It may be that humans are able to treat this discrimination as a unitary task, involving a single perceptual unit, without analysis of the elements comprising the sequence. Rats on the other hand, may have to handle the discrimination relationally—that is, they may be unable to match the elements as a unit, but be forced to treat the stimulus as three discrete elements in sequential or relational comparison.

This species difference may be based on differences in short-term memory. Humans may be able to hold the tonal sequence in short-term store with sufficient fidelity, or convert the tonal information to a symbolic and less volatile form, in order to perform a unitary or matching operation. It is likely that rats are unable to do so given their relatively poor performance on the three tone discrimination, a task posing little difficulty for humans. Further evidence for a species difference in auditory short-term or sensory store comes from recent work showing strong retroactive interference of rats' memory for single brief tones when followed by white noise having overlapping spectral energy while to human ears, the tones are clearly distinguishable (O'Connor & Ison, 1991). Short-term memory must be critically involved in the processing of sequential information, and hemispheric differences in memory dynamics when under the load of such processing may account for the species differences we find on these tasks.

In view of the differences between rats and humans, as well as between musically sophisticated and nonsophisticated subjects, it is interesting that the RE bias declined with training in Experiment 1, perhaps to some extent undergoing a reversal in favor of the LE. Extended training may produce similar effects in both rats and humans, perhaps as a result of the shift in processing strategy discussed earlier. Longitudinal experiments using human subjects, and sequences of varying complexity, are clearly needed for a proper comparison of the effects of training on processing strategy.

The present study supports the notion that hemispheric processing differences may be general across mammals. Along with other demonstrations of functional asymmetry in the auditory system of nonhuman species (Heffner & Heffner, 1984; Morrel-Samuels, Herman, & Bever, 1989; Nottebohm, 1970, 1977; Peterson, Beecher, Zoloth, Moody, & Stebbins, 1977), these results help to establish the contiguity of brain mechanisms involved in the processing of temporal information in general, and perhaps crucially involved with human language.

REFERENCES

Bever, T. G. (1975). Cerebral asymmetries in humans are due to the differentiation of two incompatible process: Holistic and analytic. *Annals of the New York Academy of Sciences*, 263, 251-262.

Bever, T. G. (1980) Broca and Lashley were right: Cerebral asymmetries are an artifact of growth. In D. Caplan (Ed.), *Biological studies of mental processes* (pp. 186-230). Cambridge: MIT Press.

Bever, T. G. & Chiarello, R. J. (1974). Cerebral dominance in musicians and nonmusicians. *Science*, 185, 537-539.

Carterette, E. C., Friedman, M. P. & Cosnides, R. (1965). Reaction time distributions in the detection of weak signals in noise. *Journal of the Acoustical Society of America*, 38, 531-542.

Chedru, F., Bastard, V., & Efron, R. (1978). Auditory micropattern discrimination in brain damaged subjects. *Neuropsychologia*, 16, 141-149.

Efron, R. & Yund, E. W. (1974). Dichotic competition of simultaneous tone bursts of different frequency I. *Neuropsychologia*, 12, 240-258.

Emmerich, D. J., Gray, J., Watson, C., & Tanis, D. (1972). Response latency, confidence and ROCs in auditory signal detection. *Perception and Psychophysics*, 11, 65.

Gordon, H. W. (1975). Hemispheric asymmetry and musical performance. *Science*, 189, 68-69.

Gordon, M. C. (1967). Reception and retention factors in tone duration discrimination by brain damaged and control patients. *Cortex*, 3, 237-249.

Green, D. M. & Swets, J. A. (1966). *Signal detection theory and psychophysics*. New York: Krieger.

Halperin, Y., Nachson, I., & Carmon, A. (1973). Shift of ear superiority in dichotic listening to temporally patterned nonverbal stimuli. *Journal of the Acoustical Society of America*, 53, 46-50.

Heffner, H. E. & Heffner, R. S. (1984). Temporal lobe lesions and perception of species vocalizations. *Science*, 226, 75-76.

Kimura, D. (1973). The asymmetry of the human brain. *Scientific American*, 227, 70-76.

Kulics, A. T. (1977). Sensory discriminability comparisons in human and monkey with implications for the study of central nervous correlates. *Annals of the New York Academy of Sciences*, 299, 244-254.

Lackner, J. R. & Teuber, H. L. (1973). Alteration in auditory fusion thresholds after cerebral injury in man. *Neuropsychologia*, 11, 409-415.

Mills, L. & Rollman, G. B. (1979a). Left hemisphere selectivity for processing duration in normal subjects. *Brain and Language*, 7, 320-335.

Mills, L. & Rollman, G. B. (1979b). Hemispheric asymmetry for auditory perception of temporal order. *Neuropsychologia*, 18, 41-47.

Morrell-Samuels, P., Herman, L., & Bever, T. G. (1989). *A left-hemisphere advantage for gesture-language signs in the dolphin*. Paper presented at the meeting of the Psychonomic Society, Atlanta, GA.

Murphy, E. H. & Venables, P. H. (1970). Ear asymmetry in the threshold of fusion of two clicks: A signal detection analysis. *Quarterly Journal of Experimental Psychology*, 22, 288-300.

Nottebohm, F. (1970). Ontogeny of bird song. *Science*, 167, 950-956.

Nottebohm, G. (1977). Asymmetries in neural control of vocalization in the canary. In S. Harnad, R. W. Doty, L. Goldstein, J. Jaynes and G. Krauthamer (Eds.), *Lateralization in the Nervous System* (pp. 23-44). New York: Academic Press.

O'Connor, K. N. (1990). *Structural aspects of auditory sequence discrimination and asymmetry of function in rats and humans* (Unpublished Doctoral Dissertation, Columbia University).

O'Connor, K. & Ison, J. R. (1991). Echoic memory in the rat: Effects of inspection time, retention interval, and the spectral composition of masking noise. *Journal of Experimental Psychology: Animal Behavior Processes*, 17, 377-385.

Peterson, M. R., Beecher, M. D., Zoloth, S. R., Moody, D. B., & Stebbins, W. C. (1978). Neural lateralization of species-specific vocalizations by Japanese macaques (*Macaca fuscata*). *Science*, 202, 324-327.

Roitblat, H. L., Scopatz, R. A., & Bever, T. G. (1987). The hierarchical representation of 3-item sequences. *Animal Learning and Behavior*, 15, 179-192.

Sidtis, J. (1980). On the nature of the cortical function underlying right hemisphere auditory perception. *Neuropsychologia*, 18, 321-330.

Simon, J. R. (1967). Ear preference in a simple reaction time task. *Journal of Experimental Psychology*, 75, 49-53.

Van Allen, M. W., Benton, A. L. and Gordon, M. C. (1966). Temporal discrimination in brain damaged patients. *Neuropsychologia*, 4, 159-167.

Vroon, P. A., Timmers, H. & Tempelaars, S. (1977). On the hemispheric representation of time. In S. Dornic (Ed.), *Attention and Performance VI*, (pp. 231-246). Hillsdale, NJ: Lawrence Erlbaum Associates.

14
Hemispheric Priming as a Technique in the Study of Lateralized Cognitive Processes in Chimpanzees: Some Recent Findings

William D. Hopkins and Robin D. Morris

For quite some time, there has been considerable interest in the relationship between cerebral dominance and cognitive functions (Allen, 1983; Beaton, 1986). Of particular interest has been the strong relation between the left hemisphere and language processing; however, later studies revealed that the right hemisphere was also dominant for a variety of cognitive and perceptual functions (Levy, 1982; Searleman, 1977).

In addition to cognitive functioning, many motor functions appear to be lateralized. For humans, it has been argued that greater than 90% are predominantly right-handed (Annett, 1985), although the notion that a person is exclusively right- or left-handed no longer seems appropriate (Healey, Liederman, & Geschwind, 1986). Of special note is that hand preference typically correlates with the hemisphere that is language dominant. For example, left hemisphere dominance for language is found in 96% of individuals with a right hand preference (Rasmussen & Milner, 1977). The remaining 4% is divided evenly between right hemisphere dominance or bilateral representation of language. About 70% of predominantly left-handed individuals are left hemisphere dominant for language processes and 15% are right hemisphere dominant. The remaining 15% have bilateral representation of language processing (Rasmussen & Milner, 1977).

Given the apparent robustness of lateralized functions in humans, the question of whether analogous or homologous functions exist in other species has been raised, particularly as it pertains to language (Harris, in press). Because many researchers have deemed the study of language impossible in animals, their focus of study has been on the presumably correlated hand preference. Despite some 50 years of research on hand preference in nonhuman animals, there still remains considerable debate on this issue (MacNeilage, Studdert-Kennedy, & Lindblom, 1987; Warren, 1980), and there is widespread disagreement on the definition of handedness, how best to measure it, and whether it exists at a population level for any species (for review, see Ward & Hopkins, in press).

The debate on whether hand preferences exist in nonhuman primates is not the focus of this chapter as it seems that handedness may not necessarily be the best behavior to focus on when studying lateralized functions in nonhumans. As some have suggested, hemispheric dominance for cognitive processes (not necessarily language) may be the driving force behind the ontogeny and phylogeny of cerebral asymmetries, rather than handedness (Hamilton & Vermeire, 1988a).

There are some behavioral data to support this notion. For example, Japanese macaques have been shown to process species-specific vocalizations better when these vocalizations are presented to the right ear (i.e., to the left hemisphere) (Petersen, Beecher, Zoloth, Moody, & Stebbins, 1978; Petersen, Beecher, Zoloth, Green, Marler, Moody, & Stebbins (1983). Moreover, in other species of macaque, right-hemisphere advantages in the processing of faces have been reported (Hamilton & Vermeire, 1988b), as well as left-hemisphere advantages for visual-spatial tasks (Hamilton, 1983; Hamilton & Vermeire, 1988b; Jason, Cowey, & Weiskrantz, 1984). These effects emerge despite the fact that subjects show a symmetric distribution of hand preference (i.e., an equal number of right- and left-handed individuals).

Although these findings are important, there are limitations in these results, which we have described elsewhere (Morris, Hopkins, Bolser, Gilmore, & Washburn, in press). Perhaps the greatest limitation in the advancement of a comparative model of hemispheric specialization has been

14. Lateralized cognitive processes

methodological and procedural factors. We know very little about cognitive functioning and hemispheric specialization in primates with neurologically intact brains. Almost all studies of laterality have employed either lesion or split-brain procedures to isolate information presented to either hemisphere. In comparison, there is a large body of literature of hemispheric specialization in normal intact human subjects using a variety of noninvasive techniques (Hannay, 1985).

One of the most widely used approaches for studying hemispheric specialization in humans has been either through dichotic listening (auditory presentation) or the tachistoscopic paradigms (visual presentation). In the case of visual presentation, stimuli are presented briefly (typically for less than 200 ms) to either the left (LVF) or right (RVF) visual half-fields while the subject fixates on a central point. After stimulus presentation, subjects typically report what information was presented or make some conditional reaction time response. A variety of procedural manipulations are used to ensure that subjects fixate on midline. These manipulations include requiring the subject to report the stimulus presented at the fixation point stimulus or alternately presenting the stimulus on either side of the fixation point so that the subject cannot predict its position.

It has long been thought that getting animals to fixate their gaze was either impossible or too difficult to train. This may have contributed to the rather limited research on neurologically intact subjects. In our laboratory, based on the earlier findings by Savage-Rumbaugh (1986) on joystick use by chimpanzees, and later studies in monkeys (Rumbaugh, Richardson, Washburn, Savage-Rumbaugh, & Hopkins, 1989; Richardson, Washburn, Hopkins, Savage-Rumbaugh, & Rumbaugh, 1990), we have developed a technique in which fixation can be sufficiently controlled by use of a cursor displayed on a computer monitor. The subjects are required to move the cursor to a central point on the screen and hold it there for a brief amount of time. If this condition is met, stimuli are presented rapidly to either visual half-field and, depending on the task, the subjects are required to make some sort of matching or conditional discriminative response, typically by moving the joystick upward or downward. Results of some studies carried out using this approach with mentally retarded children (Smith, Cash, Barr, & Putney, 1986) and nonhuman primates (Hopkins & Morris, 1989; Hopkins, Washburn, Rumbaugh, 1990) have been described elsewhere.

A second approach used in our laboratory to study cognition and laterality has been via use of hemispheric priming or warning stimulus paradigms, the focus of this chapter. To date, we have carried out several experiments examining generalized and lateralized priming effects using several different procedures and stimulus sets. The goal of this chapter is to describe some of the methodological factors that appear to be important in hemispheric priming studies and to describe some results with two language-trained chimpanzees, Sherman and Austin (see Savage-Rumbaugh, 1986, for description of language training).

METHODOLOGICAL ISSUES

Hemispheric priming trials are presented on an apparatus consisting of a video monitor and a push button. The button is located directly in front of the subject within easy reach. A button press begins the trial and its release ends the trial. On a typical hemispheric priming trial, a fixation stimulus, usually in the form of a plus sign (+), appears at a central location on the computer monitor. As soon as the subject presses the button, the trial starts with a foreperiod (typically 1-2 s in duration), followed by a warning stimulus presented either to the left or the right visual half-field (typically 150 ms in duration or less). The warning signal is then followed by a delay (1-2 s) followed by the presentation of a response cue at the fixation point. This response cue has been a 2 × 2 cm aqua blue square in our studies. The subject then responds by removing the finger from the response button as quickly as possible upon the appearance of the response cue. On some trials, for control purposes, no warning stimulus is presented. The difference in response latency (i.e., the time to remove the finger from the button) between trials in which a warning stimulus is presented, and the control trials is a measure of the degree to which a stimulus "primes", "activates" or "prepares" the subject to respond.

Before continuing, it is important to define priming or activation as it pertains to these studies. We have adopted a definition of activation used by Pribram and McGuiness (1975). They define *activation* as "the readiness to respond", "preparation for action," or "intention to respond," linked in some way to the stimulus being presented in a warning stimulus or priming paradigm. In the human cognitive literature, the concept of a prime is typically used in relation to facilitating lexical or conceptual access. For example, subjects are faster at recognizing two words as words when their meanings are related (e.g., nurse-doctor) than when their meanings are unrelated (e.g., nurse-butter; Meyer & Schvaneveldt, 1971). The first word in the pair is called the prime, and the second is called the target. Presumably, presentation of the prime word facilitates access to the target word by virtue of their semantic relation. Hence, although the terms priming and activation have been used somewhat differently,

14. Lateralized cognitive processes

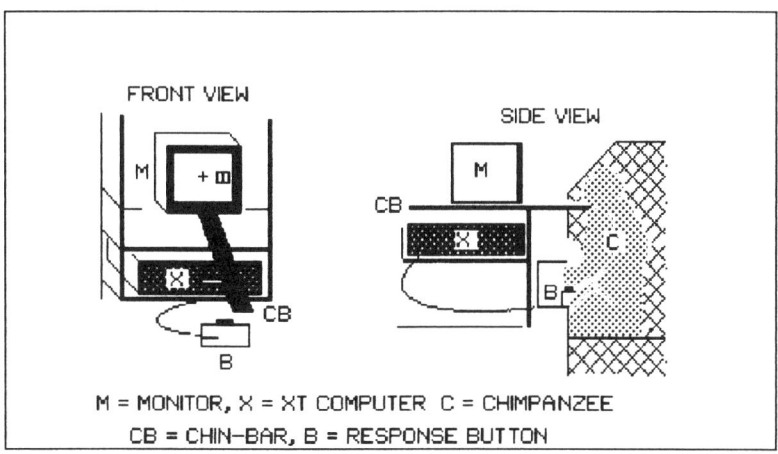

Figure 14.1: Experimental test apparatus.

in the present context they are essentially synonymous. One stimulus serves to cue or prepare subjects to make some sort of behavioral response to the second stimulus.

In our studies, we have been interested in the asymmetric hemispheric activation as described by Kinsbourne (1975), who has shown that each hemisphere is differentially activated by stimuli that are better processed by that particular hemisphere (see Bowers & Heilman, 1980).

During each trial, subjects are required to place their chin on a bar 54 cm from the screen so as to maintain a fixed distance from the computer monitor. Figure 14.1 shows the experimental test apparatus. Stimuli are presented 2 degrees off center so that there is no overlap in the visual meridian. Finally, the hand used to respond is counterbalanced across test sessions and also serves as an independent variable.

To ensure that our subjects are fixating, there are two factors built into the experimental design that foster the control of fixation. These include the location of the response cue and a response time limit. In all our studies, the response cue always occurs at the fixation point so that subjects "know" where to look for the stimulus to which they must respond. The second factor, response time limit, serves two functions. By making subjects respond within a specified time period, the subjects must look toward the fixation stimulus or

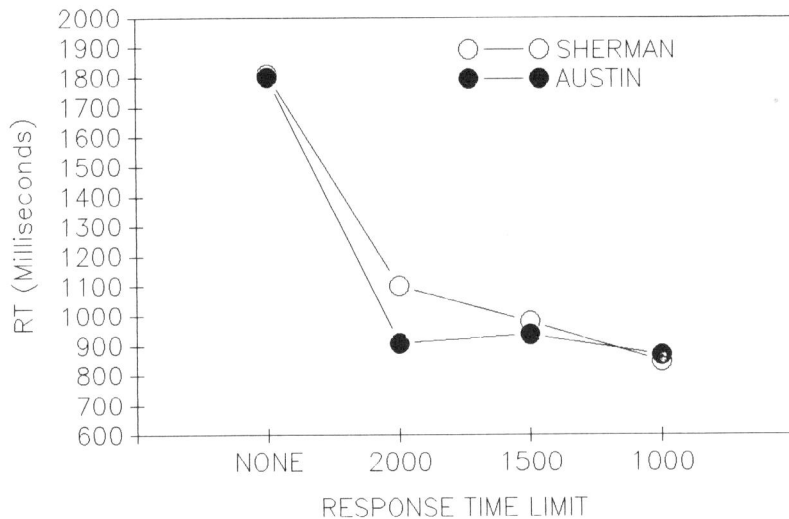

Figure 14.2: Mean reaction time as a function of response time limit.

they will be unable to respond correctly and quickly on a given trial. In addition, using a response time limit shapes the reaction time response to an asymptotic level. Thus subjects respond as quickly as possible, an important factor in the use of reaction times measures in laterality research.

Figure 14.2 shows the mean reaction times for Austin and Sherman as a function of decreasing response time limit. As can be seen, decreases in the response time limit resulted in faster responses. Unfortunately, as response latency decreased, so did response accuracy (see Figure 14.3). Choice accuracy for both chimps dropped below 80% with a 1 s response time limit. These data reflect an asymptotic level of performance and a speed of response versus accuracy trade-off for each subject.

In additional factor that may enhance fixation control, as well as limit anticipation factors, is use of randomized foreperiods and delays within the test session. Accurate anticipation of the response cue is difficult if it occurs at randomly varying times. Therefore, it becomes functionally important for the subject to look to the fixation stimulus in anticipation of the response cue in order to perform correctly.

14. Lateralized cognitive processes

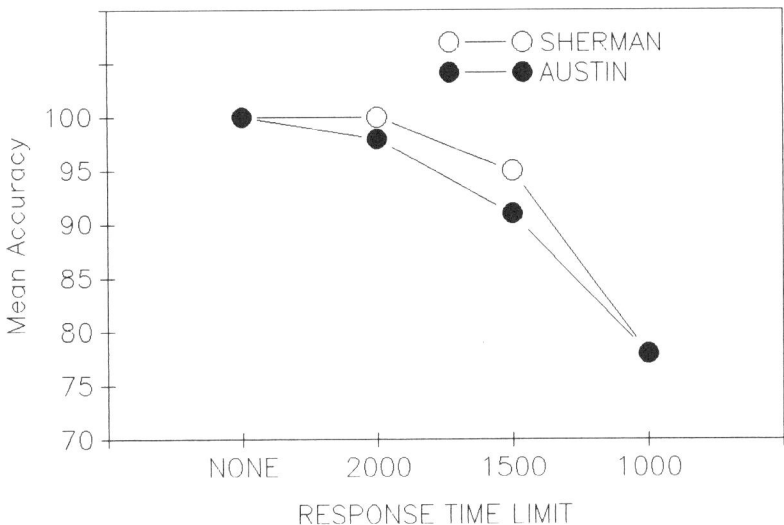

Figure 14.3: Mean accuracy as a function of response time limit.

STATISTICAL ISSUES

Given the limited number of chimpanzee subjects involved in these studies, the best way in which to present and analyze the data has been difficult to ascertain. In particular, the use of raw reaction times, mean reaction times, or differences in these times all have their limitations. In addition, because a large number of data points from each subject are needed for statistical purposes, testing must occur across days, or perhaps even months. This introduces possible confounds due to motivation, fatigue, and familiarity with previously novel stimuli. Familiarity has been found to affect visual-field advantages in human (Sergent, 1981) and nonhuman primates (Hopkins, et al., 1990).

Consistent with other studies of activation (Heilman & Van Den Abell, 1979; Shapiro & Hynd, 1985), we have primarily used a reduction value in assessing hemispheric activation because simple reaction times vary as a function of hand use, thus biasing the data for a particular hand. The reduction score is the difference in latency between primed response stimuli and nonprimed response stimuli. Suppose that the mean reaction time to primed trials was 400 ms for both the left and right hand. However, on the nonprimed trials (what we call no-warning stimulus trials), the mean reaction time for the left hand is 600 ms and 500 ms for the right hand. If you subtract the mean primed trials from the nonprimed trials for each hand, you have a difference of -200 ms for the left hand and -100 ms for the right hand. Negative values represent priming (i.e., enhanced or faster reaction times) and nonnegative values indicate no activation. Moreover, larger negative values represent greater activation. Thus, in our example, we could conclude that activation is better for the left hand compared to the right. It is important to remember that, had raw reaction time values been used, no difference would have been found. In our own studies, each raw primed reaction time value is subtracted from the mean nonprimed trials as a function of hand use and timing condition. These values are then used as the dependent measures in a repeated measures analysis of variance.

Recent Findings with Lexigrams

A series of experiments was performed with Sherman and Austin to address the issue of whether lexigrams, serving as warning stimuli, resulted in asymmetrical priming. Four warning stimulus types were utilized. One set contained meaningful lexigrams (KNOWN) that the chimpanzees could use as labels and could comprehend under blind test conditions. The second set of symbols contained stimuli that were on the chimpanzees keyboard but never language-trained. Thus, by our definition they were visually familiar (VFAM). The third set of symbols were action lexigrams used by the chimpanzees. Thus, they were familiar to the chimpanzees but it was difficult to document whether these symbols were representational (LFAM). The fourth set of warning stimuli were lexigrams constructed according to the same rules as those in the other sets, but that the chimpanzees had never seen prior to the study (UNKNOWN).

The basic test procedure was similar to that described earlier with a total of 48 trials presented each test session. Within the 48 trial test sessions, 16 trials were presented to either the left or right visual half-field (LVF, RVF). On the remaining 16 trials, no warning stimulus was presented (NWS). Using the same four timing intervals described previously [(FP = 1, D = 1 (1); FP = 1, D = 2 (2); FP = 2, D = 1 (3); FP = 2, D = 2 (4)], of the 16 trials presented to each visual half-field, one trial was presented for each warning stimulus type at each timing interval. A total of 30 test sessions was administered. During half of these sessions subjects responded with their left hand, and during the other half they responded with their right hand. Hence, each subject received a total of 1440 trials. Data were collected for Austin, Sherman and Lana in this

14. Lateralized cognitive processes

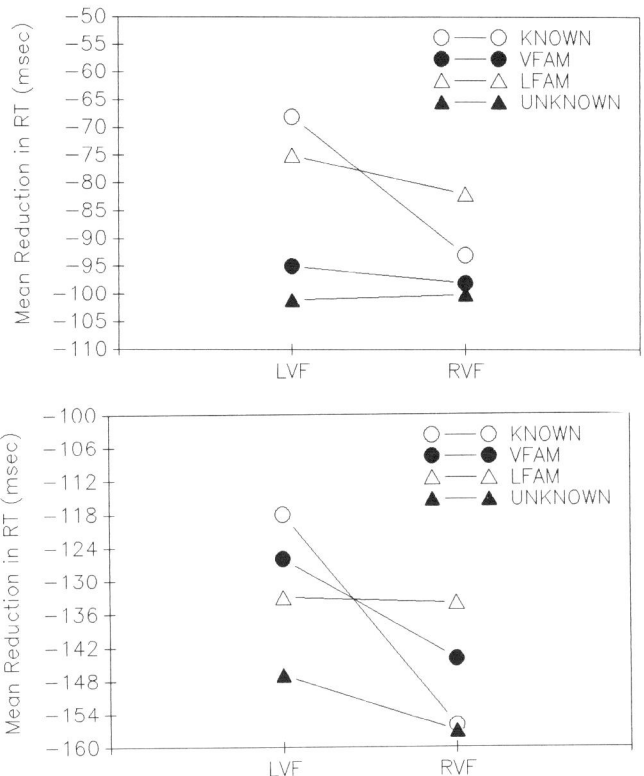

Figure 14.4: Mean reduction in RT for Austin (top panel) and Sherman (bottom panel) when using their right hand as a function of visual half-field and warning stimulus. From "Asymmetrical hemispheric priming for known and unknown warning stimuli in two language-trained chimpanzees (*Pan troglodytes*)". By W. D. Hopkins, R. D. Morris, & E. S. Savage-Rumbaugh, 1991, *Journal of Experimental Psychology: General*, 120, 46-56. Copyright, 1991, American Psychological Association.

experiment, but our earlier report focused on data only from Austin and Sherman (see Hopkins, Morris, & Savage-Rumbaugh, 1991).

The basic finding from this study was a right visual half-field advantage in priming for lexigrams that were meaningful to the chimpanzees.

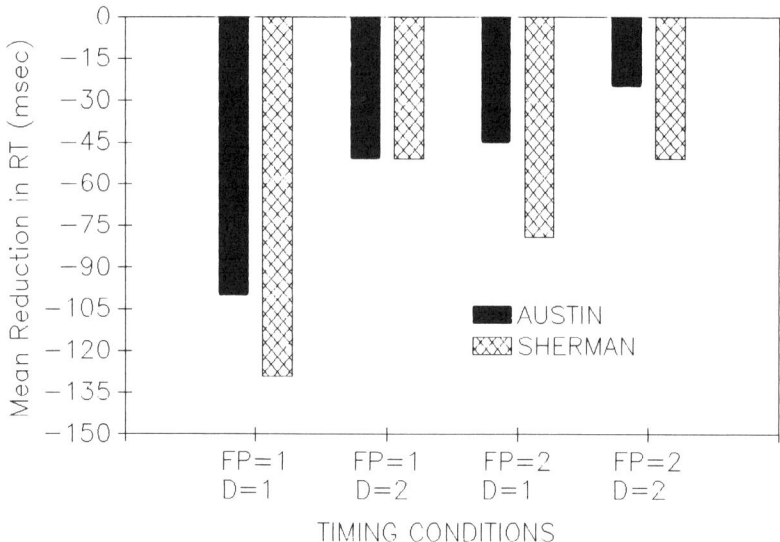

Figure 14.5: Mean reduction in RT as a function of timing interval for Austin and Sherman.

Moreover, the right visual field advantage was enhanced by use of the right hand in Sherman and Austin. Figure 14.4 shows the mean reductions in RT for each warning stimulus type and visual half-field when Austin and Sherman were using their right hand to respond. As can be seen, the reduction in RT was much greater when meaningful lexigrams were presented to the right visual field than when they presented to the left visual field. No other significant between visual half-field differences were found.

THE TIME COURSE OF HEMISPHERIC ACTIVATION

It should be pointed out that the asymmetrical hemispheric priming effects previously described have only been found in specific time conditions relative to the foreperiod and delay. When asymmetrical priming has been found in these chimpanzees, it has largely been restricted to those trials with a 1-s foreperiod and a 1-s delay. Figure 14.5 shows the overall mean reductions in reaction time (RT) as a function of timing interval. Reduction in RT for time condition 1 was significantly different from the remaining three timing conditions. These differences reflect what has been referred to as stimulus onset asynchrony (SOA) (Niemi & Naatanen, 1981). SOA is the time between the presentation

14. Lateralized cognitive processes

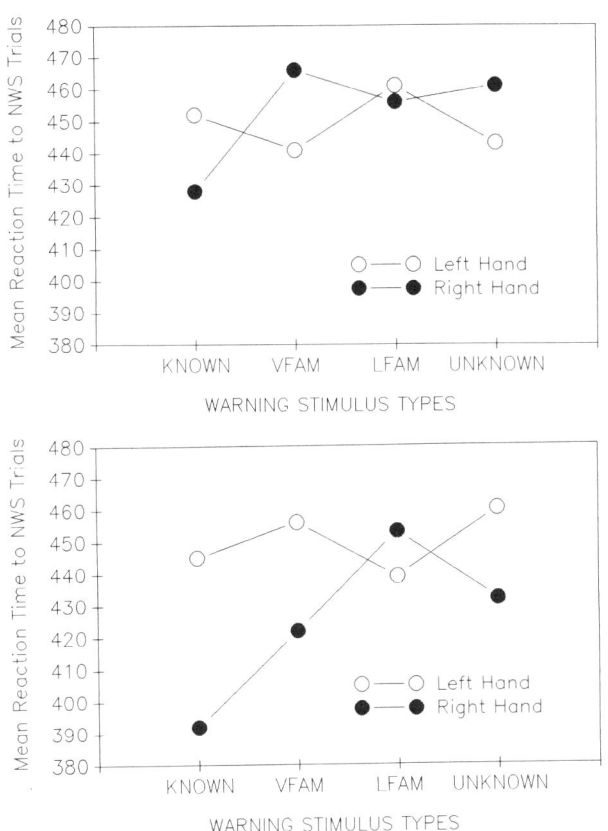

Figure 14.6: Mean reaction times to nonprimed trials as a function of warning stimulus and hand for Austin (top panel) and Sherman (bottom panel). Reaction times were determined based on the warning stimulus presented on trial $N - 1$.

of the priming stimulus and the presentation of the response stimulus. As SOA increases, the difference between primed and unprimed RTs decreases. This pattern of results indicates that the warning stimulus becomes less functional over time. It is possible that the significant hemispheric asymmetries found only in time condition 1 are due to the greater functional significance the warning stimuli serve under this condition. As the duration of a trial became longer, anticipation factors became more prevalent in response strategy compared to prepatory responses per se.

- 303 -

One additional point is relevant to the discussion of the time course of activation. In our previous analyses, we have used a reduction approach to determine the degree to which a warning stimulus speeds responding. The nonprimed trials served merely as a control, although there was a considerable degree of variability in the RTs on these trials. One source of this variance may be carryover effects from the previous warning stimulus presented on trial $N - 1$. Such an effect could be likened to proactive interference (see Edhouse & White, 1988; Hogan, Edwards, & Zentall, 1981; Jitsumori, Wright, & Shyan, 1989; Moise, 1976). For example, on trial N, the warning stimulus may be a meaningful lexigram. On trial $N + 1$, a control trial may be presented. The question arises as to whether responses to nonprimed trials are influenced by the previous warning stimulus from trial $N - 1$ as reflected by differences in reaction time for each hand.

To address this issue, the mean reaction times to nonprimed trials were calculated as a function of what the warning stimulus was on trial $N - 1$. These data were calculated for each hand, warning stimulus and visual half-field to determine whether any interactions were found among these variables. The mean reaction times for the right and left hands as a function of warning stimulus type for each subject are depicted in Figure 14.6.

From this analysis it was found that right-hand responses were faster than left-hand responses on NWS trials preceded by a trial with a KNOWN warning stimulus. No other significant between-hand differences emerged for the remaining warning stimulus types. This finding suggests that activation did persist, particularly for KNOWN warning stimuli, over longer temporal durations than those employed within a specific trial. Simply stated, KNOWN warning stimuli presented on trial $N - 1$ affected the subsequent responses to NWS trials on trial N. In addition, because this effect was specific to the right hand, it appears that the longevity of activation was due to the relationship between the meaningful warning stimulus and left hemisphere processing. Interestingly, whether the warning stimulus was presented to the RVF or LVF on trial $N - 1$ had no effect on this result. This finding is consistent with human studies, which show that hand by warning stimulus interactions emerge when warning stimuli are presented centrally, with right-hand responses faster to verbal stimuli and left-hand responses faster to human faces (Bowers & Heilman, 1980).

SUMMARY AND CONCLUSION

Collectively, the data suggest that the patterns of hemispheric activation and specialization observed in these chimpanzees are similar to those found in humans. Although further studies are clearly necessary, these are some of the first evidence of hemispheric specialization in the processing of meaningful symbols by chimpanzees. It should be noted that the patterns observed in Austin and Sherman are very similar. That Austin and Sherman reveal similar patterns is not surprising given that they have been reared in a nearly identical environment and both would be classified as right handed (Bolser, Runfeldt, & Morris, 1987).

The results of these experiments indicate that hemispheric priming studies may be useful in the study of cognition and lateralized functions in nonhuman animals. In fact, Blough (1989) recently showed that selective attention could be primed in pigeons so as to facilitate reaction time responses to previously learned conditional response cues. These data, taken together, support the view that inhibitory and facilitative processes that occur in human cognition with regard to selective attention (Posner & Snyder, 1975; Rosch, 1975) are present in other species.

ACKNOWLEDGMENT

We gratefully acknowledge the support and comments of Dr. Duane M. Rumbaugh and Dr. Sue Savage-Rumbaugh. Without their initial and continued effort this work would not be possible. Parts of this research fulfilled portions of the doctoral requirements within the Department of Psychology of the College of Arts and Science, Georgia State University for William D. Hopkins. Support for this research was provided by NICHD grant RR-00615 and HD-06016 to the Yerkes Regional Primate Research Center. Additional support was provided by the College of Arts and Science, Georgia State University.

REFERENCES

Allen, M. (1983). Models of hemispheric specialization. *Psychological Bulletin*, 93, 73-104.

Annett, M. (1985). *Left, right, hand and brain: The right shift theory.* Hillsdale, NJ: Lawrence Erlbaum Associates.

Beaton, A. (1986). *Left side, right side: A review of laterality research*. New Haven, CT: Yale University Press.

Blough, P. M. (1989). Attentional priming and visual search in pigeons. *Journal of Experimental Psychology: Animal Behavior Processes*, 15, 358-365.

Bolser, L. A., Runfeldt, S., & Morris, R. D. (1987). Handedness in language-trained chimpanzees (*Pan troglodytes*) in daily activities and assessment tasks. *Journal of Clinical and Experimental Neuropsychology*, 10, 40.

Bowers, D., & Heilman, K. M. (1980). Material specific hemispheric activation. *Neuropsychologia*, 18, 309-319.

Edhouse, W. V., & White, K. G. (1988). Sources of proactive interference in animal memory. *Journal of Experimental Psychology: Animal Behavior Processes*, 14, 56-70.

Hamilton, C. R. (1983). Lateralization for orientation in split- brain monkeys. *Behavioral Brain Research*, 10, 399-403.

Hamilton, C. R., & Vermeire, B. A. (1988a). Cognition, not handedness, is lateralized in monkeys. *The Behavioral and Brain Sciences*, 11, 723-725.

Hamilton, C. R., & Vermeire, B. A. (1988b). Complementary hemispheric specialization in monkeys. *Science*, 242, 1691- 1693.

Hannay, H. J. (1985). *Experimental techniques in human neuropsychology*. New York: Academic Press.

Harris, L. J. (in press). Handedness in apes and monkeys: Some views from the past. In J. P. Ward, & W. D. Hopkins (Eds.), *Current behavioral evidence of primate asymmetries*. New York: Springer Verlag.

Healey, J. M., Liederman, J., & Geschwind, N. (1986). Handedness is not a unidimensional trait. *Cortex*, 22, 33-53.

Heilman, K. M., & Van Den Abell, T. (1979). Right hemispheric dominance for mediating cerebral activation. *Neuropsychologia*, 17, 315-321.

14. Lateralized cognitive processes

Hogan, D. E., Edwards, C. Q., & Zentall, T. R. (1981). Delayed matching in the pigeon: Interference produced by the prior delayed matching trial. *Animal Learning & Behavior*, 9, 395- 400.

Hopkins, W. D., & Morris, R. D. (1989). Laterality for visual-spatial processing in two language-trained chimpanzees (*Pan troglodytes*). *Behavioral Neuroscience*, 103, 227-234.

Hopkins, W. D., Morris, R. D., & Savage-Rumbaugh, E. S. (1991). Asymmetrical hemispheric priming for known and unknown warning stimuli in two language-trained chimpanzees (*Pan troglodytes*). *Journal of Experimental Psychology: General*, 120, 46-56.

Hopkins, W. D., Washburn, D. W., & Rumbaugh, D. M. (1990). Processing of form stimuli presented unilaterally in humans, chimpanzees (*Pan troglodytes*) and monkeys (*Macaca mulatta*). *Behavioral Neuroscience*, 104, 577-582.

Jason, G. W., Cowey, A., & Weiskrantz, L. (1984). Hemispheric asymmetry for a visual-spatial task in monkeys. *Neuropsychologia*, 22, 777-784.

Jitsumori, M., Wright, A. A., & Shyan, M. R. (1989). Buildup and release from proactive interference in a rhesus monkey. *Journal of Experimental Psychology: Animal Behavior Processes*, 15, 329-337.

Kinsbourne, M. (1975). The mechanism of hemispheric control of the lateral gradient of attention. In R. M. A. Rabbitt & S. Dormine (Eds.), *Attention and performance IV* (pp. 239-258). London: Academic Press.

Levy, J. (1982). Mental processes in the non-verbal hemisphere. In D. R. Griffin (Ed.), *Animal mind-human mind* (pp.57-73). Dahlem Konferenzen, Berlin: Springer-Verlag.

MacNeilage, P. F., Studdert-Kennedy, M. G., & Lindblom, B. (1987). Primate handedness reconsidered. *The Behavioral and Brain Sciences*, 10, 247-303.

Meyer, D. E. & Schvaneveldt, R. W. (1971). Facilitation in recognizing pairs of words: Evidence of a dependence between retrieval operations. *Journal of Experimental Psychology*, 90, 227-234.

Moise, S. L. (1976). Proactive effects of stimuli, delays, and response position during matching to sample. *Animal Learning & Behavior*, 4, 37-40.

Morris, R. D., Hopkins, W. D., Bolser, L. A., & Gilmore, L., & Washburn, D. A. (in press). Functional lateralization in language-trained chimpanzees. In J. P. Ward & W. D. Hopkins (Eds.), *Current behavioral evidence of primate asymmetries*. New York: Springer Verlag.

Niemi, P., & Naatanen, R. (1981). Foreperiod and simple reaction time. *Psychological Bulletin*, 133, 133-162.

Petersen, M. R., Beecher, M. D., Zoloth, S. R., Moody, D., & Stebbins, W. (1978). Neural lateralization of species specific vocalizations in Japanese macaques (*Macaca fuscata*). *Science*, 202, 324-327.

Petersen, M. R., Beecher, M. D., Zoloth, S. R., Green, S., Marler, P. R., Moody, D. B., & Stebbins, W. (1983). Neural lateralization of vocalizations by Japanese macaques: Communicative significance is more important than acoustic structure. *Behavioral Neuroscience*, 98, 779-790.

Posner, M. I., & Snyder, C. R. R. (1975). Facilitation and inhibition in the processing of signals. In P. M. Rabbitt & S. Dornic (Eds.), *Attention and performance* (pp. 669-682). London: Academic Press.

Pribram, K. H., & McGuiness, D. (1975). Arousal, activation and effort in the control of attention. *Psychological Review*, 82, 116-149.

Rasmussen, T., & Milner, B. (1977). The role of early left-brain injury in determining lateralization of cerebral speech functions. *Annals of the New York Academy of Sciences*, 299, 355-369.

Richardson, W. K., Washburn, D. A., Hopkins, W. D., Savage-Rumbaugh, E. S., & Rumbaugh, D. M. (1990). The NASA-LRC computerized test system. *Behavioral Research Methods, Instruments, & Computers*, 22, 127-131.

Rosch, E. (1975). Cognitive representations of semantic categories. *Journal of Experimental Psychology: General*, 104, 192-233.

14. Lateralized cognitive processes

Rumbaugh, D. M., Richardson, W. K., Washburn, D. A., Savage- Rumbaugh, E. S., & Hopkins, W. D. (1989). Rhesus monkeys (*Macaca mulatta*), video tasks, and implications for stimulus-response spatial contiguity. *Journal of Comparative Psychology*, 103, 32-38.

Savage-Rumbaugh, E. S. (1986). *Ape language: From conditioned response to symbols.* New York: Columbia University Press.

Searleman, A. A. (1977). A review of right hemisphere linguistic capacities. *Psychological Bulletin*, 84, 503-528.

Sergent, J. (1981). Basic determinants in visual-field effects with special reference to Hanney et al. (1981) study. *Brain and Language*, 16, 158-164.

Shapiro, M. S., & Hynd, G. W. (1985). The development of functional lateralization in visual hemifield attention. *Developmental Neuropsychology*, 1, 67-80.

Smith, S. T., Cash, C., Barr, S. E., & Putney, R. T. (1986). The nonspeech assessment of hemispheric specialization in retarded children. *Neuropsychologia*, 24, 293-296.

Ward, J. P., & Hopkins, W. D. (in press). *Current behavioral evidence of primate asymmetries.* New York: Springer-Verlag.

Warren, J. M. (1980). Handedness and laterality in humans and other animals. *Physiological Psychology*, 8, 351-359.

15
Cognitive Factors Affecting Comprehension of Gesture Language Signs: A Brief Comparison of Dolphins and Humans

Palmer Morrel-Samuels and Louis M. Herman

In this chapter we examine factors affecting gesture recognition in a bottlenosed dolphin (*Tursiops truncatus*), and consider whether the nature of that recognition process is similar for dolphins and humans. We first describe the types of gesture language signs used to study comprehension in the dolphin then review a gesture recognition study where humans and dolphins were shown videotaped gestures under two viewing conditions. We then describe our recent research on cerebral asymmetry, and discuss the findings as they bear on general theories of hemispheric specialization.

ARTIFICIAL GESTURAL LANGUAGE

In our work on language comprehension, a bottlenosed dolphin named Akeakamai, has been taught an artificial language that currently contains approximately 50 individual gesture signs (see Herman, 1986, 1987; Herman, Richards, & Wolz, 1984, for reviews). The gestures of this language fall into two major groups: local commands and formal commands. Local commands typically contain a single gesture; grammatically, the gesture functions either as a transitive verb or an intransitive verb. For example, correct responses to the gesture OVER require that the dolphin jump over one object in the tank, whereas SOMERSAULT does not require involvement with an object. Local gesture signs are, in some respects, functionally analogous to the one-word holophrases characteristic of children's speech (Barrett, 1982; Dore, 1975).

Formal commands contain two to five sequential gestures and may be either nominal or relational. (Nominal commands have been called nonrelational commands in previous accounts; we have adopted the shorter term for convenience here.) In nominal commands a single object is named and a specific action involving it is requested (e.g., BALL OVER requires that the dolphin leap over a ball). Relational commands, on the other hand, require the construction of a specific spatial relationship between two named objects; for example, a correct response to the three-gesture string BASKET BALL FETCH requires that the dolphin take the ball to the basket. For both nominal and relational commands gesture order is important. For example, BALL OVER and the technically anomalous string OVER BALL are not equivalent. When an anomalous gesture order is used in nominal commands the dolphin simply ignores the object sign (BALL, in this example), treats the command as if it were the local sign OVER, and jumps over any available object. Gesture order plays a particularly important role in relational commands, because the command's meaning is entirely contingent on the order of the gestures in the string. BASKET BALL FETCH, for example, is not synonymous with BALL BASKET FETCH; in the former string BASKET functions grammatically as the indirect object, whereas BALL serves that function in the latter string.

GENERAL FEATURES OF GESTURE RECOGNITION

The dolphin's ability to respond correctly to multigesture strings such as those just described suggests that each sign in the string can be correctly recognized; however, inferences about recognition of isolated signs require analyses that control for an array of factors that lie outside the domain of semantics. To determine which variables facilitate or impede successful recognition of gesture signs for our dolphins, and to compare those findings to human performance, we showed a set of local and formal commands to a group of 21 humans and to the dolphin Akeakamai (Herman, Morrel-Samuels, & Pack, 1990). The experiment tested five groups varying in fluency with the artificial language: expert trainers, intermediate trainers, novice trainers, volunteers, and the dolphin. Group assignment was determined by an independent judge familiar with each subject's signing skill. The stimuli were 29 single-gesture holophrases and multigesture

15. Cognitive factors affecting comprehension

strings containing a total of 50 gesture signs presented via videotape under two viewing conditions. In the full display condition a human trainer was shown from the waist up signing in full illumination. In the point-light display condition, the television screen showed two bright circles of light tracing out the movement of the signer's hands; the remainder of the signer's body was obscured, so that these two moving circles were all that appeared on the blackened screen. Averaging across these two conditions, mean comprehension for the dolphin was not significantly different from that of intermediate-level trainers, a group of graduate and undergraduate students with considerable signing experience (M = 4.3 months).

The results show that the dolphin, despite lack of explicit training with video displays, was able to demonstrate good comprehension of the videotaped gesture signs. But the more specific question pertains to the variables that facilitate or impede good performance. What is it that makes an individual gesture easy to comprehend, both for the dolphin and for human subjects? To address this question we ran two exploratory multiple regressions using accurate comprehension of the 100 individual gestures (50 under each of the two viewing conditions) as the dependent variable. Covariates controlled for individual differences between subjects (coded as a class variable with 21 levels), for the sign's apparent grammatical function (coded as adjective, verb, indirect object, direct object, or holophrase), and for the viewing condition (full-torso display and point-light display). Predictor variables measured the gesture's duration (measured using slow-motion video), spatial extent (estimated by independent judges as small or large), dimensionality (coded as multidimensional, or as unidimensional if the gestural motion traveled in only one XYZ plane), number of cycles (coded dichotomously to distinguish between gestures that contained repeated sequences and those that did not contain repetitions), recency-primacy faciliation (coded as easy if the gesture was first or last in the string, and hard if it was embedded in a multiple-gesture string), and the number of gestures in the string (either one, two, or three).

The first regression results showed that comprehension accuracy was above chance and varied systematically with duration, spatial extent, dimensionality, and number of gestures in the string (Herman, et al., 1990, Experiment 2; results were essentially identical using logistic regression in place of linear regression). Thus, each of these four structural variables, when considered independently of one another, appeared to affect gesture comprehension.

The second multiple regression again tested gesture comprehension as the dependent variable, but examined whether the effect of the four structural variables was different for different subjects. The regression showed that comprehension varied systematically with these same four variables (duration, spatial extent, dimensionality, and number of gestures), but that this effect was not equivalent for experts, intermediates, novices, volunteers, and the dolphin. Specifically, the dolphin seemed to do well, if we take intermediates as a benchmark, with gestures that were small or unidimensional, but poorly with gestures that were long in duration. (For a description of similar work testing responses to novel signs, see Shyan & Herman, 1987; Shyan & Wright, this volume, chapter 19; for similar work with human subjects, see Poizner, Bellugi, & Lutes-Driscoll, 1981.)

The dolphin's ability to maintain high levels of comprehension even when the gesture was small or unidimensional may indicate that its visual system is specialized for responding to dynamic stimuli that possess these qualities. In the wild, dolphins would be well served by a visual system that can operate effectively in suboptimal viewing conditions where moving objects (such as prey) may stimulate only a small area of the retina. Such a functionalist explanation, despite its teleological features, does receive some support from physiological evidence: The dolphin's retina contains an unusually high proportion of giant ganglion cells with large receptive fields (Dawson, 1980; Shibkova, 1969), and the optic nerve contains many large-diameter axons (Morgane & Jacobs, 1972). Both characteristics are consistent with the specialization for motion detection (Dawson, 1980) suggested by the dolphin's unimpeded recognition of small and unidimensional gestures.

At least two explanations could accommodate the dolphin's poor performance with long-duration gestures: A long duration gesture may tax the capacity of the dolphin's short-term memory, or it may induce confusions between gestures that share specific features of appearance. Given that the dolphin can recall action sequences (Xitco, 1988), 3-dimensional objects (Herman, Hovancik, Gory, & Bradshaw, 1989), 2-dimensional patterns (Hunter, 1988), and gestural commands (Herman et al., 1984) for at least 30 s with little or no decrement in performance, it is not reasonable to argue that single-gesture signs having a mean duration of approximately 2 s tax the dolphin's working memory. It seems more likely that long duration induces sign confusion, as if the displayed gesture were sequentially compared to a set of templates in memory. By this explanation the dolphin recognizes the sign using a bottom-up matching process rather than a top-down process of elimination. In any event, it is clearly not the case that the dolphin's performance increases with gesture

15. Cognitive factors affecting comprehension

duration, a trend we could reasonably expect if deduction played a primary role in recognition of isolated gestures under these conditions.

In both of the regressions described earlier, the covariate classifying grammatical function was highly significant, even when other variables (e.g., number of gestures in the command, gesture order in the string) were partialed out. The findings parallel human data on recognition accuracy for the spontaneous gestures that accompany speech (Krauss, Morrel-Samuels, & Colasante, 1991), and substantiate earlier claims (Herman et al., 1984) that grammatical category affects the dolphin's ability to recognize gesture language signs. A further analysis of these data comparing all human subjects to the dolphin revealed that recognition for humans and for the dolphin differed significantly as a function of grammatical category [$F(8,2178) = 2.10, p < .03$]. Specifically, when effects associated with primacy-recency facilitation, viewing condition, number of gestures in the command, gesture length, gesture duration, dimensionality, and number of cycles in the gesture were all partialed out, the dolphin's recognition accuracy was lowest for indirect objects ($M = 33\%, B = 0.36$) whereas humans in general tended to have lowest accuracy with modifiers ($M = 58\%, B = -0.12$). Though interpretation of the interaction is complicated by a number of factors (e.g., the near-perfect performance of experts with all categories, the dolphin's requirement to retain the referent of the indirect object in memory while looking for and transporting the referent of the direct object, and the relatively low frequency of modifiers and indirect objects in training sessions with the dolphin), it is still a sound generalization that grammatical category has predictive validity for both humans and the dolphin. It is important to note that this analysis controls for the gesture's order in the command by partialing out the effects of primacy-recency facilitation and number of gestures in the command. That is, even though gesture order and grammatical function are not entirely independent in the artificial language, the performance decrement associated with modifiers and indirect objects in these data surpasses the effect that can be attributed to gesture order alone. Moreover, even when all other measured effects are partialed out (namely those associated with recency-primacy facilitation, viewing condition, number of cycles in the gesture, gesture length, gesture duration, dimensionality, and number of gestures in the command), the dolphin has poorer recognition accuracy for gestures functioning as indirect objects ($M = 33\%$) than it does for similar or identical gestures functioning as direct objects ($M = 75\%$), a difference that is statistically significant (least-squares mean, $t = 1.93, p < .05$). The analysis clearly shows that comprehension for the dolphin can be predicted by grammatical category, and suggests that the decrement associated with indirect objects may reflect either syntactic complexity, interference effects, or both.

CEREBRAL ASYMMETRY DURING GESTURE RECOGNITION

If syntactic complexity impairs the dolphin's comprehension of gestures functioning as indirect objects, then complexity-based effects should be apparent in a variety of tasks that require attention to syntax. Furthermore, if syntactic processing is mediated primarily by the left cerebral hemisphere in humans, as neuropsychological studies suggest (Christopoulou & Bonvillian, 1985; Gazzaniga & Hillyard, 1971; Zaidel, 1983; Zurif & Sait, 1970) then evidence of cerebral asymmetry associated with syntactic complexity in the dolphin would be of particular interest.

In humans, it has been found that printed words are processed better by the left hemisphere (LH) and pictographic stimuli are typically processed better by the right hemisphere (RH), though the nature of the task and stimuli can minimize or even reverse these effects (Bryden & Allard, 1976; McMullen & Bryden, 1987). For example, people respond to printed words faster when they are shown in the right visual field-left hemisphere (RVF-LH) (e.g., Bryden, 1965; Ellis & Shepherd, 1974; Geffen, Bradshaw, & Wallace, 1971; Hamers & Lambert, 1977; Poizner & Lane, 1979). Conversely, faces and pictures of landscapes are typically processed more rapidly when they are presented to the left visual field-right hemisphere (LVF-RH) (e.g., Bradshaw & Nettleton, 1983; Bryden, 1982; Levy, 1983). Though the data are relatively consistent, consensus about the nature of such asymmetries has been elusive. Different theories have suggested that the left hemisphere in humans is specialized for tasks involving symbolic language (Le Doux, 1983), fine-motor control (Kimura, 1973, 1976), high spatial frequency (Sergent, 1982), or analysis (Bever, 1975, 1980; Bradshaw & Nettleton, 1981; Levy-Agresti & Sperry, 1968), to name but a few.

In our first test of cerebral asymmetry in the dolphin, we predicted that complex analysis would be completed faster by the dolphin's left hemisphere than by its right (Morrel-Samuels, Herman, & Bever, 1989, 1991). Support for such a hypothesis comes from the finding that some cerebral structures in the LH of the dolphin are larger than corresponding structures in the RH (Cranford & Amundin, 1989; Ridgway & Brownson, 1979, 1984). The anatomical asymmetry is similar to that found in humans (Geschwind & Levitsky, 1968; Marx, 1983; Wada, Clarke, & Hamm, 1975; Witelson & Pallie, 1973; though see Carmon, Harishanu, Lowinger, & Lavy, 1972). However, encephelograph (EEG) studies show that dolphins only activate one hemisphere at a time while resting (Mukhametov, 1989; Mukhametov, Supin, & Polyakova, 1977; Shurley,

15. Cognitive factors affecting comprehension

Serafetinides, Brooks, Elsner, & Kenney, 1969), evidence suggesting the hemispheres are either independent or equivalent at least to some extent.

Gesture recognition, like some other tasks, seems to require both hemispheres to varying degrees. Static tachistoscopic displays of isolated American Sign Language (ASL) gestures are usually recognized faster (Poizner & Lane, 1979) and more accurately in the left visual field-right hemisphere (LVF- RH) (Poizner, Battison & Lane, 1979; also see Manning, Goble, Markman, & La Breche, 1977; McKeever, Hoemann, Florian, & VanDeventer, 1976). However, if tests are restricted to subjects who are fully fluent in ASL, recognition is more accurate in the RVF-LH (Neville & Bellugi, 1978). Moreover, when the left hemisphere is disabled by a barbiturate, patients cannot name pictures and objects using ASL signs (Damasio, Bellugi, Damasio, Poizner, & Van Gilder, 1986), and patients with left-hemisphere lesions show little (Heilman, Rothi, Campanella, & Wolfson, 1979; Kirshner & Webb, 1981) or no ability (Bonvillian & Friedman, 1978; Holmes, 1975) to create meaningful gesture language phrases. In general, the right hemisphere seems to carry the processing burden when signs can be processed as simple pictographic stimuli, whereas the left hemisphere seems to be engaged when sign production or comprehension entails higher-order processes associated with complex language.

To test for asymmetry we capitalized on the finding that dolphins have no ipsilateral connections between retina and optic cortex (Hatschek, 1903; Jacobs, Morgane, & McFarland, 1975; Supin, Mukhametov, Ladygina, Popov, Mass, & Poliakova, 1978). Visual information from the right eye goes to the LH first, and information from the left eye goes to the RH first. Cerebral asymmetries can therefore be tested in dolphins by exposing stimuli monocularly to each eye and comparing response time (RT) in the two viewing conditions. All other things being equal, a faster response while using the right eye suggests the LH is specialized for the experimental task, whereas a faster response with the left eye suggests specialization of the RH.

Recall that gesture order is of primary importance for relational commands because their meaning is contingent on the order of the gestures in the string. Accordingly, we assumed that nominal commands are relatively simple stimuli, whereas relational commands, because of their greater syntactic constraints, are relatively complex stimuli.

Stimuli for the experiment were 15 videotaped relational commands (e.g., HOOP BALL FETCH) and 15 nominal commands (e.g., HOOP UNDER).

All gestures were produced by an experienced signer and appeared on a video monitor placed behind an underwater window. The dolphin, Akeakamai, received no explicit training for comprehension of these monocularly presented gesture signs. Reaction time was measured from the onset of the gestural command to the moment the dolphin "snapped" her rostrum out of the stationing cup as she left the underwater window to perform the requested action. Each gestural command was shown twice, once monocularly to each eye on separate trials.

Four naive judges independently viewed videotaped records of each trial and identified the dolphin's moment of reaction (as indexed by a stopwatch readout appearing on each video frame). This frame-by-frame analysis yielded two dependent measures: reaction time (RT), and a derived measure of the difference (Delta-T) between the latency when the stimulus was presented to right eye minus the latency when the stimulus was presented to the left eye. Judges independently eliminated from consideration all trials on which they believed the dolphin might have had an opportunity to view the stimulus binocularly. A total of 26 of the 30 pairs of trials were judged as monocular in both viewing conditions by at least one judge; on these 26 trials, RT was taken as the average of all available judgments. Assessments of RT from the four judges were highly correlated, indicating suitable inter-rater reliability in judgments of the dolphin's moment of reaction.

To determine Delta-T we averaged stopwatch readouts at the moment of response across all four judges; this yielded 26 scores, 13 for simple commands and 13 for complex commands. In general, responses to simple commands were faster when stimuli appeared in the LVF-RH, but responses to complex commands were faster when presented in the RVF-LH. The general hypothesis of faster responses to simple commands in the LVF-RH, and faster responses to complex commands in the RVF-LH was confirmed in 20 of 26 cases, a difference that cannot be explained by chance alone. A full report of the method and a multivariate analysis examining the relation between RT, stimulus duration, and viewing condition can be found elsewhere (Morrel-Samuels, Herman, & Bever, 1991).

The opposing trends for simple and complex stimuli rule out a peripheral cause for the asymmetry, such as poorer visual acuity in one eye, peripheral nerve damage, or asymmetrical musculature. Our data refute the common assertion that such asymmetries are uniquely human, either in general terms (Garcia-Merita, 1984) or in reference to a specific construct such as generative capability (Corballis, 1989). The findings are consistent with a

15. Cognitive factors affecting comprehension

broadening body of evidence for nonhuman subjects showing that rats discriminate complex acoustic stimuli better when presented to the right ear-LH (O'Connor, Roitblat, & Bever, this volume, chapter 13); that macaques tend to show a right ear-LH advantage during tasks requiring recognition of conspecific calls (Peterson, Beecher, Zoloth, Moody & Stebbins, 1978; Heffner & Heffner, 1984), and that chimpanzees make faster responses to meaningful lexigraphic designs that appear in the RVF-LH (Hopkins, Morris, Savage-Rumbaugh, & Rumbaugh, 1991; Hopkins & Morris, this volume, 14). Furthermore, because handedness cannot be implicated in the current research, hand preference (with the fine-motor control and manual dexterity that this entails) cannot be a viable explanation for the development of cerebral asymmetry (Hewes, 1973; MacNeilage, Studdert-Kennedy, & Lindblom, 1987). Although some observational studies claim that dolphins have lateralized turning preferences (Ridgway, 1986), our data, like earlier results from longitudinal observational studies (Caldwell, Caldwell, & Siebenaler, 1965) found no lateral preference at the gross level. Turning was faster to the right after viewing simple commands and faster to the left after seeing complex commands.

Additional studies furnish broader evidence that the dolphin's hemispheres are specialized. In a study examining the effect of stimulus familiarity (Morrel-Samuels, Herman, & Bever, 1989; 1991) we used the procedure described above to test response latency to simple holophrastic commands comprised of one gesture. In this study both gesture duration and number of gestures in the string were constant throughout all conditions of the experiment. Again, our research duplicates the pattern found with humans viewing familiar and unfamiliar stimuli (Glass, Bradshaw, Day, & Umilta, 1985; Goldberg & Costa, 1981; Hannay, Dee, Burns, & Masek, 1981; Marzi & Berlucchi, 1977; Umilta, Brizzolara, Tabossi, & Fairweather, 1978). The effect has also been replicated in a more recent study (Morrel-Samuels, Herman, & Pack, 1990), where large 3-dimensional objects were displayed momentarily to the dolphin in a matching-to-sample task. Responses were significantly faster and more accurate when simple objects were presented to the LVF-RH. Both of these studies corroborate the claim that dolphins show evidence of a functional asymmetry. In addition, for all cases documented thus far, the pattern of those asymmetries follows the pattern obtained from human subjects.

Whatever drives cerebral asymmetry in humans, whether it is associated with complex analysis, generativity, or language-mediated symbolization, dolphins and humans clearly share features of that asymmetry. Moreover, our evidence of a functional asymmetry in the absence of speech, handedness, tool use, or language production per se strongly suggests that these factors are not necessary precursors of cerebral asymmetry in humans.

ACKNOWLEDGEMENT

Preparation of this chapter was supported by grants from the Office of Naval Research (N00014-85-K-0210) and Earthwatch Foundation. The authors would like to thank Tom Bever, Gordon Bower, Kristen Taylor, and Adam Pack, as well as the staff and students at the Kewalo Basin Marine Mammal Lab whose dedicated help made this work possible. Special thanks goes to Curtis Hardyck, Buz Hunt, Herbert Roitblat, and Eran Zaidel for comments on earlier drafts, and to Beth Rettig for her fine work with Akeakamai.

REFERENCES

Barrett, M. D. (1982). The holophrastic hypothesis: Conceptual and empirical issues. *Cognition*, 11, 47-76.

Bever, T. G. (1975). Cerebral asymmetries in humans are due to the differentiation of two incompatible processes: Holistic and analytic. In D. Aaronson and R. W. Rieber (Eds.) *Developmental psycholinguistics and communication disorders* (pp. 76-86). New York: New York Academy of Sciences.

Bever, T. G. (1980). Broca and Lashley were right: Cerebral dominance is an accident of growth. In D. Kaplan & N. Chomsky (Eds.) *Biology and language* (pp. 186-230). Cambridge, MA: MIT Press.

Bonvillian, J. D. & Friedman, R. J. (1978). Language development in another mode: The acquisition of signs by a brain-damaged adult. *Sign Language Studies*, 19, 111-120.

Bradshaw, J. L. & Nettleton, N. C. (1981). The nature of hemispheric specialization in man. *Behavioral and Brain Sciences*, 4, 51-63.

Bradshaw, J. L. & Nettleton, N. C. (1983). *Human cerebral asymmetry*. Englewood Cliffs, NJ: Prentice Hall.

Bryden, M. P. (1965). Tachistiscopic recognition, handedness and cerebral dominance. *Neuropsychologia*, 3, 1-8.

15. Cognitive factors affecting comprehension

Bryden, M. P. (1982). *Laterality: Functional asymmetry in the intact brain.* New York: Academic Press.

Bryden, M. P. & Allard, F. (1976). Visual hemifield differences depend on typeface. *Brain and Language*, 3, 191-200.

Caldwell, M. C., Caldwell, D. K., & Siebenaler, J. B. (1965). Observations on captive and wild Atlantic bottlenosed dolphins, *Tursiops truncatus*, in the Northeastern Gulf of Mexico. *Los Angeles County Museum Contributions in Science*, 91, 1-10.

Calvin, W. H. (1982). Did throwing stones shape hominid brain evolution? *Ethology and Sociobiology*, 3, 115-124.

Carmon, A., Harishanu, E., Lowinger, E., & Lavy, S. (1972). Asymmetries in hemispheric blood volume and cerebral dominance. *Behavioural Biology*, 7, 853-859.

Christopoulou, C., & Bonvillian, J. (1985). Sign language, pantomime, and gestural processing in aphasic persons: A review. *Journal of Communication Disorders*, 18, 1-20.

Corballis, M. C. (1989). Laterality and human evolution. *Psychological Review*, 96, 492-505.

Cranford, T. W. & Amundin, M. (1989). *Comparative morphology of the odontocete nose: Anatomy of a sonar signal generator.* Paper presented at the Biennial Conference on the Biology of Marine Mammals, Pacific Grove, CA.

Damasio, A., Bellugi, U., Damasio, H., Poizner, H., & Van Gilder, J. (1986). Sign language aphasia during left-hemisphere Amytal injection. *Nature*, 322, 363-365.

Dawson, W. W. (1980). The cetacean eye. In L. M. Herman (Ed.) *Cetacean Behavior: Mechanisms and functions* (pp. 53-100). New York: Wiley.

Dore, J. (1975). Holophrases, speech acts and language universals. *Journal of Child Language*, 2, 21-40.

Ellis, H. D. & Shepherd, J. W. (1974). Recognition of abstract and concrete words presented in left and right visual fields. *Journal of Experimental Psychology*, 103, 1035-1036.

Garcia-Merita, M. L. (1984). Asimetria cerebral y lateralizacion de funciones [Cerebral asymmetry and functional lateralization]. *Boletin de Psicologia*, 4, 51-75.

Gazzaniga, M. S. & Hillyard, S. A. (1971). Language and speech capacity of the right hemisphere. *Neuropsychologia*, 9, 273-280.

Geffen, G., Bradshaw, J. L., & Wallace, G. (1971). Interhemispheric effects on reaction time to verbal and nonverbal visual stimuli. *Journal of Experimental Psychology*, 87, 415-422.

Geschwind, N. & Levitsky, W. (1968). Human brain: Left-right asymmetries in temporal speech region. *Science*, 161, 186-187.

Glass, C., Bradshaw, J. L., Day, R. H., & Umilta, C. (1985). Familiarity, spatial frequency and task determinants in processing laterally presented representations of faces. *Cortex*, 21, 513-531.

Goldberg, E., & Costa, L. (1981). Hemispheric differences in the acquisition and use of descriptive systems. *Brain and Language*, 14, 144-173.

Hamers, J. F. & Lambert, W. E. (1977). Visual field and cerebral hemisphere preferences in bilinguals. In S. J. Segalowitz & F. A. Gruber (Eds.) *Language development and neurological theory* (pp. 57-62). New York: Academic Press.

Hannay, H., Dee, H. L., Burns, J. W., & Masek, B. S. (1981). Experimental reversal of a left visual fields superiority for forms. *Brain and Language*, 13, 54-66.

Hatschek, R. (1903). Schnervenatrophie bei einem delphin. *Arbeiten aus dem Neurologischen Institut an der Wiener Universitat*, 10, 223-229.

Heffner, H. & Heffner, R. (1984). Temporal lobe lesions and perception of species-specific vocalization by macaques. *Science*, 226, 75-76.

15. Cognitive factors affecting comprehension

Heilman, K., Rothi, L., Campanella, D., & Wolfson, S. (1979). Wernickes' and global aphasia without alexia. *Archives of Neurology*, 36, 129-133.

Herman, L. M. (1986). Cognition and language competencies of bottlenosed dolphins. In R. J. Schusterman, J. Thomas, & F. G. Wood (Eds.), *Dolphin cognition and behavior: A comparative approach* (pp. 221-252). Hillsdale, NJ: Lawrence Erlbaum Associates.

Herman, L. M. (1987). Receptive competencies of language-trained animals. In J. S. Rosenblatt, C. Beer, M. C. Busnel, & P. J. B. Slater (Eds.) *Advances in the study of behavior* (Vol. 17, pp. 1-60). Petaluma, CA: Academic Press.

Herman, L. M., Hovancik, J. R., Gory, J. D., & Bradshaw, G. L. (1989). Generalization of visual matching by a bottlenosed dolphin (*Tursiops truncatus*): Evidence for invariance of cognitive performance with visual or auditory materials. *Journal of Experimental Psychology: Animal Behavior Processes*, 15, 124-136.

Herman, L. M., Morrel-Samuels, P., & Pack, A. A. (1990). Bottlenosed dolphin and human recognition of veridical and degraded video displays of an artificial gestural language. *Journal of Experimental Psychology: General*, 119, 215-230.

Herman, L. M., Richards, D. G., & Wolz, J. P. (1984). Comprehension of sentences by bottlenosed dolphins. *Cognition*, 16, 129-219.

Hewes, G.W. (1973). Primate communication and the gestural origins of language. *Current Anthropology*, 14, 5-24.

Holmes, J. M. (1975). Manual signing with an aphasic patient. Paper presented at the 13th Academy of Aphasia meeting, Victoria, BC, Canada.

Hopkins, W. D., Morris, R. D., Savage-Rumbaugh, E. S., & Rumbaugh, D. M. (1991). Hemispheric activation for meaningful and nonmeaningful symbols in language-trained chimpanzees: Evidence for asymmetrical hemispheric priming using known and unknown warning stimuli in two language-trained chimpanzees (*Pan troglodytes*). *Journal of Expermental Psychology: General*, 120, 46-56.

Hunter, G. A. (1988). *Visual delayed matching of two-dimensional forms by a bottlenosed dolphin.* Unpublished master's thesis, University of Hawaii, Honolulu.

Jacobs, M. S., Morgane, P. J., & McFarland, W. (1975). Degeneration of visual pathways in the bottlenose dolphin. *Brain Research,* 88, 346-352.

Kimura, D. (1973). Manual activity during speaking: I. Right-handers. *Neuropsychologia,* 11, 45-50.

Kimura, D. (1976). The neural basis of language qua gesture. In H. Whitaker & H. A. Whitaker (Eds.) *Studies in neurolinguistics* (Vol. 2; pp. 145-156). New York: Academic Press.

Kirshner, H. A. & Webb, W. G. (1981). Selective involvement of the auditory-verbal modality in an acquired communication disorder: Benefit from sign language therapy. *Brain and Language,* 13, 161-170.

Krauss, R., Morrel-Samuels, P., & Colasante, C., (1991). Do conversational hand gestures communicate? *Journal of Personality and Social Psychology,* 61, 743-754.

Le Doux, J. E. (1983). Cerebral asymmetry and the integrated function of the brain. In A. W. Young (Ed.) *Functions of the right cerebral hemisphere* (pp. 203-216). New York: Academic Press.

Levy, J. (1983). Individual differences in cerebral hemisphere asymmetry: Theoretical issues and experimental considerations. In J. B. Hellige (Ed.), *Cerebral hemisphere asymmetry: Method, theory, and application* (pp. 465-497). New York: Praeger.

Levy-Agresti, J. & Sperry, R. W. (1968). Differential perceptual capacities in major and minor hemispheres. *Proceedings of the U.S. National Academy of Sciences,* 6, 1151.

MacNeilage, P. F., Studdert-Kennedy, M. G., & Lindblom, B. (1987). Primate handedness reconsidered. *Behavioral and Brain Sciences,* 10, 247-303.

Manning, A. A., Goble, W., Markman, R., & La Breche, T. (1977). Lateral cerebral differences in the deaf in response to linguistic and nonlinguistic stimuli. *Brain and Language,* 4, 309-321.

15. Cognitive factors affecting comprehension

Marx, J. (1983). The two sides of the brain. *Science*, 220, 488-490.

Marzi, C. A., & Berlucchi, G. (1977). Right visual field superiority for the accuracy of recognition of famous faces in normals. *Neuropsychologia*, 15, 751-756.

McKeever, W. F., Hoemann, H. W., Florian, V. A., & VanDeventer, A. D. (1976). Evidence of minimal cerebral asymmetries for the processing of English words and American Sign Language in the congenitally deaf. *Neuropsychologia*, 14, 413-423.

McMullen, P. A. & Bryden, M. P. (1987). The effects of word imageability and frequency on hemispheric asymmetry in lexical decisions. *Brain and Language*, 31, 11-25.

Morgane, P. J., & Jacobs, M. S. (1972). Comparative anatomy of the cetacean nervous system. In R. J. Harrison (Ed.), *Functional anatomy of marine mammals* (Vol. 1, pp. 117-244). London: Academic Press.

Morrel-Samuels, P., Herman, L., & Bever, T. G. (1989). *A left-hemisphere advantage for gesture-language signs in the dolphin*. Paper presented at the meeting of the Psychonomics Society, Atlanta, GA.

Morrel-Samuels, P., Herman, L., & Bever, T.G. (1991). The relation between processing demands and cerebral asymmetries in a dolphin. Manuscript submitted for publication. Technical Report 91-014, Ann Arbor, MI: EDS Center for Advanced Research.

Morrel-Samuels, P., Herman, L., & Pack, A. (1990). *Cerebral asymmetry during picture recognition: Preliminary evidence from dolphins*. Paper presented at the meeting of the Psychonomic Society, New Orleans, LA.

Mukhametov, L. M. (1989). *Sensory contact with the environment during sleep in dolphins*. Paper presented at the Fifth International Theriological Congress, Rome, Italy.

Mukhametov, L. M., Supin, A. Y., & Polyakova, I. G. (1977). Interhemispheric asymmetry of the electroencephalographic sleep patterns in dolphins. *Brain Research*, 134, 581-584.

Neville, H. J., & Bellugi, U. (1978). Patterns of cerebral specialization in congenitally deaf adults: A preliminary report. In P. Siple (Ed.), *Understanding language through sign language research*, (pp. 239-257). New York: Academic Press.

Petersen, M. R., Beecher, M. D., Zoloth, S. R., Moody, D. B., & Stebbins, W. C. (1978). Neural lateralization of species-specific vocalizations by Japanese macaques. *Science*, 202, 324-327.

Poizner, H., Battison, R., & Lane, H. L. (1979). Cerebral asymmetry for perception of American Sign Language: The effects of moving stimuli. *Brain and Language*, 7, 351-362.

Poizner, H., Bellugi, U., & Lutes-Driscoll, V. (1981). Perception of American Sign Language in dynamic point-light displays. *Journal of Experimental Psychology: Human Perception and Performance*, 7, 430-440.

Poizner, H. & Lane, H. L. (1979). Cerebral asymmetry in the perception of American Sign Language. *Brain and Language*, 7, 210-226.

Ridgway, S. H. (1986). Physiological observations of dolphin brains. In R.J. Schusterman, J.A. Thomas, & F.G. Wood (Eds.) *Dolphin cognition and behavior: A comparative approach* (pp. 31-59). Hillsdale,NJ: Lawrence Erlbaum Associates.

Ridgway, S. H. & Brownson, R. H. (1979). Brain size and symmetry in three dolphin genera. *Anatomical Record*, 193, 664.

Ridgway, S. H. & Brownson, R. H. (1984). Relative brain sizes and cortical surface areas of odontocetes. *Acta Zoologica Fennica*, 172, 149-152.

Sergent, J. (1982). The cerebral balance of power: Confrontation or cooperation? *Journal of Experimental Psychology: Human Perception and Performance*, 8, 253-272.

Shibkova, S. (1969). Structure of internal layers of the retina in dolphins. *Archives d'Anatomie, d'Histologie, et de Embryologie* (USSR), 57, 68-74.

15. Cognitive factors affecting comprehension

Shurley, J., Serafetinides, E., Brooks, R., Elsner, R., & Kenney, D. (1969). Sleep in cetaceans. I. The pilot whale, *Globicephala scammoni. Psychophysiology, 6*, 230.

Shyan, M. R., & Herman, L. M. (1987). Determinants of recognition of gestural signs in an artificial language by Atlantic bottle-nosed dolphins (*Tursiops truncatus*) and humans (*Homo sapiens*). *Journal of Comparative Psychology, 101*, 112-125.

Supin, A. Y., Mukhametov, L. M., Ladygina, T. F., Popov, V. V., Mass, A. M., & Poliakova, E. G. (1978). *Electrophysiological study of the dolphin brain.* Moscow: Nauka (in Russian).

Umilta, C., Brizzolara, D., Tabossi, P., & Fairweather, H. (1978). Factors affecting face recognition in the cerebral hemispheres: Familiarity and naming. In J. Requin (Ed.), *Attention and Performance VII* (pp. 363-374). Hillsdale, NJ: Lawrence Erlbaum Associates.

Wada, J. A., Clarke, R., & Hamm, A. (1975). Cerebral hemispheric asymmetry in humans: Cortical speech zones in 100 adult and 100 infant brains. *Archives of Neurology, 32*, 239-246.

Witelson, S. F. & Pallie, W. (1973). Left hemisphere specialization for language in the newborn: Neuroanatomical evidence of asymmetry. *Brain, 96*, 641-646.

Xitco, M. J., Jr. (1988). *Mimicry of modeled behaviors by bottlenose dolphins.* Unpublished master's thesis, University of Hawaii, Honolulu.

Zaidel, E. (1983). A response to Gazzaniga: Language in the right hemisphere, convergent perspectives. *American Psychologist, 38*, 542-546.

Zurif, E. B. & Sait, P. E. (1970). The role of syntax in dichotic listening. *Neuropsychologia, 8*, 239-244.

16 Chimpanzee Competence for Counting in a Video-formatted Task Situation

Duane M. Rumbaugh, William Hopkins, David A. Washburn, and E. Sue Savage-Rumbaugh

The emergence of new research tactics and technology in recent years is serving to demonstrate that animals' cognitive operations are generally a great deal more advanced than perspectives of the past 50 years would suggest. Research since 1979 has affirmed that chimpanzees are capable of learning the meanings of arbitrary symbols and comprehending human speech and has supported the conclusion that chimpanzees' cognitive operations are so advanced that they allow for their encroachment into areas of competence held as unique to humans (Savage-Rumbaugh, 1986, Savage-Rumbaugh, McDonald, Sevcik, Hopkins, & Rubert, 1986, 1990). Indeed, studies continue to point to remarkable cognitive operations of animals and birds in general (Roitblat, Bever, & Terrace, 1984).

Whether or not animals employ symbols, as in reason or thought to solve certain kinds of problems, remains a recurring question of high interest. That question is being addressed rather directly by research into the language and numeric skills of nonhuman primates. We argue in this chapter, for example, that if a chimpanzee counts by monitoring its intratrial performance, it can be contended that one has evidence of at least the entry-level processes of thinking. If thinking is a useful process to posit in research on human problem solving and planning, there is no reason from a comparative perspective why it might not be helpful in both researching and understanding the psychology of our nearest living relatives, the great apes (Pongidae).

The present chapter focuses on studies that have been conducted at the Language Research Center of chimpanzees' competence with numerals and quantities (for a review of animal number-relevant skills, see Davis & Perusse, 1988). Because no scientific enterprise can be better than the methods of its procedures, we begin with a discussion of research tactics.

Ideas that provide the impetus for science are advanced with varying degrees of formality, ranging from the expression of curiosity to the formulation of formal theory and hypotheses. Scientific data, of course, must be empirical and collected under conditions that permit systematic manipulation of variables and the inclusion of controls against confounds and artifacts. Validation in science rests on replication. Researchers and readers of research alike should be conservative about their acceptance of conclusions advanced until such time as replication has been obtained with other animals of a given species. Replication should, ideally, be carried out in other laboratories. With the advent of low-cost computers, it now becomes feasible to conduct experiments in more than one setting and to do so economically in well-defined conditions.

However, independent replication of some programs of research is impossible, impractical, or expensive. An added burden of responsibility for control and precision inheres these experiments, as do the added demands for describing conditions under which experimental behaviors are trained or tested.

Notwithstanding the obvious challenge of reporting the varied training experiences that an animal might have across years of work, the conditions of periodic or final tests, on the basis of which it is concluded that the subject is capable of certain skills/performances, can be operationalized in detail. The operations should be efficient and rule out all possible cuing and artifacts. In addition, they must provide data in such a quantity that the statistical risks of being correct by chance are minimized. Confidence placed in "statistically significant" findings based on a small number of observations (or in the face of a large number of failures), particularly if controls are not airtight, can be the cause of embarrassment in the long term and can serve to undermine the standing of comparative research as a field. The problems and issues noted here are exacerbated by the fact that many of these comparative investigations are based on a single subject. More emphasis must be placed on replication of findings lest a psychology be built, inadvertently, on what might be unique

16. Chimpanzee counting

interactive products of individual differences manifested in laboratory-specific contexts.

The importance of research protocols including novel tests of cognitive abilities are tested cannot be overly emphasized. They are common in studies of numeric and other skills, but all too frequently performance measures on the first of such trials are pooled with data obtained from successive presentations of those trials. Performance on each of the first trials should be reported clearly so that the reader can determine whether high-level performance (if obtained) is the result of immediate transfer/generalization apart from what might be the result of new and rapidly occurring learning. To pool trial-1 performance with those derived from other trials clouds important interpretations of subject competence.

It is a well-established fact that primates with relatively high levels of encephalization are capable of learning new discriminations within a single trial and capable of reversing a learned discrimination within a single trial (e.g., Rumbaugh & Pate, 1984). The great apes are no exception to these capacities. By definition, any given novel test trial loses its novelty once it is re-administered. Consequently, subjects' competence for the conceptual use of numbers versus rote associations between sets/arrangements of items and numbers and vice versa is best assayed by trial-1 performance on novel trials. The risks of obtaining speciously high readings of competence inheres if procedures provide for reward to be given whenever the subject is "correct" on the successive re-administration of what were novel test trials. This all-to-common procedure provides the subject, and particularly the primate, opportunity to learn anew with a facility subject to mistaken interpretation.

Blind tests should mean the subject cannot be cued either by the experimenter's pre- or intratrial activities. The risks of that happening are greatly increased when the experimenter knows what will constitute a correct response, when the subject has a small and finite number of stimuli/cards to respond to, and when those materials are manually arranged by the experimenter prior to test trials in the subject's view.

Modern technology, and particularly the use of computer-based systems, is both economical and readily available. It is highly adaptable to many of the needs of the behavioral researcher (e.g., Rumbaugh, Richardson, Washburn, Savage-Rumbaugh, & Hopkins 1989; Washburn, Hopkins, & Rumbaugh, 1989). Appropriate use can serve to objectify and to control

Figure 16.1. The apparatus used in summation studies. The subject has selected one of the pair of wells on his right and, therefore, will be able to eat the contents of that pair. Because of his selection, the pair to his left has been withdrawn from reach.

research procedures in the interests of capturing good data—the hallmark of experimental psychology.

16. Chimpanzee counting

PERCEPTIONS OF QUANTITIES

Healthy apes have voracious appetites and prefer larger rather than smaller portions of foods and drinks (e.g., Menzel, 1960). Almost instantaneously they can accurately differentiate relative mass and/or amounts of individual items. How is it that they, and other organisms that have no formal counting skills, are able to judge relative quantities? And how do they do this when the constituent items of quantities to be selected are not contiguous? Can they combine masses of various clusters? How do such skills relate to the emergence of formal arithmetic skills? We now attend to investigations of some of these questions by considering research regarding the chimpanzee's ability to choose between pairs of paired quantities of highly preferred foods: bits of chocolates.

Summation Studies with *Pan troglodytes*

When given the opportunity to select one of two pairs of piles of chocolates, two language-trained chimpanzees (*Pan troglodytes*) gradually came to choose the pair that would net the larger quantity (Rumbaugh, Savage-Rumbaugh, & Hegel, 1987; see Figure 16.1). They did not have to do so, however, in order to get chocolates. Rather, they were always allowed to eat what they chose. Their choice of the greater sum remained high (>90%) even on tests with novel arrays. As might be expected, their accuracy for the greater amount was a function of the ratio formed by the total numbers of chocolates of the two pairs. Coarse ratios (e.g., 1:2 and 2:3) were easier than fine ones (e.g., 6:7 and 7:8). Findings were tentatively interpreted to suggest that the chimpanzees first (a) subitize quantities of individual wells and then (b) summed paired subitized values so as to choose the pair that constituted the greater quantity. Summation was defined as the reliable choice of "one of a *pair* of quantities whose overall sum is greater than the sum of another pair of quantities for all possible pairs within a stated numerical range" (Rumbaugh et al., 1987, p. 107).

Subsequent research served to rule out the prospect that correct performance might have been the result of avoidance of the pair that had the single quantity or by selection of the pair which had the greatest amount in one of its constituent members, as opposed to summing across wells (Rumbaugh, Savage-Rumbaugh, & Pate, 1988). The procedures of those tests incorporated trials where the correct choice could not be made by avoiding the side with smallest single quantity in one of its wells (e.g., such as 4,3 vs 5,3 chocolates) and others where the correct choice could not be made by choosing the pair that had a well with the largest quantity (e.g., 3,5 paired with 4,5). As in the initial study, the chimpanzees always got to eat the contents of both wells of whichever pair of piles they selected.

Replication has been reported by Perusse and Rumbaugh (1989). They also found that summation was not a function of brightness associated (or confounded) with the number of chips in each pair of wells and that if the subject has only two wells, rather than two pairs of wells, between which to choose, the prospects for choice of the greater total amount are enhanced. This latter finding implies that when the chimpanzee chooses between pairs of wells it is most certainly negotiating the distance between each pair of quantities. That process of negotiation entails the operations of what we call summation.

Whether or not nonnumeric summation of the kind we have investigated is a probable precursor to the emergence of formal arithmetic operations, such as addition and subtraction, remains an empirical question that can be answered through developmental studies with children. Formal arithmetic operations require, of course, the ability to count. To pursue research into some possible requisites to formal arithmetic operations, the following research was conducted.

Can a Chimpanzee Count?

Our question was, could a chimpanzee enumerate items and thereby "produce" specific quantities of responses and changes in arrays of items in compliance with the values of numerals? This approach would contrast with those used in studies reported by others on counting or number usage that in essence asked whether an animal could learn paired associations between arrays of items and Arabic numerals. That kind of process, in our view, does not necessarily require the learning of enumeration and the meanings or values for each of several numerals. Notwithstanding, studies of that kind have yielded interesting findings that likely relate to counting in some manner.

Our selected review of such studies begins with an important study by Ferster (1964), who taught two chimpanzees to match binary digital arrangements with corresponding quantities of from one to seven items. After about 500,000 trials, the subjects could form the binary digits for corresponding quantities—regardless of the shape, size, or arrangement of items on the display. Without question, this was an impressive accomplishment. Impressive or not, Ferster refrained from claiming that his subjects were counting because enumeration of specific items was not discerned.

16. Chimpanzee counting

A relevant and more recent study by Matsuzawa (1985) with Ai, his language-trained chimpanzee, demonstrated that the chimpanzee was able to label numerically arrays comprised of from one to six items. Specifically, Ai used each of six keys, glossed as numbers, appropriate to the number of items in a given array. As in the case of Ferster, Matsuzawa did not claim, though, that Ai had literally counted. Ai's learning might have been limited to associative couplings between numbers and the complexity of patterns defined by various items displayed. There is, of course, the possibility that Ai might have learned much more than that. That Ai was able to selectively report, on request, the number of items that were, say, red and then those that were blue, when both were present in a heterogenous display, is some of the strongest evidence, we believe, that Ai might have been counting.

Davis (1984) demonstrated that a raccoon could learn to select the box that contained specifically three items of any sort from others that contained from one to five items. Sensitivity to a single, specific quantity was thus demonstrated. Several years earlier, Hicks (1956) reported the development of a concept of "threeness" in the rhesus (*Macaca mulatta*). Once again, however, the distinction between learning to perceive a specific quantity versus counting should be retained.

An impressive study by Davis and Memmott (1983) reported that rats inhibited bar pressing for food until the last of three shocks had been received, even during a 30-min time period. This result suggested that the rats were "counting" the total number of shocks—an interpretation that Davis has recently moderated. Later, Davis and Bradford (1986) reported that rats could be taught to travel to the "third" of several boxes, regardless of that box's specific spatial location relative to the other boxes.

Thus, animals can learn specific quantities, even accumulated shocks across time. Such finding are intriguing and had earlier been thought to reflect a form of counting. Alternatively, we favor a simpler explanation that recurring experiences associated with specific contexts become established as norms, (Rumbaugh et al., 1988). Then, whenever a specific context is re-encountered, the subject behaves in compliance with that norm. The subject, for example, might wait and brace itself until the final shock of a fixed and predictable quantity is experienced (so as to then eat). Or it might continue to sample/experience things (as looking in boxes of varied quantities of things or past boxes in a row) until the appropriate norm (e.g., shadows/patterns of entrances to tunnels) is reinstated. Only then is behavior substantively redirected (e.g., eating is resumed, a choice of boxes is made, an entrance is selected, etc.) toward an incentive, which, too, is part of the normative experience for a given context. But nothing within this kind of model requires counting. Rather, it entails the discerning of whether or not a current perception matches the familiar norm, based on past experience, per context.

The operations of formal counting are quite different (Gelman & Gallistel, 1978) from the behaviors discussed thus far. Formal counting is comprised of interacting and interdependent constituents. There is no such thing—either to an animal or to an experimenter—as a demonstration of "simple counting." For it to be concluded that an animal counts, the processes of enumeration of sets, things, or events (Davis and Perusse, 1988) must be demonstrated—neither a straightforward nor an easy challenge.

Enumeration must be more than just suggested by appearances (i.e, touching the items to be counted). Rather, the functional value of a presumed enumerative behavior must be validated. This point is brought home when we are reminded that simply because a child can say "one, two, three" while pointing to objects does not mean that the child can count. It remains to be established, for instance, that the child can count out just one or two as well as three items and with different kinds of items and events.

Enumeration rests on the rules of cardinality and ordinality. Cardinality refers to the use of tags or labels that enable counting with precision. By a one-to-one assignment of a tag/label to each item in a set (the one-one principle), the total count can be obtained. And that the subject "knows" that the last item's tag also defines the total items in that set (the cardinal principle) is not easy to determine. Any of many different kinds of items might be counted (the abstraction principle); however, neither the nature nor quality of items or events nor the sequence by which things are assigned tags/labels determine the total count (the order-irrelevance principle).

Each tag/label used to count has its position relative to all others. Once counted, an item can be said to be the "third" or the "fifth," and so on. The total count of a set, however, is uninfluenced by the order through which the members of that set are tagged. Each number's ordinal rank and cardinal value serve to declare the total quantity counted at each step (e.g., the item assigned "three" is the third one and, also, that three items have been enumerated).

Whether a chimpanzee could learn to count, as evidenced by the production of the appropriate number of responses/changes in accordance with the Arabic numerals 1, 2, and 3, was addressed as a question with Lana

16. Chimpanzee counting

chimpanzee serving as the subject (Rumbaugh, Hopkins, Washburn, & Savage-Rumbaugh, 1989; Rumbaugh, Savage-Rumbaugh, Hopkins, Washburn, and Runfeldt, 1989). The procedures used with Lana, at the time 17 years old, were to preclude development of associative pairings between varying quantities of things/items displayed and specific Arabic numerals to be selected as has been the case in earlier number studies. Lana would have to produce one, two, or three units—not simply label an array. Moreover, in the final test, no residual visual feedback or tally would allow Lana to determine whether she had already produced an array of one, two, or three. Rather, only her memory would be available to guide her to the successful completion of each trial. Most training and all test trials would be unique. Both the placement of the number to which she was to count (i.e., the target number) and the quantity and placement of items available with which she could count (see figures below) would be randomly determined per trial.

As with all others of our language-experienced chimpanzees, Lana (Rumbaugh, 1977) had readily learned by observing a researcher use the joystick how it should be manipulated so as to move a cursor on the monitor. Lana's training programs were broken down into three major categories: (a) Number orientation and number matching, (b) removal of perceptual or spatial relations, and (c) generalization to new shapes and colors.

A typical example of the display which Lana first saw is shown in Figure 16.2. Her first job was to take the cursor to the target number (which, in the project of reference, was always 1, 2, or 3), whereupon the items available for the count appeared in the bottom half of the screen, as shown in the lower portion of Figure 16.2. (The number of items in the bottom half of the screen varied randomly from trial to trial, and generally exceeded the number to be counted, so that no perceptual change in the pattern of that display could be used as a reliable signal for Lana to terminate counting at the appropriate point.) Lana's second job was to take the cursor to the bottom half of the screen and to make it contact one, two, or three items, in accordance with the value of the target number on that trial. After doing so, she then had to return the cursor to the target number and to thereby indicate that she had finished the count. If she did that too early or too late, it was treated as an error and she heard a raucous tone and no food reward.

Throughout the several phases of Lana's training alterations in the displays were made so that in final test, all strategies other than the counting would be obviated. In final test, Lana's ability to respond to each number without the benefit of residual, cumulative visual feedback (in the form of

Figure 16.2. Schematic of video screen mid-trial in Numath I. The numeral 3, the target number for this trial, is in the third feedback box from the left. Arabic numerals have replaced the two boxes that Lana has removed from the original array of five boxes which was present as this particular trial began. Lana now has the cursor on a third box (lower right screen). When it disappears, the number 3 will replace it. Lana will then have to return the cursor to the target number, 3, at the top of the screen. The screen will then be cleared and the next trial presented. Had the target number been a 2 or 3, they would have appeared in the second and third feedback boxes, respectively, and Lana would have had to remove two or three boxes, accordingly, before ending the trial for reward to be obtained.

feedback boxes appearing) as the selection boxes were removed from the screen. Now, only the tone sounded as each box disappeared, in turn, when touched by the cursor (Figure 16.3). Thus, Lana had only her memory of intratrial performance to discern when she should stop the count for successful completion of each trial.

16. Chimpanzee counting

To perform correctly on any given trial, Lana had first to discern the numeric value of the target number before beginning to touch and remove selection boxes from the lower portion of the screen. At some point, she had to determine that a quantity of selection boxes equivalent to the value of a given trial's target number had been removed and end the trial by returning the cursor to the target number. Because no feedback boxes appeared at the top of the monitor as she caused the selection boxes to disappear in turn, and because both the physical arrangement and the number of selection boxes changed randomly each trial, Lana could not remove boxes to create some familiar configuration. Neither could she work to the point where a familiar number of feedback boxes had been produced relative to the target number's value for that trial. Rather, she could only reference what she had done by removal of one or more selection boxes and judge that total against the trial's target number's value to determine whether to continue or to terminate the trial. Her task was neither one of matching a number label for each of several arrays nor one of creating an array reliably associated with each of three target numbers. Rather, it was one of producing selection-box removal responses in accordance with the value of a given target number.

Figure 16.4 depicts Lana's performance on the first 73 no-feedback test trials—where the composition of each was novel in that the target number's value, its position, and the number and arrangement of the boxes at the bottom of the monitor were randomly determined on each trial. Lana was well above chance on all numbers. Interestingly, she performed somewhat better, though not significantly so, on those trials that had no visual feedback than on those that did.

The results indicated that Lana was counting. We believe that her memory must have entailed processes relevant both to ordination and cardination. The act whereby enumeration progressed was clearly defined by her use of the joystick by which the cursor touched each box selected for the count as called for by the value of each trial's target number.

Her behavior strongly suggests that she kept track of what she had done and thereby discerned what had yet to be done relative to the value of the target number on any given trial. She was able to do so across a series of trials, each one of which was uniquely configured.

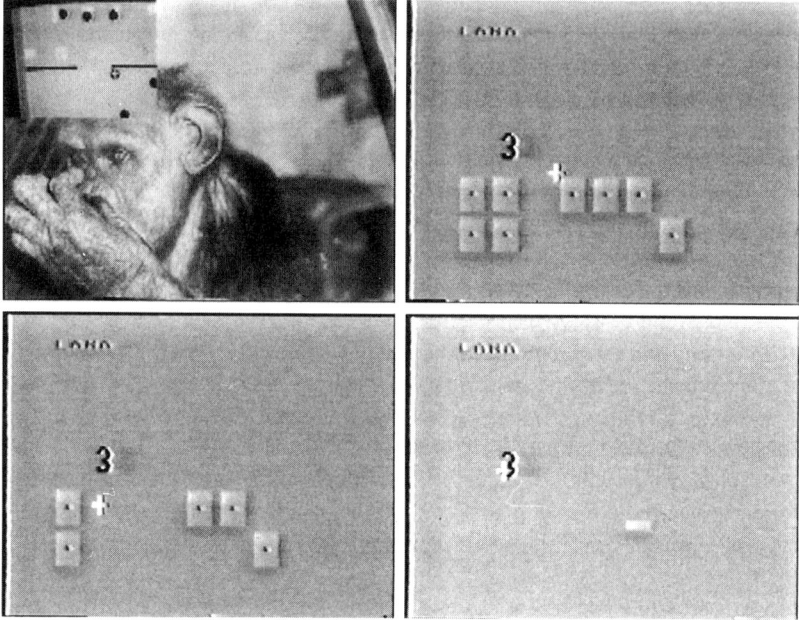

Figure 16.3. An example of the screen's appearance during a trial of final Numath 20 test of Lana's counting. Through use of her joystick-controlled cursor, Lana had to touch, and thereby remove from the screen, a quantity of boxes equalivant to the value of the target number per trial. A brief tone sounded as each box disappeared. No feedback or methods of "keep count" appeared on the screen as a correlate of the selection boxes being removed from the screen, as had been true in previous training programs. Consequently, Lana had only her memory of intratrial performance of what had been done to guide performance to the successful conclusion per trial. Upper left, Lana grooms her eye in an image reflected from glass; upper right, Lana brings the cursor to middle box, top row, after having started the trial by touching the target number, 3, with the cursor; lower left, Lana has removed a total of three boxes; and, lower right, she moves the cursor back to the target number to end the trial successfully. All boxes then disappear from the screen.)

16. Chimpanzee counting

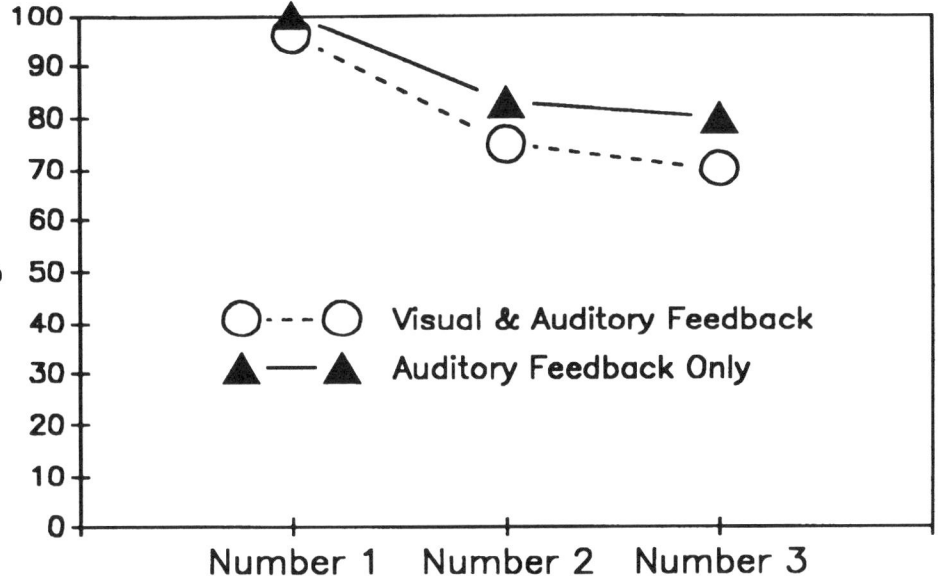

Figure 16.4. Percentage correct on visual and nonvisual feedback test trials for numbers 1, 2, and 3. (See text for further details.)

Her cognition (a) separated, in any order, the counted from the uncounted, (b) determined when the set to-be-counted, as declared by the target's value on a given trial, had, in fact, been counted, and consequently (c) determined when counting should be stopped. Recently, Lana has demonstrated mastery of the number 4, in conjunction with the numbers 1, 2, and 3, in the same training/testing situation.

Although Lana's counting was enabled by a series of training programs, quite probably not all of them were necessary. Notwithstanding, that series enabled both Lana and us to move from an initial program that by intent was rich with both numeric and nonnumeric cues to a final test where nonnumeric cues were absent. From the first to the last software program, nonnumeric cues were systematically deleted. What remained was an ability to respond to each of three Arabic numbers in a differential and productive manner—one that we term entry-level counting.

Subsequent research with Sherman, Austin, and Lana has affirmed their abilities to count out varying numbers of boxes through use of Arabic numerals in video-formatted tasks. These studies, still in progress, suggest that their counting skills extend beyond six.

In a different project, we (Washburn & Rumbaugh, 1991) have demonstrated the rhesus monkey's (*Macaca mulatta*) ability to learn the ordinal values of the Arabic numerals 0 through 9. This was accomplished in a video-formatted task where the monkey received a number of food pellets, automatically dispensed across time, in accordance with the numeral selected on a given trial (e.g., the monkeys did not have to select the larger numeral of each pair to obtain pellets.)

On test trials where seven novel pairs of numerals were presented, one of two monkeys was 100% correct. On other tests (see Figure 16.5) in which arrays of up to five numerals were presented simultaneously and in which the monkeys continued to get numbers of pellets in accordance with the numeral selected, both monkeys strongly and significantly tended to select the largest numeral that remained on the screen after successive presentations and selections. The result was that they chose the numerals in accordance with their values in a descending sequence (e.g., 9, 7, 5, 4, 2). They did so with about 85% reliability across the course of novel arrays (e.g., the numerals and their arrangement were randomly determined). Such behaviors indicated their mastery of the ordinal values of the numerals 0-9. No claim is made regarding their counting abilities, however, because enumeration of items was not involved in either their training or final testing. Notwithstanding, the ability of rhesus to do as they did is well beyond the boundaries expected of them.

Our research, assisted by modern technology, affirms the chimpanzee's ability to engage in formal counting and the rhesus monkey's ability to learn the ordinal values of numbers, a requisite to productive counting. The implications for assessments of primate's cognitive competence and as a valued life-form for studies of cognition as they apply to the definition of requisites for human competence—including thought—are clear (Rumbaugh, 1990).

ACKNOWLEDGMENTS

Preparation of this chapter was supported by grants NICHD-06016 and ARB-00165 from the National Institutes of Health to the Yerkes Regional Primate Research Center, by grant NAG2-438 from the National Aeronautics and Space Administration to Georgia State University, and by support from the College of

16. Chimpanzee counting

Figure 16.5. Rhesus monkeys reliably selected the largest numeral of those remaining on the screen after selections were made across the course of four presentations. In response to the array displayed, the rhesus first almost selected 6 (see location of cursor "+"), but reversed its choice to select 8. On subsequent presentations, with the 8 now absent from the screen, it selected the 6, then 5, 4, and 3. Selection of a given numeral resulted in the delivery of an appropriate number of pellets.

Arts and Sciences, Georgia State University. Portions of this chapter are based on our reports on summation and counting that are published in the *Journal of Experimental Psychology* and the *Psychological Record* (see references).

REFERENCES

Davis, H. (1984). Discrimination of the number three by a raccoon (*Procyon lotor*). *Animal Learning & Behavior*, 12, 409-413.

Davis, H., & Bradford, S. A. (1986). Counting behavior by rats in a simulated natural environment. *Ethology*, 73, 265-280.

Davis, H., & Memmott, J. (1983). Autocontingencies: Rats count to three to predict safety from shock. *Animal Learning & Behavior*, 10, 95-100.

Davis, H., & Perusse, R. (1988). Numerical competence in animals: Definitional issues, current evidence, and a new research agenda. *Behavioral and Brain Sciences*, 11, 561-615.

Ferster, C. B. (1964). Arithmetic behavior in chimpanzees. *Scientific American*, 210, 98-106.

Gelman, R., & Gallistel, C. R. (1978). *The child's understanding of number.* Cambridge, MA: Harvard University Press.

Hicks, L. H. (1956). An analysis of number-concept formation in the rhesus monkey. *Journal of Comparative and Physiological Psychology*, 49, 212-218.

Matsuzawa, T. (1985). Use of numbers by a chimpanzee. *Nature*, 315, 57-59.

Menzel, E. (1960). Selection of food by size in the chimpanzee and comparison with human judgments. *Science*, 131, 1527-1528.

Perusse, R. & Rumbaugh, D. M. (1989). Summation in chimpanzees (*Pan troglodytes*): Effects of amounts, number of wells and finer ratios. *International Journal of Primatology*, 11, 425-437.

Roitblat, H. L., Bever, T. G., & Terrace, H. S. (1984). *Animal cognition.* Hillsdale, NJ: Lawrence Erlbaum Associates.

Rumbaugh, D. M. (Ed.). (1977). *Language learning by a chimpanzee: The LANA project.* New York: Academic Press.

Rumbaugh, D. M. (1990). Comparative psychology and the great apes: their competence in learning, language, and numbers. *Psychological Record*, 40, 15-39.

Rumbaugh, D. M., Hopkins, W. D., Washburn, D. A., & Savage-Rumbaugh, E. S. (1989). Lana chimpanzee learns to count by "Numath": A summary

16. Chimpanzee counting of a video-taped experimental report. *Psychological Record*, 39, 459-470.

Rumbaugh, D. M., & Pate, J. (1984). The evolution of primate cognition: A comparative perspective. In H. L. Roitblat, T. G. Bever, & H. S. Terrace (Eds.), *Animal cognition* (pp. 569-587). Hillsdale, NJ: Lawrence Erlbaum Associates.

Rumbaugh, D. M., Richardson, W. K., Washburn, D. A., Savage-Rumbaugh, E. S., & Hopkins, W. D. (1989). Rhesus monkeys *(Macaca mulatta)*, video tasks, and implications for stimulus-response spatial contiguity. *Journal of Comparative Psychology*, 103, 32-38.

Rumbaugh, D. M., Savage-Rumbaugh, E. S., & Hegel, M. (1987). Summation in the chimpanzee *(Pan troglodytes)*. *Journal of Experimental Psychology: Animal Behavior Processes*, 13, 107-115.

Rumbaugh, D. M., Savage-Rumbaugh, E. S., Hopkins, W. D., Washburn, D. A., & Runfeldt, S. A. (1989). Lana chimpanzee *(*Pan troglodytes*) counts by Numath.* A video tape (15 min) with narration distributed by Psychological Cinema Register, Audio-Visual Services, Special Services Building, Pennsylvania State University, University Park, PA.

Rumbaugh, D. M., Savage-Rumbaugh, E. S., & Pate, J. (1988). Addendum to "Summation in the Chimpanzee *(Pan troglodytes).*" *Journal of Experimental Psychology: Animal Behavior Processes*, 14, 118-120.

Savage-Rumbaugh, E. S. (1986). *Ape language: From conditioned response to symbol.* New York: Columbia University Press.

Savage-Rumbaugh, E. S. (1990). Language acquisition in a nonhuman species: Implications for the innateness debate. *Developmental Psychobiology*, 23, 599-620.

Savage-Rumbaugh, E. S., McDonald, K., Sevcik, R. A., Hopkins, W. D., & Rubert, E. (1986). Spontaneous symbol acquisition and use by pygmy chimpanzees *(Pan paniscus)*. *Journal of Experimental Psychology: General*, 115, 211-235.

Washburn, D. A., Hopkins, W. D., & Rumbaugh, D. M. (1989). Automation of learning-set testing: the video-task paradigm. *Behavioral Research Methods, Instruments, & Computers,* 21, 281-284.

Washburn, D. A., & Rumbaugh, D. M. (1991). Ordinal judgments of Arabic symbols by macaques (*Macaca mulatta*). *Psychological Science,* 2, 190-193.

17 Acquisition of Personal Pronouns by a Chimpanzee

Shoji Itakura and Tetsuro Matsuzawa

The present study demonstrates that a chimpanzee can be trained to use the personal pronouns ME, YOU, HIM, and HER in a way similar to that used by humans, even when the referent individuals are shifted with respect to the "speaker". This chapter outlines the methods used to teach the use of personal pronouns and describes previous studies related to the present experiment. The subject for these experiments was first trained to discriminate the letters of the alphabet and then to name individuals with the letters (Matsuzawa, 1989, 1990). Next, she was trained to describe the actor and the receiver of the action in a videotaped scene (Murofushi, Asano, & Matsuzawa, 1986; Murofushi, Matsuzawa, & Asano, 1988).

A 12-year-old female chimpanzee named Ai was the subject. Maintenance and experimental conditions conformed to the Guide for the Care and Use of Laboratory Primates in the Primate Research Institute of Kyoto University. Ai had extensive experience in tasks involving the use of visual symbols, "lexigrams" that represented objects and object attributes. Details of some of these studies have been published elsewhere (Asano et al., 1982; Kojima, 1984; Matsuzawa, 1985, 1989, 1990).

DISCRIMINATION OF THE LETTERS OF THE ALPHABET

Ai was trained to discriminate letters of the alphabet in a matching-to-sample procedure with 26 English letters as the choice alternatives (for details see Matsuzawa, 1990). Each letter of the alphabet was drawn on a key (20 × 25 mm) in a 5 × 6 key matrix on a console. The letter format was standard Helvetica medium (Letraset No. 721, 48 point). Sample letters were presented one at a time on pieces of cardboard, and the chimpanzee was required to press the matching key among the 26 alternatives. The position of the letters on the console was changed from session to session to prevent the chimpanzee from memorizing positional cues. A daily session consisted of five blocks of 26 trials. Correct choices were rewarded with food. Ai reached the 98% accuracy level within 23 sessions.

INDIVIDUAL RECOGNITION

After the discrimination of the letters of the alphabet was established, Ai was taught to name individuals using these letters in a symbolic matching-to-sample task (see Figure 17.1). The samples were pictures of familiar individuals, each of which was paired with a letter as the correct choice. Samples included five humans and five chimpanzees (see details in Matsuzawa, 1990). Additional training was given with two humans and two orangutans (Itakura, in preparation).

As the sample was presented, 10 keys on the console were lit, each corresponding to one of the sample choices. Ai was required to press the key that corresponded to the sample individual. She learned to associate a letter with each individual within only two sessions. For the transfer test, 16 different sets of photographs of the same individuals were prepared. Each of the 10 individuals was photographed in 16 different views, such as front view, side view, face only, upper body, whole body, uniform costume, etc. Test performance on the transfer set ranged from 80% to 100% correct for the 16 sessions. Confusion between humans was more frequent than confusion between chimpanzees. Confusion between humans and chimpanzees was very rare. Moreover, when between-species confusion did occur, it was restricted to cases in which photographs of humans were named as chimpanzees, never the reverse. According to Matsuzawa (1989, 1990), this confusion must be due to perceptual similarity between the individuals, because the letters of the alphabet were discriminated perfectly by the chimpanzee.

17. Acquisition of Personal Pronouns by a Chimpanzee

Figure 17.1. The chimpanzee Ai sitting on a bench in front of the console terminal interfaced to a minicomputer in the individual recognition task.

DESCRIPTION OF THE SUBJECT AND THE OBJECT OF ACTION

The chimpanzee was next trained to describe subjects and objects as of simple episodes acted out on videotape. Human languages frequently employ word order as a syntactic device, with sentence structure designating the functions of the words in the sentence. For example, in the most common English sentence structure, we might say, "John approached Bill." In this sentence, John is the subject and Bill is the object. The chimpanzee was similarly required to select lexigram keys in the order subject, action, object. Word order was investigated to determine whether the chimpanzee was capable of using this to describe words' functions in sentences.

Training was started in a two-person condition (Murofushi et al., 1985) and a three-person condition was gradually added (Murofushi et al., 1988). The apparatus consisted of a laser disc player (TEAC Model LV200) and a TV monitor, which were used to present the stimulus, and the keyboard described

Figure 17.2. A scene from the three-person condition in the "description of the subject and object" task.

earlier. Videotaped scenes were used as stimuli (see Figure 17.2). Each 10 s scene began with two persons standing 3 m apart. As one person in the scene slowly approached the other, a row of individual name keys was lit on the keyboard. The task of the chimpanzee was to push the key corresponding to the name of the approaching person. If she chose correctly, the keys were darkened and a second row was lit. This row included a lexigram for the verb *approach*. The chimpanzee was required to push this key. She was then required to select the name of the person who was being approached from a third row of individual name keys. A correct response was rewarded with food.

As mentioned earlier, two types of stimuli were used in training. In one condition, the chimpanzee viewed two-person scenes in which one person (the subject) approached another (the object). One individual (Toshio) was labeled as T and the other (Tetsuro) as Z. Either one could serve as subject or as object. After 14 sessions (50 trials per session), the chimpanzee learned to label the persons in the correct order of subject and object and to use the *approach* key correctly (more than 90% correct). The clothing and positions of T and Z were then changed, as well as the background of the scene. Performance on these new scenes deteriorated.

17. Acquisition of Personal Pronouns by a Chimpanzee

The chimpanzee was then trained with the new stimuli until a criterion (90% correct) was reached. A third person (Kiyoko), labeled K, was then added and new scenes were constructed from all pairs of these three individuals, each serving equally often as subject and object. Performance with each new scene initially began at a low level, but reached criterion in 11 sessions (60 trials per session). In the first transfer test consisting of 12 scenes, Ai correctly named the subject of the scene 90% of the time, but achieved only 37% accuracy overall. However, she correctly named the scenes more than 90% of the time in the final fifth transfer test. These results suggested that the chimpanzee had learned to discriminate correctly between subjects and objects in the scenes.

Following testing with two-person scenes, the chimpanzee was trained to discriminate subject and object in three-person scenes. Each person in the scene occupied the vertex of a 3-m (per side) triangle. T, K, and another individual S (Shoji) appeared in each scene. One of the three then approached another. The correct response was to choose the key identifying the subject, the key corresponding to *approach*, and then the key identifying the object (the individual approached). Responses to the key of the third person (who neither approached nor was approached) were errors. Training began with one set of 24 scenes followed by generalization testing with new scenes. Choice accuracy in selecting the correct object started low during the initial sessions, but eventually reached 96% overall of 108 scenes in the generalization test sessions. This suggests that the chimpanzee was able to describe subjects and objects as determined by the word order of the sentences described in the scenes.

ACQUISITION OF PERSONAL PRONOUNS

Ai had demonstrated that she was able to acquire individual names and to describe the behavior of others by using these names. In this section, we explain how she learned to use personal pronouns instead of individual names, and also how to refer to herself. The use of pronouns would appear to require the chimpanzee to understand relative points of view. For example, in a conversation, a given person is *me* while speaking, but *you* while listening.

Two types of training were used, production training and comprehension training. In production training, a conditional symbolic matching-to-sample procedure was used. The training trial started with the illumination of a self-start key. When the chimpanzee pressed this key, a picture of an individual was presented on a TV monitor. After a 2-s delay, two rows of the keyboard were illuminated to indicate that the keys were operative. Keys consisted of letters or lexigrams designating either the individual's name and/or several personal pronouns. Touching one of the keys turned off all other key lights and turned on an end key. If an incorrect response was made, pressing this key immediately stopped the trial, causing a low tone to sound and starting a 3-s time-out period. The trial was then repeated (correction method). If a correct response was made, a high tone sounded, followed by a reward and the beginning of a 2-s intertrial interval.

The self-start key was also illuminated at the beginning of comprehension training trials. When the chimpanzee pressed this key, a letter of the alphabet or a lexigram was presented on the CRT display. Two seconds later, pictures of two individuals were displayed side by side on a touch screen. A correct response was defined as the choice of the picture that corresponded to the name or pronoun on the CRT. Incorrect responses were handled in the same way as in production trials; the correction method was used, as well as the same type of response feedback to the chimpanzee. Incorrect choices produced a low tone and correct choices produced a high tone and reward. The end key was not employed in the comprehension task.

Experiment 1. The Labeling of Personal Pronouns

Prior to this experiment, the chimpanzee received both production training (in choosing the letter of the alphabet corresponding to a pictured individual) and comprehension training (in choosing the picture corresponding to a presented letter of the alphabet). Nine individuals were used as stimuli, including three humans, four chimpanzees, and two orangutans (Itakura, in preparation).

In this study, Ai learned to use the lexigrams representing the personal pronouns ME, YOU, HIM, and HER to refer to the nine individuals. She was required to refer to the experimenter, who could be seen by the chimpanzee through the wall separating the subject and experimenter (see Figure 17.3) as YOU. The chimpanzee was to refer to herself as ME. Other individuals were to be designated with the pronouns HIM or HER, according to their respective sexes.

Training began with the production of personal pronouns. A picture was presented, two rows of alphabet keys were illuminated, and the chimpanzee was required to press the key carrying the letter name of the subject. If she chose the correct name key, the key was turned off, and the third row, which carried lexigrams for the personal pronouns, was illuminated. She was then required to select the appropriate personal pronoun. Rewards were given only

17. Acquisition of Personal Pronouns by a Chimpanzee

Figure 17.3. Schematic representation of the subject's console in the room in which the experiments were conducted. This illustration shows the situation in which role-reversal training in the use of the person pronouns was studied: 1 = self-start key; 2 = end key; 3 = keyboard for letters and lexigrams; 4 = display window; 5 = touch screen; 6 = holes for guiding responses; 7 = user's function key for the subject; 8 = user's function key for the companion. Illumination of the user's function keys could be seen through the clear acrylic partition by both the subject and the companion.

after both the correct "proper name" and the correct personal pronoun were chosen.

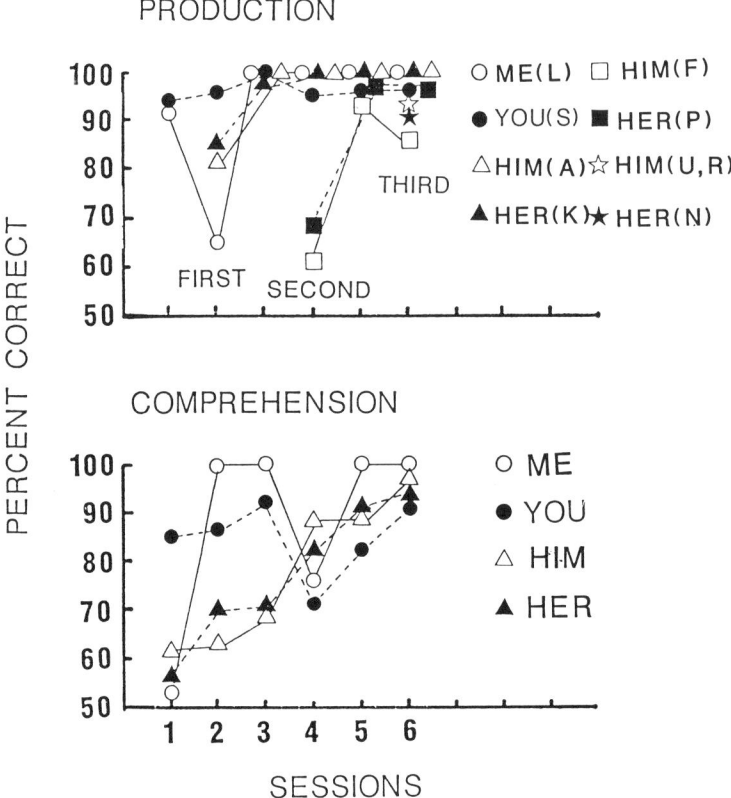

Figure 17.4. The acquisition of personal pronouns in Experiment 1. The data for production training are shown in the top panel. Third person pronouns were introduced in three steps, indicated by FIRST, SECOND, and THIRD. First A and K, then F and P, and finally U, R, and N were introduced as HIM and HER. The data for comprehension training are shown in the bottom panel.

Ai became proficient at this task by the sixth session (see upper panel, Figure 17.4). She was then tested in a single session in which only the pronouns appeared immediately following the picture instead of the proper name lexigrams. No errors were made during this probe session. In a subsequent five-session generalization test to a new stimulus set, her performance ranged from 90% to 100% correct.

17. Acquisition of Personal Pronouns by a Chimpanzee

The second phase of training was in the comprehension of personal pronouns. Sample stimuli consisted of one of the four pronouns tested earlier. For matching stimuli, pictures of the nine stimulus individuals were two at a time in random pairs, with the single constraint that two males or two females could not appear together except when the response required was ME or YOU (when one member of the pair was either the chimpanzee or the experimenter).

The first session was a symmetry test. Although this test was very similar to the one testing for naming symmetry (i.e., requiring her to select the correct picture given a name after having been trained to select a name in response to a picture), her performance on this task was initially very poor. She quickly acquired this task as well. She reached the accuracy criterion by the sixth session (see lower panel, Figure 17.4).

Experiment 2. Acquisition of Role-Reversal Usage of Personal Pronouns

In Experiments 2-4, Ai was taught that she could be either the "speaker" or the "listener". The purpose of Experiment 2 was to show the chimpanzee that the individuals designated by the first- and second-personal pronouns could be reversed if speech roles were changed, while the individuals designated by the third-personal pronouns would remain the same.

The apparatus was similar to that used in comprehension training in Experiment 1, except that the locations of two user-function keys were changed on the console. One key faced the chimpanzee and the other (the companion's key) faced the experimenter. Both the chimpanzee and the experimenter could see the two keys from their respective sides of the dividing wall in the experimental chamber. The trial began with the illumination of one of the two user-function keys. If it was the chimpanzee's key, she was required to press it, and the lexigram for a pronoun would then be displayed on the CRT. If the companion's key was lit, the experimenter had to press it. The chimpanzee could only press her own key, and the companion's key could only be pressed by the experimenter. The chimpanzee was required to respond as follows. When she pressed her key and a pronoun was presented on the CRT, she had to chose the appropriate picture from the pair presented on her touch screen. If the pronoun presented was ME, she was required to choose the picture of herself. When the pronoun she presented was YOU, she had to choose the picture of the experimenter. However, when the experimenter presented ME, Ai was required to choose the picture of the experimenter, and when the experimenter presented YOU, she had to choose the picture of herself. The chimpanzee was also

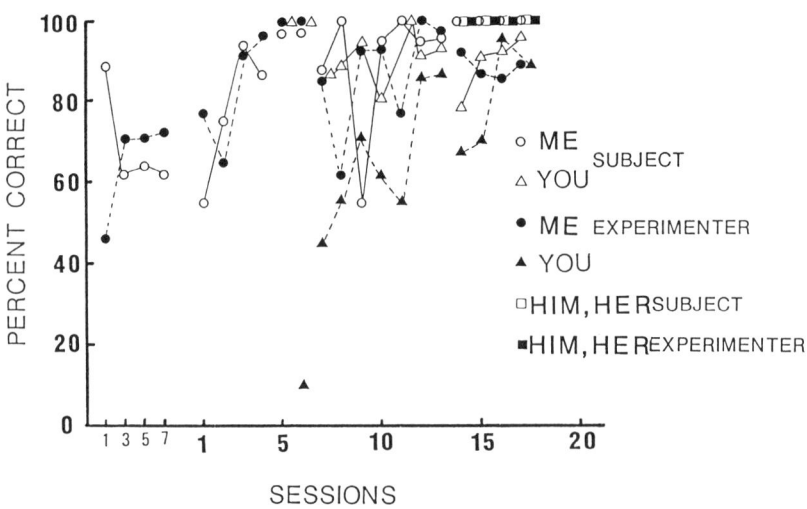

Figure 17.5. The percentage of correct responses as a function of sessions during the training in the role-reversal usage of personal pronouns. Open circles and open triangles represent the performance for the first- and second-personal pronouns with the subject as "speaker." Filled circles and filled triangles represent the performance for the first- and second-personal pronouns with the experimenter as "speaker." Performance for the third-personal pronoun presented by the subject is shown by the open squares and that presented by the experimenter is shown by the filled squares. Small numerals along the abscissa indicate seven pre-sessions in which the self-start key served as the user's key for the subject.

required to choose the picture that corresponded to the sex referred to by the third personal pronoun when either she or the experimenter presented HIM or HER. In order to illustrate to the chimpanzee that pressing the user-function key defined the speaker, the relationship was first demonstrated with ME. YOU was added later. When the experimenter began using the YOU key, Ai did initially respond correctly. This suggests that she had simply learned to choose the picture of herself when she pressed the key and to choose the picture of the experimenter when the experimenter pressed the key. When HIM and HER were presented, however, her performance was perfect, regardless of whether she or the experimenter pressed the key and displayed them. Training was completed in 17 sessions (see Figure 17.5).

17. Acquisition of Personal Pronouns by a Chimpanzee

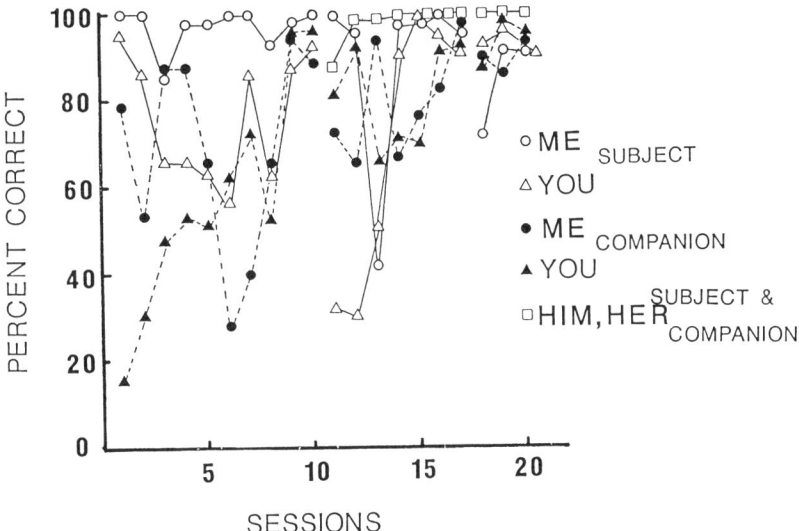

Figure 17.6. The percentage of correct responses as a function of sessions during the three hases of Experiment 3. The first phase was from the first to the 10th sessions. The second phase was from the 11th to the 17th sessions. The third phase was from the 18th to the last session. Open circles and closed triangles represent performance for the first- and second-personal pronouns with the subject as "speaker." Filled circles and filled triangles represent performance for the first- and second-personal pronouns with the second companion as "speaker." Open squares represent the combined data for the third-personal pronouns with the subject and companion as "speaker."

Ai was then given a generalization test with new picture stimuli. Her performance for each of the four pronouns as used by both the experimenter and herself ranged from 80% to 100% correct. The results of this experiment imply that the chimpanzee successfully learned that the response choice for the lexigrams for YOU and ME (either the picture of herself or the picture of the experimenter) was conditional on whether she or the experimenter pressed the user-function key.

Experiment 3. Transfer Training in Role-Reversal Usage of Personal Pronouns

In this experiment, the role of companion was assigned to a human female, whose picture had previously been the correct choice only following HER pronouns. The experimenter, whose picture had previously been the correct choice following either ME, when he presented it, or YOU when Ai presented it, remained visible throughout this experiment, but was available as a correct choice following the personal pronoun HIM. This experiment required the chimpanzee to generalize the referential function of the personal pronouns to familiar individuals in novel roles. In other ways, the procedure of Experiment 3 was identical to that of Experiment 2.

Once Ai learned to use the appropriate personal pronouns with the new companion (see Figure 17.6), she was tested to see whether she could immediately use the correct pronouns when the experimenter and the companion changed places within a session of 200 trials. The exchange occurred after 100 trials in a test session and 50 trials in another test session. Each test was conducted for three sessions. As can be seen in Figure 17.7, the chimpanzee's performance on these tests was significantly better than chance.

Experiment 4. Generalization Test for Role-Reversal Usage with a New Companion

In this experiment, the chimpanzee was tested to determine whether she could use personal pronouns correctly in referring to another new individual. This new companion was a human she knew well, but who had previously been designated only by HIM. The procedure for this test was the same as that used in Experiment 3. A new individual, a human who was familiar to the chimpanzee, acted as companion during three test sessions. Ai made no errors when ME was presented by the chimpanzee or when YOU was presented by the companion. She chose her own picture on all trials. When ME was presented by the companion, Ai correctly chose his picture on 81% of the trials in the first session. Correct responses exceeded 90% in the next two sessions. When Ai presented the pronoun YOU, the percentage of correct responses ranged from 87% to 94%. Accuracy for third-person pronouns remained high (from 80% to 100%), even when the presentation of pronouns HIM and HER called for a choice between pictures of the experimenter (first used as a companion; that is, a correct choice following YOU or ME) and the individual used as the second companion (originally a correct choice following HER, and later a correct choice following ME and YOU). These data show that the chimpanzee was able

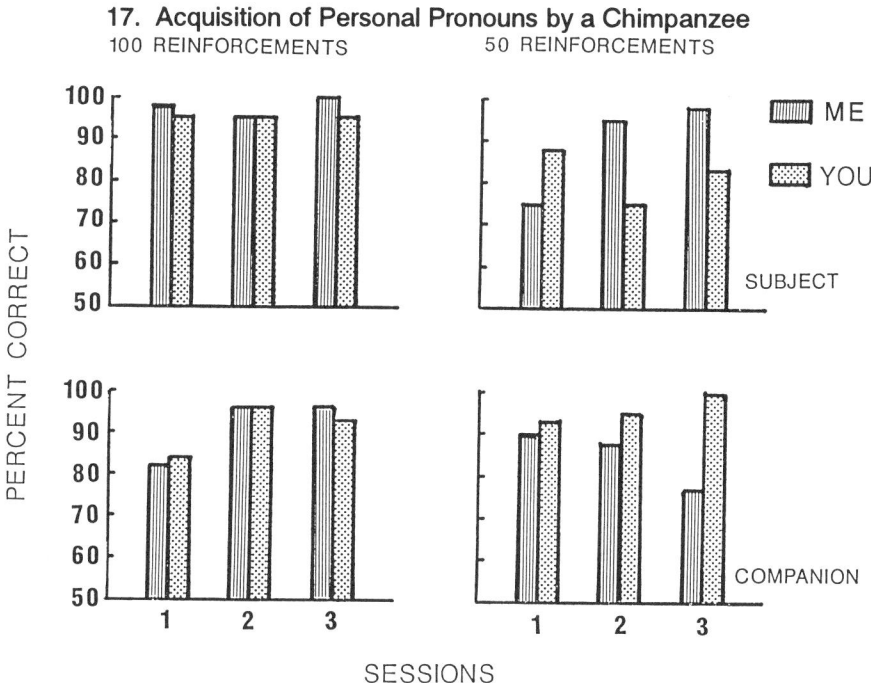

Figure 17.7. The percentage of correct responses for the first- and second-personal pronounts throught ht interchange of companions within a session in Experiment 3. The data for 100 trials per change are shown in the elft panels and those for the 50 trials per change are shown on the right. The top panels show the performance with the subject as "speaker," and the bottom panels show the performance with the companion as "speaker."

to use the pronouns correctly in the presence of still another new person (see Figure 17.8).

DISCUSSION AND CONCLUSIONS

Experiment 1 was conducted in order to teach the chimpanzee that personal pronouns can be used as substitutes for proper nouns, and that pronouns referring to first, second, and third persons are conceptual classes that express three different relationships to the chimpanzee. At this stage of training, however, the chimpanzee may formulate the erroneous hypothesis that pronouns

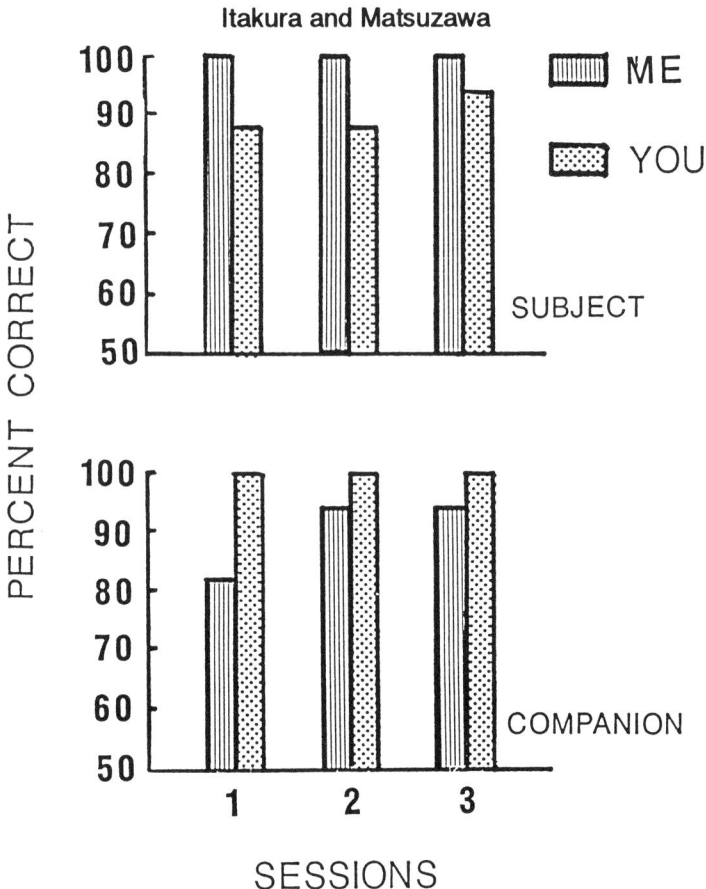

Figure 17.8. The percentage of correct responses in the generalization test with the new companion in Experiment 4. The top panel shows the performance with the subject as "speaker," the bottom panel shows the performance with the companion as "speaker."

are a type of name, as explained by Clark (1978) in her assessment of the early stages of development of the use of personal pronouns by children.

One of the special referential functions of personal pronouns is that the individual designated by the personal pronoun shifts with changes of speaker, that is, with the user of the pronoun. Viewpoints must be reversed as speech roles are exchanged. A child typically learns role-reversal usage with the

17. Acquisition of Personal Pronouns by a Chimpanzee

mother as companion (Petitto, 1987). Accordingly, in Experiment 2, the chimpanzee was trained in role-reversal usage with a single companion, the experimenter. In this study, either the chimpanzee or the experimenter could serve as speaker. The task required conditional matching-to-sample with two classes of conditional stimuli. To perform properly in the role-reversal situation, the chimpanzee had to assess the relationships between the two conditions to select the correct picture (the identity of the individual pressing the key and the pronoun that was presented). Because training began with only in the chimpanzee producing only ME, we do not know whether there are differences in learning the use of ME and YOU in role reversal. Errors in reversal of pronouns similar to those seen in children (Petitto, 1987) were observed when YOU was added.

In order to extend the chimpanzee's training in role-reversal usage, a second companion was introduced in Experiment 3. This new companion was previously known as HER, and the experimenter, who had been known as YOU, now became HIM. Petitto (1987) reported that a deaf child who was trained in ASL made no errors on 7 trials with the personal pronoun ME on a comprehension task, but she did make errors on 3 out of the 11 trials when presented with YOU. Results from the current study support these findings; however, it may have been easier for the chimpanzee to match the person who pressed the key with the first personal pronoun ME, because it was the common rule between the chimpanzee and the companion that the actor was ME. In this experiment, furthermore, the chimpanzee was trained by interchanging the companions within a session, so that each person in the experiment could either be ME or YOU when serving as companion but HIM or HER when present as a nonparticipant.

In Experiment 4 it was shown that further training was not necessary for the chimpanzee to adopt use of the personal pronouns when she interacted with a new companion. In order to respond correctly from the beginning of the generalization test, the chimpanzee must have learned the following: (a) The pictures of individuals represent real individuals. (b) The person who is interacting with the chimpanzee is the listener to be called YOU by the chimpanzee. (c) The referents of personal pronouns are determined by the relation between a speaker and personal pronouns. The chimpanzee clearly reached a solution to these problems.

The data discussed above provide clues as to the way in which the concept of YOU is established. It may be difficult to use these data to examine how the concept ME is formed, because replacement of the chimpanzee herself as the user of the pronouns was impossible. She did learn, however, that the pictures called ME by herself are the same as those called YOU by three other companions. If the chimpanzee did identify her pictures as pictures of herself then it appears that the recognized herself as YOU from the viewpoint of the companions, that is, as a social self. Similarly, if the chimpanzee did identify pictures of her companions as their pictures then she could have learned that ME referred to four different individuals (including herself) when it is used by these individuals, that is, the general self as a speaker. The "self," that is, the behavior, is established through interactions with others.

The present study suggests that a chimpanzee can understand the deictic function of personal pronouns and, in particular, that the referent individuals depend on the speaker and user of the personal pronouns.

REFERENCES

Asano, T., Kojima, T., Matsuzawa, T., Kubota, K., & Murofushi, K. (1982). Object and color naming in chimpanzees (*Pan troglodytes*). *Proceedings of the Japan Academy*, 58, 118-122.

Clark, E. V. (1978). From gesture to word: On the natural history of deixis in language acquisition. In J. S. Bruner & A. Garton (Eds.), *Human growth and development: Wolfson College Lectures, 1976* (pp. 85-120). Oxford: Clarendon Press.

Itakura, S. (in preparation). *Use of personal pronouns by a chimpanzee* (Pan troglodytes).

Kojima, T. (1984). Generalization between productive use and receptive discrimination of names in an artificial visual language by a chimpanzee. *International Journal of Primatology*, 5, 161-182.

Matsuzawa, T. (1985). Color naming and classification in a chimpanzee (*Pan troglodytes*). *Journal of Human Evolution*, 14, 283-291.

Matsuzawa, T. (1989). Spontaneous pattern construction in a chimpanzee. In P. Heltne, & L. Marquardt (Eds.), *Understanding chimpanzees*, (pp. 252-265). Cambridge, MA: Harvard University Press.

17. Acquisition of Personal Pronouns by a Chimpanzee

Matsuzawa, T. (1990). Form perception and visual acuity in a chimpanzee. *Folia Primatologica, 55,* 24-32.

Murofushi, K., Asano, T., & Matsuzawa, T. (1985). *Description of the "subject" andt he "object" by a chimpanzee: Control by word order.* Paper presented at the 49th meeting of the Japan Psychological Association.

Murofushi, K., Matsuzawa, T., & Asano, T. (1988). *Acquisition of the word-order of agentive and recipient in a three-word sentence by a chimpanzee.* Paper presented at the 4th meeting of the Primate Society of Japan.

Petitto, L. A. (1987). On the autonomy of language and gesture: Evidence from the acquisition of personal pronouns in American Sign Language. *Cognition, 27,* 1-52.

18 "Language Training" and its Role in the Expression of Tacit Propositional Knowledge by Chimpanzees *(Pan troglodytes)*

Roger K. R. Thompson and David L. Oden

A PROFOUND DISPARITY?

Premack (1983a, 1983b, 1984) has argued that there is a profound disparity in the abstract problem-solving ability of language-trained chimpanzees and those that have not been exposed to such training. Chimpanzees trained on a language in which plastic pieces symbolically serve as words (Premack, 1976) can make correct judgments not only about the resemblance of physical objects, but also about the resemblance of abstract relationships. Non-language-trained chimpanzees, however, fail problems of the latter type. For example, in a matching-to-sample task both language-trained and non-language-trained chimpanzees will place apple with apple or bottle with bottle, but not apple with bottle. The disparity is seen when the animals are asked to judge the abstract similarity of identity and nonidentity relations by matching, for example, a pair of apples to to a pair of bottles rather than to a pair of nonidentical items like a cork and a spoon, or alternatively, matching a pair consisting of a padlock and an eraser to a paired can and paperweight rather than to a pair of shoes. Although Premack's language-trained chimpanzees correctly matched the identity and nonidentity relations independently of the objects used to instantiate them, his non-language-trained chimpanzees failed the task. Interestingly, a similar, but age-related, disparity in humans is reflected in demonstrations that young children typically cannot solve relational oddity problems until they are about 5 years of age (see review by House, Brown, & Scott, 1974).

The disparities between language-trained and non-language-trained animals raise the question, what does language training do to the mind of the chimpanzee? Although the mechanism of the language training effect was not established by Premack, he has argued that language training likely facilitates the use of a nonimaginal (i.e., nonsensory) abstract form of representation, without which relational matching cannot be done (Premack, 1983a, 1983b, 1984). In contrast, Premack argued that matching on the basis of physical resemblance can be accomplished using sensory or imaginal representations which he further assumes are accessible to both language- and non-language-trained chimpanzees.

Premack's theoretical interpretation of the performance differences between language- and non-language-trained chimpanzees has not gone unchallenged, as is evidenced by the commentaries and author's response included in Premack (1983b). His claim that the ability to match relations hinges on the use of an abstract relational code, whereas objects can be matched using an imaginal system alone, has proven controversial. Perhaps this is in part because of Premack's apparent reluctance to acknowledge that an imaginal system can be abstract. However, as explained later, we believe the distinction between the representational systems mediating object and relational matching is not only reasonable but also necessary. Furthermore, we believe much of the confusion stems from an inconsistent use in the literature of the terms same and different; as shall become clear, we may have been guilty of contributing to this confusion ourselves (Oden, Thompson, & Premack, 1990).

In an attempt to avoid further misunderstanding we use the following terminology throughout the remainder of this chapter. The terms identity and nonidentity are used here to refer to the resemblance, or lack thereof, between physical objects. A pair of apples instantiates the identity relation, which can be represented as AA. Likewise, a pair of objects consisting of a padlock and an eraser is an example of the nonidentity relation, and can be represented as PE. We will use the terms same and different to refer only to judgements about the resemblance of one relation to another. For example, AA is the same as BB even though the objects making up those identity pairs differ. Likewise, CD is the

18. Expression of tacit knowledge

same as EF because they both are examples of the nonidentity relation. It follows then that AA and CD are different relations, as are BB and EF.

REPRESENTATIONAL DIFFERENCES BETWEEN PHYSICAL AND RELATIONAL MATCHING

Historically, evidence for representational processes in animals comes from tasks in which the correct choice response must occur in the absence of the discriminative stimulus (Hunter, 1913; Terrace, 1984). Such is the case in delayed matching-to-sample tasks in which an animal initially is shown a single item, the sample stimulus, to which it must attend. The sample is then removed and after a variable delay two alternative items, the comparison stimuli, are presented. The animal is rewarded for responding to the alternative that is physically identical to (i.e., matches) the now physically absent sample. In oddity matching the animal would be rewarded for choosing the comparison stimulus that is not identical to the sample. There is now good evidence that animals can remember either the predelay sample retrospectively, or a postdelay comparison stimulus prospectively (Honig & Thompson, 1982; Roitblat, 1980). A linguistically competent human subject quite possibly might represent events in both cases propositionally. However, this form of representational coding is not necessary; successful performance on delayed matching or other delayed discrimination tasks could be generated using a sensory based imaginal code.

A nonverbal animal's matching choices can be made on the sensory basis of absolute stimulus values (e.g., "see red, pick red") or on the more general, but still sensory, basis of physical resemblance. A sensory-based representational system could in principle also permit an animal to perform correctly on supposedly more conceptual categorical matching tasks such as, for example, match bird with bird and mammal with mammal. This could be accomplished by a relatively simple iconic imaginal system if the exemplars within a category share one or more invariant features. Alternatively, the imaginal system might be more abstract and based on prototypes that preserve the spatial invariants defining members of a category within the visual domain.

Evidence for an imaginal coding system based on physical resemblance rather than absolute stimulus values comes from studies demonstrating generalized matching in which animals transfer their matching abilities to novel items (D'Amato & Salmon, 1984; Herman & Gordon, 1974; Nissen, Blum, & Blum, 1948; Oden, Thompson, & Premack, 1988). From a computational cognitive perspective (e.g., Johnson-Laird, 1983), generalized matching entails learning to apply a common operator either directly on objects, as human adults might do when matching color swatches in a paint store, or on their representations. In physical delayed matching, the correct choice response can be identified and executed immediately after an animal applies the matching operator to the prospectively or retrospectively remembered stimulus and the comparison stimuli. In the case of successive matching, in which a single comparison stimulus is presented, the operator need be applied only once. If one assumes that a common matching/comparison operator is applied also in relational matching then it is difficult to see, for the reasons that follow, how anything less than a propositional form of representation (Palmer, 1978) could support judgments that AA is the same as BB and different from CD, whereas EF is the same as GH and different from JJ.

According to a computational account a standard relational matching trial proceeds as follows. First, the matching operator is applied to the pair of elements making up the sample (e.g., AA or CD). This step is the same as that involved in a single completed physical successive matching trial. However, in relational matching this operation alone can not identify the terminal response. Several more computational steps are required, beginning with representation of the outcome in working memory, which is not required in physical matching. If the relational matching trial is to proceed, then the matching operator must now be applied to the two comparison stimulus pairs, and the representational outcomes of those operations must be stored also in working memory. The terminal response still is not identified. The operator must now be applied to the stored representations generated in the preceding steps. This process of applying a common matching operator to increasingly abstract representations is outlined later. For discussions of the criteria for and distinctions between different representational systems see for example, Johnson-Laird (1983), Mehler, Walker and Garrett (1982), Pavio (1985), and Roitblat (1987).

The first two steps, applying the operator to the two-item sample and representing the outcome in working memory can be expressed as I(AA), where the sample pair consists of identical objects, or as N(CD), where the sample pair consists of two nonidentical objects. The items within parentheses stand for the sample elements to which the matching operator is applied and I and N stand for the representations of Identity and Nonidentity. The next step, in which the operator is applied to the two pairs of comparison stimuli and the resulting outcomes stored in working memory, can be expressed similarly as I(BB) and N(EF). In the case where the sample was AA, the final step in which the operator is applied to the representational outcomes can be expressed as: S{I(AA)/I(BB)} and D{I(AA)/N(EF)}. Likewise, in the case where the sample was CD, the final step can be expressed as: D{N(CD)/I(BB)} and

18. Expression of tacit knowledge

S{N(CD)/N(EF)}. Here the S and D stand for the representations of Sameness and Difference which are generated from applying the matching operator to the I and N representations. Only when S and D are generated can the correct instrumental response be identified.

If one wishes to argue that the initial outcomes of Identity (I) and Nonidentity (N) are represented imaginally then they must be abstract, possibly prototypical in nature, but definitely not pictorial or iconic. That is, the representations must be capable of encoding the isomorphic spatial properties of symmetry or reiteration for Identity (I) outcomes, and similarly, for Nonidentity (N) outcomes, they must encode the isomorphic spatial properties of asymmetry or nonreiteration. If an animal represented these outcomes on the basis of iconic element features (e.g., the A or C of AA and CD pairs, respectively) then it would fail to complete the relational matching trial successfully. An animal relying on sensory representations of the initial outcomes necessarily would fail the relational matching task because the sample and comparison stimuli pairs are constructed from objects that do not share any common physical feature.

The only viable alternative to an abstract imaginal representation of I and N is an equally abstract propositional representation. The content of a propositional code is a truth statement about a relation or function between two or more referents (or arguments). The syntax of an organism's propositional code is unspecified, but likely is a function of the species' evolutionary history and structural architecture of its brain. In principle, different species can have propositional representations which differ syntactically in a manner analogous to human discourse. For example, taking the symbolic convention just described, one can express the proposition that "Mary kissed Jim" as K(MJ).

Even if one grants that I (identity) and N (nonidentity) can be represented by an abstract imaginal system, it is difficult to see how the representations of sameness (S) and difference (D), which are generated in the final step of relational matching, can be anything but propositional. Can there be a prototype of a prototype? The argument that abstract relational Sameness and Difference" necessarily are represented propositionally is particularly compelling if an organism judges S{N(CD)/N(EF)} as being equivalent to S{I(AA)/I(BB)}. In this case, there is no imaginal isomorphism, iconic or abstract, between the representational outcomes of matching first N and N and then I and I.

EVIDENCE FOR TACIT IF NOT EXPLICIT PROPOSITIONAL KNOWLEDGE IN INFANT CHIMPANZEES

As noted previously, only those chimpanzees exposed to language training have succeeded at relational same/different matching (Premack, 1983b). The implication, then, is that these animals have the capacity to form and use abstract propositional as well as imaginal representations, whereas non-language-trained chimpanzees are capable of forming and using only the latter.

In light of the controversy it is useful to review here some recent evidence supporting certain elements of Premack's position. As described later, we have found that infant chimpanzees perceive abstract relations as being the same or different as well as perceiving that objects are identical or nonidentical. These data we believe support the view that infant chimpanzees can form at some level abstract representations of relational information. These data then are consistent with Premack's assertion that whatever language training does, it does not instil abstract representational codes. Our data suggest that these abstract codes are present even in infant chimpanzees. The same chimpanzees, however, were unable to use this information in a matching task involving relations, even though they could match objects. In this regard their performances were similar to those of non-language-trained chimpanzees reported previously by Premack (1983b). Taken together, these findings indicate that abstract codes exist prior to any language training and may influence an animal's attention, but they are not readily available for use in an instrumental situation. These findings are consistent with Premack's further assertion that language training in some unprescribed fashion facilitates the use of and not formation of abstract relational codes.

THE CHIMPANZEE INFANTS AND THEIR GENERAL ENVIRONMENT

The four captive born infant chimpanzees (*Pan troglodytes*) were 9-11 months of age at the beginning of the studies described here. There were three females, Frieda, Liza, and Opal, and one male, Whiskey. All four subjects were experimentally naive prior to the first study. The animals' daily routine was in many ways comparable to that of a normal middle-class American preschool child. The animals' free-play periods, either inside toy-filled nursery like rooms, or in a verdant outdoor environment (Premack & Premack, 1983), were interspersed with morning and afternoon experimental sessions. Human

18. Expression of tacit knowledge

caretakers typically were present during play periods and joined in the rough and tumble play or care-soliciting activities characteristic of infant chimpanzees.

The animals' evenings were spent resting or sleeping in pairs housed indoors. The chimpanzee's standard breakfast consisted of pureed monkey chow and evaporated milk. During the day they periodically received, when required by the experimental procedures, fruit, yogurt, and fruit juice as rewards and incentives. At dinner they were fed monkey chow and fresh fruits and vegetables.

MATCHING TRAINING AND TESTING

In one study (Oden et al., 1988) the infant chimpanzees originally were trained to match using only two objects, a lock and a cup. Subsequently, as shown in Table 18.1, all four animals spontaneously transferred their matching performances to novel objects, fabric swatches, and food items, in the absence of differential feedback. The overall pattern of results, including, for example, correct trial-1 performance on transfer tests, provided convincing evidence that these animals were not matching on the basis of absolute stimulus values differentially associated with reward. Instead their generalized matching ability was based on a broadly construed concept of physical resemblance.

As a control for inadvertent cuing by the experimenter, the infant chimpanzees were tested also on a relational matching task in the same study (Oden et al., 1988). On each trial, the sample consisted of either a pair of identical (e.g., AA) items or a pair of nonidentical items (e.g., CD). The two comparison stimuli consisted of one pair of identical items (e.g., BB) and one pair of nonidentical items (e.g., EF). Different objects were used to construct the sample and comparison stimulus pairs. As in the object matching task, the animal's task here was to place the matching comparison stimulus pair into a pan containing the sample pair. Hence, if the sample was an AA pair the correct response consisted of placing the BB pair into the pan, and if the sample was the CD pair, then placing the EF pair into the pan was correct. Even on those trials in which the experimenter provided subjects with explicit cues as to the correct response via body orientation looking at or pointing to the appropriate stimulus pair, they all failed to match pairs that were the same. That is, they failed to match an identity comparison stimulus pair with an identity sample pair (e.g., match AA with BB). Likewise, they failed to match a nonidentity comparison pair with a nonidentity sample (e.g., match CD with EF).

Table 18.1.
Trials to Criterion and Matching-to-Sample (MTS) Accuracy During Training Sessions and Transfer Sessions

Subject and Test Type	Number of Trials to Criterion	MTS accuracy	
		Percent Correct	Correct Trials
Whiskey	670		
Training		83	20/24
Object transfer		92	22/24
Fabric transfer		92	22/24
Food transfer		75	18/24
Liza	642		
Training		96	23/24
Object transfer		79	19/24
Fabric transfer		92	22/24
Food transfer		54	13/24
Opal	951		
Training		75	18/24
Object transfer		83	20/24
Fabric transfer		75	18/24
Food transfer		62	15/24
Frieda	1,002		
Training		88	21/24
Object transfer		88	21/24
Fabric transfer		79	19/24
Food transfer		79	19/24
Total	M = 816		
Training		86.5	83/96
Object transfer		85.4	82/96
Fabric transfer		84.4	81/96
Food transfer		67.7	65/96

Note. Training sessions were the last two 12-trial sessions before transfer tests. Each transfer category included two 12-trial sessions, each session with two novel items. Data from Oden, Thompson, & Premack, 1988.

Their failure to match relations demonstrated that these infants did not differ from other non-language-trained chimpanzees in this regard (Premack,

1983b). This result coupled with the same infants' success at generalized physical object matching is consistent with our earlier stated view that non-language-trained chimpanzees employ codes based on sensory rather than propositional representations of events in their world.

The danger at this point is to equate the conclusion that an animal does not use a particular form of representation with the claim that the representation necessarily is absent. Results from other experiments employing noninstrumental familiarization/novelty procedures provided good evidence that these same animals perceived both physical identity and relational sameness, despite their inability to match the latter. The results of the three experiments described next force the conclusion that there can be a real disparity between one's ability to perceive and propositionally represent a property of the world and one's ability to use that representation instrumentally to guide action.

PERCEPTUAL SENSITIVITY TO PHYSICAL AND RELATIONAL SIMILARITIES AND DIFFERENCES

Oden, Thompson, and Premack (1990) assessed the infant chimpanzees' perceptual sensitivity to physical and relational properties of objects. They used a familiarization/novelty procedure similar to that employed in studies of infant perception and cognitive development in human and nonhuman primates (e.g., Fagan, 1970; Fagan & Singer, 1983; Gunderson & Sackett, 1984; Gunderson & Swartz, 1986; Swartz, 1983). In the standard familiarization/novelty procedure the subject first sees a stimulus object on a familiarization trial. A novel stimulus is then paired with the now familiar object on a test trial. A preference for the novel stimulus, as expressed in relative looking time, typically is taken as evidence that the subject remembers which of the two test objects was presented on the initial familiarization trial. If a single object is presented on the both the familiarization and test trials, then attendance to the test object, as measured by either gaze duration or handling time, is proportionally less if it is identical with the familiar object than if it is not identical.

The latter variation of the familiarization task was used by Oden et al., (1990) in one experiment to measure the infant chimpanzees' ability to detect physical identity or nonidentity. First a subject was shown one object on the familiarization trial. After a brief intertrial interval either the identical or a nonidentical object was shown for a fixed duration on the test trial. The duration of time spent looking at the familiarization and test objects was recorded. As shown in Table 18.2, the infants looked significantly longer at objects if they were novel than if they were familiar. This result was consistent with those

Thompson and Oden

Table 18.2.
Mean Looking Times of all Subjects in Experiment 1 for All Sessions Under Each Condition.

Subjects	Condition	Familiarization Trial 1 (s)	Test Trial 2 (s)
Whiskey	Identity	8.71	7.08
Liza		6.78	4.12
Opal		5.15	3.61
Frieda		4.01	2.33
Mean—all subjects		6.16	4.28
Whiskey	Nonidentity	7.99	9.5
Liza		6.38	6.86
Opal		5.72	5.78
Frieda		4.76	2.91
Mean—all subjects		6.21	6.27

Note: In Oden et al., (1990) the identity and nonidentity conditions were labeled as same and different, respectively. (Data from Oden, Thompson, & Premack, 1990)

from the previously cited reports of human infant and nonhuman primate object recognition using comparable procedures. As one might reasonably expect, there was no disparity, in this case, between the infant chimpanzees' abilities to perceive and to use physical properties of the world.

In the next experiment, pairs of objects were used as the familiarization and test stimuli which the animals were permitted to handle during both the familiarization and test trials. The procedure was modified this way in order to maximize the infants' opportunity to show their sensitivity to abstract relations instantiated by the object pairs. In each session, a familiarization trial began when an animal was handed either a single pair of identical (e.g., AA) or a single pair of nonidentical (e.g., CD) objects mounted on a Masonite base. The total time an infant handled the object pair with its hands, feet, or mouth was recorded during the familiarization trial. After a brief intertrial interval the test trial began when the animal was handed a new pair of objects. The total time the animal handled the new object pair was recorded during the test trial.

18. Expression of tacit knowledge

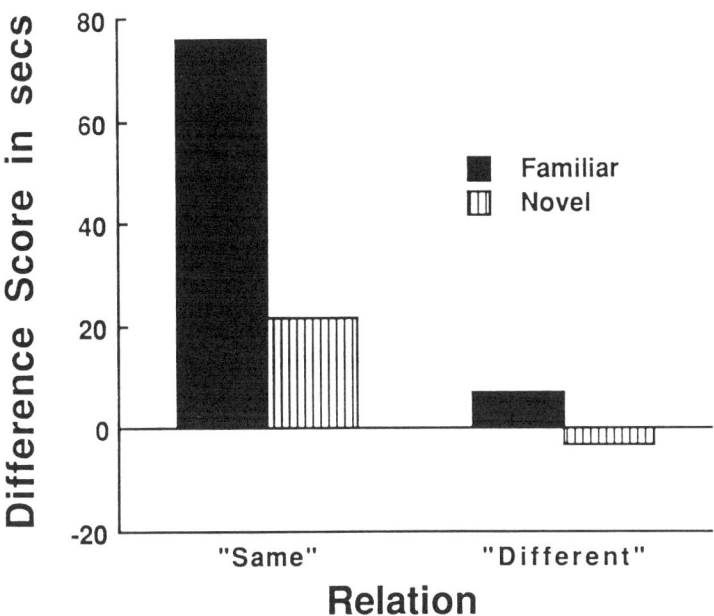

Figure 18.1. Trial 1 minus trial 2 difference scores in seconds for familiar (i.e., Same) and novel (i.e., Different) identity (BB) and nonidentity (EF) relations in experiment 2 of Oden, Thompson, and Premack, 1990). Note: the original labels have been changed to be consistent with the terminology used in this chapter.

The items making up the object pair on the test trial always differed physically from those used in the object pair presented during the initial familiarization trial. However, the identity or nonidentity relation instantiated by the object pair on the test trial was either the same as or different from that encountered on the familiarization trial. For example, relations across trials were the "same" if a BB object pair was presented on a test-trial following an AA pair on the familiarization-trial. Similarly, the relation across trials was the "same" if a CD pair on the familiarization trial was followed by an EF pair on the test trial. Conversely, relations across trials were "different" if a BB pair was presented on a test trial following a CD familiarization pair or, alternatively, if an AA pair on a familiarization trial was followed on the test trial by an EF pair. Oden et al. (1990) predicted that if the infant chimpanzees perceived abstract relations as being the same or different, then the animals would handle an object pair less on a test trial when the within-pair relation across trials was not changed and hence familiar. Similarly, they predicted that the animals would handle an object pair longer on a test trial when the relation across trials was changed and hence novel. The results of this experiment are shown in Figure 18.1 as difference scores in seconds of handling time (trial 1 minus trial 2). To be consistent with the terminology used here, we have changed the labels in this figure from those used originally by Oden et al. (1990). Here, the identity and nonidentity trial-2 relations refer to BB and EF object pairs, respectively, that were presented on the test trial.

As predicted, object pairs on test trials were handled longer when the relation (identity or nonidentity) was changed across trials than when the relation was repeated. That is to say, a BB object pair was handled relatively longer on a test trial when the identity relation it instantiated was novel (i.e., different) following a CD pair than when it was familiar (i.e., the same) following an AA pair. Similarly, an EF test trial object pair was handled relatively longer when the nonidentity relation it instantiated was novel (i.e., different) following an AA pair than when it was familiar (i.e., the same) following a CD pair. These results, showing a preference for relational novelty, provide good evidence that the infant chimpanzees perceived the relations instantiated by the object pairs across trials as being the same or different.

Recently, Tyrrell, Stauffer, and Snowman (1991) demonstrated a comparable perceptual preference for relational novelty in 6-month-old human infants, even though children typically cannot solve relational oddity matching problems until 5 years of age (House et al., 1974). Hence, both child and infant chimpanzee display a similar disparity in their ability to perceive an abstract relational property of the world and their ability to use it instrumentally as a guide for action. Whatever language training does, the pattern of results from the infant chimpanzees indicates that the experience does not create a novel propositional representation system. The propositional representational system is apparently present already in both the non-language-trained chimpanzee and the prelinguistic child. Language training then presumably alters an existing propositional representation system in a way that enhances its usefulness in instrumental situations.

18. Expression of tacit knowledge

EXPLICIT TRAINING ON RELATIONAL MATCHING

The disparity between the infant chimpanzees' ability to perceive but not match abstract relations is surprising if one assumes, contrary to the earlier argument, that past failures by non-language-trained chimpanzees to match relations reflects the absence of the abstract concept. One might argue that the present four subjects are a special case with respect to their sensitivity to abstract relations. Perhaps these particular animals could match abstract relations if they were explicitly trained on the task prior to any form of language training. To test this possibility we attempted to train the infant chimpanzees to match abstract relations by first using the same stimulus object pairs used in the familiarization/novelty procedure. When this proved unsuccessful, we tried other methods.

The original procedures were the same as those used by Oden et al. (1988) for training physical object matching. Briefly, on a given trial, pairs of objects mounted on Masonite were presented as sample and comparison stimuli. All four animals reached the matching criterion using the four training stimulus pairs (e.g., AA, BB, CD and EF) that were drawn from the familiarization/novelty experiment. However, all four animals failed to transfer matching to novel pairs of objects. Apparently, during acquisition training the animals' had learned merely to solve the relational matching task via conditional discriminations. That is to say, they learned simply to associate AA, or even A alone, with BB, or B alone. They similarly associated BC or one of its elements with the EF pair or one of its elements.

Subsequently, as described in Oden et al. (1990), various procedures were used, including, for example, trial-unique object pairs, during additional training. After 1,100 trials,the relational matching performance of all animals with novel object pairs was still at chance. These data are shown in Table 18.3. The results from this latter experiment demonstrate convincingly that the inability of these infant chimpanzees to match abstract relations did not differ substantially from that of other non-language-trained animals as reported by Premack (1983b). The non-language-trained chimpanzees' failures, and the successes of language-trained animals, cannot be attributed to individual differences in their perceptual sensitivity to abstract relations. Differences in performances on abstract relational matching tasks are attributable in some way to the history of language training.

Table 18.3.
Proportion of Correct Matching Responses with Identity and Nonidentity Stimulus Pairs in Experiment 3 of Oden et al. (1990)

Subject	Training Trials 1-24	Training Trials 517-552	Transfer1 Trials 1-36	Training Trials 751-768	Transfer2 Trials 1-36	Training Trials 1105-1128
Whiskey						
Identity	.67	1.00	.61	—	—	.67
Nonidentity	.42	.88	.28	—	—	.33
Total	.54	.94	.44	—	—	.50
Liza						
Identity	.75	1.00	.78	—	—	.33
Nonidentity	.25	.56	.22	—	—	.75
Total	.50	.78	.50	—	—	.54
Opal						
Identity	.83	.78	.56	.83	.61	.17
Nonidentity	.42	.39	.61	.72	.50	.75
Total	.63	.58	.58	.78	.56	.46
Frieda						
Identity	.33	.67	.67	.88	.50	.50
Nonidentity	.75	.67	.56	.72	.44	.67
Total	.54	.67	.61	.81	.47	.58
All						
Identity	.65	.86	.65	.86	.56	.42
Nonidentity	.46	.63	.42	.72	.47	.63
Total	.55	.74	.53	.79	.51	.52

Note. Here the terms identity and nonidentity are used where Oden et al. (1990) used the labels same and different. (adapted from Oden, Thompson, & Premack, 1990)

18. Expression of tacit knowledge

WHAT DOES LANGUAGE TRAINING DO?

Altering the Representational Hierarchy

There is likely a biological bias favoring control of action by imaginal rather than propositional representation of sensory attributes. Any experience reinforcing the instrumental use of this system will accentuate its future use at the expense of the propositional system. In the relational matching task this initial bias will promote the solving of the task via conditional discriminations, as apparently happened in Oden et al. (1990). The animals mastered the abstract relational matching task presented during training, but they failed the transfer tests. In the abstract relational familiarization/ novelty procedure their use of neither representational system was explicitly reinforced. Thus, the saliency of the imaginal representational system was not strengthened at the expense of the propositional system. Hence, in the familiarization/novelty task the animals' sensitivity to abstract relational features could be detected in a way that was prohibited in the abstract relational matching task. Obviously, there is nothing novel in any of these assumptions. One sees similar analyses involving mechanisms of selective attention in traditional theories of animal and human discrimination learning (Sutherland & Mackintosh, 1971; Zeaman & House, 1963).

We propose that language training shifts the hierarchical bias of representational systems that the animal brings to bear on novel situations and domains. Any language training procedure necessarily is designed to consistently reinforce use of propositional representations. Language training then teaches the chimpanzee that the salient aspects of its experiences are the propositionally represented relations that transcend the particular items instantiating the relations at a particular time. In other words, the language-trained chimpanzee has learned more than that a plastic token is conditionally associated with a thing or event. For a token or gesture to become a "word" the chimpanzee must comprehend the functional significance of its propositional representations as a generative means of describing its world. The propositional aspects of objects and events, which were previously simply perceived and represented, are now comprehended as the basis for action, and they displace the previously more salient physical properties. For example, the language-trained chimpanzee having used, say, a fork as a "food manipulating instrument" represents it propositionally as such. Subsequently, this animal can generalize its propositionally represented knowledge immediately to any instrument having the same functional properties, regardless of its physical similarity to the original fork.

To the extent that the disparity in relational matching between language and non-language-trained chimpanzees reflects the altered representational hierarchy in the former, then any procedure that forces attention to the instrumental use of propositional representations would have a similar effect to that of explicit language training. That is to say, the disparity may not be necessarily due to the explicitly linguistic aspects (i.e., semantics and syntax) of the training procedures used in language training programs. Perhaps even monkeys could learn to match relations if their training procedures were designed to reinforce explicitly the animals' attending to relational rather than sensory properties. New methodologies of the type described by Rumbaugh and his associates (e.g., Rumbaugh, Richardson, Washburn, Savage-Rumbaugh, & Hopkins, 1989) in which nonhuman primates use a joystick to manipulate a cursor between video-generated images suggest some interesting possibilities for future comparative research. However, such attempts would be potentially successful only if one were to first demonstrate, using familiarization/novelty procedures, that the monkeys were at least perceptually sensitive to relations.

If our hypothesis is correct, then the infant chimpanzees' failure to judge (via matching) abstract relations as being the same or different, despite their ability to perceive this distinction, may have been inevitable given their experimental history of object matching. This experience would have reinforced the hypothesized attentional bias toward associating sensory representations with action. If these same animals had been trained initially to match abstract relations rather than objects, then perhaps they might have succeeded on the former task. Conversely, an animal that has had extensive experience operating on propositional representations might be expected to experience difficulty with problems whose solutions lie in perceiving and using only simple associations between sensory properties. The data relevant to these possibilities are limited. Interestingly, however, Sarah, Premack's most proficient language-trained student of relational problem solving, experienced a surprising degree of difficulty solving simple associative problems like conditional matching to sample (Premack, 1976, 1983b).

Concrete Codes for Propositional Representations

If hypothetical experiments of the types suggested earlier were to fail, then we would be forced to conclude that language training does something in addition to, or different from, simply changing an initial bias favoring sensory representations. One possibility is suggested by the fact that the language training procedure developed by Premack (1976) contained within its token vocabulary symbols for the relational concepts identity and nonidentity. Perhaps providing concrete symbols for these abstract concepts was the critical aspect contributing to the success of the language-trained subjects on relational matching.

One possible mechanism for the effect of tokens might lie in the initial bias for action being tied to imaginal representations derived from an object's sensory properties. The tokens may have allowed the chimpanzee to portray a relational property in concrete sensory terms—that is, an initially propositional representation was translated into a imaginal one, which was accessible to action systems (Nelson, 1977; Savage-Rumbaugh, 1987). In our introductory comments on representational differences between physical and relational matching, we characterized the primary difference in terms of a common process in which a matching operator is applied to increasingly abstract representations. We are suggesting that providing a sensory code (i.e., the plastic tokens), which is consistently associated with abstract relations, permits the latter to be used in relational matching.

If we are correct, then training with tokens for only the concepts identity and nonidentity, divorced from any linguistic context, should enable abstract relational matching. Also, "language" training in which those relational concepts are not included should not enable abstract same/different judgements via matching tasks, regardless of the animal's linguistic competence. Perhaps there are data from other species or chimpanzees that speak to this hypothesis?

ACKNOWLEDGEMENTS

The research reported in this chapter was supported by a grant from the National Science Foundation (NSF: BNS 8418942) to D. Premack and grants to D. Oden and R. Thompson from the NSF program for support of small college faculty through association with faculty at large institutions. We thank T. Greene, D. Tyrrell, and the editors for their helpful comments.

REFERENCES

D'Amato, M. R. & Salmon, D. P. (1984). Cognitive processes in cebus monkeys. In H. L.Roitblat, T. G. Bever, & H. S. Terrace (Eds.), *Animal cognition* (pp. 149-168). Hillsdale, NJ: Lawrence Erlbaum Associates.

Fagan, J. F. (1970). Memory in the infant. *Journal of Experimental Child Psychology*, 9, 217-226.

Fagan, J. F., & Singer, K. (1983). Infant recognition memory as a measure of intelligence. In L. P. Lipsitt & C. Rovee-Collier (Eds.), *Advances in infancy research* (vol II, pp. 33-78). Norwood, NJ: Ablex.

Gunderson, V. M., Grant-Webster, K. S., & Fagan, J. F. (1987). Visual recognition memory in high- and low-risk infant pigtailed macaques *(Macaca nemestrina)*. *Developmental Psychology*, 23, 671-675.

Gunderson, V. M., & Sackett, G. P. (1984). Development of pattern recognition in infant pigtailed macaques *(Macaca nemestrina)*. *Developmental Psychology*, 20, 418-426.

Gunderson, V. M. & Swartz, K. B. (1986). Effects of familiarization time on visual recognition memory in infant pigtailed macaques *(Macaca nemestrina)*. *Developmental Psychology*, 22, 477-480.

Herman, L. M. & Gordon, J. A. (1974). Auditory delayed matching in the bottlenose dolphin. *Journal of the Experimental Analysis of Behavior*, 21, 19-26.

Honig, W. K. & Thompson, R. K. R. (1982). Retrospective and prospective processing in animal working memory. In G. H. Bower, (Ed.), *The psychology of learning and motivation* (vol 16, pp. 239-283). New York: Academic Press.

House, B. J., Brown, A. L., & Scott, M. S. (1974). Children's discrimination learning based on identity or difference. In H. W. Reese (Ed.), *Advances in child development and behavior* (vol 9, pp. 1-45). New York: Academic Press.

Hunter, W. S. (1913). The delayed reaction in animals. *Behavior Monographs*, 2, 21-30.

Johnson-Laird, P. N. (1983). *Mental models*. Cambridge, MA: Harvard University Press.

Mehler, J., Walker, E. C. T., & Garrett, M. (Eds.), (1982). *Perspectives on mental representation.* Hillsdale, NJ: Lawrence Erlbaum Associates.

18. Expression of tacit knowledge

Nelson K. (1977). First steps in language acquisition. *Journal of the American Academy of Child Psychiatry*, 16, 563-583.

Nissen, H. W., Blum, J. S., & Blum, R. A. (1948). Analysis of matching behavior in chimpanzees. *Journal of Comparative and Physiological Psychology*, 41, 62-74.

Oden, D. L., Thompson, R. K. R., & Premack, D. (1988). Spontaneous transfer of matching by infant chimpanzees *(Pan troglodytes)*. *Journal of Experimental Psychology: Animal Behavior Processes, 14,* 140-145.

Oden, D. L., Thompson, R. K. R., & Premack, D. (1990). Infant chimpanzees *(Pan troglodytes)* spontaneously perceive both concrete and abstract same/different relations. *Child Development*, 61, 621-631.

Palmer, S. E. (1978). Fundamental aspects of cognitive representation. In E. Rorsch & B. B. Lloyd, (Eds.), *Cognition and categorization* (pp. 259-303). Hillsdale, NJ: Lawrence Erlbaum Associates.

Pavio, A. (1985). *Mental representations: A dual coding approach.* New York: Oxford University Press.

Premack, D. (1976). *Intelligence in ape and man.* Hillsdale, NJ: Lawrence Erlbaum Associates.

Premack, D. (1983a). Animal cognition. *Annual Review of Psychology*, 34, 351-362.

Premack, D. (1983b). The codes of man and beasts. *Behavioral and Brain Sciences,* 6, 125-167.

Premack, D. (1984). Comparing mental representation in human and nonhuman animals. *Social Research*, 51, 985-999.

Premack D., & Premack, A. J. (1983). *The mind of an ape.* New York: Norton.

Roitblat, H. L. (1980). Codes and coding processes in pigeon short-term memory. *Animal Learning & Behavior*, 8, 341-351.

Roitblat, H. L. (1987). *Introduction to comparative cognition.* New York: W. H. Freeman.

Rumbaugh, D. M., Richardson, W. K., Washburn, D. A., Savage-Rumbaugh, E. S., & Hopkins, W. D. (1989). Rhesus monkeys *(Macaca mulatta)*, video tasks, and implications for stimulus-response spatial discontinuity. *Journal of Comparative Psychology*, 103, 32-38.

Savage-Rumbaugh, S. (1987). *Ape language: From conditioned response to symbol.* New York: Columbia University Press.

Sutherland, N. S., & Mackintosh, N. J. (1971). *Mechanisms of animal discrimination learning.* New York: Academic Press.

Swartz, K. B. (1983). Species discrimination in infant pigtail macaques with pictorial stimuli. *Developmental Psychobiology*, 16, 219-231.

Terrace, H. S. (1984). Animal cognition. In H. L. Roitblat, T. G. Bever, & H. S. Terrace (Eds.), *Animal cognition* (pp. 7-28). Hillsdale, NJ: Lawrence Erlbaum Associates.

Tyrrell, D. J., Stauffer, L.B., & Snowman, L. G. (1991). Perception of abstract identity/difference relationships by infants. *Infant Behavior and Development*, 14, 125-129.

Zeaman, D., & House, B. J. (1963). The role of attention in retardate discrimination learning. In N. R. Ellis (Ed.), *Handbook of mental deficiency: Psychological theory and research* (pp. 159-223). New York: McGraw-Hill.

19 The Effects of Language on Information Processing and Abstract Concept Learning in Dolphins, Monkeys, and Humans

Melissa R. Shyan and Anthony A. Wright

While some scientist and linguists still wrestle with issues of whether animals have the capacity to learn language, other questions also arise out of the numerous animal language research projects that have been developed over the years. Combining information from both animal language and comparative cognition research permits us to study what advantages having access to language produces in information processing and problem solving. Although it is obvious that language training increases communication skill between conspecifics (particularly humans; see Hoban, 1986), it seems plausible that language serves other functions as well (e.g., Bloom, this volume, chapter 6). Without entering a Piagetian versus Vygotskian debate on which came first, language or thought, we can consider the evidence and issues that suggest that language acts as an information processing mediator, improving or modifying how we encode, store, and retrieve information.

Several researchers (e.g., Forestell & Herman, 1988; Herman, Hovancik, Gory, & Bradshaw, 1989; Premack, 1983) suggest that training chimpanzees and dolphins in language-like tasks not only produces language-like behavior but also improves general problem solving abilities over those conspecifics not receiving the language training (see also Savage-Rumbaugh, 1986; Savage-Rumbaugh, Sevcik & Hopkins, 1988). They suggest that language training teaches symbolic or abstract representational manipulations and permits learning of abstract or higher order relationships. Premack (1983) goes so far as to claim that only language-trained animals are capable of learning these abstract relationships (abstract relationships refer to a subject's ability to learn concepts, rather than item or stimulus-specific responses; see Thompson & Oden, this volume, chapter 18).

There are, in fact, two issues. One is the question of how language affects information processing. The other is the question of whether abstract concept learning (learning relational rules) requires specific symbol usage training (i.e., language training) in animals, or whether animals can learn abstract concepts without language training. While this chapter is primarily concerned with the effects of language on processing, the reader will also find research throughout that addresses this second issue. Evidence is accumulating that shows that language training is not needed for abstract concept learning in animals (Wright, Santiago, Sands Kendrick, & Cook, 1985). Without taking Premack's (1983) more extreme stance, however, this chapter discusses evidence from dolphin, monkey, and human research showing that access to language mediation strategies (or perhaps, symbolic representation strategies) does, at the very least, modify the subject's processing strategies for memory tasks.

EVIDENCE FROM DOLPHIN AND HUMAN COMPARATIVE RESEARCH

Shyan (1985) and Shyan andHerman (1987) studied dolphin and human recognition of trainers' hand signals in an artificial sign language and discovered that language training, experience, and testing context all affected recognition strategies in these two species. Two dolphins had been trained in the comprehension of two artificial languages. One was a computer-generated acoustic language, and the other an artificial sign or gestural language (Herman, Richards, & Wolz, 1984). One dolphin, Akeakamai, specialized in the comprehension of the gestural language, while the other dolphin, Phoenix, specialized in the comprehension of the acoustic language. During regular gestural language training, Akeakamai occasionally made errors that did not appear to be concept errors but rather were recognition errors to individual signs. That is, she did not misunderstand the presented imperative sentence, but

19. Language Effects on Processing

instead seemed to misidentify individual words within the sentence. She would, for example, confuse the sign MOUTH[1] with the sign SPIT. A study of how dolphins recognized and identified signs began.

To study this, it was necessary to develop a methodology that would permit behavioral responses to indicate feature salience. Research on American Sign Language (ASL) with humans indicated that signs are constructed in much the same fashion as words. That is, only a limited number of physical elements (phonemes in spoken language; cheremes in gestural language; see Stokoe, 1960; 1972) are syntactically combined to produce meaningful words. The signs used in the artificial gestural language with the dolphins lent themselves to this type of cheremic analysis. Signs were analyzed into their component elements of hand shape, hand orientation, gross-motor motion, fine-motor motion, direction of motion, temporal pattern (the unfolding of a sign over time), and location of the sign. Then 15 modified signs were developed that contrasted features from different signs. Presenting these modified signs placed subjects in a forced-choice task where they were required to choose between one or more conflicting elements in order to determine their response. For example, the signs MOUTH and SPIT share elements of location, hand orientation, and gross motor motion (see Figure 19.1). They differ with respect to hand shape, fine motor motion, and direction of motion. A modified sign was developed (SPIT HANDED MOUTH) that presented the hand shape of SPIT with the direction of motion of MOUTH. If hand shape was the more salient recognition feature in signing, then subjects would respond with "Spit" (for humans) or perform the action "Spit" (for dolphins, by spitting at an object). If direction of motion was the more salient feature, then subjects would instead choose a "Mouth" response. In this fashion, 15 modified signs were developed that contrasted sign elements and forced subjects to choose responses that would indicate which were the most salient features (Shyan & Herman, 1987).

Poizner and Lane (1978), Poizner (1981), and others had noted that experienced and/or native ASL signers assigned different levels of salience and usefulness to these sign elements than did naive and inexperienced signers. It is unclear whether this was due to a first versus second language learning distinction (like that found in spoken language) as Poizner and others suggested,

---

[1] As with the conventions used in American Sign Language, gestural signs are represented by words in all capital letters. Actions performed or subject responses are represented by words in quotations. Thus MOUTH is the signed gesture, while "Mouth" is the response.

Shyan and Wright

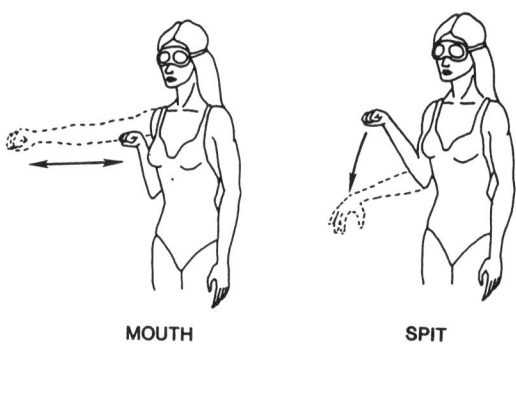

MOUTH   SPIT

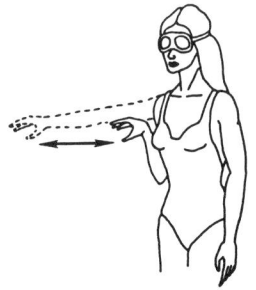

SPIT HANDED MOUTH

Figure 19.1. The handshape from sign SPIT is combined with the action from sign MOUTH to produce SPIT HANDED MOUTH.

or due to some other factors, such as testing or learning context. Like the humans in these studies, the two dolphins had distinctly different signing backgrounds. Both had over 6 years experience with signs at the time of this study, but there were differences in purpose and usage of the signs for each dolphin. While both received daily concentrated exposure to signing, the gestural specialist, Akeakamai, received signs in grammatical sentences, while the acoustic specialist, Phoenix, was not trained in signed grammatical sentences and therefore received sign training with only single signs and only in an informal setting. It was predicted that if linguistic experience had an effect on learning, then it would manifest in sign recognition strategies. Therefore, both dolphins were tested on the sign recognition task with modified signs. In the course of regular training sessions, each dolphin received two modified action signs, the gestural specialist during regular language training and the acoustic specialist during nontraining play sessions (when she usually received signs).

19. Language Effects on Processing

Eight human subjects were also tested. They were dolphin trainers who had from 1.5 to 28 months of signing experience. Trainers were matched according to months of experience and then randomly assigned to a language context or a nonlanguage context for testing. In the language context, subjects received modified action signs and other language signs. Subjects in the nonlanguage context received modified action signs, action signs, and signs that were not in the gestural language but which both dolphins knew and responded to. These nonlanguage signs were action signs that were not amenable to sentence structure, and could not be meaningfully combined with any other available words to produce semantic sentences. For example, TAIL WALK tells a dolphin to "dance" on its tail flukes. It is not meaningful to tail walk a ball, the way it is to "mouth" a ball. Both dolphins and both groups of humans received action signs, modified action signs (the test signs), and nonlanguage signs during testing. The gestural specialist dolphin (Akeakamai) and the language context humans also received other language signs (object signs and adjective signs). The acoustic specialist dolphin, Phoenix, had not been taught these linguistic signs. Her nonlanguage gestural vocabulary included over 40 action signs. The gestural specialist dolphin, Akeakami, had a gestural vocabulary of 15 language signs and the same number of action signs as Phoenix.

Each subject received four presentations of each modified sign over a 2-week (for humans) or 6-week (for dolphins) testing period. Responses (behavior for dolphins, spoken words for humans), reaction time, and, for humans, confidence ratings on a five-point scale were collected. The frequency of each response chosen was tabulated for each modified sign, based on contrasted elements. These frequencies were then analyzed using X^2, with the observed frequency of response for a given modified sign being compared to the expected frequency of response (as calculated by chance frequencies of both possible responses). Results were then graphically presented by way of statistically hierarchical importance of salient features for each dolphin (see Figure 19.2a) and for each human subject group (see Figure 19.2b).

Subjects with language experience, tested in the language conditions, tended to choose some sign features over others; that is, they developed a hierarchy of salience for individual features in sign recognition. The sign-language dolphin responded most strongly to sign location, then to the overall unfolding pattern, then to the direction of motion, gross-motor motion, and finally to fine-motor motion, hand shape, and hand orientation. The signing-context humans also used features for sign recognition in a hierarchical manner. However, the acoustic specialist language dolphin, and the humans tested in the

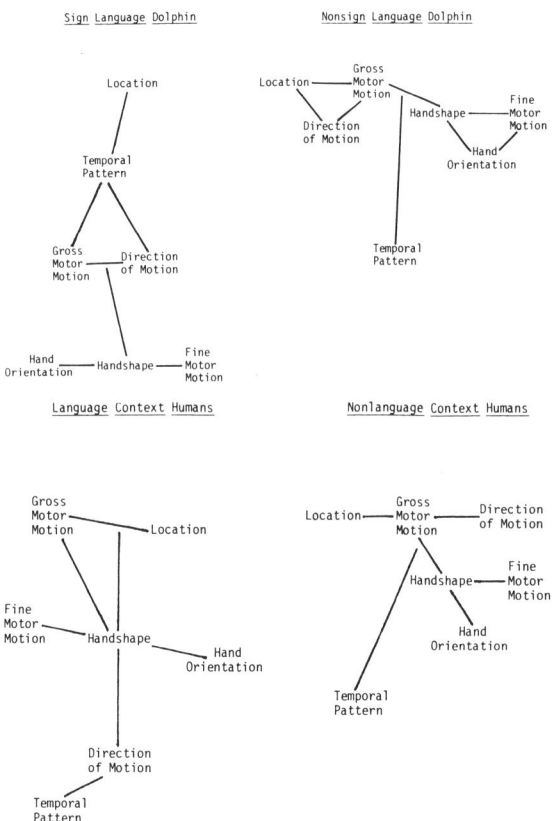

Figure 19.2. The hierarchical patterns for dolphin subjects and human subjects are presented. Triangular patterns of sign elements represent three-way interactions. Sign elements in each pattern are presented in descending order of importance. Horizontal lines represent elements of equal salience that are attended to singly and/or as interactions. Vertical and diagonal distances represent feature salience relationships, but physical lengths of lines are not quantitatively derived.

nonlanguage context, did not develop a hierarchical pattern of sign element importance. These subjects looked at the global sign, and their responses were more easily disrupted by modifications to a given sign. That is, they did not choose some sign elements as consistently more salient than others. Their answers were highly variable and indicated a general disruption in sign recognition by any changes or modifications to signs, and without any discernable patterns, which suggests a more global recognition strategy.

19. Language Effects on Processing

These findings implicate language training or language experience as a factor in processing and recognition strategies in dolphins. Here we have two dolphins with 6-years of exposure and experience in the recognition and identification of over 40 signs. The only difference in their sign experience is that one receives signs in a language-training context, is exposed to signed sentences and grammar, while the other receives signs in a nonlanguage setting and only receives individual signs at any one time. This, however, can be seen to be a major distinction because it produces different sign recognition strategies. One could possibly pass off this difference as simply individual differences between subjects, except that the findings for the humans also support this conclusion. Humans (whom we would expect to be more sensitive to language influences) were also affected by language or nonlanguage exposure to signs in a more immediate setting, that of testing context. The differences in strategy exactly parallel those found with the dolphins, with the language subjects producing hierarchies of response strategies and the nonlanguage subjects using a more global strategy. (This, of course also suggests that the different response strategies produced by the two dolphins were possibly a function of testing context. The definitive experiment would be to test the gestural specialist, Akeakamai, in the nonlanguage testing context and see if she, too, uses the global recognition strategy.) Clearly, language, whether in terms of experiential or context effects, does influence recognition strategies for both dolphins and humans.

Additional support comes from tests of dolphins on a visual matching-to-sample task (Gory, Roitblat, & Herman, 1986; Herman et al., 1989). Dolphins were shown a sample stimulus and were required to choose the matching alternative out of two simultaneously presented alternatives. Dolphins have been notoriously poor at this type of visual task. Herman et al. (1989) were able to teach a visual matching-to-sample task to Phoenix and to demonstrate abstract concept learning (that is, the ability to transfer the matching concept correctly on the first exposure to novel stimuli) by using sounds as mediating stimuli. Phoenix, the acoustic specialist, was presented with familiar objects for which she already had acoustic labels. In order to teach the visual discrimination task, Phoenix was presented with the object and its acoustic label (introduced by computer through an underwater speaker), and then was presented with the two alternative objects. If she began to make an error, a correction procedure was used before she could touch the incorrect object choice: the acoustic label was again played, directing her to the correct choice. After a large number of trials with this procedure, the sound cues were gradually faded. Phoenix was then tested on completely novel unlabeled objects, and was able to transfer the matching concept at a high (approximately

80% correct) level. Previous research in visual matching and discrimination in dolphins had been predominantly unsuccessful, leading researchers to speculate that dolphins were primarily acoustic specialists with modality-specific learning capacities, and not equipped to learn complex visual tasks. However, access to acoustic labels as bridging stimuli for this task improved performance and allowed the dolphin to develop a visual abstract concept. This again suggests that some type of symbolic or representational labeling scheme improves, modifies, or mediates information processing in dolphins.

EVIDENCE FROM MONKEY AND HUMAN COMPARATIVE RESEARCH

Cook, Wright, Sands, and Jitsumori (1985) and Wright et al. (1988) presented a series of studies looking at visual serial probe recognition in rhesus monkeys and humans that also suggest that language mediation processes affect recognition memory. Rhesus monkeys were trained to perform a visual same/different task and then were trained to an expansion of this task into a visual serial probe recognition task. Monkeys were trained to watch serially presented lists of slides. When a probe slide was presented that either matched or did not match an item from the list, subjects were taught to push a lever to the right for same or to the left for different. Wright et al. (1985) found that rhesus monkeys, pigeons, and humans all produced serial position curves with both primacy and recency effects. The primacy and recency effects for list memory have been used as evidence for the dual process memory model (e.g., Atkinson & Shiffrin, 1968; Waugh & Norman, 1965). Finding evidence of primacy and recency effects in three species would seem to confirm the model. This model claimed that rehearsal mechanisms transfer information from short-term memory into long-term memory, producing the primacy effect. However, there has been much debate over what mechanisms produce the primacy and recency effects: whether rehearsal transfers information from short term memory into long term memory or whether interference prevents the transfer of information from short-term memory to long-term memory.

To further test this, Wright et al. (1988) modified stimulus parameters in the sample list. If rehearsal and the breakdown of rehearsal were responsible for the drop in performance in mid-range list items, then increasing retention intervals for each stimulus would provide more rehearsal and thereby produce greater primacy. This was done with monkeys and humans in two ways. Some subjects were given increased viewing time for each stimulus. Other subjects were not given increased viewing time, but instead were given increased time between each stimulus (i.e., by changing the interstimulus interval, the ISI).

19. Language Effects on Processing

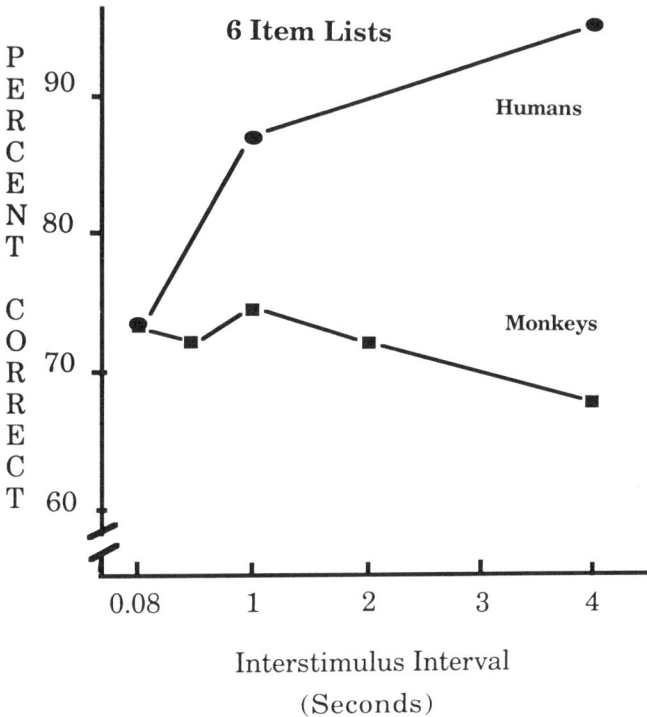

Figure 19.3. Overall performance for monkeys and humans on the visual serial probe recognition task when the interstimulus interval is systematically increased. Humans improve but monkeys do not.

Viewing time or interstimulus intervals were increased from 80 ms to 1.0 s to 4.0 s between stimuli.

Monkeys improved overall performance with increased viewing time but not with increased interstimulus intervals. Humans did improve with increased interstimulus intervals. Even though both increased viewing times and ISIs gave monkeys access to more rehearsal time for each stimulus, their performance showed no improvement on the ISI task. Two conclusions can be drawn from this research. First, the serial position curve functions were not related to rehearsal. If monkeys showed primacy and recency effects but did not improve with increased rehearsal time, then primacy and recency effects cannot be related to rehearsal. Although it is possible that monkeys do rehearse (or are capable of rehearsing) when the stimulus is physically present, this does not explain the presence of primacy and recency effects found in Wright et al. (1988). Second, and more relevant to this chapter, if humans improved with increased rehearsal time and monkeys did not (see Figure 19.3), then some additional factor to which humans had access but monkeys did not might have been responsible for the increases in performance with the humans. Although one possibility is insufficient rehearsal skills on the part of the monkeys, Wright et al. suggest that a more likely candidate is access to language processing. Perhaps the humans were using language to improve performance when given longer rehearsal times, that monkeys were unable to do.

To test this hypothesis, Wright et al. next tested humans by systematically manipulating their access to language processing functions in the same serial probe recognition task. This was done by manipulating the content of the visual stimuli. Two different types of stimuli were used. One type consisted of "travel" slides: color slides of scenery, flowers, people, and other identifiable items. These were the original test stimuli. The other type were color kaleidoscope slides, made up of geometric color patterns produced and photographed through a kaleidoscope. It was felt that these clearly distinct but unlabelable stimuli would limit the human subjects' ability to use language processing in memorizing and recognizing stimuli. (Although it is true that these stimuli also reduce familiarity of exemplars and increase similarity of exemplars by using a single category, thus increasing the likelihood of interference reducing overall performance, this factor was controlled by using a forced-labeling condition, described later.) Subjects were tested with interstimulus intervals of 0 sec., 0.5 s, 1 s, and 4 s. Results are presented in Figure 19.4.

Human subjects who were presented with kaleidoscope slides did not improve with increased interstimulus interval times. Their performance instead appeared more closely akin to the monkeys' performance. To determine whether language was in fact the delimiting factor, two other conditions were run. One group of human subjects was forced to learn arbitrary verbal labels for each kaleidoscope slide. They were presented with concrete English labels and individual kaleidoscope slides in a paired-associate task and required to memorize the pairs. The second group served as a control. They were exposed to the kaleidoscope slides for an equivalent amount of time as the labeling group, but were instead told to evaluate the percentage of each color in each slide under several different conditions. It was hoped that by giving these subjects a demanding, but nonlabeling, task, task familiarity would remain constant. Being forced to make evaluations about amounts of color in each slide

19. Language Effects on Processing

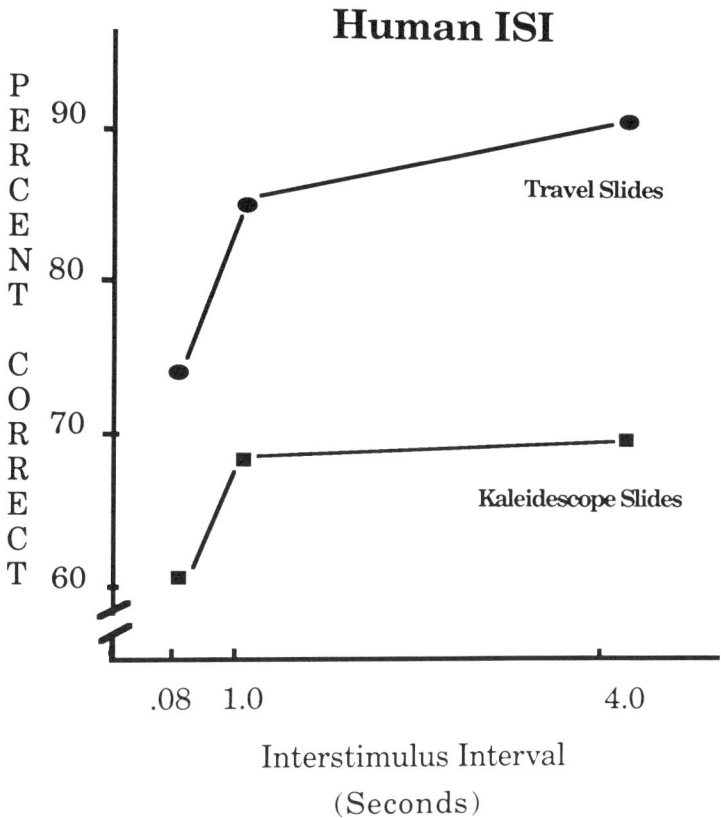

Figure 19.4: Subjects' performance on travel slides compared to subjects' performance on kaleidoscope slides with increasing interstimulus intervals.

was an attempt to equate familiarity, effort, and attention across groups. Results for the two groups can be found in Figure 19.5.

It is clear that when familiarity is kept constant, access to language mediation processing improves performance as interstimulus intervals increase. Performance for the labeling group approached the original performance on travel slides for humans. Here, again, is evidence that language mediation strategies can modify or enhance our ability to process and retrieve information.

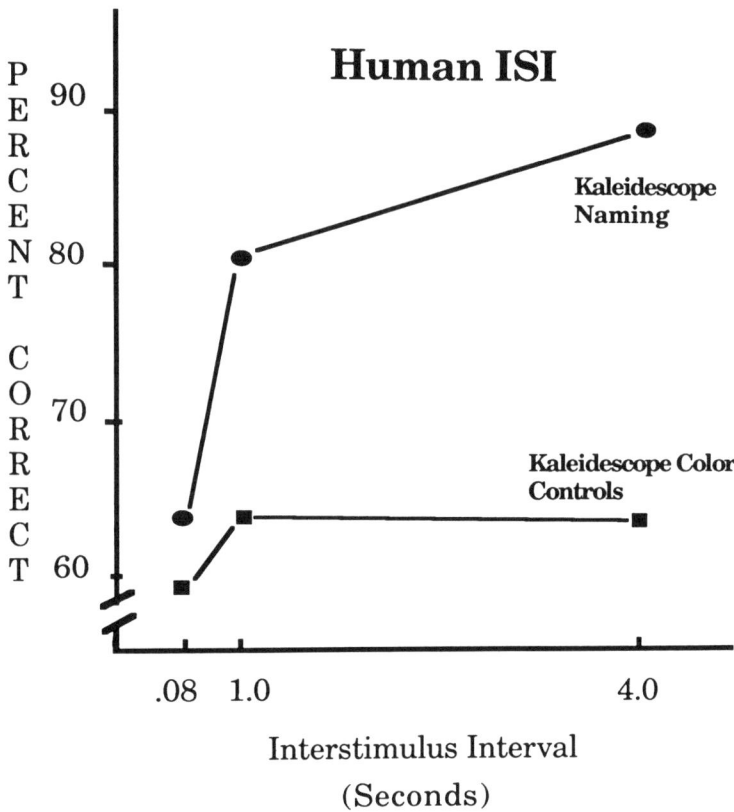

Figure 19.5: Subjects' performance on kaleidoscope slides improved dramatically when forced to learn labels. Subjects in the color control group did not improve. The labeling group's performance approached performance on the original travel slides.

WHERE DO WE GO FROM HERE?

These studies with dolphins, monkeys, and humans support the notion that language serves not only as a communication mechanism but also as an information processing mediation strategy that modifies and/or improves the

19. Language Effects on Processing

efficiency of the memory system. Additional research using dolphins, monkeys, and humans is in progress on this hypothesis, with several different approaches.

The first author is presently conducting research with native deaf signers (sign language users who learned ASL from birth) to study their processing strategies for recognition of signs. Subjects are in one of two conditions, a high language condition or a low language condition. The high language condition subjects receive modified signs within the context of complex sentences. That is, they receive one, two, or more word sentences, and some of the one-word sentences present modified signs. The low language condition subjects receive only single signs. It is impossible, or at least very difficult, to place native signers in a nonlanguage signing condition because of their extensive vocabulary and because ASL does not contain meaningful nonlanguage signs such as those used with dolphins. However, as humans are very sensitive to testing context, it is expected that the two conditions will produce differences in sign recognition strategies, much as they did with the dolphin trainers. If this occurs, it suggests that testing context is actually a more important factor in sign recognition than is experience or age of language learning in sign language.

Evidence from human research (e.g., Murdock & Walker, 1969) on modality effects in visual and auditory list memory) suggests that not only are language mediation strategies useful in processing stimuli, but the processing strategies used are identical or highly similar at least, regardless of the modality used. These findings have important implications for theories and models of cognitive processing. Contrary to what many researchers are currently suggesting, these findings propose that, while visual and auditory stimuli are processed through separate sensory and possibly preliminary or lower level cognitive mechanisms, at higher (more abstract) cognitive levels, there is a single central processing mechanism that is responsible for recognition strategies and which operates for all sensory channels. At this point it is difficult to determine which is the more parsimonious hypothesis: that there is a single central processing mechanism for higher relational processes that is unaffected by sensory channel and strengthened by language mediation strategies, or that there is redundancy in the processing systems and that each sensory/cognitive processor is sensory specific but uses similar processing mechanisms for each specific modality. It appears that the single central processor is the more likely, but more research is required before final conclusions can be drawn.

Further evidence for the single central processor model comes from recent research on species-specific processing in dolphins and monkeys. Until recently, researchers believed (e.g., Herman, 1980; Thompson, 1981) that in some species cognitive processes were modality specific. It appeared from numerous studies that monkeys learned visual discrimination tasks well but had great difficulty in learning auditory tasks (D'Amato & Salmon, 1984; Thompson, 1980, 1981). Dolphins, on the other hand, were quite capable of learning auditory discrimination tasks, but had little success in learning visual discrimination tasks. These findings were somewhat confusing because it was clear that monkeys are able to discriminate sounds in the wild, and dolphins are able to discriminate visual stimuli in the form of dynamic gestures. The modality-specific difficulties for these two species seemed to reside in the ability to learn relational concepts in these respective modalities. This would suggest, at least in nonhuman species as diverse as dolphins and monkeys, that the existence of a single central cognitive processor for relational processes is less likely than are redundant but separate modality-specific processors. However, recent success in training dolphins in visual discrimination tasks (Forestell & Herman, 1988; Herman et al., 1989), and monkeys in auditory tasks (Shyan Wright, Cook, & Jitsumori, 1987) has indicated that each species is quite capable of learning relational tasks in their "less preferred" modality. In both cases, giving the animal a mediating cue initially (an auditory cue for dolphins or a spatial localization cue for monkeys) aided in teaching the task. Later, these cues were faded, novel stimuli were presented, and both species showed complete first-trial transfer of the target concept (a visual matching-to-sample task for dolphins; an auditory same/different task for monkeys). Both species are also showing evidence of success with more complex tasks in in these modalities (see for example, Gory et al., 1986, on three-choice matching to sample in dolphins, and unpublished early preliminary evidence for auditory serial probe recognition tasks with monkeys from Wright's lab). If rhesus monkeys, dolphins, and humans do show serial position curves for both auditory and visual list memory (as preliminary data suggest), then this will provide further evidence for similar processing strategies across species and across modalities. It will then be up to additional researchers to determine whether a single central processor is responsible for these processes, regardless of modality, or whether separate but parallel processes are involved.

CONCLUSIONS

It is clear that a number of issues can be tested with comparisons between language-trained animals, non-language-trained animals, humans with access to language processing, and humans restricted from using their language processing capacities. Research is proving fruitful in helping to map the mechanisms and available strategies used in processing and manipulating information. The issue of labeling or symbolically representing stimuli in memory, the issue of a single central processor versus modality-specific multiple processors, and the issue of the nature of testing context on processing mechanisms are all finding methodological treatment through the use of animal language and comparative cognitive research. Using artificial symbol manipulation in animals (artificial language projects, according to some researchers) allows study of the processing effects of access to language-like mediating strategies that would not be possible by studying only humans.

Language does serve more than a communication function. It affects human processing strategies, and language-like training affects animal processing strategies in a similar fashion. Given the relatively late development of language in evolutionary history, researchers still wonder whether language represents a qualitative change in humans or just a quantitative difference between humans and animals. Research of the type described in this chapter suggests that animals do have some capacity for symbol manipulation or representational thought. However, it is also apparent that this capacity is used only minimally unless trained. Language training appears to provide a sufficient impetus to trigger the potentiation of this capacity.

ACKNOWLEDGMENTS

Portions of this chapter were used as dissertation material for Melissa R. Shyan in partial fulfillment of requirements for the PhD in Psychology at the University of Hawaii at Manoa. Portions of this research were funded by National Institute of Mental Health Grant MH-35202 to Anthony A. Wright and by the National Institute of Health Institutional Training Grant EY-07024. Other portions were supported by grants to Louis M. Herman from the National Science Foundation (BNS-9801653), from the Center for Field Research, and by a University of Hawaiii Marine Options Program Student Skills Project grant to Susan E. Swartz.

REFERENCES

Atkinson, R. C. & Shiffrin, R. M. (1968). Human memory: A proposed system and its control processes. In K. W. Spence & J. T. Spence (Eds.), *The psychology of learning and motivation.* (Vol. 2, pp. 90-197). New York: Academic.

Cook, R. G., Wright, A. A., Sands, S. F., & Jitsumori, M. (1985). *Rehearsal processes in monkeys and humans.* Presented at the Twenty-sixth Annual Meeting of the Psychonomic Society, November, Boston.

D'Amato, M. R. & Salmon, D. P. (1984). Processing and retention of complex auditory stimuli in monkeys (*Cebus apella*). *Canadian Journal of Psychology, 38,* 237-255.

Forestell, P. H. & Herman, L. M. (1988). Delayed matching of visual materials by a bottlenosed dolphin aided by auditory symbols. *Animal Learning and Behavior, 16,* 137-147.

Gory, J. D., Roitblat, H. L., & Herman, L. M. (1986). *Proactive interference in dolphin visual delayed matching-to-sample performance.* Presented at the twenty-seventh annual meeting of the Psychonomic Society, November, New Orleans, LA.

Herman, L. M. (1980). Cognitive characteristics of dolphins. In L. M. Herman (Ed.), *Cetacean behavior: Mechanisms and functions* (pp. 363-429). New York: Wiley.

Herman, L. M., Hovancik, J. R., Gory, J. D., & Bradshaw, G. L. (1989). Generalization of visual matching by a bottlenosed dolphin (*Tursiops truncatus*): Evidence for invariance of cognitive performance with visual and auditory materials. *Journal of Experimental Psychology: Animal Behavior Processes, 15*(2), 124-136.

Herman, L. M., Richards, D. G., & Wolz, J.P. (1984). Comprehension of sentences by bottlenosed dolphins. *Cognition, 16,* 129-219.

Hoban, E. (1986). *The promise of animal language research.* Unpublished doctoral dissertation, University of Hawaii at Manoa, Honolulu.

Murdock, B. B. Jr. & Walker, K. D. (1969). Modality effects in free recall. *Journal of Verbal Learning and Verbal Behavior, 8,* 665-676.

Poizner, H. (1981). Visual and "phonetic" coding of movement: Evidence from American Sign Language. *Science, 212,* 691-693.

19. Language Effects on Processing

Poizner, H. & Lane, H. (1978). Discrimination of location in ASL. In P. Siple (Ed.), *Understanding language through sign language research*, New York: Academic Press.

Premack, D. (1983). The codes of man and beasts. *Behavioral and Brain Sciences, 6*, 125-167.

Savage-Rumbaugh, E. S. (1986). *Ape language: From conditioned response to symbol*. New York: Columbia University Press.

Savage-Rumbaugh, E. S. (1990). Language as a cause-effect communication system. *Philosophical Psychology, 3*, 55-76.

Savage-Rumbaugh, E. S., Murphy, J., Sevcik, R. A., Williams, S. & Rumbaugh, D. M. (in press). Language comprehension in ape and child. Society for Research in Child Development Monograph Series.

Savage-Rumbaugh, E. S., Sevcik, R. A., & Hopkins, W. D. (1988). Symbolic cross-modal transfer in two species of chimpanzees. *Child Development, 59*, 617-625.

Shyan, M. R. (1985). Methodological note: Analyzing signs for recognition and feature salience. *Sign Language Studies, 46*, 87-92.

Shyan, M. R. & Herman, L. M. (1987). Determinants of recognition of gestural signs in an artificial language by Atlantic bottle-nosed dolphins (*Tursiops truncatus*) and humans (*Homo sapiens*). *Journal of Comparative Psychology, 101*, 112-125.

Shyan, M. R., Wright, A. A., Cook, R. G., & Jitsumori, M. (1987). Acquisition of the audtiory same/different task in a rhesus monkey. *Bulletin of the Psychonomic Society, 25*, 1-4.

Stokoe, W. (1960). Sign language structure: An outline of the visual communication systems of the American deaf. In *Studies in Linguistics: Occasional papers* (vol. 8, pp. 1-78). Department of Anthropology and Linguistics, University of Buffalo, Buffalo, NY.

Stokoe, W. (1972). *Semiotics and Human Sign Languages*. The Hague: Mouton.

Thompson, R. K. R. (1980). Auditory cued reversal and matching-to-sample learning by rhesus monkeys. *Anthropologia Contemporanea, 3,* 284-292.

Thompson, R. K. R. (1981). *Follow-up to auditory matching by a monkey.* Unpublished manuscript.

Waugh, N. C. & Norman, D. A. (1965). Primacy memory. *Psychological Review, 72,* 89-104.

Wright, A. A., Cook, R. G., Shyan, M. R., Neiworth, J., Jitsumori, M., Emmerton, J., Sands, S. F., Rivera, J., & Delius, J. (1988). *Concept learning by pigeons and monkeys.* Presented at the twenty-ninth annual meeting of the Psychonomic Society, Chicago.

Wright, A. A., Santiago, H.C., Sands, S. F., Kendrick, D.G., & Cook, R. G. (1985). Memory processing of serial lists by pigeons, monkeys, and people. *Science, 229,* 277-289.

20 Representational and Conceptual Skills of Dolphins

Louis M. Herman, Adam A. Pack, and Palmer Morrel-Samuels

Studies of animal language competencies bear on issues fundamental to a description of the cognitive skills and processes of animals. These skills include representational abilities, concept formation, knowledge acquisition, sequence discrimination, recall, and recognition. At the same time, these skills and processes are so broad that their scope, flexibility, and limitations cannot be judged fairly through examination of only selected portions of the data from the animal language studies. Nor can they be judged fairly through examination of only the language data. To do otherwise is to invite premature or biased conclusions. For example, Savage-Rumbaugh and Brakke (1990) and Savage-Rumbaugh (this volume, chapter 22) reach negative conclusions about the referential capabilities of dolphins by considering only a limited subset of the language-comprehension data obtained with these animals. Similar comments apply to Seidenberg and Petitto's (1987) claim that the pygmy chimpanzee Kanzi, as studied by Savage-Rumbaugh, McDonald, Sevcik, Hopkins, and Rupert (1986), was not using his lexigram symbols referentially. As Nelson (1987) stated: "[Seidenberg and Petitto's] case rests on a limited view of the evidence from children and a selective report of Kanzi's behavior as documented by Savage-Rumbaugh et al." (p. 295).

In general, the cognitive abilities of nonhuman subjects will be seriously underestimated if readers neglect to examine a comprehensive corpus of evidence. Accordingly, our goal in this chapter is to furnish a relatively broad review of our recent investigations of dolphin cognition, through studies with artificial languages as well as through studies not involving language. The findings from these varied studies contribute to a balanced view of the dolphin's representational and conceptual skills.

The work we consider is discussed within the context of three broad topics: receptive language competencies, behavioral imitation, and matching-to-sample tasks. The subjects of the studies reviewed are four bottlenosed dolphins (*Tursiops truncatus*). All were collected from the wild in the Gulf of Mexico at the age of approximately two years. Two of these, Phoenix and Akeakamai, were collected in 1978 and have been resident at the laboratory since. Both are females and are presently approximately 15 years of age. The remaining two, Hiapo, a male, and Elele, a female, have been resident at our laboratory since 1987 and are approximately 6 years of age. These ages may be put in the perspective of the typical developmental progression for this species: the young are usually weaned by 18 months; females reach sexual maturity at about the age of seven or eight and males at about ten; physical growth continues until approximately the age of 15, and in the wild or in captivity animals may live well into their 30s or even 40s (Bryden, 1986; Caldwell & Caldwell, 1972; R. Wells, personal communication, 1989; Sacher, 1980). Hence, Phoenix and Akeakamai may be classified as early adults and Hiapo and Elele as juveniles.

RECEPTIVE LANGUAGE COMPETENCIES

In earlier studies, artificial languages were constructed and used to examine in detail the receptive competencies of bottlenosed dolphins, using Akeakamai and Phoenix as subjects (Herman, 1980, 1986, 1987a; Herman, Richards & Wolz, 1984). An initial objective was to test the degree to which these dolphins could learn to understand instructions conveyed by sequences of gestures or sounds, where each unique gestural or sonic symbol referred to a modifier, or to a class of similar objects or actions. The meaning of a sequence was determined both by the particular symbols used and by the particular sequence of those symbols. The results of these studies (e.g., Herman et al., 1984) have shown substantial levels of understanding by these dolphins of both familiar and novel instructions. It is noteworthy that in organizing their responses the dolphins took account of both the sequential-order rules, the syntactical component of the constructed languages, and the meanings or referents of the individual symbols used, the semantic component. For example, Akeakamai, trained in a gestural language, understood the differences among such semantic contrasts as RIGHT

20. Representational and conceptual skills of dolphins

HOOP LEFT FRISBEE FETCH, LEFT HOOP RIGHT FRISBEE FETCH, RIGHT FRISBEE LEFT HOOP FETCH, and LEFT FRISBEE RIGHT HOOP FETCH, where the sequences mean, respectively, "take the Frisbee on your left to the hoop on your right," "take the Frisbee on your right to the hoop on your left," "take the hoop on your left to the Frisbee on your right," and "take the hoop on your right to the Frisbee on your left." Understanding was shown by the appropriate responses to each sequence. While this ability does not mirror the quality or diversity of language understanding shown by even the young child, it nevertheless illustrates that two of the fundamental components of human language sentences, the semantic and the syntactic component (Paivio & Begg, 1981), can be successfully used by dolphins to interpret the instructions given within their artificial languages.

In additional research on gestural language comprehension, an interrogative gesture and specific ordering rules were used to examine whether a dolphin might be able to report on the presence or absence of named objects in its tank (Herman & Forestell, 1985). This paradigm, the "reporting" procedure, in effect requires the dolphin to provide information about her environment. The dolphin must attend to references made to objects that are absent as well as to those that are present to provide this information. The findings (described later in this chapter) have demonstrated the dolphin's ability to understand such references, as indicated by the accuracy of her reports of presence or of absence.

The efforts with these artificial languages have been largely directed toward language understanding rather than language production, for both pragmatic and theoretical reasons. At the practical level, it is difficult to develop a simple, effective vehicle for language production by dolphins, although we have considered both vocalizations (Richards, 1986; Richards, Wolz, & Herman, 1984) and keyboard devices as potential instruments. The vocal mode suffers because of our own sensory limitations (or that of available digital signal-processing devices) for discriminating rapidly among a variety of different dolphin vocalizations that contain many high-frequency components. Keyboard devices are limited by a hostile seawater environment and by the dolphin's difficulty in readily manipulating the large array of keys required to convey significant amounts of information.

The theoretical reason for not emphasizing language production is more fundamental. There appears to be a basic asymmetry in production and comprehension abilities in animals (including humans), favoring comprehension (Herman & Morrel-Samuels, 1990). "Production" and "comprehension" are meant in the most general sense as the ability to convey (generate) information intentionally versus the ability to receive and interpret information. Metaphorically, animals are like a system of broad-band receivers coupled with a narrow-band emission system. This postulated asymmetry in animals may arise from the fundamental requirement of animals to detect, recognize, and interpret information from broad segments of the physical, biological and social worlds to insure their well-being and success. At the same time the animal needs to direct information (or signals) only toward relatively narrow segments of its biological and social worlds, and not at all toward its physical world. This asymmetry is broadly conceived as affecting cognitive structures and processes, and among other things is consistent with findings from human studies that language comprehension generally precedes language production developmentally and exceeds production capacity at any stage of development (see e.g., review in Ingram, 1989). Studies of comprehension might therefore reveal more about animal language capacities than do studies of language production.

Much of the early animal language work (Gardner & Gardner, 1975; Rumbaugh, 1977; Terrace, 1979) in fact took the opposite tack, focusing on production, with mixed and often controversial results (see e.g., Savage-Rumbaugh, Rumbaugh, & Boysen, 1980; Seidenberg & Petitto, 1979; Terrace, Petitto, Saunders, & Bever, 1979). The recent successes of Savage-Rumbaugh and her colleagues (Savage-Rumbaugh, 1986, 1988) in demonstrating language competencies of apes have in fact largely resulted from an emphasis on language comprehension. The success of animals in language understanding tasks also supports the thesis that receptive and productive asymmetries are a pervasive characteristic of animal information processing.

In the immediately following sections, we discuss some recent findings from our laboratory on the receptive competencies of dolphins. Four tasks are considered: the reporting procedure, responding to anomalous sentences, the understanding of television displays of the gestural language, and the understanding of deictic (i.e., pointing) gestures. These areas of investigation all bear on the issues of symbolic representation and reference.

Nonrelational and Relational Reporting

In the simple (nonrelational) reporting procedure (Herman & Forestell, 1985), the dolphin is shown a series of objects. After an object is shown it is thrown into the tank behind the dolphin. This seeding of the tank with objects is followed by a sequence of two gestures, one referring to an object and the second being a generic question symbol. For example, the two-gesture

20. Representational and conceptual skills of dolphins

sequence BALL QUESTION is glossed as "Is there a ball in the tank?" The dolphin can respond by pressing a paddle to her left (the "No" paddle) to indicate absence or one to her right (the "Yes" paddle) to indicate presence. Akeakamai's responses to such questions were highly accurate (mean = 81.56 in 108 trials), and absence was reported as reliably as presence (Herman & Forestell, 1985).

The initial training for the reporting procedure used a single named object, a hoop. Subsequent transfer tests showed immediate accurate performance on the initial occasions when reference was made to a different named object. Of the 10 questions (5 referring to objects that were in the tank and 5 referring to absent objects) Akeakamai responded incorrectly only once ($p < .01$ by cumulative binomial test). These transfer test results provided strong evidence that the gestural names for those objects serve as references to those objects. No response to an object was required, and references to objects present or absent were understood. Furthermore, the gestures corresponding to the different objects were understood in a context very different from the imperative constructions used during the initial teaching of the names.

Imperative constructions may also be given, however, within the reporting context. The simple (nonrelational) imperative is constructed as *Object + Action*, and requires that Akeakamai carry out the indicated action to the designated object. For example, if we state FRISBEE SPIT (through a sequence of two gestures) and there is a Frisbee in the tank, then Akeakamai should spit water at it. If there is no Frisbee present, then she should press the No paddle to indicate absence or the inability to carry out the behavior. More complex relational sequences refer to two objects and require that Akeakamai construct a relationship between the two by taking one object to another or by putting one object in (or on) another. Thus, if we form the sequence $Object_1$ + $Object_2$ + *Relational term* (e.g., FRISBEE HOOP IN, glossed as "put the hoop on top of the Frisbee") and both objects are present, Akeakamai should construct that relationship, and will do so in most cases when both named objects are present. In a minority of cases, however, she will instead put $Object_2$ on top of the Yes paddle, an invented behavior that occurred spontaneously. The meaning of this behavior becomes clearer when contrasted with the situation in which $Object_2$ is present but $Object_1$ is absent. In that case, Akeakamai will almost always place $Object_2$ on top of the No paddle, another invented behavior that occurred spontaneously (Forestell, 1988). Also, if $Object_2$ is absent, and the $Object_1$ is either present or absent, Akeakamai will directly press the No paddle. No object will be transported, because none can be. The object to be transported ($Object_2$), is absent, and therefore the relationship cannot begin to be constructed. Once again, Akeakamai's response to this situation was untaught. Through these different types of responses, Akeakamai seems systematically to indicate her ability to construct the relationship-in whole, in part, or not at all.

The ability to understand references to absent objects is vital to the issue of reference itself. It suggests that the symbol used to refer to the object is represented in memory along with representations of the class of objects for which the symbol stands. Because the dolphin can treat a broad range of objects as equivalent examples of the named concept, we can infer that the symbol stands for the class of objects, rather than for an individual example (Herman, 1989).

The spontaneous use of the Yes and No paddles as an indication of whether a requested relational construction can be executed is particularly interesting because it illustrates a common finding in our work of the dolphin spontaneously going beyond the boundaries of what has been explicitly taught to create a reasonable and informative response.

Responding to Anomalous Sequences

Studies examining artificial language acquisition by humans have revealed that subjects who do not have the underlying grammar explicitly defined for them nevertheless spontaneously invent a representation of it (Reber, 1967). After observing examples of grammatical strings in artificial languages, subjects can make reasonably accurate judgments of the grammaticality of additional novel strings. This situation mirrors the case for our dolphins: They have been exposed to many examples of grammatical strings, but have received no explicit training in the underlying grammar. Nevertheless, they appear to have generated a mental representation of the grammatical structure of their language. This implicit grammar is apparently rich enough to enable them to analyze novel sequences or build meaning by relating nonadjacent items. Like human language users (e.g., Lashley, 1951), they appear not to rely simply on associative chains or on conditional sequential discriminations in responding to their sentences.

One way to study the dolphin's mental representations of the grammatical and semantic features of the languages to which they have been exposed is to study their responses to anomalous sequences that violate the learned or inferred syntactic or semantic rules. Adult humans exposed to such anomalies may simply report that the sequences are "ungrammatical" or

20. Representational and conceptual skills of dolphins

"nonsensical." Young children given anomalous imperatives may often attempt to execute portions of the sequences, make substitutions for some of the semantic entities, or reject the sequence entirely (Carr, 1979; de Villiers & de Villiers, 1972; Gleitman, Gleitman, & Shipley, 1972; Hoban, 1983; Shipley, Smith, & Gleitman, 1969). These responses reveal the child's understanding of the semantic content and the underlying grammar of his/her language, because such responses are, in effect, judgments of grammaticality or meaningfulness. Our work has shown that the three classes of response (attempts, substitutions, and rejections) described for young children also appear in the responses of the dolphins.

Further details of the work on anomalies are reported elsewhere (Herman, 1986, 1987a; Herman et al., 1984 Holder, Herman, & Kuczaj, this volume, chapter 21). In this chapter we wish only to emphasize those anomalies that demonstrate Akeakamai's ability to construct meaning from nonadjacent gestures in a string. For example, the construction PERSON WATER HOOP FETCH is an anomalous string in that there is no rule in the dolphin's artificial language that includes three object terms. By taking the hoop to the person, a typical response with this form of anomaly, Akeakamai in effect deletes the term WATER and joins the two nonadjacent terms PERSON and HOOP. This creates the sequence PERSON HOOP FETCH, which does correspond to one of the syntactic frames within the language. In contrast, the string PERSON WATER FETCH (glossed as "take the stream of water to the person"), is syntactically consistent, but semantically anomalous, because the dolphin has no way to transport the water to the person. The dolphin typically rejects such sequences by remaining at the training station and making no attempt to carry out the instruction. The novelty of the sentence cannot account for the lack of response because the dolphin invariably responds to novel semantically and syntactically correct sequences, most often correctly (Herman et al., 1984). The different types of responses to these two different examples of anomalies add to earlier demonstrations of both semantic and syntactic processing in evaluations of grammatical sequences (Herman, 1986; Herman et al., 1984). The dolphin's ability to extract a semantically and syntactically correct subset out of a longer anomalous string suggests that the animal has constructed an internal representation of the underlying grammatical rules of its imposed artificial language.

In other work not involving anomalies, we have provided examples of the dolphin's manipulation of objects in order to make it possible to perform a named action, such as lifting a hoop off of the tank bottom in order to swim under it, in response to the command "HOOP UNDER" (described in Herman,

1986; Herman et al., 1984). Such examples, together with the results of anomalies showing the rejection of strings calling for "un-do-able" actions, suggest that the dolphin constructs mental schemas for tasks that include a broad concept of the action, an analysis of its boundary conditions, and an understanding of the relationship of objects to these actions. Thus, the symbol UNDER appears to activate a concept of "underneath" and does not simply set the occasion for swimming under any available object. Like some of the responses observed in the relational reporting paradigm described earlier, the responses to anomalies provide examples of the dolphin going beyond the limitations of what has been explicitly taught to make immediate adaptive responses to new situations.

The understanding of Gestures Displayed on a Television Screen

We have recently completed experiments documenting the dolphin's ability to recognize and interpret gestures displayed on an underwater television monitor (Herman, Morrel-Samuels, & Pack, 1990). Phoenix and Akeakamai were exposed to these gestures on a small television screen viewed through an underwater window. Neither dolphin had any prior exposure to television, and no explicit training was given in attending to television displays. The initial displays showed a signer gesturing. The signer's head, arms, and torso were visible on the screen. Both dolphins immediately understood the large majority of these gestures. Recognition accuracy for these signs was roughly equivalent to recognition for conventional signs presented by "live" signers at tankside. The gestures included simple, single-sign instructions and, for Akeakamai, two- and three-word imperatives, including relational sequences.

The television image of the signer was then successively degraded by first eliminating the view of the head and torso, and then the arms, leaving visible only a pair of white hands "floating" about the screen in black space. In the final alteration, only two flat spots of light appeared on the screen. These spots moved about the dark screen tracing out the hand movements of an otherwise invisible signer. The resulting display was similar to point-light displays used with human subjects in which lights affixed to a person's fingertips and joints are all that is visible as the person moves about (Johansson, 1975; Poizner, Beluggi, & Lutes-Driscoll, 1981). The dolphins were generally able to extract the information provided by the altered displays immediately, as shown by their appropriate responses to them. Performance accuracy was virtually unchanged through successive degradations until the point-light display was reached, but even in this condition, accuracy remained well above chance.

20. Representational and conceptual skills of dolphins

Our purpose in altering the presented images was to examine the dolphin's ability to perceive these rather impoverished displays as representations of the gestural information normally provided by live trainers, as one measure of the abstractness of the concept of a symbol for the dolphin. That is, although our previous observations with the idiosyncratic gestures of different live trainers indicated that substantial variation in given gestures could occur without affecting comprehension, we had no way previously to examine the independence of the gesture as symbol from the social agent normally providing the gesture. The problem is akin to testing the degree to which a disembodied voice can communicate effectively to the young child who is normally quite sensitive to and dependent on social cues, or to testing speech comprehension for degraded speech sounds that have no reinforcement history.

To obtain a broader perspective on the dolphin's performance with these television displays, we showed videotapes of the gestures in the initial display condition (head, arms, and torso) and in the point-light display to humans who had various degrees of fluency in the gestural language. All human subjects showed performance deficits in the point-light condition, paralleling the results for the dolphin. Further analyses revealed that the performance of the dolphin was most similar to intermediate-level trainers, that is, to college-level students averaging more than 4 months of experience with the language. However, the effects of several key formational attributes of the gestures (such as the effects of gesture duration or gesture extent) varied systematically with the artificial-language comprehension ability of the humans, just as they do in similar studies using American Sign Language (See e.g., Poizner et al., 1981). For details of these results and a discussion of their relevance to cerebral asymmetry in dolphins see Morrel-Samuels and Herman, this volume, chapter 15.

In summary, this study of responses to television displays found that (a) dolphins can easily resolve television images of the types used; (b) dolphins can recognize and interpret gesture language signs even in impoverished conditions where the image is degraded by omitting portions of the signer's body; (c) syntactic features and the structure of the gestures themselves both have systematic effects on gesture comprehension and (d) no training was necessary to evoke an understanding of televised images, even under impoverished information conditions. These data also support the hypothesis that the dolphins have developed rich representations of the symbols and that they can use these representations to make sense out of stimuli that bear little resemblance to the gestures displayed in other contexts.

The Indicative (Deictic) Gesture

Young children and chimpanzees may spontaneously point toward objects that command their attention (Bates, 1976; Savage-Rumbaugh, 1986). Bates (1976) notes that from this simple pointing response the child advances to the stage of communicative gesturing, attempting to call the attention of another person to the object of interest (e.g., by pointing and looking back at the other individual). According to Savage-Rumbaugh (1986, p. 13), common chimpanzees (*Pan troglodytes*), even those that are language trained, do not spontaneously exhibit communicative (referential) gesturing. Savage-Rumbaugh further claims that the chimpanzee does not spontaneously understand the referring function of an indicative gesture by another. Premack and Premack (1983, p. 54) also note limitations in spontaneous pointing by chimpanzees, stating that "the gesture of pointing is not natural to the chimpanzee...(but) it developed in the course of the [Woodruff & Premack, 1979] experiment [on deception]." In the Woodruff and Premack study, "cooperative" trainers shared food with chimpanzees but "competitive" trainers did not. The task of the chimpanzee was to indicate to a trainer which of two containers held food. Typically, the chimpanzees gradually developed the behavior of pointing with extended leg or arm toward a food container, or toward one not containing food, depending on whether the trainer was cooperative or competitive. In a subsequent role-reversal task, the chimpanzees learned somewhat more readily to respond (or not to respond) to the container toward which a trainer oriented, depending again on whether the trainer was cooperative or competitive. The trainer used head and body orientation as well as pointing with extended arm or leg to indicate a container. Thus, for common chimpanzees it appears that in neither the productive nor the receptive mode is there spontaneous appearance or comprehension of indicative gestures, although this function may emerge in the laboratory setting under special conditions and does seem to be part of the natural repertoire of some other nonhuman primates, pygmy chimpanzees (*Pan paniscus*) in particular (Savage-Rumbaugh et al., 1986).

An examination of the dolphin's understanding of indicative gestures is of considerable comparative interest, given the data from chimpanzees. Possibly, dolphins may be prepared to understand indicative gestures if, as some suggest (e.g., Jerison, 1986), they are capable of locating targets being interrogated through echolocation by a nearby dolphin. If one conceives of the directed sonar emission as analogous to the pointing motion of a human, then attending to another's sonar emissions or to the concordant behaviors such as bodily orientation may be functionally similar to directing ones attention to where another is pointing or looking.

20. Representational and conceptual skills of dolphins

Pointing is often used by our trainers to direct a dolphin to swim in a particular direction or to retrieve a particular object. The dolphins typically respond by moving in the direction of the point, or by retrieving the object lying in the path of the pointing gesture when it is followed by the gestural sign FETCH. Although we have not documented the history of use of these pointing gestures, we have tested whether dolphins understand an indicative gesture when combined with various gesture-language signs in simple sequences. In these sequences, the indicative gesture was followed immediately by an action term such as OVER, UNDER, or TAIL-TOUCH. The desired response was that the dolphin carry out the indicated action to the targeted object. In this use, the indicative gesture functions similarly to the demonstrative pronoun "that" in English, when it is used to refer to a specific object.

At the time of this writing, we have systematically tested these sequences only with the dolphin Phoenix. Unlike Akeakamai, Phoenix was exposed to a computer-generated acoustic language and has not been taught gestural names for objects, nor has she any familiarity with the syntactic complexities of Akeakamai's gestural language. However, Phoenix is familiar with all action signs, so that specific gestures for actions can be used in conjunction with pointing gestures.

For these tests, Phoenix was positioned near a signer who was on an elevated chair or a surfboard placed in the middle of the dolphin's tank; throughout the test the signer's upper torso was visible above the water's surface. Three objects (a hoop, pipe, and basket) were arrayed along the tank perimeter, forming the vertices of an equilateral triangle; the distance from the signer to each object was approximately 6.7 m. The signer oriented herself according to a preplanned quasirandom schedule so that she was facing one of the vertices of the triangle. The dolphin, in turn, was positioned facing the signer. The signer pointed briefly (ca. 2-3 s) toward one of the three objects and then gave an action sign. For example, if the sequence was POINT OVER, and the indicated object was the hoop, the correct response was to swim to the hoop and leap over it. A total of 21 simple sequences was given to Phoenix. She responded correctly to the indicated object 17 times (80.9%), each time with the correct action.

Phoenix seemed to interpret the indicative gesture as an instruction to proceed to an object rather than simply to swim in the direction indicated. Thus, in a follow-up test we ran 12 trials in three equal blocks using a procedure similar to that just described. After each trial, objects were repositioned. During three probe trials, one per block, one of the three objects was not replaced in the tank but remained outside and removed from view. The action was changed to either TAILTOUCH or PECTOUCH. Empty positions were different for these three trials. For the probe test, the signer pointed to the vacated position and then gave an action sign. On all three occasions, Phoenix initially swam in the indicated direction, but then immediately turned and swam to another object to perform the requested action. Thus the dolphin appears to respond to these deictic gestures as if they are indications to respond to an object at the indicated location, rather than to simply move in the indicated direction. The actions requested in these three trials (TAILTOUCH and PECTOUCH) could have been completed by touching the tank wall or even the water surface rather than proceeding to an alternative object. Phoenix's responses in these instances suggests that she makes inferences about the signer's intentions when an action gesture follows the indicative sign. The ability suggests that dolphins actively seek to resolve the meaning of the gestural commands they view much as human listeners seem to take the speaker's intentions into account during face-to-face interaction (Clark, 1985).

BEHAVIORAL MIMICRY: IMITATING THE BEHAVIOR OF A MODEL

Imitative behavior has long interested psychologists, in part because of its possible relevance to language learning by young children (Bloom, Hood, & Lightbown, 1974; Clark, 1977; Ervin, 1964; Leonard & Kaplan, 1976). However, the role of imitation in animal learning and behavior is more problematic. Galef (1988) has reviewed the literature on imitation by animals and has emphasized how difficult it is separate out true imitation from other closely related phenomena, such as social facilitation or observational learning. He stated (p. 23): "It is somewhat surprising that almost 100 years of study of social learning in animals has failed to produce a clear answer to the question of whether animals can in fact...truly imitate." The problem lies in deciding what constitutes true imitation and in measuring the degree of abstractness of any imitative ability. True imitation is generally demonstrated by the copying of an otherwise "improbable" act not in the normal repertoire of the species (e.g., Thorpe, 1963). Although an animal might be able to learn to imitate some particular behaviors or particular vocalizations, this capability may not readily generalize to other behaviors or vocalizations. In contrast, one can claim that an animal has an abstract concept of mimicry if the imitative response can be placed under stimulus control and the animal is able to generalize the response to a variety of newly observed behaviors or sounds.

20. Representational and conceptual skills of dolphins

Both vocal and motor mimicry have been studied in animals. The capability of psittacine birds and some other avian species for vocal mimicry is well established (Baylis, 1982), but prior to our work with dolphins (Richards et al., 1984), this capability had not been demonstrated under rigorous experimental procedures for nonhuman mammals. The Richards et al. study revealed the ability of the dolphin Akeakamai to imitate a variety of arbitrary sounds played through an underwater speaker. The sounds were electronically generated and most were entirely new to the dolphin's experience and unlike natural dolphin vocalizations. Akeakamai's imitative response was evoked by a 40-kHz pure tone of short duration that preceded each model sound that the dolphin was to imitate. Akeakamai attempted to copy faithfully each new sound presented to her and was successful with several on her first attempt. These results suggested that Akeakamai had acquired an abstract concept of mimicry, fully meeting the criteria for a concept as just outlined. The robustness of the concept was underscored by the immediacy with which several new sounds were imitated and by the ability of this dolphin to imitate sounds that were unlike her natural vocal repertoire.

Learning of selected motor responses through imitation has been studied experimentally in several mammals and birds. Zentall (1988) provided evidence for imitative learning of bar-pressing and passive avoidance by rats. Zentall's work showed an increased rate of learning of these responses relative to rates occurring when the subjects watched nonrelated behaviors or watched nothing. We are more interested, however, in determining whether arbitrary motor mimicry is obtainable, than in the facilitation of learning. By motor mimicry we mean the production of a behavior whose form closely resembles that of a model, and that occurs successfully after a single demonstration or after only a few demonstrations. In this sense, motor mimicry is analogous to vocal mimicry, in that both are close copies of a stimulus or of an act.

Bottlenosed dolphins and other delphinid cetaceans frequently exhibit synchronous group behaviors in the wild, such as surfacing or leaping in unison. In the settings of marine parks dolphins at times have been observed to copy the learned behavior of another cetacean spontaneously (for a review, see Herman, 1980). It was of interest, therefore, to examine motor mimicry in dolphins experimentally, much in the way that Richards et al. (1984) examined vocal mimicry. Is there a general imitative capability in dolphins that extends to the copying of both vocal and motor behaviors? To our knowledge, the imitation of both vocal and motor behaviors has not been demonstrated previously in a nonhuman. A capacity for both forms of imitation would suggest considerable representational abilities, especially under conditions of delayed imitation and the imitation of arbitrary behaviors not in the dolphin's previous repertoire. In addition to testing for simple and delayed motor imitation of a model's behavior we were interested in testing for the following: the ability to selectively imitate either a human or another dolphin, where both models are demonstrating behaviors at the same time, but each behavior is different; and the ability to imitate behaviors viewed on a television screen. Simple and delayed mimicry were studied by Xitco (1988); the remaining topics were follow-up studies to Xitco's findings and are topics in imitation that appear either not to have been studied extensively in animals previously or else not studied at all.

Simple Motor Mimicry

The behavioral mimicry paradigm (Harley, Xitco, Roitblat, & Herman, in preparation.; Xitco, 1988) required that one dolphin, the imitator, observe and copy the behavior of a model. In the initial study reported by Xitco, the dolphins Hiapo and Elele each performed imitations of a human model who demonstrated a variety of in-water behaviors, such as a backward swim, a somersault, or retrieval of a sunken object from the bottom of the tank. Both the imitating dolphin and the human model were positioned at the edge of the tank, watching a trainer standing on the adjoining deck. Using a hand gesture, the trainer instructed the model to perform some behavior. The dolphin was required to perform the same behavior simultaneous with or immediately after the demonstration by the model. The behaviors demonstrated had not been required of the dolphins previously, although in some cases they may have been performed spontaneously by one or the other of the animals. Hiapo successfully copied 7 of 13 different behaviors successfully after a single demonstration and Elele successfully copied 4 of 14. After a maximum of 8 additional demonstrations, all but 2 of the remaining behaviors were copied successfully by Hiapo and all but five by Elele. Overall, the results provided experimental evidence for true motor mimicry in dolphins as shown by the successful immediate copies of several of the novel behaviors modeled by the human. Subsequent training of Hiapo and Elele focused on placing the imitative act under control of a "mimic" hand sign. Control by this hand sign was accomplished successfully: A model demonstrated a behavior and the dolphin either attempted to copy that behavior if the mimic sign was given subsequently, or performed a different behavior if some other gestural sign was given.

The mimicry paradigm was later applied to the dolphins Phoenix and Akeakamai by Xitco. In this case Phoenix and Akeakamai acted as models for each other. No human model was used. The dolphins were able to interchange these roles successfully, each taking turns as model or as imitator. On each trial,

20. Representational and conceptual skills of dolphins

the model was given an instruction through a hand gesture or sequence of gestures to carry out some behavior. The imitator was not able to see these gestures. The mimic dolphin was then instructed through other gestures either to copy the model's behavior or to perform a behavior specifically requested by a gestural sign. Mimicking versus performing the alternative behavior was a highly reliable discrimination yielding virtually no error for either dolphin. Ten different behaviors were used to train Phoenix and Akeakamai in the mimicry task, and an additional 15 to test for transfer. Of these 15, 12 were familiar to the imitator and 3 were novel. Phoenix successfully copied 7 of the familiar behaviors, 3 on her first attempt, and 2 of the novel behaviors, both on her first attempt (a paddle press with the rostrum and pulling on a rope to ring a bell). Akeakamai successfully copied 6 of the familiar behaviors, 2 on the first attempt and 1 novel behavior. The novel behavior was copied successfully after three demonstrations and consisted of placing a ring on a short pole.

These results give further support for a capability for true motor mimicry in dolphins, with either humans or dolphins acting as models. The development of a general concept of "imitate" was shown by control of the mimic response by an arbitrary gestural stimulus, and by the ability to imitate a variety of behaviors immediately, or after only a few demonstrations. The findings on motor mimicry, together with the earlier findings of vocal mimicry of arbitrary sounds, as well as evidence that dolphins imitate one another's signature whistles (Caldwell, Caldwell, & Tyack, 1990; Tyack, 1986, this volume, chapter 7), demonstrate that imitation is a broadly developed ability in bottlenosed dolphins.

Delayed Mimicry

To test for the ability to represent a modeled behavior in memory and reproduce it subsequently, Xitco (1988) inserted delays between the end of the behavioral demonstration and the signal to mimic. The imitators were again Phoenix and Akeakamai, and they continued to serve as models for each other. Delays ranged from 0 to 80 s, and began when the model was again facing her trainer at tankside after having demonstrated one of seven different behaviors. Accuracy in imitation for Akeakamai was nearly 100% at a 0-s delay, remained above 85% correct through to a 25-s delay, and finally declined to approximately 60% at the final 80-s delay. Chance performance, based on a random selection of one of the seven behaviors, would be only 14.3%. Phoenix experienced somewhat greater difficulties with the delays. Her performance paralleled that of Akeakamai but her accuracy, while still significantly above chance, was less than Akeakamai's at each delay value.

The ability of the dolphins to copy a behavior successfully after delays implies a reliance on mental representations of the demonstrated behavior (Zentall & Galef, 1988). Because each dolphin experienced each of the seven behaviors under the zero-delay condition, before longer delays were introduced, the imitation may have been based on encoding only enough of the model's behavior to identify the proper response. The mimic need then only remember the identified response prospectively. Alternatively, once a to-be-mimicked behavior is identified, the dolphin could adopt a stereotyped posture or repetitive behavior to bridge the temporal gap between the demonstration and its performance. In additional work (Herman, Morrel-Samuels, & Brown, 1989) we ruled out the use of such behavioral mediators by requiring the dolphin to perform one of several distractor behaviors, such as swimming on her back, during the delay. The ability to mimic the modeled behavior accurately, even after performing a distractor behavior, provides strong evidence that the dolphins were forming mental representations of behaviors rather than simply using motoric cues to remember displayed behaviors. The earlier success in imitating some of the novel behaviors suggests further that, in some circumstances at least, these mental representations include specific rich details of the model's performance.

Selective Behavioral Mimicry

In further work with Phoenix and Akeakamai, a person rather than a dolphin served as a model. Imitation of the person was approximately as accurate as imitation of a dolphin, although the set of in-water behaviors that could be demonstrated by each type of model was not identical. For selective mimicry (Herman, Morrel-Samuels, & Brown, 1989), both the dolphin model and the human model were present in the tank. Simultaneously, each performed a behavior, but the two behaviors were different. The observing dolphin, Akeakamai, was directed, through a symbolic gesture signifying either PERSON or PHOENIX, to imitate only that particular model. The gestures for PERSON or PHOENIX were taken from the artificial gestural language used with Akeakamai and were given in the string PERSON MIMIC or PHOENIX MIMIC.

The test for selective mimicry consisted of 24 trials during which each model demonstrated one of 12 different behaviors. At each trial the models demonstrated different behaviors. Of the 12 behaviors, 8 were the same for the dolphin and for the human. This overlap guarded against the dolphin associating a particular behavior with a particular model.

20. Representational and conceptual skills of dolphins

Over the total of 24 trials, each behavior was demonstrated twice by each model, once as the behavior to be copied and once as the distractor behavior. Akeakamai was directed to imitate the person during 12 trials and Phoenix during 12 trials, according to a randomized, balanced schedule. While the behaviors of the models were ongoing, Akeakamai was instructed with gestures to imitate the person, imitate Phoenix, or perform some other specified behavior.

Akeakamai chose the correct model, the one specified by the trainer, on 19 (79.2%) of the 24 trials. Of these 19 occasions, Akeakamai copied the behavior being demonstrated 12 times (63.2%) by the strict criterion of an exact copy, and 16 times (84.2%) by the less-stringent criterion of an approximation of the behavior (e.g., tossing a ball in a basket rather than simply tossing it in the air). There was no appreciable difference in the ability to imitate one model or the other. Of the 5 trials in which Akeakamai chose the wrong model, that model's behavior was imitated correctly, by the strict criterion. Thus, over the total of 24 trials, Akeakamai performed an exact imitation of one of the models on 17 trials (70.8%) and performed a closely related behavior on an additional 4. The ability to select the designated model correctly on almost 80% of the trials demonstrates that the gestural signs PERSON and PHOENIX retained their referential function, despite rather substantial changes in the task and situation.

Mimicry via Television

We have recently adapted the technique of displaying gestural information to dolphins on television monitors, to the behavioral mimicry paradigm (Herman, Morrel-Samuels, and Brown, 1989). Instead of seeing gestural information, the dolphins (Phoenix or Akeakamai) viewed a scene of a human or of another dolphin performing some behavior. The behaviors included simple acts such as somersaulting and more complex acts such as throwing a ball into a basketball net. Unlike the case with displays of gestures, the dolphins did not immediately imitate the action performed in a television scene. An initial difficulty seemed to be with the small size of the images displayed. This was corrected by increasing the relative size of the model by more closely focusing the camera on the demonstration. A second, more basic, problem seemed to lie with the dolphins' lack of understanding that they were to imitate what was being displayed. This was corrected by having the human model on screen give the mimic gesture after demonstrating a behavior or by having a trainer on screen give the mimic gesture after a dolphin model completed a behavior. After this training was completed, Phoenix correctly imitated five of six different behaviors demonstrated on television by a human, and seven of eight demonstrated by

Akeakamai. In turn, Akeakamai successfully imitated three of six behaviors demonstrated by a human and five of eight demonstrated by Phoenix. Most of these different behaviors were demonstrated only once during this testing phase. These findings suggest that the dolphins were able to interpret scenes on a television display as an analog of a real-world event. Yet the dolphins distinguished between the television world and the real world. For example, if a behavior, such as tossing a ball through a basketball net, was demonstrated, the dolphin did not attempt to retrieve the ball shown on the television image, but instead retrieved a ball in its own tank and swam to the real-world net for its "lay-up."

The interpretation of television images as representations of and references to the real world is of substantial comparative interest. Savage-Rumbaugh (1986) reviewed earlier work of the responses of chimpanzees to television scenes, including the study of Premack and Woodruff (1978) with the chimpanzee Sarah. Savage-Rumbaugh argued that under the procedures used by Premack and Woodruff, there was no evidence that Sarah interpreted the television scenes she viewed as representations of real-world events; instead, Sarah's purported solution of the problems depicted in the television scenes could be interpreted as resulting from simple matching-to-sample responses, a familiar type of response for Sarah. Savage-Rumbaugh also noted the pervasive findings in the work of several other investigators, including herself, that chimpanzees seemed disinterested in television and did not respond as if they understood what was happening on the television screen. Savage-Rumbaugh went on, however, to describe procedures used to teach her chimpanzee subjects, Sherman and Austin, that television scenes were indeed representations of reality. A key factor appeared to be social facilitation. Trainers who were present with the chimpanzees during television viewing responded enthusiastically and appropriately to the various television scenes. Under these conditions the chimpanzees grew increasingly responsive to the television scenes, and began to exhibit behaviors indicating they recognized what was occurring in those scenes. It is in this context that the immediacy of response of the dolphins to the television images of a signer's gesturing, reviewed in an earlier section, takes on added importance for comparative evaluations.

Some training was necessary for the dolphins to begin to use the television scenes to direct their imitations. Some of that difficulty may have been due to the small size and poor resolution of the television displays, as we noted earlier. Additionally, the television scene provides fewer cues to the behavior than does the live situation, which may be characterized by rich acoustic information caused by splashes, slaps, leaps, and dolphin vocalizations.

20. Representational and conceptual skills of dolphins

Nevertheless, the eventual successful use of the television scenes provides further evidence that the dolphin can extend concepts acquired in one context appropriately to new and very different contexts.

MATCHING-TO-SAMPLE

The work we reviewed in previous sections on the understanding of a gestural language and on motor mimicry abilities has provided illustrations of the ease with which bottlenosed dolphins can make use of arbitrary visual information for solving problems or controlling responses in complex cognitive tasks. It is from these studies as well as those to be described below that Herman (1987b, 1990) suggested abandoning earlier images of the dolphin as primarily an acoustic specialist. A more accurate view, it seems, holds that both the auditory system and the visual system serve important biological functions, and both are important and effective sources of information for such cognitive skills as remembering, representation, problem solving, and concept formation. Such a multimodal view of animal cognitive performance is also apparent in the artificial language work with apes. Savage-Rumbaugh and her colleagues (Savage-Rumbaugh, 1986; Savage-Rumbaugh et al., 1986) reported that the pygmy chimpanzee Kanzi understands many instructions conveyed through spoken English and can also use visual lexigraphic symbols for such things as naming objects indicated by a trainer or communicating his intentions to visit particular locations. Thus, both vision and hearing appear to be effective input channels for these language-like tasks with these animals.

As a further extension of our interest in the ability of dolphins to use visual information in cognitive tasks, we recently carried out several studies of visual matching-to-sample (MTS). MTS tasks have been found to be particularly useful for examining the conceptual abilities of animals. In identity matching, the most commonly used form of MTS task, a "sample" stimulus is shown to the animal and then withdrawn. The animal is then usually offered a choice between two comparison stimuli and is rewarded for choosing the one that matches the sample. Although several different species have been shown capable of learning an MTS task, there nevertheless are substantial differences in the ease with which the task is learned, the ability to abstract the identity rule from a limited number of training problems and to apply the rule to new problems or new stimulus dimensions, and the ability to maintain a representation of the sample stimulus over relatively long periods of time before the choice among alternatives is offered (cf. D'Amato & Colombo, 1989; D'Amato, Salmon, & Colombo, 1985; Grant, 1976; Herman & Gordon, 1974; Oden, Thompson, & Premack, 1988; Pack, Herman & Roitblat, 1991; Wright,

Cook, Rivera, Sands, & Delius, 1988). Thus, pigeons developed the ability to apply the identity rule to new problems only after exposure to hundreds of MTS problems given during thousands of training trials (Wright et al., 1988). In marked contrast, chimpanzees acquired a concept of identity after an average of 816 training trials with a single pair of sample objects (Oden et al., 1988; also see Nissen, Blum, & Blum, 1948).

Our interests included an examination of the ease with which a dolphin might develop an abstract concept of matching from a series of visual MTS problems. We were also interested in examining the dolphin's ability for matching various kinds of visual materials and in testing the fidelity of the dolphin's visual memory. Finally, we wished to examine representational abilities by using the MTS task to study mental rotation. Several of these MTS studies were carried out with the dolphin Phoenix as subject (Herman, Hovancik, Gory, & Bradshaw, 1989; Hunter, 1988). The results of these studies demonstrated Phoenix's ability to match 3-dimensional (3-D) or 2-dimensional (2-D) stimuli visually, to form a general matching rule and transfer that rule to novel visual stimuli, and to maintain a briefly-displayed sample item reliably in memory for intervals of as long as 80 sec. Some of the 3-D objects had "names" within the acoustic language used with Phoenix, but other objects, equally familiar to Phoenix, did not. Phoenix appeared to categorize these two classes of objects separately in memory, in that errors in matching were greater at long delays if the distractor object of a pair of alternatives came from the same set (named or unnamed) as did the matching alternative. This is the result one might expect if the information for an item in memory included its class membership, suggesting that the dolphin can encode both functional and descriptive attributes of stimuli.

The levels of performance reached by Phoenix in these visual MTS studies were comparable to levels reached by another dolphin tested on auditory MTS (e.g., Herman & Gordon, 1974). For both auditory and visual matching, transfer of the matching rule to new problems was often immediate, indicative of the development of a strong, abstract concept of identity. Also, during delayed matching-to-sample tests (DMTS) memory for a sample item, whether visual or auditory, was faithfully retained for intervals of up to 80 sec, the longest delay tested in the visual studies, or up to 180 s, the longest delay tested in the auditory studies. From these results, Herman Hovancik, Gory, and Bradshaw (1989) suggested that cognitive performance in dolphins might be best characterized as modality independent, at least for the auditory and visual modes.

20. Representational and conceptual skills of dolphins

Extremely Rapid Learning and Transfer of Visual MTS

Oden et al. (1988) reported rapid acquisition and transfer of a matching rule by young chimpanzees after training with only two stimuli. An important procedural step leading to the rapid learning and transfer may have been the pre-exposure of the animals to a wide variety of objects. The objects used during MTS testing were those not avoided by the chimpanzees nor highly preferred. This procedure effectively guarded against the fear responses to new objects that have been observed in some MTS studies (e.g., D'Amato et al., 1985; Pack et al., 1991). The pre-exposure also allowed an opportunity for perceptual learning.

We recently applied a similar pre-exposure procedure before testing the young male dolphin Hiapo on visual MTS. During pre-exposure, Hiapo was shown eight different objects singly. We used an already familiar gestural command to require Hiapo to touch each object with his rostrum, and reinforced each touch with positive verbal and visual signals and, intermittently, with fish rewards. This procedure was repeated four times for each object. We then repeated the procedure, except that this time the object disappeared behind the tank wall after a touch, and then reappeared to one side or the other of the trainer. Hiapo spontaneously swam to the displaced object and touched it, again receiving the reinforcers described. On the basis of Hiapo's responses, we chose for subsequent MTS training a subset of six objects to which Hiapo showed the least hesitation in approaching.

At each MTS trial a trainer showed one of the six sample objects to Hiapo. After Hiapo had touched the object and then assumed a position facing the object at approximately 1 m distance, the sample object was withdrawn. The two comparison objects were then shown by assistants positioned 1.7 m left and right of the trainer. Hiapo was required to touch one of these objects to indicate his response. The assistants had no knowledge of which object had been shown to Hiapo, and the trainer had no knowledge of the correct side for a response. To accustom Hiapo to the MTS procedure, the first 4 trials of the first MTS training session presented only a single alternative (the S+), but during the remaining 24 trials both alternatives were presented. Hiapo correctly selected the matching alternative on 19 of these 24 trials (79%, $p = .003$), including 5 of the first 6 trials. During these first 6 trials each of the 6 objects appeared as sample once.

During the second and third sessions, each consisting of 24 trials, Hiapo was correct, respectively, on 21 (88%) and 23 (96%) trials ($p < .0001$). He thus met our predetermined training criterion of 80% correct responses or better on two successive sessions. Pre-exposure for transfer testing, using new objects, began at the next session.

Six new objects were chosen and pre-exposed. Each object was presented to Hiapo singly and he was required to touch each three times, once while the object was directly in front of him, once when it was to his left, and once when it was to his right. This procedure was repeated three times for each object. Transfer testing then began. The six objects were divided into three pairs. Each pair was exposed twice (the sample was changed from the first exposure to the second) during the total of 24 trials constituting a transfer session. These 6 transfer trials were embedded in random locations among the remaining 18 trials consisting of pairings of the 6 familiar objects used during training. These latter objects comprised a running baseline test against which transfer performance was compared. Two sessions of this type were run. During the second session, the left-right positions of the transfer pairs were reversed from their positions in the first session, so that over the two sessions there was complete balancing among the three pairs of the S+ or S- value of pair members, and whether the S+ occurred on the left or on the right.

The results were straightforward. Hiapo was correct on all 6 transfer trials during the first session and on 5 of 6 during the second session. Altogether, then, he was correct on 11 of 12 transfer trials ($p = .003$). He was also correct on 23 of 24 baseline trials ($p < .0001$). The difference between transfer and baseline trials was not significant ($X^2[1,36] = .07, p > .05$). These results provide the strongest evidence yet of the robustness of the identity concept attainable by a dolphin. It appears that, like the chimpanzees studied by Oden et al. (1988), the dolphin may be predisposed to discriminate identity or else can learn such discriminations with extreme rapidity, at least for three-dimensional objects of the types used.

Extensions of the Matching Concept by Individual Dolphins

Person Recognition

In our early language understanding work, we taught Phoenix an acoustic symbol PERSON and Akeakamai a gestural symbol with the same meaning. For both dolphins, PERSON was used to refer to any individual in the tank, or outside the tank but with their arms or legs in the water. Individual persons, however, remained unidentified. PERSON was used only in the generic sense of a human being. Though many anecdotes have suggested that dolphins are able to recognize particular individual humans, no formal research on this

20. Representational and conceptual skills of dolphins

capability has been reported. In a series of studies recently completed (Pack & Herman, 1989) we used an MTS procedure to study whether a dolphin could discriminate between different persons and, if so, what aspects of a person's appearance were important for recognition.

Phoenix served as the subject. She was well versed in MTS tasks through her prior experience with 3-D and 2-D matching. The procedure for person recognition was to show a sample person to Phoenix, remove that person from view, and then offer a choice between two persons, one of whom was the individual previously seen.

The sample person stood behind a closed, opaque window in a plywood panel located above the wall of the tank. When Phoenix was positioned in front of the wall facing the panel, the window was opened, exposing the person. After a few seconds, the window was closed. Two "comparison" persons then appeared at each side of the plywood panel. Phoenix was required to swim to the person who had been the sample and remain at that location for 3 s. Care was taken to avoid any useful acoustic cues resulting from movements of persons behind the screen, by padding the platform on which the individuals moved about, and by requiring movement of both comparison individuals after the window was closed.

The first experiment consisted of 1 training set and 12 transfer sets. Each set consisted of 4 persons, 1 of whom served as sample and the other 3 as distractor alternatives, with the particular distractor person selected according to a preplanned balanced schedule. A total of 31 different persons took part in the study, 13 of whom served as samples. Of these samples, 4 had virtually no training history for Phoenix and 2 were novel to her. The 18 distractors were all relatively novel, though several served in different sets.

Phoenix was correct on the first trial of 11 of the 12 transfer tests, the strongest criterion of transfer of a matching rule available and an affirmation of the ability of dolphins both to develop an abstract or generalized concept of identity and to recognize individual humans. In further work, we examined some attributes of individuals that might contribute to recognition. We explored the effects on recognition of exposing only the face of an individual versus exposing both the face and the torso. We also examined the effects of the sample person moving about in the window (as might a trainer during normal interactions) versus remaining motionless, and the effects of the sample individual speaking versus not speaking to the dolphin. The results showed that the factors contributing to improved recognition were, as might be expected:

face plus torso was better than face alone, and vocalizations were better than silence. Each factor of itself had some effect, and all three together had a cumulative positive effect. The most difficult condition was the face alone, voiceless and unmoving. Overall, the results suggest that a person is represented as a Gestalt, in that information from the body, face, voice, and behavior all aid recognition. Recognition is possible with reduced cues, but at lower levels of reliability. The study provides evidence that the dolphins have both a concept of a generic person, as shown by their responses to any individual in contact with the water when the symbol PERSON appears within their artificial language, and a concept that persons are distinguishable, identifiable individual members within the generic category.

Mental Rotation

In the classic study on mental rotation Shepard and Metzler (1971) found that humans can perform mental rotation of stimulus figures. The subjects' task was to decide whether a rotated figure was identical to an unrotated figure. The authors found that the time taken to reach a decision increased linearly with the angular disparity between the figures. Subjects reported that they turned the figures "in their heads" to make their judgments. The finding of a linear increase with angle of rotation is highly reliable, and has been observed both in adults and in children as young as 4 years of age (Marmor, 1975, 1977). Mental rotation is viewed by many theorists as support for imagistic or analog theories of mental representations (e.g., Paivio, 1986), and is consistent with the interpretations made by Shepard and his colleagues. Other investigators (e.g., Pylyshyn, 1981) argue that propositional models can also accommodate the findings.

In one of the few studies with animals, Hollard and Delius (1982) used a matching-to-sample task to study rotation invariance in pigeons. The stimuli were abstract 2-D figures. In one of the rotation tests the pigeon was required to peck a sample figure 15 times, after which two comparison stimuli appeared. The pigeon was then required to peck the comparison form, the S+, that was a rotated version of the sample. The distractor item was always the mirror image of the S+. The sample remained present throughout. The pigeons performed the task accurately, about as well as human subjects tested in a similar paradigm. Although the humans did increase their response latency as a function of angular disparity between the sample and the S+, the pigeons were equally fast at all angles. The human data supported the hypothesis that the task was performed through mental rotation. Hollard and Delius (1982) suggested that pigeons, unlike humans, might perceive a mirror image as distinctly unrelated to the virtual (unreflected) image, and hence were able to choose the remaining

20. Representational and conceptual skills of dolphins

alternative with little delay. Humans, like pigeons, do show flat and fast RT functions when the distractor item is very different from the sample, that is, when it is something other than a mirror image. The authors also suggested that the differences in human and pigeon data might reflect the aerial visual world of the pigeon, in which orientation of objects is arbitrary relative to the pigeon as it flies about through three-dimensional space. Possibly, the three-dimensional movement of the dolphin through its underwater world is analogous to the movement of the pigeon through its aerial world.

We recently carried out preliminary studies of rotation invariance in a dolphin using an MTS procedure with the young dolphin Elele as subject (Herman, Kuczaj, Shaw, & Morrel-Samuels, 1990). The stimuli were six two-dimensional patterns of the general type already familiar to Elele through her prior experience in identity matching. The sample figures were displayed in the center window of a large black board, and the two comparison stimuli were presented in windows left and right of center. The sample was always shown unrotated (i.e., in a fixed orientation). The matching comparison figure (the S+) was either also unrotated, or rotated 90° or 180°. To ensure that the dolphin was not reinforced simply for selection of a rotated figure, one of the remaining five sample figures (i.e., the one serving as the S-), was also independently rotated. No pretraining for the rotation task was given.

The dolphin chose correctly on 93% of the unrotated trials; performance declined to 76% on the 90° rotation trials and to 70% on the 180° rotation trials. There was a significant difference among these three conditions ($X^2[2, 714] = 51.1$, $p < .01$). Further, choice accuracy on unrotated trials significantly exceeded accuracy under either of the rotation conditions ($X^2[1, 641] = 32.8$, $p < .01$; $X^2[1, 560] = 35.3$, $p < .01$), but the difference between the two rotation conditions was not significant ($X^2[1,227] = 0.67$, $p > .05$). The combined performance level of 74% over all rotation trials exceeded chance expectation ($X^2[1,227] = 486.04$, $p < .01$)]. The angle of rotation of the distractor item did not have a significant effect on performance.

A preliminary analysis of differences in response time, using real-time video tape records of randomly selected trials, revealed fastest responses to unrotated figures (mean = 5.76 s, $n = 219$), slower responses to 90° rotations (mean = 6.91 s, $n = 27$), and slowest responses to 180° rotations (mean = 8.41 s, $n = 19$). These data are consistent with the activity of mental rotation, but any interpretation must be taken with caution in view of the relative imprecision of the response-time measure used. However, the data were not consistent with interpretations based on simple stimulus generalization. Trials on which the S-more closely resembled the sample than did the rotated S+ (as judged by an observer blind to the experiment's hypotheses) were no more difficult for the dolphin than were trials on which the S+ was more similar (74% correct on "easy" trials and 77% correct on "difficult trials; $X^2[2,22] = 0.1$, not significant). If stimulus generalization were operating, then such difficult trials should have been accompanied by lower choice accuracy. In further work we plan to include mirror-image distractor stimuli, and to measure response time more precisely as a function of rotation angle, so that we can more reliably determine whether a dolphin can manipulate mental representations of objects in the way that humans seem to do during mental rotation tasks.

CONCLUSIONS

Throughout this account, we have tried to present a broad view of dolphin representational and conceptual abilities. An important inference emerging from this diverse set of data is that the dolphins appeared to form, retain, and manipulate mental representations of objects and actions. There is converging evidence in support of the hypothesis that the dolphins constructed analogic or perhaps even arbitrary mental representations of the objects, events, or relationships they observed in the real world (see Paivio, 1986, or Roitblat, 1987, for a discussion of various concepts of mental representation, and Rilling & Neiworth, 1987, for a discussion of imagery as a form of representation). Thus, the demands of the behavioral mimicry and matching-to-sample paradigms appear to require that a representation of the observed stimulus object or behavioral event be formed, retained in memory, and accessed. At each trial the representation must necessarily be specific to the particular trial events, but, at the same time, these particulars must be linked to broader generic concepts about whole classes of events. These concepts represent the organized knowledge acquired by the animal about classes of events. The ability of the dolphins to match novel objects or to imitate unfamiliar or even novel behaviors when requested indicates that performance is governed both by trial-specific events and by an abstract conceptualization of the task and its requirements.

The character of the artificial languages used with the dolphins and the dolphins' responses to the languages also suggest that abstract mental representations are constructed. For example, the gestures used in signing to Akeakamai are arbitrary with respect to the form or character of the referent, and the full set of gestures comprises an arbitrary representational system. Some transformation from the physical representation of the gesture to the representation of its referent seems necessary, assuming that the gestures indeed have a referring function. The system of representations for gestural signs must

20. Representational and conceptual skills of dolphins

coordinate with the knowledge systems relating to the syntactic structure of the language and the contexts in which these structures operate. The responses to both normal and anomalous gestural sequences indicate that the dolphin evaluates strings of gestures by attending both to the meaning of individual gesture signs and to the syntactic structure of the string.

A characteristic of the dolphins in their language tasks, and one that illustrates the generality of some of the concepts they have developed, is their ability to transfer what has been learned in particular contexts to new contexts. The dolphins are also capable of rearranging a situation in order to make a particular response possible and can go beyond what was explicitly taught in order to create new and reasonable responses to new situations. Some examples, all representing untaught behaviors occurring spontaneously on first opportunity, are (a) immediate understanding of highly degraded televised images of signers; (b) moving a surfboard away from the wall of a tank in order to make it possible to carry out the request to jump over it, and lifting a hoop lying flat on the tank bottom in order to carry out the request to swim through it; and (c) transporting an object to the No paddle when the signified destination object was absent, or transporting an object to the Yes paddle when the destination object was present. These types of responses argue against explanations of performance based on simple associative-chain theories (e.g., Schusterman & Gisiner, 1988; cf. Herman, 1988) and support cognitively oriented theories of performance.

Finally, we consider reference. Bruner (1983) emphasized that "reference is a form of social interaction having to do with the management of joint attention" (p. 68). Reference may appear in many different contexts, in many forms, and at many different levels of development. Referential competence does not necessarily require that the organism be able both to direct the attention of another and to respond to the attention-seeking directives of another. Referential competence may exist within the receptive domain alone, or it may appear in both the receptive and productive domains (Herman & Morrel-Samuels, 1990). For example, there is evidence that referential understanding may precede referential gesturing in infants: An 8- to 10-month old infant will follow the caregiver's gaze, but pointing by the infant (often accompanied by vocalizations) may not emerge until 12 months of age or later (Bruner, 1975). Abilities for referential communication continue to develop through childhood, with increased age bringing a greater ability to use and understand referential terms (Krauss & Glucksberg, 1969). Reference in humans is therefore best considered as the result of an emergent process, dependent in part on communicative experience as well as cognitive endowments. This also seems a reasonable model for examining referential abilities of animals. Within the animal language work, a central issue is whether the "words" of the languages imposed on the animals are used and understood by them in a referential sense, meaning to control attention or to signify a concept. That is, do the words, when used or received by the animal, invoke concepts about their intended referents?

Thus, the relevant questions to ask about the dolphins' understanding of artificial languages seem to be: What do the symbols of the artificial languages we use with the dolphins mean to these animals? Do the dolphins understand these symbols as references to objects or to desired behavioral events? When we use the symbols are we in effect actively engaging the dolphin's attention or merely directing its behavior? To answer these questions, we must necessarily consider a diverse body of evidence, some of which has been reviewed in this chapter. Others who have developed a restricted view of the dolphins' referential capabilities have drawn their conclusions from only a limited set of the available data (e.g., Premack, 1986; Savage-Rumbaugh & Brakke, 1990; Schusterman & Gisiner, 1988, 1989; cf. Herman, 1987a, 1988, 1989).

The data described earlier concerning the dolphin's ability to understand gestural references to absent objects in the reporting paradigm provide compelling evidence for the claim that symbols refer to objects. In this situation, the dolphin does not respond overtly to an object, even if it is present, but simply indicates whether or not it is currently in the tank. Another indicant of the referring function of a symbol was the dolphin's understanding of deictic gestures offered by trainers. Still another illustration was the immediate understanding of references to objects signified by the gestures given by the television image of a trainer, or even by the degraded point-light displays of the gesture language signs.

Perhaps the clearest illustration of the understanding of the referring function of symbols and the emergence of a broader referential concept for a symbol is to consider the multiple uses and semantic functions of the gesture PERSON as used with Akeakamai, and how these multiple functions determine Akeakamai's responses or interpretations. In the early language training PERSON, when followed by an appropriate action term, could function in only one way: to direct the dolphin to take that action to a person holding his/her hand in the water. Later, additional interpretations of PERSON were added contingent on the use of the relational terms FETCH or IN. These relational terms directed the dolphin to consider a person also as an object to be transported to a destination, or as a destination to which some other object

20. Representational and conceptual skills of dolphins

should be transported. A person was now placed in the tank itself, floating on the surface, as well as merely contacting the water with his/her arm. Still later extensions of the language paradigm (reviewed earlier in this chapter) presented the gesture PERSON in new semantic and syntactic contexts, including tasks in which the dolphin's attention was directed to a person, or to the concept embodied by PERSON, without any requirement to respond directly to a person. The reporting procedure and the selective mimicry paradigm demonstrate such types of reference. Thus, today, in Akeakamai's language, a person can be referred to topically in various ways. Different gestures accompanying the gesture PERSON, different syntactic structures, and different tasks dictate different constraints on how PERSON functions grammatically or semantically within the language, and on how it may be interpreted. In Table 20.1 we list the different tasks and contexts in which the gestural sign PERSON may occur; we have included examples of how the reference to a person versus some other entity must be distinguished by the dolphin in each of these tasks.

The table shows that the gesture PERSON can be used in six different classes of command strings: nonrelational imperative, relational imperative, simple interrogative, relational interrogative, selective mimicry imperatives, and deictic imperatives. Within each form semantic and syntactic constraints govern how the dolphin is to respond to a reference to a person, or if it is to respond at all.

Within the category of nonrelational imperatives, the simple imperative refers to a single object and requires a response to that object only, such as swimming under a person in response to PERSON UNDER. The conjunctive form uses a gesture that we gloss as "and." The conjunction requires that the indicated action be taken to both of the objects signified. The gestural sign ERASE requires that the dolphin take no action to any of the preceding gestures (Herman et al., 1984). When seeing ERASE, the dolphin ceases any response or preparations for response to the preceding gestures and either returns immediately to the trainer or remains with the trainer. Thus in response to PERSON ERASE, no action should be taken to person, nor should the dolphin proceed toward a person. The more complex sequence HOOP ERASE PERSON OVER directs the dolphin to ignore HOOP and respond only to the terms following ERASE. In contrast, the sequence HOOP AND PERSON OVER requires that the dolphin leap over both the hoop and the person, in any order. Note that AND and ERASE occur in the same syntactic slot. The dolphin must therefore process AND and ERASE semantically in order to determine whether to respond to the person alone or to both the hoop and the person.

Table 20.1
The various types of gesture strings that may include PERSON in Akeakamai's artificial gestural language with examples of each sequence and response.

Objects Present in Tank	Sequence Given	Required Response
Nonrelational imperative		
Person, Hoop	PERSON UNDER	Swim under person
Person, Hoop	PERSON AND HOOP UNDER	Swim under both
Person, Hoop	PERSON ERASE	Do nothing
Person, Hoop	PERSON ERASE HOOP UNDER	Swim under hoop only
Relational imperative		
Person, Hoop	PERSON HOOP FETCH	Take hoop to person
Person, Hoop	HOOP PERSON FETCH	Take person to hoop
Simple interrogative		
Person, Hoop	PERSON QUESTION	Press YES paddle
Basket, Hoop	PERSON QUESTION	Press NO paddle
Basket, Hoop	PERSON UNDER	Press NO paddle
Relational interrogative		
Person, Hoop	HOOP PERSON FETCH	Take person to hoop or YES PADDLE
Person, Hoop	PERSON HOOP FETCH	Take hoop to person or YES PADDLE
Person, Hoop	PIPE PERSON FETCH	Take person to NP
Basket, Hoop	HOOP PERSON FETCH	Press NO paddle
Selective imperative		
Person, Phoenix	PERSON MIMIC	Imitate person
Person, Phoenix	PHOENIX MIMIC	Imitate Phoenix
Deictic imperative		
Person, Hoop	[Point to person] OVER	Jump over person

Note. Words in all capital letters indicate a discrete gestural symbol within Akeakamai's artificial language.

20. Representational and conceptual skills of dolphins

Similarly, sequential constraints determine the response to the other categories in Table 20.1. The syntactic constraints of the relational imperatives dictate whether a person is to be transported or is to be the destination of some other object being transported. Note that the only difference between the two relational imperatives illustrated in Table 20.1 is in the sequence of the terms.

In the reporting procedure the simple interrogative form (PERSON QUESTION) requires that no response be made to a person, but that, instead, the presence or absence of a person in the tank be indicated by a press of one or the other of two paddles. Akeakamai's initial responses to queries about the presence or absence of a person were spontaneous and accurate. The immediacy with which she was able to respond to the state of a PERSON provides strong evidence for a referential component to this gesture, particularly given the fact that she can respond correctly even when the referent, a person, is not present.

Similarly, in the relational reporting procedure, different responses to PERSON are required, depending on whether the objects referred to are present in the tank or not, and on the form of relational interrogative given. These various conditions can yield the transport of the person to the Yes paddle or to the No paddle, the transport of some designated object to the person, or a simple press of the No paddle. Akeakamai's various responses to PERSON in these situations were not trained and demonstrated that she immediately understood the referent of the gesture sign in novel settings, and could use the underlying concept of present-absent to guide her behavior.

In the selective mimicry paradigm, once again no response is required directly to a person. Instead, the gesture PERSON appearing before the gesture MIMIC directs the dolphin Akeakamai to imitate the person's behavior, and not Phoenix's. Finally, a person may be referred to by a deictic gesture as well as by the symbolic gesture PERSON. In addition to these various types of references to a person, the dolphin Akeakamai further distinguishes between the signer (ME) and another individual who is the referent of the gesture PERSON (or of the deictic gesture). Thus, the sequences ME TAIL-TOUCH and PERSON TAIL-TOUCH signed by the trainer determine, respectively, whether Akeakamai should touch the trainer with her tail flukes or touch another person with them. Also, although we have not tested the competency of Akeakamai for recognizing different persons, it is apparent from the work with Phoenix that dolphins can make such distinctions. This capability, together with the distinction noted between the use of ME and PERSON, suggest that references to persons can be understood both in a generic sense (to any individual who meets the defining characteristics within a paradigm) and in a particular sense.

These various uses of the PERSON or ways of referring to a person, and the different types of responses they evoke, illustrate the richness with which the symbol for a person stands for its real-world referent. It also illustrates the point made earlier that the referential property of a symbol may emerge over time and can be completely independent of context. The flexibility of this referential property is likely a function of the diversity and complexity of those contexts, and the diversity of responses or interpretations they require.

In conclusion, the studies we have reviewed here suggest that dolphins have the ability to represent objects, actions, and concepts, that the nature of those representations can be quite abstract, and that they can be used to guide behavior in a wide variety of settings.

ACKNOWLEDGMENTS

Preparation of this paper was supported by contract N00014-85-K-0210 from the Office of Naval Research and by a grant from the Center for Field Research (Earthwatch). In addition to the many students and staff of the Kewalo Basin Marine Mammal Laboratory serving as authors or co-authors on one or more of the articles cited, we thank Carolyn McKinnie, Sarah Partan, Christopher Prince, Lori Quigley, Stacy Rosen, Kristen Taylor, Eliza Wille, and Amy Wood for their assistance in the studies described.

REFERENCES

Bates, E. (1976). *Language and context: The acquisition of pragmatics.* New York: Academic Press.

Baylis, J. R. (1982). Avian vocal mimicry: Its function and evolution. In D. E. Kroodsma & E. H. Miller (Eds.), *Acoustic communication in birds. Vol. 2. Song learning and its consequences* (pp. 51-83). New York: Academic Press.

Bloom, L., Hood, L., & Lightbown, P. (1974). Imitation in language development: If, when, and why? *Cognitive Psychology*, 6, 380-420.

Bruner, J. S. (1975). The ontogenesis of speech acts. *Journal of Child Language*, 2, 1-19.

20. Representational and conceptual skills of dolphins

Bruner, J. S. (1983). *Child's talk: Learning to use language.* New York: W.W. Norton.

Bryden, M. M. (1986). Age and growth. In M. M. Bryden & R. Harrison (Eds.), *Research on dolphins* (pp. 211-224). New York: Oxford University Press.

Caldwell, M. C. & Caldwell, D. K. (1972). Behavior of marine mammals. In S. H. Ridgway (Ed.), *Mammals of the sea: Biology and medicine* (pp. 409-465). Springfield, IL: Charles C. Thomas.

Caldwell, D. K., Caldwell, M. C., & Tyack, P. L. (1990). Review of the signature-whistle hypothesis for the Atlantic bottlenosed dolphin. In S. Leatherwood & R. R. Reeves (Eds.), *The bottlenose dolphin* (pp. 199-234). New York: Academic Press.

Carr, D. B. (1979). The development of young children's capacity to judge anomalous sentences. *Journal of Child Language, 6,* 227-241.

Clark, H. H. (1985). Language use and language users. In G. Lindzey & E. Aronson (Eds.), *The handbook of social psychology*: (Vol. 2, pp. 179-231). New York: Random House.

Clark, R. (1977). What's the use of imitation? *Journal of Child Language, 4,* 341-358.

D'Amato, M. R. & Colombo, M. (1989). On the limits of the matching concept in monkeys *(Cebus apella). Journal of the Experimental Analysis of Behavior, 52,* 225-236.

D'Amato, M. R., Salmon, D. P., & Colombo, M. (1985). Extent and limits of the matching concept in monkeys (Cebus apella). *Journal of Experimental Psychology: Animal Behavior Processes, 11,* 35-51.

Ervin, S. M. (1964). Imitation and structural change in children's language. In E. H. Lenneberg (Ed.), *New directions in the study of language.* (pp. 163-189) Cambridge, MA: MIT Press.

Forestell, P. H. (1988*). Reporting on relationships between symbolically-named objects by a dolphin (*Tursiops truncatus*).* Unpublished doctoral dissertation, University of Hawaii, Honolulu.

Galef, B. G., Jr. (1988). Imitation in animals: History, definition, and interpretation of data from the psychological laboratory. In T. R. Zentall & B. G. Galef, Jr. (Eds.), *Social learning: Psychological and biological perspectives* (pp. 3-28). Hillsdale, NJ: Lawrence Erlbaum Associates.

Gardner, B. T. & Gardner, R. A. (1975). Evidence for sentence constituents in the early utterances of child and chimpanzee. *Journal of Experimental Psychology: General,* 104, 244-267.

Gleitman, L. R., Gleitman, H., & Shipley, E. F. (1972). The emergence of the child as grammarian. *Cognition,* 1, 137-164.

Grant, T. S. (1976). Effect of sample presentation on long-delay matching in the pigeon. *Learning & Motivation,* 7, 580-590.

Harley, H. E., Xitco, M. J. Jr., Roitblat, H. L., & Herman, L. M. (in preparation). *Imitation of novel behaviors by bottlenose dolphins.*

Herman, L. M. (1980). Cognitive characteristics of dolphins. In L. M. Herman (Ed.), *Cetacean behavior: Mechanisms and functions* (pp. 363-429). New York: Wiley Interscience.

Herman, L. M. (1986). Cognition and language competencies of bottlenosed dolphins. In R. J. Schusterman, J. A. Thomas, & F. G. Wood (Eds.), *Dolphin cognition and behavior: A comparative approach* (pp. 221-252). Hillsdale, NJ: Lawrence Erlbaum Associates.

Herman, L. M. (1987a). Receptive competencies of language-trained animals. In J. S. Rosenblatt, C. Beer, C. M-C. Busnel, & P. J. B. Slater (Eds.), *Advances in the study of behavior.* (Vol. 17, pp. 1-60). Petaluma, CA: Academic Press.

Herman, L. M. (1987b). The visual dolphin. Paper presented at the Seventh Biennial Conference on the Biology of Marine Mammals, Miami, FL

Herman, L. M. (1988). The language of animal language research: Reply to Schusterman and Gisiner. The *Psychological Record,* 38, 349-362.

Herman, L. M. (1989). In which Procrustean bed does the sea lion sleep tonight? *Psychological Record,* 39, 19-49.

20. Representational and conceptual skills of dolphins

Herman, L. M. (1990). Cognitive performance of dolphins in visually guided tasks. In J. Thomas & R. Kastelein (Eds.), *Sensory abilities of cetaceans*. (pp. 455-462). New York: Plenum Press.

Herman, L. M. & Forestell, P. H. (1985). Reporting presence or absence of named objects by a language-trained dolphin. *Neuroscience and Biobehavioral Reviews*, 9, 667-681.

Herman, L. M. & Gordon, J. A. (1974). Auditory delayed matching in the bottlenosed dolphin. *Journal of the Experimental Analysis of Behavior*, 21, 19-26.

Herman, L. M., Hovancik, J. R., Gory, J. D., & Bradshaw, G. L. (1989). Generalization of visual matching by a bottlenosed dolphin (*Tursiops truncatus*) evidence for invariance of cognitive performance with visual or auditory materials. *Journal of Experimental Psychology: Animal Behavior Processes*, 15, 124-136.

Herman, L. M., Kuczaj, S., Shaw, M., & Morrel-Samuels, P. (1990). Preliminary evidence of mental rotation in the dolphin. Paper presented at the meeting of the Psychonomic Society, New Orleans, LA.

Herman, L. M. & Morrel-Samuels, P. (1990). Knowledge acquisition and asymmetry between language comprehension and production: Dolphins and apes as general models for animals. In M. Bekoff & D. Jamieson (Eds.), *Interpretation and explanation in the study of behavior Vol. 1: Interpretation, intentionality, and communication* (pp. 283-312). Boulder, CO: Westview Press.

Herman, L. M., Morrel-Samuels, P., & Brown, L. (1989). Behavioral mimicry of live and televised models by bottlenosed dolphins. Paper presented at the 30th Annual Meeting of the Psychonomic Society, Atlanta, GA.

Herman, L. M., Morrel-Samuels, P., & Pack, A. A. (1990). Bottlenosed dolphin and human recognition of veridical and degraded video displays of an artificial gestural language. *Journal of Experimental Psychology: General*, 119, 215-230.

Herman, L. M., Richards, D. G., & Wolz, J. P. (1984). Comprehension of sentences by bottlenosed dolphins. *Cognition*, 16, 129-219.

Hoban, E. (1983). *Children's responses to anomalous imperative sentences.* Unpublished master's thesis, University of Hawaii, Honolulu.

Hollard, V. D. & Delius, J. D. (1982). Rotational invariance in visual pattern recognition by pigeons and humans. *Science,* 218, 804-806.

Hunter, G. A. (1988). *Visual delayed matching of two-dimensional forms by a bottlenosed dolphin.* Unpublished master's thesis. University of Hawaii, Honolulu.

Ingram, D. (1989). *First language acquisition: Method, description, and explanation.* New York: Cambridge University Press.

Jerison, H. J. (1986). The perceptual worlds of dolphins. In R. J. Schusterman, J. A. Thomas, & F. G. Wood (Eds.), *Dolphin cognition and behavior: A comparative approach* (pp. 141-166). Hillsdale, NJ: Lawrence Erlbaum Associates.

Johansson, G. (1975). Visual motion perception. *Scientific American,* 232, 76-89.

Krauss, R. M. & Glucksberg, S. (1969). The development of communication: Competence as a function of age. *Child Development,* 40, 255-266.

Lashley, K. S. (1951). The problem of serial order in behavior. In L. A. Jeffress (Ed.), *Cerebral mechanisms in behavior* (pp. 112-136). New York: Wiley Interscience.

Leonard, L. B. & Kaplan, L. (1976). A note on imitation and lexical acquisition. *Journal of Child Language,* 3, 449-455.

Marmor, G. S. (1975). Development of kinetic images: When does the child first represent movement in mental images? *Cognitive Psychology,* 7, 548-559.

Marmor, G. S. (1977). Mental rotation and number conservation: Are they related? *Developmental Psychology,* 13, 320-325.

Nelson, K. (1987). What's in a name? Reply to Seidenberg and Petitto. *Journal of Experimental Psychology: General,* 116, 293-296.

20. Representational and conceptual skills of dolphins

Nissen, H. W., Blum, J. S., & Blum, R. A. (1948). Analysis of matching behavior in chimpanzee. *Journal of Comparative and Physiological Psychology*, 41, 62-74.

Oden, D. L., Thompson, R. K. R., & Premack, D. (1988). Spontaneous transfer of matching by infant chimpanzees (*Pan troglodytes*). *Journal of Experimental Psychology: Animal Behavior Processes*, 14, 140-145.

Pack, A. A. & Herman, L. M. (1989). Person recognition by a bottlenosed dolphin. Paper presented at the Eighth Biennial Conference on the Biology of Marine Mammals. Pacific Grove, CA.

Pack, A. A., Herman, L. M., & Roitblat, H. L. (1991). Generalization of visual matching and delayed matching by a California sea lion (*Zalophus californianus*). *Animal Learning and Behavior*, 19, 37-48.

Paivio, A. (1986). *Mental representations: A dual coding approach.* New York, Oxford University Press.

Paivio, A. & Begg, I. (1981). *The psychology of language.* Englewood Cliffs, NJ: Prentice-Hall.

Poizner, H., Bellugi, U., & Lutes-Driscoll, B. (1981). Perception of American Sign Language in dynamic point-light displays. *Journal of Experimental Psychology: Human Perception and Performance*, 7, 430-440.

Plyshyn, Z. (1981). The imagery debate: Analog media versus tacit knowledge. In N. Block (Ed.), *Imagery* (pp. 151-206). Cambridge, MA: MIT Press.

Premack, D. (1986). *"Gavagai!" Or the future history of the animal language controversy.* Cambridge, MA: MIT Press.

Premack, D. & Premack, A. J. (1983). *The mind of an ape.* New York: W. W.Norton and Company.

Premack, D. & Woodruff, G. (1978). Does the chimpanzee have a theory of mind? *Behavioral and Brain Sciences*, 4, 515-526.

Reber, A. S. (1967). Implicit learning of artificial grammars. *Journal of Verbal Learning and Verbal Behavior*, 5, 855-865.

Richards, D. G. (1986). Dolphin vocal mimicry and vocal object labeling. In R. J. Schusterman, J. A. Thomas, & F. G. Wood (Eds.), *Dolphin cognition and behavior: A comparative approach* (pp. 273-288). Hillsdale, NJ: Lawrence Erlbaum Associates.

Richards D. G., Wolz, J. P., & Herman, L. M. (1984). Vocal mimicry of computer-generated sounds and vocal labeling of objects by a bottlenosed dolphin, *Tursiops truncatus*. *Journal of Comparative Psychology*, 98, 10-28.

Rilling, M. E. & Neiworth, J. J. (1987). Theoretical and methodological considerations for the study of imagery in animals. *Learning and Motivation*, 18, 57-79.

Roitblat, H. L. (1987). *Introduction to comparative cognition*. New York: W.H.Freeman.

Rumbaugh, D. M. (Ed.). (1977). *Language learning by a chimpanzee: The Lana project*. New York: Academic Press.

Sacher, G. A. (1980). The constitutional basis for longevity in the cetacea: Do the whales and the terrestrial mammals obey the same laws? In W. F. Perrin & A. C. Myrick, Jr. (Eds.), *Age determination of toothed whales and sirenians: Reports of the International Whaling Commission, special issue 3* (pp. 209-213). Cambridge: Heffers.

Savage-Rumbaugh, E. S. (1986). *Ape language: From conditioned response to symbol*. New York: Columbia University Press.

Savage-Rumbaugh, E. S. (1988). A new look at ape language: Comprehension of vocal speech and syntax. In D. W. Leger (Ed.) *Nebraska Symposium on Motivation 1987* (pp. 201-255). Lincoln, NB: University of Nebraska Press.

Savage-Rumbaugh, E. S. & Brakke, K. E. (1990). Animal language: Methodological and interpretive issues. In M. Bekoff & D. Jamieson (Eds.), *Interpretation and explanation in the study of animal behavior, Vol. 1: Interpretation, intentionality, and communication* (pp. 313-343). Boulder, CO: Westview Press.

20. Representational and conceptual skills of dolphins

Savage-Rumbaugh, S., McDonald, K., Sevcik, R., Hopkins, W., & Rupert, E. (1986). Spontaneous symbol acquisition and communicative use by pygmy chimpanzees (*Pan paniscus*). *Journal of Experimental Psychology: General*, 115, 111-135.

Savage-Rumbaugh, E. S., Rumbaugh, D. M., & Boysen, S. (1980). Do apes use language? *American Scientist*, 68, 49-61.

Schusterman, R. J. & Gisiner, R. (1988). Artificial language comprehension in dolphins and sea lions: The essential cognitive skills. *Psychological Record*, 38, 311-348.

Schusterman, R. J. & Gisiner, R. (1989). Please parse the sentence: Animal cognition in the Procrustean bed of linguistics. *Psychological Record*, 39, 3-18.

Seidenberg, M. S. & Petitto, L. A. (1979). Signing behavior in apes: A critical review. *Cognition*, 7, 177-215.

Seidenberg, M. S. & Petitto, L. A. (1987). Communication, symbolic communication, and language: Comment on Savage-Rumbaugh, McDonald, Sevcik, Hopkins, and Rupert (1986). *Journal of Experimental Psychology: General*, 116, 279-287.

Shepard, R. N. & Metzler, J. (1971). Mental rotation of three-dimensional objects. *Science*, 171, 701-703.

Shipley, E. F., Smith, C. S., Gleitman, L. R. (1969). A study in the acquisition of language: Free responses to commands. *Language*, 45, 322-342.

Terrace, H. S. (1979). *Nim*. New York: Knopf.

Terrace, H. S., Petitto, L. A. Sanders, R. J., & Bever, T. G. (1979). Can an ape create a sentence? *Science*, 200, 891-902.

Thorpe, W. H. (1963). *Learning and instinct in animals* (2nd ed.). Cambridge, MA: Harvard University Press.

Tyack, P. L. (1986). Whistle repertoires of two bottlenosed dolphins,*Tursiops truncatus*: mimicry of signature whistles? *Behavioral Ecology and Sociobiology*, 18, 251-257.

de Villiers, P. A. & de Villiers, J. G. (1972). Early judgments of semantic and syntactic acceptability by children. *Journal of Psycholinguistic Research*, 1, 299-310.

Woodruff, G. & Premack, D. (1979). Intentional communication in the chimpanzee: The development of deception. *Cognition*, 7, 333-362.

Wright, A. A., Cook, R. G., Rivera, J. J., Sands, S. F., & Delius, J. D.(1988). Concept learning by pigeons: Matching-to-sample with trial-unique video picture stimuli. *Animal Learning and Behavior*, 16, 436-444.

Xitco, M. J., Jr. (1988). *Mimicry of modeled behaviors by a bottlenosed dolphin.* Unpublished master's thesis. University of Hawaii, Honolulu.

Zentall, T. R. (1988). Experimentally manipulated imitative behavior in rats and pigeons. In T. R. Zentall & B. G. Galef, Jr. (Eds.), *Social learning: Psychological and biological perspectives* (pp. 191-206). Hillsdale, NJ: Lawrence Erlbaum Associates.

Zentall, T. R. & Galef, B. G., Jr. (1988). *Social learning: Psychological and biological perspectives.* Hillsdale, NJ: Lawrence Erlbaum Associates.

21 A Bottlenosed Dolphin's Responses to Anomalous Sequences Expressed Within an Artificial Gestural Language

Mark D. Holder, Louis M. Herman, and Stanley Kuczaj II

Two bottlenosed dolphins (*Tursiops truncatus*) have been trained to carry out instructions conveyed through artificial languages (Herman, 1986, 1987; Herman, Richards & Wolz, 1984). The instructions were conveyed through sequences of gestures or sounds and were functionally similar to imperative sentences in human languages. For one dolphin, named Akeakamai, a gestural language was employed in which the discrete gestures produced by a trainer were analogous to the words of a natural language, and referred to objects, simple actions, relationships, and indicants of spatial location. For the second dolphin, named Phoenix, an acoustical language was employed in which discrete, electronically generated sounds were used in place of gestures. Each language thus contained a vocabulary of gestures or sounds. These vocabulary items could be combined and recombined with one another according to a set of syntactic rules that governed the order in which the various semantic categories could be arranged to create expanded meanings. The syntactic rules allowed for strings of from two to five semantic entities to be constructed and for meaning to be varied by the ordering of these entities. In this way, many hundreds of unique, grammatically correct sequences could be formed from a limited vocabulary.

Both dolphins responded to novel sequences almost as well as they responded to familiar sequences. Familiar sequences were those previously given to the dolphins. Novel sequences used familiar vocabulary, but in combinations that had not previously been given to the dolphins. The dolphins also responded reliably to novel syntactic forms, which were logical extensions of familiar syntactic forms (Herman et al., 1984). Both dolphins correctly processed semantically reversible strings in which the same words in different orders conveyed different instructions (Herman et al., 1984). For example, Akeakamai reliably distinguished between sequences of the type A + B + FETCH and B + A + FETCH, where A and B may be replaced by names of objects. The sequence directs the dolphin to take the second-named object (grammatically, the direct object of the sentence) to the first-named object (grammatically, the indirect object of the sentence). The object names referred to classes of objects rather than to particular objects. Thus, balls of different sizes and shapes (e.g., a soccer ball or a football) were responded to reliably by Akeakamai after viewing the particular gesture glossed as "ball."

THE USE OF ANOMALOUS SEQUENCES IN LANGUAGE RESEARCH

In general, anomalous sequences of words given within a language violate some semantic relation, or a grammatical rule, or may employ nonsense words in place of some of the real words of a sentence. The use of anomalous sequences has been fruitful in the study of human language, particularly the study of the grammatical systems used by children or their knowledge of or competency in adult forms of grammar (see, e.g., Carr, 1979; de Villiers & de Villiers, 1972; Frasure & Entwisle, 1973; Kuczaj & Maratsos, 1975; Tyler & Marslen-Wilson, 1981). It is perhaps unfortunate that there has been no substantive attempt to exploit this technique in any of the projects attempting to tutor apes in sign language or in artificial languages, given the disputes about the level of grammatical competency of these animals.

Anomalous sequences have been given to the dolphins Akeakamai and Phoenix, as reported in part in several papers (Herman, 1986, 1987; Herman et al., 1984). In the present study we extended this previous research by further tests of the responses of the dolphin Akeakamai to sequences that violated semantic relations or syntactic rules within her artificial gestural language.

21. Responses to anomalous sequences

AKEAKAMAI'S LANGUAGE AND THE CONSTRUCTION OF ANOMALOUS SEQUENCES

The major word-order rules of the artificial gestural language to which Akeakamai was exposed were that modifiers preceded the object modified, and objects preceded actions. Grammatically correct, two-word strings were thus constructed as Object + Action. For example, BASKET OVER instructed the dolphin to select the basket from among the different objects available in her tank and leap over it. Three-word sequences were of two types: those involving modifiers of object location and those instructing the dolphin to construct some relationship between two objects. The syntactic rule for modifier strings was Modifier + Object + Action. Thus, RIGHT WATER TAIL-TOUCH instructed Akeakamai to go to the stream of water flowing into the tank from her right, and by implication not the one flowing in from her left, and place her tail flukes within it. The rule for relational constructions can be given in general form as A + B + Relational term. The relational term may be either FETCH or IN. FETCH requires that one object be brought to the side of (next to) another object. IN requires that one object be placed inside of or on top of another. Thus, SURFBOARD BALL FETCH requires that the ball be placed next to the surfboard, but SURFBOARD BALL IN requires that the ball be placed on top of the surfboard. Behaviorally, FETCH and IN result in distinctively different responses by the dolphin.

Four- and five-word relational sequences are constructed by placing modifiers before the first object term, before the second, or before both. For example, LEFT HOOP PIPE FETCH instructs the dolphin to take a pipe to the hoop on her left, but HOOP LEFT PIPE FETCH instructs her to take the pipe on her left to a hoop.

In the present study, anomalies were defined as sequences of gestures that were either inconsistent with the syntactic rules of the language and/or that violated a semantic relation by requesting a physically impossible response. For example, WATER SPEAKER IN, a syntactically correct construction, nevertheless violates a semantic relation because it instructs the dolphin to transport the speaker, which is firmly attached to the side of the tank, to the stream of water and fling it into the stream. Many anomalies consisted of syntactically incorrect sequences of gestures, but did contain subsets of gestures that were syntactically and semantically correct when extracted from the entire anomalous sequence. For example, the sequence PHOENIX WATER PIPE FETCH is anomalous on the whole, because no extant rule allows for three

object names in a row, but embedded within are the correct sequences
PHOENIX PIPE FETCH and WATER PIPE FETCH.

TESTING RESPONSES TO ANOMALOUS SEQUENCES

Akeakamai lived and was tested in two interconnected circular outdoor seawater tanks, each 15.2 m in diameter and 1.5 m deep. During each session eleven different objects were in the tank in which the dolphin was tested: a black-and-white soccer ball (BALL), a plastic white 160 g Frisbee (FRISBEE), a brown plastic laundry basket kept afloat with four small buoys (BASKET), a surfboard (SURFBOARD), a 117-cm length of a 1.9-cm diameter plastic pipe (PIPE), a square hoop made from four 81-cm-long pieces of the same piping (HOOP), a person sitting on the edge of the tank with both feet in the water (PERSON), a garden hose tied to the side of the tank that poured water into the tank (WATER), an underwater speaker attached to the side of the wall (SPEAKER), an underwater window (WINDOW), and the dolphin Phoenix (PHOENIX).

Between sessions the location of all objects except the window varied. During a session Phoenix and the window, person, water and speaker were fixed in a given location (i.e., they could not be moved by Akeakamai). All other objects were transportable, floating freely in the tank. During each session, 2 of the 11 objects were paired: For example, in addition to the 9 other objects present in the tank there might 2 hoops and 2 pipes. One member of each pair was always on the dolphin's left and the other on her right. The objects that were paired were balls, Frisbees, pipes, hoops, persons, and water. The objects selected to be paired varied between sessions with the restriction that each object was paired for the same number of sessions as every other paired object and a particular object was never paired for two consecutive sessions.

Seven of each week's 20 testing or training sessions were dedicated to the study of the anomalous sequences. Each of these seven sessions was approximately 40 minutes in duration. A trainer stationed himself or herself at the side of the tank, and using gestures signed to Akeakamai. While signing, the trainer wore opaque goggles to guard against eye-gaze cues and to limit the trainer's knowledge of what responses were being made by Akeakamai. Akeakamai's responses were judged by an observer having no knowledge of which gestures had been given to Akeakamai. The observer was able, however, to observe Akeakamai's subsequent responses, and labeled these responses in English using the vocabulary and grammar of the artificial gestural language. For normal (nonanomalous) sequences, Akeakamai's response was scored as

21. Responses to anomalous sequences

correct only if the blind observer's labels coincided exactly with the gestural sequence given the dolphin. Correct responses were followed by a whistle blast by the trainer and a fish reward. These were omitted after incorrect responses.

During each session the dolphin was given 17 normal sequences: six 2-word sequences; four 3-word modifier sequences, including 2 with the modifier LEFT and 2 with RIGHT; three 3-word relational sequences including at least one with FETCH and one with IN; and four 4-word relational sequences including 2 with FETCH and 2 with IN, and 2 with the direct object modified and 2 with the indirect object modified.

In addition to these normal sequences, five of every seven sessions, selected at random, contained two anomalous sequences. In this study, anomalous sequences never referred to objects that were currently paired. The low proportion of anomalies to normal sequences was intended to reduce the probability that Akeakamai would learn to expect anomalies or would develop some stereotyped response to them. Each anomaly was unique and was presented only once. The anomalies were presented to the dolphin in three series. Only a selected subset of the anomalous types given within each series is reported here: 5 from the first series of 10 different types; 1 from the second series consisting of 6 different types; and 2 from the final series consisting of 7 different types. These 8 different types selected from the 3 series are described in Table 21.1.

Generally, anomalies were presented in 3 blocks of 10 and then 3 blocks of 9 such that within each block all types were presented in random order. A restriction was that each pair of anomalies presented in a session shared no more than 1 gesture in common, but in practice such overlap was rare, occurring in only 3 of the sessions containing anomalous sequences.

None of the gestures in the three normal sequences that immediately preceded an anomaly were contained in the subsequent anomaly. No anomaly was presented in the first or last three sequences of a session, and pairs of anomalies were separated by a minimum of five normal sequences. To avoid reinforcing specific responses to anomalies, no whistle or fish was given after the dolphin's response. Instead, the dolphin was called back to the trainer by gently splashing the water in the tank. After the dolphin returned, the trainer resumed normal interactions with her.

The completion of the first series of anomalies took 6.5 weeks, the second 3.5 weeks, and the third 4 weeks. Series 2 immediately followed the

Table 21.1
The Eight Types of Anomalies Reported Here

Type of Anomaly	Example
SSR	WATER PHOENIX IN
SSRA	WATER SPEAKER IN TAIL-TOUCH
STSR	WATER HOOP PHOENIX IN
SSTR	WATER PHOENIX BASKET IN
TSR	BASKET SPEAKER FETCH
OA (action not physically possible)	SURFBOARD THROUGH
OAA	PIPE UNDER TOSS
OAOA	PIPE TOSS BALL UNDER

Note. Abbreviations: S = stationary (nontransportable) object; T = transportable object; O = either S or T object; R = relational action term (FETCH or IN); A = nonrelational action term (e.g., OVER, TAIL-TOUCH).

completion of Series 1, and Series 3 followed Series 2 by a gap of only 2 weeks. At the conclusion of the three series, eight additional anomalies were given using the same procedures as in the three preceding series. However, the individual giving the gestural signs to the dolphin had no knowledge of the meaning of the gestures or of the grammar of the language. This procedure tested whether the dolphin's responses to the previous anomalies may have been influenced by the signers distinguishing normal and anomalous sequences and somehow presenting the two types differently.

The trainer giving the anomalous sequences, the dolphin's responses, and the location of all objects immediately before and after the trial were videotaped. The video operator pretended to film all trials so that the blind observer did not know whether the current trial was anomalous or not. After each anomalous sequence was completed, and after the blind observer had labeled the dolphin's response he or she drew a map of the location of all objects in the tank and the path the dolphin took in its response. The accuracy of this

21. Responses to anomalous sequences

drawing was confirmed, and modified as necessary, by reviewing the videotape record. If the dolphin remained close to the signer and did not direct a specific response to any object then this was recorded as a rejection.

RELATIONAL ANOMALIES

Six types of relational sequences were considered semantic anomalies because the total sequence, or a portion of the sequence, instructed the dolphin to transport nontransportable objects. One such anomalous type, symbolized as SSR in Table 21.1, consisted of a sequence of two nontransportable or stationary (S) objects followed by a relational term, either FETCH or IN. Specifically, the SSR sequence instructed Akeakamai to transport the second-occurring nontransportable object (S2) to the first-occurring nontransportable object (S1), and place it beside the first object (FETCH) or in or on it (IN). We have previously given an example of an SSR sequence: WATER SPEAKER IN. Akeakamai rejected five of six of the SSR sequences given her, including the example illustrated, attempting no response in each case. In the sixth case, WATER PHOENIX FETCH, a sequence requesting a transport of the dolphin Phoenix to the stream of water, Akeakamai instead transported the hoop to the water.

With SSR sequences, not only is the entire sequence semantically anomalous, but there is no normal embedded subset available to which the dolphin might respond. A second type of anomaly was used to test whether an available embedded normal subset might produce a response. This type of anomaly, symbolized as SSRA, adds the A term to the previous SSR type, where A is a nonrelational action such as OVER or UNDER. The addition of the A term in principle allows for two nonadjacent normal subsets to be formed: S1A and S2A. For example, given the anomalous sequence WATER PHOENIX FETCH OVER, the two embedded normal subsets are WATER OVER and PHOENIX OVER (jump over Phoenix or jump over the stream of water). Despite the presence of these embedded sequences, in all six cases Akeakamai rejected the sequence.

These rejection responses show that the two types of anomalies, SSR and SSRA, were discriminated from normal sequences. Previous research (Herman et al., 1984) has shown that normal, but unfamiliar (novel), sequences are almost never rejected. However, all types of anomalies were not rejected.

For the two types of anomalies just discussed, the dolphin could not respond to the relational term because neither object referenced in the anomalous sequence was transportable. Would the dolphin perform a relational response when a gesture referring to a transportable object was added to the SSR anomaly? With this addition, the sequence becomes syntactically anomalous. However, the addition of a transportable (T) object creates normal subsets involving a relational instruction, even though the gestures that formed these subsets were not always adjacent in the sequence. One such anomaly is symbolized as STSR (e.g., WATER FRISBEE SPEAKER FETCH). The normal subset STR (WATER FRISBEE FETCH) is embedded within this sequence. As with the previously discussed anomalies, the anomalous subset SSR (WATER SPEAKER FETCH) was also present. Thus, as before, rejections might occur. The results were, however, that only one rejection occurred among the six cases given. In three of the five cases of a response, Akeakamai responded to the embedded STR subset. In a fourth case she again responded to the STR component, but constructed an inappropriate relationship, taking the transportable object to the side of the first S object (a FETCH response) instead of putting it on top of that object (an IN response). In the fifth case, she took the ball, which was not referred to in the anomalous sequence, and transported it to the T object that was referenced in the anomaly.

Another type of anomaly adding a T item was expressed as SSTR. Here the second S object and the T object are in reversed order to that of the previous anomaly. This placement resulted in two possible normal subsets: S1TR and S2TR. For example, given WATER PHOENIX BASKET IN, the dolphin might choose to place the basket in the water, if the initial gesture was of importance, or she might place the basket on top of Phoenix, if the adjacency of gestures was more important. Again, only one rejection occurred among seven cases. The S1TR subset was selected in four cases and the S2TR subset in one case. In a sixth case the T object was transported to a destination object not mentioned in the anomaly.

The collection of results for the SSR, SSRA, STSR, and SSTR sequences thus indicate that only anomalies that contain a relational term but no transportable object were typically rejected. Only 2 rejections out of 13 instances occurred when a transportable object was available within the sequence.

Anomalies of the type TSR were also tested. These contained a transportable object, but in an anomalous sequence. Though syntactically correct, this type of sequence instructs Akeakamai to transport a nontransportable object to one that is transportable. If the order of the T and S objects were reversed, the normal sequence STR would occur. Would the

21. Responses to anomalous sequences

dolphin reorder such anomalous sequences, transforming TSR into STR? If the dolphin had strongly incorporated the rules of word order (i.e., the first object is the destination of transport and the second the object to be transported), word-order reversal would be unlikely. This was in fact the case: Word-order reversals never occurred. Two of six TSR anomalies were rejected. In another two cases, Akeakamai transported a T object not present in the anomaly to the one that was present, in effect substituting a T object for the specified S object. In still another case, two objects were used that were not specified in the anomaly, and in the final case, Akeakamai carried out a nonrelational response, a rare failure to respond to a relational term.

Based on the responses to these five types of anomalies, we can begin to develop a model of the "on line" processing of sequences by the dolphin. The language was constructed such that a sequence was anomalous if it referenced two objects and the second object was not transportable. Suppose that the dolphin used a simple serial-order processing strategy to encode the sequence of gestures. If the second object referenced in a sequence was not transportable, the sequence could be immediately detected as anomalous. Consistent with this strategy is the finding that the dolphin overwhelmingly rejected anomalies of the type SSR and SSRA. However, the anomalous sequences SSTR and TSR were not typically rejected. Therefore, processing of sequences does not terminate when the second object referenced is not transportable. Furthermore, nonadjacent gestures that form normal subsets can be extracted from anomalies. Therefore, the dolphin's processing of sequences is not accurately described by a simple model involving the serial processing of each sequential gesture.

Additionally, when the dolphin could respond to either the initial gesture or the second gesture as the indirect object (the destination object), the dolphin generally responded to the initial gesture even though the second gesture was adjacent to the remainder of the normal subset. This suggests that primacy was more important, or more controlling, than was adjacency. Lastly, word order was also highly controlling. In no case, did the dolphin reverse the word order to "correct" an anomaly.

NONRELATIONAL ANOMALIES

Several types of anomalies were constructed containing no relational (R) term. One type was symbolized as OA, where O refers to some object and A, as before, to a simple (nonrelational) action. Although OA may be used to form a normal sequence, it can generate a semantically anomalous sequence when the action specified cannot be applied to the object referenced. This type of anomaly might be rejected entirely. However, if a response is made it is of interest to see whether the object term or the action term may be more controlling of responses. Six semantically anomalous OA sequences were given to the dolphin: SURFBOARD THROUGH, FRISBEE THROUGH, PHOENIX TOSS, WINDOW TOSS, SURFBOARD TWIRL, and WATER TWIRL. The first two instructed the dolphin to swim through solid objects. The second two requested that objects be tossed that will not or cannot be tossed, and the final two asked Akeakamai to spin objects on her rostrum that cannot be so manipulated. Only WINDOW TOSS was rejected; the remaining anomalies yielded substitution responses, or in one case resulted in an apparent approximation to the request. Thus, in response to the two THROUGH commands, Akeakamai in each case swam through a hoop, the only available object permitting that response. The apparent approximation occurred in response to PHOENIX TOSS. Akeakamai swam beside Phoenix and waited in a bodily position similar to that used just prior to tossing an object, although she never actually attempted to toss Phoenix. Finally, for both TWIRL sequences, Akeakamai twirled a frisbee on the tip of her rostrum, a frequently requested behavior. When given SURFBOARD TWIRL she simply went to the frisbee and twirled it. However, when given WATER TWIRL she brought the frisbee, while twirling it, to the water and continued to twirl it there. Her responses to PHOENIX TOSS and WATER TWIRL suggest that in some cases both the action and the objects can determine responses to these anomalies, but that, on average, actions dominate objects. This latter finding is consistent with the dolphin's responses to normal OA sequences. When the dolphin makes an error in response to a normal OA sequence, it is much more likely to be to the object term than to the action term (Herman, 1986, 1987; Herman et al., 1984).

The OA anomalies are all syntactically correct but semantically anomalous. In contrast, two other types of anomalies given to Akeakamai were syntactically anomalous but preserved appropriate semantic relations. These sequences were symbolized as OAA and OAOA. These are syntactically anomalous sequences because there is no rule allowing for two terminal action terms, or for two successive OA sequences. Examples of each type are BASKET OVER TAIL-TOUCH (OAA) and BALL UNDER FRISBEE PEC-TOUCH (OAOA). Rejections of these sequences could conceivably occur, but responses to embedded OA subsets would also be possible. It is also possible that conjoined responses could occur, such as leaping over the basket and then touching it with the tail in the OAA example, or going under the ball and touching the frisbee with the pectoral fins in the OAOA example. Seven OAA and six OAOA examples were given. In each case, only a single rejection occurred. All of the remaining OAA sequences were responded to by applying

21. Responses to anomalous sequences

the final indicated action to the first named object. Thus, given BASKET OVER TAIL-TOUCH, the response was BASKET TAIL-TOUCH. For the five OAOA sequences yielding responses, all again incorporated the final indicated action. However, the choice of object was more arbitrary: In two cases the dolphin responded to the first-named object, in another case to the second-named object, and in the two remaining cases an object not contained in the sequence was chosen for response.

Responses to the OAA and OAOA anomalies add to the development of a model of on-line processing of sequences. Simple strategies of serially processing of the elements of sequences do not easily account for the dolphin's responses. Given anomalies that begin with the normal sequence OBJECT ACTION, the dolphin might terminate processing after the first two gestures and respond to this sequence because it is complete. Alternatively, any gesture following the OBJECT ACTION sequence necessarily makes that sequence anomalous so that the sequence can be rejected. Neither of these response patterns were typical. Instead, following anomalies of either OBJECT ACTION ACTION or OBJECT ACTION OBJECT ACTION the dolphin responded to the last ACTION term in 11 of 13 cases (the remaining two cases were rejected). This indicates that the last gesture is particularly emphasized and that processing did not end following either a normal sequence or following the first gesture that made the sequence anomalous. The responses are compatible with a model that views the processing of gestures and responding to gestures as a function of the gestures that precede and/or follow them.

RESPONSES TO SEQUENCES GIVEN BY A NAIVE SIGNER

All the sequences discussed so far were given by signers familiar with the dolphin's language. The finding that anomalous sequences were recognized and discriminated by the dolphin from correct sequences is based on the rejections occurring to many of the anomalous sequences (depending in part on the type of sequence) but to none of the normal sequences. However, the possibility exists that the signers, who because of their familiarity with the language were aware that a sequence was anomalous, somehow presented such sequences in a different manner from normal sequences. Although none of the authors could discern such differences, perhaps the dolphin did and treated anomalous sequences differently because of the signers' behaviors and not because of the structural or semantic differences occurring.

To test for any effect of prior knowledge of a trainer on the responses of the dolphin, naive signers were used who presented signs without any knowledge of the language, including the meaning of individual gestures and the underlying grammar. Thus, they could not distinguish a normal sequence of gestures from an anomalous one. To these naive signers, all sequences were equally nonsensical. The results were that the percentage of correct responses to normal sequences was very high for sequences given by the naive signers, as it was for sequences given by knowledgeable signers. Also, responses to anomalies presented by naive signers were similar to responses to the same types of anomalies given by informed signers. For example, following OAOA anomalies, in three of four cases the dolphin performed the action indicated by the final action term to one of the two objects mentioned. In the fourth case she rejected the anomaly.

SUMMARY

A bottlenosed dolphin was proficient in responding to instructions given through multigestural sequences within an artificial gestural language. Her responses to sequences that violated semantic relations and/or syntactic rules of the artificial language were studied. Responses to these anomalies revealed an understanding of how objects stand in relation to one another, and an understanding of the structure that governs combinations of gestures. Serial-order relations were very important but adjacency of items was not, as long as serial-order was maintained. The dolphin took account of all items in the sequence and of their serial order in organizing a response, or in deciding not to attempt a response.

ACKNOWLEDGMENTS

This research was supported in part by grants to LMH from the Office and Naval Research and from Earthwatch. MDH and SAK were on sabbatical leave at the Kewalo Basin Marine Mammal Laboratory at the time of these studies. The authors wish to thank the many students and staff at KBMML, and the Earthwatch volunteers who assisted in the research.

REFERENCES

Carr, D. B. (1979). The development of young children's capacity to judge anomalous sentences. *Journal of Child Language*, 6, 227-241.

21. Responses to anomalous sequences

Frasure, N. E. & Entwisle, D. R. (1973). Semantic and syntactic development in children. *Developmental Psychology*, 9, 236-245.

Herman, L. M. (1986). Cognition and language competencies of bottlenosed dolphins. In R. J. Schusterman, J. Thomas, & F. G. Wood (Eds.). *Dolphin cognition and behavior: A comparative approach* (pp. 221-252). Hillsdale, NJ: Lawrence Erlbaum Associates.

Herman, L. M. (1987). Receptive competencies of language-trained animals. In J. S. Rosenblatt, C. Beer, C, M-C. Busnel & P. J. B. Slater (Eds.). *Advances in the study of behavior* (Vol. 17, pp. 1-60). Petaluma, CA: Academic Press.

Herman, L. M., Richards, D. G., & Wolz, J. P. (1984). Comprehension of sentences by bottlenosed dolphins. *Cognition*, 16, 129-219.

Kuczaj, S. A. II, & Maratsos, M. P. (1975). What children can say before they will. *Merrill-Palmer Quarterly*, 21, 90-111.

Tyler, L. T. & Marslen-Wilson, W. D. (1981). Children's processing of spoken language. *Journal of Verbal Language and Verbal Behavior*, 20, 400-416.

de Villiers, P. A. & de Villiers, J. G. (1972). Early judgments of semantic and syntactic acceptability by children. *Journal of Psycholinguistic Research*, 1, 299-310.

22 Language Learnability in Man, Ape, and Dolphin

E. S. Savage-Rumbaugh

Language is viewed by many linguists as an intrinsic property of the human brain (Chomsky, 1988). On view, the language faculty, though not evident at birth, develops according to a prescribed program, which permits the child to decode the elemental structural aspects of language. These structural elements are needed in order to "break the linguistic code," and without them there can be no language proper. Proponents of this "strong nativist" perspective maintain that these elemental structural rules do not reside in the language input data available to the child; and thus it follows that the rules must reside in an innate *language module* within the child. Experience serves to activate this module but it does not shape its contents.

There are two alternative perspectives to the strong nativist argument and both rely on the fact that complex brains are capable of acquiring, integrating, and processing complex information effectively and rapidly. The first of these, termed the *modified nativist* position, suggests that language is indeed learned, but that it can be learned only by a human brain (Bever, Carroll, & Miller, 1984). Accordingly, language does not unfold as though it follows a specific program, nor is it located in a specific cognitive module. Instead, language emerges as a function of the typical kinds of interactions between the totality of the human brain and the human environment.

The nativists, both strong and modified, base their respective claims on four common observations that they take to be fact. (a) Humans are the only species that appears to have language. (b) Animal communication systems are believed to be devoid of either reference or syntax. (c) Animal communication systems do not seem to be modifiable or open to the incorporation of new sounds. (d) Animal systems lack syntax. All of these assertions were widely accepted 10 years ago; however, they are currently under attack by primatologists studying the natural communication systems of monkeys (Gouzoules, Gouzoules, & Marler, 1984; Seyfarth & Cheney, 1982, this volume, chapter 10; Snowdon, 1988; this volume, chapter 9).

THE STRONG-L LEARNING VIEW

The second view, termed the *strong-L* (learning) position, maintains that although language is found only in humans (as far as we have presently determined), other complex brains should also be capable of some simple language given the proper experience. Indeed, in principle, some other species may well have a language that is very different from our own and consequently is not yet recognized as a linguistic system. This view suggests that a simple language, with reference and syntax, could exist in a species that lacked the ability to engage in long-range planning, group coordination, representational art, knowledge of parenthood, complex formalized kinship structures, and the recognition of mortality that characterize *Homo sapiens*. Because children demonstrate reference and simple syntax before they are able to deal with concepts such as these, it seems reasonable to assume that reference and syntax may exist in animals who do not exhibit other behaviors that *Homo* has traditionally associated with language.

According to the strong-L view, the only innate capacity that humans bring to the language acquisition task is the ability to imitate long and complex novel vocal sequences. All other aspects of language are dependent on generalized cognitive structures, which humans share with the great apes and perhaps with other social mammals that have large brains.

Prerequisite Mental Capacities

The strong-L view asserts that there are prerequisite mental capacities that must be in place before language can be learned. The strong-L stance does not assume that these prerequisites are innate or peculiar to humans, but it does assume that language requires special ways of handling information that are not within the abilities of most animals. These include (a) the ability to engage in cause-effect reasoning from a single example, (b) the ability to imitate purposively (that is, to achieve the same effect as the party being imitated, not just the same actions), and (c) the ability to equate stimuli as functionally

22. Language learnability in man, ape, and dolphin

similar (stimulus equivalence) even though the behavioral history with those stimuli is not equivalent (Sidman, 1986; see also Schusterman, this volume, chapter 12).

Even if the capacities for plasticity, reference, and syntax are demonstrated in the natural communication systems of animals, two questions remain. First, in what ways, if any, are these aspects of animal communication functionally similar to human communication? Second, if animals are taught a human language, do they use these capacities in the same way that we do? Specifically, do they, for example, use the capacity for plasticity to constantly expand and enhance the kinds of things they can say to one other? Do they use the capacity for reference to communicate about events that are removed in time and space, to plan for the future, and to reminisce about the past? Do they employ syntax to allow for more efficient expression, such that a single concept can be multiply embedded within others and yet the listener knows which words refer to certain other words and in what way?

REFERENCE AND SYNTAX

To answer these questions with animals, procedurally grounded theories of the development of reference and syntax are required. Development of such theories is likely to be difficult, however. For example, the concept of *reference* has a long and variegated history within the fields of philosophy and psychology that is fraught with difficulties (Skinner, 1957; Gauker, 1990). Many of these difficulties can be avoided, however, by treating reference as a process or set of expectancies that arises between individuals as a function of past experience, rather than as a mental entity residing within a single individual. On this view, reference is primarily a social function, rather than a mental entity, and it is more appropriate to ask whether an individual uses this function than to ask whether it has some specific mental structure.

The Concept of Reference

Reference as traditionally used in the child language literature denotes the emergence of the ability to use words to convey ideas, feelings, desires, and so forth to others. Words are assumed to represent specific things. Key questions in the field of language acquisition focus on the manner in which the child acquires categorical concepts that are similar to those of adults (Clark, 1983). In previous discussions of reference, I have followed the standard usage of the word as it is employed in the field of developmental psychology. The term *reference*, as used in the child language literature, is not procedurally defined, however, and it carries along with it some conceptual baggage that is inappropriate to the procedural definitions of reference being developed with apes (Savage-Rumbaugh, 1984; 1986; Savage-Rumbaugh, Pate, Lawson, Smith, & Rosenbaum, 1983; Savage-Rumbaugh, McDonald, Sevcik, Hopkins, & Rubert, 1986; Savage-Rumbaugh, in press).

When two individuals engage in the process of reference, one of them uses a word, a sign, a gesture, a posture, or some type of symbol to point out or to draw attention to a specific thing, idea, goal, or a particular activity that is desired, etc. Generally, the act of reference is assumed to be an intentional act that is carried out for a specific purpose. It is also assumed that such acts are executed by a sentient party who is aware of their purpose. That is, when one speaks, one has some idea of the impact ones communication will have on the listener. The *perceived intent* is critical to the issue of reference. For example if someone bumps into you forcefully on the subway, it is important to assess whether the intent was to do so or not. If the bump was accidental, it will be assumed that there was no message intended.

The act of referring occurs most often with regard to things that are not obvious from circumstances. For example, one frequently says, "I am hot," "I am cold," "I am hungry," "I am sick," etc., because it is not possible for others to know such things. However, one rarely says "I am male" or "I am white," because there is no need to refer to things that are self-evident. Because words, or groups of words, tend to be used in similar ways across many circumstances, they are sometimes characterized as "referring" to certain things. Words themselves however, obviously do not refer, only speakers who intend to produce a behavior or state of belief in the listener can "refer" (Strawson, 1950/1971; also see Roitblat, Harley, & Helweg, this volume, chapter 1). Words are the vehicle of that process. This does not mean however, that reference resides in the communicator anymore than it resides in individual words. Reference as a process can occur between individuals sentient of the nature of the communicative system that they employ. However no specific word actually refers to a limited set of things as a dictionary definition suggests.

Reference versus Association

Teaching an animal to form associations between words and symbols does not result in the type of representational function that one normally ascribes to children (Savage-Rumbaugh, 1986). Animals may be said to engage in the process of reference if they emit a gestural or vocal signal with the obvious intent of producing a specific response or belief on the part of the recipient,

22. Language learnability in man, ape, and dolphin

though this is generally not what is happening when animals are taught to pair symbols and behaviors. For example, when a dolphin is trained to retrieve a Frisbee (in response to a computer-generated sound code or a visual signal), those symbols that precede the behavior are produced by the experimenter for the purpose of "referring to" the Frisbee. That is, the experimenter intends to draw the dolphin's attention to the Frisbee (which is one of many objects in the tank) and to cause the dolphin to act on the Frisbee in a certain manner. To the extent that the dolphin forms an associative connection between the Frisbee and the symbol, the symbols used by the experimenter will result in the desired or referenced action on the part of the dolphin.

Whether or not the dolphin "knows" that the symbol is being used to refer to the object is a separate question. When human parents communicate with infants, before the infant is capable of intentional referential communication, the parent treats the infant as a competent communicative partner by attributing intent, which is, in fact, not evident in the infant's behavior (Bruner, 1974/1975). It is believed that this attribution of communicative intent and reference fosters the emergence of these processes in the infant (Lock, 1980) and that without such attribution, language as a functional system for conveying one's desires by means of symbols would never arise. Lock (1980) argues effectively that language does not arise within the child, but rather as a function of the way in which the child is responded to by others who are attempting to bring the child into the language-using community.

Both dolphin and child may need to experience being treated as a sentient recipients of referential communications, before they are actually capable of becoming effective participants in the process. Bruner (1974/1975) observes that in most early communicative play, the mother takes on the role of the responder for the infant. Thus she might ask the rhetorical question, "And what goes bow-bow?" then wait a moment before answering for the infant, "The doggie." Through such interchanges the infant comes to learn what is expected of him or her. Nothing comparable occurs with dolphins, however, as the goal of the dolphin training program has not been to make the dolphin a communicator (Herman, 1986).

When an experimenter holds up an orange and requires a chimpanzee (a parrot, a retarded child, or any organism) to produce a particular sign or symbol, the difference between this training paradigm and that just described is clearly more than a simple reversal of the direction of an associative chain. In this paradigm the experimenter can no longer be characterized as engaging in an act of reference. The object that is being displayed (a hat, a banana, etc.) is not being used (by the experimenter) to refer to anything. By displaying the object, the experimenter is attempting to evoke an association between object and symbol, but that is all.

RECEPTIVE AND PRODUCTIVE COMPETENCE

At first glance it often appears that reception and production are complementary processes, both requiring the development of similar associative connections, albeit the directionality of the associative response is different. However, this view overlooks the fact that objects have concrete properties while symbols do not. Objects can be physically manipulated, carried from one place to another, and used for many different purposes. Symbols have a singular function, that of indication of some type. Signs made to a dolphin cannot be touched, smelled, or manipulated. They must function and exist in the special realm of indication. The direction of the referential process is from symbol to object or event, for it is in this direction alone that it has communicative power for the dolphin.

Language Learning Paradigms

The object-labeling experiences of the child and the dolphin reflect two different types of receptive paradigms. One paradigm typifies the way in which the child acquires language processes, and the other typifies the way in which the dolphin acquires the ability to follow the experimenter's instructions. In the first paradigm, words are not taught individually, indeed they are not taught at all. They are parsed from the stream of ongoing speech, and the subject selects what to learn and when to learn it. The child is not required to produce a response in order to learn. In the second paradigm, the subject is taught to give the correct item when a particular symbol is selected. Because these two receptive paradigms are fundamentally different, their outcomes might be expected to produce different results, and they do.

Before focusing on the differences in receptive paradigms however, it is worthwhile to look at the productive paradigm more closely. The purpose of the productive paradigm is to teach "words." Yet it doesn't really do so. Rather, it teaches the subject to select a particular symbol when a specific object is displayed. This is rarely what happens when a child uses a word (Lucariello, Kyratzis, & Engel, 1986). Talking is not a matter of someone holding up objects and asking a child to say a word. Talking is a matter of a child using words to tell the parents things that they might not otherwise know, for example that he or she wants a "cookie", needs to go to the "potty", does not like the bad "dog", is leaving "Goodbye," etc. (Greenfield & Smith, 1976).

22. Language learnability in man, ape, and dolphin

While middle-class parents may ask the child to name things, there is no evidence to suggest that this behavior serves to teach the child words, or how words are really used.

The use of words for communicative ends, as contrasted with the selection of symbols because someone has displayed an item, evokes significantly different cognitive schema. When a child uses a word communicatively, quite often the referent is absent (which is why the word has a communicative function beyond that given in the context). Additionally, the child's communicative partner does not prompt word usage by displaying items. If the partner prompts at all, it is by questions such as "What do you want?" "How do you feel?" "Do you like this?" etc. Such questions may be answered in any number of ways and the various answers are not necessarily provoked by object-symbol associations elicited by the display of an object. The productive paradigm should not be expected to enable an organism to "communicate with symbols," because it incorporates none of the normal situations in which children use words.

The receptive paradigm, as employed with dolphins and sea lions (Herman, 1986; Schusterman & Krieger, 1984), suffers from similar difficulties in that it lacks important aspects of the linguistic communicative process as employed by *Homo*. The receptive language input that the dolphin and the child receive differs in four fundamental ways. I argue here that these four differences constitute the critical and sufficient conditions for language acquisition in any species capable of observer-based cause-effect reasoning. (The ability to engage in observer-based cause-effect thought requires that an organism be able to watch the actions of another and interpret the significance of these actions for him or herself.)

On clarifying the nature of these differences it is shown how the strong-L stance predicts that when and if the linguistic input is equated for dolphin, child, and ape, the dolphin and the ape should, like the child, invert the receptive paradigm and spontaneously produce referential language output. Data already published for the pygmy chimpanzees constitute an important confirmation of the view that comprehension leads spontaneously to production (Savage-Rumbaugh et al., 1986; Greenfield & Savage-Rumbaugh, 1991).

Savage-Rumbaugh

CRITICAL DIFFERENCES BETWEEN DOLPHIN AND CHILD LINGUISTIC EXPERIENCE

Medium

The first and most obvious difference between the receptive input received by the sea lions, the dolphin Ake, and a child is that of the medium. The child's input occurs via a medium (spoken sounds) in which the child is capable of producing symbols easily and fluently on its own, once its motor and vocal system have matured sufficiently. The dolphin Ake receives language input in a gestural mode that she cannot produce. The input received by the dolphin Phoenix is acoustical in nature and is produced by a computer that generates 1 second whistles that are similar to the dolphin's natural sounds (Herman, 1987). Phoenix could conceivably imitate the input stimuli, but she does not. Instead, her performance has fallen steadily with increased experimental demand.

Communication of New Information to Predict Important Events

The second and less obvious difference is that the type of input that the child receives contains important characteristics not found in the communications directed to dolphins. To the extent that the child comes to understand what is being said, the linguistic communications directed to the child frequently serve to make his or her world increasingly predictable. For example, a mother may say, "Oh, here comes Daddy." When the child can understand this, he or she knows that someone will approach soon and who that person will be. On the other hand, if the child hears, "Oh look, here comes doggie bow-wow" he knows that in a moment a very large and furry creature may be licking his face.

The knowledge of what will happen next in our lives is important to all of us, but particularly to young children. If one knows what is about to happen, there is opportunity to plan one's reaction. In a rapidly changing social and physical environment, knowing what is going to happen next, and why, is of fundamental importance to our capacity to carry on normal social engagements. Thus, because of the nature of the information carried by the linguistic code, there exists a powerful and intrinsic motivation to understand linguistic communications.

By contrast, none of the linguistic input that the dolphin receives carries information about events of significance to the dolphin that may be about

22. Language learnability in man, ape, and dolphin

to occur. Instead, the linguistic signal encodes only what the dolphin is to do if it wishes to receive a fish. The information carried by the linguistic signal that the dolphin sees (or hears) never carries information that is intrinsically salient to the dolphin; rather, it carries information that is of importance to the teacher's evaluation of the dolphin.

Error Correction

A third unique characteristic of the child's input is that failure of the child to understand a linguistic request is not typically associated with punishment, failure, or the omission of extrinsic reward. For example, if a child is told to "help carry your toys" and does not understand, the caretaker does not keep repeating the sentence, or refuse to give the child a reward. Instead, he or she places toys in the child's hand and shows the child what needs to be done. Similarly, if a child is told to "Throw the ball" and does not, hear she will be shown how to do so. Such error correction serves to reveal to the child the intent behind the linguistic communications directed to him or her. It also serves to show the child that the speaker wants something to happen for a particular reason.

The child does not carry out many different requests in order to effect a common outcome. Rather, toys must be picked up because Mom wants them off the floor. Balls are thrown because they are fun to catch and the speaker's words indicate that he or she is ready to catch one. The essence of linguistic communication is revealed to the child as a means of making many different things happen. Each different sort of linguistic communication becomes associated with a different outcome in the mind of the child.

Thus, the child hears linguistic token A, carries out action A1, and in so doing, brings about a particular state of affairs A*. Then the child hears linguistic token B, carries out action B1, and brings about B*. If A is "Throw the ball," A* is the catching of the ball by the partner. If B is "Give Grandma a hug," then B* is the feeling that arises while engaging in this action. If C is "Eat your vegetables," then C* is the state of having a clean plate in front of you. Thus, the response to the linguistic token creates a state of affairs that is different for each token and that is intrinsic to that token.

It is informative to contrast this set of events with that experienced by the dolphin. From the dolphin's perspective, the linguistic input directed to it is associated with a single salient outcome, the receipt of a fish. For the dolphin, responses to the linguistic tokens A, B, or C all bring about one set of events (a fish), and these events are extrinsic to the linguistic token itself.

The child, but not the dolphin, thus has reason to attempt to determine the intent of the speaker. That is, the child seeks to comprehend the state of affairs that the speaker intends to bring about by utterances such as "Give Grandma a hug" or "Throw the ball." To the extent that the linguistic token is not clear to the child, the adult prompts the child with regard to the correct set of actions, and in so doing, makes their own intent manifest. However, if the dolphin does not carry out the correct response to a token such as "Pectouch the Frisbee," no one leads the dolphin to the Frisbee and places its peck on it. Additionally, when a child grasps the link between linguistic tokens such as "Throw the ball" and the associated expected set of actions, he or she does so because the act of throwing is, in itself, intrinsically motivating. Consequently, once the connection between token and action is made, the child can use the token "Throw the ball" to ask the speaker to throw the ball to him! Even if the dolphin could sign, it is not likely that it would ask the speaker to "Pectouch the Frisbee," since that action was done not for its intrinsic interest, but to receive a fish. Thus, it becomes clear that a key difference between the dolphin and the child is in the nature of their motivation to decode the linguistic tokens presented to them. The child has many reasons to attempt to invert the receptive paradigm and use what others have said to him or her to communicate with them. The dolphin's training provides no similar motivation. As noted earlier, the child's comprehension of linguistic input is motivated by many factors, but all of the them share the fact that increased comprehending skills give the child more control over its environment, and the potential to manipulate that environment him- or herself by using the linguistic code. At least a large part of the input received by the child is of the sort that the child, as initiator could benefit from inverting. For example, a child who hears "Let's drink some juice" may later want to initiate juice drinking herself by saying "Let's drink some juice." However, it is difficult to imagine Ake wanting to invert the experimenter's behavior and ask him to "Take the hoop to the Frisbee". Indeed, the problem is that relatively little that Ake and Phoenix have learned to do is something that they would want to ask of another! Coupled with this is the fact that their purpose in correctly carrying out instructions is to receive a fish. (Should Ake and Phoenix develop any concept as to why another being might be willing to carry out their instructions, their concept would surely impute to that other party a desire to obtain a fish.)

22. Language learnability in man, ape, and dolphin

A THEORY OF LANGUAGE ACQUISITION

The theory set forth here is that the acquisition of the linguistic code is fundamentally a receptive process. When the process of acquisition becomes sufficiently sophisticated to permit the child to understand the nature of interindividual reference, he or she will spontaneously attempt to control the behaviors of others via the linguistic code, just as they have been controlled in the past by this code and just as they have observed others being controlled by it. In other words, comprehending the way in which the linguistic code operates will result in attempts at production. While these initial attempts may reflect poor pronunciation and may be limited to halting single word expression, they appear to be motivated by past experiences in comprehension, and the child's knowledge of what similar communications achieved for others in similar circumstances.

The implication of this theory for animal language training paradigms is that the most effective teaching strategy is predicted to be one that provides the animal with information about his environment that he will find useful. Moreover, this information must be variable and serve a predictive function. To the extent that this information is social in nature and predicts the behavior of other individuals, it will be potentially useful if and only if the animal can utilize the input in future exchanges for its own ends.

Support for this perspective is found in the language acquisition patterns of four chimpanzees (three *Pan paniscus*, and one *Pan troglodytes*) (Savage-Rumbaugh et al., 1986; Savage-Rumbaugh, 1988; Savage-Rumbaugh, Sevcik, & Brakke, 1991) who were exposed to the linguistic code solely through receptive input, with no explicit receptive training (i.e., drills) or demands for specific productions). Their receptive input was made as similar as feasible to that which would be received by a normal child, with the exception that vocal communications were accompanied, when possible, by pointing to graphic symbols. These apes were raised in a social group by human caretakers who spoke to them as they would to a child. Topics of conversation were varied, spontaneous, and at the discretion of the caretaker. They included descriptions of the chimpanzee's behavior, characterizations of the chimpanzee's desires, descriptions of what was to happen next, simple requests of the chimpanzee, expression of pleasure and displeasure with the chimpanzee's actions, stories, etc.

Unlike the chimpanzees who were required to produce lexical symbols (Sherman, Austin, and Lana) prior to comprehending their meaning or the communicative process of reference (Savage-Rumbaugh, 1986), these four apes (Kanzi, Mulika, Panbanisha, and Panzee) began to use lexigrams for the purpose of communicating with no specific training and no arbitrary extrinsic rewards. Also unlike the earlier subjects, these four apes demonstrated comprehension of spoken English words, again without explicit training or reward. Most important, for the present theory, all four apes demonstrated receptive competencies that greatly exceeded and preceded their productive competencies (Brakke & Savage-Rumbaugh, 1989). At 69 months of age, formal tests showed that Kanzi comprehended 150 English words. That is, whenever he heard one of these words, he could select either the photograph or the lexigram that corresponded to it. However, it was not until Kanzi made evident the importance of comprehension as a driving force in language acquisition that we became aware that such data should be collected from the other apes prior to the onset of productive competence. This was first done with Kanzi's younger sister Mulika. Formal tests of Mulika began at 2.5 years of age and revealed that she comprehended 70 spoken English words, even though she was regularly using only symbols. Appendix 22.1 illustrates the hypothesized steps of symbol acquisition for Kanzi and Mulika as well as for Panbanisha and Panzee. Appendix 22.2 depicts all of the actual uses of the words "bubbles" for Panbanisha and Panzee as this word passed through the stages outlined in Appendix 22.1.

In contrast with the dolphin Ake, the input mode directed to these four apes (lexigrams and spoken English) could at least be partially imitated, that is, the apes could easily point to the lexigrams, though the ape vocal tract made it impossible for them to produce human speech. Also unlike the dolphins, the input directed to the apes functioned to make their world predictable. They heard things like "Let's go to the A-frame." "We will visit Matata." "We are going to take our bath now," etc. The range and variety of utterances directed to these apes on a daily basis approximated the range and variety of utterance addressed to a 2-3 year old child each day (Savage-Rumbaugh, in press). These apes, like children, were intrinsically motivated to try to understand the linguistic input directed to them because it provided valuable information about their social and physical environment. It told them how the caretaker felt about them, what they were going to do next, and what others around them were doing. When the chimpanzees did not understand a particular communication, they were either shown what to do, or the action was carried out for them. For example, if the chimpanzee did not respond to a request such as "Would you please wash with soap?" the soap was picked up and put in their hand and they were shown what to do with it. When the communication was about a place or activity that they could not understand, because they did not know a particular

22. Language learnability in man, ape, and dolphin

word or symbol, the caretaker often found a picture of what he or she was talking about and used the photo to clarify the topic.

Many of the communications directed to these four apes were ones that they were motivated to use in turn as a means of gaining control over the behaviors of others. Consequently, when they, like the human child, achieved sufficient motor and neuronal control, they also inverted the paradigm and became spontaneous producers of lexical symbols. They began to use the keyboard with no training, no prodding, and no extrinsic reward. They decided, for example, that they wanted a certain food, that they wanted to play a certain game, or that they wanted to go to a particular place, and they began to communicate these desires by pointing at symbols. As with young children, they sometimes overgeneralized or undergeneralized words, but they did not go through periods of incorrect symbol use, as had previous subjects (Savage-Rumbaugh, 1986). Additionally, they rarely confused symbols that they chose to use, although their usage was often somewhat idiosyncratic. For example, Panbanisha used "goodbye" to indicate that she wanted to leave the person she was with and go to someone else, as opposed to the conventional salutation on departure (for this she employed a particular vocalization.) She also used "tree" as a verb to connote that she wanted to climb on any object or person (derived from the fact that the common activity in trees was that of climbing.) Other chimpanzees similarly formed idiosyncratic usages, some of which overlapped while others did not. Idiosyncratic uses differed from errors in that the apes intended to use the lexigram they selected. They made this evident by resisting suggestions to the contrary, and by continuing to use the lexigram for its idiosyncratic referent in many different contexts. Errors were treated quite differently by them. If they selected the wrong lexigram by mistake, they readily changed to the correct lexigram when it was shown to them.

SUMMARY

The essential condition for language acquisition can readily and easily be understood as the presence of a model who talks to the learner. To the extent that what the model says makes the immediate events within the world more predictable, there will arise an intrinsic drive to understand the model's language behavior. To the extent that the model provides the potential to learn things that can be useful in terms of not just predicting events, but controlling them, then the learner will also spontaneously begin to produce symbols, given that there is an output mode sufficiently similar to that of the model to permit this to happen. The model must, of course, respond and allow the child, ape, or other sentient party to take charge of some things and begin to make decisions. This caveat regarding motivational variables applies most poignantly to apes, dolphins, and other creatures larger and more powerful than we, because, as *Homo sapiens* we are not accustomed to giving animals that might be capable of dominating us the right to decide our activities.

The strong-L stance thus predicts that linguistic reference will be acquired and spontaneous symbol production will follow if (a) the language input conditions are appropriate, (b) there exists a compatible output mode, and (c) the learner is capable of high-level imitation and cause-effect hypothesis formation on the basis of single-trial observational input.

ACKNOWLEDGMENT

The work described in this chapter and its preparation were supported by National Institutes of Health Grant NICHD-06016, which supports the Language Research Center, cooperatively operated by Georgia State University and the Yerkes Regional Primate Research Center of Emory University. Research is also supported in part by RR-00165 to the Yerkes Regional Primate Research Center of Emory University.

REFERENCES

Brakke, K. & Savage-Rumbaugh, E. S. (1989). Speech comprehension in an infant bonobo (*Pan paniscus*) and chimpanzee (*Pan troglodytes*). Paper presented at 5th annual meeting of Language Origins Society, Austin TX.

Bever, T., G., Carroll, J. M., & Miller, L. A. (1984). *Talking Minds: Study of Language in Cognitive Sciences*. Cambridge, MA: MIT Press.

Bruner, J. S. (1974/1975). From communication to language-A psychological perspective. *Cognition*, 3, 255-287.

Chomsky, N. (1988). *Language and problems of knowledge: Manaugua Lectures*. Cambridge, MA: MIT Press.

Clark, E. (1983). Meanings and concepts. In P. H. Mussen (Ed.), *Carmichael's manual of child psychology, Volume 3: Cognitive development*, J. H. Flavell & E. M. Markman, (Eds.) (pp. 787- 840). New York: Wiley.

22. Language learnability in man, ape, and dolphin

Gaulker, S. (1990). How to learn language like a chimpanzee. *Philosophical Psychology*, 3, 31-53.

Gouzoules, S., Gouzoules, H., & Marler, P. (1984). Rhesus monkey (*Macaca mulatta*) screams: Representational signalling in recruitment of agonistic aid. *Animal Behavior*, 23, 182-193.

Greenfield, P. M. & Savage-Rumbaugh, E. S. (1991). Imitation, grammatical development, and invention of protogrammar by an ape. In N. Krasnagor, D. M. Rumbaugh, M. Studdert-Kennedy, & D. Scheifelbusch (Eds.), *Biological and behavioral determinants of language development* (pp. 235-258). Hillsdale, NJ: Lawrence Erlbaum Associates.

Greenfield, P. M. & Smith, H. (1976). *Structure of communication in early language development.* New York: Academic Press.

Herman, L. (1987). Receptive competencies of language trained animals. In J. S. Rosenblatt, C. Beer, M.-C. Busnel, & P. J. B. Slater (Eds.), *Advances in study of behavior* (Vol. 17, pp. 1-60). Petaluma, CA: Academic Press.

Herman, L. M. (1986). Cognition and language competencies of bottlenosed dolphins. In R. J. Schusterman, J. Thomas, & F. Wood (Eds.), *Dolphin cognition and behavior: A comparative approach* (pp. 221-252). Hillsdale, NJ: Lawrence Erlbaum Associates.

Lock, A. (1980). *Guided reinvention of language.* London: Academic Press.

Lucariello, J., Kyratzis, A., & Engel, S. (1986). Event representations, context, and language. In K. Nelson (Ed.), *Event knowledge: Structure and function in development.* Hillsdale, NJ: Lawrence Erlbaum Associates.

Savage-Rumbaugh, E. S. (1984). Verbal behavior at a procedural level in chimpanzee. *Journal of the Experimental Analysis of Behavior*, 41, 223-250.

Savage-Rumbaugh, E. S. (1986). *Ape language: From conditioned response to symbol.* New York: Columbia University Press.

Savage-Rumbaugh, E. S. (1988). A new look at ape language: Comprehension of vocal speech and syntax. In D. Leger (Ed.), *Comparative perspectives in modern psychology. Nebraska Symposium on Motivation, 1987* (vol. 35, pp. 201-256). Lincoln, NE: University of Nebraska Press.

Savage-Rumbaugh, E. S. (1990). Language as a cause-effect communication system. *Philosophical Psychology*, 3, 55-76.

Savage-Rumbaugh, E. S., Murphy, J., Sevcik, R. A., Williams, S. & Rumbaugh, D. M. (in press). Language comprehension in ape and child. Society for Research in Child Development Monograph Series.

Savage-Rumbaugh, E. S., Sevcik, R. A,, & Brakke, K. E. (1991). Symbols: Their communicative use, combination, and comprehension by bonobos *(Pan paniscus)*. In L. P. Lipsitt & C. Rovee-Collier (Eds.), *Advances in infancy research*, 7, Norwood, NJ: Ablex.

Savage-Rumbaugh, E. S., Pate, J. L., Smith, S. T., & Rosenbaum, S. (1983). Can a chimpanzee make a statement? *Journal of Experimental Psychology: General*, 112, 457-492.

Savage-Rumbaugh, E. S., McDonald, E., Sevcik, R. A., Hopkins, W. D., & Rubert, E. (1986). Spontaneous symbol acquisition and communicative use by pygmy chimpanzees *(Pan paniscus)*. *Journal of Experimental Psychology: General*, 112, 211-235.

Schusterman, R. & Krieger, K. (1984). California sea lions are capable of semantic comprehension. *Psychological Record*, 34, 3-23.

Seyfarth, R. M., & Cheney, D. L. (1982). How monkeys see world: A review of recent research on East African vervet monkeys. In C. T. Snowdon, C. H. Brown, & M. R. Peterson (Eds.), *Primate Communication* (pp. 239-252). Cambridge: Cambridge University Press.

Sidman, M. (1986). Functional analysis of emergent verbal classes. In T. Thompson & M. D. Zeiler (Eds.), *Analysis and integration of behavioral units* (pp. 213-245). Hillsdale, NJ: Lawrence Erlbaum Associates.

Skinner, B. F. (1957). *Verbal behavior.* New York: Appleton-Century-Crofts.

22. Language learnability in man, ape, and dolphin

Snowdon, C. (1988). A comparative approach to vocal communication. In D. Leger (Ed.), *Comparative perspectives in modern psychology. Nebraska Symposium on Motivation, 1987* (vol. 35, pp. 145-200). Lincoln, NE: University of Nebraska Press.

Strawson, P. F. (1950/1971). On referring. In P. F. Strawson, *Logico linguistic papers*. London: Methuen.

APPENDIX 22.1
DEVELOPMENT OF COMMUNICATIVE COMPETENCE WITH THE SYMBOL "BUBBLES"

1. Imitative Touching

Panbanisha   Panzee

13 Months 6 Days   14 Months 6 Days

2. Displays comprehension of relationship between spoken word and object, or symbol and object.

Panbanisha   Panzee

13 Months 6 Days   19 Months 29 Days

(Word, symbol, and object)   (Symbol and object)

3. Uses communicative request in context of blowing bubbles and after teacher has used symbol. Use is essentially that of getting the teacher to continue to blow bubbles.

Panbanisha   Panzee

17 Months 5 Days   20 Months 21 Days

4. Uses communicative request after teacher has mentioned bubbles, but is not already engaged in the routine to blowing bubbles.

Panbanisha   Panzee

17 Months 2 Days

5. Uses communicative request spontaneously out of context. The teacher has no bubbles out and has not mentioned bubbles.

Panbanisha   Panzee

22. Language learnability in man, ape, and dolphin

17 Months 5 Days	29 Months 21 Days

6. Uses symbol to comment on the object of actions of another, rather than to request something.

Panbanisha	Panzee
17 Months 10 Days	

7. Uses communicative request to alter planned activity.

Panbanisha	Panzee
17 Months 10 Days (possibly)	30 Months 27 Days

8. Uses comment to indicate agreement with teacher, after teacher has commented.

Panbanisha	Panzee
20 Months	30 Months 3 Days

9. Uses comment for types of bubbles other than those typically referred.

Panbanisha	Panzee
20 Months 24 Days	

APPENDIX 22.2
PANBANISHA
DEVELOPMENTAL HISTORY OF THE USAGE OF "BUBBLES"

13 Months 29 Days (01/15/87) During a game of bubbles the teacher draws Panbanisha's attention to the bubble lexigram. Panbanisha approaches and tries to say "bubbles" after the teacher, however she accidentally touches the lexigram "oil" which is located next to bubbles. The teacher asks "Do you want oil or bubbles?" and Panbanisha responds by rushing over to the bubble jar and mouthing it.

Comment: Panbanisha is imitating the teacher, and saying "bubbles" as part of what is done during the bubble blowing routine. At this early age imitation often occurred. However, Panbanisha also shows comprehension of the spoken word by mouthing the bubble jar after she hears the teacher mention bubbles.

16 Months 30 days (05/18/87) Panzee (the common chimpanzee coreared with Panbanisha) is playing with the keyboard, touching lexigrams that interest her. Panzee does not appear to be attempting to communicate as she activates the symbols "Flatrock" and "bubbles." However, her teacher decides to treat it as a communication and replies that they cannot go to Flatrock, but they could play with bubbles. Panzee makes no response. However, Panbanisha observes this exchange, then goes to the keyboard, says "bubbles," and looks toward Panzee's teacher. The teacher interprets this as a response to her question and gets out some bubbles and plays with bubbles with both chimpanzees.

Comment: The bubbles routine is not yet in progress and bubbles are not present, but Panbanisha now uses "bubbles" to initiate the routine. She does not initiate it completely on her own yet, but only after the teacher has already suggested the activity.

17 Months 2 Days (05/19/87) Panbanisha and the teacher are seated in front of the keyboard playing with toys. The teacher is showing Panbanisha some new lexigrams. They have not been talking about bubbles. Panbanisha all at once carefully points to bubbles and looks at the teacher. The teacher interprets this as a request and looks in the backpack where she finds some bubbles for Panbanisha. The teacher notes that this is the first time she has seen Panbanisha ask for bubbles.

Comment: Again the bubble blowing routine is not in progress, however, now the teacher has not previously mentioned bubbles. Panbanisha seems able to think of this on her own and to encode the request symbolically.

17 Months 5 Days (05/21/87) Panbanisha and the teacher are getting ready to take a bath when Panbanisha spontaneously asks for bubbles. There are no

22. Language learnability in man, ape, and dolphin

bubbles present. The teacher agrees that they can play with the bubbles and begins looking through the backpack to find some bubbles. While the teacher is looking, Panbanisha comments bubbles twice, remarking on the target of the teacher's search.

Comment: Panbanisha again spontaneously requests to play with bubbles even though they are not present and the teacher has not initiated the routine. Additionally, she comments on the target of the teacher's search even though the bubbles are not visible.

17 Months 5 Days (05/21/87) The teacher is blowing bubbles, then stops for a little bit and looks at something else. Panbanisha says "bubbles" to ask him to continue.

Comment: This is the first time Panbanisha has used "bubbles" to ask that a routine, which is in progress, continue.

17 Months 9 Days (05/25/87) The teacher is outdoors in the woods with Panbanisha. They are walking along the trail when Panbanisha stops and asks to play with bubbles. There are no bubbles in the backpack, so she is told that maybe she can do so later when they go back inside.

Comment: This is the first time Panbanisha has used the bubbles lexigram outdoors. Generally, though not always, bubbles has been an indoor game.

17 Months 10 Days (05/26/87) Panbanisha is again walking with the teacher out in the woods. They are traveling through a dense scrubby area toward the raisin site. It is necessary that they walk on a footbridge here because of the wet ground. Panbanisha does not want to go this way and keeps heading back toward the lab. The teacher insists they continue on to raisins but Panbanisha refuses, then says "bubbles" and looks back toward the lab. The teacher interprets this an expression of why Panbanisha wants to go back to the lab. She is told that they need to continue on now, but that they can play with bubbles when they return.

Comment: Panbanisha now uses "bubbles" to try to change the planned activity from one she does not like to one that she would rather do and one that would return her to the lab.

Savage-Rumbaugh

17 Months 15-21 Days Panbanisha asks for bubbles on five occasions as she and the teacher are working with other things. Each time she seems to enjoy playing with them very much. Each of these requests is spontaneous and is not preceded by the teacher showing or talking about the bubbles. Panbanisha seems very interested in her ability to bring about the "playing with the bubbles" routine. After these 6 days, she seems to lose interest in bubbles and this word does not occur again for two months.

Comment: This does not mean that Panbanisha does not play with bubbles for 2 months, just that the word does not occur again in the daily notes for 2 months.

20 Months (08/17/87) The teacher is getting ready to go outdoors. Panbanisha wants to stay inside and play. She asks for "bubbles" and then for "balloons." These are two things that are usually played with indoors. The teacher refuses the request and tells Panbanisha that they are going to go on outdoors now anyway.

Comment: Again Panbanisha used "bubbles" to attempt to get the teacher to do something different than what had been announced.

20 Months (08/17/87) As the teacher is looking through a cabinet, she comes across some bubbles and comments on this. Panbanisha agrees, commenting bubbles herself. Panbanisha does not attempt to play with the bubbles, nor indicate that she wants to by reaching out for them.

Comment: This is the first usage of a comment in a situation that clearly reveals that Panbanisha does not have an interest in obtaining the bubbles.

20 Months 14 Days (08/31/87) Panbanisha is touching different words on the keyboard, seemingly practicing the activation of ones that she knows. She includes "bubbles" during this self-initiated practice session.

20 Months 24 Days (09/10/87) Panbanisha is playing with the dogs outside the lab. She stops and activates the "bubbles" symbol and looks at the teacher. The teacher interprets this as a request to play with bubbles while also playing with the dogs. This is not something that Panbanisha has done before but something she appears to have thought of on her own. The teacher agrees and goes to the

22. Language learnability in man, ape, and dolphin

lab and retrieves some bubbles. Panbanisha them plays happily with the dogs and the bubbles for over half and hour.

20 Months 28 Days (09/14/87) Panbanisha asks the teacher for some bubbles. The teacher has a bin of toys and bubbles are in this bin. The teacher gives Panbanisha the bubbles and she plays happily.

21 Months 5 Days (09/23/87) Panbanisha stares at her bath water as it is foaming up very high in the sink, as the teacher has inadvertently poured in a lot of soap. It has made a very tall pile of bubbles, not the kind we blow from the jar, but small foamy bubbles. Panbanisha looks at this large pile of soapy foam and comments "bubbles."

14 Months 6 Days (02/05/87) Panzee is watching as the teacher blows bubbles. The teacher draws Panzee's attention to the lexigram on the keyboard and says "bubbles" at the keyboard several times. Panzee watches, then touches the bubbles lexigram also.

Comment: This usage is an imitation of the teacher's behavior. At this age, both Panzee and Panbanisha often pointed to any lexigram that the teacher drew their attention to, as if they enjoyed imitating what we said. Such imitation was always immediate and spontaneous. They touched the lexigram right after the teacher with no urging to do. In the same manner, they wanted to touch almost any object that the teacher touched during this period. By about 16 months this interest had dropped out. In its place appeared an interest in self-directed pointing. Both chimps would take the keyboard and point to a number of lexigrams in sequence that they knew. They made no attempt to communicate during this time, but simply pointed to different lexigrams for the interest in so doing. If the teacher attempted to point also, they would move away. Panzee's early imitation differs from Panbanisha in that she shows no evidence of making a connection between the word, the lexigram, and the object at this stage.

14 Months 14 Days (02/13/87) Panzee is watching as the teacher blows bubbles. The teacher holds up the bubbles symbol on a plaques and points to it. Panzee watches and points to it after the teacher, and then touches the tool used to blow bubbles.

Savage-Rumbaugh

Comment: Panzee here seems to be imitating for the sheer joy of doing so. Panzee also begins to give some evidence of realizing that there is a correspondence between the symbol and the object. However, the bubbles symbol is not on the keyboard, but singled out by being placed on a plaque.

17 Months 18 Days (05/18/87) Panzee is exploring sounds that symbols make as she touches the keyboard. One of the symbols that she touches is bubbles.

18 Months 28 Days (05/28/87) Panzee keeps trying to take the jar of bubbles because she wants to play with them. The teacher places her finger on the symbol and helps her say bubbles.

21 Months 29 Days (09/26/87) Panzee and the teacher are playing with bubbles when the teacher comments bubbles at the keyboard. Panzee then places her lips on the bubbles lexigram.

Comment: This is reminiscent of the earlier imitation, but differs in that Panzee uses her mouth, something she never did earlier while engaging in simple imitation.

21 Months 26 Days (09/26/87) Panzee again seems to be exploring the keyboard, touching a number of symbols, but not attempting to communicate. One of these symbol is bubbles.

22 Months 11 Days (10/11/87) The teacher is blowing bubbles and asks Panzee if she can name bubbles. Panzee does not respond. The teacher points to the bubbles lexigram and Panzee imitates, saying bubbles.

22 Months 21 Days (10/11/87) Panzee and the teacher are playing with bubbles and the teacher has commented bubbles at the keyboard. Panzee then also touches the bubbles lexigram and then points to the teacher's mouth, wanting her to blow more bubbles.

Comment: This is Panzee's first truly communicative usage of the bubbles lexigram. While it was imitative in the sense that the teacher had said "bubbles" earlier, this imitation was deferred but contrast with the earlier imitation. Imitation now does not occur until Panzee wants to communicate something about bubbles. Earlier, it was simply driven by the teacher's touching behavior.

22. Language learnability in man, ape, and dolphin

23 Months 18 Days (11/18/87) The teacher and Panzee are blowing bubbles. The teacher says bubbles then asks Panzee if she can say this also. Panzee repeats bubbles after the teacher.

Comment: The teacher here begins to urge Panzee to say bubbles. Teachers are asked not to use this method as an general acquisition strategy. When it does occur it is generally directed toward Panzee, who seems, at this point by contrast with her age-mate Panbanisha, somewhat slow. It is difficult for the teachers not to try to press Panzee at least a little.

27 Months 28 Days (03/28/88) The teacher is blowing bubbles with bubble gum and commented "bubbles" as she does so. Each time one pops Panzee wants to see her do this again and points to her mouth to get her to do so. After several times, Panzee spontaneously touches the "bubble" lexigram to ask the teacher to blow another bubble.

Comment: Again Panzee uses bubbles in a communicative format to request repetition of an action on the part of the teacher. Again her usage reflects deferred imitation.

27 Months 29 Days (03/29/88) The teacher tells Panzee she is going to blow a bubbles. Panzee says "bubble" after the teacher to indicates that she agrees with this idea, then waits and watches as the teacher does so.

29 Months 21 Days (05/21/88) One teacher playing with Panbanisha blows bubbles toward Panzee and her teacher. Panzee's teacher had commented on this activity several minutes earlier. She now picks up some bubbles and blows them for Panzee and then asks "What are we playing with?" Panzee touches the "bubbles" lexigram in reply.

Comment: For the first time Panzee begins to show evidence that she comprehends the relationship between the spoken word and the lexigram. However, she may have seen Panbanisha's teacher say bubbles and be engaging in deferred imitation that appears to coincide with the teacher's utterance.

29 Months 21 Days (05/21/88) Panzee and her teacher are visiting various rooms in the laboratory. (They have just traveled to the observation room where others are working on data and observing.) Panzee spontaneously says "bubbles." Her teacher agrees and looks around the observation room but finds no bubbles.

Comment: Here for the first time, Panzee uses bubbles out of context. The teacher has not previously said "bubbles," nor have they been playing with bubbles. Bubbles is not a toy that is generally found in, or played with in, the observation room. Panzee thus, after demonstrating comprehension just a few days earlier, now exhibits her first context-free nonimitative usage.

29 Months 22 Days (05/22/88) Panzee is leaning out of her chair attempting to play with Panbanisha who is nearby. Her teacher tries to distract her from playing with Panbanisha by asking "Why don't you play with the bubbles?" In response to the question, Panzee turns and activates the bubbles lexigram, indicating that she understands something about what the teacher has said. (The teacher did not activate the lexigram herself, she spoke the word.)

30 months 3 Days (06/03/88) The teacher is again blowing bubble gum bubbles and Panzee is attempting to catch them before they pop. The teacher is using the bubble lexigram to comment on this activity. Later after the teacher stops, Panzee says "bubble surprise" and approaches the teacher and touches and looks closely at her mouth, waiting for her to blow bubbles again.

30 Months 10 Days (06/10/88) The teacher is blowing bubbles with bubble gum, but has not commented on the activity. When she stops Panzee says bubble to ask her to start the activity once again. She wants the teacher to blow bubbles so that she can pop them.

30 Months 10 Days (06/10/88) A bit later Panzee stops trying to pop the bubbles and just watches the teacher blow them. While she is watching the teacher comments that she is going to blow a bubble. Panzee responds to the teacher's remark by saying bubbles, apparently to indicate her agreement that the teacher do so.

Comment: Panzee now, for the first time, uses bubbles to comment on the activities of another rather than to request something.

30 Months 27 Day (06/27/88) Panzee spontaneously comments "Yes." The teacher asks her "Yes. What?" and Panzee answers "Yes bubbles." The teacher

22. Language learnability in man, ape, and dolphin

tells her that they cannot play with bubbles right now, but perhaps will get some later.

31 Months 29 Days (07/29/88) There is a variety of objects lying around on the floor and Panzee is ask to retrieve the bubbles (the bubble bottle is among those objects.) She is able to do so without help.

32 Months 24 Days (08/24/88) The teacher is again blowing bubbles with bubble gum and commenting to Panzee on this activity. This time the teacher calls these bubbles "surprise bubbles," following Panzee's earlier usage. (The word surprise is often used to refer to novel foods for which we have no name; thus its usage here reflects the fact that bubble gum bubbles are eaten while regular bubbles or "soap bubbles" are not.) Five minutes later, after another activity has intervened, Panzee asks the teacher to reinstate the bubble game by saying "bubbles" and looking closely at the teacher's mouth.

Comment: Panzee reinitiates a routine, but sometime after it has stopped and while the teacher has already gone on to something else.

32 Months 31 Days (08/31/88) Panzee starts to grab the bubbles out of a bin of play toys without asking. She is told not to grab, but rather to ask. She then uses the keyboard to say bubbles. To determine how well Panzee understands the word, the teacher then lays out 5 photos of objects in front of Panzee and asks her if she can select the picture of bubbles. Panzee does so.

Comment: The teacher is now confident enough of Panzee's comprehension of bubbles to insist that she use it to communicate when she is otherwise engaged in an activity. The teachers are asked not to require that the chimpanzees name things until they are certain that they understand the word.

34 Months 13 Days (10/13/88) Panzee is near the NASA building when she begins to fuss. The teacher asks her what is wrong and she answers "bubbles".

34 Months 22 Days (10/22/88) Panzee is riding around in the car looking at various things when she spontaneously says "bubbles." The teacher, who interprets this as a request for bubbles, looks in the backpack and finds none, then takes Panzee back to the group room and gets some bubbles.

Savage-Rumbaugh

35 Months 7 Days (11/07/88) The teacher is testing Panzee and she is playing with toys between trials. The teacher (not part of the test) then asks Panzee if she can go get some bubbles as there are none present in her toy bin. Panzee goes to the adjacent room and points to the bubbles, then carries them back.

Comment: For the first time Panzee is able to respond to request for bubbles when they are not present, though, had the teacher requested this sooner, Panzee might have been able to do so sooner.

AUTHOR INDEX

Abrahamsen, A. 73, 75
Alexander, R.D. 142
Allard, F. 316
Allen, M. 293
Altmann S. A. 31
Amundin, M. 316
Anderson, J. R. 12, 37, 38
Annett, M. 293
Arnold, M. 101
Asano, T. 347
Atkinson, R. C. 392
Au, W. W. L. 162
Awbrey, F. 54
Axelrod, R. 121
Baptista, L. F. 125, 140, 222
Barr, S. E. 295
Barrett, K. 101, 103, 312
Bartecki, U. 186
Bastard, V. 276
Bates, E. 31, 98, 412
Batteau, D. W. 154, 155
Battison, R. 317
Bauers, K. 179
Baylis, J. R. 415
Beaton, A. 293
Bechtel, W. 4, 66, 73, 75, 76
Beckwith, R. 102, 103, 105
Beecher, M. D. 178, 290, 294, 319
Begg, I. 38, 405
Bellugi, U. 130, 317, 410
Benigni, L. 98
Bennett, J. 144
Benton, A. L. 276
Berlucchi, G. 319
Berntson, G. G. 239
Berryman, R. 249

Bever, T. 8, 140, 184, 221, 280, 288, 289, 316, 319, 329, 406, 457
Bloom, L. 101, 102, 103, 104, 105, 385, 414
Blough, P. M. 305
Blum, J. S. 252, 367, 422
Blumenthal, A. 99
Blumstein, S. E. 237
Bolser, L. A. 294, 305
Bonvillian, J. 316, 317
Borys, R. 58
Bower, G.H. 90
Bowers, D. 297, 304
Bowlby, J. 125
Boyd, R. 213
Boysen, S. 35, 36, 239, 406
Bradford, S. A. 232
Bradshaw, G. L. 86, 93, 314, 316, 319, 385, 422
Braine, M. D. S. 7, 14
Brakke, K. 403, 430, 467, 468
Brentano, F. 76
Bretherton, I. 31, 98
Brizzolara, D. 319
Brooks, R. 317
Brown, A. L. 31, 33, 166, 366, 418, 419
Brownson, R. H. 316
Bruner, J. S. 429, 461
Bryden, M. M. 316, 404
Bullock, T. H. 131
Burghardt, G. M. 50
Burns, J. W. 319
Cable, C. 140
Caldwell, D. 131, 132, 135, 153, 154, 155, 319, 404, 417
Camaioni, L. 98

Campanella, D. 317
Campbell, C. B. G. 7, 13
Campos, J. 101
Canaday, R. A. 123
Cantor, G. W. 13
Capatides, J. 102, 103, 107
Carder, D. A. 160
Carmon, A. 276, 316
Carpenter, P. A. 28
Carr, D. B. 409, 444
Carroll, J. M. 457
Carter, D. E. 249, 260
Carterette, E. C. 278
Case, R. 228
Cash, C. 295
Catania, A. C. 252
Chedru, F. 276
Cheney D. L. 31, 54, 55, 117, 130, 141, 144, 181, 186, 187, 196, 197, 198, 200, 203, 204, 205, 206, 208, 210, 211, 213, 214, 221, 458
Chiarello, R. J. 288
Chomsky, N. 31, 46, 86, 457
Christopoulou, C. 316
Church, R. M. 15, 16, 17
Churchland, P. S. 5
Clark, E. 360, 414, 459
Clarke, R. 316
Cleeremans, A. 74
Cleveland, J. 57, 178, 179, 180, 182, 185, 188
Colasante, C. 315
Cole, M. 103, 125
Colombo, M. 421
Connor, R. C. 133
Cook, M. 48, 187, 392, 398, 422
Corballis, M. C. 318
Cosmides, L. 120, 122
Cosnides, R. 278
Costa, L. 319
Cowey, A. 294

Cranford, T. W. 316
Culver, C. 103
Cumming, W. W. 249
D'Amato, M. R. 367, 398, 421, 423
Dalheim, M. 54
Damasio, A. 317
Danto, A. 97
Darwin, C. 122
Dasser, V. 115
Davis, H. 232, 330, 335, 336
Dawson, W. W. 314
Day, R. H. 319
Deacon, T. W. 118, 123
Dee, H. L. 319
Delius, J. 239, 422, 426
Dennett, D. 97
Descartes, R. 66, 67, 74
Deutsch, D. 127
Diehl, R. L. 181
Dittus, W. P. J. 187
Dixon, L. S. 256, 261
Dore, J. 14, 312
Dorsky, N. P. 13
Dreher, J. J. 153, 157
Dufty, A. 183, 188
Eaton, R. L. 130
Edhouse, W. V. 304
Edwards, C. Q. 304
Efron, R. 276
Eimas, P. 203
Elawson, A. B. 188
Ellis, H. D. 316
Elman, J. 78
Elsner, R. 317
Emmerich, D. J. 278
Engel, S. 462
Entwisle, D. R. 444
Ervin, S. M. 414
Essock, S. M. 227
Evans W. E. 153, 155, 200
Ewing, G. 15, 17
Fagan, J. F. 373

Fairweather, H. 319
Fauconnier, G. 97
von Fersen, L. 239
Ficken, M. S. 178, 184
Fiorelli, P. 130, 267
Florian, V. A. 317
Fodor, J. 67, 74, 75, 76, 97, 117, 118
Ford, J. 54, 57
Forestell, P. 18, 30, 54, 55, 224, 385, 398, 405, 406, 407
Fouts, R. S. 30
Fragaszy, D. M. 214
Franklin, M. 14
Frasure, N. E. 444
French, J. A. 178
Friedman, M. P. 278, 317
von Frisch, K. 51
Funk, M. 223
Galef, B. G. 414, 418
Gallistel, C. R. 336
Garcia, J. 117
Garcia-Merita, M. L. 318
Gardner, B. T. 28, 30, 54, 117, 127, 221, 224, 406
Garrett, M. 368
Gauker, C. 77, 459
Gazzaniga, M. S. 316
Geffen, G. 316
Gelman, R. 336
Geschwind, N. 293, 316
Gildea P.M. 28
Gill, T. V. 10, 227
Gish, S. 130, 267
Gisiner, R. 17, 223, 224, 227, 233, 235, 249, 254, 255, 257, 267, 269, 429, 430
Glass, C. 319
Gleitman, H. 409
Gluck, M. A. 90
Glucksberg, S. 429
Goble, W. 317

Goldberg, E. 319
Goldsmith, H. 102
Goodall, J. 115
Gordon, H. W. 276, 288, 367, 421, 422
Gordon, M. C. 276
Gory, J. D. 314, 385, 391, 398, 422
Gould, J. 51, 119
Gouzoules, H. 54, 458
Granier-Deferre, C. 225, 226, 238
Grant, T. S. 421
Gray, J. 278
Green, D. M. 139, 178, 212, 278, 294
Greenbaum, S. 28
Greenfield, P. M. 229, 462, 463
Grice, H. P. 210
Griffin, D. R. 144, 240
Gunderson, V. M. 373
Gyger, M. 183, 188, 210
Hafitz, J. 103
Hailman, J. P. 184
Halperin, S. 143, 276
Hamers, J. F. 316
Hamilton, C. R. 116, 294
Hamm, A. 316
Hanggi, E. B. 227
Hannay, H. 295, 319
Hansen, E. W. 204
Harishanu, E. 316
Harley, H. E. 184, 416, 460
Harris, L. J. 294
Hatschek, R. 317
Hauser, M. D. 200
Hayes, C. 115, 129, 186
Healey, J. M. 293
Hearst, E. 224
Heffner H. 290, 319
Hegel, M. 333
Heider, F. 99
Heilman, K. 297, 299, 304, 317
Helweg, D. A. 184, 460

Hennessy, D. 200
Herman L. M. 7, 9, 18, 30, 54, 55, 57, 76, 77, 78, 79, 89, 124, 130, 131, 135, 154, 222, 223, 224, 227, 235, 238, 251, 253, 267, 270, 290, 311, 312, 313, 314, 315, 316, 319, 367, 385, 386, 387, 391, 398, 404, 405, 406, 407, 408, 409, 410, 411, 415, 416, 418, 419, 421, 422, 425, 427, 429, 430, 431, 443, 444, 449, 452, 461, 463, 464
Herrnstein, R. 140
Hewes, G.W. 319
Heymann, E. W. 186
Hillyard, S. A. 316
Hinton, G. E. 73, 77
Hintzman, D. L. 91
Hoban, E. 385, 409
Hockett, C. F. 31, 32, 197
Hodos, W. 7
Hodun, A. 181
Hoemann, H. W. 317
Hogan, D. E. 304
Holder, M. 312
Holmes, J. M. 317
Honig, W. K. 367
Hood, L. 414
Hopkins, W. 240, 294, 295, 299, 301, 319, 329, 331, 337, 380, 386, 460
House, B. J. 366, 376, 379
Hovancik, J. R, Gory, J. D. 314, 385, 422
Hoyningen-Hüne, P. 115
Hulse, S. H. 13
Humphrey, N.K. 121
Hunter, G. A. 314, 367, 422
Hynd, G. W. 299
Ingram, D. 406
Irvine, A. B. 131
Ison, J. R. 289

Jacobs, M. S. 314, 317
Jason, G. W. 294
Jenkins, H. M. 167
Jerison, H. J. 412
Jitsumori, M. 304, 392, 398
Joch, E. 232
Johansson, G. 410
Johnson-Laird, P. 97, 102, 106, 367, 368
Jones, M. 58
Juno, C. 222
Jusczyk, P. 203
Just, M. A. 28
Kamil, A. C. 115, 116, 221, 226
Kaplan, L. 414
Karakashian, S. J. 183, 210
Kassin, S. M. 13
Kawai, M. 196
Kendrick, D.G. 386
Kenney, D. 317
Kihlstrom, J. F. 142, 144
Kimura, D. 288, 316
King, A. P. 222
Kinsbourne, M. 297
Kirshner, H. A. 317
Klima, E. S. 130
Kluender, K. R. 181
Kodratoff, Y. 225, 226, 238
Koelling, R. A. 117
Kohler, W. 38
Kojima, T. 347
Kozak, F. A. 222, 223, 230
Krauss, R. 315, 429
Krebs, J. R. 116, 123
Krieger, K. 89, 224, 250, 252, 254, 257, 270, 463
Kritzler, H. 134
Kroodsma, D. E. 123, 178
Kuczaj, S. 55, 58, 409, 427, 444
Kuhl, P.K. 118, 139
Kuhn, T. S. 26
Kulics, A. T. 278

Kummer, H. 115
Kyratzis, A. 462
La Breche, T. 317
Lackner, J. R. 276
Ladygina, T. F. 317
de Laguna, G. 98, 99
Lahey, M. 101
Lakatos, I. 3, 4
Lakoff, G. 10, 11
Lamb, M. 101
Lambert, W. E. 316
Lane, H. 316, 317, 387
Lashley, K. S. 408
Lavy, S. 316
Lawson, J. 30, 55, 76, 124, 136, 224, 460
Le Doux, J. E. 316
Leech, G. 28
Leger, D. 54
Lein, M. N. 178
Leonard, L. B. 414
Levine, L. 102, 106, 107
Levitsky, W. 316
Levy, J. 293, 316
Lewis, S. 13
Lewontin, R. C. 119
Lieberman, P. 48, 118, 119, 129, 237
Liederman, J. 293
Lightbown, P. 414
Lillehei, R. A. 178
Lilly, J. C. 154, 155
Limber, J. 31
Lindauer, M. 51, 54
Lindblom, B. 294, 319
Lindburg, D. G. 196
Lock, A. 461
Loveland, D. H. 140
Lowinger, E. 316
Lucariello, J. 462
Lutes-Driscoll, B. 410
Mackay, H. A. 267

Mackintosh, N. J. 379
Macmillan, N. A. 181
MacNeilage, P. F. 294, 319
MacWhinney, B. 14
Malatesta, C. 103
Malinowski, B. 98, 99
Mandler, J. M. 224
Manning, A. A. 317
Maratsos, M. 7, 444
Marentette, P. F. 128, 130
Markey, P. R. 154
Markman, R. 317
Marler P. 54, 56, 57, 123, 126, 178, 183, 185, 188, 197, 200, 210, 294, 458
Marmor, G. S. 426
Marshack, A. 6
Marshall, J. C. 7
Marslen-Wilson, W.D. 444
Martinich, A. P. 11
Marx, J. 316
Marzi, C. A. 319
Masek, B. S. 319
Mass, A. M. 317
Massaro, D. W. 181
Matsuzawa, T. 224, 347, 348
McBride, A. F. 134
McCall, R. 107
McClelland, J. L. 70, 73, 74, 87, 90
McConnell, P. B. 183, 186
McDonald, E. 329, 460
McFarland, W. 317
McGuiness, D. 296
McIlvane, W. J. 256, 270
McKeever, W. F. 317
McMullen, P. A. 316
Mehler, J. 368
Meier, R. P. 130
Melnick, D. 196
Menzel, E. 143, 222, 333
Meyer, D. E. 296
Miles, H. L. 30, 224

Miller, G. 12, 14, 28, 237, 457
Mills, L. 276
Milner, B. 293, 294
Mineka, S. 187
Minsky, M. 70, 87, 88, 90
Moise, S. L. 304
Moody, D. 178, 290, 294, 319
Moran, G. 232
Morgan, C. L. 7
Morgane, P. J. 314, 317
Morrel-Samuels, P. 290, 312, 313, 315, 316, 319, 405, 410, 411, 418, 419, 427, 429
Morris, R. D. 294, 295, 301, 305, 319
Morse, D. H. 178
Mukhametov, L. M. 316, 317
Murdock, B. B. Jr. 397
Murofushi, K. 347, 349
Murphy, E. H. 276
Musgrave, A. 3, 4
Naatanen, R. 302
Nachson, I. 276
Neiworth, J. 428
Nelson K. 223, 381
Nettleton, N. C. 316
Neville, H. J. 317
Newell, A. 38
Newman, J. 129, 224
Neyman, P. A. 186
Niemi, P. 302
Nissen, H. W. 252, 367, 422
Norman, D. A. 392
Nottebohm, F. 290
O'Connor, K. 279, 289
O'Sullivan, C. 141
Oatley, K. 102, 106, 107
Oden, D. L. 35, 209, 366, 367, 371, 373, 374, 376, 377, 378, 379, 386, 421, 422, 423, 424
Ogden, C. 98
Owings, D. 54, 200

Pack, A. 312, 313, 319, 410, 421, 423, 425
Paivio, A. 405, 426, 428
Pallie, W. 316
Palmer, S. E. 368
Papert, S. 70, 87, 88, 90
Pate, J. 15, 30, 331, 333, 460
Patterson, F. G. 30, 222
Pavio, A. 368
Pawlukiewicz, J. 178
Payne, K. 50, 127
Pearl, M. C. 196
Penner, R. H. 160
Pepperberg, I. M. 222, 223, 224, 225, 226, 227, 228, 229, 230, 231, 232, 233, 234, 235, 236, 237
Perusse, R. 330, 334, 336
Peters, A. M. 14, 15
Petersen, M. R. 178, 294
Peterson, M. R. 290, 319
Petitto, L. 15, 128, 130, 184, 221, 223, 361, 403, 406
Petrinovich, L. 125, 140, 222
Piaget, J. 102
Pickert, R. 183, 188
Pierce, J. R. 185
Pinker, S. 12, 73, 93
Poizner, H. 317, 387, 410, 411
Pola, Y. V. 179, 180, 181
Poliakova, E. G. 317
Pologe, B. 14
Polyakova, I. G. 316
Popov, V. V. 317
Posner, M. I. 305
Premack D. 1, 3, 17, 35, 36, 37, 58, 124, 144, 184, 201, 209, 210, 221, 223, 224, 226, 227, 228, 230, 239, 240, 365, 366, 367, 370, 372, 373, 377, 378, 380, 381, 385, 386, 412, 420, 421, 430

Pribram, K. H. 296
Prince, A. 73, 93
Putney, R. T. 232, 295
Pylyshyn, Z. 66, 67, 426
Quine, W. 54
Quirk, R. 28
Ralls, K. 130, 267
Ramer, A. 14
Rasmussen, T. 293, 294
Ratcliffe, L. 185
Reber, A. S. 12, 13, 408
Recchia, C. A. 134
Rescorla, R. A. 90
Richards D. G. 9, 30, 57, 89, 98, 130, 131, 133, 135, 136, 144, 154, 155, 156, 164, 170, 171, 235, 251, 311, 386, 404, 405, 415, 443
Richardson, R. C. 66, 295, 331, 380
Richerson, P. 213
Ridgway, S. H. 131, 155, 316, 319
Rilling, M. E. 428
Ristau, C. A. 31
Rivera, J. 422
Robbins, D. 31
Robinson, J. 57, 185, 186
Rogoff, B. 228
Roitblat, H. L. 4, 5, 6, 7, 8, 9, 14, 49, 58, 116, 184, 221, 226, 240, 250, 257, 280, 329, 367, 368, 391, 416, 421, 428, 460
Rollman, G. B. 276
Rosch, E. 35, 305
Rosenbaum, S. 30, 124, 460
Rothbart, M. 106
Rothi, L. 317
Rubert, E. 240, 329, 460
Rumbaugh, D. 10, 15, 35, 36, 54, 55, 76, 136, 222, 224, 227, 295, 299, 319, 331, 333, 334, 335, 337, 342, 380, 406
Rumelhart, D. E. 70, 73, 87, 90

Runfeldt, S. 305, 337
Russell, B. 11
Ryle, G. 65, 68, 69, 81
Sacerdoti, E. D. 38
Sacher, G. A. 404
Sachs, J. 38
Sackett, G. P. 373
Sade, D. S. 196
Sait, P. E. 316
Salmon, D. P. 367, 398, 421
Sampson, G. 98
Sands, S. F. 386, 392, 422
Santiago, H.C. 386
Saunders, R. J. 140, 184, 406
Savage-Rumbaugh, E. S. 27, 30, 31, 35, 36, 37, 55, 76, 77, 79, 124, 136, 142, 143, 223, 224, 240, 295, 296, 301, 319, 329, 331, 333, 337, 380, 381, 386, 403, 406, 412, 420, 421, 430, 460, 463, 467, 468, 469
Sayigh, L. S. 131, 132, 133, 153
Schiefelbusch, R. 59
Schusterman, R. 17, 89, 223, 224, 227, 233, 235, 249, 252, 254, 255, 257, 267, 270, 429, 430, 459, 463
Schvaneveldt, R. W. 296
Scopatz, R. A. 14, 280
Scott, M. D. 131, 132, 153, 366
Scribner, S. 125
Scronce, B. L. 160
Searle, J. 76, 95, 97
Searleman, A. A. 293
Sebeok, T. A. 39
Seidenberg, M. 15, 221, 223, 403, 406
Sells, P. 31
Serafetinides, E. 317
Sergent, J. 299, 316
Servan-Schreiber, D. 12, 74, 78
Sevcik, R. 240, 329, 386, 460, 467

Seyfarth, R. 31, 54, 55, 117, 130, 141, 144, 181, 186, 187, 196, 197, 198, 200, 203, 204, 205, 206, 208, 210, 211, 213, 214, 221, 458
Shannon, C. E. 185
Shapiro, M. S. 299
Shaw, M. 427
Shepard, B. 103
Shepherd, J. W. 316
Sherman, P. W. 210
Shettleworth, S. J. 123, 138
Shibkova, S. 314
Shiffrin, R. M. 392
Shipley, E. F. 409
Shurley, J. 316
Shyan, M. R. 304, 314, 386, 387, 398
Sidman, M. 249, 250, 251, 252, 267, 269, 271, 459
Sidtis, J. 276
Siebenaler, J. B. 319
Simon H. A. 38, 66, 276
Singer, 373
Siqueland, P. 203
Skinner, B. F. 67, 85, 459
Slobin, D. 256, 270
Smith, C. S. 30, 54, 55, 76, 124, 136, 178, 200, 224, 295, 409, 460, 462
Smolker, R. A. 133
Snowdon, C. 52, 57, 115, 126, 178, 179, 180, 181, 182, 183, 185, 186, 188, 458
Snowman, L. G. 376
Snyder, C. R. R. 31, 305
Sorenson, L. 232
Sperry, R. W. 316
Sroufe, A. 107
Staddon, J. E. R. 239
Stauffer, L.B. 376
Stebbins, W. 178, 290, 294, 319

Stein, N. 102, 106, 107
Stenberg, C. 102
Stephens, D. W. 116
Stern, C. 97, 99
Stoddard, L. T. 256, 270
Stokoe, W. 387
Strawson, P. F. 10, 460
Streeter, L. A. 51
Stromer, R. 261
Struhsaker, T. T. 197, 203
Studdert-Kennedy, M. G. 294, 319
Sullivan, K. 210
Supin, A. Y. 316, 317
Suppe, F. 4
Sutherland, N. S. 379
Svartvik, J. 28
Swartz, K. B. 373
Swets, J. A. 278
Symmes, D. 129
Tabossi, P. 319
Tailby, W. 249, 250, 267, 269, 271
Tanis, D. 278
Tannenbaum, P. L. 188
Tavolga, W. 54
Taylor, C. 96, 97, 99, 101
Tempelaars, S. 276
Terrace, H. 28, 33, 55, 58, 140, 184, 221, 223, 329, 367, 406
Tesman, J. 103
Teuber, H. L. 276
Thomas, R. K. 271
Thompson, C. R. 15, 16, 17, 35, 209, 366, 367, 373, 378, 386, 398, 421
Thorpe, W. H. 414
Tierney, A. J. 121
Timmers, H. 276
Tinbergen, N. 120, 122, 130
Todt, D. 222
Tooby, J. 120, 122
Touretzky, D. 73
Trehub, S. E. 51

Trivers, R. L. 121
Tule, N. 205
Tyack, P. 127, 129, 132, 134, 135, 139, 153, 155, 417
Tyler, L. T. 444
Tylor, E. B. 99
Tyrrell, D. J. 376
Umiker-Sebeok, J. 39
Umilta, C. 319
Van Allen, M. W. 276
Van Den Abell, T. 299
Van Gilder, J. 317
Van Valen, L. 240
VanDeventer, A. D. 317
Venables, P. H. 276
Vermeire, B. A. 294
Verner, J. 123, 127
Vigorito, J. 203
de Villiers, J. G. 199, 409, 444
de Villiers, P.A. 199, 409, 444
Visalberghi, E. 214
Volterra, V. 98
Vroon, P. A. 276
Vygotsky, L. 98
de Waal, F. 141
Wada, J. A. 316
Wagner, A. R. 90
Walker, E. C. T. 368, 397
Wallace, G. 316
Ward, J. P. 294
Warren, J. M. 294
Washburn, D. A. 294, 295, 299, 331, 337, 342, 380
Waters, 107
Watson, C. 278
Waugh, N. C. 392
Webb, W. G. 317
Weiskrantz, L. 294
Weisman, R. G. 185
Wells, R. S. 131, 132, 133, 153, 404
Werner, T. J. 249, 260
West, M. J. 222
White, K. G. 304
Witelson, S. F. 316
Wittgenstein, L. 98
Wolff, J. G. 224
Wolfson, S. 317
Wolz, J. 9, 30, 57, 89, 130, 131, 154, 235, 251, 311, 386, 404, 405, 443
Wood, F. G. 134, 153, 154
Woodruff, C. 36, 37, 184, 210
Wright, A. A. 304, 386, 392, 394, 398, 421, 422
Wynne, C. D. L. 239
Xitco, M. J. 314, 416, 417
Yates, J. 205
Yeager, C. P. 141
Yund, E. W. 276
Zahn-Wexler, C. 103
Zaidel, E. 316
Zeaman, D. 379
Zelazo, P. 107
Zentall, T. R. 304, 415, 418
Zoloth, S. R. 139, 178, 290, 294, 319
Zurif, E. B. 316

SUBJECT INDEX

Abstract concepts 386, 391, 392
Abstract relationships 25, 365
Abstract representation 386
Abstract rules 8, 14
Acoustic communication 135, 153, 154
Acoustic labels 391, 392
Activation 88, 89, 304
Age of language learning 397
Akeakamai 78, 311, 312, 386, 389, 391, 404, 407 - 410, 413, 415 - 420, 424, 428, 430, 431, 433, 443 - 447, 449 - 452
Alarm call development 197
Alarm calls 54, 183, 184, 186, 187, 197, 200, 203, 204, 208, 210, 211
All-or-none questions 19
Amboseli National Park 196
American Sign Language 388, 397
Animal cognition 34, 35, 39, 40, 115, 128, 145, 249, 268
Animal communication 85
Animal language 2, 6, 25 - 30, 32, 34 - 37, 39, 40, 45 - 48, 51, 53, 54, 57 - 59, 66, 116, 118, 119, 123, 124, 126, 128, 129, 131, 135, 138 - 144, 249 - 251, 256, 403, 406, 430, 467
Animal language research 2, 65, 68, 75, 76, 81
Animal thought 118
Apes 85, 86
Aphasia 118
Arithmetic skills 333
Artificial language 1, 55, 57, 119, 126, 128, 141, 254, 257, 260,
263, 311, 312, 315, 408, 409, 411, 426, 454
Associationism 69, 74, 75, 81, 116
Associationist learning 87
Associative symmetry 251
Audience effects 183, 184, 210, 211, 213
Auditory sequence learning 275
Austin 27, 36, 37, 76, 77, 79, 296, 298, 300 - 303, 305, 342, 420, 467
Back propagation 90
Bait shyness 117
Behavior 86
Behavioral contrast 10
Behavioral ecology 115
Behaviorism 67, 69
Beliefs 144, 209, 214
Beluga whales 130
Birds 35, 117, 118, 120, 123, 126, 127, 129, 177, 178, 329, 415
Bonobos
  see pygmy chimpanzees
Bottlenosed dolphins 78, 86
California Primate Research Center 196
California sea lions 86
Callitrichidae 177
Canalization 121
Capuchin monkeys 186
Cardinality 336
Categorical matching 367
Causal relations 195
Cause-effect reasoning 458, 463
Central processor 397, 398
Cercopithecus aethiops
  see vervet monkeys

Cerebral asymmetry 275, 277, 278, 281, 282, 288, 289, 293-305, 311, 316 - 320, 411
Cerebral dominance 293
Cheremic analysis 313, 386 - 392
  defined 387
Chickadees 185, 189
Chickens 35, 183, 184, 189
Children 28, 31 - 33, 51, 55, 59, 118, 124, 127, 143, 199, 256, 270, 312, 334, 360, 366, 376, 403, 409, 412, 414, 426, 444, 458, 460, 463, 464, 468, 469
Chimpanzees 15, 27, 36, 37, 76, 77, 80, 86, 115, 140, 176, 184, 201, 209, 221, 223, 224, 253, 263, 271, 296, 298 - 300, 319, 329, 330, 333, 334, 338, 339, 341, 343, 348, 350, 355 - 359, 361, 365, 366, 370 - 374, 376, 377, 380, 381, 386, 412, 420, 422 - 424, 461, 463, 467, 468, 469
Cistothorus palustris 123
Classical conditioning 8, 9, 90, 169
Classification rules 88
Cognition 34, 35, 39, 40, 49, 50, 65 - 68, 70, 74, 76, 81
  abilities 118, 119, 124 - 126, 129, 136, 139, 140, 144, 221 - 224, 226, 237, 240, 329, 331
  adaptations 119
  capacities 58, 222
  competence 342
  development 373
  ethology 115
  evolution 119, 120, 123
  levels 397
  mechanisms 121, 122

Commands 128, 135, 141, 142, 144, 154, 311, 312, 314, 317 - 319, 414, 452
Communication 29 - 33, 35, 39, 40, 45, 46, 48, 50, 53, 57, 58, 115, 116, 118, 119, 126, 128, 130, 135, 138 - 144, 153, 154, 210, 404, 457 - 461, 463, 465, 468
Communication context 182, 183, 184
Comparative cognition 221, 385
Comparative language research 45, 47, 49, 50, 56, 58, 59
Complex language 317
Complexity 27, 33, 47, 48, 127, 139, 144, 155, 157, 177, 276, 277, 282, 288 - 290, 315, 316, 335, 434
Comprehension 26, 56, 57, 118, 124, 127, 135, 249, 250, 252, 254, 255, 257, 261, 263, 270, 271, 311, 313 - 318, 351, 386, 403, 405, 406, 411, 412, 463, 466, 467, 468
Concept learning 387
Concepts 35, 50, 130, 140, 271, 381, 386, 421, 428 - 430, 434, 458, 459
Conditional discriminations 5, 251, 252, 263, 267 - 271, 377, 379
Connectionism 70, 74, 81, 87
Connectionist models 65, 74, 77, 89
  see also PDP models
Consciousness 142, 144
Context 39, 54, 131, 139, 142, 143, 155, 170, 250, 254, 256, 257, 269, 270, 335, 336, 381, 390, 404, 407, 420, 421, 434, 463

Contingent discrimination 89
Cooperation 121, 142
Correspondence theory of meaning 11
Criticism 4, 39
Cross-modal processing strategies 398
Cross-species comparisons 46
Deictic function 362
Desires 143, 144, 209, 461, 467, 469
Development of antipredator behavior 211
Discourse 95, 369
Discrimination 87, 89, 90
Dolphin vocalizations 405, 415, 420
Dolphins 9, 25, 39, 47, 57, 78, 85, 86, 125, 128 - 138, 141, 144, 153 - 171, 176, 222, 223, 251 - 253, 261, 267, 270, 311, 312, 314, 316, 317, 319, 386 - 392, 396 - 398, 403 - 406, 408 - 422, 424 - 426, 428 - 430, 433, 434, 443, 444, 461 - 466, 468, 470
Dual process memory model 392
Eagles 35, 197, 211
Echolocation 131, 412
Elele 404, 416, 427
Empiricism 66, 67
English 28, 51, 52, 54, 56, 73, 78, 79, 138, 140, 267 - 270, 413, 421, 446, 468
Enumeration 334, 336, 339, 342
Equivalence relations 250, 251, 269, 271, 459
Error correction 90, 465
Ethology 115, 119, 120
Evolution 115, 119, 120, 122, 123, 126, 144
Evolutionary precursors of language 177

Exclusion 251, 256, 261, 265, 266, 270, 271
Experimental paradigms 25, 27
Feature detection 88
Feature salience 387
Fixed action patterns 120, 184
Flaky entelechy 7
Food calls 183, 187, 188
Foraging 116, 121, 153
Formal systems 87
Foundations of human nature 2
Frieda 370, 372, 378
Generative grammar 189
Gertie 255, 256 - 258
Gestural language 404 - 406, 411, 413, 418, 421, 443 - 446, 454
Gesture comprehension 313, 314, 317, 411
Gesture duration 313 - 315, 319, 411
Gesture recognition 311
Gestures 129, 252, 255, 257, 311 - 319, 398, 404, 406, 407, 409 - 414, 417 - 419, 428 - 431, 443, 445 - 448, 450, 451, 453, 454
Grammar 12, 14, 28, 29, 31, 46, 74, 78, 89, 118, 124, 128, 129, 184, 185, 408, 409, 444, 446, 448, 454
    Finite-state 9, 12, 13, 14, 74, 78, 129, 184
Grammatical category 315
Granny 137, 138
Ground squirrels 54, 210
Habituation 203, 207, 215, 254, 256
Handedness 294, 319, 320
Hiapo 404, 416, 423, 424
Hidden units 71, 72, 78, 88
Hippocampus 123
Holophrases 9, 312
Horizontal integration 15

Human children 295
Human language 28 - 30, 33, 34, 39, 40, 45 - 59, 115, 116, 118, 119, 123, 124, 126 - 128, 143, 144, 153, 195, 275, 290, 405, 444
Humans 27 - 30, 36, 37, 39, 47 - 50, 53, 56, 66, 67, 74, 75, 78, 79, 85, 86, 93, 95, 118 - 120, 123 - 130, 135, 138, 139, 141, 144, 153, 256, 261, 270, 271, 275, 277, 282, 284, 288 - 289, 311, 312, 315, 316, 319, 320, 329, 366, 386 - 392, 394 - 399, 405, 408, 411, 417, 424 - 429, 457, 458
Humpback whales 127
Implicit rule learning 87
Imprinting 117, 120
Individual differences 313, 331, 377, 391
Individual recognition 348
Information processing 385, 386, 396, 406
Innate releasing mechanism 120
Instance-based learning 87, 91
Intelligence 117, 123, 140, 143, 201
Intentionality 76, 96, 123, 143, 144
Interference 289, 315, 392, 394
Interstimulus intervals 393
Japanese macaques 196, 212
Jesse 37
Justificationism 2
Kanzi 79, 80, 250, 403, 421, 468
Kinship 116, 133
Knowing how versus knowing that 68
Knowledge 29, 36 - 38, 59, 209, 379, 403, 415, 423, 428, 429, 444, 446, 448, 454, 458, 464, 467
Lana 15, 76, 300, 336 - 342, 467
Language 85, 93, 385, 394, 396, 457 - 459, 461 - 464, 467, 469, 470
  acquisition 28, 31, 47, 53, 85 - 87, 93, 95 - 108, 118, 120, 125, 129, 457, 459, 467, 468, 469
  acquisition mechanisms 86
  as a mediation strategy 396
  as information processing mediator 385
  competency 28, 32, 34
  definition of 86
  functions 46, 47, 57
  instrumental function 95, 96
  learning 32, 33, 41, 93, 458
  mediation processes 386, 392, 395, 397
  modularity 117, 118, 458
  processing 293, 394
  production 26, 128, 320, 405, 406
  production versus reception 463
  training 58, 124, 135, 138, 142, 143, 270, 366, 370, 376, 377, 379 - 381, 385, 430
Language of thought 67, 72
Language theory 46
Language training, effects of 223, 386, 391, 397, 399
Lateralization 293
Laws of learning 86, 87
Learning 87, 90, 92
Learning algorithms 90
Learning mechanisms 86, 87
Leopards 197

Lexemes 9
Lexical syntax 185
Lexigrams 37, 76, 77, 79, 250, 251, 269, 270, 347, 468
Linguistic capacities 75, 176
Linguistic competence 5, 381
Linguistic comprehension 89
Linguistic ethology 177
Linguistic precursors 177
Linguistic processing 394
List memory 392
Liza 370, 372, 378
Locke 67
Logic network 73
Long-term memory 392
Macaca mulatta see rhesus monkeys
Macaca fuscata see Japanese macaques
Macaques 139, 196, 294, 319
Marmosets 177, 179 - 184, 189
Marsh wrens 123
Marshall 200
Matching to sample 222, 250, 255, 256, 257, 259 - 261, 263, 264, 266 - 271, 367, 391, 398, 380, 421 - 423, 425
Mathematical logic 89
Mean length of utterance 30
Meaning 9, 11, 12, 37, 38, 45, 52 - 57, 154, 199 - 201, 271, 312, 317, 404, 407 - 409, 414, 424, 429, 430, 443, 448, 454, 467
Memory 53, 117, 258, 289, 314, 315, 337, 338, 339, 340, 368, 397, 408, 417, 422, 428
Memory models 392
Mental capacities 458
Mental contents 95
Mental states 36, 37, 144, 209
Methodology 2

Mimicry 131, 135, 170, 171, 414 - 419, 421, 428, 431, 433
Missionary versus anthropological approach 175
Modalities 398
Modality effects 397
Modality-specific learning 392
Modality-specific processors 398
Models of cognitive processing 397
Monkeys 185 - 187, 189, 196, 197, 201, 210, 215, 386, 392 - 398
Morgan's canon 7
Morphemes 33, 52 - 58
Naming 76, 118, 251, 261, 268, 270, 421
Nativism 457
Natural communication skills 189
Natural selection 120, 122, 123, 143
Neural net modeling 87
   see also PDP models
Nicklo 136, 137, 138
Nim 33, 76
Nonhuman primates 294, 295
Nothing-but-ism 5
Novel stimuli 267, 398
Numerical competence 330
Nutcrackers 138
Occasion 9
Opal 370, 372, 378
Operational definition 11
Orangutans 224
Ordinality 336
Output 88
Paired-associate learning 16, 265, 394
Pan troglodytes 140, 333, 412, 467
   see chimpanzees
Panthera pardus 197
Parallel distributed processing (PDP) 87

499

Parrots 39, 125, 138, 140, 141, 221, 223, 461
Parsimony 7, 8, 116
Pattern recognition 87
PDP models 70, 73, 76, 87, 89, 91, 92, 93
  see also neural net modeling
Perception 87
Personal pronouns 347, 351 - 353, 355, 357 - 359, 362
Phoenix 141, 389 - 391, 404, 410, 413, 414, 416 - 420, 422, 424, 425, 433, 443, 444, 446, 449, 450, 452, 464, 466
Phrase structure 78, 79
Phrase structure grammar 89, 184
Pigeons 86, 138, 140, 141, 392, 422, 426, 427
Playback 133, 141, 203
Polemaetus bellicosus 197
Positivism 11
Primacy effects 392, 393, 394
Primates 129, 141, 144, 178, 329, 331, 373, 380, 412
Priming 295, 296, 302, 305
Proactive interference 304
Problem solving 38, 39, 58, 329, 380, 365, 385
Processing strategies 288, 397
Production 52, 56, 351, 462, 463, 467, 470
Productivity 31, 56, 67
Propositional knowledge 68, 71
Propositional logic 72
Propositional representation 69
Propositions 37
Protolinguistic capacities 190
Proximate mechanisms 115, 116
Psittacus erithacus 221
Psychology versus ethology 176, 189

Pygmy chimpanzees 79, 86, 176, 250, 412, 463
Python sebae 197
Raccoons 335
Rationalism 66, 69, 74
Rats 13, 14, 85, 86, 275, 277, 280, 283, 284, 285 - 289, 319, 335, 415
Reasoning 37 - 39, 66, 67, 74
Recency effects 392 - 395
Recognition memory 392
Reductionism 5
Reference 10 - 12, 27, 143, 176, 186, 195, 201, 270, 318, 337, 339, 406 - 408, 429, 431, 458 - 461, 467, 468, 470
Referential communication 188, 429
Referential relations 195, 270
Reflexivity 268, 269, 271
Rehearsal 392 - 394
Relational features 379
Relational matching 366, 368, 369, 371, 377, 379, 380, 381
Relational oddity matching 376
Representation 36 - 38, 54, 66, 69, 73, 91, 117, 119, 141, 142, 251, 366 - 370, 373, 376, 379 - 381, 386, 399, 406, 408, 409, 421, 428
Representational capacity 195
Representational labeling 392
Representational status of tokens 10
Representational thought 399
Representations 36, 37, 39, 186, 195, 408, 411, 418, 420, 426, 428, 434
Requesting 76, 445, 449
Res cogitans 66
Res extensa 66

Resemblance 2, 6, 155, 161, 163, - 168, 201, 286, 365 - 367, 371, 411
Response strategies 391
Response units 88
Rhesus macaques 187
Rhesus monkeys 54, 196, 212, 335, 392, 398
Rio 262 - 266
Rocky 252 - 255, 257 - 258, 260, 264, 265
Role-reversal 360, 412
Rule systems 69
Rule-based processing 65
Rule-learning models 90
Same/different task 392
Sarah 184, 201, 380, 420
Schemata 14, 37
Scientific progress 4, 116
Scotty 134, 135, 139
Sea lions 25, 39, 86, 138, 141, 224, 252, 253, 260, 261, 263, 266, 270, 271, 463, 464
Seals 130, 267, 270
Semantic grades 9 - 11, 197, 200, 209
Semantic signals 214
Semanticity 197, 201, 249, 250, 271
Semantics 9, 57, 95, 128, 201, 269, 312, 380
Sensory versus cognitive mechansims 397
Serial anticipation 13, 14
Serial position curves 392, 398
Serial probe recognition 392, 394, 398
Sherman 27, 36, 37, 296, 298, 300 - 303, 305, 342, 420, 467
Short-term memory 249, 289, 314, 392
Sign elements 387, 389

Sign Language 140, 317, 397, 411, 444
Sign recognition strategies 388, 397
Signature characteristics 30, 32, 33, 34
  learning 31
Signature characteristics approach to language learning 30, 34
Signature whistles 131 - 138, 141, 144, 417
Signing 33, 312, 313, 388, 428, 446
Signs 140, 141, 143, 255, 261, 269, 311 - 315, 317, 318, 388, 410, 411, 413, 419, 428 - 430, 448, 454, 462
Simple language systems 75
Skills 116
Slot and frame grammar 14 - 17, 184
Snakes 197
Social behavior 115, 116, 141, 142
Social cognition 142
Social context 182, 189
Sociobiology 122
Sociology 2
Song learning 117, 120, 121, 123
Song structure 185
Sparrows 125, 140
Spatial memory 123, 138
Species-specific mechanisms 86
Speech roles 360
Spontaneous gestures 315
Spray 134, 135, 139
Spreo superbus 206
Starlings 206
States of mind 95
Stephanoaetus coronatus 197
Stimulus equivalence 267, 268, 270, 459

Stimulus-response mechanisms 88, 91
Stimulus-specific responses 386
Subject, action, object 349
Symbol processing 66, 74, 75
Symbolic labeling 392
Symbolic representation 69, 251, 386, 387
Symbols 27, 54, 176, 186, 250, 267, 271, 329, 381, 386, 403, 404, 411, 421, 430, 460 - 464, 467, 468, 469
Symmetry 251, 268 - 271, 369
Symmetry test 355
Syntax 14, 56 - 58, 89, 95, 118, 126 - 130, 140, 176, 184, 185, 189, 316, 349, 369, 380, 458, 459
Systematicity 67, 75, 76, 80, 81
Tamarins 177, 183, 185 - 188
Task familiarity 394
Theory of mind 210
Titi monkeys 185
Token-specific rules 8
Tokens 9, 128, 381, 466
Toque macaques 187
Transitivity 268, 269 - 271
Trill vocalizations 181
Turn-taking 182
Tursiops truncatus
   see dolphins
Variable binding 73, 74
Verbal labels 3945
Vertical integration 15, 17
Vervet monkeys 54, 130, 186, 196 - 216
Video displays 313
Vocal communication 135, 154, 177
Vocal imitation 135, 136, 139
Vocal labels 136

Vocal learning 118, 129 - 131, 133, 138, 139, 141
Vocal mimicry 131, 268, 415, 417
Vocalight 134
Vocalizations 128 - 131, 202, 208, 405, 414, 421, 426, 429
Washoe 76
Whiskey 370, 372, 378
Whistle exchanges 132
Whistles 131 - 138, 153 - 155, 157, 163, 417
Word order 57, 349, 451
Words 27, 28, 53, 56, 57, 95, 118, 127, 138, 186, 250, 252, 267 - 270, 316, 365, 379, 387, 430, 443, 444, 460
Working memory 66, 78, 314
XOR problem 71, 72, 77, 89